AF735576

Roberto Moro Visconti

From Microfinance to Business Planning:

Escaping Poverty Traps

Roberto Moro Visconti

FROM MICROFINANCE TO BUSINESS PLANNING:

Escaping Poverty Traps

ibidem-Verlag
Stuttgart

Bibliografische Information der Deutschen Nationalbibliothek
Die Deutsche Nationalbibliothek verzeichnet diese Publikation in der Deutschen Nationalbibliografie; detaillierte bibliografische Daten sind im Internet über http://dnb.d-nb.de abrufbar.

Bibliographic information published by the Deutsche Nationalbibliothek
Die Deutsche Nationalbibliothek lists this publication in the Deutsche Nationalbibliografie; detailed bibliographic data are available in the Internet at http://dnb.d-nb.de.

∞

Gedruckt auf alterungsbeständigem, säurefreien Papier
Printed on acid-free paper

ISBN-13: 978-3-8382-0662-2

Printed in Germany

INTRODUCTION – Poverty is a complex matter

> In some circumstances escape may not be possible. Especially in the urban slum, race or poverty may confine individuals to an area of intrinsically limited opportunity. And once again the environment perpetuates its handicaps through poor schools, evil neighborhood influences, and bad preparation for life.
>
> John Kenneth Galbraith, *The affluent society*

Poverty is a complex matter, requiring a holistic approach

Poverty goes beyond social inequalities and it is concerned with the failure of the underserved, due to their social condition and to asset deprivation, to acquire and maintain a minimum set of basic capabilities–such as nutrition, instruction, clothing, housing needs, basic healthcare–which prevent the poor from fully participating in labor and credit markets–hence the importance of microfinance.

Dehumanizing poverty goes also beyond low levels of current income and consumption, being concerned with the inability to freely access the market economy. Social exclusion from the benefits that others can enjoy is typically an enduring phenomenon, which is hard to eradicate, together with vulnerability to adverse shocks, due to the absence of social safety nets[1].

> According to the DAC Guidelines for Poverty Reduction[2]:The concept of poverty includes different dimensions of deprivation. In general, it is the inability of people to meet economic, social, and other standards of well-being. The multidimensionality of misery–with a not competing plurality of overlapping poverty traps–is now widely accepted, requiring nuanced visions, beyond oversimplified single-minded approaches. […] It covers measures of *absolute*

1 Mookherijee in Banerjee, Benabou, Mookherjee (2006), p. 234.

2 OECD (2001).

poverty such as child and infant mortality rates, and *relative poverty,* as defined by the differing standards of each society.

The ›poverty soup‹ is a cocktail of different–typically not tasty–ingredients, which compose the multicolored and instable condition of the poor, like a kaleidoscope where different interacting colors mix and split, simply fine tuning its detecting lenses.

Abandoned, withdrawn, and forgotten poor are daily frustrated and humiliated by their hard and starless hell-on-earth life and they have constantly to fight through eccentric and not conformist choices against colorless resignation and desperation, which derives from perception that the world is hardly likely to change, and there is no prospective, in spite of one's–useless?–efforts. Living in an empty and paralyzing darkness, the resigned, voiceless, and apparently (e)motionless poor show a fantastic talent for endless waiting.

Maladaptive and unhealthy behaviors, so common for many emarginated poor, cause personal distress and social impairment, destroying self motivation and reinforcing misery. Such a misery–with its social and anthropological interpretation–has a deep impact on the psychology of the poor, who are often deluded, depressed, unempathic, and vulnerable. The poor also show a disorganized behavior (evident in their dressing, body posture, personal hygiene ...) that segregates them from any wealthier status and prevents any clear life goal, bringing to boredom, monotony, and hopelessness. Extreme poverty is a dreamless mental status, silently breathing and whispering its feelings, while mirroring a self-image of destitution. Self-reliance and motivation, albeit being a key ingredient of development, are hardly present in the ›diet‹ of the poor.

Quintessential poverty is the living state for the majority of world's and nations' people and it may so tend to be confused with the study of humanity. Chronic, stubbornly persisting and path dependent poverty brings to vulnerability, which can trap in its intricate maze entire nations and social groups, with durable social inequalities, due to a destabilizing wealth gap. Diffidence against an unforgiving external world can bring to fear and aggressiveness while pain quickly becomes an integral part of life.

Persistent pockets of severe poverty are untouched by worldwide development and created by an ill conceived social system and they shamefully resist in a pitiless and selfish world – either we forget that others are suffering or we decide to open our heart to love and longing for the poor, unlocking it from its prison of selfishness. Much is possible for those who love, going beyond the idolatry of reason, and they do not need to measure the result of their efforts, remembering that the opposite of love is indifference, not hate.

Many factors are crucial to understanding the reason why people are poor and a multivariate and interdependent analysis of multifaceted poverty seems necessary, with an anthropological holistic and poor-centric approach to intertwined

poverty issues – always remembering that one-size-fits–all development strategies do not work. Trying to link and to distill largely disconnected disciplines is a hard but fruitful effort and it requires a mastering of complexity, digging inside the intricate array of connected poverty issues and favoring an inspiring vision of the question. Everybody–rich or poor–represents many different things, inside and altogether, with his predictable irrationality and different tastes. As Voltaire said in 1750 »minds differ more than faces«.
According to Sen (1999), p. 126 »The case for taking a broad and many-sided approach to development has become clearer in recent years, partly as a result of the difficulties faced as well as successes achieved by different countries over the recent decades«. The Nobel Prize winner also suggests a »comprehensive development framework«, rejecting a compartmentalized view of the process of development, avoiding the search for a single all-purpose remedy, which has proved largely ineffective in the past.

Walking with Socrates inside the poverty issues

Following a well established and functional Socratic method, open questions will tend to outweigh, by frequency and importance, fragile assumptions and questionable answers.
Walking with Socrates, who modestly lived as a poor man, while being incredibly rich inside, and being constantly accompanied by his maieutical questioning, is probably the best way to approach consciousness. And while trying to extract innate ideas from our minds, it is important to remember that apparently simple questions are even more important than uneasy answers.
Philosophers and thinkers have a huge impact on culture, and an example is given again by the Greek master of life, among the greatest contributors of the Western thought, who used to say to his disciples »Know yourself!«.
Socrates was the fascinating master of Plato, who in turn has inspired Aristotle, whose syllogism–every man is mortal; Socrates is a man and so Socrates is mortal–synthesizes the cause-and-effect relationship, a key mental category, able also to explain, from a logical perspective, the origins and the consequences of the poverty traps.
In Socrates, knowledge is a life reason, well beyond more human temptations like power, money or success, and the great philosopher has spent all his life by learning and teaching how to learn, starting from ourselves, and trying to extract the hidden truth inside us. Socrates digs inside our soul, by saying »I know that I don't know!« and making deep questions, rather than giving superficial answers. In this way he empties our mind with his irony and then progressively fills it up with apparently trivial questions, in order to wake up our sleeping reason and to learn how to self master our emotional storms. Socrates helps his

counterpart to get free of his ignorance and superficiality by learning by his own contradictions.
Our veil of ignorance and superficiality about deep poverty, its causes, traps, and unfortunate consequences, needs a constant presence of an inspiring Socrates inside us – poor outside but rich inside, beyond the contradictions of a plain and conventional life, where a selfish superficiality suffocates any questioning about misery.
Beyond the cause-and-effect relationship, poverty is also a non-comparative transcendent and metaphysical issue, being not only a living condition but also a mystic state of mind, mysteriously going well beyond our material comprehension.
The poor may follow Socrates more than the rich, if what Bertoldt Brecht says– »Poverty makes you sad as well as wise« –is at least partially true.

Breadth over depth

This book has an incredibly wide perimeter, attempting to tackle intricate poverty issues with a multidimensional and interdisciplinary approach, trying to link in an uneasy marriage topics that are apparently unrelated and culturally segmented.
Cross disciplinary approaches range from history to philosophy and geography, from medicine and technology to other sciences, from politics to anthropology and, in the second part, considering the economic and financial problems and opportunities for the poor, eventually arriving–a bit exhausted but still alive–to microfinance. With its porous and wide perimeter, the conglomerate theory of poverty traps finds its gravitational point in the anthropological concept of misery, putting the poor, with their human dimension, at the centre of any investigation. Poverty has to be investigated with its kaleidoscopic nuances, far beyond a Manichean black-and-white vision, bringing to an aggregated knowledge framework.
There are many sided approaches to development, bringing to a comprehensive development framework consistent with the encyclical letter Caritas in Veritate (§ 22), where Benedict XVI affirms that: »today the picture of development has *many overlapping layers*. The actors and the causes in both underdevelopment and development are manifold, the faults and the merits are differentiated«.
The advance of knowledge discourages broad surveys and scientific advances are increasingly based on narrower subjects, to be investigated as deeply as possible, blending the Western analytical tradition with other complementary cultures.
There should so be little wonder that such a broad analysis is incredibly superficial, as even a reader uncomfortable with these issues may immediately discov-

er, simply turning the pages or looking at the contents of this book. On the other extreme, we increasingly find overspecialized scholars who know everything … about nothing. Should the reader feel a bit embarrassed about his ignorance, we may just congratulate with him for joining the above mentioned Socrates club, of which we are enthusiastic members.
Trying to soften the intrinsic superficiality of this book is difficult, but it is not completely impossible, and the best remedy seems a constant reference to specific bibliographic sources and –for technological and impatient readers–to web sources.
Being the Socratic purpose of this book to raise common sense questions–starting from the apparently simple ones, which in reality are the trickiest–we feel that even the less interested reader has enough to reason about for the rest of his life … and so should urgently start thinking!

Poverty is neither a sin nor a fatality

In ancient times, for instance in Palestine at the time of Jesus (… once upon a time in the Middle-East), illnesses and related poverty were ancestrally and improperly considered as punishment from God for misbehavior or guilt, up to the point of becoming a permanent and shameful social stigma.
Many poor are physically or mentally handicapped and they resignedly accept their miserable condition. They believe in fixed predestination and in sinful fatalistic determinism, reinforced by closeness to nature, and they consider the course of their life as mapped out from birth–paying a tribute to the problematic behavior of their past–and impossible to be changed, especially in places where social mobility is a chimera and poverty, with its litany of grievances, traps in even the dreams. Suffering and stormy feelings cathartically temper our souls, while spicing our life.
With their miserable condition and their tortured ideals, the weeping poor incarnate the mystery of life. The poor nevertheless share with other wealthier individuals a transcendent and spiritual destiny, with equal eschatological dignity. And we are increasingly less convinced that poverty is an ineluctable destiny.
Passive fatalism is concerned with the view that ›whatever will be, will be‹ and hence that action–starting from self willingness up to collective strategies–makes no difference against a bizarre destiny. Idleness and disillusion are a typical corollary, suffocating free will and emancipation with the iron hand of an already written destiny. According to the Koran »what God writes on your forehead, you will become«. Reinhold Niebuhr used to say »God, grant me the serenity to accept the things I cannot change, the courage to change the things I can, and the wisdom to know the difference«.

The vituperated poor often think that the world belongs to somebody else and that they are hardly part of it. While they may tend to accept with ancestral resignation their exclusion, the sorrowful and dropped out underserved are likely to suffer from psychological consequences well beyond any superficial first impression. Subjective perception of poverty, remembering that everyone is different, makes the issue uneasy to generalize and treat.

Josh Billings used to say: »I am a poor man, but I have this consolation: I am poor by accident, not by design«. And also »Poverty is the step-mother of genius« or again »Remember the poor, it costs nothing«. Looking for consolation, it shouldn't be forgotten what Napoleon said: »The surest way to remain poor is to be an honest man«.

The disillusioned poor often miss the vital energy and motivation to change their alienated and emotionally flat life, which makes them feel strangers even in their motherland, wasting the incredible talents and potentialities that are inside every human being, exploiting his different keystone abilities and multiple intelligences.

Among the Socratic questions that we may raise, we might ask ourselves:

- What fault have the poor committed for deserving their miserable condition?
- Which is their responsibility for their unfortunate existence?

We may concentrate our attention not on finding out difficult answers–such as the well known statement that poor are lazy, sometimes partially true but hardly explaining the whole issue–but rather on some unconscious and subliminal consequences of these beliefs. Prejudices are still widespread and they are often the cause for which so many poor feel ashamed of their unlucky condition, with severe mental drawbacks that may induce resignation, fatalism, indolence, and lack of stimuli for sorting out the labyrinth of interconnected poverty traps.

Fight to poverty starts from inside the poor, within their heart and their mind–no hope and self esteem, no rescue, remembering that psychology matters. Poverty–extreme need–may tentatively and roughly be defined by adverbs such as (physical and psychological) grief, discouragement, and its synonyms[3] include abjection, aridity, bankruptcy, barrenness, beggary, dearth, debt, deficiency, deficit, depletion, destitution, difficulty, distress, emptiness, exiguity, famine, hardship, impecuniousness, impoverishment, inadequacy, indigence, insolvency, insufficiency, lack, meagerness, necessitousness, necessity, pass, paucity, pauperism, pennilessness, penury, pinch, poorness, privation, reduction, scarcity, shortage, starvation, straits, underdevelopment, vacancy …

3 See http://thesaurus.com/browse/poverty.

While we do not believe in predestination or fatalism, we are a bit sympathetic with some Murphy's rules–according to which luck is blind, … whereas misfortune is perfectly sighted–sharing also the paradoxical opinion of Finley Peter Dunne, who says that »One of the strangest things about life is that the poor, who need the money the most, are the ones that never have it«.
The ›black box‹ of poverty can also lead to (mental) alienation and even if there isn't any predestination in misery, who does listen to the desperate cry of the poor, drying their tears?
Happiness and well being derive from positive thinking, but also from a material dowry below which even mere subsistence is endangered by backslash ness.
Poverty may also be a metaphysical state of mind and, as it happens in India or within Western ascetics, there are those who leave everything and renounce to material life, to get ready for the next spiritual one, gradually detaching their body from their soul. According to Martin Heidegger, death–our later companion–is the salary of our sins.

Poverty traps are self fulfilling, if left unsolved

A poverty trap is concerned with many possible different self-reinforcing mechanisms which cause misery to persist in a vicious circle. This trap soon becomes cyclical and it begins to reinforce itself and unfortunately not to self-correct itself–due also to poor expectations–unless adequate steps are taken to break this perverse and enduring cycle.
Detecting, softening, and then breaking away the vicious circle of poverty is an exhausting and long lasting achievement and an uphill task, requiring both compassion and empathy towards the poor.
Extreme poverty is mostly concentrated where it shouldn't, in tough places which are landlocked (see Chapter 2), subject to extreme climatic adversities and far from the world's main trade routes[4].
The reason of self-fulfillment is mainly concerned with inertial features of each trap and with its perverse synergic interactions with other traps. Some few examples may clarify the concept. The demographic trap (dealt with in Chapter 4) is concerned with the nutritional and health trap (Chapter 7), since the fertility rate is higher within the poor and is linked with higher mortality, due to poor nutrition and health, lower instruction (Chapter 9), interacting with a more violent (Chapter 5) and polluted (Chapter 8) environment. No or little financial access (Chapter 17) exacerbates most of these traps.
Breaking the trap chain is a complex and multidimensional task, which requires a holistic approach to be effective and long lasting.

---

4 Sachs (2008).

The invisible soul of the poor represents their elusive and intangible self and the ghost within them–up to ›metaphysics‹ of poverty–and thus it is permanently suspended between an ideal transcendent hope for a better future and immanent despair about their current living condition. Every man dies, but not every man lives.
Self esteem and motivation, to be decoded and made conscious, may greatly help the poor on their road towards emancipation, together with their emotions, belonging to a largely unexplored continent of affective blindness.

The poverty tree

Due to their interactivity, poverty traps may be ideally represented by a tree–poverty itself–with many connected branches, each representing a trap.
Some branches are big, others are smaller than the previous ones and they may be close or distant among themselves, but they all belong to the same tree. Such a tree figuratively represents the poor, while neighboring trees symbolize the other poor living close to him. The tree gets its nourishment from the ground roots but it interacts even with the environment around and above it, accompanying the poor all along the parable of their miserable lives.
Poverty is a complex concept, that goes well beyond the economic level of personal income and it is a consequence of unfulfilled market potentials; it is not a mere by-product of power and domination or of biased political attitudes towards the production and reproduction of wealth and capital.
Each poor is diverse, because each one has his own history; individuality and undifferentiated homologation of the poor's problems need to be avoided. An individual approach–similar to a tailor made suit–albeit tiring, is strongly needed, since it simply fits better. Massification of problems is simpler and it allows economies of scale, but it is too superficial to be long lasting and analytically sound.
Digging inside the deep roots of poverty is the key to understand where its branches come from, analyzing the putative causes of misery in order to find out possible solutions. Fully eradicating the poverty tree is so the dreamy ultimate goal, that is hard to achieve but necessary to conceive, remembering that poverty is nowadays a global drama of the enlarged human family.
Contemporary incarnation of poverty places additional psychological burden to the underserved, less segregated from the wealthy than they used to be and so continuously subject to painful comparisons.

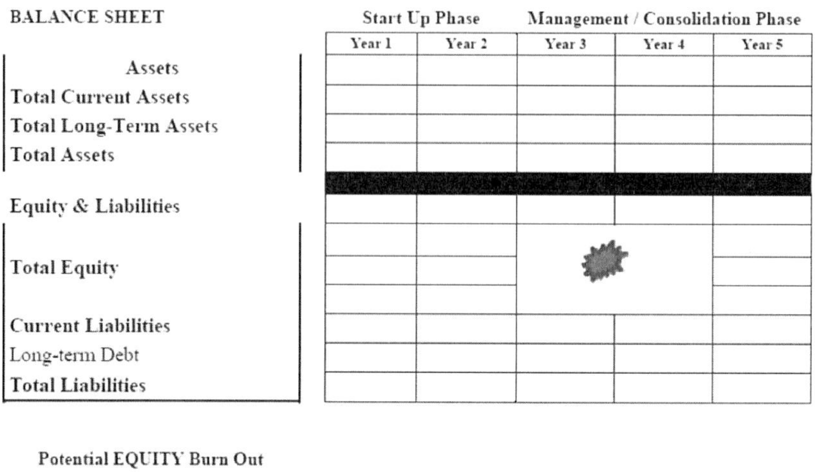

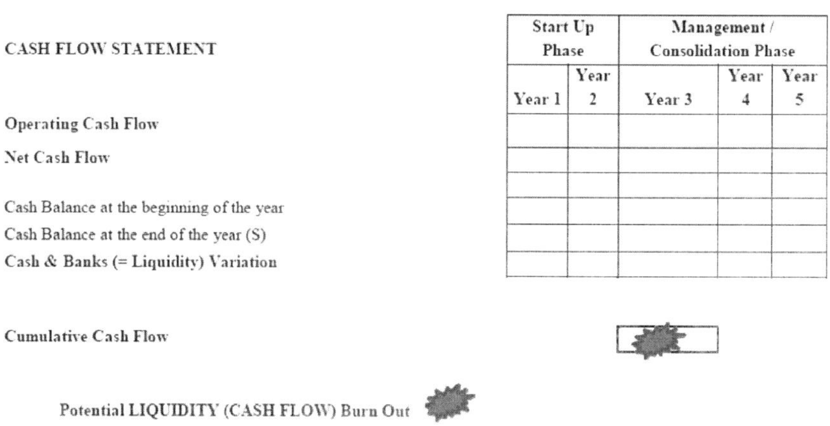

The rich with the poor: living together, sharing opportunities

The beyond rich and the behind poor ultimately share a common fate that is transcendental and not comparative, even though the former and the latter are separated by an astonishingly different standard of life, in a world where obscene and amazing poverty contrasts with fabulous wealth. Wealth gravity, measuring the distance between prosperity and misery, is an ephemeral concept, while–like it or not–the sour smell of poverty is ubiquitous and lasting. In a selfish-conformist and distracted-world, the plight of the poor largely remains unaddressed and at the grass roots of society, life is simply different and surrounded by ignorant prejudice. In his encyclical letter Caritas in Veritate[5], § 35, Benedict XVI points out that »the poor are not to be considered a ›burden‹, but a resource«.

The poor, with their social profile, are different from those who live in the shadow of plenty because they are desperate and vulnerable, having too little to lose.

According to Abraham Maslow[6] and irrespectively of the level of affluence, physiological necessities (food, water, and sex) and safe shelter cohabit in order to secure self survival and, possibly, happiness. They also command a priority over love and belonging, esteem (comfort about one's accomplishments) and need for self-actualization, which occurs when individuals reach a state of harmony and understanding. This ranking, albeit being questionable, gives anyway a rough idea of what the rich and the poor need and desire, showing that money isn't everything and remembering that the subjugated poor, abandoned to the social control of misery, desire happiness as anybody else.

The rich often don't know the poor and meeting them is a real lab of life. The undeserving rich have to weigh their conscience, shaking their naked emotions and avoiding abandoning the weakest to their cruel and unfair destiny. Even the rich can learn from the poor – they may open up to a dimension they don't have, softening material juxtapositions.

When the home of a poor is burning, it's better to intervene as soon as possible – it may well happen to our own, since fire is highly contagious. Solidarity and reciprocity are key ingredients of a pluralist world, beyond the empty sadness of any status division. Mutual sharing of a common destiny is based upon taking responsible care of the weakest, beyond any dialectic confrontation, with an emphatic cultural anthropology of otherness – the Adriane's thread that brings out of the labyrinth of greed and selfishness.

---

5 See also: http://www.coc.org/system/files/Precis+of+the+Encyclical+Caritas+in+Veritate-Truth+in+Charity.pdf.

6 *The Developing Person through the Life Span*, (1983).

Human altruism, beyond Darwinian Mother Nature

Animals tend to behave as intrinsically selfish and reasonless creatures, imposing their own personal interests in the daily Darwinian struggle for survival, under the cruel rules of a heartless Mother Nature, fighting at the expense of other weaker species. Similarly to other animals, human beings, so harmful for other living entities, show innate egoistic behaviors, well symbolized by the attachment that children demonstrate towards objects – try to take a toy away from them, and they shall cry and struggle for getting it back. Sharing comes later, conditionally upon teaching of cultural values able to distinguish mankind condition from that of other more brutal animals.

Philosophers have observed this lack of altruism since ancient times, starting with the Athenian sophists, who in the 5th Century B.C. argued for ethical egoism, continuing with Socrates, who assumed that human benevolence towards others was only an appearance. In more recent times, Thomas Hobbes took it for granted that people are in constant strife with others, looking for their own conflicting interests, while the nihilist German philosopher Friedrich Nietzsche–not a … diplomatic guy–condemned charity and selfless altruism, saying, in 1888, that »the weak and ill-constituted shall perish: first principle of our philanthropy« and regarding benevolence as a »tyranny against nature«.

The biological path-breaking theories of Charles Darwin about the (selfish) evolution of species assert that only the strongest and the fittest may have a chance to survive in our cruel world, being able to adapt to a hostile and changing environment and these theories are more or less consistent with the philosophical cynical denegation of altruism.

Animals, looking after one's own, are intrinsically selfish and they don't hesitate to kill even their similar in their struggle for survival, as it happens with the praying mantis, a cannibal insect, or with young hippopotami that may kill elder mates looking for social predominance.

In this gloomy scenario, the weakest human beings, mostly represented by the poor, should have little or any chance of survival and–applying Darwinian selection theories–they should tend to disappear.

Actually, albeit coping with their unpleasant condition, most poor succeed to survive and multiply, showing amazing resilience to difficulties. Sometimes they also take benefit of the altruism of those who don't follow the cynical insight of the mainstream philosophers. These people are indeed among those who are good-hearted and sympathetic, spreading a culture of sharing and togetherness that is continuously fueled by transcendent religious beliefs, able to lift our conscience above immanent and selfish material worries. Secularization of the transcendent concept of poverty, more and more immanently considered as purely material and deprived living condition, reduces the poor to soulless entities, with a suboptimal output and consumption.

Altruism can help to restore hope, going beyond an anemic relationship with the poor, bypassing radical injustice and fostering adaptability and remembering that there is more joy in giving than in receiving. Nobody is so rich to have nothing to receive and nobody is so poor to have nothing to give. Mutuality and gratuity are the true glue of social capital.

Microfinance, a partial solution to (some) poverty traps

After the pioneer experiment of Grameen Bank almost 30 years ago, microfinance has entered the adult age and thousands of mostly small microfinance institutions (MFIs) are competing in a market where demand for financial services from the poorest is potentially unlimited, while supply isn't.

While the success of microfinance has gone beyond any expectation, enormous problems are still on the ground and the road towards what is now considered microfinance's optimal goal-maximization of outreach to the poorest, combined with financial self-sustainability of MFIs–is still full of obstacles.

Academic research is wide, both on theoretical and empirical grounds, and it is proving useful in a field where flexibility and financial innovation are highly needed, in order to overcome problems that make the poorest unbankable according to commercial banking standards.

However local experiences are showing a difficult universal application and what works in Bangladesh is not always successful in Bolivia or in Sub–Saharan Africa, even if international cross pollination plays a substantial role. Empirical evidence from hundreds of micro-cases is represented in models that often have just a local application: exactly the contrary of the fundamental rules of a scientific approach, from Galileo onwards! This is a disappointing but healthy lesson for those who believe that science alone is a solution to every problem, while the poorest need and deserve much more. So learning comes more from confusion and trial and error than from dogmatic certainties.

Even in microfinance, the last mile to the client seems the most difficult, requiring a flexible cultural and technical adaptation to local habits and needs.

From empirical evidence and academic research we might however draw precious indications for policy issues, such as for instance the determination of the optimal level of interest rates. While high rate charges, in order to cover high operating costs that derive from small unitary loans and weekly on field money collection, are an evident obstacle to borrowing, rate ceilings or endless subsidies are–perhaps surprisingly–an even worse remedy.

The life cycle growth of MFIs that are surviving Darwinian selection allows them to reach commercial banking status, being enabled to collect deposits and–in the best cases–to have links with international funders, mainly through Microfinance Investment Vehicles. For the few MFIs that until now have been

able to jump on the train of global financial markets, smart opportunities of lower funding costs and more sophisticated financial services are on hand.
The empirical evidence that microfinance has real impact in reducing poverty is less clear–cut than expected, disappointing those who place excessive expectations in this device – a mere instrument, behind which there is always a human being commanding a priority, especially if poor. Mixed results have however to consider that microfinance is probably unfit for the poorest, who are not ripe to front any financial experience, and it shows to be a complementary part of the poverty traps solution, rather than the only and lonely one.
Microfinance can help to reduce poverty, even if it is not a one-fits-all solution or a silver bullet for its complete eradication, even because not every poor is a potential entrepreneur waiting and wanting to be discovered and financed.
Further research and on field application is strongly needed in order to make substantial progress in meeting the basic needs of the destitute and underserved. Since the poorest are naturally humble, even scientists and practitioners addressing their problems should accordingly be.

* * *

I wish to thank my beloved daughter Elisa for Her help in writing some paragraphs of Chapters 8, 13, and 14, and my MBA students from all the continents for their insightful comments. The usual disclaimer applies. Comments and emails (to: roberto.morovisconti@morovisconti.it) from readers are welcome.
This book is dedicated to the poorest of the poor, to those who silently remain behind, suffering from financial exclusion and other often lethal poverty traps.

CHAPTER 1 – History matters: from asymmetric development to diverging cumulated growth

> How and why did we get where we are? How did the rich countries get so rich? Why are the poor countries so poor?
> I propose to approach these problems historically.
>
> David Landes, *The Wealth and Poverty of Nations*

Historical roots of (under)development

Any question about the various causes of development cannot refrain from asking why some countries are so developed while others aren't[7]. Historical roots and causes of development are a key starting point for all those who try to understand which are the ingredients that–combined together often in a casual and unpredictable way –start up the engine of growth.
The grandest question of all, following courses and ... curses of history, concerns the causes of the (so far) divergent destinies from primordial equalities–according to which the rich are often likely to get richer and the poor poorer–and relative prosperity levels of different national economies, comparing still developing with already affluent countries.
History represents the notebook of life and is full of surprises, which hardly follow a deterministic pattern, according to which every event has a prior cause. Historical processes are indeed not ineluctable and they do not inexorably proceed on their own, because they are influenced by contingent and unpredictable events and by human often irrational choices and behaviors. But even if history does not automatically replicate events, useful lessons can be taken from past happenings. Thanks to non deterministic trends, each country is entitled to overcome its historical original sins.
As George Santayana used to say, those who cannot remember the past are condemned to repeat it. Wondering if humans can learn from their mistakes, history collides with economics in describing development erratic patterns.
When social amnesia pushes a country to forget its past and characters–burning the value of historical memory–any reference point gets lost and falling into rel-

7 See Helpman (2004), p. 1, and http://www.theworldeconomy.org/.

ativism is an easy temptation: when there are no values to remember, every behavior is simply allowed.

Countries all around the world have experienced, especially in the last two centuries, a highly asymmetric growth pattern, which has brought them to increasingly diverging levels of development and to growing inequalities, representing the wealth gap able to destabilize nations. Such a pattern is mainly due to a different cumulated path of growth that albeit with alternative phases of ups and downs (economic booms and golden ages versus recessions and wars …), has contributed to shape each country's level of development. Long term cumulated growth is what really makes the difference and development is a long, painful, and always imperfect goal, difficult even to assess and define. Progressive catching up is a long term strategic trend.

Income per capita across countries showed little differences until the 19th Century, starting to widen with the Industrial Revolution[8]. It began by showing a polarization effect, according to which the rich are becoming even richer and the poor poorer, following diverging development patterns. Convergence[9] and catch up with richer countries is also possible and sometimes takes place, if properly driven by the lucky interaction of several growth factors. Is the great curve of history touching also the poor?

The overriding reason for lack of sustained growth was that in pre-modern world, production technology improved only slowly and capital was hardly used to replicate itself, preventing wealth from being generated and diffused. While the scientific achievements of the ancient Mediterranean civilizations and China were remarkable, in general there was little attempt to apply science to economic problems of the peasants, following a still missing Galilean scientific approach. Entrepreneurship and invention have long been hardly rewarding[10].

According to Maddison[11], over the past millennium, world population rose 22-fold. Per capita income increased 13-fold, world GDP nearly 300-fold. These figures contrast sharply with the preceding millennium, when world population grew by only a sixth, and there was no advance in per capita income.

The wealth … and poverty of nations

Understanding historical causes of development is a key point in order to get useful recipes for the promotion of worldwide growth, particularly in underdeveloped areas. Each analysis conducted without any historical perspective is condemned to be short sighted, severely biased, and often useless – if not misleading. Also the historical approach, if considered alone, is fatally limited.

---

8 Helpman (2004), p. 2.

9 For an analysis of convergence and divergence in growth, see Chapters 14, 15 and 16.

10 Azariadis, Stachurski, in Aghion, Durlauf (2005).

11 Maddison (2001).

So the best method seems based on an interdisciplinary multicultural combination of different approaches, linking history with geography, sociology, economics, and natural sciences and so on.
According to Stiglitz (2007), p. 57 »as globalization and new technology reduce the gap between parts of India and China and the advanced industrial countries, the gap between Africa and the rest of the world is actually increasing«.
In this synthetic survey of the historical reasons behind development and–conversely–underdevelopment, we shall mainly refer to a book by David Landes, ›*The Wealth and Poverty of Nations*‹. The title echoes Adam Smith, but Landes is interested in both the wealth *and poverty* of nations, examining the roots of relative–and absolute–economic failure or success. Capitalism is seen as the triumph of Western culture and the determinants of modern economic prosperity are found in geographical advantaged position–of Western Europe and also the U.S. –and in the key characteristics of the Western culture.
Economic historians have either paid a tribute[12] to Landes or confuted[13] his book[14] and ideas[15], which–like them or not–have anyway an unquestioned utility. They raise exceptionally important questions with unprecedented clearness and this fact stands out as a precious contribution on its own.

From nomadism to the dawn of agriculture

Civilization began roughly 10,000 years ago, coinciding with the ending of the glacial era and the beginning of the Neolithic revolution. At that time there was a progressive shift in human activity away from nomadic hunting, leaving the Stone Age and moving towards a primitive form of agricultural farming. At the dawn of agriculture, about 8,000 BC, population of the world was approximately 5 million[16] and till then hunters were keen enough to kill the megafauna–large mammals and birds–sparing forests and sea life.
In his original book ›*An Edible History of Humanity*‹, 2009, Tom Standage writes that »Domesticated plants and animals form the very foundations of the modern world«. Most of the important decisions about food were made thousands of years ago–in Standage's view–and most of our food is the result of »selective breeding« and »genetic engineering«.
The historical passage from nomadism to agriculture is particularly important in the analysis of the poverty traps, for many complementary reasons:

---

12 See Joel Mokyr, Eurocentricity Triumphant, in http://www.historycooperative.org/journals/ahr/104.4/ah001241.html.
13 See http://www.riseofthewest.net/thinkers/landes01.htm; http://www.rrojasdatabank.info/agfrank/landes.html.
14 See http://www.historycooperative.org/journals/ahr/104.4/ah001241.html.
15 See J. Mokyr, cit.
16 See www.census.gov/ipc/www/worldhis.html.

- nomadic populations, albeit not numerous, are still present in any continent, and they represent almost everywhere the weakest and poorest caste;
- capital accumulation, indispensable to foster growth and development, is nearly impossible for nomads, that by definition do not own land or homes and just have transportable belongings (mainly, horses and cattle and other nearly valueless items);
- instruction and healthcare are difficult and precarious for non sedentary pupils or–respectively–patients;
- financial inclusion–and microfinance–are hardly conceivable for nomads;
- conflict is a frequent companion of nomads, especially when they come into contact with sedentary populations, crossing their territory and depleting their resources;
- discrimination and prejudice often accompany wandering populations, everywhere seen as strangers, not assimilated with other sedentary clans and characterized by different cultures and languages.

In spite of all these difficulties, nomadism is still alive and its traditions resist the corruption of time, dating back to the very beginning of human history.

The European miracle

Landes explains with anecdotic cure the ›European Miracle‹, or why European societies, within their geohistorical boundaries, experienced a period of explosive growth when the rest of the world did not. By doing so, he revives–at least in part–several theories he believes have been unfairly discarded by academics over the last 40 years. Among them:

- the ›cultural thesis‹ or ›Protestant work ethic‹ of Max Weber[17]– according to it the rise of capitalism is essentially a cultural phenomenon rooted in religion. According to Landes, the protestant advantage »gave a big boost to literacy, spawned dissents, and heresies, and promoted the skepticism and refusal of authority that is at the heart of the scientific endeavor. The Catholic countries, instead of meeting the challenge, responded by closure and censure«. The Calvinists, believ-

17 Max Weber in his (nowadays somewhat surpassed) masterpiece of 1905, *The Protestant Ethic and the Spirit of Capitalism,* argues that Puritan ethics and ideas strongly influenced the development of capitalism.

ing in predestination, were induced to personally contribute to their own development;

- the ›climate thesis‹ – it posits that tropical climes are, *ceteris paribus*, poor candidates for development[18]. Hot climates are indeed enervating and they breed a wide variety of dispiriting and incapacitating diseases, underlining the slow, soft, and quiet rhythm of tropical life, where even history takes a rest. When not dominated by deserts, their weather patterns alternate between drought and torrential downpours that are inimical to farming and living. Almost all the advanced countries are in temperate zones and a large majority of underdeveloped countries are in the tropical zone, but geography does not explain all[19];

- ›comparative advantage‹ described by Adam Smith in 1776 in his ›*Wealth of Nations*‹–the ability to produce most efficiently, given all the other products that could be produced–can change over time, and also that developed countries, typically developed in an environment of protectionism against foreign trade.

According to the climate thesis, Western Europe is located in a favorable temperate zone, with equable supply of water and it takes also benefit, in its Western part, of the warm current called Gulf Stream.

Hardwood forests prevented Europe to develop at the golden age of Egypt and Sumer, with a delay of thousands of years, and only iron cutting tools, allowed to clear the fertile land north of the Alps in the first millennium B.C. No surprise that people, before getting able of trespassing forests, preferred lacustrine, and seaside settlements.

The pertinent geographic difference between Europe and other temperate regions was the fragmented nature of European topography. Overland transportation and communications were simply too difficult. It proved impossible, after the fall of the Roman Empire, for any nation or autocrat to conquer all of Europe. However, they kept trying. The obvious downside was 1,500 years of interminable and bloody conflict[20].

Due to his relatively favorable environment, Europe commanded a strategic advantage, if compared with other places, especially central Asia and Middle East, with which there was the longest and most ancient confrontation. America was indeed completely unknown before Columbus and Africa, apart from Egypt and its Mediterranean cost, was a mystery: some two hundred years ago the German

---

18 This theory is consistent with the ›10/40 window‹ theory, according to which regions of the Eastern hemisphere located between 10 and 40 degrees north of the equator, have the highest level of socioeconomic challenges. See http://www.ad2000.org/1040broc.htm.

19 Harrison, Huntington (2000), p. xxix.

20 http://www.futurecasts.com/Landes,%20Wealth%20&%20Poverty%20of%20Nations.html

philosopher Hegel used to say that Africa was a continent all nature and without a history[21]. A milder climate and more fertile lands meant also fitter animals, to be used as livestock or for transportation or in battles – European horses were simply bigger and stronger than others.

Nevertheless Europe's differences were not confined to geography or agriculture and the very reasons of its success were due to a lucky ›cocktail‹ of many ingredients, including also private property and a sense of justice. Such a ›cocktail‹ derives from enlightened Christian principles (combining justice with freedom and love) and Greek and Roman philosophical background (with the path breaking works of Aristotle and Plato), which helped them to distinguish between what was proper and what was improper. Free press, at least in some of the European countries, helped to transmit these ideas, somewhat revolutionary in the Middle Age till the Illuminist golden age in the 18th Century, and hardly present in other continents – not a trivial particular. As it will be shown[22], there is a strong causal link between freedom in its varieties (of thinking; social, economic …), and economic development.

In the relatively tiny Western Europe, people were allowed to travel and choose among the variety of political powers that were locally diffused in extremely fragmented areas–if we only think about what were at those times territories that we now identify with Germany or Italy or Switzerland–each with its different ruling lord or king. Commercial interests became important players in political power struggles. Kings continuously needed money for themselves and their expensive wars and they brought with them need for freedom and compromises between ruling and ruled parties. Each of them needed support from the other, this being a precious laboratory for future democracy, especially after the ›earthquake‹ of the French revolution, a serious matter not locally confined as usual.

Since the Middle Age there was in Europe an embryonic competition between political systems. Its fragmentation also allowed competing religious attitudes to carve out places for themselves, with similar beneficial results. »Europe was spared the thought control that proved a curse in Islam«, Landes asserts.

At each moment, there were political and religious leaders in much of Europe who tried to control events and throttle dissent or innovation. A sad example was that of Inquisition, particularly strong in Italy and Spain.

China, a glorious and (once) sleeping giant

The world was not only Europe: there was a highly civilized country in Eastern Asia, where the Venetian explorer Marco Polo eventually arrived, reaching

---

21 See Hegel J.F., *The Philosophy of History*, http://www.philosophicalmisadventures.com/?p=18.

22 Mainly in Chapter 13.

China through the Silk road in the 13th Century. Even at those times coastal China was–like and even more than Western Europe–a lucky, fertile, and prosperous place, where people lived overcrowded since ancient times, letting the place become the most precocious and the most successful developer of all.
Chinese civilization had a clear half–millennium as the world's leader in technological innovation from 500 to 1000 A.D. Yet somehow China's technological lead–impressive in printing and the handling of gunpowder in the 13th Century, in shipbuilding in the 15th Century, in porcelain–making in the 17th Century–turned into a significant technological deficit in those same centuries that China's pre-industrial population quadrupled[23].
In the symbolic year 1000 A.D., Europe was a barbaric backward continent, well behind the civilizations of China, India, and the Islamic world.
However, invention and commerce were limited by the absence of freedom[24]. As Landes points out, in China and India, there was »an absence of incentive to learning and self improvement«.
In the Islamic world, there was religious opposition to anything new. In China there was lack of competitive pressures on the autocratic rulers. The peasant belonged to the emperor – a form of possession so far from the Christian belief in Europe, according to which men only belong to God. A citizen had only very limited rights in land or personal property, and no incentive to improve the land or productive tools – this being the real and unavoidable stimulus behind economic development.
Being China usually a single, unified, great empire, there was no exit for those who felt stifled in their economic ambitions. Also India suffered from religious taboos, autocratic governments, and lack of rights in land or personal property. Any wealth could be expropriated. As Landes says: »In short no one was trying. Why try?«.
Early in the 15th Century, China launched grand fleets, which circumnavigated the Indian Ocean all the way to East Africa, decades before the coming of the Portuguese. But although they did conduct trade, the emperor felt little economic incentive – backward mentality was present even in China.

The colonial adventure

On the contrary, European expansion was profit-driven, and thrived. By the 15th Century, Europe had the upper hand in economic power and weaponry. With the cruel attitudes of those times, Europeans drove forward towards empire-building, with disastrous results for native peoples in the backward regions of Africa and the Americas.

---

23 See http://econ161.berkeley.edu/Econ_Articles/Reviews/landes.html#anchor2077092.
24 See http://www.futurecasts.com/Landes,%20Wealth%20&%20Poverty%20of%20Nations.html.

Ruthless Europeans conquered empires because those empires were despotic and oppressive in nature, with no real interest or loyalty extending from the subjects to their rulers. Their strength might have been hard, but it was always brittle. Repeatedly, the populace ingenuously welcomed the strangers who came to overthrow the indigenous tyrants, just in order to replace them – from worse to worst.

In synthesis, Landes's account of why Eurasian[25] civilizations like Europe, Islam, and China had an edge in technological development over non-Eurasian (and southern Eurasian) civilizations, rests heavily on climate. It is impossible for human beings to live in any numbers in ›temperate‹ climates before the invention of fire, housing, tanning, and sewing (and in the case of northern Europe iron tools to cut down trees), but that once the technological capability to live where it snows has been gained, the ›temperate‹ climates allowed a higher material standard of living.

A similar thesis comes from John Maynard Keynes[26]. According to the great English economist, the combination of unprecedented accumulation of capital, self fulfilling with compound interests and technical inventions, produced a remarkable raise in the standard of life, in spite of the dilution induced by population growth, overcoming apocalyptic Malthusian worries.

Euro centrism and the development gap

Discussing on asymmetric development, Landes[27] raises the question if »the gap between rich and poor is still growing today«. The answer is particularly important: »At the extremes, clearly yes. Some countries are not only *not* gaining; they are growing poorer, relatively and sometimes absolutely. Others are barely holding their own. Others are catching up«[28].

Europe's cultural development was also characterized by the beginning of individuality, bringing to individual economic freedom and entrepreneurship – something that in many other cultures is nowadays still missing. This phenomenon stands at the very root of capitalism. Labor, goods, and capital are traded in ›free‹ markets, whereas profits are distributed to private owners of capital or invested in new technologies and industries and wages are paid to labor.

---

25 Diamond (1997) attempts to explain why Eurasian civilizations, as a whole, have survived and conquered others.

26 *Economic Possibilities for our Grandchildren*, (1930), integrally reproduced in http://www.eco.utexas.edu/facstaff/Cleaver/368keynesgrandchildren.html.

27 Introduction, p. xx.

28 Introduction, p. xxi.

From the geographical to the cultural approach

A fascinating but controversial thesis of Landes concerns nature's inequalities and–in broader terms–the so called ›geographical approach‹[29]. It regards climate matters and in general the discomfort of heat exceeds that of cold. In order not to sweat excessively, keep still and don't work when it's too hot. *Siesta* is a wise social adaptation and in British India, the saying had it, only mad dogs and Englishmen went out in the noonday sun. The natives knew better.

Year-round heat encourages the proliferation of life forms hostile to man: insects such as the tsetse flies or malaria's mosquitoes, parasites …, harvested in warm and stagnant water, wild reptiles, spiders, and mammals and so on. Malaria still is a big worldwide killer. Tropical medicine has billions of potential patients, often trapped in technically backward societies. Unpredictable and irregular rains pose the problem of water, often abundant but hardly manageable. Drought is less forgiving in tropical areas and semitropical deserts that are continuously expanding. Catastrophes are much more frequent in tropical areas, especially with climatic changes, and–as Landes notes–life in poor climes is precarious, depressed, and brutish.

Yet it would be a mistake to see geography as destiny and this appears a wise suggestion for many poor, especially Africans, often still depressed by their tortured history and naturally inclined to fatalism and passive acceptance of their often cruel fate. Science and technology are the key: the more we know, the more can be done to prevent disease and provide better living and working conditions.

Nowadays, within an increasing global and speedy changing world, it's again history that teaches us–day after day, with growing momentum–that Euro centrism, justified or not in the past, is eventually fading and that a new mental and cultural approach is urgently needed.

Looking at historical examples, the Indian Nobel prize economist Amartya Sen (1999) argues that »Western traditions are not the only ones that prepare us for a freedom-based approach to social understanding« and that diversity and pluralism are the norm, not the exception.

These cultural approaches and states of mind, silently forging the mentalities of so many people, are often misunderstood or underestimated and they represent a much more powerful and subtler threat that what we may superficially guess. Culturally rooted ideals drive actions and behaviors and they contribute to make history, together with destiny and doom. Landes demonstrates that cultural characteristics of a society's history are the key to explaining success, particularly economic success.

---

29 For an opposing viewpoint that emphasizes geography rather than culture as the main cause for differences of prosperity among peoples, see Diamond (1997).

Even for what concerns (under)development, the cultural approach has a crucial and predominant importance in the understanding of its deeper causes. This belief has strong practical implications, since cultural changes–differently from technical upgrades, typically much quicker to absorb–are extremely slow, painful and uncertain. It takes generations to change some deeply rooted and psychologically hidden ›ancestral‹ habits and that's may be why development in many backward areas is so slow and disappointing.

Industrializing inventions

Introducing the topic of the Industrial Revolution–important even for our issue, in order to detect from history what has ignited development, hoping to find some useful pattern for the future–Landes explains why the Industrial Revolution took place in England and not elsewhere.

The reasons are manifold and, as it always happens, they have somewhat casually interacted. Causes of this extraordinary and unprecedented development–after millenniums of relative stagnation where human conditions have shown little improvements–range from the *Magna Charta* of 1215 (the first shy attempt to give political and civil freedoms at least to the nobles, which is considered the primordial root of democracy and the parliamentary system), to the Protestant Ethic, later celebrated by Max Weber.

The European love of mechanical mechanism, linked with what Landes insightfully calls ›the invention of invention‹, recalls innovations such as the water wheel, eyeglasses (useful with printed books, diffused after the invention of paper and printing in China, for mechanical precision working and many other things), the mechanical clock, gunpowder (again, a Chinese invention)[30].

The replication of Galileo's path breaking scientific method has had enormous and unprecedented effects in reshaping the world we are living in, thanks to the search for the universal application of the method, refined by Isaac Newton and other scientists, to serial industrial production.

Europe's industrial revolution is the heart of the story of how some–largely Western Europe and northwest Europe's settler ex-colonies have grown rich, following the principle of self determination. Relative poverty elsewhere is the result of failure on the part of political, religious, and mercantile elites.

Even geography–unsurprisingly, considering Landes' elective affinities–played its part and the very fact that England is surrounded by the sea and naturally positioned towards the new world (like Spain, Portugal and Holland, the other biggest colonial powers), is another cause of comparative advantage.

---

[30] Francis Bacon was writing around 1600 of how three inventions - the compass, gunpowder, and the printing press - had totally transformed everything, and that all three of these came to Europe from China.

Even the path breaking industrial revolution did not however occur magically or for free. It was a long, tiring and painful process of stops-and-go, alternating successes and failures, with a profound and unprecedented social impact on the population. It was indeed not a joke to transform so many peasants into workmen, moving them and their fragmented patriarchal families from the countryside to polluted and noisy factories, as millions of Chinese are hardly experimenting nowadays.

In Chapter 2, we shall examine the sad fate of so many landlocked underdeveloped countries, far from the sea, and surrounded by bad neighbors, and this might let us better understand while England was and still is, from that aspect, so lucky and privileged. The very fact that underdeveloped countries got in contact with these discoveries so late–often after some centuries–is a powerful cause of their much slower growth pace together with their technological backwardness, again to be seen also as a deeply rooted cultural aspect,.

According to Landes's narrative, other keys of success have shown to be: openness (willingness to borrow whatever is useful from abroad), politics, with a government strong enough to properly manage the affairs of its citizens and, in particular at that time, the rising bourgeoisie, being concerned for the well-being of a new business class with a strong and conscious interest in rapid economic growth.

Among the different additional lessons that emerge from Landes's story of the wealth and poverty of nations:

- try to make sure that your government enables innovation and production, rather than maintaining power by massive redistributions of wealth from its enemies to its friends;
- recognize that the task of a less-productive economy is to imitate rather than innovate, for there will be ample time for innovation after catching-up to the production standards of the industrial core. Japan has shown to be a master example in imitation and improvement;
- recognize that things change and that we need to adjust accordingly, so that the mere fact that a set of practices has been successful or comfortable in the past is not an argument for its maintenance into the future – history is normally not self repeating;
- there is no reason to think that what is in the interest of today's elite–whether political, religious, or economic–is in the public interest, or even in the interest of the elite's grandchildren.

Looking for a new global common wealth: from war games to post colonial heritage

The Commonwealth of Nations is an old and a bit nostalgic voluntary association of former British colonies with the once motherland and now dethroned U.K. They cooperate within a framework of common values and goals, including the promotion of democracy, human rights, good governance, the rule of law, individual liberty, and egalitarianism, free trade, multilateralism, and world peace.

Almost everywhere, as time fades away, colonial ties are evaporating, as well as their historical legacy.

History can give some useful lessons about phasing out from the colonial experience.

The question whether colonizers played a decisive role in the development of their overseas colonies, far beyond the historical limits of the colonial experience, is hotly debated. While some researchers find differences between the British and the Spanish (or Portuguese, French, Belgian, Dutch, German, Italian …) colonies[31], others[32] claim that factor endowments were much more important than colonizers. The last explanation seems more intuitive, if only we think that both the U.S. and Sudan were under the British rule, with so remarkable differences in terms of development.

The different degree of presence of colonizers was unsurprisingly influenced by local conditions and extractable rents (in order to maximize the proceeds minimizing the effort – some call it productivity … others cynicism): the harder the place, the lower the colonizers' presence. Hardly anybody was willing to live in Central Africa when tropical illnesses were unknown and hardly curable, whereas people were queuing up to go to the U.S. or other countries of the New World.

The intoxicant blowing wind of independence

Reversing history, the impact of decolonization on poverty has proved to be mixed–being the changing of the guard an engaging but tempting laboratory of freedom and democracy for new nations–with successes alternated by failures and hopes balanced by dismay. Independence and self-determination, albeit accompanied by a modest sense of guilt from ex colonizers, have given to many a deep sense of dignity, self-respect and hope for a better future, even if most colonies were ill prepared for starting ruling themselves from scratch.

31 See Helpman (2004), p. 122.

32 See Acemoglu, Johnson, Robinson (2002).

The impact of colonization on the territories where it took place has on average been profound and long lasting and it's difficult to say if it was good or bad, since both aspects are true and false at the same time and cohabit, together with many other contradictions of history. Colonization has often destroyed, or kept frozen, ancient kingdoms, and tribal groups, while with decolonization old interethnic ties suddenly come up again, contributing to forge a new nation but also igniting new conflicts.

Despite its disturbing brutalities, colonial experience has also had positive aspects, with the introduction of new technologies, healthcare, education.

To the extent that a society's culture reflects its entire historical heritage[33] and self awareness shapes its identity, the influence of colonial ties–trespassing the Master–and–Slave logic–is still alive in most former colonies several decades after independence.

The passage of many decades since independence from Western colonizers–in Africa often more than fifty years[34] and elsewhere even more–has however removed most of victimization and defeatist excuses with which so many African corrupted and ruthless leaders have long tried to cover up their failures. Unluckily the victimization approach is still well rooted in the mentality of so many Africans–and in the propaganda of their leaders–and it has created an enduring psychological dependency, often being also an excuse for demoralization and underachievement. Victimization, resentment towards past colonizers and passive resignation are characteristics of many colonized countries, creating a fragile psychological background, unfriendly for self development. Resignation is common within the poor, unable to dream a better future and often blind towards chance to change.

Psychological attitudes are incorporated in historically rooted cultural values, contributing to shape the future. Forgiveness about the past and hope for a better future are much welcome.

Statehood in history

A particularly complex topic is concerned with the size and the borders that countries find themselves to have, often involuntarily or capriciously, as a result of many complex interacting historical reasons. Such a topic here is just recalled for its impact on many poverty traps, starting from geographical ›landlockedness‹[35] of countries with no direct access to the sea.

Even if it is impossible to ascertain which would be the ideal dimension of each single State, some brief considerations about their size may be worth to be at

[33] See Harrison, Huntington (2000), p. 86.

[34] http://africanhistory.about.com/library/timelines/blIndependenceTime.htm.

[35] See Chapter 2.

least synthetically mentioned, with the reasons that are behind its current borders and their geopolitical consequences.
Fragmentations and unifications of communities forming a State are so frequent and have such a profound impact on their citizens' life–as well as that of communicating people, starting from neighbors–that history is largely, albeit not univocally, dedicated to this intriguing topic.
Collier (2010), Chapter 8–concerned about the economic impact on poverty of State and nation building–gives us some smart clues, worth to be summarized. According to the renowned economist, the boundaries of modern States emerged as a result not due to ethnic primordial solidarity, but rather as »the solution to the central security issue of what size of territory was best suited to the creation of a monopoly over the means of violence«.
A Darwinian process of State selection, in a violent and often conflicting contest has accompanied humanity since its inception, at least after settling down after the primordial nomadic experiences. When countries split, as it is happening in 2011 in Sudan, after the referendum for independence of the south division of assets, reallocation of people and new geopolitical equilibrium stand out as hot and uneasy issues.
Most underdeveloped countries–listening to the insightful Collier's provocation–are simply too small to be autonomous States, since they are not large enough to ensure a minimum set of public goods, starting from an essential internal security. Is there a minimum optimal size?
Excessive fragmentation–forgetting unity in diversity–brings to inefficiencies, lack of coordination, and missing economies of scale, if only we think about transports, basic functions such as justice, public healthcare, and instruction and institutions and their facilities, whose minimum fixed costs are hardly bearable and inefficiently spread within tiny communities. Being too little to survive is a challenge and a problem, often more serious that being too large to be manageable.
Fragmentation is a typical feature of micro-nations, whose boundaries tend to be identified with those of the prevailing ethnic group, in the attempt to shape and rule homogeneous communities. But micro-nations are often coalesced, forming multifaceted bigger countries, such as Tanzania, composed of over 120 micro-nations[36], in a Babel of different languages and habits.
Forced cohabitation and turmoil bring to diverging geostrategic ambitions, incarnated by divorcing nations, unwilling to share their existence and a common identity »when life together becomes hell«, as Riccardi (2008) p. 22, recalls. Coalesced groups of people tend to form nations, whereas random collection of heterogeneous ethnic groups, regardless and disrespectfully of shared cultural identities bring to artificial States where nobody really feels at home.

---

[36] Maathai (2009), p. 216.

Re-fixing State borders is a long and complex task, that typically requires unwelcome fighting shocks and so mitigation strategies preferably have to address themselves elsewhere, looking for lighter but more feasible and less invasive solutions, in order to preserve national sovereignty, whose symbolic value often goes well beyond its intrinsic emptiness.
Regional cooperation, up to federation, shows that pooling and renouncing to a bit of sovereignty has clear advantages, allowing to share costs–dividing some defense expenses, coordinating trade policies, transports, migration, harmonizing markets, sharing technologies and expertise–and to increase efficiency and productivity, with potentially valuable reciprocal advantages.
Cooperation is however difficult to conceive, put in place, manage, and monitor, especially if its candidates are weak or Stateless countries, suspicious about the real covered intentions of bordering politicians, whose only common denominator is often confined to unreliability, being divided by their struggle for power but united in their similar lies.
With multilateral cooperation, acknowledging that nations can achieve more by working together, governments are also forced to restrain the power that they want to preserve so jealously, pooling a part of their sovereignty. This is a difficult thing to ask to ruthless dictators, who are too selfish to care about a superior common good and obsessed by a predatory and possessive ruling attitude. Only well established democracies might–still painfully–try to make it.

Why nations fail? An institutional explanation

Institutions are a backbone of human societies, gathering individuals and governing their targets with cooperative rules, often with formal organizations. While the institutional poverty trap will be better described in chapter 5, some historical anticipation is here summarized, being inspired by the seminal book of Acemoglu & Robinson (2012) about the origins of power, prosperity, and poverty.
The question addressed by the two authors, following Adam Smith's wealth of nations debate, is fully consistent with the contents of this chapter: why are some nations rich and others poor, divided by wealth and poverty, health and sickness, food and famine? Is it culture (see chapter 9), the weather (chapter 8), geography (chapter 2), migration (chapter 12) or other complementary poverty traps described in the first part of this book? Simply, no, since according to Acemoglu, Robinson, none of these factors is either definitive or destiny: it is man-made political and economic institutions that underlie economic success (or the lack of it). Differences in institutions, from political governance to the inclusiveness of the political and economic system, explain the huge differences in economics success across nations and over time.

As Boldrin, Levine and Modica synthetize[37], the authors theorize that political institutions can be divided into two kinds-"extractive" institutions in which a "small" group of individuals do their best to exploit–in the sense of Marx–the rest of the population, and "inclusive" institutions in which "many" people are included in the process of governing hence the exploitation process is either attenuated or absent. They argue that for any economic success political institutions must be sufficiently centralized to provide basic public services including justice, the enforcement of contracts, and education. Given that these functions are carried out, inclusive institutions enable innovative energies to emerge and lead to continuing growth as exemplified by the Industrial Revolution. Extractive institutions can also deliver growth but only when the economy is distant from the technological frontier. These extractive institutions will ultimately fail, however, when innovations and "creative destruction" are needed to push the frontier. Hence, while success may be possible for a while under extractive institutions continuing success is possible only under inclusive institutions.
Accordingly, Ferguson (2013) shows that the great Western degeneration is due to a deep institutional crisis, with a dwindling role played by associations (trade unions, guilds, and charitable and public interest groups) compared with that of the state, within a Darwinian environment which continuously affects and reshapes institutions. Breathtaking technological discoveries create less jobs than infrastructural investments such as railroads, highways, and bridges or heavy industries such as steel or automotive.

Making poverty a history … is better than telling the history of poverty

The topic we are examining, concerning the historical roots of underdevelopment, would certainly deserve further analysis, considering also the complex problem of poverty throughout history, with its black holes of untold tales and hidden memories of the past. Dealing with such a topic would bring the reader too far, but some preliminary considerations deserve anyway some attention.
Poverty is so deeply rooted and widespread in human history that a history of it would in most cases coincide with history itself. There are many poor today, more than one billion, according to some metrics, but there were proportionally many more in the past and almost everybody, with few exceptions, was poor, especially before the Industrial Revolution and its slow-developing but increasingly consistent effects on wealth. The eclipse of poverty is still long awaited.

---

37 A Review of Acemoglu and Robinson's *Why Nations Fail, http://levine.sscnet.ucla.edu/general/aandrreview.pdf*

The endless history of poverty is actually a painful collective biography of humanity, since its inception and–pessimistically–forever, in spite of the long waited sunset of indigence.
Instead of telling the history of poverty, it seems much wiser to contribute to make poverty a history, trying to relegate this atavistic problem to a painful remembrance of the past.
According to an optimist Muhammad Yunus »One day our grandchildren will go to museums to see what poverty was like«.

The condensed Chapter

Historical roots of (under)development are a key starting point in order to analyze causes of poverty of nations and their different level of development. History matters, even if it doesn't follow a predictable deterministic pattern, based on a static projection of current trends over time.
Cumulated growth over a long time span, fueled by path breaking inventions and out bursting productivity, is what really matters for development, explaining why some countries perform better than others and whether those who lag behind may eventually catch up.

Out of Poverty Tips

Unephemeral (historically cumulated) growth, combined with wealth centripetal convergence–i.e. decrease of social inequalities – is what mostly matters for structural poverty reduction, combining benign development with its fair distribution.

Selected Readings

LANDES D.S., (1998), *The Wealth and Poverty of Nations: Why Some Are So Rich and Some So Poor*, Norton & Company, New York.

FERGUSON N., (2011), *Civilization: The West and the Rest*, Penguin, London.

VAN DOREN C., (1991), *A History of Knowledge,* Ballantine books, New York.

CHAPTER 2 – Geography matters: the misfortune of landlocked countries

> Landlocked developing countries continue to face steep challenges due to their geographical handicap and face serious constraints in their efforts to achieve the goals of poverty reduction and elevating living standards of their population.
>
> Anwarul K. Chowdhury[38]

Sea less countries with unnatural borders

Landlocked countries are enclosed or nearly enclosed by land and they don't have a direct access to the sea. As of 2010, there are 44 landlocked countries in the world. Only North America does not have any landlocked country among the major landmasses that have more than one country, while Africa includes a total of 15 landlocked countries, Asia includes 12 of them, Europe 15, and South America 2[39].

Approximately one–fifth of the world's countries is landlocked and has no direct access to an ocean or ocean–accessible sea (such as the Mediterranean Sea) with the result of being in the disadvantageous situation of needing to rely upon neighboring countries for access to seaports. For example, Ethiopia relies on Eritrea for access to the Red Sea, and recent conflicts have made that access difficult[40] – as a matter of fact, conflicts tend to exacerbate problems concerned with being landlocked, making isolation even harder.

Since the very fact of being landlocked is in most cases an evident handicap, it seems unwise to be in such a situation. Even if some regions are also particularly far from the sea–think about Central Asian countries–others are sufficiently close and they wouldn't be landlocked, if only they could be part of a larger and geographically sounder State. But borders are hardly fixed following these wise

38 United Nations Under-Secretary General and High Representative for the Least Developed Countries, Landlocked Developing Countries and Small Island Developing States at the United Nations in July 2006; http://mediaglobal.org/article/2006-07-25/landlocked-developing-countries-a-new-book-raises-issues-and-concerns.

39 For a full list of landlocked countries, see http://www.nationsonline.org/oneworld/developing_countries.htm; http://www.wisegeek.com/what-countries-are-landlocked.htm.

40 http://geography.about.com/od/politicalgeography/a/landlocked.htm.

strategies and history, with its capricious complicacies, often predominates above geography, synthesizing along its course the human problems and their often irrational solutions.

Countries are often originated by divide and rule old fashioned strategies, following the Latin motto ›*divide et impera*‹. The consequence is a drawing up of eccentric and arbitrary porous political boundaries, which often don't have any geographical or ethnic sense, lacking any homogeneity of culture or tribal coherence. This is particularly the case for countries coming out of Western colonization (in Africa, the Middle East, with the rough division of territories, irrespective of any historical or geographical criterion ...) or Soviet imperialism (in Central Asia), with a recent history that is too weak to be able to enforce their legitimate aspirations of a more properly shaped territory.

Figure 2.1. is not updated with the split of Sudan; its Southern part reached independence in 2011, becoming landlocked and increasing its troubled relationship with North Sudan, whose principal access to the sea is still represented by Port Sudan, in the Read Sea. Independence of South Sudan, a young and fragile State still shaken by violence and a slippery civil war (even as recently as December, 2013), dating back to more than 60 years, is also threatened by the presence of oil, especially close to the borders with North Sudan, which are hardly surprisingly disputed.

Figure 2.1. – Landlocked nations[41]

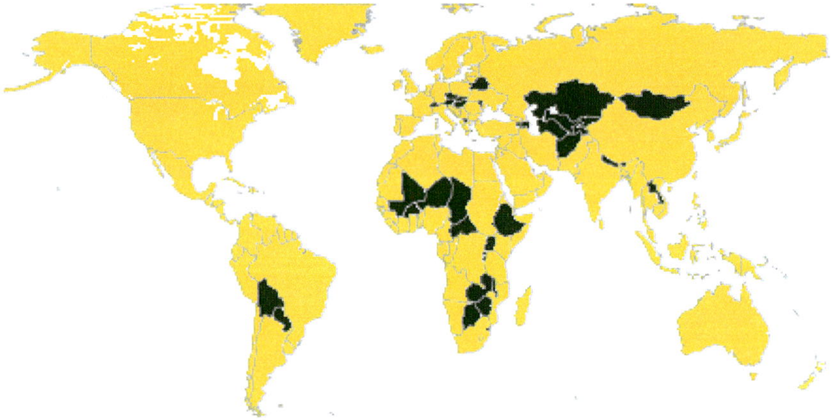

[41] These graphs are created by the author freely using http://www.29travels.com/travelmap/index.php.

Figure 2.2. – Heavily Indebted Poor Countries[42]

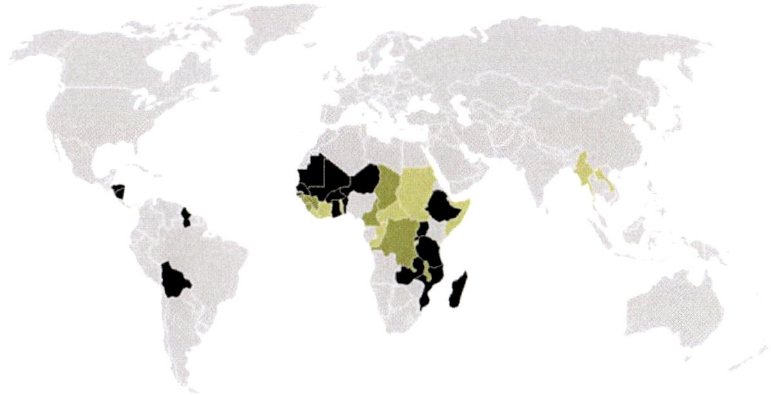

This point adds fuel to burning vindications, which procure unhappiness and unrest, scaling up to a destabilizing rebellion which can be among the primary causes of prolonged civil wars[43]. Emigration and Diaspora become also more likely in such an environment, where patriotism is hardly felt and poverty unsurprisingly finds a proper habitat where to develop.

If landlocked countries can be objectively identified, poor countries can be selected according to many different criteria. A map of the heavily indebted poor countries, this being one of the many possible classification criteria, allows us to catch at a glance, with a simple comparison, the extraordinary overlap between countries that are simultaneously landlocked and poor (over indebted).

Burdening geography

Connectivity to global markets and vital centers may be puzzled by unlucky geographic positioning, especially if huge landmasses are far from the sea and suffer from poor linking infrastructure.

Even historically, being landlocked was regarded as a disadvantageous position. It cuts the country off from sea resources such as fishing, and–more importantly–it cuts off access to seaborn trade which, even today, makes up a large percentage of international trade. Coastal regions have always tended to be wealthier and more heavily populated than inland ones. Losing access to the sea is generally a great blow to a nation, politically, militarily, and particularly with

---

42 web.worldbank.org/WBSITE/EXTERNAL/TOPICS/EXTDEBTDEPT/0,,content MDK:20260049~menuPK:528655~pagePK: - Color Key:
Black: Countries which currently qualify for full HIPC relief.
Olive: Countries which currently qualify for partial HIPC relief.
Beige: Countries which are eligible for HIPC relief but have not yet met the necessary conditions.

43 See Chapter 5.

respect to international trade and therefore economic security. Landlocked countries are hardly a preferred venue for foreign investments, unless they show up with some peculiar competitive advantage (as Switzerland or Luxembourg for financial services).

Considerations about landlocked countries can be extended even to their hosting continents. Even if all continents are surrounded by the sea, some are less lucky than others. Both Central Africa and Central Asia are far from the sea, having the highest concentration of landlocked countries, considering also their distance from the sea and the relative shortage of navigable rivers.

In particular, according to Calderisi (2006), p. 29 »Africa has an unfortunate shape. It is the second largest continent after Asia (11.7 million square miles) and five times the size of Europe, but its coastline is barely a quarter as long. South of the Sahara there are few natural harbors and rivers navigable from the sea«.

Aspirations to some greater unity can greatly contribute to solve the problem of being landlocked, together with a federation of States, which is often prodromal to uneasy unification[44] and supported by better infrastructures.

Since artificially set borders are porous and poorly controlled, a natural result is unchecked migration. In addition, cross border externalities matter, while other positive externalities deriving from the access to the sea may be missing, especially in small and remote landlocked countries.

Poor mountains

The classification of landlocked countries shouldn't be too dogmatic, since the perverse effects of such a trap do not fully depend on the mere geographical evidence that the country has or has not a direct access to the sea. Other ancillary particulars matter, such as the infrastructural framework or the degree of friendship with neighboring countries. Among them there is a further geographical aspect, that is the fact that isolation seems (and in fact it is) deeper in the mountains.

Mountains, especially in Asia or in Africa, are often far from the sea (even if it is not always the case, as it happens with the Andes cordillera in South America, almost parallel to the Pacific ocean) and they suffer from ›landlockedness‹ typically much more than flat regions, The causes can be found in transports which are made difficult by nature, infrastructures such as road connecting or energy transmission, which are expensive to build and keep and isolation, which is an often evident geophysical handicap.

Even cultivation is more difficult if compared to flat areas, since at high latitudes Mother Nature changes and both flora and fauna rarefy–and breathing be-

[44] See Chapter 1.

comes more difficult–whereas economies of scale made possible by extensive cultivation are hampered by the characteristics of a sloping ground. Again, once the harvest is collected, it is difficult and expensive to transport.
Mountaineers are typically poorer than those who live in flat areas and they tend to be more introverts, like the nature surrounding them, even if they can benefit from a fresher climate, more abundant water, and a marvelous panorama. Mountainous areas are typically much less populated and it is not always good news, since schools and hospitals, wherever existent, are more far away and travel to reach them is more arduous and sometimes even impossible. Illiteracy, isolation, and related side effects on poverty are simply more common in the mountains than elsewhere.
As Collier (2010), p. 136, points out, mountains matter in war games and grieving mountaineers are more likely than others to storm down to flatter areas to redress their discontent. Mountains are also an excellent place to hide rebels (Al Qaeda terrorists are for instance mostly hidden in the impenetrable mountains between Pakistan and Afghanistan) and to train them, with a mutual sharing of limited resources.
Used to cope with adversities, rocky mountaineers are also typically hard minded and strong tempered. When fighting, they may command a physical or psychological superiority over soldiers living in more relaxed and richer flat areas, because anger and desperation are a basic component of stamina and aggressiveness. They also know their impervious territory better than anybody else, like those who live in thick forests, and in this way they have a competitive advantage at home against intruders, even if now modern technologies, such as satellites, soften these information asymmetries.
But poorer mountains also play a strategic and fundamental role in preserving our delicate ecosystem, since most of water and rain come from there, and if the sources are already polluted since their inception, then problems flow down everywhere. As a matter of fact, mountain ecosystems are continuously ravaged by irresponsible deforestation–easing soil erosion–and its consequential illegal logging, together with improper cultivations. So, considering also our self interest and going beyond a mere solidarity approach, it seems anyway rewarding to keep mountains clean and alive, without forgetting their poor inhabitants. Positive externalities–spillovers of an impact on a party not directly involved–derive also from the role of mountains in proving a natural defense system and a natural border for surrounding territories, making however transport harder and so being a double edged sword.
Volcanic mountains may however represent a threat, even if erupted land is particularly fertile. But Mother Nature may be even more unfriendly, because if glaciers continue to melt down, water reservoirs are going to shrink, temporarily increasing the water supply from melt snow, but eventually drying up even

the mountains, with dramatic changes in their ecological equilibriums. The buffering effect of mountain snow, collected in winter time, and released during the spring, may be puzzled by changing temperatures, with still unknown but probably unfriendly side effects.
Mountains and uplands represent the majority of the Food and Agricultural Organization's (FAO) ›critical zones‹ – those areas of the world that are not able to grow enough food to feed their inhabitants adequately.

Landlocked development

United Nations term ›*Landlocked Developing Countries*‹ describes countries with serious constraints on the overall socio-economic development, due to lack of territorial access to the sea and therefore remoteness and isolation from world markets, which cause high transit and transportation costs. These countries are among the poorest and sixteen of the thirty landlocked developing countries in the world are classified as being least developed[45].
The least developed countries are a group of countries that have been identified by the UN as ›least developed‹ in terms of their low gross national income, their weak human assets and their high degree of economic vulnerability[46].
The least developed countries that are also landlocked are the following:

- Africa (12): Burkina Faso; Burundi; Central African Republic; Chad; Ethiopia; Lesotho, Malawi, Mali, Niger, Rwanda, Uganda, Zambia[47];
- Asia (4): Afghanistan, Bhutan, Laos, Nepal.

45 http://www.nationsonline.org/oneworld/developing_countries.htm.

46 The term ›Least Developed Countries (LDCs)› describes the world's poorest countries with the following three criteria: Low-income criterion based on a three-year average estimate of the gross national income per capita (under $750 for inclusion, above $900 for graduation); Human resource weakness criterion involving a composite Human Assets Index based on indicators of: (a) nutrition; (b) health; (c) education; and (d) adult literacy; Economic vulnerability criterion based on indicators of the instability of agricultural production; the instability of exports of goods and services; the economic importance of non-traditional activities (share of manufacturing and modern services in GDP); merchandise export concentration; and the handicap of economic smallness. Source: http://www.nationsonline.org/oneworld/least_developed_countries.htm.

47 South Sudan, after the referendum for independence of January 2011, is soon due to become another land-locked country.

The graph is the following:

Figure 2.3. – Least developed landlocked countries

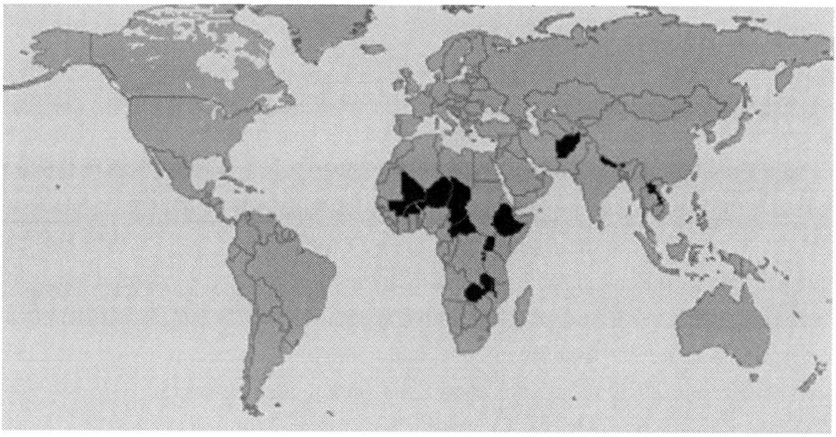

Sub-Saharan Africa is the unfortunate leader of this sad classification. Some poor countries are not geographically landlocked (e.g. Haiti, Cambodia or Democratic Republic of Congo …) and some few European landlocked countries are rich or very rich indeed: Switzerland, Austria, the double landlocked tiny Liechtenstein, Luxembourg.
Smart economists have deeply studied the phenomenon and Collier (2007), includes the problem within his four misery traps (the conflict trap[48], the natural resource trap[49], landlocked with bad neighbors, bad governance in a small country[50]). Being landlocked does not necessarily condemn a country either to poverty or to slow growth, but 38% of the bottom billion people live in landlocked countries, and this figure poses a real challenge to development.
Being landlocked doesn't have to be a disaster, as long as neighbors have decent infrastructure and they allow you to use their ports. Collier gives the example of Switzerland, which can trade through Italy, France or Germany. If neighbors are unfriendly, it becomes difficult to find a trading way out. Without dependable ways to export, landlocked countries such as those in central Asia or even more Africa are unable to participate in the global economy.
30% of Africa's population lives in landlocked countries. Colonial powers have a lot to answer about it, because they drew up the borders naively, completely forgetting historical, cultural, and ethnic background, or duplicitously following a cynical »divide and rule« strategy. »A reasonable case can be made that these places should never have become countries« says Collier. »However: the deed is done. These countries exist and they will continue to do so«. The best we can

48 See Chapter 5.
49 See Chapter 3.
50 See Chapter 5.

do is making sure that landlocked countries are prioritized in aid, also in the form of a moral compensation from exploiting powerful nations.

Lack of infrastructures

Lack of infrastructures to carry goods to the market (mostly needed when the sea is far and difficult to reach) is one of the biggest problems and it brings to several drawbacks, which are difficult to eradicate. Integration with global markets is problematic and in some cases extremely difficult (think for instance of hardly accessible rural areas of Chad), unless expensive air trade–needing often non existent airports and roads around them–is intensively used. Nature and geography, with or without physical barriers such as mountains, hills, rivers to cross, and a hostile or friendly climate, can make the task harder or simpler. The first case is obviously more common in poor landlocked countries.

Expensive transport costs can be justified mainly–and sometimes, only–in landlocked resource-rich countries, because natural resources are so valuable. Oilfields and mines are a powerful incentive to build roads and establish connections. Lack of transport infrastructures is an expensive and long lasting problem to solve. Each single State has to build its own roads, but the effort has to be twofold, since half a road towards the sea is almost useless. Getting appropriate funding for road building is a big problem in resource-scarce poor landlocked countries, hardly able to collect taxes domestically for infrastructural investments.

International organizations such as the World Bank can help, even if it is not easy to coordinate and sponsor multi-country projects. Road density and dimension and capillarity of the railway network are key parameters to consider when assessing such a problem. Rapid growth of cars and trucks on roads often unpaved–and hardly passable through during the rainy season–dramatically increases road accidents, because people are not used to drive safely and passers–by, often represented by bare feet children walking to school, are not accustomed to watching carefully before crossing the road. The social cost is high, even considering ancient habits according to which in many backward rural areas–for example in Sub-Saharan Africa–drivers who stop to rescue the wounded after a car accident seriously risk being lynched, irrespectively of their responsibilities.

Bicycles remain one of the most popular and cheap mean of transport, while motorbikes are the safest shelter against land mines, since those calibrated for the weight of a lorry don't explode and those targeted against men do but normally don't hit sufficiently speed motorbikes.

When war is over, road traffic normally explodes and hospitals get rid of wounded soldiers but get full of injured people, in a wild context where safety

rules are not a priority and ambulances typically offer a private service only to the few who can afford it.
Geography matters also in shaping development, not only within land-locked countries–with the uneven comparison between rich coastal areas versus laggard and backward internal ones–but also considering the profound disequilibria always existing between different regions. They are indeed characterized by a diverse socio-economic development, with strong and unbalancing inequalities that find it hard to cohabit and are likely to cause disrupting unrest, sooner or later due to come out. The tide of history washes out people and events, solving old problems while ineluctably presenting new ones.

Bad neighbors

All countries are influenced by their neighbors–for the good or for the bad–and by wars, territorial disputes, epidemics but also by economic growth. Problems easily cross the borders, often artificially designed, following a ›divide and rule‹ strategy (as it happens in many colonial countries) and changing, as history evolves. For instance, independence of Eritrea and Montenegro, brought about by successful separatist movements, has caused Ethiopia and Serbia respectively to become landlocked.
Being landlocked with bad neighbors, stuck in one or another growth trap, is a misfortune which hits in particular resource-scarce countries, whose appeal is typically weak, failing to attract foreign interest. Opportunities are few and they are difficult to take. Border clashes and proxy wars are frequent with bad neighbors, being the ›appetizer‹ of straightforward invasions, unless the answer to provocations is immediate and adequately tough.
Coastal countries are naturally open to sea trade and they can address themselves potentially everywhere, whereas landlocked countries are condemned to be linked to neighbors they were not enabled to choose.
When the sea is your neighbor, there are no roads to build or diplomatic relations to keep – You just need good sailors and ships.

Regional integration and other mitigation strategies

Collier (2007) gives some hints to overcome or, at least, to soften this development trap. Key issues for landlocked countries are regional integration[51] through federation or other unifying policies and reduction of the external barriers of the region, together with a strengthening in the transport infrastructure and eased transit on both sides of the border. If economies are better integrated, economic performance of neighbors matters more. Segmentation (due to many causes, al-

[51] This concept is linked with Statehood in history, a topic analyzed in Chapter 1.

so racial, linguistic or cultural), which sometimes represents a form of protection, is a brake against development.

Both countries can benefit from a close integration and complementarities of their economies, but the poorer landlocked country often has an asymmetric disadvantage and it has to pay its tribute. Following the well known Murphy's rule, problems are shared much more than opportunities.

Improving coastal access is a must, again with asymmetric incentives, since it matters much more for the distant country. Landlocked countries have stronger incentives in becoming more skilled and specialized in some fields, such as financial or other intangible services, which do not need many physical transportation costs-finding something new or different to sell, hardly interesting for luckier and spoiled countries, can be a matter or life or death.

Another partial solution is represented by technology, referring in particular to TLC. Mobile phones and wireless communications allow countries to overcome physical obstacles almost everywhere. Thanks to the Internet, geography simply doesn't matter and remarkable success even in poor areas is hardly surprising. Should you travel along small villages in rural Africa, you shall always find small food stores, mobile phone or Internet shops, and cafés and hardly anything else. Isolation decreases with these new devices, even if many impediments are still in place (lack of energy; unskilled users; costs of hardware, and maintenance, hard to overcome in poor and isolated rural areas; primitive regulatory, and competition policies …).

Landlocked countries are not necessarily air-locked or, even more, e-locked. Technology flattens the world and it reshapes geography, changing its role and softening its lucky or perverse effects – location still matters, but less than in the past.

People emigrate more easily from landlocked countries and if this is normally an impoverishment for the country, remittances coming back home are an important source of funds, especially for rural development, a key issue in countries unlikely to become soon highly industrialized.

Geopolitical handicap

Landlocked countries are evidently not all the same. What counts in order to detect their degree of isolation is not only the distance from the closest harbor, but also–even more–their communication network (airports, enabling the country to ›fly over‹ problems; railways and especially roads, which are often unpaved, corrugated, potholed, muddy in rainy seasons, dusty especially in desert zones …).

Harbors matter for their intrinsic basic transport function, even if their effective role depends on a variety of elements which include their geographical posi-

tion–considering the territories behind them, the presence of alternative sea places, the geographical location strategic or not for the main trading routes, etc.–and their dimension, remembering that critical masses matter, producing consistent economies of scale, and are uneasy to build up shortly.
Landlocked countries find much harder not only to export but also–unsurprisingly–to import almost everything they need, starting from foodstuff and energy. Diversification of sources is a key geopolitical issue, especially if neighbors are untrustworthy, and it is strategically important but also often hard to put in place. The anxiety is multiplied in places where choices are much more restricted and opportunities, wherever existent, very limited.

Unifying water

The sea always unites distant places and it is not a barrier, but a bridge, especially where roads are bad or not existent. Phoenixes, starting from actual Lebanon, were blessed by the Mediterranean Sea and they could reach Cartago in actual Tunisia, Sardinia, and other coastal places. The industrial revolution unsurprisingly took place, for a variety of reasons synthesized in Chapter 1, in England, that is surrendered by the sea and naturally oriented towards the New World. The other main colonial countries, from Portugal to Spain and the Netherlands, are all coastal. Modern but also ancient China is much more developed in its coastal part that in the inside territory, as well as Brazil or the U.S.A.
Water is a powerful communication device not only considering the sea, but also taking into account navigable rivers ending in the sea, unsurprisingly hardly present in the poorest landlocked countries. When roads are bad, water and air are the only other transportation alternatives. Synergies between the three means are obviously highly welcome and diversify transport risk.
The United Nations Convention on the Law of the Sea[52] now gives a landlocked country a right of access to and from the sea, without taxation of traffic through transit States.
Problems of landlocked countries require an inter-disciplinary approach, starting from geopolitical strategies, which take into account issues and prospects of vast continental areas, increasingly intertwined with the rest of more and more global world, up to micro interventions and tools, where even microfinance can find its place.
Landlocked sinless citizens, often among the poorest of the poor, eventually deserve to get out of a natural or artificial cage where they were born, because they are too weak to sort out on their own this geographical trap. And like when someone tries to get out of quicksand, he cannot avoid an external help.

---

52 http://www.un.org/Depts/los/convention_agreements/convention_historical_perspective.htm.

According to the Millennium Development Goal number 8 (develop a global partnership for development)[53], target 1 is dedicated to landlocked countries, requiring to »address the special needs of least developed countries, landlocked countries, and small island developing States«.

The condensed Chapter

Landlocked countries without access to sea are geographically handicapped, especially if they border with bad neighbors, which trap them in a closed territory, making trade difficult.
Albeit airports and web communications ease aloneness, geopolitical isolation matters, hampering development, and asking for international alliances to overcome unnatural borders of ill conceived States.

Out of Poverty Tips

Forward-looking investments in physical and intangible infrastructures reshape geography, together with increasingly porous national borders, within a flattening global world.

Selected Readings

ACEMOGLU D., JOHNSON S., ROBINSON J.A., (2002), *Reversal of Fortune: Geography and Institutions in the Making of the Modern World Income Distribution*, in Quarterly Journal of Economics, 117, November, pp. 1231–1294.

COLLIER P., (2007), *The Bottom Billion: Why the Poorest Countries are Failing and What Can Be Done about It*, Oxford University Press, Oxford.

DIAMOND J., (1997), *Guns, Germs, and Steel: The Fates of Human Societies*, Random House, New York.

[53] See http://www.un.org/millenniumgoals/bkgd.shtml.

CHAPTER 3 – Disgraceful opportunities: the natural resources curse

> The first challenge facing any resource-rich country is to ensure that the public gets as much of the value of the resources that lie beneath its land as possible.
>
> Joseph Stiglitz, *Making Globalisation Work*

Unlucky bingo

Imagine that in a poor country, oil or gold or diamonds are occasionally discovered. It would seem and it should naturally be a blessing from God, like winning the lottery, with floods of easy money suddenly pouring into the country. In most cases however it soon appears (to the dismay and incredulity of many) as a fake or–even more–a nightmare, exactly like when, after making bingo and becoming suddenly reach, a poor man is overwhelmed and suffocated by greedy relatives and friends, who soon transform his ephemeral joy into an unbelievable nightmare, a sort of winner's curse.

For many poor but rich-in-commodities countries, natural resources represent a unique–unforgettable and unforgivable–chance for social and economic development.

There is a curious and counter–intuitive phenomenon that smart economists such as the Nobel Prize winner Joseph Stiglitz or Jeffrey Sachs or Paul Collier call the ›resource curse‹, also known as the ›paradox of plenty‹. The reason for such a name is that, on average, countries and regions with an abundance of natural resources (such as oil, gas or metals, and minerals like gold, diamonds, copper, cobalt, manganese, bauxite, chromium, platinum, silver, coltan …), specifically concerning point-source non renewable resources like minerals and fuels, tend to have less economic growth and worse development outcomes than countries with fewer natural resources[54].

Abundant natural wealth often creates rich countries with poor people. Yet some blessed countries with abundant natural resources do perform better than

[54] This theory has some critics. John Tierney (*Rethinking the oil curse*, in http://tierneylab.blogs.nytimes.com/2008/05/05/rethinking-the-oil-curse) is skeptical of some of the alleged evils of petroleum.

others, and some have done well. Why is the spell of the resource curse cast so unequally?

According to Collier (2007), misuse of natural resources is simply another poverty trap, together with the conflict trap[55], being landlocked with bad neighbors[56] or being exposed to bad governance in a small country. Proper management is more valuable than minerals, if we just look at the example of resourceless countries such as Japan or Taiwan or Germany.

For example, once oil is discovered, the demand for infrastructure and business development in that area will immediately trump any other concern. As the oil is pumped, other sectors of the economy wither, since their costs rise as a result of both increased wage competition and the sudden rush of foreign currency into the country that is unfairly shared across the country. Even the demand for land is likely to increase, pushing up prices, to the detriment of the penniless poor.

Countries like Angola prove this point. The government and the elite are making a fortune out of the oil, while common people–including the needy poorest–are simply out of the game, and they don't belong to that privileged and exclusive private club. There is no incentive for them to invest in the country more broadly, so Angola's oil is a greedy curse and not a blessing.

Many hopes lie down in the underground, resting in peace with their huge potential and waiting for troubled exploitation. When the country is poor and too many rivals quarrel for its hidden resources, a stalemate is among the likeliest options.

The best antidote against natural resources curse is represented by a complex framework of institutional devices, where fossil fuel is progressively being replaced by environmental–friendly renewable, and fair sharing incentives both participation and democracy, following a development–friendly strategic pattern[57].

The worldwide economic growth, fueled by a growing population and increasing living standards, is putting unprecedented pressure over resources appropriation, pushing prices up–even due to speculation–and increasing the disparities between resources haves and haves-not. The latter obviously concern mainly the discriminated poor, ironically even within resource-rich countries (oil is here, but not for those who can't exploit it!).

Geopolitical disputes for the control of fuel, gas, steel, other minerals or soft commodities, such as cereals and other foodstuff, are getting tougher, with selfishness and predation sadly prevailing over sharing, enhancement of renewable

---

55 See Chapter 5.

56 See Chapter 1.

57 For the microfinance applications of renewable sources of energy, see Chapter 24.

and mutual cooperation – even if as far as physical limits to full exploitation are becoming closer, realistic compromises increasingly look unavoidable.

The Dutch disease

The natural resources curse isn't just a problem of badly managed African or South American nations. The phenomenon is known as ›*Dutch Disease*‹, after Holland's initial mismanagement of natural oil and gas stocks, discovered in the 1970s in the North Sea.

The question is crucially important for the destiny of so many poor but potentially rich countries, which are currently being depleted from their not renewable resources. Resource of a country is its natural endowment – once it is removed, the asset is gone forever and it cannot be replaced. These scarce assets should be accounted for and adequately depreciated in the nation's accounting framework[58], in order to fairly reflect their depletion. Also environmental degradation is a liability that is to be accounted for, looking for Green net national product. Rich-in resources countries have a unique opportunity to invest and manage well the proceeds: a good clean up of the spoiled territories and adequate infrastructural investments in growth and education, first of all concerning local people, are certainly the top priority.

As Stiglitz (2007) says, it is immensely important to understand why developing countries that are resource-rich perform so badly: first because so many developing countries are economically dependent on natural resources and second because resource-rich countries tend to be wealthy places with poor people, broadening social inequalities, which traditionally fuel unrest and discontent.

The potential for growth of these resources, if properly used, is still in many cases enormous, with a positive spill over even on neighboring countries.

The natural resources curse is hypothesized to happen for many different reasons.

First of all, a decline in the competitiveness of other economic sectors (caused by appreciation of the real exchange rate as resource revenues enter an economy), brings to deindustrialization and the country's currency, normally not convertible and sometimes pegged to the euro or, more frequently, to the dollar, rises in value against other currencies. Especially if resources represent an important fraction of the country's GDP, other export activities–already intrinsically fragile–tend to become uncompetitive[59]. In principle, it is easy to avoid currency appreciation – keep the foreign exchange earned from oil exports out of the country, invest the money in the US or Europe and bring it back only

58 Stiglitz (2007), p. 153.
59 See Collier (2007), p. 39.

gradually. But in most developing countries, such an ›unpatriotic‹ policy is viewed as using oil money to help someone else's economy.
Competitive devaluations of local currency are aimed at discouraging imports and fostering exports, even if they also puzzle foreign investments and produce instability, together with higher inflation. With currency appreciation, imports are cheaper and exports are more expensive and the trade balance gets under stress, for what concerns non oil products. Once the oil bonanza is over, due to natural exhaustion of resources or boost periods, it is uneasy and not immediate to readdress an ailing industrial system – the deeper the loss of competitiveness, the longer it takes to gain it back, involving also cultural and motivational issues, fallen asleep in the golden age. A distorted vision of what real and enduring development should be about, does not help, and natural resources may have uneasy-to-remove hallucinating effects – »when money can be extracted from the ground, people simply don't develop the DNA of innovation and entrepreneurship«[60] and the smartest flee away, in search of better opportunities abroad, contributing to a long term damaging brain drain[61].
Another often underestimated collateral effect is represented by the fact that de-industrialization induced by the Dutch disease is particularly harmful not against product and services with a high added value–less price sensitive but hardly existing in poor countries–but rather against typical basic industries of underdeveloped countries, such as the textile or the agricultural sector, where women are mostly occupied. Such a fact creates an asymmetric gender bias, where already weak women are disproportionately hit and they tend to become even weaker. Besides, natural resources booms, often accompanied by easy bank loans, tend to incentive infrastructural jobs – in the construction industry only men are typically present.
In Nigeria, oil exports boomed in the 1970s and the country's other exports such as peanuts and cocoa became unprofitable and production rapidly collapsed. Natural resources sooner or later evanish, while the damage to the rest of the economy can even be more long lasting, due also to intangible losses in innovation, accumulated experience, and industrial productivity – which become evident much later on, if and when the country tries to fill the gap with other apparently not so lucky competitors, forced to work hard by the absence of resources.
Countries that rely on natural resource exports may tend to neglect education because they see no immediate need for it.
The induced decrease in the industries exposed to international competition consequently causes even greater dependence on natural resource revenues, and it leaves the economy extremely vulnerable to commodity price changes, nor-

60 Friedman (2009), p. 137.
61 See Chapter 12.

mally driven by international speculation, against which single States typically have little or any power.

Volatile revenues: the boom-and-bust cycle

Natural resource revenues are intrinsically volatile and they can lead to crises. Resources are both a source of conflicts to grab them and a way to finance these conflicts[62], which typically occur when people scramble for scarce resources. Turbulence takes its toll, hitting in particular the unsheltered poor.
Boom-and-bust business cycles, albeit painful, seem unavoidable corollaries of capitalistic systems. The prediction of the path of commodity prices is more concerned with faith than common sense – bubbles tend to blow, as a consequence of irrational exuberance, followed by unjustified depression, remembering that expectations, albeit often senseless, do matter in economics. A key target for central bankers and policymakers is leaning against the wind, trying to soften erratic and volatile trends – an uneasy task in developed countries, relegated to science fiction aspirations in underdeveloped places where financial institutions and think tanks are not part of a bare survival landscape.
Problems are coming also from the intrinsically high volatility of revenues from the natural resource sector due to exposure to global commodity market swings, government mismanagement of resources, or weak, ineffectual, unstable or corrupt institutions (possibly due to the easily diverted actual or anticipated revenue stream from extractive activities). Undiversified over-reliance on commodities amplifies volatility issues.
Volatility is among the worst enemies of microfinance development and outreach, since it endangers its harmonic development, with stop-and-go cycles that are hardly bearable and manageable by the poorest. During the boom, discrimination softens and everybody finds it easier to get unchallenged credit, while during the subsequent crash, the weakest and most vulnerable is the easiest target for cut off. Boom-and-bust periods need strong social shock absorbers, hardly ever present in poor countries. When commodities boom, human rights bust[63]. Energy supplying and economic interests typically command a cynical priority on human rights. When geopolitical interests prevail, Western or Chinese politicians tend to become crazy about them, forgetting anything else, starting from the poorest of the poor, unable to catch votes domestically but even more uninteresting thousands of miles away.
Volatile prices are concerned with oil abundance or shortage, depending on the contingent demand and supply balance (due to over-consumption or little re-

---

62 Stiglitz (2007), p. 135
63 Khan (2009), Chapter 8.

quest in recession periods – free or restricted availability, but also competition from alternative sources, increasingly depending on innovation).
Especially in volatile scenarios, reliable forecasts are increasingly harder to make, particularly in underdeveloped countries with unskilled economists and managers, whereas public expenditure and budgeting requires stability, fine tuning and long term plans. Whereas it is obviously easy to increase public spending during boom periods–with hardly anybody complaining for the bonanza–it is very difficult and politically unpopular to cut it during the subsequent crash, especially in the absence of adequate ›cushion‹ reserves and when problems are accumulating – when it rains, it pours.
Public spending and financing of infrastructural investments is also a long debated Keynesian measure to help countries sort out of depression.
The boom-and-bust cycle also makes it very hard for electors to detect which politicians have performed well and which have not. Mistakes are easy to conceal and the first thing that every politician learns (not only in resource-rich countries) is to attribute to himself and his party undeserved merits, claiming that any mistake belongs to the opposition. Governments are addicted to debt, especially if it lasts long enough to be inherited by the next generation of politicians and voters.
Big confusion can distort reality, especially in countries with no or little free press, where illiterate citizens are easily manipulated and their votes are bought with few peanuts. Checks and balances, that are made possible by free elections, are hardly the case, as well as strong opposition parties and deeply rooted democratic habits.
Boom periods are often accompanied by a real estate surge in prices, which is backed by easy loans guaranteed by their increasing collateral value. Price of commodities plummets, revenues to pay home mortgages or to sustain boom quotations fall short, with dramatic decreases in the value of properties, followed by a weakening banking system, suffering from both higher delinquency rates and lower value of collateral, to the detriment of the real economy, with a spiral effect difficult to interrupt, which directly brings to recession. Recovery sooner or later takes place, but it can be slow and painful – it takes much more time and effort to build than to destroy.
It is difficult to find social and market stabilizers such as diversification of output (so as not to be too much depending on commodity prices), progressive tax brackets, wages for unemployment, and other social safety nets, that on the contrary are typically present in Western countries (especially in Western Europe, where their cost and abuses are a well known obstacle to development), because the poorest are used to live with little or any parachute.
Stabilization funds that are accumulated in boom periods and that are carefully used in downward phases, are a wise example of forward looking economic

policy–as it happens for instance in Norway–but they prove difficult to be put in place in developing countries.
Even international bank loans are highly cyclical, because they are abundant in boom periods and they are subject to credit crunches in hard times, when repayments are stressed and new money is hard to find. This pro-cyclical behavior, so typical with banks, which love to lend money to those who don't need it– think about it, they are the best customers! –exacerbates economic trends, worsens crises, and helps their gloomy transformation into recession or depression.
Economic diversification, that is so useful to reduce the risk of price volatility or resources exhaustion (which represents the end of the dream or, more realistically, the nightmare), often tends to be neglected by authorities or delayed, in the light of the temporary high profitability of the limited natural resources. The diversification attempts that occur are often grand public works projects which may be misguided or mismanaged. However, even if authorities try to diversify the economy, this is made difficult because the resource extraction is vastly more lucrative and out-competes other industries. Successful natural resource-exporting countries often become more dependent on extractive industries over time. Resource sectors which tend to provide large financial revenues often provide relatively few jobs, and tend to operate as enclaves with few forward and backward connections to the rest of the economy.

Spoiling rents, mixing windfall oil with ruthless repression

The Western oil addiction, that burns increasing quantities of non renewable fossil fuels, involuntarily contributes to fix and support oil backed undemocratic regimes, providing them with precious financial resources, that otherwise would not be available – fuel and democracy are seldom synonyms and enriching the enemy is hardly a wise strategy. In such a context, running out of oil may not completely sound as bad news, since it may encourage political reforms, abandoning undemocratic rents.
Resource rents tend to weaken men and democracies, often already fragile on their own, improperly mixing oil with repression and unfreedom. Undeserved rents are harmful even for the psychology of workers and citizens. Oil wealth leads to larger patronage careless spending, dampening pressures for democratization and modernization[64].
Collier (2007) again recalls that in the presence of large surpluses from natural resources, autocracies outperform democracies. Blessed resource-rich countries often experiment a repression effect and its dictators, eager to loot the treasury at the expense of their own citizens, are prone to overspend in security. Tyrants look for friendly army in order to remain in power, diverting money from in-

---

64 See Friedman (2009), p. 135.

vestments in schools, public hospitals or other projects with a positive social impact. In such a context, human rights are just an optional.

Another reason is given by the fact that many resource rich countries–e.g. in the Arabic peninsula–do not need to collect taxes and consequently to give evidence of how they spend public money – no representation without taxation. This is known as the paradigm of *rentier* states, where rulers don't need to tax their citizens because they have a guaranteed source of income from natural resources, to be stored in their personal fiefdoms. So the intrinsically troubled relationship between rulers and subjects–representing a core issue of democracy–definitely breaks down.

In addition, those who benefit from mineral resource wealth may perceive watchful civil society as a threat to the benefits that they enjoy, and they may take steps to thwart them. Countries whose economies are dominated by resource extraction industries tend to be more repressive, corrupted, and badly-managed[65], spreading insecurity and injustice. Wado (2013) confirms, with proper empirical evidence, that natural resources breed corruption and reduce educational attainments, affecting the incentives to invest in education and so dampening economic growth.

Taxation sharply varied across time[66] and it was more systematically conceived as a mean to finance wars and its consequent huge expenses. Such a matter happened in particular in Europe during the Napoleon wars and it involuntarily contributed to the birth of modern democracies, since angry citizens forced to pay taxes, unsurprisingly wanted to … know more about the destiny of their money.

Resource surpluses induce an excessively large public sector, giving ruling politicians the chance to hire friends, relatives or clan members, buying their votes forever, in exchange for jobs and protection. Autocracy develops particularly well in countries with an ethnic predominant group, this luckily being hardly the case in most societies of the bottom billion[67] – resource rents are however likely to induce autocracy, highly detrimental for economic development.

During resources-boom periods, both public and private sector tend to expand their debt, whereas in hard times tax revenues collapse. Following the sharp decrease of taxable incomes, the balance deficit explodes (due to the difficulty to match growing public expenses with lower incomes), the trade balance deteriorates (as a consequence of the exports' sharp decrease, not fully compensated by anyway lower imports), together with a depreciating currency, causing a

[65] See www.globalpolicy.org/security/natres/generaldebate/2003/12curse.html, *Lifting the Natur al Resource Curse.*

[66] See for example the peculiar tax system of Imperial Spain; the extraordinary tax burden levied on the Dutch mercantile economy by the cumulated debt of having had to spend from 1568 to 1714 fighting to achieve and preserve independence.

[67] Collier (2007), p. 49.

surge in inflation and capital rationing of financial resources lent from banks. In such a gloomy scenario, governments unfit to cope with combined stressing factors are likely to default.

Medium and long term planning is often biased by irrational projection of the current situation, bringing to over optimism or excessive pessimism, both damaging for proper and realistic budgeting. Ordinary life does need volatility smoothing – people simply can't survive passing from four meals in happy times to zero in hard ones, even if their average sounds good.

Public money is often embezzled out of official budgets into slush funds. Money laundering, with the complicity of international tax heavens and corruption, become so organic and endemic with the system that they tend to be even morally accepted – especially by those who are part of the game. Secret bank accounts and cash payments not only support terrorism, but they also facilitate the corruption that undermines development. Computerized international banking payments–where physical transport of money has almost completely disappeared–and conservation of electronic track records are now powerful devices against dirty money laundering, even if much still waits to be done.

Resource-rich countries have unique comparative advantages that are hardly exploited for the best. According to Lindsay[68], this fact is due to the natural resources that tend to be commodity products, with little value added and little control over the prices to be charged.

Unfriendly multinationals

Multinational firms are typically part of this bonanza, since they concur to exploit the natural resources, turning a blind eye to human rights abuses. They inappropriately share extra revenues with top politicians, warlords or whoever controls strategic mines or oilfields – the group of beneficiaries is typically restricted, in order not to excessively dilute wealth, and newcomers are admitted and co-opted only if absolutely necessary.

It is much cheaper to bribe a government to provide resources at below-market prices than to invest and develop an industry, so it is no surprise that multinationals colluding with local firms succumb this temptation, competing for limited and expiring resources at the expense of the poorest. Unscrupulous politicians that make unfair long term agreements with greedy foreign multinationals, mortgage the future of their typically unaware citizens, by selling off not renewable national assets at bargain prices[69] and what is depicted as a historical agreement looks in reality more like a tombstone than a milestone.

---

68 In Harrison, Huntington (2000), p. 285.

69 Collier (2010), p. 76.

In equilibrium, foreign firms–carefully chosen with an international tender–should be fairly remunerated for searching, engineering, extraction, and marketing costs, leaving the rest to local people. Refinery and other added-value transformations may well be conducted locally, to the extent that domestic citizens are given the right rewards and skills to carry them on.

Unless duly challenged by fair competition or public opinion, greedy multinationals are often tempted to grab the resources away from the poor, permanently depleting their habitat, with little or any refunding.

Corruption and lack of transparency and public accountability, fueled by dirt money, discourage competitive bidding for public investments, increasing costs at the expense of quality. Damages are hard to detect, especially in the short run, and they come out when the tide goes down and liquidity dries up or badly built infrastructures collapse.

According to Stiglitz (2007): »The first challenge facing any resource-rich country is to ensure that the public gets as much of the value of the resources that lie beneath its land as possible«.

There is an ongoing struggle by oil, gas and mining companies to seize as much of the wealth for themselves as possible. They are organized in powerful lobbies, against which dispersed and not properly informed citizens fight a difficult battle, considering also that the central government is more subject to corruptive pressures of power multinationals' interests, unless citizens prove to be enough powerful to contrast them. Such a task is easy in well established democracies with a mature public opinion and a free press, whereas it is hardly ever the case in underdeveloped countries.

Bribery, cheating, and imbalanced negotiating all cut into what rightfully ought to go to the developing country. The rent-earning countries get less than they should, while the oil, gas, or mining companies get more[70].

Citizens cannot bribe the government, as multinationals may do, and they can just vote against it, but the threat is typically much less effective than real and immediate money in the pockets, that can be used even during polls for unfairly diverting votes.

The negative impact goes well beyond bribe itself, since it undermines the democratic process, as well as the market. Meritocracy is destroyed for years to come and excess gains of oil companies are offset by smaller local gains, addressed to the pockets of politicians and businessmen, who invest this money in corruption, that seems to be an investment with high yields, to the detriment of poor people, who are out of the game and suffer for wild exploitation of their land, stealing non reproducible resources, polluting the environment and destroying the rest of the economy – and since only a happy few are admitted to

---

[70] Stiglitz (2007), p. 141.

the banquet, spillovers are carefully controlled, in order to avoid curiosity and temptations.

Public opinion in host countries can be a precious ally in the struggle for transparency and fairness–sunshine is the strongest antiseptic against corruption[71]–and deserves support from Western human rights activists. Transparency would be encouraged if only fully documented payments from foreign companies exploiting local resources were fully tax deductible. Citizens have the right to know.

Mitigation of this collusive sharing of local resources is promoted by initiatives such as:

- the Voluntary Principles on Security and Human Rights–the principles provide guidance to companies operating in zones of conflict or fragile States so that they can ensure that security forces–public or private–protecting the companies' facilities and premises operate in a way that protects the company's assets while respecting human rights and fundamental freedoms[72];
- the Extractive Industry Transparency Initiative, which promotes the application of principles such as the management of natural resource wealth for the benefit of a country's citizens[73].

It is difficult–or even impossible–to resist to bribery, cheating, imbalanced negotiating, superior legal and technological skills, financial soundness, economic power, availability of international networks, specific experience, together with a borderline foxy behavior – often formally correct but ruthless and greedy in substance.

Empowerment of local communities–with their active participation–eases the promotion of human rights, since it fosters transparency and accountability, avoids unfair wealth concentration and contributes to social and economic development[74].

Blood diamonds

Disorder and civil wars may sometimes endanger the exploitation of resources, even if normally they are a powerful obstacle against transparency, fairness, and democracy – that is exactly what bribers and ruthless politicians, together with their multinational partners, typically long and look for. The cause-effect rela-

---

71 Stiglitz (2007), p. 151.

72 http://www.internationalalert.org/pdf/Voluntary_Principles_on_Security_and_Human_Rights.pdf.

73 http://eitransparency.org.

74 See Khan (2009), p. 193.

tionship is obviously twofold and it operates in both directions, each supporting the other: war is financed by predatory exploitation of resources but at the same time it makes this exploitation much easier. Blood diamonds coming from war zones and children soldiers are just an example of this sad relationship. Once violence has begun, it proves hard to stop, with countries falling in a downward spiral[75]. The Kimberley treaty for ethically sourced jewelry and the Extractive Industries Transparency Initiative[76] sets a global standard for transparency in oil, gas, and mining, with an effort to make natural resources benefit all.

The level of instability can be detrimental for foreign investments, especially in early stages such as prospecting and surveying, and multinationals may face a difficult trade off between mighty rewards and high risks (such as: early expropriation, inability to exploit the deposit due to lack of infrastructures, transport, and security challenges, difficulty to hire staff ...).

In resource-rich but democracy-poor countries, most of the income that is extracted from oil or other mineral exploitation is unsurprisingly spent in weapons and army. The aim is to keep (if necessary with force) the established authority, preventing not only democratic regimes but also-mostly-coups or wars that may change the ruling politicians, who are well aware that their place is highly rewarding but also extremely risky–up to the point that the most forward–looking tyrants tend to accumulate treasures abroad and to have foreign supporters, just in case they need to flee their country.

Violent conflicts are often fed by Western governments' massive and ›confidential‹ sales of arms to developing countries, especially former colonies, in a perverse swap of oil and minerals against weapons. Both counterparts are happy about the deal, whereas the bill, with its death tolls, is paid by an anonymous mass of destitute, which is too poor to be interesting.

Conflicts and bad policies are both a powerful incentive to the heavy dependence on exports of natural resources, already easygoing on itself. The economy of a country becomes skewed when chaos and economic policies of that country scare off ordinary foreign investors and send local entrepreneurs abroad to look for better opportunities. Factories may close and normal businesses may flee, but oil and precious metals remain for the taking. Resource extraction becomes the last resort sector that still functions after other industries have stopped working – being unable to invest, produce, and export.

It is again Stiglitz (2007) who explains that just as there is often conflict between haves and haves-not, there can be a conflict between regions with or without resources, with the former eager to break away (e.g. Kurdistan from Iraq, Ogoniland in Nigeria, Angola's oil-rich Cabinda province, an enclave between Congo Brazaville and Democratic Republic of Congo, apparently unim-

---

75 See Chapter 5.

76 See http://eiti.org.

portant but in reality plentiful with resources, South Sudan from the North, Bolivian mining regions …).
Also Collier (2007) remarks that natural resources can–and sadly often do–provoke conflicts within societies, as different ethnic groups and factions fight for their possession, since they are unwilling to share it.
There are several main types of causal relationships–in both directions–between natural resources and armed conflicts[77]:

- resource curse effects can seriously undermine the quality of governance and economic performances, thereby increasing the vulnerability of countries to conflicts (the ›resource curse‹ argument);
- conflicts can occur over the control and exploitation of resources and the allocation of their revenues (the ›resource war‹ argument);
- access to resource revenues by belligerents can prolong conflicts (the ›conflict resource‹ argument).

Myopic underinvestment

Resource-rich countries tend also to under-invest and the reason is again the lack of strategic vision, together with not careful budgeting, whereas investments are the true engine of long lasting economic growth. A key challenge for volatile resource-rich countries is indeed spending money well and at the right timing, in order not to miss the way to development.
According to Stiglitz (2007), rich-in resources countries don't need more foreign aid[78], but more help in getting full value for their resources and in ensuring that they well spend the money they get. Technical assistance, training, and education are far more important and long lasting than money, even if they are much more difficult and more tiring to provide and to receive. A fishing rod given to a poor is much more useful than a fish – it is not for immediate consumption and one needs to learn how to use it, but in the long term, he will be much happier and more responsible.
An even superficial analysis of human psychology tells and teaches much about this point. In his remarkable analysis, Stiglitz (2007) points out that selling off their natural resources in order to get immediate personal advantages, crooks governing rich-in-resources underdeveloped countries get less money to pay for infrastructures, hospitals, schools, administration of justice – the very basic pillars of social and economic development. In such a context, democracy is a threat to be carefully kept away.
When resource fields are privatized, exploitations become even easier.

---

77 See Ross (2004) and Le Billion (2006).
78 See Chapter 14.

Choice, not fate

According again to Stiglitz (2007), p. 149, the natural resource curse is not fate, it is choice. It is neither an unavoidable and automatic event nor an act of God (recalling from the Greek mythology Zeus' primitive intervention against humans), but it is simply a clear-cut and voluntary choice. It depends on both the interests of extractive resource industries, mainly in the hands of Western multinationals, and the willingness of a handful of greedy local politicians and businessmen, sometimes transformed into warlords. The fatalistic belief that is so diffused within resigned poor peasants contributes to ease the phenomenon, often bringing to a passive and silent acceptance of what in reality is a robbery.
Some possible solutions to the articulated problem regard the opportunity to set up transparent and efficient governmental institutions, in order to reduce corruption and ensure the best possible investment of the proceeds. The issues about the correct use of natural resources–and resources in general, even those collected with taxes–are well known common problems even in solidly established democracies, while in developing countries the task to ensure that the fruits of a country's wealth are equitably and well spent sounds even more challenging, since they are often too poor to afford any waste of money and they tend to forget that resource prices are extremely volatile and not everlasting.
Abundant natural resources can and should be a blessing, not a curse.

The condensed Chapter

Instead of being a blessing from God, exhaustible mineral resources often tend to weaken resource-rich countries, favoring laziness, corruption, and mismanagement.
Oil, tribalism, corruption, and weapons are the natural lubricant for a combustible mix.
Commodity prices are extremely volatile, favoring boom and bust cycles, timely exploited by unfriendly multinational and their local accomplices, trapping the excluded poor and unfairly forever exploiting their not renewable resources.

Out of Poverty Tips

Intangible sources, starting from proper instruction, are potentially not exhausting and self fulfilling, if only properly ignited, even by burning fossil resources. For poverty reduction, knowledge, more than oil, proves to matter.

Selected Readings

COLLIER P., (2007), *The Bottom Billion: Why the Poorest Countries are Failing and What Can Be Done about It*, Oxford University Press, Oxford.

WADO W.A., (2013), *Education, Rent Seeking and the Curse of Natural Resources,* in Economics and Politics, November.

CHAPTER 4 – Poverty multiplication: the demographic spiral

Your children are not your children.
They are the sons and daughters of Life's longing for itself.
They came through you but not from you and though they are with you yet they belong not to you.

Kahlil Gibran, *On Children*

Poor fertility

It is widely known that poor people have many more children than rich ones, even if such a statement is somewhat counterintuitive, since a poor environment with high infant mortality rates and gloomy life perspectives should discourage massive reproduction.

This intertwined and well known question concerns the causal link between poverty and fertility. Since the poor tend to make many more children, this self fulfilling demographic spiral (according to which, more children simply and quickly tend to make many children on their own, from puberty along their fertile shorter lives) erodes the few available resources, making the poor even poorer.

If the pie does not grow, more hungry people unsurprisingly get smaller slices of it. In underdeveloped areas, demography typically ends up multiplying the poor, and so leveraging up poverty both in absolute and in relative terms. A worrisome aspect of demography is that population is growing where it shouldn't, in already crowded, illiterate, insalubrious, and poor areas, which are less able to absorb further increases of inhabitants. Low-lying coastal areas, increasingly exposed to rising sea level due to climatic changes, are roughly five times more populated than the average[79]. All these unbalances threaten global stability.

Higher levels of economic prosperity soon lead parents to reduce the number of desired children but the problem is to slow down fertility trendy effects, being fertility choices a cultural issue associated with mortality rates and poverty. Convergence to sustainable levels may take generations, waiting for a positive

79 Sachs (2008), p. 28.

development dividend but considering the dragging effect of demographic tendencies.

In poor areas, cultural choices tend to be strongly pro-natal and nearly all girls get married young, often just after puberty, with the mission of procreating.

What is important to consider in demography is not only the level of population, but also–mainly–the population's likely trend. High population growth often leads to deeper poverty, and deeper poverty contributes to high fertility rates. Like the other ones, even the demographic trap is avoidable.

It is not the demographic spiral on its own to be interrupted–unless we share Malthusian worries about an overcrowded world–but rather the detrimental link between demography and poverty – the real enemy being the poverty spiral, so often linked with overpopulation.

Poverty is not necessarily a chronic condition, and individuals and families may be able to move into or out of poverty over their life-cycle, often as a result of demographic events.

In order for Gross Domestic Product per capita to grow, its overall increase has to outperform population's growth. Wealth dilution is otherwise quite likely, even if some economies of scale may occur, and depletion of natural resources can be a typical by-product of uncontrolled demographic expansion.

High fertility is typically linked with high child mortality, which is so common in backward poor areas. But when the child mortality rate declines, parents tend to perceive that excess fertility is unnecessary and they slowly change their habits, with a consequent decline of population growth. Child mortality rates–and subsequent fertility and demographic choices–significantly depend on the extent of discretionary spending on children's nutrition and healthcare[80]. Health trends are influenced by demographic development and the main point are the survival rates, since they are inversely proportional to the fertility rates.

In traditional poor societies, fertility is also influenced by early, universal, and typically combined marriage, followed by immediate and continuous child bearing[81]. Children are conceived being considered as a reliable and cheap labor force and a sort of pension, for the lucky poor who reach the elder age. While children are procreated to guarantee their parent's old age, they are condemned to impoverishment if they are too many in places where resources are scarce.

When demographic equilibrium is reached, it will be easier to acknowledge that the best renewable natural resource is represented by people, with their largely unexploited potential.

---

80 Eswaran in Banerjee, Benabou, Mookherjee (2006), p. 153.

81 Munshi in Banerjee, Benabou, Mookherjee (2006), p. 396.

Cassandra Malthus

According to Thomas Malthus, a political economist who wrote his controversial ›*Essay on the Principle of Population*‹ in 1798 (while being concerned about what he saw as the decline of living conditions in 19th Century England), in nature plants and animals produce far more offspring than can survive, and also man is capable of overproducing, if he is left unchecked.
Malthus' Iron Law of Population suggested that exponential growing population rates would contribute to a rising supply of labor that would inevitably lower wages. In essence, Malthus[82] feared that continued population growth would lend itself to poverty, which would ultimately rebalance upward demographic trends, downsizing population to lower subsistence levels and heading for inevitable and catastrophic self-annihilation.
History–and the industrial revolution, with its geometric advances in productivity, beyond those in population–has followed a different evolutionary pattern and so Malthus may luckily be nicknamed a Cassandra, like the Greek disbelieved prophetess. The statement that population grows exponentially, following a deterministic trend, is false and it is contradicted by a natural tendency to level off – once become affluent, humans tend to reproduce less. What remains true is the law of marginal diminishing returns, which explains also the natural proclivity of the poorest to work harder.
Malthus, being worried about the failure of human rationality in contrasting the overpopulation trend, pessimistically concluded that–unless family size was regulated–famine would become globally epidemic and it eventually consume Man. His single minded view that poverty and famine, together with war and disease, were natural outcomes and counterweights of population overgrowth and food insufficient supply was not popular among social reformers, who believed that all ills of man could be eradicated[83] with proper social structures. Hunger and illnesses are two major poverty traps, analyzed in Chapter 5, which contribute together with migrating diseases to stabilize population, with their lethal impact. The terminal of Malthus somewhat fascinating–but also old fashioned and terrifying–idea is represented by famine and its consequent Darwinian selection of the fittest (and fattest …)[84].

---

82 See http://www.ucmp.berkeley.edu/history/malthus.html

83 See http://www.ucmp.berkeley.edu/history/malthus.html.

84 The Malthusian hypothesis regards famine as a temporary escape valve from extreme privations, from the point of view of the survivors of famine. By contrast, the first post-Malthusian hypothesis views famine as having been the principle perpetuator of endemic poverty in the pre-modern world. The next hypothesis takes the extreme opposite view that famine has no significant long-term effect on poverty. The final hypothesis covers the middle ground and contends that even though famine may not be the principal perpetuator of poverty, it does have the potential of accentuating endemic poverty. http://ideas.repec.org/a/wly/jintdv/v8y1996i5p597-623.html; see also Chapter 7.

Demographic issues are intrinsically related to agriculture and food availability. Shrinking farm sizes, due to excessive population increases, produce diseconomies of scale, making the already poor even poorer. The decisive increase in human population came when once nomadic people decided to settle down; they started crop cultivation and began to alter–forever and increasingly–the balance between humans and the rest of the biosphere[85] with land transformation. The big jump in population occurred since the industrial revolution, which greatly contributed, with its technological discoveries and consequent upside potential, to soften Malthusian worries.

The demographic-economic paradox[86] is the inverse correlation found between wealth and fertility within and between nations. Roughly speaking, nations or subpopulations with higher GDP per capita are observed to have fewer children, even though a richer population can support more children. Malthus held that what he called ›moral restraint‹ (which included abstinence) was required in order to prevent widespread suffering, from famine for example. The demographic-economic paradox suggests that reproductive restraint arises naturally as a consequence of economic progress.

The higher the degree of education and GDP per capita, the fewer children are born in any industrialized country. In 1974 at a UN population conference in Bucharest, Karan Singh, a former minister of population in India, illustrated this trend stating that »development is the best contraceptive«. Also Condorcet, a protagonist of the French Enlightenment, insightfully understood that an educated society, in particular if concerning women, would reduce and invert population growth – not coerced human reasoning proves effective in reducing family size[87].

The ghost of overpopulation, which sometimes materializes, is often present in our worries, producing irrational anxiety. The effect of a rising population depends on how much people produce and consume, following or not a sustainable–environmental friendly–pattern of development. The psychological effect of considering that the pie–representing our resources–is not going to grow, whereas people competing for a slice of it are increasing, is likely to produce apprehension and, eventually, irrational violence for survival.

It is hypothesized that the observed trend has come about as a response to increased life expectancy, reduced childhood mortality, and improved female literacy and independence.

Overpopulation does not depend only on the size or density of the population, but on the ratio of the population to available sustainable resources, and on the

---

85 Sachs (2008), p. 58.

86 See Weil (2004).

87 Sen (2009), p. 102.

means of resource use and distribution used by that population[88]. There cannot be any infinite growth in a finite system and even if the world's resources are often–but not always–renewable and nature often shows a surprising resilience, a sustainability limit is not far from being reached.
Neo-Malthusian prophecies sometimes reappear, when the demographic bomb is considered a threat that may go out of control, if population grows more than sustainable resources.
Technology is one of the best friends of demography, helping it to pass unharmed through many Malthusian worries, since on one side it increases both survival rates and life expectancy, and on the other side it provides more abundant food and other resources. While we lift the crossbar, we may wonder if there is a physical limit to human growth and nature exploitation and–if so–whether we are close to it (with deforesting, over pumping, depleting soil, overgrazing …).

The demographic trap

The demographic trap, according to which poor families tend to have lots of children, is one of the main poverty traps, complementary to others (the conflict trap[89], the natural resource trap[90], being landlocked[91] with bad neighbors, being subject to bad governance in a small country[92] …).
Links between poverty, conflict, demography, and environment are increasingly a topic of discussion and investigation. Demography is just one side of the problem, which however greatly contributes to give substance to the matter, starting from its numbers (how many people are involved in the issue? Is over–or under–population leveraging or decreasing the problems? …).
Demography is concerned not only with actual numbers of people, but also–mostly–with their evolutionary trend and with the composition and concentration–both actual and expected–of population. The poor are not only many and growing, but–due to a high fertility rate–they are also young and concentrated in overcrowded big cities or rural areas. They are looking for enough food, decent housing, basic healthcare, education, and employment. Since these basic needs are unmet, these young poor may easily be attracted by violence, civil unrest, and extremism[93], being tempted to export their rage–and their broken dreams and hopes–wherever they can. Every other place is–or, at least, seems–a

88 It can result from an increase in births, a decline in mortality rates due to medical advances, from an increase in immigration, or from depletion of resources.
89 See Chapter 5.
90 See Chapter 3.
91 See Chapter 2.
92 See Chapter 5.
93 See Friedman (2009), p. 66.

better one to stay and global mobility is hardly anymore a surprise, if only we wonder about its main causing factors.
From ›*Too Poor For Peace?*‹[94], an initiative of the Wilson Centre, we can draw the following insights:

- *Poverty is a Security Issue*

Poverty claims life of millions of people each year by increasing their vulnerability to hunger, disease, and natural disasters. Poverty not only causes insecurity in individuals' life, but it can also contribute to broader political instability, as demonstrated by failed States.

- *Natural Resources and Conflict: Scarcity or Abundance?*

Demography and environment play a role in linking poverty and conflict. The neo-Malthusian deprivation hypothesis argues that environmental and population pressures lead to resource scarcity and poverty, causing people to become frustrated and therefore more likely to rebel[95]. A second neo-Malthusian theory, the State failure hypothesis, posits that population and environmental pressures are more likely to cause conflict in weak States, which are unable to address their populations' grievances.

We already know from Chapter 3 that natural resources can be a disgraceful opportunity; the conflict issue will get a broader coverage in Chapter 5.

- *The Challenge of Youth Bulges*

A youth bulge can increase the likelihood that poverty will lead to conflict. Young people who are impoverished and lack educational and employment opportunities have unsurprisingly little reason to support the *status quo*, and they are therefore more willing to rebel, as it happens in 2011 in North Africa and elsewhere.

---

94 http://www.wilsoncenter.org/index.cfm?topic_id=1413&fuseaction=topics.event_summary&event_id=274774; the link to the book ›*Too poor for peace*› is http://www.brookings.edu/press/Books/2007/toopoorforpeace.aspx.

95 However, according to Kahl (www.wilsoncenter.org/), the deprivation hypothesis »dramatically over predicts the incidence of violence. If poverty and inequality were enough to lead to civil strife, the entire world would be on fire«.

A cruel Spartan selection

When children are many, poor families hardly ever can afford to fully invest in the nutrition, health, and education of all.
Choice is often arbitrary and always cruel. Sometimes preference is given to the first born child, as it used to happen in Western Europe till the Modern Age, while in other cases the strongest and healthiest children are selected, to the detriment of others, whose destiny (may be not as sad as that of Spartan handicapped children in ancient Greece, who were thrown down from the Tarpeia precipice) is anyway gloomy.
If life for many poor children is sad, life of handicapped babies is even worst, since they often are not even given a chance to survive, in societies where pity and compassion are often overwhelmed by hunger and despair. To those who say that Darwinian selection, according to which only the strongest survive, is one of the basic rules of nature, it should always be reminded that human beings have the capacity and the rights to overcome these brutal laws, differentiating themselves from other animals.
Even the destiny of nearly half of the population, represented by young girls and eventually women, for the lucky who arrive to adult age, suffers huge and ancestral gender discriminations, as we shall see in Chapter 10. Whereas girls are not the first desire of a couple, selective abortion–a crime against defensless living fetus–becomes a tragic but frequent choice.

Literate women and the book of life

According to Amartya Sen (1999)[96], there is considerable empirical evidence that women's education and literacy tend to reduce the mortality rates of children. Countries with basic gender inequalities, such as India, Pakistan, Bangladesh, China, Iran, those in West Asia, in North Africa and others more, often tend to have higher female mortality of infants and children. Employment empowers women, increasing their role and power, with positive effects on child care.
Men are typically known for being reluctant to do housekeeping and if their emancipated spouses are busy with an external job, the pressure to have more children naturally decreases.
Sen explains also that there is a close relationship between female literacy and child survival in many countries in the world, reducing also gender bias-more children survive but also the percentage of non surviving female decreases. Actually, the effect of female literacy on child mortality is extraordinary large, while male literacy or general poverty reduction has a comparatively ineffective

96 Chapter 8. Since this topic is related with gender problems, see also Chapter 10 of this book.

role. This is an important statement to think about, with huge practical applications for aid strategies.
High birthrates also include the denial of substantial freedoms that are routinely imposed on many Asian and African women, who are too often considered as mere reproducing ›machines‹. The social shame that many sterile women carry is another sad example of a backward mentality according to which the woman is frequently considered an object rather than a human being with her dignity and rights.
The questions we are addressing have high interdisciplinary links, embracing topics discussed in other Chapters[97]. Here we should underline that compulsory education raises the cost of children to parents–banning child labor and increasing the quantity and quality of time dedicated to each child–and so lowers fertility[98].

Trendy demography

When we discuss about the future of our planet and about the possible outcomes of the actual trends, one of the first topics to be analyzed (together with climatic changes) is demography. Many developing countries have population growth rates well in excess of 2 % per year and at this rate population is due to double in 35 years. While trends are subject to temporal changes and they tend to converge to more sustainable levels, it takes time to slow down any population increase, considering also its inertial drift.
Sooner or later, even poor countries, getting wealthier and more literate, undergo the demographic transition and they pass from a phase of high fertility–somewhat softened by high mortality, especially concerning children–and consequent high population growth, to a subsequent phase of lower fertility, lower mortality, and marginally decreasing population growth. Trends in demography[99] are concerned about a variety of interlinked issues. Among them, the dynamics of gender and poverty can for instance be analyzed under four demographic scenarios[100]

97 See Chapters 10 and 13.
98 See Eswaran in Banerjee, Benabou, Mookherjee (2006), p. 145.
99 See also http://www.unicef.org/sowc09/statistics/tables.php.
100 Source: http://www.geohive.com/default1.aspx http://web.worldbank.org/WBSITE/EXTERNAL/TOPICS/EXTGENDER/0,,contentMDK:21773978~menuPK:336874~pagePK:148956~piPK:216618~theSitePK:336868,00.html.

1. Populations that are growing rapidly due to high fertility

This fact has implications in women's health and labor force participation, as well as in the resources available to invest in children.

2. Populations in which fertility has fallen and dependency ratios are low

The extent to which women contribute to the potential gains of this ›demographic dividend‹ depends on policies that seek to invest in their human capital and facilitate their labor force participation.

3. Rapidly aging populations

Women are especially vulnerable because they live longer than men, but they tend to have lower lifetime earnings, due to lower labor force participation – with implications for their private savings and access to pensions and other sources of old age support linked to earnings.

4. Populations that have lost significant proportions of young adults due to factors such as HIV or sex-selection

Women may be more affected by factors such as HIV, through their greater involvement in caring for sick young adults and their children. By contrast, a shortage of adult women due to sex-selection has implications for male well being, especially in old age.

Table 4.1. – World most populated countries (millions)[101]

	1950	**2012 April**	**2050* estimate**
China	555	1,347	1,478
India	358	1,241	1,529
USA	158	312	349
Indonesia	80	238	312
Brazil	54	197	244
Pakistan	40	177	345
Nigeria	30	162	279
Bangladesh	42	151	265
Russia	102	143	121
Japan	84	128	105
World	**2,521**	**7,058**	**8,909**

Demographic trends are driven by the surviving (in)balance between fertility and mortality rates. The total fertility rate[102] (TFR)–the engine of demography–

[101] See http://www.nationsonline.org/oneworld/world_population.htm and http://www.photius.com/rankings/world2050_rank.html.

is a measure of the fertility of an *imaginary* woman, representing the number of children a woman would have if she was subject to prevailing fertility rates during her reproductive life from a single given year, and survives throughout all her childbearing years. It is a more direct measure of the level of fertility than the crude birth rate, since it refers to births per woman. TFR depicts the population inertial momentum, depending on its youth bulge, consequent to a baby boom or bust, which is profoundly likely to affect the population's composition. Mortality rates tend to decline before the total fertility rate, showing a demographic transition initial lag, culturally rooted within consolidated societal norms and needing time to be modified, acknowledging a recognition lag. When high fertility rates are not offset by high mortality rates, the imbalance brings to population growth.

The replacement fertility rate is roughly 2.1 births per woman for most industrialized countries, but it ranges from 2.5 to 3.3 in developing countries because of higher mortality rates. Below the replacement fertility rate, declining birthrate processes take place, with not trivial problems brought by an aging population. Taken globally, the total fertility rate at replacement is 2.33 children per woman. At this rate, global population growth would trend towards zero. When the TFR exceeds 5, as in much of Africa today, the population roughly doubles each generation[103]. Even slight changes in the total fertility rate can have a big–multiplier–impact on the population's trend and consistency.

The debate over population issues is flamed by ideological inclinations and by more objective differences of opinion and–like in many other disputes–the optimist cohabit both with the pessimist and the neutral.

As Sachs (2008), pp. 160-161, illustrates, population optimists rely on technology, which can provide the adequate means for unbound population growth, reminding the spectacular advances in food production and disease control and their welcome consequences in falling child mortality and rising life expectancy. Technology relies on path-breaking inventions made possible by geniuses' ignited minds and their no rival ideas, which–hopefully–represent a fairly constant proportion of the population and should accordingly grow together with it. Pessimists argue that growing humans are not nourished by ideas but rather by the depletion of natural resources, including fossil not renewable, while moderates are somewhat in the middle, acknowledging the importance of technology but also recognizing that their impact may not fully support the current massive population increase.

The demographic transition–driven by choice, not fate–should ideally bring to a soft landing where the population's inertial increase slows down, as a conse-

---

102 See https://www.cia.gov/library/publications/the-world-factbook/docs/notesanddefs.html ?countryName=France&country Code=fr&regionCode=eu#2127.

103 Sachs (2008), p. 165.

quence of interacting factors such as the improved child survival, the education and empowerment of girls and women.

Demography and poverty

Demography and poverty are increasingly recognized as intertwined problems. From a conference in Florence about this issue[104], we draw some useful insights. The relationship between demographic behavior and poverty is a central issue in economic demography but it is also a topic that has a tendency to be dominated more by ideology and preconception than by empirical evidence.

At first glance, being poor is a relatively simple concept, but poverty assessments are typically subjective and clouded in conceptual and methodological uncertainties[105].

There are also long-term issues. While alleviation of poverty and inequality is generally considered a high priority in the development process, there is considerably more debate about the impact of population growth to this laudable goal.

The poor are often blamed for a large share of environmental damage but this characterization is unfair because, individually, the poor have the least amount of power to damage the environment. In urban areas the poor are indeed avid recyclers–without their efforts the environmental degradation might be much worse (Satterthwaite).

David explored the evidence that high fertility and short spacing of births have negative consequences for the life-chances of family members, especially of children. These negative outcomes include higher morbidity and mortality, and worse nutrition.

For a variety of reasons, teenage mothers tend to be disproportionately represented among the poor and among those dependent on public assistance. Gage's paper addressed the social implications of adolescent pregnancy and childbearing, that it has been a topic of intense debate and controversy in recent years. Gage reviewed evidence on the potential negative consequences of adolescent fertility including, *inter alia*, low educational attainment, poor employment opportunities, low social mobility, and poor wages. Gage also reviewed some of the medical consequences of teenage pregnancy for both mothers and children, including unsafe–sometimes fatal–abortions in many countries where abortion is illegal or restricted.

Garcia documented the most common family survival strategies in Latin America, which include, *inter alia*: increased labor force participation of family members (particularly women), increased mean number of jobs held per family

---

104 http://www.iussp.org/Activities/scp-pov/pov-rep95.php.

105 If one uses a measure based purely on income, where should the poverty line be drawn? Should other dimensions of poverty be considered? There are many pitfalls to using cross-sectional data on income to measure poverty and well-being (Murdoch, Anand, 1999).

member, modified patterns of family consumption, internal and international migration of family members, and establishment or reactivation of networks of assistance between neighbors and relatives. At the same time the decline in living standards has also been associated with growing domestic violence– a phenomenon that Garcia argued is more widespread than is often realized –and increasing family instability.

One example of the complexities involved in jointly modeling demographic and economic behavior is the relationship between household mortality and poverty. Most studies that focus on the effect of poverty on mortality concentrate on the attempt of better understanding how household income or maternal and paternal education affect the probability of a child's survival.

As it was noted above, poverty does not necessarily have to be a permanent state.

Another issue concerns the demographic effects of coping mechanisms by which individuals, households and communities handle the problem of chronic or transient poverty and vulnerability. Another common coping response to poverty is migration[106]. Wery identified two types of adaptation: through out-migration and through changes in labor force participation. In turn, these changes affect rates and timing of demographic events or strategies. For example, Wery documented how out-migration can affect, *inter alia*, production and consumption patterns in household, labor force participation of other household members, dependency ratio, and local price of dowry. In turn, these changes can drive up the age at first marriage and the timing of childbearing.

Hunger and malnutrition remain the most devastating problems that the majority of the world's poor has to face. Poverty can lead to nutritional insecurity, which in turn can trigger a number of adaptive biological responses, both voluntary and involuntary, including weight loss, reduced physical activity, and increased metabolic efficiency. At the same time, food deprivation can cause temporary or irreversible deterioration of the productive capacity in man, creating a feedback loop to more permanent poverty.

Another link has to be found in deeply-rooted rural habits, according to which children are considered as a natural form of saving, since daughters and sons are bound to take care of their elder parents. Such a habit has little consideration for the demographic impact or the depletion rate of unbalanced demographic choices.

Population growth often pushes up innovation and investment and denser population can substantially alter the social and economic environment, increasing both problems and opportunities. Urbanization is likely to grow up and new markets open up, full of opportunities and challenges. The world's population increase on aggregate amplifies our planet's global growth.

---

[106] See Chapter 12

Life expectancy

The demographic spiral issue is linked with the most common demographic problems, such as life expectancy–the average number of years of life remaining at a given age[107].

In countries with high infant mortality rates, life expectancy at birth is highly sensitive to the rate of death in the first few years of life. In these cases, another measure such as life expectancy at age 5 can be used to exclude the effects of infant mortality to reveal the effects of causes of death other than early childhood causes.

Infant mortality and fertility are not independent but rather they are jointly determined. A decline in infant mortality that is due to an increase in per capita real income triggers a subsequent decline in fertility. This dynamic nexus between changes in infant mortality and fertility lies at the heart of the demographic transition.

Humans live on average 39.5 years in Swaziland and 81 years in Japan (2008 estimate). This is referred to as the ›life span‹, which is the upper boundary of life, the maximum number of years an individual can live. Life expectancy rises sharply in all cases for those who reach puberty. During the Industrial Revolution[108], life expectancy of children increased dramatically, showing a powerful and direct link between economic development and social conditions.

The Healthy Life Years indicator is a disability-free residual life expectancy, which has dramatically increased in the last decades almost everywhere, with the notable exception of Sub-Saharan Africa, where AIDS and recrudescent malaria are among the biggest responsible for life shortening and worsening.

Public health measures are credited with much of the recent increase in life expectancy[109].

There are great variations in life expectancy worldwide, mostly caused by differences in public health, medical care, and diet from country to country. Much of the early death in poorer nations is due to war, starvation, or diseases (AIDS, malaria …).

Significant differences still remain in life expectancy between men and women in developed countries, with women outliving men by five years or more. On average women tend to live until 80 years old whereas men are only expected to live until 74. These gender differences have been increasing in recent years.

Poverty, in particular, has a very substantial effect on life expectancy[110]. Life expectancy may also be reduced for people exposed to high levels of pollution.

---

107 See Sullivan, Sheffirn (2003) from which the next sentences are extracted.

108 See Chapter 1.

109 During the 20th century, the average lifespan in the United States increased by more than 30 years; 25 years of which can be attributed to advances in public health.

Occupation may also have a major effect on life expectancy. Well-educated professionals working in offices have a high life expectancy, while coal miners (and in prior generations, asbestos cutters) do not. Other factors affecting an individual's life expectancy are genetic disorders, obesity, access to health care, diet, exercise, tobacco smoking, and excessive drug and alcohol use. Even if obesity is very rare in underdeveloped countries and drugs are often hardly present, alcoholism can be a real problem, also because it is eased by the fermentation of many different fruits. AIDS has recently had a strong negative effect on life expectancy, especially in Sub-Saharan Africa.
Women tend to have a lower mortality rate at every age.

The population pyramid

The population pyramid evidences the distribution of various age groups in a population. In developing countries it shows a much larger base represented by young people, who are more eager to accept the challenges of a global world and who represent a great resource of human capital, with the enthusiasm and unconsciousness that only the young still have. Different age cohorts, showing the balance between young and elder people, have huge implications both on development and on national stability, which is weaker where a young population bulk is present.

[110] In the United Kingdom life expectancy in the wealthiest areas is on average ten years longer than the poorest areas and the gap appears to be increasing as life expectancy for the prosperous continues to increase while in more deprived communities there is little increase.

Figure 4.1. – The population pyramid

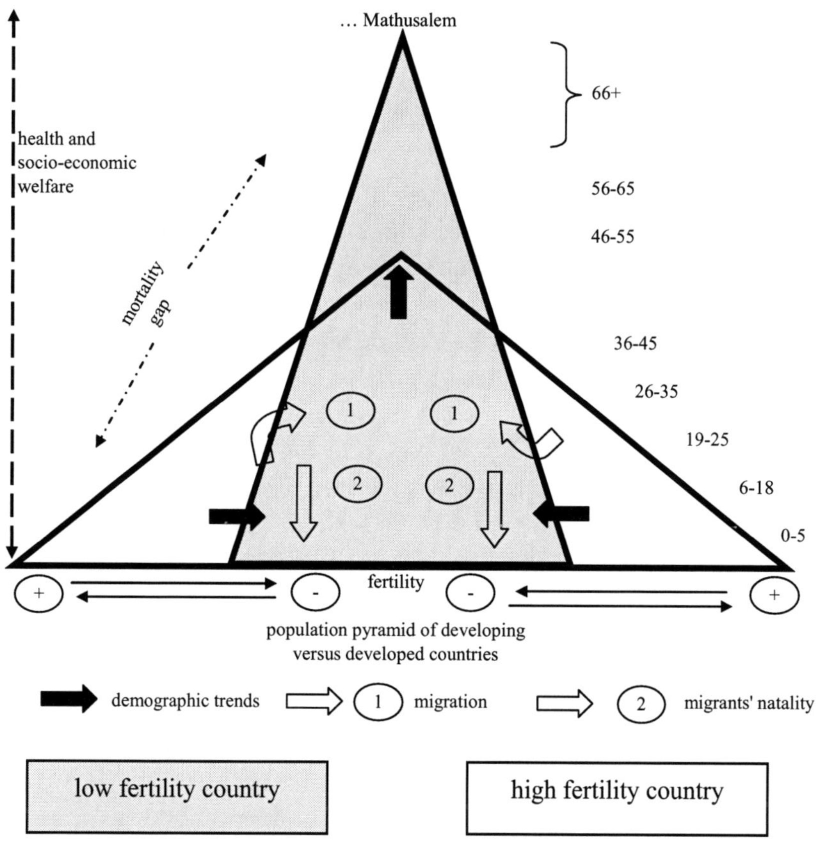

Converging fertility rates among different countries decrease the diversities of the population pyramid, typical of high or low fertility countries. The former are characterized by a pyramid with a broad base and a narrow peak, while the opposite applies to the latter.

Demographic imbalances may have destabilizing effects if young people represent an excessive proportion of population or a too limited part of it. Young's inability to vote and to matter poses big political challenges and it may severely hamper their freedom, as it happens for instance in Iran, where the young are an unrepresented majority of the population, as a result of a baby boom of some 20 years ago that is now converging to more stable fertility ratios.

Is growing population an opportunity, instead of a problem?

This whole Chapter is pervaded by a creeping pessimism about overpopulation, due to concomitant and interacting factors such as:

- gloomy–but–trendy apocalyptic Malthusian prophecies;
- the evidence that countries with a growing population trend are typically poorer;
- sustainability worries about over-consumption of the limited resources of our overcrowded planet.

Whereas these worries are sometimes justified–especially the sustainability ones–they however seem unable to capture and fully synthesize the complex nature of the problem. The main point in demography is not only–or not mainly–the population number, but rather its increasing or diminishing trend. A perspective movie–a forecast–may be more meaningful than a photography of the current situation, reminding that marginal growth typically has a decreasing pace, bringing to an inertial maximum and then slowly declining from that apex.

If these are well known considerations, their economic consequences are somewhat less trivial, as it is showed by evidence from developed countries–from Japan to Western Europe–where the population is stable or declining and especially getting older, due to a growing negative birth rate. Such consequences, far from being benign, are often even more worrying than those concerning the opposite case of growing birthrate.

When less and less people go to work and more retire, the pension system and the welfare state (which is so complex and capillary in developed countries) gets troubled, since pensions tend to outweigh workers' contributions. With an increasingly elder population, fixed social costs–from pensions to healthcare and caring–tend to grow and, in order to finance them, fiscal pressure is forced to increase accordingly.

As a matter of fact, downward demographic trends pose challenging threats that are not less problematic than those caused by demographic growth. Even if pressure on natural not renewable sources' exploitation softens–mitigating ecological wonders–other often underestimated and misperceived problems arise. This fact is mainly due to decreasing fertility rates, but sometimes also to higher mortality rates, which change the demographic structure of the country: with a population that is getting older and a correspondent reduction of the workforce, there is a progressive and cumulated loss of competitiveness.

Ethnic composition also changes, since demographic trends are never synchronous among different clans. Examples are given by ageing Russia or Japan, the latter being also a more homogeneous ethnic environment. Since in some countries population is decreasing while in others it is increasing, immigration in the former is often unavailable and, by the wisest, even welcome – are the numerous poor going to save the childless rich?

As we shall see elsewhere–for example in Chapters 19 or 22–demography has a huge impact on savings rate, which psychologically depends on the willingness to delay consumption, in order to harvest future generations. Low fertility is unsurprisingly associated with decreasing saving attitudes.
Demographic trends also play a fundamental complementary role, since changing savings' lifecycles tend to adapt to population modifications.

The condensed Chapter

The poor multiply themselves and their misery, while the rich experiment demographic decline. The world is getting increasingly crowded, threatening our fragile ecosystem albeit with a marginal decreasing trend, despite gloomy Malthusian worries about deathly balancing of exuberant population growth, contradicted by technological advances.
The best antidote against excessive fertility and its induced poverty traps is represented by women instruction and emancipation, softening old fashioned tendencies of over-procreation.

Out of Poverty Tips

Sustainable fertility, albeit difficult to envisage and fine tune, is a key target for balanced development and its fair distribution, transforming demography from a trap to the liveliest resource.

Selected Readings

BANERJEE A.V., BÉNABOUR R., MOOKHERJEE D., (2006), *Understanding Poverty*, Oxford University Press, Oxford.

CHAPTER 5 – Misery, conflicts and bad governance back themselves

> War is the mother of every poverty.
>
> Andrea Riccardi, *Living together*

Poverty and conflict trap: years of pain ahead?

Among poverty traps, conflicts and bad political governance play a fundamental role, magnetizing other problems and amplifying their long term perverse effects. Around the world, extreme poverty, especially if induced by conflict strategies, fuels a volatile and hardly manageable mix of desperation and instability, which is easily exported outside the weak and porous borders of failing States.

Poverty is often a synonym of dehumanizing violence and, according to the Mahatma Gandhi »poverty is the worst form of violence«. Are the underserved too poor for peace?

Poor countries tend to be intrinsically insecure and the poor are often besieged by an escalating bloody violence. Violence behaves like a drug–the more you use it, the more you get addicted–but is however hardly a solution to violence and instinctive revenge needs to be overcome, as culture is teaching us, trying to bypass the drama of fratricide conflict, from Cain and Abel onwards.

The destabilizing effect of fruitless wars is well known even in today's developed countries and historical memory[111] can be very helpful, even in this case. History is full of wars and a history of wars is simply history itself, even if it may be severely biased, especially if legends are written by the winners. The complete eradication of wars is among the mightiest–but still unfulfilled–dreams of humanity, even if claiming that wars reduce needs to their true essence, there are those who stress the cathartic effect of conflicts.

According to Wangari Maathai (2009), Kenian Nobel Prize for peace »cultures of peace take the form of fairness, respect, compassion, forgiveness, recompense, and justice«.

The link between war and poverty is so evident that it hardly needs any demonstration, even if it has many different and often hidden consequences, which are worth to be analyzed.

---

[111] See Chapter 1.

The conflict trap is one of the four main obstacles to development illustrated by Paul Collier (2007), together with bad governance in a small country, the natural resource trap[112] and being landlocked with bad neighbors[113]. It is not surprising that countries suffering from protracted armed conflicts occupy the lowest ranks of the Human Development Index[114].

»Wars and coups are not tea parties: they are development in reverse«[115]–it may take years to build what can be destroyed in a few hours. But the conflict trap is possibly the worse of the many examined in this book, due to its huge, immediate, and contagious impact on other traps, such as undernourishment, famine, forced migration and displacement, property destruction, and other long lasting intangible–but not less dangerous–psychological traps, such as traumas, despair, and hopelessness.

Synergic and self fulfilling perverse links within the traps[116] are sadly common. Wars and insurrections are nourished and often anticipated by dysfunctional bad governance, which weakens the democratic institutions, wherever present. The geographical handicap of being landlocked pushes towards the conquer of a sea access, especially if neighbors are not ›friendly‹ and the trapped country remains at odds with them, risking to be engulfed in a ruinous conflict. The natural resources trap is fed by bad governance and often distracting conflicts … and so on. When communal and mechanical mass violence–somewhat even hate-less–becomes endemic, so does economic decline.

Poverty makes a country more prone to conflict and also continuous conflicts keep a country poor, following a biunique causal pattern of causes and consequences that can easily become a self fulfilling loop. Repressive measures from military powers have a big impact on unfreedom and they typically target the haunted poor, violating their human rights and strongly contributing to their enduring underdevelopment. When things go wrong, tyrants need to find a scapegoat and the weaker they are, the easier it is to attack and destroy. The poor are an obvious and likely target of dissatisfaction and dismay, whose causes are however originated elsewhere.

The situation is difficult above all for young people. Teenagers, often orphans, walk with bare feet through bombed huts, in backward and brutal environments. How could those who represent the age of innocence, dream of a better and peaceful world, if they have known only war in their short life, being unable to cash the peace dividend?

---

112 See Chapter 3.

113 See Chapter 2.

114 The HDI combines three dimensions: life expectancy at birth, as an index of population health and longevity; adult literacy rate and standard of living. See http://hdr.undp.org/en/

115 Collier (2009), p. 9.

116 See Chapter 24.

As Paul Collier[117] magisterially explains, the first and most ›deflagrating‹ of the four traps is conflict; 73% of those in the poorest billion of the world's population are either involved in the civil war or are recovering from it. In the fight against poverty civil war, erupting within one country and its broken society creates a vicious circle: war causes poverty, and low income contributes to tension.

Low growth means high unemployment and thus means plenty of angry young men ready to fight. Conflict then destroys infrastructure and it scares away domestic and foreign investors, leaving even fewer opportunities for development. Building lasting peace–both practical and attainable–has to be a major part of any poverty solving strategy. Past incidence of conflict is one of the best and unluckiest predictors of poverty.

Two costly forms of political conflict are short termed violence, in the form of an often bloodless coup d'état, and long lasting dreadful civil or regional wars. Both are often repetitive because convalescent countries are often too weak to fully recover and it is easy for them to get ill again. Conflicts, in whatever form, can trap a country in poverty for long – it is a healthy economy that protects peace. To the extent that conflict causes are often deeply and culturally rooted, it is hard to try to eradicate them, becoming a tiring and often frustrating task. It might take ages to rebuild what you can destroy in a few seconds (is it easier to bomb a house or to build it?), and irrational violence is much more difficult to control than enduring peaceful intentions.

War is the first and most evident enemy of development, because it is–in any sense–the most powerful destroyer. Historical wounds are often much more damaging and longer lasting than destroyed villages, which are easier to rebuild. The memory and spirit of dead relatives live for long in their descendants, often struggling for their whole life between appeasement and revenge, fighting an interior psychological conflict, in a tragic dilemma suspended between war and peace, agony, and ecstasy. Social and civil amnesia are hardly synonyms of peace building and keeping.

Most of the poorest countries have reached the point of being more or less always in war, since they frequently pass through many civil wars, as Sudan sadly exemplifies, with its ethnic conflicts in Darfur or opposing the North to the secessionist South. This fact is in contrast with the historical experience of the Spanish, American, Russian, French or British civil wars, which were tough but occasional.

Lack of spontaneous and unbiased feedback (the essence of democracy) prevents dictators from realizing about their mistakes. Dictators are increasingly paranoid with their hegemonic dreams and they are detached from reality, espe-

---

117 See http://makewealthhistory.org/2008/12/08/why-some-countries-remain-poor-paul-colliers-four-poverty-traps/ and, for a complete description, Collier (2007).

cially if surrounded by pleasing yes-men. Their actions easily escalate in an endless spiral of tremendous insanity, violence, and vengeance, destroying both the economy and the civil society.

War games and killing fields

Causes of war are manifold and they are often due to apparently trivial psychological causes, such as conflicting and envious personalities, hatreds, betrayals, jealousy, mistakes or even–at a macro level–rival nationalisms or small ethnic clashes, which degenerate and bring societies to a disruptive meltdown. The roots of war are intrinsically within us, in the violence of our continuous conflicting relationship with the others.

Thucydides[118], the father of ›scientific history‹, recalls that »war takes away the easy supply of daily wants, and so proves a rough master, that brings most men's characters to a level with their fortunes«.

There are also many ways to conduct a war: through international invasion, with a subversive rebellion that drives to civil war or even with surgical coup. Conflicts are often destructive, even if in some limited cases they may be welcome, should they succeed in replacing bad dictators without much bloodshed. In poor countries colonialism has long kept the lid on boiling internal wars, since they imposed a fragile artificial peace. Different ethnicities were indeed all equally subject to a foreign dominating ruler and they were unable to settle ancestral tensions that were simply waiting for the first chance to angrily reappear.

Dictators and their puppets dislike democracy and free elections, and the sacredness of their undisputed power is hard to challenge, since they tend to be self referential. What challenges dictators, even more than a coup, is the potential threat that it may eventually take place at any time and typically with no preventive notice. Differently from free elections, coups are indeed not publicized and fixed in advance and dictators know that their allies and the army that have to defend them against coups can soon revolt the situation, developing a predatory attitude and becoming the worst enemy.

Potential coups should in theory keep dictators quiet and make them cautious. However countermeasures such as strengthening the army are dangerous and expensive, above all considering that aspirant dictators may succeed only if they pay soldiers more or make them larger undemocratic promises.

According to Collier (2007), (2009), there is a link between risk of war and initial level of income. Civil war is much more likely to break out in low-income countries–halving the starting income of a country, the risk of a civil war dou-

118 ›*History of the Peloponnesian War*‹, 3.82.2.

bles. Civil wars tend to be more persistent than international conflicts and they typically last more than ten times as long, structurally being difficult to halt[119].
Rebel movements, which recruit hopeless and fearless desperate poor, romantically nicknamed ›freedom fighters‹, tend to justify themselves and their actions with noble grievances such as repression, exploitation, and exclusion–easily forgotten if and when they conquer power. A global supermarket of deadly weapons, increasingly available at bargain prices, leverages up conflicts and their potential mortality toll.
War, often conceived by criminal minds, has always been cruel and ruthless, everywhere, today and even in ancient times – opening the door to hell. Merciless winners, overwhelmed by the sadness of evil, like devils with an angel's face, often throw anonymous dead in mass graves, excited by wild and uncontrolled violence.
Retaliation against the powerless defeated, which incarnate a physical scapegoat, to be tortured up to killing, is common outburst for a dissatisfaction whose reasons should instead be found elsewhere. Blood spilling, coming out of accumulated hatred, is often an unavoidable by-product of uncontrolled and irrational violence, whose poisoned arrows bring time back to the dark Middle Age of history.

History is littered with tragic conflicts

Great historical watersheds are often triggered by destabilizing conflicts, inventing horrors, often from scratch. Lessons from tragedies are hardly enough for those who constantly look for enemies, fueling a culture of contraposition, paying a tribute to collective hysteria, in an escalating sad gallery of instinctive violence–and sanctuaries of violence cool down in mass graves.
Regime survival is often backed by an expansion of political patronage of the ruling ethnic clan, at the expense of meritocratic and impartial growth, causing stagnation and social unrest that sooner or later foment rebellion. Rebellion occurs especially if the discriminated ethnicities–which are often victims of collective and selective violence–are many and their repressed discontent is great. Sorrow and mourning are a tragic epilogue of deadly wars. War has to be exorcized with a cultural effort, understanding its impact, learning from painful historical experience. Pacificators–more than pacifists–are hardly needed, together with their irenic utopia.
Recruiting new rebels may be easy and cheap. Even remittances from relatives abroad can help the cause of rebellion and rebels are soon learning international marketing and public relations. Examples range from the Irish immigrated to

---

119 Collier (2009), p. 3.

the U.S., financing rebellion against the English in Northern Ireland, to Cubans escaped in Florida trying to kick off the too long lasting dictator Fidel Castro.
Political repression is however–may be surprisingly–not directly linked with the risk of a civil war[120]. Segregated ethnic minorities, with their hidden and sleepless history of discrimination, are just as likely to rebel with or without clan or racial prejudice, experimenting sad contradictions such as foreignness at home.
Violence stands out as the rudimentary voice of inequality and exclusion and ›purifier‹ genocides and cleansing eliminate interethnic worries, exterminating unwanted minorities, even if hardly up to the point of erasing the wounded memory of survivors. International treaties such as the Convention on the Prevention and Punishment of the Crime of Genocide[121] have the uneasy task to prevent mass murdering, a typical by product of the scourge of war.
There is a self fulfilling spiral even with wars, since war makes a country poor and poverty makes war more likely. Civil war reduces income, contributes to an environmental decline and makes resources scarcer. And low income increases the risk of civil war. Chain bilateral causes and effects are hard to stop and to prevent, especially if they are deeply culturally rooted, as we have seen before. Violence is a shortcut for problems, much more direct and simpler than dialogue and painful peacekeeping. It takes time to confuse differences.
Like in economics, expectations are very important and often self-realizing. Slow growth or, even worse, stagnation and decline make a country prone to civil war, but it is also the anticipation of war that causes a socio-economic decline, since people feel unsafe, uncomfortable, and not eager to invest in a gloomy future – would you build a home or start up a business knowing that it can soon be bombed?
A moribund economy is unsurprisingly hosted in a weak country, where the State is hardly present and often powerless: few–or any–public services such as infrastructures, public hospitals and schools, a fair justice, artificial borders, hardly present order and police, unemployment and diffused misery, hunger, and discontent within the army. All these points depress the immune defenses of a State, easing unsurprisingly rebellion.
Wars disrupt human capital and it may take generations to fully recover from it. War and peace, the two alternating states of the world which has inspired Tolstoj's masterpiece, continuously remix, with transitory periods where uncertainties about the outcome prevent any proper development planning.
In modern times a new cultural attitude is painfully starting to consider war as neither necessary or inevitable nor useful. According to John Kennedy »mankind must put an end to war, or war will put an end to mankind«.
Epitaph on a tombstone »I was nobody, now I am myself«.

---

120 See Collier (2007), p. 23.
121 www2.ohchr.org/english/law/genocide.htm.

(Un)civil wars

According to the Heidelberg Institute for International Conflict Research (HIIK)[122], conflicts are clashes of interest (differences of position) concerning national values (territory, secession, decolonization, autonomy, system/ideology, national power, regional predominance, international power, resources, other). These clashes are of a certain duration and scope and they involve at least two parties (organized groups, States, groups of States, organizations of States) which are determined to pursue their interests and to win their cases. Conflict intensity is defined according to the state of violence and its intensity. HIIK also publishes every year a conflict barometer[123], which well evidences the width and breadth of conflicts.

The risk of a civil war is also increased by dependence upon commodity exports, from polluting oil to bloody diamonds and it is a somewhat counterintuitive bad surprise, since bonanza resources should make the country richer and more stable–as we have learnt from Chapter 3.

Another illusion–still according to Collier–is that civil wars largely depend on ethnic strife. Many multiethnic societies, such as Brazil, substantially–even if difficultly–live in peace while others ethnically pure countries, such as Somalia, suffer an enduring civil war.

The risk seems higher whereas an ethnic dominant group is accompanied by strong minorities–as for example Rwanda, where the bloodshed between the Hutu majority and the Tutsi minority got its peak in the genocide of Spring 1994.

Even geography somewhat matters and vast countries with dispersed ethnicities, such as again Democratic Republic of Congo, or with many forests, such as the Amazonas in Colombia, are riskier than flat and densely populated States. Guerrillas find indeed it easier to form and hide and central government is weak and far.

Another by now unsurprising relationship is between the country's income at the onset of a conflict and its potential time extension: the lower the income, the longer the war.

Civil wars–again following Collier–are highly persistent and they continue with stops and go just because they become normal and ›institutional‹. The experience of having passed through a civil war roughly doubles the risk of another conflict. In low-income countries relapses are very common and history in the aftermath of a conflict is still troubled and volatile and it normally takes time, up to a decade or more, to cool it down. Each coup surreptitiously tends to legitimize the following one, especially if people understand that it may be easy to

---

122 http://hiik.de/en/index.html.

123 http://hiik.de/en/konfliktbarometer/pdf/ConflictBarometer_2008.pdf.

organize, so infecting their hot minds of power seekers with dangerous temptations.
Politicians in power accordingly know that the situation is unstable and when recovering from conflict, they use most of the money they have (that is often improperly leaking from foreign aid for humanitarian relief and help in reconstruction) to keep the army ready against another likely coup or war. Armies are expensive and often unreliable, since soldiers require to be well paid to (pretend to) be loyal, magnetized by wealth.
Army factions are often divided and they share the risk of being on the wrong side, nobody's knowing which is going to prevail, and such factions are those which almost always gain, sharing power and money with politicians (and oil and mining companies in resource-rich countries), to the detriment of the uninteresting poorest, for which the game nearly always ends up with a defeat.
Civil war is acutely defined by Collier as »development in reverse«.
As the Guns N' Roses sing »I don't need your civil war–It feeds the rich while it buries the poor«.

Contagious conflicts

If naughty neighboring countries have a well equipped and large army, it seems wise to build up appropriate countermeasures to avoid a domino effect, which may bring to cross border conflicts. Behind an external threat there are always economic reasons, concerning both the wealth potentially graspable and the rate of growth that domination can guarantee. Civil wars impose direct and hidden costs on unlucky neighbors, as well as long lasting territorial disputes.
The peace dividend, in spite of its consistency, is often unable to show its real appeal, because senseless war seems often more seductive. Strategists concerned about preventive measures often favor a neighborhood arms race, both escalating and exponential.
The only feasible alternative is to be federated with other allies, in order to share costs of a common defense system, such as the NATO. However, the mutual assistance in case of attack needs to be trustworthy and it is anyway expensive and uneasy to set up and keep. Military escalation[124] is difficult to stop, and single steps from one country have to be neutralized by appropriate counter defensive actions.
Every conflict damages both the country and its unlucky neighbors, since it is economically expensive. Globalization encourages the risk of spreading conflicts well beyond the national boundaries where they typically start. This case occurs especially when borders are porous–as it still happens in many Stateless

[124] For an analysis of military expenditure, conflict management and related issues, see the website of the Stockholm Peace Research Institute, http://www.sipri.org/.

countries of Sub-Saharan Africa–and when violence can be easily exported in an increasingly interconnected world, where transports, money flows, and trading of weapons are much easier than in the past.
Refugees may export or cause conflict in recipient countries, stimulating a cross-border reaction from their former country or clashing with locals, due also to emergency settlement in already occupied territories.
During a conflict, economic activity gets stuck and if the country is already poor and landlocked, its problems become desperate, often bringing to famine and unrest. If the country in war borders in particular landlocked ones, it suddenly exports its problems.
There are also conflicts which might block a big river going to another country. What would Egypt do with its unique source of life coming from the Nile in case of an obstruction caused by a war in Sudan or Ethiopia or Uganda? The same may apply to Brazil with the Amazonas River coming from Colombia and the Andes, but the list is long and certainly not limited to rivers.
Wars between neighbors were almost always the case in the past, unless conducted by sea, but are nowadays not necessarily the standard cases, because aircraft and long distance missiles can easily bypass geographical barriers. Unbalanced military power is an ideal propellant behind conflict – you go to war with the soldiers you have, but differences with your rival may be substantial.
Many of the costs of conflicts are born in neighboring countries and war easily exports its nasty by-products, typically not being particularly respectful of law and order. Roughly 95% of the global production of hard drugs comes, for instance, from conflict countries such as Colombia or Afghanistan. Diseases quietly travel everywhere without any passport and they are often transported by soldiers, as it happened in 1527 with the Lanzichenecchi venture soldiers bringing the plague to Rome while sacking it or, more recently, with mercenaries and other soldiers who rape women and spread AIDS all across Sub-Saharan Africa–a war was probably the first vehicle for random dissemination in the late 1970s of the then unknown illness.
To those who haven't known the war they parents suffered, a sign to remind it is often left with landmines – a patient killing device which can make his dirty job even decades after the end of a war.
Technology, so useful elsewhere, has inevitably raised the death toll and new weapons, symbolized by nuclear bombs, make havoc much more easily. The difference is not negligible and it deserves deeper reflections on the issue.
Poor people distressed by war often export the only valuable thing they've got, that is themselves and their dearest. This is not an easy task, because these people have often to walk long distances with bare feet and little water and food, towards bordering nations or other countries that are willing to accept them as refugees. Survivors carry back painful souvenirs of deadly wartime.

During wars or under dictatorships, mass deportations follow the ›*divide et impera*‹–divide and rule–that is a well known strategy, weakening ethnic clans with preemptive purges, diluting their concentration, and cutting their ancestral social links among themselves and with their native lands. The long lasting cultural and psychological effect may be devastating even for the luckiest who are able to survive unfair displacement and it may take generations to recover from it. Deliberate humiliation of the poor, instilling inside them a permanent sense of inferiority and fear, is a ruthless–albeit common–form of control, which is not compatible with the rule of law and with the respect of basic human rights but anyway widely practiced by careless tyrants.

Since countries bordering conflicting States are typically poor and unstable on their own, mass migration is often the last desperate attempt to survive, albeit knowing that a warm welcome in the host country is highly unlikely. Relatives abroad can sometimes help, and migration to safer and richer countries continues well after the war is over. Never knowing what destiny is about, it is widely acknowledged that relapses to another conflict are highly frequent and uneasy to avoid.

Poverty can spread instability and terrorism well beyond the boundaries of its native location and it is in the interest of everybody–even that of distracted and distant developed nations–to settle and solve the problem. Ghost-Stateless-countries are a safe harbor for terrorism, due to their weak controls, easy complicity in exchange for little support and facility to recruit cheap and desperate supporters.

Let it bleed: counting the damages, when the war is over

Most of the economic costs of a civil war–perhaps as much as half, as Collier (2007) suggests–accrue when the war is over and transition towards pacification is still a fragile option. This shouldn't be surprising, if only we think that during the conflict many economic activities are indeed suspended, traveling is difficult, the media are hardly working. When the smoke of destruction is over, you can better see and assess the damages.

Internationally coordinated recovery approaches to post-conflict situations, even in order to prevent relapses, are still in their infancy, as Collier (2009), p. 75, recalls. The awareness of their strategic importance is still far from being properly understood–but this is always the case with prevention, a cultural value that finds it difficult to be recognized as it should. Economic recovery, with progressive baby steps to development, is possibly the best antidote against civil war relapses, because it contributes to enduring peacekeeping, even if it is uneasy to invest in a cloudy scenario.

Hyper-inflation during conflicts and afterwards is a typical corollary of war, since many desperate governments print money, putting a hidden future tax on their unaware citizens, often unable to recognize its long term perverse effects. Inflation destroys both the accumulation of wealth, soon devaluating it, and any trust in the economy, bringing to balancing competitive devaluations of the local currency and to a consequent sharp decrease in the purchasing power of already poor citizens.

Wars are expensive ›investments‹, always looking for financial coverage, with different graduations, depending on their extent, duration, and sophistication of weaponry used. They tend to go on to the extent that they can find money, often coming from unofficial ›dirty‹ circuits. Second hand markets for armies are more frequent than we may think – business is business and many developing countries are eager to buy older weapons at … ›fire‹ sales.

Blocking the influx of money and arms to warlords is a highly recommendable strategy, which is often characterized by embarrassing fiascos. The latter occur since weapons and money follow international parallel markets and wars are often unofficially backed by regional or international powers which often have an edge on the U.N. or other agencies, being close, more committed with self interests, and more used to exhausting dirty games.

Not only conflict management is typically proving to be a hard job–as foreign peacekeepers can sadly report–but also post war strategies are possibly even harder to conceive and implement. It is easy to win the war and to subsequently lose the peace. And destroyed places take ages to recapture their historical soul, often lost forever.

Among the economic traps that according to Collier can ease a civil war, there are low income, slow growth, and dependence about primary commodity exports. The best antidote is probably represented by cumulated growth over time, as it helps the general level of incomes (considering those directly positively affected by growth but also the positive spill-over on the rest of the economy) and the diversification of exports, particularly for commodity exporting countries.

The combinations of negative factors that, together, bring to rebellion and later on to civil war, follow a probability factor, much more likely in poor countries.

Civil wars leave a legacy of woes, revenges, killing lists, unrest, and legal problems (with seized properties claimed back by original owners …) which are more difficult to set than coups, which often represent just a political change of the guard, of course … without democratic polls. Forgiveness is always difficult and it depends also on cultural and religious habits of different ethnic groups.

On their side, coups tend to be much more frequent because they are easier and normally less dramatic than civil wars. When war is officially over, following an armistice or an undisputed victory, a collateral conflict is likely to continue, even for years, albeit softened and classified as a low-level period of violence.

In such a case–so unluckily frequent–the impact on the vilified population is typically devastating and it suffocates any optimism about a better future, hindering reconstruction and reconciliation of those who can't forget and forgive and fomenting revenge, especially if ethnic disparities are involved. As von Clausewitz admonishes »victory is purchased by blood«. Relapses are frequent in a fragile environment and a new war may be looming on the horizon, with all the social and economic costs of a return to conflict. It is often easy–as history teaches us–to win the war and lose the peace.

When institutions are weak, criminal gangs–the slum lords–can easily penetrate the poorest areas, violently keeping insecurity and unrest alive and strongly hindering development. According to the charismatic and controversial former secretary of Amnesty International, Irene Khan (2009), p. 92 »crime prevention and public security are extremely complex challenges but they are inextricably linked to human rights protection and are of crucial importance to people living in poverty«.

The real costs of a war have to be detected considering its length and depth – the shorter, the lower.

War has also a catastrophic impact on education, reducing government public spending, destroying schools, and killing both the students and their teachers. Orphans, especially if they have to take care of younger sisters and brothers, are much less likely to attend school, considering it not a priority in survival times.

The phase out from traumatic conflicts is a delicate restoration passage that may hopefully bring to peace, but it is both dangerous and hazardous, bewaring of (likely) relapses. Discounting the future is however difficult when life expectancy is shortened by external events.

Peace needs to be built gradually–step after step–and sudden miracles are by definition hardly likely, whereas long termed enduring efforts are less spectacular but much likelier to pay off.

It is always difficult, albeit important, to try to forgive–going beyond crime impunity–and to forget. And it takes time for smoking guns to cool down.

Dialogue reduces hatred and diffidence, looking for the uneasy conscience of peace and trying to discover and share common ideals, forgetting divisions and remembering that »poverty is the parent of revolution and crime«, as Aristotle used to say. Diplomatic transitions towards a possible peace come from dialogue, meetings, mediation, sharing and agreeing, informally bridging fractures with friendship. and flexibility.

Bad governance and kleptocracy

According to Confucius »in a country well governed, poverty is something to be ashamed of. In a country badly governed, wealth is something to be ashamed of«.

Bad governance is another big issue, closely related to conflicts, once again with two-way side effects, according to which weak governance makes wars easier, but conflicts prosper within a bad governance context–where the legal and regulatory system is moribund–and have it as a natural by-product, leaving a challenging ›intangible‹ legacy for the post war reconstruction of lawless and ungovernable countries.

Poor countries are so even because they tend to have a poor governance system, falling into a vicious circle that is difficult to be interrupted. When endemic predation and corruption offer greater rewards than providing stable administration, State leaders are strongly tempted to undermine their country, dilapidating and dissipating common wealth, and showing the disastrous impact of fair leadership deficits. On a lower hierarchical level, corruption is often a by-product of hunger and desperation. When the belly is empty, also moral values begin starving.

Ruthless politicians are eager to put up kleptocratic governments where bribes and rampant corruption–a way of life–are the core issues, together with supportive cronyism, in an attempt to fully exploit the lucky coincidence of being in power. Looking for the asymmetric reward of the ruling ethnic group or coalition, the relatives and those belonging to the enlarged clan are the natural beneficiaries of mass robbery, which often completely depletes the government's safe box, leaving little or any cash for public services.

Corruption is even more detrimental to domestic growth when money is brought away in complacent foreign banks, instead of being spent locally. The army is always a key component of the mechanism, since dictators and their puppets need continuous military support in a volatile environment where aspirant dictators are frequent, and they are often looking for a somewhat ›democratic‹ tribal rotation system. According to such a system, each tribe should alternatively be given its chance to rob, following an awkward ›distribution‹ system.

The ruling party is an irresistible magnet for the corrupt, not just the talented[125]. If someone succeeds, his relatives or friends are very likely to insist on sharing in the fruits of his success, since they belong to the same enlarged ›big family‹, often arriving to the point of transforming a successful position into a nightmare. Brothers, cousins, friends, and their relatives queue up looking for patronage, recommendations, and material support. And while politicians quarrel about the booty, the poor suffer.

---

[125] Calderisi (2006), p. 74.

Bad governance can be present everywhere but in poor countries it is simply much more likely and it is responsible for slower growth much more than initial poverty.

Paul Collier[126] examines the problem, jointly with the other mentioned poverty traps (including the natural resources trap, typically misused to support puppet regimes).

Governance is concerned with decisions that define expectations, grant power, or verify performance and it conveys the administrative and process-oriented elements of governing. Pillars of good governance imply a fair, honest, transparent, and efficient use of resources, for the sake of stakeholders that pivot around the organization (in our case, the citizens of a State). Conversely, bad governance is concerned with the absence of accountability and transparency in public affairs. Rules make governance enforceable, balancing the trade off between an increasing set of complicated norms and the necessity to keep them ›simple and stupid‹ – too many rules equal no rules.

Ethnic polarization in a win-win scenario is often accompanied by a weak and predatory governance system, which tries to fully exploit the ruling opportunity, maximizing short term accumulation, with a consequent asymmetric partitioning where only clan members are invited to share the pie – try to take profit of your turn, when it comes. Narrow interests, according to which those in power leave little representation and limited rights to the opposition, automatically exclude the many poor.

Misery is always caused by bad governance, again with a two-way causal effect, since it is also poverty that induces poor and inadequate governance. Bad governance is, in its simplest terms, an intangible but powerful misery trap.

The lack of reliable and working social infrastructures (that is the institutional and government policies which provide unavoidable economic incentives) is another characteristic of bad governance. Its deep causal effects are discouraging innovation and capital accumulation, which are among the two most powerful ingredients of growth–falling into rent–seeking, corruption, and theft[127] and remembering that parasitic rents of few privileged crooks, the sycophants supporting the tyrants and looking for personal patronage, suffocate the growth of all, with bribes, asymmetric public spending, and cash diversions. Idolatry for money is at the very heart of abuse of power.

Again, it takes time and pain to build up a good social infrastructure within the complex long run development process. A difficult learning process, by trial and error, and a continuous fine tuning of checks and balances are required, since fairness and honesty are a necessary but not sufficient ingredient.

---

[126] See, extensively, Collier (2007), Chapter 5.

[127] Helpman (2004), p. 128.

Good governance is, on its optimistic side, a precondition without which the State cannot be trusted, with enormous negative consequences. Well established international investors stay far away from a weak-governance country (would you play a game without knowing its rules, being aware that they are arbitrarily set and conveniently changeable at any time by your counterpart?). Honest citizens are scared and discouraged from making business, while–on the other side–when corruption becomes endemic and unpunished, profiteers are attracted, injustice proliferates, and meritocracy, so important for growth, is set apart as a useless and disturbing particular. And corruption hurts the poor most, also because they are hardly protected by mercenary and intimidating judicial systems.

Bad governance is not only a condition that pertains just to developing countries, but it can also, with its various degrees of intensity, contribute to worsen their picture, representing an enormous obstacle to growth and eventually bringing to a complete lack of trust.

It takes time and pain to develop a good governance system, bringing up civil servants and teaching them properly how to look for common good. A decent pay … keeps bribes away, since those who are wealthy enough, simply don't need to steal and everybody knows how temptations are difficult to resist. Corruption is fatalistically endemic in all the poorest countries, since it is so deeply rooted that it becomes culturally accepted and often hardly challenged. Pressure groups for transparency and democracy seldom exist and when they do, they are often weak, failing to collect massive support.

The institutions that determine governance are difficult to reform, especially from inside. Almost everyone agrees that corruption is bad for growth, but still it remains pervasive.

Ailing countries typically lack civic sense, that is a virtual stock of capital which improves the overall performance of a society. It takes ages to accumulate it and a short time to dissipate it, even because it proves expensive to sacrifice particular interests for collective good.

The World Bank has built an index – the Country Policy and Institutional Assessment (CPIA) which measures the extent to which a country's policy and institutional framework supports sustainable growth and poverty reduction, and consequently the effective use of development assistance[128].

Bad governance is intrinsically nurtured by information asymmetries, and misbehaviors such as corruption have to be disguised in order not to end up in scandals. E-government makes it possible to publish on the Web much public and relevant information with no restrictions and so it represents a powerful and cheap way of softening misgovernment. The Internet can have indeed a big im-

---

128 See http://web.worldbank.org/WBSITE/EXTERNAL/EXTABOUTUS/IDA/0,,contentMD:20941073~pagePK:51236175~piPK:437394~theSitePK:73154,00.html.

pact on transparency and democracy and that's why dictatorial governments so strongly oppose it.

Failing banana republics

Failing States[129] in war torn and sliding backward societies–those defined by Collier as low–income countries with poor governance and ailing economic policies-hardly ever can turn around on their own. It is again the problem of an external help needed to get out of quicksand.

Governments should be first of all concerned about providing basic education, legal frameworks, and administration of justice, infrastructure, and some elements of a social safety net, regulation of competition, banks, and environmental impacts. Such elements are the basic building blocks of a good governance system that gets its financial resources mainly from fair taxation, with a system of ›checks and balances‹, an intangible public good that enhances transparency and accountability.

Developmental States are characterized by institutional integrity and organizational capacity, able to achieve a good level of cooperation, accountability, and flexibility[130], whereas imploding countries systematically lack these intangible features, which are uneasy to detect but able to make the difference, for the better or the worse.

Preconditions for recoveries from bad governance and disrupting sovereignty[131] give high probabilities to countries with a large and instructed population, perhaps coming out from the civil war, a powerful ›disinfecting‹ experience, somewhat easing the build up of new and fairer reforming rules from scratch. Large and educated populations make it better.

Democracy–surprisingly and disappointingly–doesn't seem to help policy turnaround. But, again, the Western concept of democracy is often hardly applicable to developing countries, because it is linked to localized culture and values. Even if the core ideals–taken from the U.N. universal declaration of human rights–should be the same everywhere, the devil is always in the details ... and an adequate transition period is necessary, together with local adjustments.

Indeed it took thousands of years to the Western countries to develop and apply the concept of democracy, starting from the ancient Greeks, passing through the Magna Charta in England and the cathartic experience of the French Revolution. So we should really wonder why Westerners are so impatient of seeing

---

129 For a statistical analysis, see *Failed States index score*, http://www.fundforpeace.org/web/index.php?option=com_content&task=view&id=229&Itemid=366.

130 See Evans (1995).

131 See Ghani, Lockhart (2008).

democracy ruling even elsewhere, in countries with a completely different cultural background[132].

According to Jacobsen[133], democratization has often enhanced the likelihood of civil war, in conjunction with low levels of socioeconomic development and ethnic fragmentation. Empty societies sooner or later collapse.

Recoveries are always at risk of setbacks, more likely if the patient (country) is weak and an erratic stop-and-go pattern is highly likely to happen, reminding that civil strife is often persistent.

Failing States losing their legitimacy have sharply reduced growth possibilities and they often make very bad use of foreign aid[134], which should be much more committed to teaching and giving a replicable good example – a much tougher and longer task than just giving plain money.

State decay, degradation, and political instability cause economic decline, in a mutually backing spiral, aggravated by bad governance in a gloomy environment.

Transforming a violent society into a peaceful place requires complex actions such as the establishment and respect of a legal order, with working institutions and cooperation from the international community. Much is to be accomplished within the country, contrasting often recalcitrant governments, and multi-ethnic reconciliation can help to progressively reach, step after step, this painful and far sighted target.

Building a nation, by overcoming the banana skins of fake republics, is a long term key issue, based on national identity, sense–and pride–of belonging, common and shared ideals and symbols (such as the flag or the national football team) which have to go beyond ethnic or religious differences, finding their equilibrated synthesis for the sake of a peaceful living.

Country and political risk

Another way of synthesizing the level of governance is to consider country and political risk of each nation – a key parameter for foreign investors and insurers (would you invest in an unsafe country, risking arbitrary confiscation at any time, or insure it?).

Country risk[135] is concerned with the likelihood that changes in the business environment will adversely affect operating profits or the value of assets in a specific country. Closely linked to country risk[136], complementary political risk is a

---

132 For a deeper analysis of this concept, see Chapter 13.

133 Quoted in Nafziger, Väyryen (2002), p. 151.

134 See Chapter 14.

135 For an impact of country risk on microfinance, see Chapter 23.

136 Country risk is periodically measured. See for example the International country Risk Guide. See www.countryrisk.com.

consequence of complications that businesses and governments may face as a result of what are commonly referred to as ›political decisions‹. This is the risk of strategic, financial, or personnel loss for a firm, due to non-market factors as macroeconomic and social policies (fiscal, monetary, trade, investment, industrial, income, labor, and developmental) or events related to political instability (terrorism, riots, coups, civil war, and insurrection …).

Bad governance is obviously a core component of both country and political risk. The threat of being neglected from the international community should be–and often represents–a stimulus for improving the country's governance. Anyway this fact is much more likely to happen if there is an effective pressure from the exhausted population to go in this direction. The way governors respond to these solicitations is obviously of crucial importance to determine the path and the speed of reforms.

Factors that statistically increase the risk of conflict include:

- weak or declining economic growth;
- heavy dependence on natural resources for livelihoods;
- drop in per capita income;
- the presence of large youth cohorts;
- substantial decline in rainfall.

The institutional poverty trap

Institutions are established organizations that set the legitimate ›rules of the game‹ of a society, promulgating rules which coordinate, regulate, and mediate individual actions, gathered together, towards a common goal. Institutions are also human constructions, with self enforcing conventions, and their adherents conform to a common strategy and behavior.

Institutions are the basic building blocks of each State, since they are structures and mechanisms of social order and cooperation, aimed at fostering stability and mutual confidence, and even because they are deemed to design, implement, and monitor economic policies, regulating also the relationships among citizens. When they are dysfunctional, ailing, capricious or not properly performing, they provide a bad institutional framework for development, allowing predatory rulers to act unchallenged, extracting public wealth for personal selfish purposes.

The idea that institutions are impartial public goods–going beyond closed systems of power–is not evident everywhere as it and unresponsive bureaucracies should interact with weak institutions and sclerotic courts.

Prolonged periods of political instability weaken already frail institutions–which become denied and neglected–depriving them of skilled manpower and putting at risk their authoritativeness and credibility, weakening their vital relationship with citizens.
Ethnic fragmentation brings to poorly integrated communities, where representatives of different tribal clans often violently alternate in power. In this way they forget about popular legitimacy and they cause prolonged instability which prevents the formation of a large middle class, whose role is fundamental in softening social inequalities. Extreme poverty disrupts exhausted institutions, depleting their tangible and immaterial resources, weakening political leaders and bureaucrats, and crushing the hopes of those, including the poor, who rely on these institutions.
Unequal and partial institutions, biased in favor of a selected group of interest, can be very harmful towards the misrepresented poor.
The legal and judicial system provide a set of (possibly) impartial rules, checks, and balances, that have an enormous impact in shaping the level of cohabitation of the citizens.
According to Banerjee, Benabou, Mookherjee (2006), p. xxiii »societies that inherit poor institutions may be stuck with them for long spans of time (...). Many of these institutional failures involve denial of essential inputs and services to the poor, such as voting rights, education, land, or finance, so that they have neither the resources nor the skills–or, indeed, the social status–to be full participants in the economy«.
Efficient and fair institutions are the natural defense against scandals, expropriations, and uneven distribution of common resources. Formal and informal institutions are meant to allow a peaceful living and an interactive framework of individuals, who typically try to pursue personal objectives, while contributing to the general welfare.
Institutions normally have to be able to synthesize and politically manage conflicts, in order to restore democracy, while in practice they are seriously damaged by corruption and pervasive clientelism, which limit investment and growth, leading to ineffective government.

Corruption and underdevelopment

Patronage patterns and systematic favoritism produce a corrupted, rent seeking economy, with distorted competition that generates huge inefficiencies and hidden costs. Corruption artificially increases entry barriers in a market, keeping honest incumbents out of the game and increasing penetrating fees, distorting competition and consequently reducing value for money, represented by the price for quality equation. With corruption, the formal sector–described in

Chapter 20 while comparing formal versus informal financial institutions–shrinks and finds it increasingly difficult to survive.

Greed and malpractice are inversely proportional to the risk of being discovered by a proper system of checks and balances. Public procurement of goods and services is one of the main areas at risk of corruption, especially in underdeveloped countries.

Incentives to fight corruption may be expensive, since it is not easy to know in advance which the indemnity request from potential bribers. As a matter of fact, corruption is a hidden tax, with extremely negative collateral effects, since it also destroys meritocracy.

Since corruption grows up together with the complexity of institutions–having primitive societies fewer opportunities for it–it is likely to increase with development, being an obstacle to the growth potential. Corruption brings with itself hidden costs, in terms of lost resources and systematic distortions, bringing to talent misallocation.

Resources to fight against corruption increase when development reaches a certain stage and new technologies, such as computerized recordings of money transfers, may play an important part, leaving hard evidence of mismanagement. A well functioning democracy is the best antidote against briberies, where politicians are constantly subject to public scrutiny.

A high level of ethnic diversities can also increase corruption, creating segmentation between different clans.

When institutions and markets are smoothly performing without the need of government interventions, the invisible hand invoked by Adam Smith and nurtured by self interest, makes its discrete but efficient job, but when they are corrupted and poorly acting, a grabbing hand intervenes. According to Shleifer, Vishny (1998) »in many countries, public sector institutions impose heavy burdens on economic life: heavy and arbitrary taxes retard investment, regulations enrich corrupt bureaucrats, State firms consume national wealth, and the most talented people turn to rent-seeking rather than productive activities. As a consequence of such predatory policies, entrepreneurship lingers, and economies stagnate. De-politicization of economic life emerges as the crucial theme of the appropriate reforms«.

Ending impunity is a major challenge and a signal of disruption with the past. Democracies, based on shared consensus, often generate incentives that make politicians and statesmen more sensitive to public welfare, in part because they need to be re-elected, but democratically elected politicians typically do not maximize social welfare either. In particular, the winning majorities in democ-

racies often pursue highly wasteful policies of redistribution from losing minorities[137].
Formalized institutions go beyond informally built up ethical or family ties, needing impartial regulations and so bearing contracting costs that in a familiar context are seldom necessary and when existent are only embryonic. The process of passing from non-market to formal institutions may however also bear some benefit, to the extent that it reduces exclusion to those who are not part of the clan and it can ease the relationships with other external realities. Subjectivity is also reduced, favoring rationality and impartiality. This last one is the necessary background of meritocracy.
Family foundations or legacies and endowments can become institutions. This is often the case in richer countries, while in poorer ones the initial bequest may be too limited and the culture of accumulating wealth for social targets even outside the family clan is not yet diffused, possibly needing not ephemeral prosperity to come up.

Racial discriminations and the ethnic trap

Ethnic different belonging–racial otherness–is among the causes of unrest and conflicts (e.g. in Rwanda or former Yugoslavia or in disrupting Soviet Republics in the Caucasus area …). Ethnic divisions may lead to slow economic growth and persistent poverty in underdeveloped countries. Polarization hardens conflict, bringing to a discriminatory ethnology of violence. Humanitarian foreign aid[138] may bring in some temporary relief, even if it is however unable to solve deeply rooted local problems, which can easily trespass local borders, bringing unrest even abroad (an example is again given by the Tutsi – Hutu confrontation, a primer cause of unrest not only in Rwanda and Burundi, but in the whole area of the Great African lakes, from southern Uganda to the Central Western part of Congo, to northern Tanzania). Among the many treaties and conventions concerning ethnic issues, the following are worth considering:

- the UNESCO Declaration on Race and Racial Prejudice[139];
- the Convention on the Elimination of All Forms of Racial Discrimination[140];
- the Convention against Torture and other Cruel, Inhuman or Degrading Treatment or Punishment[141].

---

137 Notes on The Grabbing Hand by Shleifer and Vishny, David Andolfatto October 2004 http://www.sfu.ca/~dandolfa/sv.pdf.
138 See Chapter 14.
139 http://www2.ohchr.org/english/issues/racism/rapporteur/docs/Declaration_on_race_and_racial_prejudice.pdf.
140 http://www2.ohchr.org/english/law/cerd.htm.

Challenges all around our world are living together, sterilizing the ethnical trap and paranoid racial inequalities and looking for a peaceful solution of conflicts, but in some underdeveloped areas this task looks harder. As John Kennedy used to say »let us not be blind to our differences – but let us also direct attention to our common interests and to means by which those differences can be resolved«. Confucian ethics, Taoism, and Buddhism together with Christianity favor the cohabitation of different ethnic groups.

Fundamentalism–when orthodox faith becomes fanatic–is a backward Manichean black-and-white vision, which is often mystified with messianic and apocalyptic religious propaganda, depicting heaven or hell on earth, not friend of democracy. It preaches a conservative and authoritative set of teachings, to be followed to the letter, which lacks the basic insights of a multicolored world, where different opinions should peacefully cohabit.

Nation building policies try to forge a national common and shared identity across different ethnic groups[142], which often brought together by artificial colonial borders. They should conveniently follow a long termed bottom up approach, raising a broad popular consensus and starting from education at school, and being complemented by sound economic policies, in a democratic framework where different ethnicities are carefully represented and respected, easing a cultural blending where differences are both accepted and synchronized in a reconciliation pattern.

When racial blending is successful, it produces a new multiethnic society, beyond the nowadays old fashioned borders of homogeneous community of people, within the same territory and sharing a common language, history, and culture.

The problem with nation building common policies is that they tend to uniform different cultures, trying to reach a unifying synthesis even where the historical cultural heritage is profoundly different. A flexible adaptation policy is highly wanted, cooling down rivalries and de-escalating anger, with compromises able to preserve ethnic cultural differences, but it is uneasy both to envisage and to put in place.

Social capital and racial identities, described in Chapter 9, have an important cultural impact on peaceful cohabitation, together with different languages, habits or religious beliefs, which should overcome the lack of confidence and sometimes racism – hate, especially against suffering minorities, is often a byproduct of ignorance.

Plural institutions, considering different needs and tastes, unsurprisingly become more complex to create and to run and they need an extra portion of fairness and transparency to find undisputed acceptance. From the employees that

---

[141] http://www2.ohchr.org/english/law/cat.htm.

[142] See Miguel in Banerjee, Benabou, Mookherjee (2006), Chapter 12.

they rent, you can easily detect if the ethnic blend is appropriate or skewed in favor of one group.
Community social sanctions and pressures can play an important role in reconciling ethnic diversities, while economic disparities within different communities may be softened with public spending targeted to the poorest, provided that the country has the political willingness and some cash to fund mindful projects of social inclusion.
Dialogue, confrontation, and interaction are the natural premises to broader inter-ethnic cooperation, in a pluralist society where all the interests are carefully balanced and represented.
An increasing harder challenge is living together and coping amid increasing diversities in a multicultural society. Such a challenge requires a growing sense of fraternity, an extended brotherhood beyond blood and family ties.

The condensed Chapter

War is an astonishingly evident poverty trap, even if its long term consequences, including the probability of relapses from a conflict to another, are frequently underestimated.
Contagious conflicts nourish warlordism, bad governance, and kleptocracy, spreading corruption and undermining the establishment of democratic institutions, damaging in particular the excluded poor.

Out of Poverty Tips

Full understanding of the inconvenience of war, in any sense, is the first cultural step towards its complete removal. It takes a few seconds to destroy what may take decades to build, not only physically, and nothing produces poverty more than war and its often underestimated side effects. Poverty is the only war which deserves to be fought and won.

Selected Readings

CASSESE A., (2008), *International Criminal Law*, Oxford University Press, Oxford.

COLLIER P., (2010), *Wars, Guns & Votes. Democracy in Dangerous Places*, Vintage, London.

FUKUYAMA F., (2005), *State building. Governance and World Order in the Twenty–First Century,* Profile books, London.

GHANI A., LOCKHART C., (2008), *Fixing Failed States*, Oxford University Press, Oxford.

CHAPTER 6 – Water and diamonds

> Nothing is more useful than water: but it will purchase scarce any thing; scarce any thing can be had in exchange for it. A diamond, on the contrary, has scarce any value in use; but a very great quantity of other goods may frequently be had in exchange for it.
>
> Adam Smith, *An Inquiry into the Nature and Causes of the Wealth of Nations*

Water, the true jewel of a thirsty world

The problem the Scottish economist and moral philosopher Adam Smith posed in 1776 has come down to us as the ›*Paradox of Diamonds and Water*‹. As Smith observed, water is very useful–indeed it is necessary for life–whereas, by contrast, diamonds have little practical utility–they are only useful for adornment. It is possible to do without diamonds entirely, and most people do–yet diamonds are very costly, while water is very cheap. Difference in price between water and (superfluous) diamonds is due to their marginal perceived utility and contingent scarcity.

This–in peanuts–is Smith's ›paradox‹. If demand depends upon the usefulness of the product, then we would expect the more useful product, water, to command the higher price–but yet diamonds are much more expensive. Not only do we know that water is cheaper as a matter of fact, but most people would agree that they would not pay as much for diamonds as for water.

Diamonds extracted in war zones, such as Sierra Leone, are often bloody and they represent one of the worst examples of the natural resources curse described in Chapter 3, softened by the Kimberley Process Certification[143].

Yet freshwater is the key issue for life and survival, which is often neglected whereas it is abundant and its presence considered quite obvious, underestimating the importance of conservation and care. So this paradox serves just as an

[143] A legally binding treaty, signed by seventy-four countries. Its purpose was to create a trail of custody in the supply chain of diamonds that eliminated diamonds being used for illicit purposes: the funding of regional conflicts. In a nutshell, the goal of the treaty is to regulate the diamond trade, tracing diamonds from mine to market through a clear and documented chain of custody. See http://www.fairjewelry.org/archives/1582.

introduction, and it is useful, too, in order to show that the hierarchy of values that we have is often profoundly biased by selfishness (how much water could be supplied to thirsty neglected poor renouncing to one of our useless diamonds?). From now on, we shall abandon diamonds and concentrate just on water, a really vital issue that baptizes life and it is so concerned with poverty.

As a supreme–albeit increasingly scarce and so, expensive–public good, water should be a gift for everybody, needing to be accessible without exclusions, even if–unlike ai –its consumption makes it unavailable to others.

An increasing imbalance between the demand and the availability of drinkable water is a big threat for human development, worsened by demographic trends and especially by climatic changes. Water is the blue gold, more valuable than the black gold–oil–or the precious metal. And drought is to be beaten with a flood of innovative ideas, starting with just a drop of water after the other in an empty sea. Nomadic wandering in arid zones, looking for a sip of water, sadly witnesses the desperate fight for survival of the thirsty poorest, surrounded by an unfriendly and often deadly environment.

Salted sea water covers some 75% of the earth's surface, but freshwater represents only 2.75% of earth's water and it is mostly stored in melting glaciers and overexploited groundwater. Water also represents in weight some 70% of the human body and it is essential for life. Is there anymore doubt about the importance of water?

The main problem that concerns water–as well as other environmental issues, described in Chapter 8–is that its demand is increasing, while its supply is shrinking. The result is not only an economic surge in price, but rather its growing unavailability, which mostly damages the poor.

On one side, demand is increasing mainly as a combined consequence of demographic up–going trends and quality improvements–the world's population is growing in both number and aspirations. On the other side, supply of fresh water is not unable to keep it up with a surging demand, being rather likely to decrease. The main reasons are climatic changing and hotter temperatures, which increase heavy rainfall where they shouldn't, with the consequence of making arid places even drier and–last but not least–being particularly unfriendly where the poor tend to live and increase in number.

Water imbalances concern not only quantity but also quality, which is deteriorating, too, as salinity grows and freshwater is more and more contaminated, soon becoming undrinkable.

Safe drinking and sanitation are basic human rights

Water is both a public good of first necessity and a basic human right.
»The right to water means the fundamental human right of access to Water for Life, i.e. water of a quality, quantity, and accessibility sufficient to satisfy the basic human needs for drinking, hygiene, cleaning, cooking, subsistence agriculture for local food consumption, and sanitation«[144].
The right to water is explicitly enshrined in two UN human rights treaties:

- the Convention on the Elimination of all Forms of Discrimination against Women; according to Article 14 »[…] States Parties shall ensure equal rights of men and women to participate in and benefit from rural development, and shall ensure to rural women the rights to: […] have adequate living conditions, particularly in relation to […] sanitation […] and water supply […]«;
- the Convention on the Rights of the Child; according to article 24.2.c. »State Parties shall pursue full implementation of this right and, in particular, shall take appropriate measures: To combat disease and malnutrition […] through the provision of […] clean drinking-water […]«.

The topic is also dealt with in one regional treaty – the African Charter on the Rights and Welfare of the Child[145].
In addition, the right to water is an essential part of the right to an adequate standard of living. Governments must recognize that all people, without discrimination, have the right to enjoy access to safe, affordable, and sufficient water services. Quality of water, even more than quantity, is a key issue for drinking and health related issues – in poor countries with poor water, diarrhea, which is apparently a trivial disease, kills more than AIDS or malaria.
Water is also essential for animals and plants needed by humans for their survival. Thirsty cattle looking for precious drops of water die from lack of grazing lands and of drinking water. Only their skeleton remains to witness their unlucky end.
Even if the right to water does not mean that it is to be provided completely free of charge, individuals are entitled to water that is affordable – this being a big economic and social problem, especially in dry, overpopulated, and poor areas. Water should conversely be considered as a social and cultural public good of common utility, which has sustainable and affordable access, going beyond its economic importance.

---

144 http://www.watertreaty.org/faqs.php#1.
145 http://www.africa-union.org/official_documents/Treaties ...

The trade off between drinking versus dirty water is a question of survival for everybody, most noticeably the poorest.
Water itself is not enough for living. It has to be potable, so free of pathogenic micro organisms that can cause waterborne diseases when the contaminated water is consumed. Waterborne diseases are among the leading causes of morbidity and mortality in low–and middle–income countries. The quality of water is compromised by both biological and chemical disease agents, that can cause diseases such as diarrhea, bilharzias, schistosomiasis[146]... Diarrhea is among the most common causes of (easily avoidable) death in poor countries and–incredibly and shamefully–it is the second most common cause of infant deaths worldwide. The spread of this disease is directly linked to water availability.

Table 6.1. – Making water drinkable in poor countries

Technique	How It Works	Result And Eventual Problems
Water Filters	Removes impurities from water by means of a fine physical barrier, a chemical process or a biological process.	Some disease organisms are eliminated, but not others, especially the smaller creatures that can easily slip through the pores of the filtering mechanism. Viruses are a special problem because of their extremely small dimensions, since water filters are often unable to trap them.
Chemical Treatment	Chlorine bleach, iodine and a number of other chemicals can be poured into the water.	Some disease organisms will have been destroyed, so the water will be, at least partially, purified. A frequent problem is that some chemicals used in the treatment of water have expiration dates and they can lose effectiveness over time. Another potential problem with chemically treating water to make it safe to drink is the chemical itself, which may actually be a health hazard. A further problem is the immunity of some pathogenic micro organisms to the chemicals used.

146 See Chapter 7.

Technique	How It Works	Result And Eventual Problems
Solar Water Disinfection[147]	Is a method of disinfecting water using only sunlight and plastic PET bottles.	Exposure to sunlight has been shown to deactivate diarrhea-causing organisms in polluted drinking water. Three effects of solar radiation are believed to contribute to the inactivation of pathogenic organisms.

Whatever method is used to make water potable or, at least, to eliminate the most harmful bacteria inside, technical ability and resources (chemicals, filters …) are always required. This is a basic but very important point to bear in mind when dealing with poverty.

Smelly and dirty water, that is unpleasant and nasty, is a frequent and unwanted companion of hundreds of millions of poor, living around them with his unhealthy friends, such as microbes and pollution.

Proper sewage treatment (the process of removing contaminants from wastewater and household sewage) is increasingly spreading and it is by now capillary in developed countries, but in underdeveloped areas it is instead becoming an increasing problem, especially within rapidly urbanizing towns, where population randomly grows, typically at a speed much quicker than (hydraulic) infrastructures. The catch up is difficult, due to chaotic and wild urbanization, lack of proper planning and budgetary constraints. Water pollution is an increasing problem, together with salinization, with the consequence of deepening water crisis mostly in already endangered places.

Clean water is an essential element for hygiene. Close to 3 billion people do not have unrestricted access to adequate sanitation facilities, lacking the possibility of washing themselves or their clothes, as a matter of personal hygiene. As a matter of fact, lack of latrines means also lack of dignity. Proper hand washing before eating–a wise and old habit, deeply rooted in the Jewish culture–greatly contributes to prevent pathogen germs, which are intrinsically present in our dirty hands, from silently contaminating our body, with at the moment invisible but potentially lethal consequences.

Dry and cry: the misfortune of poor water

Most of the poorest countries are located either in dry land areas, where rainfall is extremely scarce, or in tropical zones, where abundant precipitations are volatile and seasonal. So there is little no wonder that water rarity or variability is so strictly associated with misery. Such an assumption is consistent with the

[147] See http://www.sodis.ch/index_EN.

tropical theory of underdevelopment examined in Chapter 1 or the higher tensions behind the conflict trap described in Chapter 5, together with other factors, such as likelier diseases. Combining adequate precipitations with fertile soils is even more difficult and it can bring to the malnutrition trap that will be examined in Chapter 7. According to Sachs (2008), p. 120 »in total, the drylands cover roughly 41 percent of the Earth's land area and support 35 percent of the world's population«.
According to the World Water Council[148] »While the world's population tripled in the 20th Century, the use of renewable water resources has grown six-fold. Within the next fifty years, the world population will increase by another 40 to 50 %. This population growth–coupled with industrialization and urbanization–will result in an increasing demand for water and will have serious consequences on the environment«.
Today, one third of the world's population is suffering from a lack of adequate drinking water and/or sanitation. International organizations, governments, local authorities, financial institutions, private corporations and indeed all members of society are responsible for redressing this situation and ensuring the right to water for all[149].
According to the United Nations' World Health Organization (WHO) more than one billion people in low and middle-income countries lack access to safe water for their most basic needs. These figures represent more than 20 percent of the world population.
Another complementary source comes from the World Bank[150]: »More than 1.1 billion people lack access to safe water, and 2.6 billion lack accesses to basic sanitation. The costs of inadequate water supply and sanitation (WSS) are high: 1.6 million children die every year from diarrhea, mainly as a result of inadequate sanitation, water supply, and hygiene. And the economic costs of lost time in fetching water and environmental degradation from wastewater pollution are high «.
At the heart of this crisis there is an increasing imbalance between availability and demand for fresh water. In this increasingly tense contest from the local to the regional, it is the poorest people who invariably lose out. Water is an essential resource on earth and it is used for many human activities such as drinking, sanitations, agriculture, fire extinguishing, chemical uses, hydroelectricity ... We will concentrate on the first three vital uses, in order to draw attention to the actual water crisis in terms of poverty:

- drinking;

---

148 http://www.worldwatercouncil.org/index.php?id=25.

149 http://www.watertreaty.org/faqs.php.

150 http://web.worldbank.org/WBSITE/EXTERNAL/TOPICS/EXTWAT/0,contentMDK:21706928~menu PK:4602430~pagePK:148956~piPK:216618~theSitePK:4602123,00.html.

- sanitations;
- agriculture.

The overall situation where there is not enough water for all uses can also be called water stress, whose main causes are considered being population growth, increased affluence, climate change, urbanization, pollution, depletion of aquifers and conflicts.
»The importance of water in poor people's lives goes far beyond the significant health-related outcomes to broader issues of livelihoods and well-being. In particular, poor management of water resources has led to degradation of the environment and loss of natural resources on which the livelihoods of so many of the rural poor depend«[151].
Privatization of water rights, albeit introducing some form of market efficiency with a pay-for-use system, may lead to greedy overexploitation or to a frequent discrimination of the poor. They may indeed be likely to be underserved because of to their limited paying capacity, and this fact will have an impact on current water availability and on infrastructural investments in aqueducts, which may be economically inconvenient – water is a vital public good. To the extent that water may already be a monopoly–and increasingly is due to become it–its privatization may worsen both its pricing and its distribution, once again to the detriment of those who can't afford it.

The big mess … of the water stress: a vital resource often unavailable to the thirsty poor

Water is intrinsically characterized by what Sachs (2008), p. 115, calls ›hydrological interdependence‹, meaning pervasive spillover effects and externalities, which are intrinsic within the water's physical state of liquidity. They favor pouring, washing, and fluid transmission, less but more pervasively than the air but consistently more than in the case of solid materials. This rather obvious statement is full of vital implications, often good but sometimes menacing, especially for the poor.
We shall deal with water conflicts later on in this Chapter, whereas in Chapter 8 we shall refer to the issue of environmental problems concerning also sea or drinking water. Again, in Chapter 16 we shall refer to the ›tragedy of commons‹, concerned with the selfish depletion of shared resources, of which water is the first and possibly most important one.
Water stress–an imbalance between water use and water resources–occurs when the demand for water exceeds the available amount during a certain period or when poor quality restricts its use and causes deterioration of fresh water re-

151 http://www.ourplanet.com/imgversn/122/short.html.

sources in terms of quantity (aquifer over-exploitation, dry rivers, etc.) and quality (eutrophication[152], organic matter pollution, saline intrusion, etc.)[153].
The water crisis is an increasingly worldwide critical issue, which is faced by poor people on a daily basis. The sustainable management of water is crucial to efforts to eliminate poverty. Poor people's lives are closely linked to their access to water and its multiple uses and functions.
In countries hardly kissed by luck, water is not a luxury or a superfluous device – it's merely a matter of life or death. In such countries, aqueducts and pipes, which are so developed in Western countries from the ancient Romans onwards, are hardly present – giving an example of the complexity of water distribution. Where they aren't, wells have to be properly dug in often arid soil, with a careful balance of the extraction capacity and a continuous threat of getting out of order or simply dry. Wells do not solve the problem of sewage, especially in urban areas – the vital separation of ›white‹ from ›black‹ water is far less obvious that it would seem.
When water is scarce and it is controlled by water-lords who sell it at exorbitant prices to thirsty farmers, a typical monopolistic rent takes place, deeply damaging the underserved, forced to overpay a vital resource.
Not everyone has access to usable water for their most basic needs and water unavailability for the poor is often caused by lack of water as a commodity. However, in some cases the resource is in theory present, but there is not the required infrastructure to carry and purify it, so making it practically unavailable. In other cases water can be involved in resource wars and it ends up with not being available because of mismanagement and corruption in water politics (hydropolitics). So water poverty's causes can be split into three main groups:

- lack of water;
- lack of infrastructure;
- mismanagement.

Proper storage (conservancy) of water stands out as a major issue for bare survival. The water stress acts on dry lands, and it makes their aridity even more extreme, whereas in already wet equatorial areas precipitations become more violent. The net result is however not a win-lose zero sum game, since both situations are worsening, with the result of bringing to lose-lose pattern.
Managing water stress in thirsty environments is indeed a huge task. Already narrow poor households' survival options are very limited at times, and in places, of water scarcity. Being highly vulnerable to economic and climatic shocks and with negligible access to finance, the poor greatly suffer from lack of water

[152] Increase in the concentration of chemical nutrients in an ecosystem.
[153] http://www.greenfacts.org/glossary/wxyz/water-stress.htm.

supplies. And the thirsty burden–immense and exhausting–is getting even more complicated.

When the rain dance hardly works anymore: trendy water shortages due to climatic changes

Due to worsening climatic changes, it hardly rains where it should and when it does, it pours when and where it shouldn't – the result is far from an apparently harmless zero sum game.

Ubiquitous threats come not only from the sky, but also they are concentrated under our feet, as it has been shown by ground-water progressive exhaustion. Glaciers are the most evident example of this phenomenon, as timely photos show up their progressive retirement–with no pension bonus–downsizing also their precious sponge effect. Thanks to glaciers, water is kept refrigerated, since it fell into lethargy in winter time and it is ready to be smoothly released during springtime. Should water seasonality be permanently puzzled, we may face unprecedented ecological problems. If either Malthusian demographic worries[154] or Darwinian selection rules are right, the weak and thirsty poorest will once again be the first to suffer. Feel a bit worried and thirsty? Enjoy a glass of fresh water before going on reading – and just remember that it may be increasingly difficult to do so.

Due to the global heating ongoing process, worldwide rainfalls are overall decreasing–albeit increasing where they shouldn't–and this worrying phenomenon, accompanied by augmented pollution and overpopulation is already severely damaging the most exposed populations, which are typically concentrated in poor desert or tropical areas and which are already miserable and vulnerable on their own.

Increasingly needed and less available water stands out as a key problem of our times. Due to water decreased and unevenly distributed quantity, also its quality is unsurprisingly worsening, becoming more and more dirt, polluted and overexploited.

Water can be absent or scarce as a resource itself. This problem is backed up either by the geography of a nation, that can find itself in an arid area (e.g. nations in sub Saharan Africa), or by overpopulation, which means that the same quantity of finite supplies of drinkable water need to satisfy the needs of a larger amount of people, and other man-caused problems, such as desertification and climate change.

Desertification is the degradation of land in arid and dry areas, which is primarily caused by man-made activities and influenced by climatic variations. These include overgrazing, over pumping of groundwater and diversion of water from

---

[154] See Chapter 4.

rivers for human consumption and industrial use, with unnatural dams whose complex ecological costs are typically underestimated.
The most obvious example is Lake Chad, somewhat in the middle of Saharan Africa. It was one of the largest lakes in the world, in a very strategic position, once upon a time strongly contributing to soften the region's intrinsic aridness. But it has shrunk considerably since an increased and uncontrolled demand on the lake's water from the local population has accelerated its downsizing over the past 40 years.
Another sad example of ecological disaster is Lake Aral in Central Asia, where overexploitation, for water-intensive cotton production needs, has now reduced it to a … pissing spot, because of the stupidity of an unwisely conceived and backward Soviet planned industrialization.

Irrigation and hydraulic infrastructure: hell without well?

Scarcity of water increases the need of irrigation for agriculture, posing several problems, which are related again to water shortage. Irrigation is an expensive and energy consuming infrastructural investment, to which many peasants are not accustomed to and it is difficult to find a proper financial coverage, since marginal returns are intrinsically narrow and long termed. River systems are often being deviated and dammed for irrigation purposes, altering natural equilibriums, with complex ecological costs.
Some 70 % of surface water use (mainly from rivers) is agriculture – while 20 % is roughly for industry and the remaining 10 % for household use[155]. So the poor, almost entirely occupied in the primary activity, suffer more for water scarcity, considering also that it mainly occurs in already underdeveloped areas. When collected rainwater is not enough to satisfy the consumption needs–and it is the standard case, especially in dry seasons–additional water is pumped from ground-water, through manual or mechanized wells. The problem is that ground-water is not always a renewable resource and when it isn't, extracting it from beneath the soil, it looks like depleting a limited resource. Such a circumstance recalls the problems concerned with fossil fuel, even if here we do not have to consider its uniqueness, since water is ubiquitous (even if in asymmetric quantities, and so without generating the natural resources curse described in Chapter 3), but rather we have to consider its environmental negative side effects, that will be synthetically examined in Chapter 8.
Over-pumping of ground-water has serious side effects, which go well beyond its due disappearance, since land can subside in the case of lack of cushion-

[155] Sachs (2008), p. 116.

water below or in the case in which aquifers may more easily be exposed to salinization or poisoning, so making the little water left completely useless[156].
A remarkable example of senseless and myopic exploitation of ground-water is given by the Pharaonic big Libyan project to pump water from the desert ground reserves, so as to serve thirsty coastal cities.
Irrigated agriculture is at a crossroads, because irrigated lands now account for about 20 percent of the world's farmed area and 40 percent of global food production. Increases in irrigated area, cropping intensity, and crop yields have helped to stabilize food production per capita, even though population and per capita food intake have grown significantly. Investments in irrigation and drainage have driven rural growth in many developing countries, with the result of creating jobs and reducing poverty[157].
Agricultural water management is a key factor in farmer incomes, in agricultural growth and exports, and–this being the predominant job of the poor–in misery reduction[158].
Water itself is present as a resource in case of lack of hydraulic infrastructure, but it is unavailable for the population, since a considerable amount of expensive infrastructure is needed to both clean and filter water and to send it to consumers. This equipment includes:

- system of pipes, pumps, valves, **filtration**, treatment equipment and meters, including buildings and structures to house the equipment, used for the collection, treatment and distribution of drinking water;
- sewage collection and disposal;
- drainage systems (storm sewers, ditches, etc..);
- major irrigation systems (reservoirs, irrigation canals);
- major flood control systems (dikes, levees, major pumping stations, and floodgates).

Water mismanagement and hydro-politic problems

Water mismanagement is incredibly common, for simple reasons that range from its apparently endless and free availability to the difficulty to claim money for what is and should universally be considered as a public good. As soon as the problem gets under an even superficial scrutiny, it becomes immediately ev-

---

156 Sachs (2008), p. 122.
157 http://web.worldbank.org/WBSITE/EXTERNAL/TOPICS/EXTWAT/0,contentMDK:21752798~menu PK:4602436~pagePK:148956~piPK:216618~theSitePK:4602123,00.html.
158 http://siteresources.worldbank.org/INTARD/Resources/DID_AWM.pdf.

ident that, albeit often neglected, appropriate water management is a tough–and deserving–issue.

While we shall analyze in the next paragraphs ›hydrological interdependence‹ and other related issues, it may be anticipated here that water mismanagement brings to spillovers and negative externalities–unwanted priceless external consequences–and to irresponsible exploitation, within the framework known as the ›tragedy of commons‹. Such concepts, illustrated in Chapter 16, argue that multiple individuals, selfishly acting on their own, have an irresistible tendency to deplete common resources, such as water, even when it is clear that it is not in anyone's long-term interest for this to happen.

Water lack and poverty are both causes and effect. Water shortage brings to poverty and is a symptom of it, but the poor are also typically waterless.

Because of overpopulation, mass consumption, misuse and water pollution, the availability of drinking water per capita is inadequate and shrinking. For this reason, water is a strategic resource in the globe and an important element in many political conflicts.

Water mismanagement is an increasingly serious matter. When a resource as important as water isn't properly considered, its availability can seriously decrease. Managing problems come out when the same water source is shared between two groups, as it happens during interstate conflicts, that occur between two or more neighboring countries that share a trans-boundary water basin (river, lake, groundwater basin). Conflict is inevitable when the two competing users aren't able to decide in a diplomatic way how to share a common resource. The problem may somewhat be similar to landlockedness, a topic examined in Chapter 2 that concerns countries with no access to sea water, which strongly and asymmetrically depend on their neighbors' friendliness or, as a second best, forced cooperation.

Water is increasingly a geopolitical issue, especially wherever shared by different countries – an example is represented by the river Nile, with complex agreements among Egypt, Sudan, Uganda, and Ethiopia. It is absolutely vital for Egypt, which depends on the other aforementioned countries for its water income – an equivalent of the Aswan dam is unlikely to be built in other Nilotic countries without an improbable Egyptian consent.

The largest international rivers (such as Amazon, Rhine, Nile, Danube, Zambesi …) are shared by many countries, with complex harmonization issues.

The wolf and the lamb: from hydrological interdependence to water conflicts

According to Aesop's tale, a wolf was drinking at a spring on a hillside. On looking up, he saw a lamb just beginning to drink lower down. »There's my supper« he thought »if only I can find some excuse to seize it«. He called out to the lamb »How dare you muddle my drinking water?« »No« said the lamb; »if the water is muddy up there, I cannot be the cause of it, for it runs down from you to me«. »Well, then« said the wolf »Why did you call me bad names this time last year?« »That cannot be« said the lamb; »I am only six months old«. »I don't care« snarled the wolf; »if it was not you, it was your father« and with that he rushed upon the poor little lamb and ate her all up.

The moral of the fable is that the despot will always find a pretext for his tyranny – and reference to water is just a pretext to deal with wider topics.

Water refugees, who are desperately escaping from drought, often trigger violent conflicts for bare survival, when they compete with thirsty neighbors, wherever water is present but already scarce before their arrival. Weak institutional frameworks due to instability, wars, underdevelopment, and other poverty traps, can only contribute to worsen water shortage problems, making their detection and solution even harder. Water stress and induced drought worsen food insecurity, due to marginally decreasing crop yields, up to harvest failures, affecting both humans and their feeding animals. Insatiable thirst may bring to madness – a desperate condition of the mind where any (mis)behavior becomes possible.

There is already mounting empirical evidence–for example in Darfur, Ethiopia or Somalia–that growing aridity is correlated with conflicting attitudes. It is often triggered by despair, as more people struggle for drinking from the same shrinking or leaking bottle.

Thirsty environments are a hotbed of instability, especially if they are mixed with other ready-to-explode bombs such as uncontrolled demography or related problems of other Mother nature creatures, starting from thirsty cattle and edible plants, through consequent induced hunger to health diseases and so on, following a worrying Rossinian crescendo.

Interstate conflicts occur between two or more neighboring countries that share a trans-boundary water basin, whereas intrastate conflicts take place between two or more parties within the same country. Some examples are the conflicts between farmers and industry (agricultural vs. industrial use of water). Three important points to be taken in consideration when dealing with a water conflicts are the following:

- water alone is not usually a cause of war. Normally there is a conflict background or other causes of conflict. Gradual reductions over time in quality and/or quantity of fresh water can add to the instability of a region by having negative effects on the health of a population, obstructing economic development, and causing larger clashes;

- there must be a minimum interest for cooperation between the parties, otherwise they would refuse even the existence or the problem/conflict;
- presence or absence of international treaties for the basin. The possibility of a conflict is generally reduced when there is an international treaty about managing the water of the basin.

Water treaties also concern the sea and the territorial waters, i.e. the distance between the shore and the sea beyond it that is considered part of a nation's territory. Such a question is not trivial, because of to its implications on enforceable jurisdiction and exploiting capacity, concerning fishing, oil and gas offshore extraction, etc.

In his Encyclical letter Caritas in Veritate, § 51, Benedict XVI remembers that »the hoarding of resources, especially water, can generate serious conflicts among the peoples involved«.

We have mainly concentrated on the first aspect of water crisis, which is its unavailability, whereas water pollution is the second element to consider, which can also be seen as a further cause of the lack of available water.

Becoming–or remaining–a waterless country causes instability, together with unrest and conflicts. Equitable allocation of water resources provides an important opportunity for social and environmental justice, eliminating the risk of a conflict.

The Nile Basin Action Plan teaches that an excuse for conflict has been turned into a basis for cooperation, providing a hugely important example to other regions facing competition over water.

A vital drinking … for the sober

Water is an essential element for the human body, which contains large quantities of it. It is not clear how much water intake is needed by healthy people, though most advocates agree that 7-8 glasses of water daily (approximately 2 liters) is the minimum to maintain proper hydration. Much bigger amounts are needed in hot and humid environments–which are typically concentrated in the tropical poor areas–where water conspicuously evaporates from the ground and from the body.

Observant Muslims who live in hot places know how inspiring and demanding is waterless (and foodless) Ramadan practice during the day, especially if it occurs in summertime.

Access to drinking water is measured by the number of people who have a reasonable means of getting an adequate amount of water that is safe for drinking, washing, and essential household activities.

No crop without drop: H2O for agriculture

Agriculture, other than being one of the most important human activities for providing food, is also by far the largest water absorber, and it accounts to some 70 % of the overall consumption of fresh water. Water-intensive irrigation is needed in expanding drier areas, differently from rain-fed agriculture, where crops can capture all the water they need from natural rainfall.

Technology can greatly help to soften the water stress issue, thanks to a variety of solutions ranging from proper–less water absorbing–crop variety selection, using either traditional breeding techniques or transgenic modifications[159]. The latter represent a promising new scientific frontier, which is hotly debated not only by worried traditionalists but also (in poor countries forced to import it from abroad) by those who fear that foreign multinationals can use a well known ›Troy horse‹ gift strategy. They may indeed donate the first seeds and complementary instruments but then, once they are deeply rooted, they may introduce a toll system that may create dangerous dependence concerning a vital issue – the poor need to be overcautious, since survival can hardly cope with ingenuity.

Suitable plant varieties are just a component of the set of mitigating solution, being usefully complemented by appropriate agronomic irrigation system – such as the constant drip irrigation device so successfully engineered by smart Israelis agronomist in their Negev dry lands. Water distribution via main aqueducts and small irrigation structures often needs extensive and expensive initial infrastructural investments, with continuous maintenance and fixing necessities, in order to minimize water losses and abusive consumption. While writing these few trivial sentences, I am unwisely inspired by a leaking air conditioning system in my campus bedroom in Chennai, India. Water is impolitely dropping on the floor, but the external humidity is so oppressive that I feel reluctant to switch it off, as I probably should.

Even humidity is concerned with water, since it is an effect of its air condensation, to be released with rains and recreated with evaporation in a continuous circle whose unstable balance so deeply influences human, other animals, and vegetal life in our complicated planet.

Rainwater harvesting, learning from the *impluvium* (literally meaning ›raining–inside‹) of the ancient Romans, is a simple device to collect roof rainwater in jars and it acts as a stabilizing sponge (similar but not in competition with glaciers, being most useful in arid places or with discontinuous seasonal rainfall), to be used as a supplementary water supplier in dry and especially in drought moments, trying to limit evaporation and excessive stagnation, which may soon make the water undrinkable, even if still suitable for agricultural use.

---

159 See Sachs (2008), p. 132.

Crop diversification, alternating water-addicted with less thirsty varieties, may well soften risky dependence on uneven water availability, which may induce monoculture countries to painfully decrease their food exports and/or to increase their subsistence imports, in extreme cases of floods or dryness. Crop insurance, that can be possibly linked with microinsurance devices, described in Chapter 19, may well be a suitable component of synergic and diversified mitigation strategies. Should however the risk be systemic within a region–as it is in continuously flooded Bangladesh or intrinsically dry Saharan countries–then the insurance premium may become expensive and international risk diversification a necessary strategy for the insurer.

The condensed Chapter

Water is the often neglected basic component of life and it is apparently freely available potentially to everybody but in practice it is increasingly rationed by penury and mismanagement.
In our overcrowded and polluted world, the poor are getting thirsty and in need of proper sanitation, since they are often unable to afford the increasing price of a scarcer access to water, that is the true life jewel, much more precious than useless diamonds and increasingly recognized as a vital human right.

Out of Poverty Tips

Professional surveying of available drinking resources is the first step for their careful protection, in a sustainable evolutionary pattern where complex variables (hydro geological, demographic, etc.) capriciously interact. Requested investments are huge and unaffordable by the poorest, but nothing should be more stimulating than survival risk.

Selected Readings

ÜNVER I.H.O., GUPTA R.K., KIBAROGLU A., eds., (2003), *Water Development and Poverty Reduction*, Kluwer Academic Publishers, Dordrecht.

CHAPTER 7 – The dark side of the spoon: (mal)nutrition, healthcare and biblical plagues

> Behold, seven years of great abundance are coming in all the land of Egypt; and after them seven years of famine will come, and all the abundance will be forgotten in the land of Egypt, and the famine will ravage the land. So the abundance will be unknown in the land because of that subsequent famine; for it will be very severe.
>
> Book of Genesis 41: 29-31

Illness, undernourishment and poverty

Paraphrasing the Pink Floyd's famous album of 1973, the dark side of the … spoon here symbolizes empty cutlery–providing little or any food–or a dispenser with no syrup, a metaphor for missing healthcare treatment.

Illness and malnutrition are unanimously recognized as two of the most important causes and consequences of poverty, and they frequently triangularly interact – since emaciated poor are often both ill and hungry and poverty has such a critical role in the incidence of so many diseases. Infectious diseases, nutritional deficiencies, and unsafe childbirth unsafely cohabit in poor areas, with an impressive synergic death toll.

Diseases and hunger–which are a primary cause of migration[160] towards safer places–are also linked with other traditional poverty traps, such as misuse of natural resources[161], the conflict trap[162], being landlocked with bad neighbors[163] or bad governance in a small country[164] and they can find temporary relief from remittances[165] or international aid[166], even if their structural causes normally require deep internal involvement and self consciousness to be eradicated.

---

160 See Chapter 12.
161 See Chapter 3.
162 See Chapter 5.
163 See Chapter 1.
164 See again Chapter 5.
165 See Chapter 12.

Any development strategy normally starts from basic food and health problems, even if an interdisciplinary approach to so complex underdevelopment issues is increasingly acknowledged. Improving food security–from both a quantitative and qualitative side–can greatly contribute to reduce related health problems. Poverty, malnutrition, permanent ill-being and starvation are closely interdependent, being also linked with ›biblical‹ plagues:

Figure 7.1. – The interaction among health, poverty and hunger

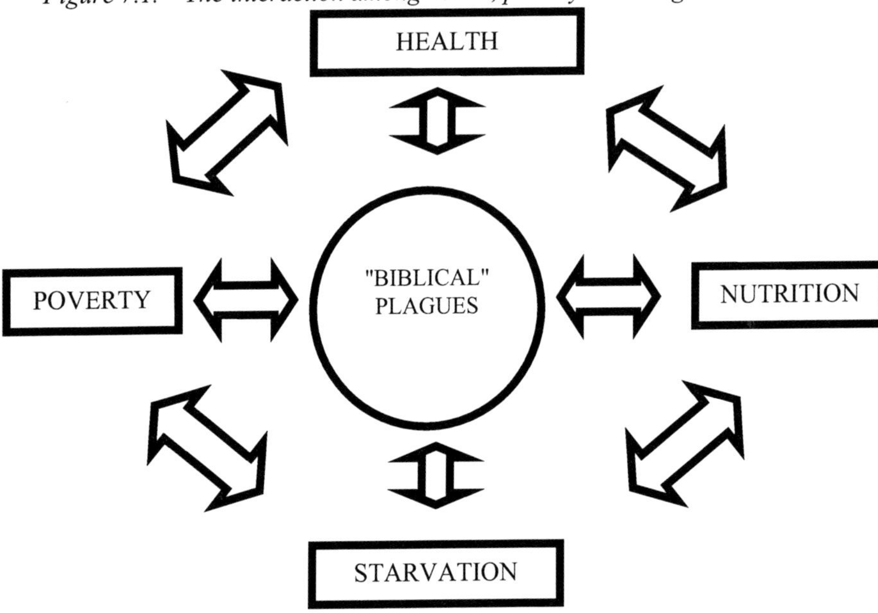

Even microfinance can play its part in softening these problems, while enhancing human development, to the extent that it can promote basic development of the unbanked poor.
According to article 25 of the U.N. Universal Declaration of Human Rights[167]:

> Everyone has the right to a standard of living adequate for the health and well-being of himself and of his family, including food, clothing, housing and medical care, and necessary social services, and the right to security in the event of unemployment, sickness, disability, widowhood, old age or other lack of livelihood in circumstances beyond his control.

Health and nutrition are basic and vital human rights as well as a key input to poverty reduction and social and economic development.

---

166 See Chapter 14.

167 See http://www.un.org/en/documents/udhr/index.shtml#ap.

The interaction of ›Biblical‹ plagues with illness and hunger

The biblical plagues of Egypt, which are recognized by the book religions of Jews, Christians, and Muslims, literally are the ten calamities imposed upon Egypt by God, to convince Pharaoh to let the poorly treated Israelite slaves go. In their metaphoric popular meaning of ancient and recurring disgraces (floods, drought, hail, uncontrolled proliferation of locusts or other diseases on plants, and livestock …) they also play their part and they are often a primary cause of both illness and hunger.

The fight against undernourishment and starvation seems still far from being won and it is amazing, in an unprecedented rich world, where there is enough food for everybody – and to the shame of the rich, each year tens of millions of desperate poor prematurely die[168], even if they could be saved, often with little effort or expense. Each time it happens, a part of our conscience dies with them. The problem is not food, whose quantity is enough for everybody, but its needed capillary and equitable delivery.

As it will be shown on later, collective hunger–famine–undernourishment or even starvation are not an automatic consequence of lack of foodstuff, but rather of its unequal distribution (with a ›scarcity in abundance‹ paradox), often for intentional Machiavellian purposes, which are exacerbated by dictatorships and civil wars that devastate the economy, uprooting its development pattern.

And even if this drama takes place each single day far from rich countries and it is continuously reported by the news, we get so used to it that most of us simply don't care about it – what eyes do not see, heart does not grieve over. As Albert Schweitzer used to say »happiness is nothing more than good health and a bad memory«.

In his encyclical letter Caritas in Veritate, §17, Benedict XVI talks about »situations of underdevelopment which are not due to chance or historical necessity, but are attributable to human responsibility«. This is why »the peoples in hunger are making a dramatic appeal to the peoples blessed with abundance«. And again (§25): »The problem of food insecurity needs to be addressed within a long-term perspective, eliminating the structural causes that give rise to it and promoting the agricultural development of poorer countries«.

Food insecurity–and consequent malnutrition–may be caused by the unavailability of food, insufficient purchasing power, inappropriate distribution or storage, or inadequate use at the household level.

A body weakened by hunger unsurprisingly gets much more easily ill, and diseases can deathly interact with malnutrition. Even if health and nutrition are so strongly linked, from now on we shall mainly deal with each topic separately,

168 According to Hunger and World Poverty (www.poverty.com) about 25,000 people die every day of hunger or hunger-related causes, according to the United Nations. This is one person every three and a half seconds.

synthetically considering some of the main interactions between illness–or, respectively, hunger–and poverty.
The historian David Landes has given an original explanation of underdevelopment[169]: hot climates are enervating and they breed a wide variety of dispiriting and incapacitating diseases. According to his ›climate thesis‹, tropical climes are, *ceteris paribus*, poor candidates for development. What deserves attention in the tropical thesis is in particular the tremendous cocktail of synergic problems that cause poverty: enervating climate not encouraging labor, numerous and more lethal diseases, which are tropical and occasional for the rich living else where but endemic for the poor and their animals, under the capricious direction of an extremist weather (often too hot and dry but ... when it rains, it pours), increasingly worsened by global warming[170]. Geography and luck matter.
Technology is often a powerful device for health and nutrition, since new medicines, cures, fertilizers or curing and cultivating techniques can greatly help. Unluckily they are not for free, since they are both risky for their often unknown side effects and they are also typically jealously reserved only to those who can afford them – hardly ever the poorest, as we are experiencing, for example, with expensive anti-AIDS treatments, well beyond the economic possibilities of so many ill Africans. Is it right that those who cannot pay simply die?
Health experts, economists, and international development advocates cite the inextricable link between poor health, poverty, and under-development. For the poorest, every day of their life is a survival challenge.
Lack of food is another example of multidisciplinary issue and according to the United Nations Development group[171] »attention to hunger and under-nutrition requires integrating technical and policy interventions with broader and more integral approaches which incorporate perspectives from agriculture, health, water and sanitation, infrastructure, gender, education, good governance, and legal, judicial, and administrative protection«. Mitigation measures concern:

- equitable economic growth, promoting development (see Chapter 15), and dismantling the poverty traps (Chapter 16);
- outreach to vulnerable and poor, even through microfinance (see in particular Chapter 21);
- social protection and disaster risk reduction, through public expenditure and prevention measures, initially backed by foreign aid (see Chapter 14);

---

169 See Chapter 1 and Landes (1998).
170 See Chapter 8.
171 ›*Thematic papers on the Millennium Development Goals*‹, 2008, http://www.un.org/millenniumgoals.

- investments in sustainability, again recurring to microfinance, considering the possible trade-off with outreach, referring again to Chapter 21 (lack of sustainability hampers outreach, whereas excessive outreach endangers sustainability).

From little wealth to … poor health

Health, which is something more than a simple absence of sickness, is a well evident primary need. According to Hippocrates, the prominent Ancient Greece doctor (460 – 377 B.C.), a wise man should consider that health is the greatest of human blessings, and he should learn how by his own thought to derive benefit from his illnesses[172]. Going to modern times »if you trust Google more than your doctor, then maybe it's time to switch doctors«[173].
The very fact that also health is not everlasting, like anything concerning human nature, is well evidenced by Robert Orben: »Quit worrying about your health. It'll go away«.
But poor health, even if it is fronted with a bit of humor, remains a very serious issue, especially when associated with other typical poverty traps. We know from Western countries that health spending absorbs a great fraction of the Gross Domestic Product in each country, mainly because the lengthening of life multiplies the number of elderly people, much more prone to get sick. The budget spending is much lower, both in absolute and relative terms, in underdeveloped countries, where the pockets of citizens are empty, like the safe boxes of their Government.
Technology and scientific discoveries are continuously changing, normally for the better, and the healthcare system and its users are strongly taking benefit of these developments. But a large part of humanity is entitled to receive little or any health care – a complex, expensive and labor intensive process, which takes time to be put in place, requiring a continuous fine tuning. Many are so poor that they can't even afford medicines or vaccinations or cheap devices such as bed nets, so useful against malaria. The death toll is impressive and passing away, the unlucky poor definitely abandon their body – our material envelope due to become an empty shell. The tragedy and comedy of life eventually find in death their leveling synthesis.
Primary sanitary education and basic hygiene also play an extremely important role in prevention of illnesses, but they are hardly followed or known in many backward rural places, where strongly needed doctors are hardly available or, if present, they often severely lack proper equipment and facilities. Dispensaries for drug distribution or hospitals for acute treatment can be too far or expensive

172 Hippocrates, ›*Regimen in Health*‹.
173 Cordova (2006).

or unskilled. Proper networking with disseminated hard presence in the territory is highly wanted and it is often desperately missing, together with a professional and efficient organization. In many underdeveloped countries, even ambulances do not provide a public service, to the extent that they can reach injured people in unpaved roads – unless you have money, they don't pick you up to the hospital.

Undernourishment and bad sanitary conditions (with smelly open air toilets, built around a simple hole dig in the ground) and bad water, that is often undrinkable, are a natural environment for poor health. Superstition and ancestral belief in witchcraft also play their part and medicines or treatments provided to sick poor are often refused, also because they are not immediately effective (no immediate miracles, no medicine). Those who deny the scientific cause of illnesses such as AIDS in some parts of Austral Africa also share a big burden for the absurd death toll of so many innocent that could otherwise be saved. And teaching HIV patients to take antiretroviral pills each day is often a daunting task.

Poor health is also concerned with mental illnesses and handicaps, which are highly diffused and largely preventing the possibility to live a decent life frequent within the poor. According to Emerson (2007) »epidemiological studies have consistently reported a significant association between poverty and the prevalence of intellectual disabilities«.

In poor countries, overwhelmed by survival problems, handicaps are typically a taboo and their social acceptance and care is often a mirage. Illnesses can be a social stigma which often brings also social exclusion or self embarrassment, together with incapacity to accept a different condition and severe psychological drawbacks. AIDS is nowadays a typical example, as leprosy used to be in ancient times – and still somewhere today. In some cultures illness is also fatalistically and improperly linked to guilt and those who are sick and poor are often unfairly stigmatized as sinners[174].

Black Death deriving from bubonic plague and the pale memory of its induced tragic mass mortality should also contribute–symbolically better than anything else–to remember our cruel and selective past, waiting for the shadow of overcoming death, while putting an end to the mask of life.

Especially infective diseases, like plague, require a minimum threshold of population density to spread[175] and they are so related with the demographic issues–and Malthusian worries–depicted in Chapter 4.

---

174 As it has been shown in the introduction.

175 Sachs (2008), p. 62.

Global health … needs an affluent help

Global health is concerned with the health of populations in a worldwide context, beyond the perspectives and concerns of individual nations. On the one side, it is an opportunity for those who rightly advocate a worldwide improvement in the general health conditions – with a positive spill over for everybody and externalities such as general economic growth, social progress, improved well being and so on. On the other side global health is also a threat, if only we think about global diseases, such as the 1918 Spanish flu pandemic, which severely hit those who survived World War I and with a worldwide death toll estimated from 50 to 100 million people, infective diseases such as the plague, with its devastating impact in Middle Age Europe.
Bacteria, viruses, and other pathogen agents are ›discourteously‹ irrespective of … borders, and they need no passport to spread everywhere, while quarantine to prevent uncontrolled diffusion of illnesses is always recommended but increasingly difficult to put in place, in a global world where people chaotically move everywhere.
Supranational institutions and agencies are indispensable to deal with such global issues – such as the World Health Organization (WHO), UNICEF, World Food Program (WFP), the World Bank or other less formal networks, often driven by charities or NGOs. Global health is unsurprisingly an interdisciplinary topic, since it is a research field at the intersection of medical and social science disciplines–including demography, (macro)economics, epidemiology, and sociology–concerning in particular:

- an epidemiological perspective, which identifies major global health problems;
- a medical perspective, describing the pathology of major diseases, which promotes prevention, diagnosis, and treatment of these illnesses;
- an economic perspective, which addresses the cost-effectiveness and cost-benefit approaches for both individual and population health allocation.

Among the parameters and indicators which can broadly contribute to define the uncertain perimeter of global health, we shouldn't forget:

- life expectancy[176], a statistical measure of the average life span (average length of survival) of a specified population – its expected time remaining to live;

[176] See Chapter 4.

- disability-adjusted life year (DALY), a summary measure that combines the impact of illness, disability and mortality on population health[177];
- quality-adjusted life years, or QALYs, a way of measuring disease burden, including both the quality and the quantity of life lived, as a means of quantifying in benefit of a medical intervention;
- infant mortality and under-five child mortality, more specific in representing the health in the poorest sections of a population;
- morbidity (sickness) measures.

Babies with abnormal and distended bellies sadly witness one of the latest stages of malnutrition due to marasma or kwashiorkor, up to probable death, mirroring a disintegrating and dysfunctional society where they have the bad luck to be born and live.
Mobility of morbidity is concerned with pandemic diffusion of infective illnesses, which are globally spreading in a connected world where quarantine proves increasingly difficult.

Neglected tropical diseases and (elsewhere) trivial illnesses

Poor countries experiment both peculiar illnesses (which are hardly known in richer countries, due to climatic differences and different standards of hygiene and nutrition, commonly known as–often neglected–tropical diseases) and harder and much more frequent diseases than in developed countries (to name a few, diarrhea, tuberculosis, often associated with AIDS, measles, pneumonia, leper, cholera …).
Neglected tropical diseases[178] are a symptom of poverty and disadvantage. The most affected ones are the poorest populations often living in remote, rural areas, urban slums or in conflict zones. With little political voice, neglected tropical diseases have low profile and status in public health priorities. The neglected tropical diseases express this link between health and development in an explicit, almost visual way – a way that is more compelling than statistics alone. Although neglected tropical diseases are medically diverse, they share features that allow them to persist in conditions of poverty, where they cluster and frequently overlap. Over 1 billion people–about one sixth of the world's population–suffer from one or more neglected tropical diseases.

---

177 The DALY combines in one measure the time lived with disability and the time lost due to premature mortality. One DALY can be thought of as one lost year of ›healthy‹ life and the burden of disease as a measurement of the gap between current health status and an ideal situation where everyone lives into old age free of disease and disability.

178 http://www.who.int/neglected_diseases/en.

Awkward diseases, often harmful even for livestock and other animals, include African trypanosomiasis–sleeping sickness induced by tsetse flies–or other often unheard of illnesses such as–just to name a few–leishmaniasis, yellow fever, ebola, dracunculiasis, onchocerciasis or river blindness, dengue fever, hookworm, strongyloidiasis, trichuriasis, helminthes, chagas disease, schistosomiasis or bilharzias, treponematoses, sickle cell disease, buruli ulcer, food-borne trematodiases, neurocysticercosis, flavivirus infections ...

Where love and care proved stronger than Ebola ...[179]

At the beginning of October 2000, the St. Mary's Hospital Lacor in Gulu, Northern Uganda, founded by Piero and Lucille Corti, observed inexplicable deaths amongst its patients and staff occurring after a brief but intense illness, occasionally with hemorrhage. The Ebola virus causes the victim to die from massive hemorrhaging.

Following these deaths the hospital advanced the hypothesis of hemorrhagic fever and gave the alarm. Blood samples of some patients were sent to a specialized lab in South Africa and on the 14th of October the results revealed hemorrhagic fever caused by the EBOLA virus.

At the end of the outbreak the hospital had to pay tribute to the battle against the virus: of the 90 staff members who volunteered to care for patients affected by EBOLA, twelve lost their life, amongst those Dr. Matthew Lukwiya, an unforgotten hero.

Malaria is the quintessential ›tropical‹ vector-borne infectious disease caused by protozoan parasites. It is widespread in tropical and subtropical regions, including parts of the Americas, Asia, and especially Africa. Each year there are approximately 350-500 million cases of malaria, with the death of one up to three million people, the majority of whom are underweight children in Sub-Saharan Africa[180]. Mortality can be sharply and cost-effectively reduced by use of insecticide–treated bed nets, prompt artemisin–based combination therapy and it can be supported by intermittent preventive treatment in pregnancy. While full prevention seems still far off–and definitive vaccination a mirage–cheap devices (such as the aforementioned bed nets) prove highly effective, even if they are much less popular than they should be.

Just to make an example of elsewhere normally trivial illnesses, diarrhea infections are responsible for 17 % of deaths worldwide among children under the age of five, making them the second most common cause of child deaths global-

179 Source: http://www.lhospital.org/eng/storia_ebola.shtml.

180 http://www.cdc.gov/malaria.

ly[181]. Poor sanitation can lead to increased transmission through water, food, utensils, hands and flies. Rotavirus is highly contagious and a major cause of severe diarrhea and death (ca 20%) in children.

The case for universal healthcare: a hardly affordable right?

Is universal health care a human right? The question is not exactly addressed in these terms by the above quoted article 25 of the U.N. Declaration of Human Rights.

Before shortly considering some of the main pros and cons of this major issue, a preliminary practical caveat should concern our analysis: just in case that we come up with a positive answer, who does pay? It shouldn't be forgotten that developing countries have little resources for health and–to the extent that they can afford to cover the costs–many of them provide basic public healthcare assistance, which cohabits with private hospitals. The latter have normally higher quality standards than the former, at least for what concerns the comfort, but they have also unattainable costs for most of the citizens and unaffordable access for the poor, unless they are subsidized by aid agencies, religious institutions or other donors.

According to the World Health Organization (WHO)[182], there are cost-effective interventions for controlling major diseases, but serious lack of money for health and a range of system constraints hamper global and national efforts to expand health services to the poor. The high burden of preventable diseases in poor countries and communities calls for strategic planning of investments across health and health-related sectors in order to improve the lives of poor people and promote their development. WHO, working closely with governments and their partners, advocates for a more prominent role for health within countries' macroeconomic agendas. It also offers technical expertise to support country efforts for developing long-term multi-sector investment plans. The work is carried out in line with three themes:

- achieving better health for the poor;
- increasing investments in health;
- progressively eliminating non-financial constraints.

Pros and cons of universal healthcare are summarized in the following table[183].

[181] http://www.childinfo.org/709.htm.

[182] Macroeconomics and Health, http://www.who.int/macrohealth/en.

[183] The main concepts are taken from http://www.nhchc.org/humanright.html and Goodman J., (2005), ›*Five Myths of Socialized Medicine*‹, Cato Institute, Cato's Letter, Winter, 2005.

Table 7.1. – Pros and cons of universal healthcare

Issue	Pros	Cons
Is medical care a right?	The U.N. Universal Declaration of Human Rights asserts that medical care is a right of all people. Many religions also impose an obligation on their followers to care for those in less favorable circumstances, including the sick. Humanists too would assert the same obligation and the right to medical care have been enshrined in many other ways too.	Laissez-faire capitalists assert that providing health care funded by taxes is immoral because it is a form of legalized robbery, denying the right to dispose of one's own income at one's own will. They assert that doctors should not be servants of their patients but rather they should be regarded as traders, like everyone else in a free society.
Which should be the involvement of Government?	Universal health care requires government involvement and oversight. There is a public interest besides the Government's involvement. Removing profit as a motive will increase the rate of medical innovation.	A concern is that the right to privacy between doctors and patients could be eroded if governments demand power to oversee health of citizens. Another concern is that governments use legislation to control personal freedoms. Removing profit as a motive will decrease the rate of medical innovation.
Which is the economic impact of universal health care?	It reduces wastefulness in the delivery of health care by removing the middle man, the insurance companies, and thus reducing the amount of bureaucracy. Supporters note that modern industrial countries with socialized medicine tend to spend much less on	Socialized medicine suffers from the same financial problems as any other government planned economy. They argue that it requires governments to greatly increase taxes as costs rise year over year. Universal health care essentially tries to do the eco-

Issue	Pros	Cons
	health care than similar countries lacking such systems.	nomically impossible. Opponents of universal health care argue that government agencies are less efficient due to bureaucracy. Universal health care plans will add more inefficiency to the medical system through additional bureaucratic oversight and paperwork, which will lead to fewer doctor patient visits.

Health policy is a complex interdisciplinary topic, since it ranges from medicine and other sciences (biology, chemistry …) to philosophy (with its ethical debate about individual rights), economics, and even further. Many governments around the world have established universal health care, which attempts to provide the same level of access to every person in a country, while some citizens are against universal health care for a variety of reasons.

From the vaccination puzzle to the drugs free riding

In Western countries, healthcare is increasingly concerned with prevention and, when this strategy is not sufficient, with proper treatment, using more and more sophisticated medicines and hospitalization. This rather obvious pattern is easier said than carried through. What makes the real difference is the quality of treatment, enabling the lucky ones to live longer and better. Prevention is a (non trivial) cultural concept and it takes ages to promote it, as Western countries are still experiencing. In many backward realities, if the vaccine or the drug does not have an immediate effect, people may prefer to go back to the sorcerer or the wizard – ignorance and superstition are still widespread and damaging.
A huge amount of public and private resources is dedicated to healthcare–it is even due to the aging factor–and there is an increasing pressure for continuous quality upgrading.
Both vaccines and drugs are conceived, manufactured, and sold by private companies, which look for profit maximization, often without regard to the needs of those who can't afford to buy them. In Western countries this problem is mitigated by public healthcare and social safety nets, financed by taxation,

while in underdeveloped ones the safe box is typically empty and little or any money is left to support proper medical treatment. The quality of public hospitals–wherever they are present!–in underdeveloped countries is often impressively lower than that of richer ones. Prevention is hardly considered a cultural value to share and promote in places where bare survival worries absorb most of the poor's resources, leaving little room and fancy for upgrading their miserable condition.

When Western pharmaceutical multinationals approach poor countries, the different objectives of producers and potential clients soon appear difficult to combine, since the former want to maximize their returns and the latter want to get vaccines and drugs paying the little they can afford. Expensive R&D financing of new drugs is unlikely to be properly covered by destitute clients and patents breaching or softening is a dangerous policy for multinationals, not only because it may sharply reduce their profits in poor markets, but also since it may elsewhere ignite an imitation effect uneasy to control.

Patent holders bear monopolistic rights which reflect in a typically rigid supply function, with a market price that is unaffected by the demand and hardly interested in serving the moneyless poor.

What multinationals probably underestimate is the very fact that potential clients, living in underdeveloped countries, are poor but they are many and growing, and they so represent a formidable chance for creating new markets, with lower margins but consistently higher volumes and consequent impressive scaling opportunities. In addition, to the extent that the poor are helped to improve their starting miserable condition, they can become wealthier, with a growing spending power.

Within this broad context, it shouldn't be surprising that the debate is hotly flamed, considering also its deep ethical implications–while the rich discuss about the issue, the poor continue to die.

Strange and rare illnesses are present everywhere in the world and they unsurprisingly receive little attention from private R&D labs, always looking for lucrative new blockbuster drugs. Tropical diseases are certainly strange–at least for the Westerners unused to manage with them–but unfortunately they are not rare, if only we think about malaria, and typically more virulent, living in a warmer environment. Economic incentives are always needed and without them it is difficult to solve the puzzle. Who is going to pay the bill?

Should the healthcare problem in poor countries be addressed as it deserves, approaching Western standards, the resources to be spent would be enormous. A second best but more viable and realistic strategy is gradual upgrading and outreach, that is still posing impressive challenges.

Aid is increasingly addressed at sponsoring and subsidizing ›ethical‹ R&D, otherwise neglected by profit-seeking companies. Other mitigation measures en-

visage a more intense use of preventive vaccination. Unfortunately they are still missing for malaria, AIDS and other big killers. Scientific improvements bring to positive outputs, which are represented not only by new drugs, but also by cheaper techniques and materials.
A liberal approach to the problem of drugs availability is encouraged by the Millennium Development Goal n. 8 (develop a global partnership for development)[184]. According to Target 4 »in cooperation with pharmaceutical companies, [it is needed to] provide access to affordable essential drugs in developing countries« (Poor availability and high prices are barriers to access to essential drugs in developing countries).
Illnesses synergistically interact with poor nutrition, bad sanitation and weak institutional framework, which are highly dysfunctional even in satisfying basic needs. The outcome of these unwanted interactions is typically gloomy, resulting in consistently higher mortality rates, accompanied by a lower quality of life.

Dead unless properly fed: is hunger … an exaggerate diet?

Despite Malthusian gloomy prophecies of some two hundreds years ago, nowadays food seems to be enough for everybody, even in an increasingly populated world. The problem lies in its profoundly unequal distribution – too much for increasingly fat Western populations and too little, up to starvation, for the misfortunate poorest in underdeveloped countries.
Western countries' intervention in the poorest areas produces ambiguous results, because sometimes it rescues starving populations from certain death, but in other cases it contributes to their needy situation with the refusal to import agricultural or textile products (exceeding self consumption) from poor countries. The last cases block possible exports, to the very detrimental volatility of food prices, induced by international greedy speculation, which hardly damages the poorest, as we have witnessed in the much harmful foodflation (i.e., food price rise) of 2007-2008, linked with the recession of 2008-2009 – the twin crises.
Gross prices are coming down from their speculative peaks but inelastic and hardly adaptive retail prices are slow to react to changes in costs, making intermediaries even richer. Market inefficiencies place indeed a heavy burden on the poor, typically unable to find viable alternatives.
Food self sufficiency is an old autarchic target, that is less justified in an increasingly integrated world but it is still popular and with a high propagandistic effect. Cooperation and trading across countries, each focused on its specialized

---

184 See http://www.un.org/millenniumgoals/bkgd.shtml.

activities, are a much safer parachute against adversities than a nominal self sufficiency, always threatened by calamities and wastes.

Problems related with food show an unsurprising graduated pattern–as it happens for illnesses or many other issues–which, following a Rossinian crescendo, ranges from under nourishment to hunger till starvation. The sad death toll becomes even gloomier if we consider that those who are intrinsically weaker and more vulnerable to food scarcity are the first to succumb. In addition, among them we find needy babies and children or even teenagers, who are blocked in the most delicate phase of their growth by lack of nutrition and who are too young or weak to contrast an unfriendly environment. In order to cope with such a difficult situation, they need a hint.

Hunger is an unpleasant feeling experienced when one has a desire to eat, originated in the hypothalamus and released through receptors in the liver. Due to its inextricable link with poverty durable hunger alleviation should not only be concerned with the distribution of emergency food to starving population, but also–mainly–with structural policies aiming at removing the causes of poverty and consequent under nourishment.

Like a drug, aid can anyway create dependency, as we shall see in Chapter 14. If efforts are only directed at providing food, or improving food production or distribution, then the structural root causes that create hunger, poverty, and dependency would still remain.

Ross Copeland[185] claims that hunger is essentially a question of poverty. People, who are vainly looking for meet on the bones, are starving simply because they cannot afford to buy food. The current situation is nothing less than criminal, because it sees the best agricultural land in the bulk of the world's poorest countries used for the growing of cash crops that only benefit the wealthy. At the heart of any real solution, therefore, is the question of land reforms[186].

Land currently used for mono cropping cash crops must be made available to the dispossessed. The landless rural poor and the urban unemployed and small farming should be encouraged. There is a real need, therefore, for the imposition of trade restrictions, imposing tariffs that would render imported foodstuffs more expensive than those produced locally and exporting only genuine surplus.

Even if the problem of hunger is not a question of overpopulation at the present time, as human numbers continue to grow, there can be little doubt that we will have to face genuine shortages in the not too distant future. All available evidence demonstrates that as the wealth in a society increases, population growth slows accordingly[187]. Addressing the problem of poverty will therefore not only

---

185 The ›*Politics of Hunger*‹, http://motspluriels.arts.uwa.edu.au/MP1500rs.html.

186 See Chapter 15.

187 See Chapter 4.

provide everyone with an adequate food supply now, but it will also ensure the security of our food supply for the future.
According to Kapuściński, hunger is the quietest and most docile kind of death, which progressively suffocates its unlucky clients with its anesthetizing tentacles, pushing them from behind. On the other side, food–bread–symbolizes not only the necessary ingredient for eating, but also a social aspect of sharing.

Famine and the tragedy of mass starvation

Many underdeveloped countries carry on with endemic malnutrition, that is a situation of improper diet or nutrition that has a severe impact on health and it may occasionally bring to mass death, especially if it is associated with other health problems.
The outlook worsens when malnutrition becomes a permanent hungry season, up to starvation, that is a state of exhaustion of the body, caused by a severe lack of food. It may precede death, largely announced by its ubiquitous phantom. Malnutrition is paradoxically concerned not only with food deprivation but also with overeating (in rich countries), remembering how difficult it is to keep an equilibrated diet. Actually, famine is often more related to food displacement and its inefficient delivery than to real scarcity and it occurs when mass hunger knocks at the door of already ailing places.
History records a sad gallery of tragic famines, even in recent times, such as the Gorta Mór (Great Hunger) which devastated Ireland in 1845-1952 or the 1932-1933 Holodomor (Death by Hunger) in Ukraine or the more recent 1984-1985 famine in Ethiopia.
Famine is a widespread scarcity of food which applies to man, livestock, or other animals and it can follow all the steps from malnutrition to lethal starvation, especially if prolonged in time. Humanitarian relief[188] is often the only solution to the problem and it calls for promptness and efficient coordination in a context of emergency, where little help can normally come from inside the over troubled hit area. When famine is occurring, emergency foreign aid is urgently wanted, but often it is not admitted for reasons of prestige of ailing regimes, whose dictators tend to consider their pride more valuable than the life of their unlucky subjects.
Amartya Sen in much of his writings on poverty, famines, and malnutrition, argues that democracy is the best way to avoid famines partly because of its ability to use a free press:

188 See Chapter 14.

> Famines are easy to prevent if there is a serious effort to do so, and a democratic government, facing elections and criticisms from opposition parties and independent newspapers, cannot help but make such an effort. Not surprisingly, while India continued to have famines under British rule right up to independence ... they disappeared suddenly with the establishment of a multiparty democracy and a free press[189].

Famines do not occur in democracies since they are extremely easy to prevent, if only there is such a political willingness – considering the mess they do when they occur, in multiparty democracies no politician hoping for reelection could afford to let it happen. Freedom to escape from starvation and famine's mortality unsurprisingly is core and vital economic forms of liberty[190].

Sen summarizes some of his best-known work on famines[191]. These are usually caused by a lack of purchasing power or entitlements, not by actual food shortage–famine–struck areas sometimes continue to export food–and they are easy and cheap to avoid. Large–scale famines have never happened in a democracy and, Sen argues, are unlikely to. They can only happen in authoritarian systems lacking openness of information and transparency. A similar analysis may be applicable to the Asian monetary crisis at the end of the 1990s.

Famine prevention finds an obstacle in poverty and cultural inability to program[192]. Good farming with proper incentives (such as land titling[193]) is among the best antidotes against famine as well as agrarian reforms are one of the best antidotes against famine, but they have to democratically distribute the land to its natural users.

The Malthusian hypothesis[194] regards famine as a temporary escape valve from extreme privations, from the point of view of the survivors of famine. During famines, people are desperate and in need at the point that they may be willing to sell land, properties and cattle for the very first time – a real bargain for vulture profiteers.

Drought and famines reinforce economic decline by lowering agricultural output and productivity, with a consequent growing need of imports, which is hardly managed by a weakening State, which is indeed unable to respond to the population grievances.

---

189 *Democracy as a Universal Value*, Journal of Democracy - Volume 10, Number 3, July 1999, pp. 3-17.

190 See Chapter 13.

191 For a critical comment, see Myhrvold-Hanssen (2003).

192 Sen (1999) p. 168.

193 See Chapter 15.

194 See Chapter 4.

The condensed Chapter

Poor health and malnutrition are both a cause and a consequence of misery, hitting the poor like the symbolic biblical plagues of Egypt. Underdeveloped countries cannot afford an expensive public healthcare system and they must rely on foreign donors, even for what concerns nutritional programs.
Undernourishment and (tropical) illnesses reduce productivity, hampering development and famines, which are disappeared from democratic countries, but they still impose their deathly toll in the poorest regions.

Out of Poverty Tips

The shame of hunger causes poverty amidst plenty, due to unequal and unfair wealth redistribution. Full and conscious understanding that the poor are a resource, not a burden, is the spring for proper and enduring action against malnutrition. Once properly ignited and culturally rooted, healthy development may eventually become affordable and self sustainable.

Selected Readings

SACHS J.D., (2008), *Common Wealth: Economics for a Crowded Planet*, Penguin Books, London.

CHAPTER 8 – Apocalypse soon? Warnings from global warming

Modern technology
Owes ecology
An apology.
Alan M. Eddison

The weather has no passport: worrying and warnings from global warming

Global warming is an unprecedented threat to the limited resources of the planet and it is also the most damaging environmental problem in the history of humanity, both on broad and deep terms, remembering how important it is to properly read the signs of our times. Everybody talks about the weather, but nobody does anything about it[195]. And the weather is the most global issue, with no passport and frontiers – we all share the same atmosphere, and we just have one, within the colored alphabet of a larger universe.

In a very brief and general way, global warming is defined by climatologists and earth scientists as the increase in the average temperature of the Earth's near-surface air and oceans, mainly as a consequence of human activities, such as burning fossil fuels or destructing natural resources for industrial production, overexploiting limited resources. The market economy and Mother Nature have to reach a living compromise, for the sake of the entire humanity.

Climatic issues and turbulent changes well symbolize the complex symphony of nature, with its ›mathematical language‹–as Einstein used to say–that is so difficult to fine tune and understand. Surprising and capricious nature often goes far beyond any human control – is there a beautiful order underneath the apparent chaos of nature?

Our planet is warming, species are migrating, rainfall patterns are changing and seasons are shifting, while lands are increasingly becoming sandy–due to ongoing desertification of degraded lands–or salty, as a consequence of the ocean level uprising[196]. Earth cannot keep unchanged if we continue littering it. And even if we personally don't like extremists, we fear that climate is becoming so. Threshold effects, so abundant in nature, may have devastating effects[197]: slight increases in temperature can melt down icebergs, augment the diffusion of ma-

195 Quotation attributed to Mark Twain.

196 For an updated survey of climatic issues, see the Global Environment Outlook, http://www.unep.org/geo/geo4/media/.

197 Sachs (2008), p. 78.

laria and other once tropical-only diseases, dry up sources of water, destabilize rainfall, etc.

To have an idea about the connection between this sort of climate change and world poverty, it is sufficient to follow a very short argument. Increasing temperatures cause big parts of the polar ice on the North and South Pole to melt. Through the melting of polar ice but also as a consequence of warming oceans causing seawater to expand, sea levels rise so that big parts of land are flooded and damaged by salinity intrusion. This fact notably decreases the amount of low-lying coastal land where it is possible for people to live and grow food on. Typically it is the most valuable soil, as it is demonstrated indirectly by the curse of landlocked regions, depicted in Chapter 2 or directly by their higher population density (of the many who live within the shoreline) or economic activities such as tourism, fisheries or transports through sea harbors. Coastal setting is both growing and more endangered by climatic changes, with a multiplication of synergic risk factors.

Another consequence of global warming is desertification that, just like floods, will notably decrease the amount of spaces suitable for people to live in. The main consequence of this process is overpopulation (people concentrate themselves in the only suitable areas, that are becoming fewer and fewer) and forced migration, due to catastrophes or no more supportive farming, of environmental refugees dislocated to safer places, even abroad, so becoming a destabilizing geopolitical issue. Failed States are going to export their instability and poor governance, with potentially serious implications for global security and world prosperity[198]: a warmer world is likely to become a more violent one, especially in increasingly concentrated urban areas.

The particular vulnerability of many poor countries–starting from those concentrated in the tropics–is partly a capricious accident of geography, but it is also a consequence of human (in)actions and of a combination of social, economic, and environmental factors, including a cultural unconsciousness about ecological issues, fragile and hazardous locations, with improper housing, little knowledge, and poor technological means. The poor are disproportionately hit by the capricious hazards of changing weather and they typically lack the capacity and resources to cope with its unwanted impact.

If left free to make its damages, climate change may compromise human development, reversing it, especially where growth is weak and still uncertain. The unwanted outcome may resemble the Penelope's loom metaphor, according to which the faithful wife of Odysseus worked each day at her loom and she unraveled the cloth each night, trying to delay the suitors that wanted her to remarry, taking profit of the long absence of her beloved husband. Even if Penelope was eventually happy, with Odysseus definitively coming back and reuniting

---

[198] See Brainard, Jones, Purvis (2009), p. vii.

with his bride, the impact of climatic changes on socio-economic growth is likely to be much less fortunate, seriously risking unraveling the loom of development.

The long term strategic target has to be addressed to bringing more and more people out of poverty. The ideal solution would be everybody, if complying with the somewhat utopian and dreamy, but anyway still useful, Millennium Development goals so authoritatively advocated by Jeffrey Sachs. It is also necessary to act in a sustainable way, without despoiling our only but not lonely planet.

Since greenhouse gases warm the earth for many years after their emission, they are deemed to have a long term legacy, contributing to shape a gloomy future outlook. Due to inertia in the climatic system, consequences of global warming are likely to bypass the gas emissions peak, progressively slowing down – it's just like stopping a fast train.

Longing for Noah's protecting ark

Preserving local biodiversity is among the most illuminated mitigation strategies, following the Biblical example of Noah and his ark, where biodiversity was carefully selected and sheltered in the garden of creation, due to God's intervention, refraining from totally destroying the earth after completely flooding it. »The book of nature is one and indivisible – beware of an uncareful reading«[199] and show gratitude for this gift, as saint Francis of Assisi did in his Canticle of Creatures[200]. It is also important to remind that global strategies need a physical on site implementation, understanding and fixing local problems.

Biodiversity can soften ecological problems, if it is enabled to overcome its current deep crisis which brings to its pervasive drop. Complementary and synergic attacks to biodiversity are man-induced pollution, population unbalanced increase, and consequent over–harvesting and over–exploitation of not renewable resources, predominance of invasive species and habitat undermining. They damage pervasively fisheries, corals, amphibians, pollinators, great apes, etc., up to their possible extinction[201]. Biodiversity is asymmetrically endangered, since large animals or slower growing and weaker plants face a consistently larger risk.

According to Al Gore »The warnings about global warming have been extremely clear for a long time. We are facing a global climate crisis. It is deepening. We are entering a period of consequences«. We so have to redesign our lifestyles and our socio-economic policies before we deploy our only planet.

199 Encyclical letter Caritas in Veritate, § 51.

200 See http://www.appleseeds.org/canticle.htm.

201 Sachs (2008), 141.

There is an escalation and self fulfilling of ecological disasters–in the form of often irreversible damage to terrestrial and marine ecosystems–and of an induced potential reduction in global food production, caused by a capricious combination of natural, climatic, and human processes, such as mass deforestation, land degradation (soil erosion and growing infertility), over cultivation, or overgrazing, unless properly managed. When imperiled ecosystems are harvested faster than they can recharge, depletion is the unsurprising outcome.
Planet earth is increasingly exposed to a polarized effect, according to which extremist scenarios are increasingly common: exposure to droughts, floods or storms–meaningfully defined as ›acts of God‹–is growing both in intensity and frequency, exacerbating the severity of extreme weather events. In the ancient Greek mythology, the Gods were acting through nature, punishing the humans for their misbehavior, and thunder was the metaphoric voice of Zeus, but nowadays, as Friedman (2009) recalls, no human anxiety about nature is back, forgetting the romantic attitude to consider nature the mirror of our soul.
Ecological disasters are becoming so frequent and shocking that many people are starting to reconsider their careless ideas, painfully acknowledging that the power of Mother Nature, together with man-induced disasters, still goes beyond our often unwise human control. According to some pessimist experts, the threshold of an ecological catastrophe is likely to be reached soon, with unknown side effects. It has indeed never happened before on such a large extent and we hardly know what can take place, even if scientists are trying to model the effects. Side effects may cause an unprecedented halt in human development and standard of living. The nonlinearity of the climate system may lead to abrupt changes, either milder or harsher than expected by conflicting scientists. Climate change (and its impact on the world's environment, our economies and our security) is a key issue of our era and every delay makes its consequences more irreversible. Other scientists are more optimistic about the outlook, confuting catastrophic forecasts. It is still difficult to say who is right and mixed outcomes may also be possible.
In any case, climate unwanted changes may retard or even reverse development, affecting also human rights, especially in the vulnerable poorest areas where resources are extremely limited and there is no proper shelter against weather degradation. Extreme weather is difficult both to forecast and to smooth, making survival much more volatile and intrinsically riskier, as it is shown by cases like droughts or floods due to heavy precipitation, heat waves, cyclones or hurricanes.
There is–and increasingly should be–a strong ethical commitment behind the conservation of our planet, back to nature and aware of the effects of overconsumption and unsustainable development. According to Sachs (2009), p. 3, forging nationwide commitments to reduce pollution is harder in composite so-

cieties such as the U.S., where the temptation of selfish unilateralism is an underlying cultural attitude. Worldwide connected problems need global answers, even if the existence of a ›free-rider‹ temptation makes international negotiations about climate changes difficult. According to ›free-rider‹ temptation, individual countries may have an incentive in letting others cutting emissions, taking profit from somebody else's efforts.

Monitoring, interventions and mitigation measures are highly wanted – the sooner, the better … and the cheaper.

Diverging economic interests also play an important part in slowing down the process of contrasting global warming, while alignment towards a shared common goal is increasingly necessary.

Countries have different industrialized and polluting models and Mahatma Gandhi once reflected on how many planets might be needed if Indians were due to follow Britain's pattern of industrialization. According to the entomologist Edward Wilson »destroying a tropical rain forest and other species-rich ecosystems for profit is like burning all the paintings of the Louvre to cook dinner«.

Unless the current trend is soon slowed down and reversed, a gloomy legacy may be awaiting future generations, too used to be thankful for the material wealth that they have received but often unaware of the intangible badwill of disrupted ecosystem.

Both underestimation and overrating of climatic issues are wrong–now that catastrophists are increasingly challenged and their alleged impartiality put under scrutiny–even if it is difficult to detect their real immediate but also long term effects. Correct timing of actions and measures–bewaring of early warnings–is crucial but also uneasy to detect. Climatic issues are complex, non linear, and often unpredictable because they involve infinite possible interactions and altered equilibriums between natural sciences such as physics, chemistry, and biology, as Friedman (2009), recalls. He reminds also that Mother Nature is completely amoral – the oceans have no memory, washing away everything, and it proves difficult to negotiate with nature, as we tend to do with other human beings, looking for compromises. And climatic mutations changes can interact among themselves, even thousands of miles away, especially if they are put in connection by the common atmosphere or by water (melting icebergs in the Poles are raising sea tides everywhere).

Climate is a complex issue also because nature is far from being simple–as Blaise Pascal used to say »nature is an infinite sphere of which the center is everywhere and the circumference is nowhere«.

Causes and consequences of global warming

The ecological disaster is a double edged sword and it is a paradoxical outcome of the very fact that people want to extract from nature the most they can, trying to transform it into wealth, while this strategy, brought to its extreme consequences, is on the long run an implacable resource destroyer.
Global warming is caused by numerous factors, which can be split into two main groups:

- natural causes – they are not linked to human activities. The main natural cause of global warming is methane release from the arctic tundra and wetlands. Methane is a dangerous, greenhouse gas, which has been very damaging for the world's climate. However, we have to bear in mind that natural causes of global warming have a very small impact on climate change, if compared to those produced by human activities;
- man-made causes–they are doubtlessly the most damaging. In the last 50 years, development and economic growth have had an extremely negative impact on the environment, and global warming is one of the most damaging problems that have been caused by the continuous burning of coal, gas, and oil to power our lives.

The use of fossil fuels, such as oil and coal, is the main cause of global warming because, when these resources are burnt, they produce large amounts of CO_2. However, a mining process is needed to make them available, since fossil fuels very often find themselves underground. This human activity frees a considerable amount of methane from the ground, another greenhouse gas. Fossil fuels are irreplaceable and not renewable, polluting, increasingly expensive–due to growing demand, unable to meet decreasing supplies–and politically incorrect, if they produce the natural resources curse described in Chapter 3. In a world where natural resources, mostly being not renewable, are intrinsically limited and increasingly scarce, economic growth is increasingly forced to follow alternative sustainable patterns.
The following list shows the human activities that produce the largest amounts of greenhouse gases and other elements that contribute to worsen the damaging effects of global warming:

- extraction of coal and oil;
- transportation;
- increasing world population;
- manure;
- deforestation;

- building structures. Both heating and air conditioning release indeed greenhouse gases.

Westerners should be deeply concerned with global warming and its effects on poverty. The problem often is that many affluent citizens do not have to cope with its most dramatic consequences that the poor world is going through. The media obviously play an important role in spreading awareness for this phenomenon, but on many occasions it doesn't make people realize how serious it is.
Many studies on the effects of climate change on the world population have been made, and two main contrasting models have recently come out:

- the ›catastrophic model‹, according to which there will be sudden migrations that will bring extremely large numbers of refugees into More Economic Developed Countries. Floods and hurricanes will happen all of a sudden and it will become harder and harder to forecast these cataclysms, with extremely damaging effects. (It is sufficient to think that, if we won't be able to forecast these natural disasters, the evacuation of areas exposed to risk will hardly be possible and many people will die). It will become very hard to control the migration trend, and NGOs will be overwhelmed by extremely large numbers of people needing assistance[202];

- a more ›optimistic‹ model, according to which the consequences of climate changes will come out in a very gradual way, and so people will get a chance to learn to cope with them. The poorer countries will consider the contrast of climate change part of their developing program, and they will build their economy considering global warming (this means growing a certain type of food, building homes and industries in certain places – an overall adaptation to the changing climatic conditions).

Climate changes and misery: are the poorest paying the bill for the richest?

An evolutionary pattern of development has to take into account not only the current progress in poverty eradication strategies, but also the threats that are being posed by ongoing and emerging problems, such as global warming. To the extent that global warming is caused by human industrial pollution, the poor (who hardly contribute to this process and who are often displaced from their native territories, especially if natural resources are being exploited without

---

202 See Chapter 12.

their participation[203]) are the first real victims of industrial development, being disproportionately affected by adversities. Poverty reduction and sustainable resource management are different sides of the same strategy.

Climate changes are closely linked with poverty, especially in underdeveloped regions, which are highly exposed to weather modifications. Growing temperatures bring big parts of polar ice to melt, increasing the sea level and threatening low coastal areas. Due to irregular rains, desertification advances and violent floods, many places are becoming inhabitable, causing overcrowding of populations forced to abandon the native territories they can no longer live in.

Malthusian worries about the impact of the demographic spiral[204] on the environment may raise further concerns about long term development sustainability, especially in the presence of a weak institutional framework. Environmental sustainability is strongly linked to quality of life and social justice.

Another debated issue is concerned with the impact of climatic disasters on civil conflicts. As Busby reports[205], someone think that disasters could help to diminish conflicts (may be, cooling down overheated moods and characters with heavy rains), since antagonists are forced by the emergency situation to stop quarreling, trying to urgently solve together common problems. Others argue that disasters foster competition between opponent groups with atavistic rivalry for shrinking basic resources. In both cases conflict management during emergencies seems a very challenging issue and out-warding externalities may well be positive but also negative, being a consequence of economic activities experienced by unrelated third parties.

The consequences of climatic changes are already dramatic for some of the poorest populations, who are hardly able to defend themselves and too weak to put in place expensive mitigation measures, which require a global coordination, within international institutions where the poorest countries have a very limited power of influence. Fair, serious, and effective multiple commitments, albeit strongly needed, are still far to come.

The most polluting countries–the U.S., the European Union, Brazil, Russia, India, and China (the last four with their ›BRIC‹ acronym) but also Mexico, Indonesia, Turkey, and other newcomers to this unfortunate club–are well aware that they should bear heavy costs to cut emissions, with the risk of undermining industrial competitiveness. Politicians are unsurprisingly hardly willing to promote actions with immediate unpopular effects and distant benefits, uninteresting for their careers, since they are too concerned about short term perspectives, within the time span of their electoral mandate.

---

203 See Chapter 3.
204 See Chapter 4.
205 Brainard, Jones, Purvis (2009), p. 160.

According to Diringer[206] »effective climate change mitigation commitments can take three basic forms: greenhouse gas emission targets, policy-based commitments, and sectorial agreements«, with economy-wide emission targets, like those set up by the Kyoto protocol.

Climate changes may have a malign repercussion on the poor's livelihood means, limiting options and potentialities, with impact on food shortage, increased morbidity, access to clean drinking water, and home security. In many cases, the poor are victims of the violence of man and nature. Even the already ailing and inelastic infrastructures may be weakened by exposure to climatic adversities. The synergic effect of these interactive negative factors can be potentially harmful, as well as their often asymmetric inequitable impact, which unsurprisingly mostly affects the weakest. Such fact requires a coordinated mitigation and adaptation strategy to soften and delay its effects.

Efforts to reduce extreme poverty can be jeopardized by climate changes and the two problems have to be jointly considered, with flexible and adaptive strategies. The poorest–locked in their long term misery traps–are currently the first to pay the rich nation's polluting bill, but sooner rich countries will join them, unless proper action is quickly taken. Climate changes deepen poverty.

The poor are bearing problems they hardly contributed to create and this unwanted legacy is transmitted to new generations. Today, humanity faces the intertwined challenges of obscene levels of poverty and a rapidly warming global climate, uneasy to coordinate and mitigate.

As Astrid Heiberg says, climate change is no longer a doomsday prophecy, but it is a reality, even if nature intrinsically has an extraordinary capacity to regenerate.

World's equilibriums are already changing–slowly and haphazardly but constantly–as a consequence of the climatic heating, which is already having a tangible impact on growth, downsizing long term development opportunities.

From the Human Development Report 2007/2008[207] we identify five key transmission mechanisms through which climate change could stall and then reverse human development.

- *Agricultural production and food security.* Climate change will affect rainfall, temperature, and water availability for agriculture in vulnerable areas;

- *Water stress and water insecurity.* Changed hydrological and rainfall patterns and glacial melt will add to ecological stress, compromising flows of water for irrigation and human settlements in the process. Water availability, accessibility, and demand are affected by climatic

[206] Brainard, Jones, Purvis (2009), p. 70.
[207] http://hdr.undp.org/en/media/HDR_20072008_EN_Complete.pdf.

changes, hardly ever for the better. Water quality is also threatened, due to overexploitation, saltwater intrusion, and tidal inundation in coastal areas, depletion and contamination due to inefficient sanitation, and other complementary causes;

- *Rising sea levels and exposure to climate disasters.* Sea levels could rise rapidly with accelerated ice disintegration, with melting icebergs. Being a fluid, water easily flows and it is difficult to stop;
- *Ecosystems and biodiversity.* Climate change is already transforming ecological systems, compromising biodiversity, a precious resource which helps us to adapt and that we tend to care about only when it is definitely lost. But even the economy can be considered a (not natural) ecosystem, strongly interacting with its surrounding environment;
- *Human health.* The greatest health impacts will be felt in developing countries because of high levels of poverty and the limited capacity of public health systems to respond. Major killer vector-borne and zoonotic diseases (malaria, dengue fever, cholera …) are likely to expand their action, incubating in a hotter and–just for them …–friendlier environment. Enhancing the resilience of poor countries and vulnerable communities to illnesses has become an unmissable priority and reducing greenhouse gas emissions can have a significant health benefit.

The development of an ecological culture is particularly important, since action has to be urgently taken from complementary top down and bottom up approaches, mobilizing masses about the issue. Disaster awareness and community consciousness of the problems is the first step towards their solving, both in rich and in poor countries.

Vulnerability to humanitarian emergencies[208] is increased by land degradation and climatic issues, while proper environmental care and regeneration may soften increasingly worrying problems. Raised disaster risk may seriously slacken future development.

A solution to the problem has to come from complementary sources, such as supranational agencies, governments, public and private corporations, and institutions, citizens–each according to its of her possibilities–and to integrate complementary issues to climatic changes, such as human rights, sustainable development within the community and the environment, and corporate social responsibility.

[208] See Chapter 14.

According to Jeffrey Sachs[209] »the climate-change problem is not a trade negotiation. It is simply the most complex engineering, economic, and social problem humanity has ever faced«.

Cooperative agreements for adaptation and mitigation measures: who pays the toll?

Since climatic issues are a recognized global problem, unilateral engagements (albeit useful on a micro level) are hardly likely to solve the problem of global warming and they may be easily counterbalanced by non-cooperative behaviors of other countries, fueled by lack of trust and short-sighted selfish targets. The game may however be cooperative, and groups–coalitions–of players are strong enough to enforce mutual behavior, with an international coordination based on shared consensus. In extreme cases such as climate agreements, it is essential to look for an all-or-none unanimity, since even few exceptions from disagreeing countries may make others' efforts ineffective.

Climatic global issues may be interpreted with the ›tragedy of commons‹. It is a metaphor that describes a situation in which multiple individuals act independently and solely and rationally they respond to their selfish own interest. They will ultimately deplete a commonly shared limited resource even when it is clear that it is not in anyone's long-term interest for this to happen[210]. The issue becomes much more difficult to address to the extent that individuals don't care about polluting a common environment, looking for their immediate self advantage and misunderstanding and minimizing its long term side effects. Waiting for crises to happen substantially increases the price to be paid for their solution.

According to the Intergovernmental Panel on Climate Change (2007), adaptation is definable as the »adjustment in natural or human systems in response to actual or expected climatic stimuli or their effects, which moderates harm or exploits beneficial opportunities«. Man is an opportunistic animal, able to adapt even in extreme circumstances.

Progressive and gradual adaptation to the changing global environment is strongly needed. It is the first mitigation measure, within the transition process towards eco-sustainability, which has to go together with disaster risk reduction. But when the need for a massive adaptation is urgent–too much and too fast–human beings or the ecosystem may not make it. The choice is between mitigation and resilient adaptation to external shocks, providing a cushion against adversities–the sooner, the better, properly choosing the correct timing–versus longer term suffering. A multidisciplinary approach to the problem is needed to

---

209 http://www.unctad.org/Templates/Page.asp?intItemID=4768&lang=1.

210 For a more detailed description, see Chapter 16.

understand the scientific, technical, environmental and social aspects of climate changes.

Various types of adaptation exist, e.g. *anticipatory* and *reactive*, *private* and *public*, and *autonomous* or *planned*.

According to a Chinese proverb »when the wind changes direction, there are those who build walls and those who build windmills«. Even adaptation–with sustainable business models–may be transformed from a problem into a mighty opportunity.

Farsighted mitigation, trying to prevent more climatic changes, may substantially improve disaster response mechanisms and strategies, minimizing malign consequences of climatic changes, and remembering that disasters are also security problems, easily exported abroad if not properly fixed locally.

Since we are aware that a complete solution of climatic problems is a chimera, we have to take in account second best solutions such as adaptation and mitigation, following a progressive strategy of slow down, stop, and then reverse. Mitigation and adaptation are however not meant to be considered competing trade offs–one excluding the other–even if in some cases this is more than a temptation. Mitigation is formally an anticipatory strategy, trying to soften the effects of ecological problems so as to prevent new ones while adaptation is an ex post partial remedy to get used to an unfavorable environment. In practice they tend to overlap and interact, with a precious synergic impact. Adaptation activities are increasingly recognized as a synonymous of sustainable growth[211], because they are incorporated in projects design and implementation, where the ecological factor is a key input, concerned with an environmental friendly natural resource management.

The alternative between top down versus bottom up approaches, so crucial in foreign aid strategies[212], may conveniently bring to compromising mixed results. Since climatic changes are a worldwide problem with no frontiers, on the one side a top down approach seems necessary, and it should be globally shared and implemented, so to allow also economies of scale and experience (sharing knowledge, expertise, and funding) and minimize duplications and lack of coordination. On the other side a grass-rooted bottom up strategy, involving local communities and enhancing shared participation, is needed to duly take into account specific aspects, looking for community tailor-made interventions.

Adaptation funding is a form of compensation, from those who can afford it and so typically coming from the West … to the Rest–following the ›polluter pays‹ principle[213]–that tries to indemnify the innocent poor for being contaminated by the industrialized rich.

---

211 Huq, Ayers in Brainard, Jones, Purvis (2009), p. 143.

212 See Chapter 14.

213 See Bapna, Mcgray in Brainard, Jones, Purvis (2009), p. 195.

A participatory local process is strongly needed and it should bring to a community-based adaptation, that should be culturally accepted, agreed, and shared by local people–possibly with decisions made at the lowest appropriate level, following a subsidiarity approach[214], with learning-by-doing strategy, based on a knowledge platform open and accessible.
Maladaptation of vulnerable communities, which simply cannot cope on their own, has to be duly taken into account and an external help is needed. Ecology is typically not concerned with immediate survival issues, unless a catastrophe is undergoing, and consequently the problem is hardly a priority for those who have to front other daunting daily life challenges.
The poor have traditionally low adaptive capacity, often lacking the means and the skills to change their habits and to protect themselves from new adversities –but they do not lack the psychological attitude to sacrifice. The dimension of the ecological problems often tends to be underestimated, until their impacts suddenly come clear, with catastrophic events, which are likely to occur more frequently than in the past.
Trade-off between costs and ›benefits‹ of pollution (cost of renouncing to filthy activities), mainly in contaminated industrial areas, is hardly present in the poorest countries but it is more concentrated in young developing nations, such as China, where growth comes before environment care. Social ecology increasingly matters, even if in the short run mitigation can increase poverty, through its economic impact.

Blowin' in the wind: cutting emissions and solving the energy dilemma

›*Blowin' in the Wind*‹ is a celebrated song written by Bob Dylan in 1963, which may indirectly recall renewable wind energy, a clean answer to our polluting queries. The refrain »The answer, my friend, is blowin' in the wind« has been described as »impenetrably ambiguous: either the answer is so obvious it is right in your face, or the answer is as intangible as the wind«[215]. But even the responses to our energy problems (in order to go beyond polluting fossil fuel) are ambiguous, since they appear at hand (the wind, the sun, the tide, flowing water …) but are difficult to grasp, store, engineer, and make suitable for energy production.
Single countries are reluctant to move the first step in cutting emissions of carbon dioxide, knowing that if other countries don't cooperate, their efforts are going to be painful for the local economy but hardly effective on a global scale. Cutting emissions of carbon dioxide–with greenhouse gas mitigation commit-

[214] For an application of the subsidiarity principles to foreign aid, see Chapter 14.
[215] Gold (2002), p. 43.

ments–is indeed likely to have a negative impact on development, at least in the short run, forcing to limit or stop the production of obsolete polluting factories. Furthermore unilateral cutting of emissions and production in the short run can limit competitiveness on a relative basis, to the extent that other countries can take profit of this action, with a compensative increase of their polluting plants. Opportunistic behaviors and free riding strategies (where single States may have an incentive in a wait-and-see policy) are unsurprisingly dividing the polluting world, with traditional big polluters–such as the U.S.–and newcomers – such as China, which are unwilling to sign and respect international agreements about cutting emissions. Non cooperative countries may not only override joint efforts of virtuous nations, but also gain an unfair competitive advantage over them, being able to produce without bearing any ecological extra cost.

Poor countries are in a paradoxical situation: they are normally small polluters, because their industrial production is typically limited, but they are likely to increase their emissions to the extent that they develop. New technology, limiting ecological impacts, is now available, but it is typically expensive and most underdeveloped countries cannot afford it.

Incentives to adopt improved ecological standards have to be supported by foreign richer countries, since poor countries are unable to finance them with their limited budgets. Pollution from poor countries can come also from deforestation and demographic growth. Whereas they unwillingly import uncleanness from richer countries, they may also sooner or later react by exporting ecological problems induced from outside, with mass migrations and overexploitation of local natural resources.

This myopic and selfish strategy, which places widespread global burden, is difficult to contrast and it may go on up to the point of irreversible consequences, when local damages start to outweigh the benefits of an opportunistic behavior. But at that time the clean up toll may become unbearable, while pollution gets out of control.

Where environmental problems are dealt with locally, bottom-up strategies have to strongly interact with macro top-down interventions. It is a standard micro-macro link, and a global understanding and setting of the issue commands a priority, for the aforementioned reasons. Adaptation is essentially locally rooted, requiring specific territorial knowledge, even if it needs to be coordinated across frontiers–due to the borderless impact of climatic changes.

Sustainable development reflects the environmental friendly capacity of an economy to grow without compromising the welfare, the consumption, and the investment possibilities of future generations, which may involuntarily inherit negative endowments. Progress can help to better cope with global warming but it has to be sustainable. In poorer regions, starting later in some cases may be an advantage, since newcomers can learn from the mistakes of first movers, but

they need to be enabled to share advanced and environmental friendly technologies.
Each economic activity has an impact on climate and it may contribute to CO_2 emissions. A zero impact behavior is an ideal target–that is nice to call out but difficult to put into practice–according to which human actions should have no effect on global warming, reducing emissions and compensating their effect.
Sustainable development is also due to maintain stability, health, and productivity of water resources[216] (including rivers, lakes, groundwater, and wetlands), which are essential for the livelihoods of people, the growth of the economy, and the sustenance and health of all species. Freshwater–rainwater or water coming from glaciers, rivers, and lakes–sustains the integrity of ecosystems and their hydrological functions. Growing and unbalancing demands for water threaten water reservoirs around the world, with a bigger asymmetric impact on the poorest, who are also more exposed to water quality degradation.
Natural ecosystems are a precious and delicate source of protection against erosion, storms, and they act as a sponge that absorbs and slowly releases precious rainwater or store other precious and vital substances.
The energy market is less competitive than other industries, because the demand in a resource constraint world is never missing and marketing is not a primary concern for oil companies or utilities. In some cases, natural monopolies (already examined in Chapter 3 while dealing with the natural resources missed opportunities) go beyond extractive places and they cause huge damages to the consumers, not only with the higher and unchallenged prices they impose, but also with their lack of innovation, that may go against their current interests.
Governments can intervene in many ways to soften these problems and incentive opportunities, stopping monopolies, subsidizing research and consumption of green energy, taxing more polluting fuel, etc. But to do all this Governments need lot of money–raised with taxes–and massive popular consensus, together with a long term vision that typically goes well beyond electoral mandates.
Clean energy has another underestimated but powerful advantage: it is much less geographically focused and concentrated, since it is mostly unlinked to current natural resources, so reducing the otherwise unbridgeable gap between resource–rich and resource–poor countries. The idea of reducing dependence from the several blackmailing oil tyrants looks fascinating and deserving, even if it is also hard to put into action-renewable energy is both ecologically and geopolitically friendly.
Renewable sources of energy tend to be less exposed to international speculation, to the extent that they are mainly local, as it is wildly exemplified by the volatility of the oil's price. Large-scale use of technology will enhance produc-

[216] See Chapter 6.

tivity and innovation, lowering the cost of the energetic output due to competitive pressures.
Fighting pollution also enables to stop unwanted negative externalities, mostly born by the poor, also remembering that pollution is a synonym of inefficiency and waste of resources, materials, time and–mostly–energy.

Climate refugees and vulnerability

Flatlands close to the sea, the Netherlands, Bangladesh (the latter is a sad and poor symbol of environmental fragility), Ghana or the Maldives are four examples of countries that are extremely vulnerable to the rise of sea levels, induced by global warming. Their vulnerability is partly due to an accident of geography, which has been worsened by human imprudent choices.
These countries' population is exposed to many risks that may originate the phenomenon of climate refugees. A climate refugee can be defined as a person displaced by climate change induced environmental disasters. Such disasters are evidence of human-influenced ecological change and disruption of the earth's climate system.
Climate refugees, with their migration issues (analyzed in Chapter 12), escape from rural unlivable lands, increasing urban migration–typically without any proper planning–and stressing the already weak existing facilities and infrastructures. They end to find a precarious shelter in growing slums, at the outskirts of disordered and dangerous megalopolis, ironically also overexposed to climatic threats.

Mother Nature versus Father Profit

The main issue about the necessity to reconvert the world to a green energy program is technical and scientific, substituting dirty fossil fuel with renewable and clean sources of energy. Alternative sources of energy are still expensive and unfit for large scale consumption, while innovation in this field is slow, painful, and incremental, and we would need a path breaking exponential invention. Required investments in R&D are enormous and what is missing is certainly not the potential market for free energy, but rather proper economic incentives to continue long and uncertain research, in order to combine the needs of Mother Nature with those of … father profit, as Friedman (2009) puts it.
Paradoxically the poor are doubtlessly the most vulnerable to climate change, although they are the ones with the smallest impact on it. Global warming is indeed a negative consequence of the economic development that has taken place in many More Economically Developed Countries (MEDC). The impact is big, because development means people with cars, industries, energy produced from

fossil fuels, homes provided with heating and air conditioning … In Less developed countries, underdevelopment makes it hardly possible for these ›greenhouse gas producing‹ activities to take place.
However, there is one side of poverty that contributes to the world's average temperature rise: lack of electricity. Electricity itself causes global warming when made from limited resources such as coal, and lack of electricity forces people to find more polluting alternative ways to heat water, light up, cook food. In developing or even more underdeveloped country, the alternative to electricity is burning wood, an activity that produces considerable amounts of greenhouse gases.
The African continent is an example of how climate change can dramatically affect poor and developing countries. Multiple stresses make most of Africa highly vulnerable to environmental changes, and climate change is likely to increase this vulnerability. Impacts include desertification, sea level rise, reduced freshwater availability, cyclones, coastal erosion, deforestation, loss of forest quality, woodland degradation, coral bleaching, the spread of malaria, and impacts on food security.

Reshaping poverty traps in a polluted planet

Some poverty traps may be reshaped and modified by climatic changes, especially if they are so acute to consistently changing human habits.

Table 8.1. – Impact of climatic changes on poverty traps

Poverty trap	Impact of climatic changes
Landlockedness	Unless extreme climatic changes concur to cause a change in geographical borders of countries, there is no impact, even if low-lying coastal areas (which are highly populated and risk being submersed by rising sea level) are by definition not present in landlocked countries, which may eventually host migration from threatened areas.
Natural resources curse	Overexploitation and mismanagement of not renewable fossil fuels are among the main causes of global warming. Poor countries, rich in natural resources, may face both expropriation of resources and collateral causes of pollution deriving from their usage in richer countries and brought by the shared atmosphere.
Demographic growth	Climatic changes often hit overpopulated areas, such as coastal regions, up to the point of inducing mass migration to safer but less convenient places. Extreme climatic

Poverty trap	Impact of climatic changes
	changes may ease unwanted outcomes of gloomy Malthusian prophecies.
Conflict trap	If climatic changes cause imbalances in the use of vital resources, such as water or food or energy, they may trigger conflicts for appropriation or redistribution.
Water and food shortage, illnesses	The impact of climatic changes on water is becoming dramatically evident nowadays, since it causes over–flooding in some areas and extreme drought in others (with consequent water shortages, increased risk of fires …). Hydraulic imbalances and related food shortages–or price increases, due to their higher volatility–may negatively affect human and animal health.
Illiteracy and language trap	There is no immediate and direct impact, even if illiteracy favors ignorance, also for what concerns causes and remedies against pollution. Particular languages do not favor the transmission of scientific know how about adaptation to climatic changes and mitigation of the problems.
Property and ›registry office‹ trap	The impact is not direct, even if unrecorded poor find it more difficult to move and adapt elsewhere. Untitled properties are difficult to sell in case of migration. Long-term, secure rights to land set the stage for environmental stewardship and sustainable farming practices. Moreover, in specific settings such as Brazil, Indonesia or the Philippines, reallocation of secure rights to existing cultivated land may also have an important environmental impact through forestalling landless peasants from descending on, cutting down, and burning the forest in the desperate search for a piece of land to farm. The latter is a form of escape parallel to the desperate flight to cities.

According to the DAC Guidelines for Poverty Reduction[217]:

> Environment and poverty are linked in many ways. Environmental degradation, in both rural and urban areas, affects poor people the most. Conversely, it is also a result of poverty. Sustainable development and poverty reduction require maintaining the integrity of natural ecosystems and preserving their life-supporting functions. Critical factors linking environment and poverty in-

[217] www.oecd.org/dataoecd/47/14/2672735.pdf.

clude security of access to the natural resources on which many poor households depend, and environmental health risks that particularly affect women and children.

The condensed Chapter

Global warming due to carbon dioxide emissions is dramatically changing the world's climate, threatening biodiversity, and hitting in particular coastal and poor regions, where the underserved are mostly concentrated, in spite of their limited contribution to global pollution.
Mitigation and adaptation measures are too expensive and sophisticated for the poor and innovative recourse to renewable sources of energy (to be backed and managed by richer countries) stand out as the only, uneasy, and long termed solution to the issue, reminding that environment underlies all human activities, strongly advocating sustainable development strategies in a friendly environment.

Out of Poverty Tips

Nothing is potentially more contagious and borderless than pollution, a silent but lethal threat which ping pongs from the rich to the poor. Shared solutions, together with disenchanted consciousness, are so the prerequisite for any viable intervention scheme. Long, costly and difficult, but unavoidable, for all. Poverty reduction and environmental protection are two global tasks for sustainable development.

Selected Readings

AGOLA N.O., AWANGE J.L., (2014), *Globalized Poverty and Environment,* Springer Verlag, Berlin.

BRAINARD L., JONES A., PURVIS N., eds., (2009), *Climate change and global poverty*, Brookings Institution Press, Washington.

VON BRAUN J., GATZWEILER F.W., eds., (2014), *Marginality. Addressing the Nexus of Poverty, Exclusion and Ecology,* Springer Verlag, Berlin.

ZHEN N., FU B., LU Y., WANG S., (2014), *Poverty reduction, environmental protection and ecosystem services: A prospective theory for sustainable development*, Chinese Geographical Science, February 2014, Volume 24, Issue 1, pp 83-92.

CHAPTER 9 – Underdevelopment and the cultural trap

The wise are instructed by reason, ordinary minds by experience the stupid by necessity and brutes by instinct.

Marcus Tullius Cicero

Culture matters

The relationship between culture and development is fiercely debated, paying a tribute to … cultural differences of opinion. Even if it seems evident to many, included the author of this book, that culture does have an impact on development and growth, this statement seems particularly hard to prove (and conversely, even to confute), since culture is a broad concept, difficult to define and uneasy to measure.

Man nature is intricate and complex, as well as culture and its multiple facets, even for what concerns the poor, apparently less sophisticated but in reality characterized by hardly detectable problems and features.

Culture–from the Latin *cultura*, cultivation–is an anthropological concept concerned with human knowledge and its symbolic image, mentality, customs, and ideas, representation, interpretation, and classification of events, influencing behavior and strategies, both for single human beings and collectively. Culture is also concerned with a binding set of control mechanisms and rules that shape behavioral patterns with a comprehensive articulation of norms, instructions, prescriptions, and moral sanctions – behind each legal system, there is a cultural approach. Culture models our will and it contributes to shape our destiny, capriciously melting with external unpredictable events.

Culture is concerned with the history and the tradition of ideas–shaping our mental archetypes–and it is synthesized by the capacity of symbolic thought, describing a set of shared attitudes, values, visions, beliefs, orientations, underlying assumptions, and goals that characterize institutions or organizations. On an individual basis, easing self understanding, culture shapes the mind-set or mental construct and orientates interaction and behavior with others[218].

Lack of cultural values and of consolidated mental attitudes produces empty societies, whereas a solid cultural base can strongly help to front difficulties and

[218] The Polish anthropologist Bronislaw Malinowski argues that culture functions to meet the needs of individuals rather than society as a whole. When the needs of individuals, who comprise society, are met, then also the needs of society are met.

to promote not ephemeral development. Culture–the architecture of our mental life–is the software behind intelligence, whereas the brain symbolizes an empty blackboard or, in modern times, hardware to be started with proper programs. Thought is a symbolic synthesis of the unpredictable interaction of different individuals, shaping both reason and behavioral attitudes. Culture is what we ultimately are able to retain, after we have forgotten all what has been taught to us, enabling us to sharpen our views and grasp otherwise undetectable connections.

To the extent that not copyrighted ideas are public goods, their dissemination has an influence on culture, with hardly predictable consequences, which are often enriching but sometimes even harmful.

Culture[219] is also the totality of socially transmitted behavioral patterns, arts, beliefs, institutions, and all other products of human work and thought, considered as the expression of a particular period, class, community, or population, or even the predominating attitudes and behavior that characterize the functioning of a group or organization or are prevalent among people in a society. Culture can be oral and/or written but also–thanks to technology–visual and so also its transmission, that is now characterized by innovative ways of information storing, easy to retrieve but not to decipher. Spreading web idioms marginalize oral culture, deepening the digital divide.

The definition of culture also embraces intellectual and artistic activity, as well as the development of the intellect through training or education. Culture needs to be met, assimilated, and elaborated through a long term mental and behavioral process.

Culture has (positive or negative) impact on poverty, to the extent that it influences our life and, together with it, economic and social events concerned with development and growth – in their broadest ›cultural‹ sense. However, according to De Soto (1999) »The disparity of wealth between the West and the rest of the world is far too great to be explained by culture alone«.

The search for cultural roots of underdevelopment, coming out from the midst of ancestral times, remains however difficult and it is sometimes back-slashed by wrong and dangerous racist opinions, nurturing a sense of inadequacy towards supposedly inferior cultures.

A society's culture reflects and synthesizes its entire historical heritage[220] and culture is also concerned with the history of ideas. Cultural changes are path dependent and typically slow – they may take several generations to become effective, unless traumatic circumstances (wars, invasions …) suddenly change the environment, forcing those who want to survive to adapt. Human beings show high flexibility and resilience, when they are put at stress. The changing

219 See http://www.thefreedictionary.com/culture.

220 See Harrison, Huntington (2000), p. 86.

environment–due to modernization, globalization, environmental issues …–is reshaping culture. Also deeply rooted, enduring, and path dependent cultural traditions (which are still shaping the society with their historical heritage and nostalgic mythology) are adapting to the new global framework, not always smoothly.

Societies are transforming as also culture is doing, being a fore runner or, in other cases, a follower. Cultures are painfully changing, with different speeds, to accommodate the global economy. Those who are not able to continuously wonder themselves, adapting their beliefs to a changing environment, are old both in their heart and in their mind. Cultural integration is typically slow and difficult, often ending up in a fiasco – human history is full of disastrous xenophobic weddings, ill conceived since their inception.

Culture–going beyond a static mental quicksand–is also modified by an intergenerational shift, which is affected by many factors often randomly interacting. Different inputs combined together in a capricious way, unsurprisingly produce an unpredictable output.

The demographic trend is one of the key ingredients of cultural modifications, since countries with a growing population and a high percentage of children and young are more subject to cultural transformations than others, especially if they live in a global world or if they are changing their settlement (e.g. moving from the countryside to town), disrupting ancestral family ties. Western influence is very strong–and often polluting–especially in big towns of underdeveloped countries, while it is quite absent in the countryside. Culture is leveraged–or unleveraged–also by demography, since even quantity matters, with its growing influence.

New ideals fostering women empowerment, democracy, and environmental care are increasingly accepted on a wider international base: even if it may take time (even several generations, looking at the Western experience, but now changes are faster even if less stable), to modify settled cultural models, the trend seems unstoppable.

According to Muhammad Yunus »Culture is a dynamic thing. If you stay with the same old thing over and over, you don't get anywhere«. But culture is also like water in a desert: wherever it is present, life flourishes, metaphorically representing blossoming ideas. Culture also comes from a proper blending of reason and emotion, respectively representing knowledge and empathy.

Biased ideology and intolerance frequently obscure the analysis of cultural changes and culture itself is a slippery concept, with different side aspects (psychological, political, racial, geographic, religious …) that interact in mixed ways, with potentially infinite outcomes.

Managing cultural melting pots, beyond battle of idea(l)s

When different civilizations meet and–according to Huntington–clash, they produce compromising cultural melting pots, which can have many different outcomes, from forced cultural assimilation and submission to dialogue and mutual enrichment, with a cross fertilization process, based on an intellectual heterodoxy of beliefs and reasoning. Elective affinities and tolerance of diversities matter and they ease this osmotic process, whereas cultural differences are uneasy to focus and idealize. Path-breaking ›Copernican‹ cultural changes abruptly change well tried mental habits, going beyond the surpassed geocentric Ptolemaic vision of the universe.

According to Kapuściński, civilization is a material and external concept, whereas culture is an intimate and spiritual feeling. The former is expanding, while the latter is a defensive mental anchor. Patriarchal tradition meets rootless modernity in an awkward melting pot.

Globalization, exalting cultural commonalities, is just speeding up a multicultural process that, with ups and downs, has always characterized human history and cultural fusion, up to syncretism, that is the attempt to reconcile and combine disparate or contrary beliefs, relying just on the non violent strength of complementary ideas. Globalization[221] has a deep impact on adaptive cultures, acting as a conveyor belt across different civilizations, easing cultural exchanges on one side but weakening different cultures on the other side, deviating from the mainstream way of thinking, and acting as a powerful centripetal force, trying to homologate concepts and traditions, often regardless of their precious differences. Wealth is hidden in diversities.

An irresistible and traumatic temptation for many poor is often characterized by the passive assimilation of Western models, which intrinsically attract the poor with an alleged–but fake–superior culture, discarding their traditional one, and forgetting that cultures and civilizations are full of internal–intestine–conflicts. As a matter of fact, technology is separated from culture and the success of Western technology brings to a partial colonization of minds unused to it, even if it does not automatically imply the supremacy of Western culture over the spiritual being of man. Science is more easily culturally accepted than religions or philosophies, which deeply shape different customs and habits.

Humans are intrinsically curious to experience unknown varieties of sounds, colors, and tastes, so favoring cultural exchanges and pollination of ideas, even if they tend to retain a strong sense of identity with their original culture, customs, and history. Curious cultures are thirsty to understand each other, with intertwined thoughts and mutually inspiring exchanging of opinion. Cultural anthropology is dedicated to studying different populations, with relativism and

---

[221] See Chapter 11.

possibly tolerance. Multicolored and ›spicy‹ poverty stands out as a privileged subject.

Ideological confrontation and competition, starting from a different cultural heritage, has long influenced human conflicts. But when power is unrivaled, the winners tend to lose their focus and decline is likely to start. It is indeed competition that keeps us alive.

The cultural assimilationist approach argues that dominant powers–from the *pax Romana* onwards–tend to impose their culture wherever they go, and it typically ends up in a net cultural impoverishment with a toxic synthesis of imposed ideological principles that try to instill an inferiority complex, while multiculturalism sounds as a much richer and longer lasting approach, remembering that repressed cultures are hard to extirpate. Free creativity, nourished by confrontation and inspiring differences, takes its time to properly develop.

Culture is also differently spread among each population and democracy is an important referee of cultural interactions. In countries where democracy is present and effective, a free press and transparent elections allow cultural differences of opinion to be expressed and discussed, while in undemocratic regimes values and beliefs of ordinary citizens are constantly challenged and obscured by autarchic elites. It is like a football game without the referee, where the strongest arbitrarily set the most convenient rules for them and make them compulsory, forbidding any dissidence.

Culture is also concerned with different geographical declinations and–just to make an example–the European idea of progress is not African.

A prevailing male-dominant culture–machismo–is pervasively common in most underdeveloped countries, where the atmosphere in which most women and their children daily live has severe drawbacks to their emancipation[222]. The negative impact on development, even if hardly detectable, is far from being negligible. Women and men do not inevitably see their culture through the same eyes[223] and male dominance burns out a precious source of differentiation, originality and complementarities. Cultural gender bias, so acutely perceived in Western countries, is still a taboo in many developing countries, where unlucky women represent the silent majority, especially among the poorest of the poor.

Confucian values such as the emphasis on the future, work, achievement, education, merit, and frugality play a crucial role in Asian development[224]. Western ideals have been traditionally–but not exclusively–divided in Protestant versus Catholic values, following the intriguing but somewhat old-fashioned and Manichean Max Weber's classification[225]. Culture is also concerned with ethics,

---

222 See Chapter 10.

223 In Harrison, Huntington (2000), p. 183.

224 See Harrison, Huntington (2000), p. 296.

225 See Chapter 1.

which regulates internal behavior with norms, beliefs, habits, attitudes, and values, each influencing the other.
Confrontation between different cultures is always challenging but enriching, representing a place of reason and dialogue. Cultural values also have to be concerned with economic aspects–because culture is an asset and lack of culture a liability–and so financial illiteracy is among the causes of misery, generating economic impoverishment.
Fundamentalism, refusing doctrinal compromises, is the fanatic output of biased faith and extremist virulent differences, often becoming an instrumental use of religion, in order to get and keep power. It destroys dialogue and cultural exchanges, because it is dogmatically influenced by the insistence on the truth of one's principles, with a concomitant unwillingness to consider the enriching views of others.
Since fundamentalism is a byproduct of bigotry and conservatism as well as of neglecting and denying voices and opinions from elsewhere, it is an ideological alibi for avoiding confrontation, bringing to constrained thought, and imposing the violent pervasiveness of unreason. Fundamentalism goes also against the International Covenant on Economic, Social and Cultural Rights[226] or the Declaration on the Elimination of Any Form of Intolerance Based on Religion or Belief[227]. Tetragon gatekeepers of faith forcefully impose their ideas, misusing religion as an excuse to enforce their secular power.
Ethnocentrism brings to close-minded conservatism and prejudices against the others, with a strong tendency to reject other ideas, without any preventive unbiased confrontation, whereas the absence of respect for different cultures bears a consequential loss of self confidence. Trivialized cultures weaken any sense of identity, pushing disoriented people to uncritically embrace alternative–and allegedly superior–cultural models, often unfit for their needs and inconsistent with their traditions.

Economic progress is a cultural process

Progress generally indicates forward moving (from the Latin *Progressus, a going forward, advance*) and it refers to the improving–step after step–of one's life conditions, often but not exclusively measured from a material aspect, in terms of satisfied needs or increased standards of living.
Progress, going beyond basic survival values, is concerned with the enhancement and upgrading of life quality and it is normally linked to growth and poverty reduction. Such a concept is closely related to innovations and technolo-

[226] www2.ohchr.org/english/law/cescr.htm.
[227] www2.ohchr.org/english/law/religion.htm.

gies[228] and it typically depends on new available discoveries, which ease up life (e.g., availability of drinking water, possibility to use energy and its applications, new medicines or electronic technologies …).
According to Lidsay[229] »culture is a significant determinant of a nation's ability to prosper because culture shapes individuals' thoughts about risk, reward, and opportunity«. And again »cultural value matter because they form the principles around which economic activity is organized«.
The relationship between culture and progress is typically two-way, since culture (scientific attitudes …) can ease–or prevent–progress, but also the degree of progress has a great impact on culture. As an example, let's consider the availability of the Internet, which is made possible by technological advances and which can deeply influence culture of web navigators.
A positive cultural attitude to growth is an essential part of development, since it helps to accept and to adapt to the changing environment, leading to progress, that is represented by a longer, less burdensome, healthier, richer life, symbolized by a higher and unprecedented standard of living.
Progress is increasingly a universal value, even if its boundaries are far from certain and cultural attitudes greatly contribute to define its perimeter. Economic development brings to gradual cultural changes, with a transformation that is neither easy nor automatic. Adaptation to new paradigms brings to new mental equilibriums, which have to cope with a volatile environment because changes are nowadays much faster than before and routine behaviors are increasingly challenged, even if people tend to change not when they should, but rather when they must.
A not ephemeral development, avoiding a dangerous boom–and–bust cycle, can be attained preserving one's cultural historical roots and traditions, while trying to smoothly adapt them in uneasy catch up with a changing environment.
Porter[230] acutely points out that hard work, education, and savings are necessary but not sufficient conditions for growth, since they need to be rightly driven and shaped. It is the type of done work, the kind of education and the effective deployment of savings that matters.
Seeking to isolate the sources of successful development, Harrison (1985) concludes that the principal determinant is culture, defined for this purpose as values and attitudes. In each of the successful countries »the world view of the society has expressed itself in ways that have affected the society's cohesion, its proneness to justice and progress, and the extent to which it taps human creative potential«. Development is strongly influenced by a society's basic cultural values.

228 See Chapter 15.
229 In Harrison, Huntington (2000), p. 282.
230 In Harrison, Huntington (2000), Chapter 2.

Culture shapes economic development but development changes culture, too. The goal is to reduce cultural obstacles to development, such as corruption, laziness, lack of discipline and strategy, fickleness, injustice, irrationality, fatalism ... There is a trade off between development prone and development resistant (unproductive) cultures and what really makes the difference is productivity[231].
The role of culture in development is however hotly debated. According to Landes »culture makes all the difference«, while Michael Porter[232], acknowledging that culture influences economic development and competitiveness, stresses the impact of globalization in homogenizing culture, overcoming gaps and disadvantages. On the contrary, Jeffrey Sachs[233] argues that culture is an insignificant factor by comparison with the environment (geography and climate). The economic side of culture–uneasy to define–is hard to measure and to separate from other psychological, political, geographical, religious or institutional factors, but not up to the point of making it useless.
Culture is adaptive to the changing environment but both its pace of change and its direction are uneasy to forecast and they do not always converge to proactive targets of development.
Cultural legacies become institutionalized when, being transmitted across generations and codified in voluntarily shared and customary uses, they are transformed into compulsory laws.

Unproductive cultures

Illiterate *barbaritas*–the cultural emptiness of barbarians approaching the gate of civilization–as well as unproductive cultures cited by Porter[234], are short termed attitudes that reflect wrong beliefs about the development targets. Flawed but captivating ideas and mentalities–for example about autarchic self-sufficiency–have a major impact on keeping the economy stagnating.
Social policies have a strong impact on cultural attitudes towards working and personal saving behavior. Too much protection disincentives job seeking and it destroys motivation, as the experience of many Western countries shows.
International isolation is another factor that prevents ideas, wealth, goods, people, and investments from circulating, highly impoverishing the autarchic country, as it happened to Spain during Franco's dictatorship or to Albania during the Cold War or to Myanmair even today.
Porter again admonishes that globalization is a powerful source of discipline on unproductive behaviors. Cultural differences can contribute to the specialized

---

231 See Chapter 15.
232 In Harrison, Huntington (2000), Chapter 2.
233 In Harrison, Huntington (2000), Chapter 3.
234 In Harrison, Huntington (2000), Chapter 2.

advantages in order to improve the prosperity of nations, even if they risk being washed out by unselective globalization, which tends to standardize and trivialize ideas and concepts, in order to make them interchanging and comparable.
The insight of Grondona[235] is that economic development is a cultural process, which is ultimately driven by non-economic factors that can protect from dissipating temptations.
Individuals are considered as an often not conformist and a bit heretic Prometheus set free from its chains. Trust in the individual fosters the work and creativity of individuals, who are the principal intangible engine of economic growth. Since neither submission nor rebellion foster development, as Grondona points out, free invention and faith in the individual are a really needed ingredient of progress. Conformists and followers stay always behind and they hardly contribute to growth.
Wealth can also be considered in a static way–what already exists, such as land, natural resources and their proceeds–or in what does not yet exist and may be created following a pro growth paradigm, through continuous innovation.
As we shall see later on in this Chapter, culture is also very much affected by the concept of time–so strongly linked to productivity–and by the attitude to focus on the past, with its nostalgic legacy, or to be projected towards a challenging future.
A scientific approach is increasingly adopted for the interpretation and modeling of economics, concerning in particular neo-liberalism. The disasters of such a cultural approach are well evident, especially in the Western world, after the recession of 2008-2009. The biggest ›philosophical‹ mistake is probably considering the ›*homo oeconomicus*‹ as a fully rational subject, whose behaviors can be modeled and predicted according to an aseptic Cartesian rationality, following a scientific–i.e., replicable–pattern.
But human beings are too complex to be reductively interpreted just with a rational approach, which is unable to fully grasp the variety of unpredictable behaviors and cultures, often skewed towards irrationality or, as Erasmus admonished, folly.

Falling down from the tower of Babel to the language trap

The Tower of Babel, according to the Book of Genesis, Chapter 11, was built by the descendants of Noah at the city of Babylon. But God, in order to punish the arrogance of men that wanted the tower to reach heaven, confounded their tongue, so that they did not understand one another's speech, and thus he scattered them from that place into all lands, and they ceased to build the city.

---

[235] In Harrison, Huntington (2000), Chapter 4.

This biblical tale well exemplifies the incommunicability problems, which are a sign of division that derives from speaking so many languages or dialects, often completely different among them, even if belonging to neighboring ethnic groups.
The topic concerning currently spoken languages in the world is controversial: »It is difficult to give an exact figure of the number of languages that exist in the world, because it is not always easy to define what a language is. The difference between a language and a dialect is not always clear-cut. It has nothing to do with similarity of vocabulary, grammar, or pronunciation. Sometimes, the distinctions are based purely on geographical, political, or religious reasons. It is usually estimated that the number of languages in the world varies between 3,000 and 8,000«[236].
Far from going into further details, it may suffice to remind that the ›language trap‹ is a major segmentation factor, and it is a form of cultural and ethnic identity and belonging. It represents a form of defense against intruders, but also–as a double edged sword–a strong impediment to communication and sharing, and it severely hampers cultural and economic exchanges and, in synthesis, it substantially downsizes growth potentials.
Neighboring ethnicities speaking different idioms need a translator or facilitator that knows both languages, this being an uneasy intermediation, since the translation's quality is often poor, whereas the illiterate underserved hardly speak any English or other *lingua franca*. My uneasy own experience in rural Ugandan villages has taught me how these apparently trivial communication problems may impact on growth, hampering development, exports, geographical scaling, technological diffusion (how can locals read an instruction manual of an electronic device, unlikely to be translated in their own dialect?). So the language trap is also an educational trap.
In countries where many local languages are spoken, there is growing need for a common idiom, when people from different ethnic groups travel and meet. This necessity was well evident even in ancient times and the Greeks used a *κοινε'*, a term that stands for common language spoken in their Mediterranean area of influence. *Κοινε'* was the first common supra-regional dialect in Greece and came to serve as a *lingua franca* for the Eastern Mediterranean and ancient Near East throughout the Roman period.
Nowadays the common language is mainly English, being the first idiom simultaneously spoken by the two superpowers U.S. and (once upon a time) U.K. Today predominant common languages are changing, because of many others factors such as immigration–Spanish being the second language in the U.S.–or religion, with the Arabic diffused in Muslim countries, or economic influence, with a rising importance of Chinese (Mandarin or Cantonese).

236 http://www.ling.gu.se/projekt/sprakfrageladan/english/sprakfakta/eng-sprak-i-varlden.html.

The illiterate poor however hardly know any other language except their local one, this increasingly being a poverty trap, especially in a globalized world where communications and information are rapidly exchanged in a common idiom, discriminating all those who are not part of the global network. Hardly anything is more differentiating than language, that is on the one hand a protection for ethnic identity and cultural values and on the other hand it is also a strong impediment to connection and interchange. According to the Declaration on the Rights of Persons Belonging to National or Ethnic, Religious and Linguistic Minorities[237] of 1992, art. 2.1.:

> Persons belonging to national or ethnic, religious, and linguistic minorities (hereinafter referred to as persons belonging to minorities) have the right to enjoy their own culture, to profess and practice their own religion, and to use their own language, in private and in public, freely and without interference or any form of discrimination.

Language–so important for cultural and social identity–is also another key aspect of culture and ethno-linguistic differences (so common in fragmented and artificially born African States, as a powerful segmentation factor) act as a defense device but also as a brake to development and cultural exchanges, especially where a common idiom is hardly spoken, as a consequence not only of illiteracy but also of local pride and suspicion towards the central national government. Examples can be taken from Catalonia, where Catalan is preferred to the Spanish Castilian or in Tamil Nadu, where Hindi is hardly taught and known, even if English can soften the problem. When somebody is forced to speak a language that is not his own, or when another idiom is commanded as a national language, he feels both humiliated and superimposed – and no wonder that rebellion just waits for its first chance to be put into action.

In an Internet-dependent world, language can be even more unifying or, conversely, discriminating. A big obstacle to development and growth is the apparently trivial but in reality crucial fact that so many ethnic languages (spoken in a geographically narrow territory by a limited number of people) are not properly codified (with grammars, dictionaries …) and do not have digital applications – starting from lack of keyboards, up to the absence of websites. Basic body language is nice and it may be somewhat helping, but only to some extent and where physical interaction is possible and so not in an increasingly virtual world.

With the SMS and touch screen revolution, young Asians are forgetting ideograms and their writing traditions, following an unprecedented ›digital amnesia‹ pattern, a side effect of technology and globalization with a mass sociologic impact of evolving–simplifying–culture.

---

[237] http://www2.ohchr.org/english/law/minorities.htm.

English is not the mother tongue of the author of this book, who would probably be jobless shouldn't he have been given the privilege to study this foreign idiom, a necessary linguistic standard in the scientific community.

A cultural approach to prosperity

Prosperity[238] is the state of flourishing, thriving, success, or good fortune, and it often encompasses affluence but also includes other factors which are independent of wealth to varying degrees, such as happiness and health. In broader terms, Ray (1998), p. 9, notes that »prosperity is the ability of an individual, group, or nation to provide shelter, nutrition, and other material goods that enable people to live a good life, according to their own definition«.

Prosperity is a state of mind, being a qualitative as well as a somewhat measurable issue, highly depending on personal feelings. Culturally eradicated impediments to prosperity and growth always have a cultural background and so once again culture matters for development. According to Mariano Grondona[239], when people feel richer they may fatally feel sated and inclined to work less, since they are able to enjoy some of the fruits of their labor and the proceeds of reinvestment. Consumption can erode some of the accumulated surplus, making also wealth circulating and spreading prosperity. New investments of the surplus are however not automatic and it may be diverted elsewhere, even looking for utopian plans of welfare, wars of prestige or outright corruption – crucial temptations are difficult to resist.

Economic development is intrinsically linked to an unending sequence of decisions favorable to investment, differentiation, productivity enhancing innovation, competition, in an environment where mission drifts[240] for social justice are always likely. Unending development is based upon an accumulation process that is not suffocated by its own success. In order to make it possible, non-economic cultural values matter: well-being, happiness, freedom, security, religion or philanthropy (the so called ›third sector‹), which are not completely satisfied by economic success. They can foster new development, to the extent that they are pro-economic and ease the process of accumulation.

Culture and subsequent prosperity are also based upon what Grondona calls the ›lesser virtues‹–a well done job, tidiness, courtesy, punctuality–so important to smooth and ease human relations.

Lindsay, cit., notes that a country's comparative advantage, given by the presence of natural resources or low labor costs, is typically unable to create high and rising standards of living, having little or any effect on productivity. But

---

238 http://dictionary.reference.com/browse/prosperity.

239 See Harrison, Huntington (2000), Chapter 4.

240 See Chapter 22.

this is hardly culturally rooted evidence and much effort is wasted looking for unproductive strategies, being unaware of the circumstance that they simply don't work.

Only competitive mind–sets–with culturally rooted pro-growth attitudes and beliefs-can shape development strategies. In order to achieve growth, mental models continuously need to be reoriented[241], promoting progressive cultural changes.

Prosperity is hardly likely or possible without hard work–a necessary but not sufficient condition–which is considered a central value in progressive cultures and a burden in static ones. According to Harrison[242], in progressive cultures »work structures daily life; diligence, creativity, and achievement are rewarded not only financially but also with satisfaction and self–respect«. Distaste for work–so common in many backward cultures, even in Western countries–is a strong impediment to growth and development.

Social capital

Social capital derives from social gatherings such as family or ethnic clan and it refers to local connections and forms of association that express trust and norms of reciprocity and support within and between communities. It includes also social networks, that is an opportunity deriving from structures of linked individuals, increasingly even on the Internet, by several different possible kinds of interdependency. People that are engaged in forms of association develop a social framework of common cultural values, ties, and beliefs, and they develop a common social anesthesia that, with its membership entitlement, partially relieves them from a painful existence. Social–associational–capital is concerned with the mutual interaction of social and economic life[243], where gifting, sharing, solidarity and reciprocity are considered as core values and the clan acts as a defensive and protective structure. Partial vested interests of a clan bring however to parochialism and exclusion for non members.

Togetherness scans the step from personal to collective action and responsibility. In each clan there is a respectful leader. Pride concerning one's position–especially if prominent, together with the cult of the personality–is common especially in backward environments, where authority is both recognized and respected, following complex cultural habits. Societies are increasingly becoming more open and connected, so reducing cultural backwardness.

Culture–as well as shared cultural norms and behaviors–are also greatly influenced by family ties, whose perimeter is variable and changing, because of the

---

241 Lindsay in Harrison, Huntington (2000), p. 294.

242 Harrison, Huntington (2000), p. 299.

243 Bordieu (1977).

disrupting social impact of migration, demographic changes or instruction. Family ties are formed and changed with marriage and–later on–fertility rate impacts. Especially in traditional societies, each union strengthens existing network ties and forges new ones, as Munshi[244] reports, since marriage is a permanent bond and divorce is hardly an exit option.

Intra-community ties, connected with bonding social capital, are particularly strong and pervasive in closed rural environments, where contacts with the external world are rarefied. In such a context, a backward culture is particularly likely to perpetuate intergenerational poverty, difficult to eradicate from its ancestral legacies.

The social ›glue‹ of capital depends on the degree of cohesion, affiliation and sense of belonging within the clan members – as Reinikka reports[245] »fractured, heterogeneous communities [...] have little capacity for collective actions«. Mutuality and gratuity of love are the true lasting glue of social capital.

Both social capital and cultural values are so different not only within underdeveloped countries, but also comparing the Rest with the West, where autonomy and individualism are core cultural aspects – in poor countries, being alone is an unaffordable habit, putting survival even more at risk. In Western countries unbound individualism is often projected towards selfish and empty goals, and it disrupts social values and self-nourishes with a solipsistic ego, that is so different from the rural mutuality of most underdeveloped countries. It is the ephemeral triumph of the unbound Prometheus, passing from old physical chains to new intangible ones, concealed by an apparent freedom.

Moyo (2009), p. 58, claims that »social capital, by which is meant the invisible glue of relationships that holds business, economy, and political life together, is at the core of any country's development. At it's most elemental level, this boils down to a matter of trust«.

According to Fukuyama[246], social capital is an informal norm that promotes cooperation between two or more individuals, going beyond the cruel Latin motto ›*mors tua vita mea*‹ – your death is my life. If members of a group come to expect that others will behave reliably and honestly, they will come to trust one another – and trust acts as a lubricant that speeds up and eases human relations (even if mistrust of those outside the family, considered as intruders, is highly diffused). The norms that produce social capital substantively include virtues like truth telling, meeting obligations, and reciprocity, with a ›radius of trust‹. Life is better staying together.

---

244 Banerjee, Benabou, Mookherjee (2006), p. 397.

245 In Easterly (2008), p. 187.

246 See http://www.imf.org/external/pubs/ft/seminar/1999/reforms/fukuyama.htm or Harrison,Huntington (2000), Chapter 8.

Harrison[247] points out that »societies with a narrow radius of identification and trust are more prone to corruption, tax evasion, and nepotism« and a shortsighted and limited environment, that is suspicious and mistrustful towards innovation, openness, and transparency, hardly looks development friendly.

Family clan survival legacies

In hard environments where struggle for survival leaves little space for other more sophisticated worries, people, who typically belong to a common family or tribe, live together in clans, scattered over vast and hostile territories. Nurturing the family stands out as the first commandment, reminding that its perimeter and concept gets wider in non European cultures, going far beyond the elsewhere dysfunctional nuclear entity of mother-father-children. Small groups allow to flee danger more easily and to flexibly adapt to perils, constantly moving to allegedly safer places. Tribalism is questioned to be a stumbling block to progress[248] and ethnic ties in Africa or elsewhere are a magnified expression of family loyalty, since they work as a safety net in times of distress and they somewhat soften the effort towards growth.

Sharing and solidarity come out as culturally rooted survival values within clans, standing out as a supreme ethical canon, out casting with a permanent ostracism those who don't comply with these unwritten codes of conduit. Individualism, which is so highly prized in the Western world, in poor environments symbolizes unhappy and often lethal exclusion. The popularity of group lending–as a key microfinance feature–in underdeveloped countries is a cultural consequence of different life styles, with an intrinsic and often underexploited potential.

Within a community, social learning process let information, knowledge, and behaviors to be diffused among its members, following an imitative pattern within the social network where the process takes place. The degree of openness of the community towards the outside world shapes the level and the intensity of social learning but also its cultural stability, since new ideas and habits have to interact with the historical background, possibly in a smooth and gradual way. Unprecedented models and experiences may bring to cultural shocks and loss of identities, especially if such models and experiences are suddenly imposed by the neighbors within the community or the outside changing environment, even with traumatic events (natural calamities, epidemics, wars …). Such models and experiences are hard to detect at the moment but they have long lasting side effect, preventing integration.

---

247 In Harrison, Huntington (2000), p. 299.

248 See Calderisi (2006), p. 85.

Harrison (1985) notes that »there is evidence that the extended family is an effective institution for survival but an obstacle to development«. And Lipset and Lenz[249] add up that »solidarity with the extended family and hostility to the outsider who is not a member of family, the village, or perhaps the tribe can produce a self-interested culture«. If only we think about so many underdeveloped countries and their socio-economic ethnic ties, that are culturally so deeply rooted, we may begin to understand why progress and development are so difficult to start up and keep going.
Social capital is strongly–but not exclusively–linked to ethnicity, a concept that encompasses tribes, enlarged family clans, races, and nationalities and it broadly refers to a group identity, speaking the same language, typically being native from the same place, often showing somatic differences with other ethnicities, with rooted culturally distinctions and different ritual traditions.
The stronger the ties within the family clan, the weakest the relationship outside it – trusting strangers becomes difficult and interacting with them requires high transaction costs, whereas within the family entourage nepotism and corruption are the norm. In the *Republic*[250], Plato abolishes the family for the guardians, to avoid nepotism and amassing of private wealth. Like it or not, family ties, especially those between parents and children, are the main forces that underline institutionalized social classes.
Banfield (1958) writes that »in a society of amoral familists, no one will further the interest of the group or community except as it is to his private advantage to do so« – corruption and deviance from meritocracy grow up an automatic and unsurprising effect. Family is a value to preserve, to the extent that it does not fall into amoral familism, so harmful even in developed countries and being a primary cause of their stagnation.
When community belonging is more important than individual merit, it is hard to approach a market economy – both parasitism and selfishness are easy temptations. Transactions always bear social costs and are difficult to design, regulate, and check, especially outside the perimeter of the social network.
Meritocracy becomes a very relative concept and it seriously risks being drowned in static cultures which pursue an egalitarian *status quo*. People are selected according to their membership, not to their intrinsic value or merit, and this fact favors a brain drain of the smartest that have a strong incentive to get out of the backward and–sometimes–brutal family clan. Civic sense is also neglected and common good outside the family boundaries is hardly recognized as a cultural value. Bad choices are often persistent and culturally rooted.
Castes represent the deepest formal and substantial division between ethnic groups, each with its own social capital ranking position in the society, as it is

---

[249] In Harrison, Huntington (2000), p. 119.

[250] Book 5, 464.

sadly exemplified by Brahmins, the architects and the guardians of the Indian caste system, which is difficult or even impossible to disrupt, due to its ancestral pervasiveness and inculturation.

Social capital and networks are good and they can have positive externalities on outside parties to the extent that they are not discriminatory, otherwise they can promote intolerance, racism (a ›cultural‹ influence afraid of diversity?), exclusion and even violence to non-members. Indifference is a silent and subtle form of violence, especially towards the poor.

From corruption to trust

Social trust is a by product of social capital. Fukuyama (1995) argues that a society's ability to compete globally is conditioned by high–trust or low–trust, and the latter is typical of underdeveloped countries less effective in shaping and governing large and complex social institutions.

Even family ties can loosen and disrupt with separations, breakdowns, betrayals, disenchantment – and consequently social groups continuously tend to change their perimeter. They can play a role in microfinance, where group lending–typically within the same social network–is a celebrated form of collective guarantee. Cooperative actions often operate within the theoretical frame of game theory, describing social behavior in strategic situations, in which an individual's success in making choices depends on the choices of others.

Corruption, that is responsible for bad country governance at an aggregate level[251], is an evident violation of social norms, and it is detrimental to social capital, since it is so deeply rooted and omnipresent in so many places around the world that it deserves to be considered a cultural ›value‹ – more precisely ... a disvalue. This fact is true probably since the beginning of humanity: according to the Bible, it started in the Garden of Eden with Eve, who corrupted Adam with her sex appeal.

According to Lipset and Lenz[252] »corruption has been ubiquitous in complex societies from ancient Egypt, Israel, Rome, and Greece down to the present. Dictatorial and democratic polities; feudal, capitalist, and socialist economies; Christian, Muslim, Hindu, and Buddhist cultures and religious institutions all experienced corruption but not, of course, in equal measure«. Unfortunately, corruption is not a passing or ephemeral dysfunction and feudal group bondage is still widespread.

Corruption has highly unbalanced effects on the stakeholders that, willing or not, pivot around it. And private gain at public expense is the most probable gloomy outcome – »all animals are equal, but some animals are more equal than

---

251 See Chapter 5.

252 In Harrison, Huntington (2000), Chapter 9.

others« is the well known statement of George Orwell in his ›*Animal Farm*‹ novel.
Corruption is nurtured by asymmetric family or clan ties and it develops in secrecy, within a private club where only the strict beneficiaries, necessary to develop it, are carefully admitted – the larger the association, the higher the danger that embarrassing information leaks out.
Antidotes again corruption are represented by scandals (made public by a free press), moral reprimand, social, and judicial sanctions, from embarrassment and loss of future job prospects to imprisonment. These countermeasures are unsurprisingly much more likely and effective in deeply rooted democracies, where common good is a shared value and private clans and lobbies are not particularly influential.
Education and democracy–with its rules of law equal for everybody–increase the possibility of catching abuses and even technology can help out. To the extent that corruption is often represented by dirty money anonymously circulating, controls of bank transfers are increasing, together with devices against money laundering, internationally set up mainly against terrorism. Globalization and the degree of a country's integration within the world economy should negatively be associated with corruption, taking also profit of powerful means of information circulation, now represented by the Internet.
The poor and underserved, being almost by definition powerless, are unsurprisingly severely hit by corruption and its highly detrimental effect on development, with its well known negative impact on investment and consequent lower economic growth.
According again to Lipset and Lenz[253], corruption is harmful to development also because it concentrates resources where bribes are more efficiently collected and managed (larger, hard-to-manage projects such as big infrastructures or natural resources exploitation fields, nurturing the curse described in Chapter 3), diverting funds from other traditional pro-growth areas, such as education, where expenditures, efforts, and results are more visible and accountable, making corruption much more difficult to spread and prosper.
A key strategy for development is eradicating corruption and promoting universalism, instead of particularism and loyalty to private interests. It is also an antidote against the erosion of social capital, harmful even if hard to detect.
Microfinance is a good tool in order to go beyond family ties, as it has proved effective even outside the clan boundaries. Group lending, a basic building block of microfinance[254], is a well known example of jointly liable social network, where the poor help themselves, struggling together for survival.

---

[253] In Harrison, Huntington (2000), Chapter 9.
[254] See Chapter 18.

Culturally inherited poverty traps

Poverty is often persistent across generations, up to the point of becoming chronic, with miserable heritage difficult to reverse and likely to condemn newcomers to the same sad fate of their parents and ancestors.

Cultural heritage, far from being neutral, is very much concerned with the environmental history of the social clan where the poor are born and live. Cultural (dis)values are transmitted across generations and they have an enormous impact in shaping their attitude towards progress and development, which are to be considered as cultural values.

Role models, concerned with examples of adults with a different degree of success, have an imitation impact on children. Children's aspirations are often depending on the archetypes they have in front of them and that they are induced to replicate. Parents' aspirations concern not only their own working life, but also the opportunities for their children. When aspirations are low, investments in education are likely to be limited wherever present, ignoring that the ›grammar‹ of the poor increasingly matters.

The surrounding environment, with its social (un)mobility patterns, also contributes to shape the evolutionary trend and it may either worsen the prospects of future generations, if the socio-economic situation becomes more troublesome, or provide new stimuli for growth and catch up.

When the future is perceived as uncertain and volatile, development models downsize.

When adults and their children are stuck in chronic poverty trap, they are likely to consign to their descendants and neighbors a similar underdeveloped pattern, which is characterized by the absence of positive role models.

Durlauf[255] has described this scenario in his membership theory of poverty, which depends on the influence on individual outcomes of the socio-economic groups they belong to.

Our wealth strongly depends on the cultural heritage of our ancestors, and even if physical endowments (capital, housing, land …) matter, in a knowledge economy the soft–intangible–aspects are increasingly important.

From poor illiteracy to the primacy of education

According to the Millennium Development Goal number 2 (achieve universal primary education)[256], the key target is to »Ensure that, by 2015, children everywhere, boys and girls alike, will be able to complete a full course of primary schooling« (political will, coupled with targeted investments, have yielded

---

255 See http://www.econ.wisc.edu/archive/wp2014.pdf.

256 See http://www.un.org/millenniumgoals/bkgd.shtml.

widespread progress in primary school enrolment; poverty's grip keeps children out of school; the quality of education is as important as enrolment). A boost in education and literacy has shown to be able to open up opportunities for employment and exports, pulling growth.

Illiteracy or analphabetism–the inability to read and write–is intuitively linked with poverty, as we shall see in Chapter 10, dealing with the topic of child labor, which is a sad and painful alternative to school. Child labor is often a forced option for the poorest whose income is too low to afford education, with its long term results. Literacy is a fundamental human right and people who are quite literate decide all policies, good or bad they are. Analphabetism is a form of segregation and discrimination, that keeps the poorest excluded from the decision process, likely to be much less democratic and representative of their interests. Public investment in schooling has a major positive impact on the distribution of the benefits of growth.

Falling illiteracy rate–more children in school–has substantial positive effect on development. Among the key factors behind economic development there is indeed education, which contends the first place with survival issues such as decent nutrition and basic healthcare. In poor environments, these factors are frequently intertwined and many poor tend to be at the same time illiterate, hungry and ill. On the one side hunger and illness can be temporary (albeit serious) problems, while on the other side illiteracy and its consequences–low skill, lack of self confidence, inability to access increasingly sophisticated labor markets …–are deeply rooted problems, and they are difficult to solve and they require long term structural interventions. A literate work force is typically much more productive than an illiterate one and literacy can also positively contribute to the quality of life.

Schooling is associated with health improvements, and fitter students are more likely to have a better track record and more ›healthy‹ time at their disposal to learn and to enjoy greater returns of education. Bringing electricity–and consequently computers–to rural classrooms, is an effective albeit uneasy strategy to reduce the digital divide with other places. According to Erasmus of Rotterdam, the first hope of a nation lies in the correct education of its youth.

It is widely known that social and economic returns to basic and advanced education are very high and the expected returns far exceed the costs, boosting productivity, even if they are uneasy to detect–especially in the short run–and to measure. Poor societies with a weak governance system often have other survival priorities and they tend to waste money elsewhere, even if rational societies should invest public resources in educating their citizens, giving them proper incentives and waiting for positive externalities, being education a public good. A question so becomes unavoidable – why should parents have to pay for the basic education of their children, especially if they are poor? Why shouldn't

parents be paid to have their children educated? Proper incentives can be very effective, but the biggest problem in poor countries is concerned with … who pays, being resources limited and misspent.
Education is inversely linked to the fertility rate, as we can see in Chapters 4 and 10, since literate women are emancipated and they have better opportunities which prevent them to be exclusively dedicated to procreation and child bearing. This is again a cultural relationship, which reflects the historical heritage, where women live, and the changing environment, where new social and cultural paradigms interact with old habits, in a bizarre and often unpredictable way, different from place to place.
Illiteracy is a cultural problem because it contributes to shape the culture of individuals who are unable to read and write, keeping it segregated from a fast changing world where many information and solicitations are written and they need at least basic schooling to be understood and used.
In knowledge-based society, analphabetism puts illiterate individuals at a growing competitive and comparative disadvantage, making it hard for them to develop and catch up.
The impact of education to higher wages is evident, even if far from straightforward, as they also depend on other factors, such as family or clan connections–making use of the ›social capital‹ described above–entrepreneurship, initiative, a bit of luck and, on the supply side, availability of better jobs. In meritocratic environments, education tends to have a higher impact, while corruption stresses other ›values‹.
Children education has a public good component, since it is able to forge a new mentality, which should be more open to other cultures and increasingly linked to a global and fast changing world. Children are respectively more or less likely to be allowed to go to school, to the extent that the concept of public good–which goes beyond selfish private rents, confined to the family and its ethnic clan–is or is not culturally accepted.
Investments in education can give large returns, even if the pay-off is far from being immediate and it leads to substantial improvements in productivity–the key factor behind growth–only if the environment is ›development friendly‹. It means that is able to offer good job opportunities and to attract talents, who otherwise are an incentive to flee away, following a well known ›brain drain‹ pattern[257].
Instruction has a strong collective aspect and students share their time in large classes–with even more than 100 pupils per class, contrary to the Western model where some 20-30 students per class represent the norm–but teaching does also have a strong personalized function and there is an individualistic component in learning. The students are not all equal and the smartest ones are seldom

257 See Chapter 12.

appreciated in a system where meritocracy is not considered a cultural value. A proper blending of healthy individualism (bringing to entrepreneurship …) and compassionate sharing with the weakest can have an enormous social impact, with the result of fostering development.
Statistics and information about the worldwide literacy rate can be taken from several sources on the web[258].
Role models play an important part in influencing the instruction pattern, since new generations or clan members typically follow an imitative approach, according to which the degree of instruction of peer members represents a model for others, with a strong social and environmental interaction. The decision to attend school–and its gradation, up to a certain level of instruction–is strongly related to the percentage of literate peer within the community.
Instruction is difficult to spread in places where analphabetism is common, since people tend to be unskilled and poor, they lack the monetary resources to send their children or relatives to school, and they are also unaware of the real importance of instruction. School attendance is also more intermittent and drop out rates are higher. The consequence[259] is a durable and pernicious poverty trap–once again difficult to extirpate–and social influences tend to be high within groups, especially if they are closed, bringing to persistent cultural patterns that are uneasy to be modified The right to education concerns particularly children and it greatly affects their culture and their future[260].

The cultural concept of time

An essential–even if often neglected–dimension of culture is represented by the concept of time and by its psychological perception, to be conveniently investigated with a neuroscientific approach. Lonely time and passive living are a hopeless major feature of the poor.
Harrison[261], talking about time orientation, says that »progressive cultures emphasize the future; static cultures emphasize the present or past. Future orientation implies a progressive worldview – influence over one's destiny, rewards in this life to virtue, positive–sum economics«. According to Lowenthal[262]: »the past is essential – and inescapable. Without it we would lack any identity, nothing would be familiar, and the present would make no sense«.

258 See for example http://www.newworldencyclopedia.org/entry/Image:Literacy_rate_world.svg; for illiteracy in Africa see http://www.afdb.org/fileadmin/uploads/afdb/Documents/Publications/African%20Statistical%20Yearbook%202009%20-%2000.%20Full%20Volume.pdf.
259 See Durlauf in Bowles, Durlauf, Hoff (2006).
260 See Chapter 10.
261 In Harrison, Huntington (2000), p. 299.
262 ›*The Past is a Foreign Country*‹, 1985, Cambridge University Press, Cambridge.

Nothing ages faster than future, which represents today's expectation, while tomorrow belongs to the young and never dies, being continuously replaced by a new timeless frontier. Reconciliation between origin and future may help to explore still indefinite and slippery time dimensions, with a Proustian research of the impassive and oblivious lost time, passing through an immanent present.
As Albert Einstein used to say »I never think of the future – it comes soon enough«. The Beatles used to sing that »life is very short and there is no time«, while according to the French poet Paul Valéry »the future is not what it used to be«. The roman emperor Adrian, a refined esthete, used to say ›*festina lente*‹ – a subtle paradox meaning ›hurry up slowly‹.
Time is the key parameter to examine the duration of misery, discriminating between chronic and transitory poverty[263], represented by a different level of depth and persistency and bearing important implications for exit strategies. Chronic poverty is characterized by income permanently below the poverty line, and it is typically transmitted across generations and innocently inherited, being often considered ineluctable and accepted with passive resignation. Chronic poverty is a timely concept that is related to the duration of deprivation, whereas extreme poverty refers to the magnitude and depth of intensity of misery.
Every culture has its concept of time[264], and no study of a culture is complete without attention being given to this fundamental topic. Elapsing time is the intangible bridge that retrospectively links past to present, and in prospect present to future – before, now and after.
The concept of time is profoundly linked to economic development, since it influences targets, strategies, timing, and achievements. In economics, time preference–measured with mathematical discounting–quantifies the premium a consumer will place on enjoyment nearer in time over more remote pleasure. Those with a high time preference are focused substantially on their well-being in the present, while others with low time preference are more orientated towards the further future.
In Western mentality, time and its intrinsic urgency and alertness are an obsession and a tyrant, too precious to be misallocated. And the same anxiety, driven by trendy over-expectations and timeless avidity, pushes to save time up, paradoxically ends up wasting it (how may you wisely employ the time that you have so painfully saved?), while in Africa time is principally represented by events – and posh watches are often used for decoration, not to tell the time.
For Africans, whose attitude towards time seems more relaxed, the future is concerned with the possibility to be remembered as long as possible by other people. According to an African proverb »the best time to plant a tree is twenty

[263] See http://www.chronicpoverty.org/page/index.
[264] See Hawking, Mlodinow (2005).

years ago. The second-best time is now«. In the African vision time flows toward us from the future–instead of being a projection of our past, passing through the present–and the more or faster our activity, the faster time flows. Time is created, it is not something in itself, and it is made up of connected events. Time is not actually passing, it is rather simply waiting for us and happenings fall within natural (seasonal) rhythms. Time has to be experienced in order to make sense and to be culturally perceived. Since what is the future has not been experienced, it does not make sense – it cannot, therefore, constitute part of time, and people do not know how to think about it. Time and reality end now, the future is unreal and there is no future yet, still to come out of the interaction of all forces in the world.

Beyaraza[265] challenges Mbiti's thesis[266] that for Africans »time is a two-dimensional phenomenon, with a long past, a present and virtually no future. The linear concept of time in Western thought–with an indefinite past, present, and infinite future–is practically foreign to African thinking«.

To an African as compared to a Westerner the present is larger and the future is smaller. Are long term efforts worthwhile? This apparently rhetoric question depends on the culture of time, with important consequences on savings predisposition, investment horizons and debt schedules and repayments, strongly influencing most of the microfinance issues analyzed from Chapter 17 onwards. The cult of ancestors links time with historical legacy, representing a unifying cultural bond within clan members with the same genealogic roots.

From recurring cycles to the cosmological arrow of time

Western time is linear, cardinal, and mechanical, being ideally represented by an arrow that ineluctably goes from a point (instant) to the following one. Classical traditional African time is neither linear, nor cardinal, nor mechanical. Neglected cultural differences bring to misunderstandings and failures.

In his masterpiece ›*The Shadow of the Sun*‹[267], the great Polish war reporter Ryszard Kapuściński noticed that »the European and the African have an entirely different concept of time. In the European worldview, time exists outside man, exists objectively, and has measurable and linear characteristics [...]. Africans apprehend time differently. For them, it is a much wider concept, more open, elastic, and subjective. It is the man who influences time, its shape, course, and rhythm (man acting, of course, with the consent of gods and ancestors) [...] Time appears as a result of our actions, and vanishes when we neglect

265 How, he wondered, could such great societies as the Ashanti, the Zulu, the Kitara, and the Mwenemutapa - to mention just a few - could have developed into such powerful centres of civilization with no concept of progress, planning, or future? See Beyaraza (2000).

266 Mbiti J., (1969), *African Religions and Philosophy*. Heinemann, London.

267 Penguin books, London, 2001, p. 16.

or ignore it. […] The absolute opposite of time as it is understood in the European worldview«. No way to understand Western versus African differences in development, productivity, and related issues, concerning also microfinance and its timely applications, if we do not first apprehend that the philosophical concept of time is so different – and so crucial.

Our very existence restarts every morning, following a cyclical trend, but any single day represents a unique chance, according to the Western culture, or it may show up in different ways, following the Indian reincarnation beliefs. According to the Indian culture–in its broadest and so superficial sense–time is cyclical and limitless and events represent themselves continually (daily, monthly, seasonally …). Time is also eternal, since everyone is called to share the eternity with God. Practical consequences of this cultural and philosophical concept of time immediately follow–don't hurry up (wondering why the silly Westerners are so anxious …), live peacefully, no chance is definitely lost and should you miss something today, you may well wait till tomorrow or any other countless future days. People are more important than time and it is time that is at the service of people, not people who are slaves of their time.

In general, Western time can be conceived and interpreted in the form of a line–the arrow of time[268], with an absolute beginning and a certain end (biblically represented from the Genesis, representing the act of creation by God, to the end, symbolized by the Apocalypse)–or in a circular rhythmic way, endlessly expressing alternating seasons or recurring days, sunrises and sunsets, tides, repeating over and over again. An animal sense of time–the difference between day and night; hibernation in winter time …–is also likely to influence rural peasants' life, much more than life of citizens.

The concept of time is present also in mythology and religion and it strongly affects the cultural approach to growth and development. The concept of time as a circle is an ancient one that has been incorporated into mythology and religion of numerous ancient cultures such as the Babylonian, Ancient Greek, Hindu (with ›lost in time‹ metempsychosis), Buddhist (with their reincarnating ›karma‹), Jainist, or the Incan, Mayan, Hopi, and other Native American Tribes. These populations share a somewhat similar concept of a wheel of time, which regards time as cyclical succession of repeating events. Though different in the description, each believes in some form of continuous time, either through life after death or rebirth[269].

Hinduism has little to do with the linear concept of history, time, and life. Hindus have a cosmic perspective of time and they believe that the process of crea-

---

268 The arrow of time is a complex concept that can be declined in several distinct forms, following a thermodynamic or a cosmological or a causal or even a quantum approach. The term has been coined in 1927 by British astronomer Arthur Eddington.

269 http://library.thinkquest.org/06aug/01010/linearCircular.html.

tion moves in cycles and that each cycle has four great epochs of time[270]. Since the process of creation is cyclical and never ending, it »begins to end and ends to begin«. In Indian thought, time is conceived statically rather than dynamically.

As a cultural category, time has always attracted the attention of philosophers[271] and thinkers – just to name a few:

- Confucius (551–479 BC) said »Study the past if you would define the future«;
- Heraclitus (ca. 540–ca. 480 BC) wrote that you couldn't step into the same river twice, for the waters are ever flowing new upon you. All is becoming, an understanding somewhat similar to the teachings of Buddha;
- Aristotle (384–322 B.C.) has realized that the motion of two objects could be confronted by comparing the elapsed amount of time while the objects were moving;
- St. Augustine (354–430). In Book XI of his ›*Confessions*‹, he was the first to posit that perpetual 'present' in time, did not exist. No time is truly present, and the present never takes up any space; time for him was an enigmatic entity, and also for the entire human race!
- René Descartes (1596–1650) rationalized that anything that existed had to have spatial extension (length, width, and height) but not temporal endurance (it only existed in the present, not the past, nor the future);
- Gottfried Leibniz (1646–1716) believed that without events, time would not exist;
- Isaac Newton (1643–1727), in his ›*Principia Mathematica*‹ described »absolute, true and mathematical time«;
- Immanuel Kant (1724–1804) simply found human comprehension of time itself to be impossible. He felt however that even though we could not define time, we could experience things in time;
- Søren Aabye Kierkegaard (1813–1855), reflected about the infinite succession of time and the illusory distinction between past, present

270 *Satya Yuga, Treta Yuga, Dwapar Yuga and Kali Yuga.*

271 See http://library.thinkquest.org/06aug/01010/famousPhilosophers.html.

and future[272] – a strong mental category, at least in the Western culture;

- Martin Heidegger (1889–1976), contrary to the tradition of philosophy, argued that time does find its meaning not in eternity, but in death;
- Stephen Hawking (1942–living), a British theoretical physicist, coauthor of ›*A Brief History of Time – From the Big Bang to Black Holes*‹, a popular science book which timely attempts to explain a range of subjects in cosmology.

Synchronizing global time

In Western cultures time is a limited, expiring, and precious resource. Money cannot buy or recover time and any possible effort has to be addressed to fully exploit its unrepeatable occurrence, acknowledging that unexploited past opportunities are lost forever. Time is money–but with money, you cannot buy time …–and the value of money, in its many forms and aspects (interest rates; timing debt facilities …) is indissolubly linked to the elapsing time. In other cultures from the South or the East of the world, time is not considered a tyrant and choices are just recurring. This different cultural concept has a strong impact on economic performance.

When microfinance issues will be dealt with, in the second part of this book, we are going to be deeply influenced by the (Western) concept of time, linked to financial covenants and conventions – time is money and the poor have to acquire a real consciousness about their repayment timing and schedules. Capital rationing or other sanctions induce borrowers to comply with timely lending rules. All human activities involve a dimension of time and so does microfinance.

The meeting of different cultures, which is eased by the ongoing worldwide globalization, has a strong impact on the different concepts of time. Western attitude to measure time and to make economic choices according to it, is gaining momentum and it is strongly influencing other cultures, even if harmonization of different cultures … has to take its due time. Globalization, still culturally dominated by Western standards, imposes time measurement and coercive deadlines. This aspect is a core point of productivity, being time a costly resource to be used in combination with other resources for output maximization – and there is little wonder that such an imposing concept finds so many cultural and practical resistances wherever time is a completely different concept.

272 See http://www.jstor.org/pss/1461656.

Painful convergence to the Western cultural concept of time is under way, mainly because those who do not comply with the settled rules of the game (about timely deliveries, time measurement …) are simply not admitted to play. Time concept strongly influences the attitude towards life and its challenges. By and large, Africans are contingently worried with the here and now and this short sightedness prevents budgeting, slows down maintenance and makes long-term progress difficult. Africans tend to enjoy life as it is–now–rather than worry about an uncertain future, even if in the long run lightheartedness and disorganization can be severely challenged by an unfriendly environment. Africans are patient and stoically long suffering to an extent probably unparalleled on earth, with the exception of Buddhist countries[273]. ›Count down‹–a familiar concept in the West, not only for starting rockets–is not so (spare) well know in Africa.
Time discipline is a concept representing a set of socio-economic habits, rules, customs or conventions, typically with a legal enforceable value. The estimate of the time needed to perform a task is part of a discipline called ›time management‹, with deep organizational and practical consequences. Time is a convention that is routinely used in transports: e.g., the airplane is due to take off at a certain scheduled time, on a fixed day from an assigned place – forget about just one of these complementary details and you are going to miss it!
Time concept is somewhat transformed by technology and–most of all–by the Internet: if a download is possible, a movie can be seen at any wished time, without being conditioned by the television palimpsest. Again, with Mobile or Home banking, being linked to a cellular phone or a PC modem, money transfer operations can be performed at any time, possibly anywhere. The space and temporal dimension of time are changed by technology, with a big impact on the management of our life. Time stops to be a tyrant, to the extent that a TV program is not missed if you can retrieve it at any time from the Web.
According to Bert Hamminga[274]: » ›Future‹ is a word that both Westerners and Africans know […]. The difference between the Western mechanical and African emotional time consciousness is a highly instructive one: it explains a lot of intercultural differences and problems of intercultural contact in any kind of business. […] What time does is ordering events. You have before, simultaneously, and after. […] Africans do not adhere to the Western dogma of cardinality of time. Africans have different aims in life. They want to ›live‹ their own way. Traditionally, Africans have no concept of historical progress«.

---

273 Calderisi (2006), p. 85.

274 ›*The Western versus the African Time Concept*‹ in http://www.mindphiles.com/floor/teaching/timeafr/timeafri.htm

The condensed Chapter

Economic progress is a cultural process and culture (so difficult to define and measure) is a mental category, which is influenced by social clan belonging, especially in backward environments. Oral culture greatly differs from its written transmission, the latter being increasingly important in our world.
Cultural melting pots, eased by globalization, favor confrontation and mutual enrichment, but also flatten homologation. The cultural concept of time, so different if comparing the West with the Rest, is reflected in different attitudes towards productivity and growth, with a strong impact on development.

Out of Poverty Tips

Reshaping our minds and fine tuning them towards sustainable development is possibly the most painful and slippery achievement for both the rich and the poor. Continuous re-engineering of shared ideas and ideals, through confrontation of ideas and mutual enrichment, is the humble background of any form of development. Culture matters.

Selected Readings

HARRISON L.E., HUNTINGTON S.P., eds., (2000), *Culture Matters*, Basic Books, New York.

HAWKING S., MLODINOW L., (2005), *A Brief History of Time*, Random House, New York.

CHAPTER 10 – The silent majority of humanity: gender and age discrimination of disdained women and neglected children

> The education and empowerment of women throughout the world cannot fail to result in a more caring, tolerant, just and peaceful life for all.
>
> Aung San Suu Kyi

Motherhood and childhood: a symbiotic and discriminated relationship

When a baby is born, for the first years of his life the mother represents the whole world around, after having been the passport to life. This symbiotic relationship permanently contributes to shape–for the better or for the worse–the psychology of the child and his attitude in progressively approaching and discovering the external real world, interacting with others and painfully learning, day after day, how to face difficulties and challenges, while gradually detaching from the protective mother's womb. Trust towards the others, that is so crucial for social interaction, is inspired by the degree of confidence that a baby finds when he is kept in his mother's protective arms. Mothering modes matter, as well as fatherly cares.

When this vital relationship, that is shared also by other animals, is disturbed or challenged by deprivation, illnesses, and other poverty traps of either the mother or child–or even both–then it is very likely to have everlasting consequences on the child's emotional and physical equilibrium, perpetuating his intangible and material poverty.

The role of the sensitive and supportive mother is even more fundamental in places where the biological father may be unknown, due to polygamy and to the unwillingness to bear any responsibility and financial cost in the child's upbringing.

The Latin proverb ›*mater semper certa*‹–mother is always known–albeit being nowadays puzzled by new technologies, seems to resist in backward places, linking at least the biological mother to her lovely creature.

The importance of the father, not to be underestimated, will be felt more later on when the age of innocence is over, while fronting a hard adult world, often unfit for children. Mother and father, with their gender roles and family codes,

respectively symbolize protective creation and passport to emancipation, from the family to the external world.
The mother is the first to welcome the birthing child, while sending the child to the external world is typically a father's assignment. The father's role is so fundamental for the psychic development of the child, as a ›third party‹ able to break the umbilical cord that over-protective mothers are reluctant to renounce to.
Goleman (1996) underlines that parental sacrifice for their progeny witness altruistic love in human life. But when the father is missing–being dead, gone away or permanently addicted to alcohol or drugs–the teenager lacks a fundamental psychological support, that is strategically vital in an unfriendly environment, experimenting the cardinal fear of a permanent loss. It's again Goleman (p. 235) who remembers that »isolated children are highly sensitive to injustices«. Affective poverty is caused by a biased and unbalanced emotional alchemy of feelings and thought, and it may date back to birth time, since »many potent emotional memories date from the first years of life, in the relationship between an infant and its caretakers. This is especially true for traumatic events, like beatings or outright neglect« (p. 22). Unforgiving lives often start with their very beginning.
According to art. 25 of the U.N. Universal declaration of Human Rights[275]:

> Motherhood and childhood are entitled to special care and assistance.
>
> All children, whether born in or out of wedlock, shall enjoy the same social protection.

The problems that are dealt with in this Chapter seem absolutely relevant, if only we consider that women and children represent the vast, albeit often silent, majority of humanity. In spite of this undisputed solar evidence, these crucial questions are often neglected, underestimated, disdained, or simply ignored. Motherhood and childhood are commonly subject to special oblivion and indifference, exactly the contrary of the U.N. Human Rights intention.
The relationship between gender discrimination and poverty is unsurprisingly strong. Disdained women are often at the very bottom of the social pyramid, among the poorest of the poor, and they share their desperate condition with their beloved children – a bitter consolation indeed. Gender discrimination of women and their children (especially if girls) traps them in poverty, often permanently, even if biology is not destiny. ›Women and children first‹ is an often misunderstood act of politeness, which instead may open up a prioritizing door to hell.

---

[275] See http://www.un.org/en/documents/udhr/index.shtml#ap.

Women are often weak, quiet and resigned to their condition, especially in backward and masculine rural societies as well as children who, so loved and spoiled in birth declining Western countries, are often seen like a burden in underdeveloped societies.
As a counterweight, in patriarchal and traditional societies, male impose their undisputed political and economic power, leaving little room for opinion sharing and compromise. Men driven social institutions, biased by cultural backwardness, tend to perpetrate gender inequalities, subjugating women and girls. »Low-income parents tend to have less time and resources to invest in their children«[276].
Another difference between rich and poor countries concerns the elderly, respected and considered wise. In poor countries, even if few people get old enough to get elderly mental diseases (today's life extension increasingly presents the problem also in underdeveloped places). Wise old people are respected as it used to be with the ancient Romans, but conversely they are often considered a burden in Western societies. Children and elderly follow a ›paradox of plenty‹ rule, being mostly desired where they are missing. Scarcity and abundance follow even here a well known economic rule in setting the ›price‹, even if we are dealing with human beings, not to be confused with tradable goods.
Discrimination of women and children unsurprisingly brings to a much more likely probability of being and remaining poor, with dire consequences even for the most basic freedom – bare survival[277]. And »when race intersects with gender, the disparities are even more pronounced«[278]. Deeply rooted social barriers still affect women, especially in backward cultures.
According to the Koran (§2:228) »(women) have rights similar to those (of men) over them in kindness, and men are a degree above them«. And again (§ 2:282) »A woman is worth one-half a man«. Religions often consider women as inferior beings, either theoretically or practically.
The by-products of discrimination and abuses are manifold and they range from child labor to prostitution or raping, escalating up to children soldiers (typically boys)[279] or sexual slaves (mainly girls) – one of the saddest features of many wars. Slavery, bondage and sometimes deliberate killing are strict relatives of the aforementioned phenomena.
In most cases, women and children live symbiotically, starting from fetal life up to full age – and love, tenderness and compassion represent the noblest part of

276 Pick, Sirkin (2010), p. 9.

277 See Chapter 13.

278 Khan (2009), p. 51.

279 Poverty, the proliferation of small and cheap weapons, and the changing nature of warfare have increased both the use and the roles of child soldiers. Using children as soldiers robs them of their families and their education; surviving children often have difficulty rejoining their communities. See http://www.child-soldiers.org; http://www.amnesty.org/en/children; http://www.bbc.co.uk/worldservice/people/features/childrensrights/childrenofconflict/soldier.shtml.

their silent existence. Poverty influences this bondage, which is often dramatically interrupted by premature death, either of the ailing mummy or of the child, especially whereas child death is still common and socially accepted with resignation, as it used to be even in Western countries while they were still developing towards progressively higher survival rates, especially thanks to path breaking inventions in medicine, since the end of the 19th Century.

Fernando (2006), p. 23, notes that »the majority of world's poor are women. Despite the fact that women constitute approximately 50 percent of the world's working population, and do roughly 67 percent of the world's work, they earn only 10 percent of the world's wages, and hold 1 percent of its wealth«.

According to UNICEF »Having a child remains one of the biggest health risks for women worldwide. Fifteen hundred women die every day while giving birth. That's a half a million mothers every year. The difference in pregnancy risk between women in developing countries and their peers in the industrialized world is often termed the greatest health divide in the world« [280].

Safe motherhood is concerned both with the right of becoming a mother when the girl herself chooses it (typically well after puberty) and with the survival of both mother and baby, often in places where the magnitude of maternal mortality is still a human rights calamity. According to Khan (2009), p. 123 »maternal mortality figures are the strongest indicators of inequality between men and women and between rich and poor«, representing a human rights abuse and reminding us how gender discriminations still matter. It's again Khan, p. 125, who reminds that »maternal mortality is a story of prejudice, discrimination, inertia, and inaction, denying women their right to life, health, and safe motherhood«.

The causes of maternal mortality are many, especially in poor environments, and they range from illegal abortions to lack of proper hygiene and medical care, from violence, rape, and sexual harassment (up to female genital infibulation, still a common practice in Africa) to malnutrition, fueled by ignorance, superstition, and powerlessness in an unequal and discriminatory environment. Khan, p. 130, reminds also that »pregnancy is life–threatening for many poor women in times of peace; in times of war it can become a death sentence«. Unwanted pregnancies are a by-product of gender–based rape, with women acting like innocent victims, unable to negotiate safe sex with their stronger mates.

Violence is ubiquitous in poor environments and many unlucky women are continuously beaten and harassed by their drunken companions, silently suffering and typically being unable to rebel or to ask for justice, freely accessing discriminating and corrupted courts.

Motherless babies, if they are lucky enough to survive to parental death, are often abandoned orphans, especially if females, and a dark and unwelcome future

---

[280] http://www.unicef.org/sowc09.

is likely to wait for them. In addition, considering child mortality, it shouldn't be forgotten–even if the poor are used to it–that there is no greater pain than surviving one's children.

Women duties ... and rights

Women have a pivotal role within the family, which is often underestimated but in many cases enhanced by the absence of the father, due to his premature death or to his chronically drunk state, with a consequential addicted personality, often with his core interests well outside the family. As Seneca reminded »drunkenness is simply voluntary insanity«. So women are in (sometimes exclusive) charge of children raising up and home running.

Reintroducing man in his family–so that he can properly provide much needed emotional and physical security[281]–is a trivial but effective pro-development strategy. Burdens of survival are enormous in poor environments but those of women are typically even greater, often reaching physical and mental exhaustion.

According to article 16 of the U.N. Universal Declaration of Human Rights:

> (1) Men and women of full age, without any limitation due to race, nationality, or religion, have the right to marry and to found a family. They are entitled to equal rights as to marriage, during marriage and at its dissolution.
>
> (2) Marriage shall be entered into only with the free and full consent of the intending spouses.
>
> (3) The family is the natural and fundamental group unit of society and is entitled to protection by society and the State.

More specific principles are found in Convention on the Elimination of All Forms of Discrimination against Women[282] (CEDAW) or in the Convention on the Rights of the Child[283] (CRC).

The CEDAW Convention defines discrimination against women in the following terms:

> Any distinction, exclusion, or restriction made on the basis of sex which has the effect or purpose of impairing or nullifying the recognition, enjoyment, or exercise by women, irrespective of their marital status, on a basis of equality of men and women,

281 Maathai (2009), p. 275.
282 http://www.un.org/womenwatch/daw/cedaw.
283 http://www2.ohchr.org/english/law/crc.htm.

> of human rights and fundamental freedoms in the political, economic, social, cultural, civil, or any other field.

CRC is an international convention setting out civil, political, economic, social, and cultural rights of children. The Convention acknowledges that every child has certain basic rights, including the right to life, his or her own name and identity, the right to be raised by his or her parents within a family or cultural grouping and to have a relationship with both parents, even if they are separated.

Brave and sharable statements are the equal rights of husbands and wives, full consent (possibly driven by true love) about getting married, protection by society and the State. Even more than 60 years after the declaration of 1948 such rights are hardly respected, even in many developed countries.

Violence and abuses within the family are incredibly common and women are unsurprisingly the most likely victim, with their children often assisting as silent witnesses and getting accustomed to violence, a bad and often replicated example. Sexual violence has a disproportionate impact on poor women. Shame, confidentiality, backwardness, lack of empowerment and a fatalistic acceptance of ancestral bondage are the worst accomplices of these women's rights continuous breaching. Alcohol is often stronger than love and misery plays its part, in stateless slums where a civil society has never existed.

According to Khan (2009), p. 94 »gender violence is essentially an abuse of power. For families living in poverty, some people feel that the easiest way to establish power is physically«. Machismo is hard to eradicate and it is still very damaging, considering also the often underestimated impact of psychological violence. And violence keeps women poor.

Changing this situation is a tremendous and difficult challenge, especially if women are too ashamed to open the door of their problems. But women's rights are human rights.

Orphanage, another disrupting threat for the family, is so common that often it gets unnoticed, especially since AIDS got its death toll in Sub Saharan Africa or elsewhere, like the silent weep of a child missing his daddy or/and mummy, with interior invisible psychological scars.

Enlarged rural families provide a precious and well trained ancestral social network, with unregulated adoptions that may guarantee survival, however often bringing to other well known problems (malnutrition, lack of proper education and care, legal problems starting from the identity of the orphan and their inheritance onwards, just to name a few), which are often typical by products of misery.

The agency of women is very much concerned with bringing up children. Mortality tolls are still high in underdeveloped countries and we have already seen in Chapter 4 that women's education and literacy have an inverse proportional link with demographic boom and infant mortality. Alphabetized and emancipated women live indeed more outside home and they tend to have fewer children and to care more about the ones they jointly decide to procreate. Such education brings to a better quality of life for everybody, starting from the children. Women's literacy and employment levels are the best predictors of both child survival and fertility rate reduction[284] and they may benefit from the application of the UNESCO Convention and Recommendation against Discrimination in Education[285].

According to Jewkes[286] those women who try to earn an income and gain a degree of autonomy face paradoxically more violence from the men in their lives and the communities in which they live. In cases where a woman is working but her partner is not, or in patriarchal societies in which men traditionally hold most of the power, women can find that their efforts to improve their situation increase the likelihood of violence, as men resent their efforts to assert their freedom.

The cost of time to women has a strong impact on demography and the decision to spend all the time at home, making and raising children, that is often imposed by a backward cultural heritage, is increasingly challenged by new possibilities, such as instruction or out-of-door employment, and the result is a decline in fertility. Higher values attributed to women's time are linked to lower fertility rates, raising the opportunity cost of childbearing. Economic and social development stands out as the best contraceptive.

Dignity, equality, respect, and possibly love are all necessary ingredients in the relationship between men and women, naturally complementary during all their lives.

Sen (1999) has focused on women role in development, arguing that, while improving their well-being is important, enhancing their agency is just as critical.

According to a World Bank report[287] societies that discriminate by gender tend to experience less rapid economic growth and poverty reduction than societies that treat males and females more equally. To promote gender equality, the report proposes a three part strategy, emphasizing:

1. institutional reforms that promote equal rights for women and men;
2. policies for sustained economic development;
3. active measures to redress persistent gender disparities.

---

[284] See Chapter 4.

[285] www.unesco.org/education/pdf/DISCRI_E.PDF.

[286] Jewkes (2002), quoted in Khan (2009), p. 95.

[287] ›*Engendering Development - Through Gender Equality in Rights, Resources, and Voice*‹ http://www-wds.worldbank.org/external/default/WDSContentServer/WDSP/IB/2001/03/01/000094946_01020805393496/Rendered/PDF/multi_page.pdf.

Women freedom to seek employment outside the family is a major issue in many developing countries and both education and outside earning can increase women's decision autonomy, enabling them to know and to get what they need and deserve. Microfinance can help out, not only because it mainly focuses on women, but also because it represents a natural bridge between domestic activities and the surrounding world.

From unfreedom to emancipation

Women unfreedom and gender bias have serious drawbacks, following a well known spiral of self enhancing problems. Backwardness, lack of proper education and of job opportunities fatally keep women imprisoned in their homes–often represented by stinky slums–where they asymmetrically bear most of the unpaid domestic labor, often being reduced to the role of ›reproductive machines‹, causing serious demographic imbalances that fuel poverty[288].

Even within the poorest, there are discriminations and women and their children are likely to be positioned at the very bottom of the social pyramid.

Women's organizations play an important part in removing ancestral attitudes, which are so disdainful towards women and their dignity, but much is still to be done: the role of women is not fully emancipated even in developed countries.

Old matters such as women's right to vote have been solved almost everywhere during the last Century. Women's degree of emancipation is represented by their active participation in political, social, and economic roles.

Sen (1999), p. 201, again explains that a reason for the relatively low participation of women in day-to-day economic affairs in many countries is the relative lack of access to economic resources. In developing countries, indeed, the ownership of land and capital is very heavily biased in favor of males. And to run businesses or to be elected passing through expensive polls, one needs some initial resources, as well as an education that is often denied to girls.

Microfinance, as it will be seen later on, represents an embryonic lab of political involvement thanks to its empowerment of women, enabling them to participate to meetings and to freely express their opinions and strategies. The step from credit to political meetings is not so long, especially in unsophisticated rural environments.

Women progressive empowerment and their pivotal role in the decision making process is the central issue of their emancipation–›*A long and winding road*‹, as the Beatles used to sing–and it should conveniently start from the new generations, acknowledging that we are all born free of prejudices, that are simply transmitted by biased cultural heritages. Building from scratch is often easier

[288] See Chapter 4.

that restructuring, but the men at work have to be careful, illuminated, and forward looking.
Women emancipation is also linked to better exploitation of natural resources, bringing to lower birthrates[289], rising demand for education, and better farming techniques and more investment in the land and villages[290]. In addition, women emancipation fosters democracy and it favors a bottom up approach in development, easing foreign aid reception.
According to the Millennium Development Goal number 3 (promote gender equality and empower women)[291], Target 1 is to »Eliminate gender disparity in primary and secondary education, preferably by 2005, and in all levels of education no later than 2015«. The state of the art is that:

- girls still wait for equal primary school access in some regions, attending ›road schools‹ whenever they are prevented from joining an organized education, missing the aggregation effect of schooling;
- women slowly gain ground in political decision-making, but progress is erratic and marked by regional differences;
- targeted action is needed to help girls from poor, rural areas stay in school;
- job opportunities open up, but women often remain trapped in insecure, low-paid positions;
- women slowly gain ground in political decision-making, but progress is erratic and marked by regional differences.

We can get useful indications also:

- from the Millennium Development Goal number 4 (reduce child mortality), Target 1: Reduce by two thirds, between 1990 and 2015, the under-five mortality rate (despite progress, deaths of under five children remain unacceptably high; vaccinations have however slashed deaths from measles);
- from Goal number 5 (improve maternal health), Target 1: Reduce by three quarters the maternal mortality ratio (The high risk of dying in pregnancy or childbirth continues unabated in sub-Saharan Africa and Southern Asia; Little progress has been made in saving mothers' lives; Skilled health workers at delivery are key to improving outcomes); Target 2: Achieve universal access to reproductive health (Antenatal

289 See Chapter 4.
290 See Harrison, Huntington (2000), p. 179.
291 See http://www.un.org/millenniumgoals/bkgd.shtml.

care is on the rise everywhere; Adolescent fertility is declining slowly ; an unmet need for family planning undermines achievement of several other goals).

Culturally rooted gender inequalities

Gender inequalities and women discrimination are culturally deeply rooted and they follow ancestral stereotypes that are difficult to change, forgetting that women's rights simply are ... human rights[292]. Traditional cultural attitudes towards women are often highly humiliating and discriminatory.

Women's uneven exploitation enforces well known poverty traps, such as the demographic spiral (women are often considered just as ›procreating machines‹) or environmental drawbacks. Better woman education and empowerment not only decreases the birth rate to more manageable levels but can also improve farming techniques, children upraising, and healthcare.

Women have a peculiar cultural sensitivity, which is often overwhelmed and hidden by the male's outstanding and suffocating dominance, with enduring values such as resilience, loyalty, dedication (to the children, home keeping ...), and a savings capacity that makes them natural candidates for microfinance. Women can well balance men thanks to their complementarities, if only they are given the chance to do so.

Female autonomy is everywhere a matter of the relative power within couples, which is in the complex relationship between men and women. It is typically skewed in favor of stronger males, who are more likely to work outside home, earning more money and being the owners of properties, in particular land. Women tend to be in a weak bargaining position[293], because of deeply rooted social norms, which make female autonomy harder and continuously challenged.

Forced underage marriage represents a by product of gender inequalities, since it often happens little after puberty, meaning an abuse of child's rights. It is frequently linked with high maternal mortality ratios, which prevent girls from being normal teenagers[294], with serious drawbacks on their education and development. Economic convenience, cultural customs, and the desire to get rid of a daughter make early marriage a recurring option, especially in backward rural areas. Love is just an independent variable, far from being considered in these bridal agreements, often with a much elder man.

---

292 See also http://humanrightshouse.org/Articles/9367.html.

293 Eswaran in Banerjee, Benabou, Mookherjee (2006), p. 153.

294 See Khan (2009), p. 137.

According to the OECD's DAC Guidelines for Poverty Reduction[295], gender inequality concerns all dimensions of poverty. Cultures often involve deep-rooted prejudices and discrimination against women. Female poverty is more prevalent and typically more severe than male poverty.
Women play a crucial role in the livelihoods and basic human capabilities of poor households. By providing for their children, they reduce the risk of poverty in the next generation. But women in general have less access than men to assets that provide security and opportunity. Such constraints on women's productive potential reduce household incomes and aggregate economic growth. Gender inequality is therefore a major cause of female and of overall poverty.

Avoid child labor and let children play

Demography in underdeveloped countries has a great impact not only on the number of children, but also on the way they are brought up. To the extent that poverty encourages high fertility, having to do with old-age security, future poverty is also likely to increase.
Child labor is a symptom of current–and future–poverty and economic growth can reduce the problem, which is a consequence but also a cause of underdevelopment. Poverty and child labor are mutually interacting and they create a vicious circle, according to which poor parents keep their many children out of school and they grow up poor, so perpetuating misery. The outcome of under investing in children is not immediate and its long lasting damaging effects are hardly visible in the short term, especially if parents follow a backward dominant culture, according to which it is fair and normal that children have to work, instead of studying. Immediate modest benefits of child labor often outweigh long-delayed insidious problems for exploited and illiterate children.
Child labor is particularly diffused in rural areas and children are basically employed in agriculture. The negative effects of this lack of proper intellectual training become evident when children grow up and try to enter the adult job market, since they are confined at the margins of it by their low skills – in poor environments, child labor displaces schooling.
The choice between sending children to work or to school depends on opportunity costs and expectations, with a trade off between deferred versus immediate gains – it's again the Aesop's history of the hard-working ant versus the lazy grasshopper. On the one side, costs depend on several factors, including school fees, availability and nearness of teaching resources, and the latter is not a trivial particular, especially in unpopulated territories of Africa, where schools are far away and teachers are desperately needed. On the other side, there are returns of child labor – higher wages of adults are typically reflected by similar

[295] Source: http://www.oecd.org/dataoecd/47/14/2672735.pdf.

increases for children and they make the whole family wealthier, decreasing the need to keep children out of school but at the same time increasing the opportunity cost of instruction.
Is the choice of sending children to work or to school driven by ignorance, selfishness or simply state of need? Decisions are typically made without considering its full implications, especially if parents themselves have a low degree of literacy, which typically makes them unaware of the full consequences of their often draconian decisions. In such context, proper and forward looking counseling is strongly needed, together with a system of smart incentives, which is difficult and expensive to set up, but highly rewarding when properly established.
Little or any attention is typically paid to the psychological impact of child labor, especially if it concerns arduous or exhausting employment. To the extent that children are taught to work hard, obey, and shut up, it seems difficult to disclose their emotions, dreams and nightmares.
In many backward cultures, children are simply considered assets to exploit–sometimes to full physical and mental exhaustion–especially as parents get older and need assistance, in places where public social safety nets are still missing. Adult children can help, in societies where the respect for elder people is deeply culturally rooted.
Banning child labor is a straightforward and draconian solution to the problem, even if it is hard to be enforced in backward rural areas, where poor households are resorting to child labor out of desperation. Children are working for survival purposes, to help the household make ends meet and, according to Udry[296], effective bans on child labor would make these destitute households.
Child labor is a particularly relevant factor, especially in poor countries where child mortality rates are high and where it proves expensive to let children study, if they have a short life expectancy. According to Eswaran[297] »legislation that bans child labor is virtually unenforceable in the midst of poverty«. And again (p. 154) »since mothers bear a greater proportion of the cost of children, they prefer to have a few children and ensure their survival by devoting resources to them. Fathers, on the other hand, prefer to have many children and to devote little by way of resources to each of them«.
Malnutrition in children is thought to have adverse long-term consequences for their learning and hence their future incomes, while higher income inequalities raise the incidence of malnutrition[298].
The distressing issue of child labor, which is still frequent in many underdeveloped countries, is increasingly seen and interpreted as a question of unacceptable slavery and bondage. The reason is that unwilling children are forced to

296 In Banerjee, Benabou, Mookherjee (2006), p. 252.
297 In Banerjee, Benabou, Mookherjee (2006), p. 145.
298 Ravallion in Banerjee, Benabou, Mookherjee (2006), Chapter 14.

work often till exhaustion, depriving them from the most essential freedoms, such as the possibility to receive a proper education and training, to get basic health services and, last but not least, to live a cloudless infancy, playing football instead of producing footballs with tiring hand job.
According to Article 24 of the U.N. Universal declaration of Human Rights »Everyone has the right to rest and leisure, including reasonable limitation of working hours and periodic holidays with pay«. Even if poor children are not taught to play, they often show a natural happiness that is unknown to their spoiled correspondents in richer countries. Playing is a fantastic form of evasion from the hard outside world.

Invisible children and the birth (un)registration trap

Many children[299] are not only illiterate and often orphans, but also excluded from any birth registration program, especially if born in uneducated backward rural areas, living in a sort of unofficial limbo – being there but officially nowhere. Birth registration is child's first right, as enshrined in Article 7 of the UN Convention on the Rights of the Child of 1989.
In modern global times, consequences of missing registration are increasingly heavy and they strongly limit the potentialities of invisible unregistered children. The trap is likely to be transmitted across generations, since unrecorded parents may be unused to register their children. They may typically lack proper facilities and they may be culturally unaware of the strong impediments of such a hidden trap. Such trap is indeed hardly visible also because it is based on a silent omission, that is unlikely to produce immediate effects but it is potentially harmful in the long run, across all the existence of unrecorded poor.
Invisible children are easier to kidnap and abduct, transforming them into street boys, young soldiers, or sexual slaves, even beyond porous national borders of failing and ailing States. Suffering from a Stockholm syndrome (according to which the kidnapped may be infatuated by the kidnapper), fascinated abductees tend to become docile soldiers. And children soldiers are soon taught to hide their teary eyes, disguising any emotional empathy towards an unwelcoming external world.
The ›unregistration‹ trap that concerns invisible children somehow resembles the property trap described in Chapter 15, according to which many real estate properties are unfit to be given as collateral guarantee for a loan, simply because there are untitled and so nobody can claim back a legal property certificate. Their invisible identities are strongly linked with unofficial financial mar-

[299] According to UNICEF estimates, the number of unregistered children every year has increased from 48 million (2003) to 51 million (2007). Statisticians love recordings - their informational database - and when they are missing, their research job gets harder and less precise.

kets or a blackmail labor system, where clandestine workers are exploited and deprived of their basic rights.
The Community of Sant'Egidio[300] has launched its global program BRAVO!–Birth Registration for All versus Oblivion–in view of the growing concern about unregistered children and its implications on peace and stability of States in the developing countries. The programmatic approach to address the issue involves the concerned Government ministries and departments, in order to assist them in building capacity of the civil registration systems, to create awareness by educating parents and children, and to adopt an approach that will create balance between service provider (Government) and the beneficiaries (people/children).
An institutional approach to the issue is necessary, combining a top down strategy with a capillary bottom up retail network, in order to create proper culture and suitable facilities. ICT and biometric devices are increasingly necessary, also in order to create multipurpose databases.
In addition, there are also inabilities to travel with a passport, to use a–mighty–credit card, to formally buy durable goods such as a real estate property, to have a driving license, etc. Security reasons are also important. Even from a psychological perspective, lack of registration prevents invisible poor to reach a full citizenship status, weakening their feelings about national belonging and identity and making them feel segregated from wealthier and properly recorded ›first-class‹ citizens.

The right to education

Education is not a natural activity–like eating–and it has to follow an intentional cultural project, starting from teachers and their training – who does educate educators? Instruction and knowledge are not enough and they have to follow a suitable pedagogic pattern, while methods of education may always represent a lab of innovative ideas.
Education and the social perimeter of instruction are difficult to implement in big groups and they can be a cornerstone of group lending activities, following an anthropological perspective that is consistent with the contingent environment, and creating self fulfilling learning networks, ignited by optimistic educators. Another problem of education is concerned with its frequent poor matching to the rhythm of daily rural (or even urban) life.
Invisible children with no identity and no proper birth record are institutionally nonexistent and they find it difficult to go to school or to get healthcare services – albeit nobody can deny them the right to exist. The problem is particularly complicated with lonely children, transformed into little orphans looking for

[300] See http://www.santegidio.org/index.php?pageID=1730&idLng=1064.

adoption and relying, if they can, to relatives or members of the enlarged family clan.
Skilled parents educate their children and send them to school, since they are typically not poor and they are well aware of the importance of instruction. So the problem lies with the unskilled, whose children face the risk of perpetuation of ignorance, which is a synonym of unawareness. And illiterate parents are those who are most likely to transmit analphabetism to their children, and this fact is a typical and resilient poverty trap, especially for girls.
A problem with opportunity costs is the fact that they are often misrepresented and they bring to sub optimal–wrong–decisions, since they are biased by backward cultural habits and by a short sighted consideration of the discounted value of wealth. They tend to be substantially underestimated, especially if families are unable to borrow in order to finance delayed consumption, to the extent that the benefits of further schooling are not immediately evident.
Choices take place at individual levels, but single families are highly influenced by their clan's typical behavior. These influences have broader effects at an aggregate level, creating districts or clusters where development can be hindered or fostered by the kind of education and assignments that parents tend to give to their children. A critical mass of literate versus illiterate children does make the difference.
Proper access to education is often critical and typically gender biased, impeding schooling to many girls. When families are poor and they have to select who can go to school and who can't, girls are typically excluded and they are kept at home cooking, delivering illiterate children.
It proves much wiser and effective to encourage school attendance, by improving the quality of teaching–a difficult task where resources are scarce–and subsidizing families with grants, in the form of current resources that compensate missed earnings taken away from child labor and postponed to future bigger earnings by better-trained scholars. Since instruction brings net benefits, these subventions should be a sort of ›bridge financing‹, which is uneasy but not impossible to be repaid. The cost of school grants is a substitute of child wages and it should not be unreasonably expensive, to the extent that children are poor and poorly paid. As it happens with foreign aid[301], grants need to be properly targeted and reach the real beneficiaries – children and their poor families, not politicians or soldiers.
When children are many and decisions are not clear cut, some may be allowed to go to school, at least at primary levels, while others may be not, creating discriminations and disparities within the family.
Even if many children formally go to school, their true attendance and frequency is often irregular, following both the working needs–which may be seasonal,

[301] See Chapter 14.

with peaks during the crop season–and the general economic outlook. When such a situation is gloomy, many children are simply withdrawn from school, abruptly interrupting a learning pattern that is difficult to restore later on. Transitory income shocks may have permanent effects on children education.
Along their whole life (hopefully getting longer), children absorb resources, imposing a cost on their parents, especially if when they grow up they are allowed to study and exempted from early job occupation. Then they become productive and, getting old and/or ill, they become again unproductive, with a social toll to be carried typically not by their parents, who are already passed away, but by their own children. Each child now is a potential cost for future generations, typically ignored or underestimated by his parents.
The cultural attitude towards children and the value attributed to their very existence has an incredible importance in shaping their destiny. Child mortality, that is possibly the saddest grief for tenderhearted parents, is too often accepted as unavoidable and the reaction is not how to avoid it, but rather how to replace the dead child with another one.
Children are too often considered as a short term investment and fully exploited, regardless of their basic human rights. Parents myopically do not consider that their productivity is low and it may be much greater if only properly trained. The turning point is considering education not a dead cost without immediate return, which decreases today's resources, but a medium to long term highly rewarding investment.
When a population succeeds in getting out of poverty, the issue of child labor gets smaller and it soon vanishes, but the very point is that this is a solution which is often lacking a benign background and an initial push behind.
Let children study is the best investment for development, remembering that future is young.
School fees and related instruction costs are a common barrier to education. These charges–which may be called ›voluntary‹ quotas, matriculation fees, or examination costs–are a great and often unaffordable burden for children from poor families, and they disproportionately affect racial and ethnic minorities, members of indigenous communities and migrants.

The denied childhood of young soldiers

In wartime, women and children–being considered harmless–are sometimes spared from mass killings, but this fact has to be considered more as a matter of simple disinterest, rather than of deliberate mercy. However, throughout history and in many cultures, children have been extensively involved in military campaigns–as fighters' messengers, spies, porters, cookers, sexual slaves …–even when such practices were supposedly against basic cultural morals, weakened by the dramatic context of war.

As a matter of fact, children have always been used in war. Present-day war, though, triggers those conditions most likely to pressure a child to become a soldier: lack of education and stability, internal displacement or refugee flight, separation of families, and poverty. Under these circumstances, it is difficult to distinguish between a forced and a voluntary child soldier. Children are also, albeit involuntarily, psychologically fit for fearless behaviors and undisputed obedience to authority, and they are typically unused to receive and give love, in the hard environment where they are brought up. Young minds are easy to manipulate.

Kidnapped children, who are forced to leave their family and education program to join the army, tend to forget that school tales are nicer than war tales. Infancy is a one-way-only train and when somebody grabs it, recruiting young soldiers, it is stolen forever.

Some children join armed forces because of food, survival, or to avenge atrocities in their communities. Armed forces and paramilitary groups use both girls and boys in many roles. Children commonly start out in support positions, acting as porters, cooks, spies, or sexual slaves. Often, though, these children end up on the front lines of combat, e.g., planting or detecting landmines or participating in first-wave assaults.

Wars and displacements have a catastrophic impact on education, with enduring negative side effects on development and human rights.

Child soldiers are frequently subject to extreme abuse and manipulation during training and combat, and they generally suffer higher casualty rates than adults. Child soldiers are often plied with drugs and given promises of food, shelter, and security, and they are at times forced to commit atrocities against other armed groups and civilian populations, including sometimes their own families and communities[302].

When children of war see foreign soldiers killing people and they acknowledge that even the military have their own family elsewhere, they find it hard to understand why they simply don't stay at home, peacefully enjoying their own children. It is hard to explain a senseless war to children – how can they understand what we personally don't?

In addition, child soldiers often have nothing to go back to, when the conflict is over, since they were abruptly eradicated from their native land and separated from their family clan.

Child soldiers are one of the most tragic, shameful and cruel aspects of poverty and human rights violation. The phenomenon is still tragically widespread in

---

[302] http://www.fpif.org/briefs/vol4/v4n27child.html.

several countries in the world, where civil wars have condemned many children to be deprived of their childhood and to remain traumatized for their whole life.
The United Nations Convention on the Rights of the Child, that is the most widely ratified human rights treaty in history, encompasses civil rights and freedoms, family environment, basic health and welfare, education, leisure, and cultural activities and special protection measures for children. In article 38, (1989) the Convention states that: »State parties shall take all feasible measures to ensure that persons who have not attained the age of 15 years do not take a direct part in hostilities«.
Social reintegration of children soldiers, when they come back home, several months or years after their abduction, is a painful task and psychological wounds are the hardest to treat, since they are deeply hidden within the mind and the soul of these unlucky children.
The apex of this humanitarian tragedy is possibly reached when months (or years) after the abduction the luckiest children soldiers succeed to get home, often after having been forced by ruthless warlords to kill their brother or sister or daddy. When they eventually meet their desperate mummy, she has in front of her the most atrocious dilemma: are they going to be considered a beloved and missing child or the killer of other equally beloved children? Even girls who have been raped and forced to have children with their kidnappers and murderers of their relatives, don't have easy choices.
Sometimes they remain, even if they can escape, because they now have a new family, albeit with an awful companion, while in other cases they succeed to go back, not knowing who and what is waiting for them.
Here below we summarize the reasons why children face abduction and subsequent transformation in the most cruel war machines at this rate:

- they are far too weak to rebel, and very often they are too young to fully understand what is happening;
- it's psychologically much easier to brainwash a 10 year-old boy and turn him into a ruthless killer that an adult. Children need a little time to become obedient and docile;
- when children are given drugs (the main strategy used to make them fearless to war cruelty) they may even not realize how dangerous these substances can be;
- weapons are rapidly evolving: guns and grapeshot's are becoming increasingly cheap and easy to carry, making them accessible to children. Arm smuggling and poor monitoring of legal arm trade drastically increases this traffic.

Children are taken away from their homes mainly in two ways:

- deception: often a promise for a piece of bread is enough to convince children to follow recruiters, especially if they are street children, who are deeply convinced that they won't have anything to lose;
- abduction: Children are violently kidnapped from their villages, mainly during the night hours, and driven to armed basements.

The trauma children go through makes the rehabilitation an extremely hard job. It is not just about giving children food, water, and a proper medical treatment, but it is mostly about helping them to re-integrate in the society.

The condensed Chapter

The inexorable economic law about the value of scarcity cynically applies also to children, who are mostly appreciated in western countries, where declining birth rate is largely spreading, but not in the poorest countries, where they are mostly abundant.
Both children and their mothers are significantly discriminated: the formers in the saddest cases end up being recruited as young soldiers or sexual slaves, while the latter tend to be unfree and not emancipated, living in silence, poverty, and despair, albeit this condition, with its local differences, sadly applies to more than half of the world's population. Enduring progress has to start from here.

Out of Poverty Tips

Caring mothers are the present and needy children our mighty future: nothing is more crucial for development. A tough but rewarding investment against poverty.

Selected Readings

MOORE K.A, REDD Z, BURKHAUSER MBWANA K,, COLLINS A., (2009), *Children in Poverty: Trends, Consequences, and Policy Options*, Child Trends Research Brief, Washington.

CHAPTER 11 – Globalization and poverty: not a zero sum game

Globalization is a fact of life. But I believe we have underestimated its fragility.

Kofi Annan

Looking for sustainable globalization in a flattening world

Globalization describes an ongoing process by which local economies, societies, and cultures are becoming more and more integrated and cosmopolite, through globe-spanning networks of exchange. The result is that the world is becoming flatter and increasingly connected, compressing distance and time and widening the virtual library of our shared knowledge.

Globalization and interconnectedness shake cultural identities and frontiers, making them relative and fluid. Through multipolar vision, material differences are corroded and melted down into an unknown blending, opening up new horizons and unprecedented scenarios, which stand out as a potential threat but also as an unmissable opportunity. The world is flat but also–as David Smick (2008) pessimistically admonishes–curved.

As Marshall McLuhan used to say in 1962 »Time has ceased, space has vanished. We now live in a global village«. Should compression of space and time reach a merging point, we would enter a context ideally similar to Einstein's relativity, where conventional coordinates such as mass, space, and time vanish, evaporating and becoming relative together with our old fashioned ideas. Compression of space and time is synergic (close distances reduce time) but also asymmetric, since time is an elapsing parameter, which depends on cultural interpretations[303]. Time is less squeezable than space and it is influenced by the global compass and its connecting impact on distant geographical places.

The term globalization[304] is sometimes used to specifically refer to economic globalization, that is the integration of national economics into the international

[303] See Chapter 9.

[304] According to the United Nations ESCWA »globalization is a widely-used term that can be defined in a number of different ways. When used in an economic context, it refers to the reduction and removal of barriers between national borders in order to facilitate the flow of goods, capital, services and labor [...] although considerable barriers remain to the flow of labor [...]. Globalization is not a new phenomenon. It began in the late nineteenth century, but its spread slowed during the period from the start of the First World War until the third quarter of the twentieth century. This slowdown can be attributed to the inward looking policies pursued by a number of countries in order to protect their respective industries. However, the pace of global-

economy through trade, foreign direct investment, capital flows, migration[305], and the spread of technology[306], enhanced by the ›human web‹ of increasingly connected people.

However, globalization is usually recognized as being driven by a (random?) combination of economic, technological, socio-cultural, political, and biological factors, melting commodities with people and their ideas. So the term can also refer to the transnational dissemination of ideas, languages, or popular culture. The uneasy attempt to harmonize global issues with local peculiarities has produced the ›glocal‹ neologism. Optimist and confident cosmopolitan strategies, coming from citizens of a common world, increasingly follow the motto »think globally and act locally«.

Is globalization a benign form of cosmopolitanism? This intuitive question has many possible answers, biased by the degree of optimism and by so many unpredictable facts that the question itself may lose part of its insight potential. Benedict XVI notes in his Caritas in Veritate encyclical letter, § 33, that:

> The *explosion of worldwide interdependence*, commonly known as globalization, [...] originating within economically developed countries, [...] by its nature has spread to include all economies. It has been the principal driving force behind the emergence from underdevelopment of whole regions, and in itself it represents a great opportunity.

From a geopolitical perspective, the end of the Cold War and of the ideological confrontation between the West and the East is a strong global flattener[307]. So it seems unsurprising that the last big globalization wave has started in the 1990s, with the habitual ups and downs, however characterized by an evident trend of increasing openness and interdependence. We now currently experiment an unprecedented worldwide promiscuity, to which nobody was used or prepared. But scenarios, far from following a deterministic pattern, may change fast, like in a video game.

We all live under the stars of a common sky and our global destinies are intertwined as never before.

---

ization picked up rapidly during the fourth quarter of the twentieth century [...]«, in http://www.escwa.un.org/index.asp.

305 See Chapter 13.

306 See Chapter 16.

307 See Friedman (2009), p. 67.

No global or go global?

The most globalized factors are undoubtedly weather and climate[308]. Irrespective of national borders, they have a worldwide impact, with a contagion effect of pollution, greenhouse effect, or global warming, taking a natural revenge against senseless exploitation of the planet. Poor countries are normally the victims of the polluting developed nations, which export their ecological problems without taking particular care of their consequences.

We are–willingly or not–entering an era of unprecedented social, political, and economic change, where nothing is going to remain as it was. Now, when it is universally acknowledged that only a continuous growth pattern can give an indispensable contribution to eradicate poverty, we are also becoming increasingly aware that global development has to be sustainable and environmental friendly.

Is globalization increasing or reducing poverty? Does it have a perverse or a good impact on the underserved? Do trade reforms that cut import protection improve life of the poor? Has increasing financial integration led to more or less poverty? How do the poor fare during currency crises, global recession, and food price increases, known as ›foodflation‹?[309]

These intriguing questions are probably mainly due to remain Hamletic, since they unsurprisingly tend to have mixed and ambiguous answers.

The first path in order to try to give some answers to the above quoted questions, is to start from the socio-economic relations between underdeveloped countries and the rest of the world, represented in particular by the most developed nations – such as those being part of the OECD[310] ›club‹ or to the even more exclusive, but increasingly less representative, G8.

Globalization (driven by rich nations), and poverty (endemic ›by definition‹ in developing countries) interact together, unsurprisingly following a well known bilateral causal relationship, each influencing the other. Cause-effect relations, linked to the aforementioned questions, are however here particularly complicated to find out and to interpret.

Economists[311] claim that globalization acts as a »rising tide which will eventually lift all boats«, with a positive spill over even on poor regions, but the evidence is mixed and optimistic views are often not supported by empirical evidence. The new global economic order is often pitiless with the poor, considered useless or even disturbing.

---

308 See Chapter 8.

309 Many of these questions and of the statements of this chapter are taken from Harrison (2007), introduction.

310 www.oecd.org/.

311 See Rodrigo De Rato, http://www.imf.org/external/np/speeches/2006/052206.htm.

With delocalization to poorer areas where the labor cost is cheaper, power shifts elsewhere and opportunities arise for underdeveloped areas, even if they are not automatically caught by the poorest, waiting for positive spillovers from more skilled local entrepreneurs. Decentralization and outsourcing, which are induced by globalization, favor the developing countries, with low labor costs, that already have adequate infrastructures and a proactive educational system, so creating a deepening division between the poor countries who succeed to catch up and those who fail to do so.
Globalization is by itself unlikely to spread the benefits of business evenly around the globe and it appears as a worldwide phenomenon which forces managers to rethink their markets and strategies, while the poor seriously risk lagging behind, passively reacting to epochal changes that they are barely aware of. Other companies attract entrepreneurs and industrial or trading clusters act as a magnet, since they provide infrastructure, collateral services, specialization, and skilled workforce. Less Developed Countries are highly integrated into the global economy through international flows of goods, services, capital, and people (i.e. migrant workers and their remittances)[312]. During international recessions, migrant workers may be resent home and their remittances tend to decrease, sometimes dramatically.
Technological innovation is flattening an increasingly interconnected world, with ICT networks, high-speed travel and unprecedented mobility of capitals, people, and ideas. Local poverty is a global issue and segmentation factors between the haves and haves not are weaker than in the past – interdependence now matters. The technological revolution, decreasing space and time barriers, is leveling the global economic playing field[313], lowering the entry barriers and opening up new markets. However, as Kevin Watkins says »contrary to the received wisdom, global markets are not unregulated. They are regulated to produce inequality«.

Openness and growth

Frédéric Bastiat, a 19th Century French economist who fought against autarky and protectionist relapses, reminded that »when goods cannot cross borders, armies will«.
As Harrison (2007) brilliantly points out, most economists expect openness to trade to be associated with higher diffused growth, in order to be listened to use the aforementioned cautions, and we do know how growth is good for the poor. Consequently, following a sort of Socratic syllogism, since trade enhances growth and growth reduces poverty, open trade (i.e., globalization) is good for

312 Unctad (2008).
313 Friedman (2009), p. 63.

poverty reduction. Her conclusion (page 13) is nevertheless puzzling: »to summarize, there is no evidence in the aggregate data that trade reforms are good or bad for the poor«. Empirical evidence suggests that globalization positively affects growth, but it is not clear if the poor in developing countries are benefiting for it or not (some probably yes, others certainly not – and the overall result is mixed …).

Paul Samuelson admonished that »globalization presumes sustained economic growth. Otherwise, the process loses its economic benefits and political support«.

This would be certainly the case if every poor can get the same symmetric benefit from trade openness, having a similar growth pattern if compared with his peer. But we do know that each poor is different from others: some can take profit from trade openness while others simply don't and they can be seriously damaged by it.

Openness to trade is often detrimental for the poorest, who are typically too weak and unskilled to take profit of the liberalization. And growth gains from trade are likely to bring to increasing and potentially destabilizing inequalities, with little or any positive spill over at the very bottom of the social pyramid. When the train of development and liberalization passes by, some are simply too weak to jump on it – and regret grows when people understand that missed chances are limited or even one-shot.

Some broad themes emerge out of the complex issues dealt with in Harrison (2007):

1. *The poor in countries with an abundance of unskilled labor do not always gain from trade reform*

According to the famous Heckscher, Ohlin model[314], international trade liberalization should raise the incomes of the unskilled in labor-abundant countries. Similarly, the Stolper, Samuelson model[315] in its simplest form suggests that the abundant factor, such as unskilled labor in underdeveloped countries, should see an increase in its real income when a country opens up to trade.

Like a devil that is always hidden in the details, the problem with the Heckscher, Ohlin model lies in its unrealistic assumptions. Labor is in reality much less mobile and capacity to move out from contracting sectors into expanding ones is highly wanted, but it is often missing or, at least, slow to be developed. In addition, since developing countries are typically protecting sectors that use unskilled labor, such as textiles and apparel, trade reforms reduce these protections and unskilled workers become even poorer, because they are too weak to compete in an open market.

---

314 Heckscher, Ohlin (1991).

315 Stolper, Samuelson (1941).

In conclusion, penetrating global markets even in sectors that traditionally use unsophisticated labor require more skills and quality standards than the poor in underdeveloped countries typically possess[316].
As a consequence of the aforementioned models, trade reforms in underdeveloped countries should be pro-poor, since poor unskilled workers are the competitive advantage of these countries, enabling them to have a cost advantage in production.

2. *The poor are more likely to share in the gains from globalization in presence of complementary policies*

Globalization is more likely to benefit the poor if trade reforms are implemented together with a reduction of impediments to labor mobility and efficiency – access to credit, even through microfinance, and to technical knowledge, the presence of social safety nets, selective income support of the disadvantaged, good targeting of food aid are an example of necessary complementary policies to accompany trade reforms.
Other reforms include macroeconomic policies such as exchange rate stabilization (a titanic task for countries with not convertible currencies, requiring also stabilization of key macroeconomic parameters such as inflation and interest rates) or privatization.

3. *Export growth and incoming foreign investments have reduced poverty*

Export growth brings precious cash, especially if it is denominated in hard currencies, and it is one of the most effective ways of starting up the engine of development, especially if exports are diversified and not (only) commodity dependent. Incoming foreign investments–attracted by specialized labor, good infrastructures and a positive governance framework[317]–are typically highly welcomed, unless they spoil the environment without any benefit for the populations (an event that often occurs with oil and mining exploitation[318]). This recommendation is consistent with the Millennium Development Goal n. 8 (develop a global partnership for development)[319]: according to Target 2 (Develop further an open, rule-based, predictable, non-discriminatory trading and financial system), market access for most developing countries is little improved; domestic agricultural subsidies by rich countries overshadow money spent on development aid and trade-related assistance needs to be increased.

---

316 Harrison (2007), p. 3.
317 See Chapter 5.
318 See Chapter 3.
319 See http://www.un.org/millenniumgoals/bkgd.shtml.

4. Financial crises and recessions are costly to the poor

Since the poorest fly with no parachute (no safety nets and little saved cash for emergencies[320]), they can much more easily precipitate to desperation. Financial crises are often born in Western countries, but the illness is soon contagious even for the poorest with no antibodies, especially if they are increasingly linked with the international markets because of globalization. Backwardness and segmentation represent, in such a case, a curious shelter against imported shocks. According to the structure of the economic system within one country (oil based; agricultural intensive …), the reaction to external shocks is very different and it can be mitigated by resilience, mobility and proper diversification (uneasy in an underdeveloped and unsophisticated environment).

5. Globalization produces both winners and losers among the poor, but is not a zero sum game

Poor wage earners in sectors that open up to exports see globalization as a form of God's blessing, whereas on the other side previously protected and weak sectors which become exposed to import competition suffer and are often hardly likely to survive. Even comparing winners with losers, it is difficult to say that it is a zero sum game, especially in the absence of stabilization funds and compensation schemes, which are examples of good governance, but they are difficult to put in place and hardly present in unsophisticated and underdeveloped countries.

6. Trade liberalizations can have mixed effects on the prices that regard the poor

The poor are obviously very price-sensitive to the primary goods they need for survival. Trade liberalization can have an impact on exported as well as imported goods. Domestic production of the poor is unaffected by international competition, to the extent that imported goods are complementary and not competing with domestic goods. In such a case, the poor should gain from new exports without being directly affected by imports. If imported goods are competing with domestic products, the poor producing these products have to face competition. And on the one side they may claim a marketing and transport advantage, knowing local customers' habits, already having trading channels and saving on importing costs, and on the other side they often suffer from weak organization, little economies of scale, financial unsoundness, and often low quality, being highly exposed and ill prepared to competition. Many of them, being already close to their break-even point, simply don't make it anymore and soon disappear.

---

320 See Chapter 17.

Everybody should specialize in what he/she is better for, provided that the market provides a sufficient demand for what he/she makes.
Competition of imported goods with existing domestic products should in theory always be welcome (let's think about the positive effect of foreign banks or cars in the economy of the developed countries), because it represents a major stimulus for price reduction and quality enhancement. Nevertheless, within an underdeveloped context, the dilemma is that increased competition can drive off the market domestic poor producers unable to face it. The world is increasingly competitive ... what about the poor?

Painfully converging to common standards

With their bizarre and unpredictable blending, geography, history, demography, languages, culture, and religion profoundly shape each country's originality, and they create profound segmentation factors, that are however increasingly challenged by globalization and its flattening impact, confusing the established socio-economic rules of the game, with a Schumpeterian destruction and beyond a shared global heritage.
Globalization can be a powerful equalizer, softening or even eliminating the segmentation factors between countries, which keep them apart, to the extent that comparisons between similar products (or services, wages, conditions ...) are easy and possible. That is the reason why the convergence to common standards–starting from the English language, up to international accounting principles, shared legal issues such as those of patent protection or product quality and liabilities, technological standards ...–is so powerfully pushed by the centripetal force of globalization. Those who don't comply with the internationally settled rules of the game, are simply not allowed taking part to it.
An equalizing effect can be helpful if the poor have similar levels of productivity but lower endowments. In such a case, an arbitrage effect takes place and comparisons between similar products induce an increase in the lowest priced products, which are offset by a correspondent decrease of the overpriced items – the poor with lower wages profit of the situation.
If quality is different, arbitrage between apparently similar products may be blocked by market segmentation which obstacles comparisons. This fact is the safety net for many producers from developed countries, who find it increasingly hard to compete on costs (let's think about the Chinese challenge) and so they try to strategically position their products in a higher quality shelf. Differentiation is the other competitive advantage and uniqueness is a strategic differential asset, which is potentially able to generate monopolistic rents.
In an increasingly global world, the strategic questions that all countries, even developing ones, should make are more or less the following: what are we good

at? Where do we have competitive and comparative advantages, wisely mixing specialization and free trade? What are we universally known for? In which way the other nations need us or look for our products? They are simple questions, with difficult answers – but an important step of the long road to development passes from these demands.
Poor countries, in most cases, are ill equipped and trained to handle an increasingly competitive international environment, facing drastic and radical changes in a world where life symbols change, cultural cornerstones move elsewhere and orientation points fade away.
Technology is driving the world towards a converging commonality, leveling and synchronizing existing differences. But many poor countries find it increasingly difficult to catch up, since the technical international standards and rules are becoming more and more complicated, sometimes raising the suspicion that they are set so awkward just to prevent competition. It was much easier 20 or even more years ago than now, when the game has become tough. And in a context where many people scream, it is often difficult to hear their plaintive voice. The poorest, ashamed by their condition and resigned, are often shy and voiceless.
Globalization can eventually increase productivity, if the poor can specialize thanks to a bigger market, that is made possible by exports, or if they can synergistically combine their raw products with others imported, especially those technologically advanced, and this can raise long-run growth and progressive accumulation of capital – the two preeminent economic keys of sustainable development.
Easterly[321] and Milanovic and Squire[322] disgracefully find out that increasing trade integration is associated with falling inequality within developed countries, but with greater inequality within developing countries. This fact is due to differences in productivity in developing countries with developed ones, since the former lead to outflows toward the latter, exacerbating inequalities in the poor countries, or to lack of labor mobility (due to weak infrastructures, cultural reasons such as ancestral willingness of staying close to home, economic problems …) and the weak power of trade unions – may be not a real damage, if we only think about the problems they often cause in Western countries.
Tougher domestic competition, which is caused by import of foreign goods similar to the ones produced at home, increase unemployment and informality. Unprotected workers become poorer and they fall back to the black market, where moneylenders and usury typically replaced microfinance. Temporary complementary policies are so highly wanted to minimize the adverse effects of trade

321 Harrison (2007) pp. 109-142.
322 Harrison (2007) pp. 143-182.

reforms on some of the poor. The impact varies according also to the prevailing macroeconomic scenario.
Even within a country, the poor are not all the same and they can be divided in many categories, according to their level of poverty but also to the place where they live – indeed rural poor are different from urban poor: the former are net producers of agricultural products, while the latter are net buyers. If the net effect is positive, may be for some products and not for others, there is room for exports, otherwise the country has to import food. Natural calamities, famine, and other disgraces can sharply decrease the amount of available food. The trading from the countryside to cities is booming, since urbanization is rapidly growing everywhere in the world.

International speculation and food price volatility

Agricultural and textile products and, wherever existent, oil or minerals, are the most frequent output of poor countries. The former meet many restrictions in international trade–since Western farmers are strongly protectionist–and they are ›poor‹ unsophisticated products, which are often not domestically processed (raw coffee non toasted …), while the latter are typically highly wanted even if they generate the somewhat surprising curses that we have seen in Chapter 3.
International prices of food represent a reference point for exports and they strongly influence the redistribution of wealth within the poor. No country on its own is strong enough to dictate international prices, even if cartels for some products–such as OPEC for oil–are somewhat effective. International pricing for standardized commodities takes place in specific Stock exchange (the biggest ones being Chicago and London), strongly influencing developing countries, typically highly exposed to international speculation.
A sad example was the dramatic surge in food prices in 2006-2008, which was nicknamed ›foodflation‹, because of many causes, which referred not only to a growth in the typical demand for food, but also to the alternative use of some food products for bio-fuel, in search of alternatives to increase oil prices, driven by an unprecedented surge in the demand, as a consequent of the long phase of worldwide economic expansion.
Speculative investments on commodities make prices highly volatile and they typically find an incentive in derivative products (futures, options, swaps, forwards …). Investments grow together with market liquidity (which should much more conveniently be addressed at financing the real economy) and risk attitudes of greedy investors typically concern metals, oil, and gas but also some standardized food stuff (rice, corn, wheat …). Speculative bubbles periodically grow and sooner or later they burst, with explosive side effects that are particularly harmful for the unprotected poor. Advocates of commodity speculation

claim that it provides liquidity and price visions and outlook, favoring also real intermediation between producers and consumers. Increasing the deposit margins on open derivative positions makes them more expensive, softening speculation.

If food prices grow, normally farmers and importers from abroad (for the foodstuff not produced locally), are expected to gain, at the expense of citizens living in urban compounds. Should prices fall, the opposite would otherwise happen.

There is also a big difference between gross and retail prices. Even when the former go down, as it has started to happen from the second half of 2008, the latter–those who really count for final consumers–often show a much lower decreasing pattern, making the fortune of intermediaries, at the desperation of poor consumers. The more inefficient the distribution chain, the higher the arbitrages between gross and retail prices.

Another hot issue, debated in Chapter 14, is concerned with food aid – is it right or wrong? Again, the answer is ›it depends‹: for emergencies, food aid may be amply justified, but if it is structural, it can seriously damage poor farmers, who are unfairly to compete against them, to the joy of urban poor, who may however have big problems, should aid expire in the long term, with a rural class by the time downsizing its production to a mere self sustaining output.

The best aid strategy is to buy food from local producers and to distribute it to poor consumers. But aid funding governments often prefer to ›soften‹ their real effort buying food from their own domestic producers, strongly lobbying not only in order to avoid unwanted competitive imports but also to sell their own products.

Free capital and financial integration

Another key aspect of globalization is represented by financial liberalization, lifting capital controls. Freedom to flow capitals to underdeveloped countries is not a bad or harmful strategy on its own, but again it can hide some threats, if it is improperly managed.

Greater financial integration allows poor countries to have higher and better (cheaper) access to capital–that is much needed for development–even through microfinance: Microfinance Investment Vehicles[323], represented by closed end funds typically owned by Western financial intermediaries, increasingly invest in local Microfinance Institutions, proving to them more sources of funds to be used for lending to the poor, aimed at fueling development.

---

323 See Chapter 22.

Technology normally follows capital, since new technological start-up investments are typically funded from abroad, at least initially and especially if the hosting country is not only devoid of technology, but also unable to pay for it. The impact of increased financial integration on poverty reduction through the growth effect is however »likely to be small«, as Harrison (2007), p. 20, puts it. Among mostly bad news, a mildly positive note emerges from globalizing financial markets, since they bring with them a natural increase in foreign direct investments, which are less volatile than other flows and significantly effective in poverty reduction.

Trade and capital flows are frequently associated with an increase in the demand for skilled workers. Again it is not automatically a bad news for the unskilled ones–to the extent that the country attracts foreign investments, spillovers are much more probable–even if it should be noted that when developed countries choose to invest in underdeveloped areas, selecting them carefully, they preliminary look for necessary, even if not sufficient, preconditions. Such conditions can be summarized in: availability of airports where to land and roads to travel, presence of English speaking intermediaries who act as facilitators with indigenous populations and basic infrastructures, including basic education.

Worldwide inequalities: globalization makes us neighbors, not brothers

In the global market, resources move following economic convenience, without social protections or privileged relationships, getting close to an idealized world of complete liberalization, even if market failures are however always possible. The poor, who are culturally influenced by their local habits, find it unsurprisingly difficult–if not impossible–to compete, since clan mentality and social capital[324] structures find it mentally uneasy to face and cope with unprecedented scenarios.

The ethnic trap segregates the poor, keeping them split from the globalized economy and, on the one side, preventing developmental key factors, such as impartial institutional facilities, shared countrywide services, connections beyond the tribal birthplace and, on the other side, impeding other factors, such as the inability to confront and share different cultures and ideas – too sudden changes threaten identities and push back to ›safe harbor‹ traditions. Nationalism and chauvinism–so concerned with irrational self pride–suffocate jointly liable globalization.

[324] See Chapter 9.

Since globalization is characterized by openness, impartiality, and disregard for local values and cultures, the more the poor live in backward and timeless environments, the more is mentally difficult for them to catch up.

The skill level that is required by the labor market follows a classical trade-off: on the one side unskilled workers are typically much cheaper than skilled ones, but there is a big question mark about what they are really able to do and–especially–to learn.

If productivity is too low, they soon become uninteresting and after some pilot unsuccessful investment, foreign investors get bored and fly away, looking for nicer places. On the other side, skilled workers are more expensive but also more productive: the investor's preference often goes to them, especially if they are many and if they can interact in clusters, becoming specialized in a particular industry (for instance, IT in Southern India, whose impetuous growth was inadvertently favored by the unexpectedly lucky firing of many Indians once working in Californian's Silicon Valley after the New Economy Crash of 2000-2001).

Critics to globalization are often biased by prejudices and by a myopic short term approach. Aggregate poverty often declines, even if some can become even poorer, indicating once more that inequalities matter.

Empirical evidence is still missing to fully answer important questions, as Harrison (2007) suggests (p. 24). According to the Aristotle's syllogism application, since openness (globalization) is positively related to growth and since growth reduces poverty, then openness should reduce poverty. Yet evidence supporting this conclusion is fragile, either because of incomplete country data or, more worryingly, because the poor are more asymmetrically hit by trade reforms.

The relationship between trade liberalization–the first economic pillar of globalization–and poverty reduction is complex and it strongly depends on the casual interaction of many variables, that are uneasy to predict – somewhat like when playing shanghai, the movement of one stick causes unpredictable chain movements of other sticks.

Globalization in developing countries increases inequalities. Even if the general level of poverty is reduced, and there are clear winners, there are also losers who become even poorer. From this fact we can draw the general conclusion, which has inspired the title of this Chapter: the impact of globalization on poverty cannot be reductively interpreted, summing up wins and losses, as a zero sum game. According to Joseph Stiglitz »it takes more than free trade to end poverty«.

Brotherhood is a long term cultural process that has to be developed with a progressive civilized cohabitation, ›living together‹, following the insightful provocation of Andrea Riccardi (2008).

Is globalization an orchestra without director?

According to John Naisbitt[325] »Globalization is a bottom-up phenomenon with all actions initiated by millions of individuals, the sum total of which is ›globalization‹. No one is in charge, and no one can anticipate before the result manifest what the sum of all the individual initiatives will be. A global economy can only be the result of ›spontaneous order‹«.

Actually, globalization also follows a complementary top-down approach, since it is directed and addressed from global groups of power (multinationals and governments behind them; opinion groups …), who are hardly respectful of the disoriented poor.

The factors behind globalization seem to interact in a fortuitous way, without any proper planning and well beyond the boundaries of any consistent strategy of harmonic development – but this should not come as a surprise, since it is the footprint of our erratic historical development, where randomness plays a key role, denying any deterministic path dependence.

Unless properly driven and regulated, globalization is a trust-less strategy of liberalization that may soon become an economic nightmare for the poor – but who is in charge of this complex issue of systems thinking, requiring an overall picture?

Insecurity is the–unwanted?–side effect of global vertigo, which corrupts traditional cultural values, producing dangerous consequences such as the secular disintegration of the family, weakening social values and cultural identities. Conformity–according to which everybody should be as alike and compliant as possible–suffocates uniqueness and originality.

In the cultural melting pot[326] that has been induced by globalization, it is increasingly harder for economically weak indigenous cultures to retain their identities, seriously risking to be left aside, especially if they find it hard to understand and practice rules-of-the-game imported from abroad and ill-adapted to local necessities.

In front of globalization, most of the underserved are poor spectators of a changing world, who are waiting for closeness and inclusiveness against worldwide poverty.

The historical pendulum of globalization, from autarky to openness, reminds that there are always winners and losers.

325 http://blog.gaiam.com/quotes/authors/john-naisbitt.

326 See Chapter 9.

Making globalization work with fair trade

Fair trade is a commercial partnership that is based on respect, cooperation and transparency and it aims to make all producers benefit from global commerce. Recent phenomena of globalization and free trade have been indeed extremely advantageous for big exporters such as multinational companies, but they have notably damaged small and medium-sized businesses, trapping into poverty many commodity-producers in developing countries.

Many organizations were created to support the Fair Trade movement. Their objective is to sell different kinds of goods (such as coffee, tea, cloths, nuts, cocoa ...) that are produced in decent working conditions and for which the producers receive a fair amount of money. The Fair Trade movement also works on a global campaign to ›make trade fair‹, mainly by making pressure on the WTO to have trade rules changed and by spreading awareness about how influent Fair Trade can be in eradicating poverty.

One of the key aspects of trade policies is that every nation must have the right to ensure itself food, the right to food sovereignty (claimed as one's right to define their own food, of an adequate quality and produced in a socially fair condition, in contrast to having food that is subject to international market forces), and every nation must have the chance to protect the most important sectors of its economy. However this is often not possible, for several reasons:

- subsidies and consequent dumping: rich countries continuously protect and support their own farmers with subsidies[327];
- commercial liberalization and structural adjustment policies generated a supply that was excessive if compared to the demand for many agricultural primary goods. The result has been a drastic decrease in the price that producers get paid, and sometimes the producing prices have exceeded over the actual product prices!
- developed countries are pressurizing for abolishing high custom duties that some poorer countries have established to protect small rising industries;
- extensive monocultures: one of the biggest mistakes made by the developed world that has caused the ongoing food crisis is to have destroyed the developing country's regional agricultural fields.

These phenomena have had a big influence on the lifestyle of third-world producers, and they are inevitably causing poverty. Organizations such as the

[327] Most subsidies are paid by the government to producers or distributors in an industry either to prevent the decline of that industry or to encourage it to increase its prices or to hire further labor.

WFTO (World Fair Trade Organization) have developed partnerships with the world's poor who have been weakened by the international trade system, to export and sell their products at a fair price.
Fair Trade groups set prices that can guarantee producers a minimum profit independently from market fluctuations. The price is decided together by the organization and the producer: the producer suggests a price that is then discussed and the organization must ensure that the price, a part from being fair, is kept competitive. A fair pay means the provision of socially acceptable remuneration considered by producers to be fair and which takes into account the principle of equal pay for equal work. Fair prices take account of commodity costs, apparatus used, labor, social and environmental expenses that a product requires. The profit must be partially used for local development projects.
There is a lot of evidence that Fair Trade has contributed to decrease poverty levels in many places around the globe. This fact is attested by research carried out by Fair Trade organizations. The interest to know if the Fair Trade system is really effective is shared between firstly producers, who must evaluate the advantages of this kind of marketing, secondly importers, who propose a different way of trading, thirdly consumers and NGO voluntaries, who want to see the positive results of their decision to consume fairly traded products, and finally also institutions, who must see how successful Fair Trade is in order to support organizations economically, as a means of tackling poverty. The impact is measured by interviewing the producers and their families and by carrying out surveys.
The book ›*50 Reasons to buy Fair Trade*‹, written by Miles Litvinoff and John Madley and first published in 2007, lists the main positive consequences of buying products with a Fair Trade label. The following list shows a few of the consequences, which are described in this book, that are having an extremely positive impact on the Human Rights situation in many poor villages and for many producers:

- ensuring plantation workers a fair wage (Article 23.2 – Everyone, without any discrimination, has the right to equal pay for equal work);
- empowering women and girls;
- sending children to school (Article 26.1 – Everyone has the right to education. Education shall be free, at least in the elementary and fundamental stages. Elementary education shall be compulsory …);

- improving health conditions (Article 25.1 – Everyone has the right to a standard of living adequate for the health and well-being of himself and of his family, including food, clothing, housing, and medical care and necessary social services …);
- preventing child labor;
- working in environmentally safe conditions (Article 23.1 – Everyone has the right to work, to free choice of employment, to just and favorable conditions of work and to protection against unemployment).

Fair Trade must no longer be restricted to fair trade shops. We can now find Fair Trade-labeled products in the aisles of every day supermarkets and shops, but much more must be done. On the one side consumers can play an important role by buying fair trade labeled products, and on the other side producing companies must evaluate their efforts in ensuring that they sell goods that are produced in safe and adequate conditions, paying a fair wage to primary producers and getting their products labeled by organizations such as the FLO (Fair-trade Labeling Organization). The Western world is a world of consumerism, and consumers have a notable power in conditioning trade rules. How? Thanks to products we buy every day. The more often we decide to buy Fair Trade – labeled products, the more progress will be done to ensure fairer retribution and poverty eradication.

The condensed Chapter

The world is rapidly flattening, becoming increasingly connected and moving capitals, goods, people, and technology as never before, with a mixed impact on poverty, creating unprecedented opportunities for those who can export to new markets but conversely increasing the gap–and the digital divide–between the haves and haves not.

Openness encourages growth but also contamination and instability and globalization makes us neighbors, not brothers, trapping the poorest in their misery and stressing inequality patterns, unless fair trade is adequately diffused.

The possible adverse effects of globalization bring to a polarized debate on the plight of the world's poorest: through greater openness to trade and foreign investment, the process of globalization could affect poverty in the developing world. On the other hand, a policy of excessive openness to external trade without complementary support mechanisms is negatively related to the depth of poverty.

Out of Poverty Tips

A disordered orchestra with unfit directors: this is the drama of globalization, whose trends are driven and imposed by the wealthiest, at the expense of the harmless poorest. Careful lifting of trade barriers, encouraging complementary specialization of countries and social classes, may eventually tune up the orchestra.

Selected Readings

BHARADWAJ A., (2014), *Reviving the Globalization and Poverty Debate: Effects of Real and Financial Integration on the Developing World*, Advances In Economics And Business vol. 2, n. 1: pp. 42-57, http://www.hrpub.org doi: 10.13189/aeb.2014.020107.

FRIEDMAN T.L., (2009), *Hot, Flat, & Crowded*, Penguin Books, London.

HARRISON A. ed., (2007), *Globalization and Poverty*, NBER, University of Chicago Press, Chicago.

SACHS J.D., (2008), *Common Wealth: Economics for a Crowded Planet*, Penguin Books, London.

STIGLITZ J., (2007), *Making Globalization Work: The Next Steps to Global Justice*, Penguin, London.

CHAPTER 12 – Wandering poor: is migration a dream or a nightmare?

> Our task (the rich countries), in our own interest as well as theirs, is to help the poor become healthier and wealthier. If we do not, they will seek to take what they cannot make; and if they cannot earn by exporting commodities, they will export people. In short, wealth is an irresistible magnet; and poverty is a potentially raging contaminant: it cannot be segregated, and our peace and prosperity depend in the long run on the well-being of others.
>
> David Landes, *The wealth and poverty of nations*

Exodus out of poverty?

When the poor realize that they are unable to solve their problems locally and that fight for survival may have an unhappy end, they unsurprisingly try–if they can–to move to healthier, wealthier and safer places.
Desperation often pushes the poor beyond man's sedentary nature–with all means, even on foot–to unknown places, where they typically arrive without money and with little idea of what to do, homelessly sleeping under the stars, migrating out of desperate regions. Relatives and friends attract and host newcomers, to the extent that they can help. Unsafe journeys of tired travelers are common, but the desire or necessity to sort out places that in some cases are open-sky prisons, is so strong that it brings poor migrants even in places that they should rationally avoid. With their traveling shoes or even barefoot, the desperate go somewhere and they hardly come back.
Permanent migration towards nowhere in the form of nomadic wandering was prevalent in ancient times, especially before the invention of agriculture, while now it is limited to gypsies, such as the Roma, mainly coming from the Balkans, or to nomadic pastoralism practicing transhumance, moving in constant

and erratic search of new pastureland, mainly in Central Asian steppe or in thirsty African countries.
According to the Human Development Report 2009[328] »there is a range of evidence about the positive impacts of migration on human development, through such avenues as increased household incomes and improved access to education and health services. There is further evidence that migration can empower traditionally disadvantaged groups, in particular women. At the same time, risks to human development are also present where migration is a reaction to threats and denial of choice, and where regular opportunities for movement are constrained«.
Migration is a core pillar of globalization, together with trade openness, capital mobility and sharing of technology[329] and it represents one of the hardest challenges of living together in an increasingly flat world[330]. No surprise that the topic is so crucial, controversial, and hotly debated – it is much easier and quicker to move capitals or goods or technology than people.
Since migration is such an unsurprisingly complex issue, we shall focus–coherently with our target–only on a small part of this vast topic, concerning its causal links with poverty, especially from the point of view of underdeveloped countries, which often involuntarily export their poor, with their ideals, worries, and hopes.
Is migration to dreamland–following a flight over fight paradigm–an escape from the misery trap and, if so, does it work? Is it poverty that causes migration or vice versa? Which is the nexus between migration and development? Can migration to richer places help native countries, through remittances or increased exchange?
Migration is often an expensive choice and migrants may be forced to save up for years in order to cover travel expenses. They have to mortgage their houses and run into debt their remaining relatives, who become involved in the hopeful business, expecting remittances and helping from abroad, but risking to be suffocated by indebtedness.
The psychological mood of migrants is a topic that is hardly going to be covered here, but that has an incredible–albeit often underestimated–importance. To name a few of them: are they happy in their new destination or incredibly homesick? Do they feel welcome and accepted or treated with suspicion and subject to racist discrimination? This last question has much to do with the degree and quality of their integration in host countries, among the most crucial topics of migration.

328 http://hdr.undp.org/en/reports/global/hdr2009/.
329 See Chapter 16.
330 ›*The World is Flat: A Brief History of the Twenty-First Century*‹ is an international bestselling book by Thomas L. Friedman that analyzes globalization.

And migration is a core pillar of the ongoing globalization process. It is a hot issue that can represent either a nightmare or an incredible opportunity, depending on how it is managed and dealt with. Making migration sustainable is the real challenge, one of the most defying of our joined lives.
According to art. 13 of the U.N. Universal declaration of Human Rights[331]:

> (1) Everyone has the right to freedom of movement and residence within the borders of each State.
>
> (2) Everyone has the right to leave any country, including his own, and to return to his country.

Combining the two commas of art. 13, it comes up immediately that the right to freedom of movement and residence wherever, outside one's own State, is not contemplated. But even with these limitations, migration–especially immigration–is still a hot issue, which closely depends on geopolitical factors, speeded up by globalization, which determine the path and the trends of individuals or populations that decide–or sometimes only unsuccessfully try–to move to better places.

The complexity of global migration problems

Migration towards wealth tends to reduce the arbitrage between the poorest and the richest, who represent two corner contexts with many possible intermediate gradations. This attempt is sometimes successful, especially if it adds value for the poor but also for the rich – a shared happiness is much easier to deal with. »Searching opportunities and a better life, migrants can speed up the developing process«, says UN Secretary–General Ban Ki–moon.
According to Rahman, Mizanur[332], poverty is seen as a motivating factor for international labor migration from many developing countries. Conventionally, international temporary labor migration is believed to be contributing to poverty reduction, because the remittances sent back by migrants are supposed to improve the economies of migrant families. However, recent trends suggest that ›the age of the great honey pots‹ is over, especially for unskilled migrant workers in Asia. In many cases, economic costs of migration even outweigh economic benefits. Now more migrants and their families are more worried about the economic outcome of labor migration than ever before. The existing migration literature does not adequately document this trend[333].

---

331 See Chapter 13 and http://www.un.org/en/documents/udhr/index.shtml#ap.

332 ›*Migration and Poverty: Ironies and Paradoxes*‹ paper presented at the annual meeting of the International Studies Association, Hilton Hawaiian Village, Honolulu, Hawaii, March 5th, 2005. http://www.allacademic.com/meta/p70165_index.html.

333 To capture the recent trend in labor migration, the paper introduces another type of interrelationships, that is, 'poverty as a result of migration'. Focusing on Bangladeshi temporary labor

The current literature identifies three types of interrelationships between migration and poverty:

1. poverty as a root cause of migration;
2. migration as the result of poverty;
3. migration as a cause of poverty.

Page and Adams (2003) have examined the impact of international migration and remittances on poverty in a broad cross-section of developing countries. Four key findings emerge:

1. International migration–defined as the share of a country's population living abroad–has a strong statistical impact in reducing poverty;
2. Distance to a major labor-receiving region–like the United States or Western Europe–has an important effect on international migration. Developing countries that are located closest to the United States or Western Europe are also those countries with the highest rates of migration;
3. Developing countries with low or high per capita GDP produce smaller shares of international migrants than middle-income developing countries do. Because of considerable travel costs associated with international migration, international migrants come from those income groups which are just above the poverty line in middle-income developing countries;
4. International remittances–defined as the share of remittances in country GDP–have a strong statistical impact in reducing poverty and they represent the human side of globalization.

According to Collier (2013), while low levels of immigration add some variety to life, large, unassimilated, and culturally distant blocs of immigrants reduce what the author calls ›mutual regard‹ and trust within a society-vital for the cooperation and redistributive taxation upon which rests the welfare state, thereby putting »these achievements of modern societies at risk«. At the same time, large numbers of incomers exert pressure on public goods like schools and social housing.

Migration and demography are close relatives, since imbalances in demographic trends can induce to arbitrage migration from overcrowded and overexploited areas to less populated ones with declining fertility rates, especially if labor force is required in the latter–typically richer–countries. Local economic growth

---

migration to Singapore, the paper demonstrates that labor migration causes the extension of poverty for a substantial number of migrants and their families in Bangladesh.

is the best antidote against migration, and it concerns in particular the ›brain drain‹ problem, illustrated later in this Chapter.

Migration is also increasingly concerned with global labor mobility, as a consequence of globalization. Shifts in types of industry create new work opportunities, while development and democratization in poorer economies have created a labor force that is more eager, and able, to migrate to take advantage of these opportunities. The result has been a significant expansion of global mobility[334].

Among the key factors concerning globalization[335], labor is more difficult to move than capital, goods, or technology, due also to more coercive covenants, frictions, costs of travel, and subsistence in a foreign country, including sunk costs of assimilation, etc.

Types of migration

Migration is a complex and manifold issue, with different varieties that create variegated problems. Migrants are typically complementary workforce in the host country, and they are not in competition with native workers – hence the strategic importance of migration.

The migrant is the human link that relates the source country with the host one. In the following table, the taxonomy of the main migration types[336] is briefly represented, in order to present an explanatory framework to the following considerations.

Table 12.1. – Types of migration

Types of migration	Characteristics
forced	It may be due to war, oppression, discrimination, famine, natural disasters, and displacement, bringing to migrant refugees and ousters, particularly vulnerable and looking for asylum. Mass migration often becomes a destabilizing avalanche.
voluntary	It is the unforced search for better job opportunities of any kind (from high to low skill), often temporary and possibly unrestricted in the host country (even if clandestine are typically volunteers … albeit undesired).
return	It means going back to the motherland again, driven by homesickness.

334 http://www.migrationdrc.org/research/typesofmigration/global_labor_mobili.html.

335 See Chapter 11.

336 See http://www.migrationdrc.org/research/typesofmigration/global_migrant_origin_database.html.

Types of migration	Characteristics
skilled	It refers to the brain drain phenomenon, due to which skilled migrants emigrate in search of better job opportunities, pauperizing their origin countries. It is typically legal, sometimes temporary, if homesickness and improved opportunities call migrants back.
internal	It is from countryside to town (rarely vice versa), following a chaotic urbanization trend, often seasonally.
abroad	It is typically long termed, sometimes with no return. It faces bureaucratic, linguistic, and logistic challenges. If concerned with skilled workers, it produces brain drain.
temporary	It is seasonal. Governments in both origin and destination economies are devising policies, independently, bilaterally, and multilaterally, that respond to this shifting global demand for labor. However, fears about the practical and political consequences of permanent settlement of migrants have led to renewed interest in temporary, rather than permanent mobility[337].
permanent	Distance discourages return and quality of life makes the difference.
lonely / with the family or clan	Migration impacts on social clusters. Clan abroad eases naturalization, providing first survival shelter.
for health purposes	It is typically temporary, depending on curses and recovery time.
for job purposes	It implies social mobility because of unemployment.
legal / illegal	The poorer the emigrant, the likelier illegal immigration is.

337 See http://www.migrationdrc.org/research/typesofmigration/.

Basic migration patterns are represented in Figure 12.1.

Figure 12.1. – Migration patterns

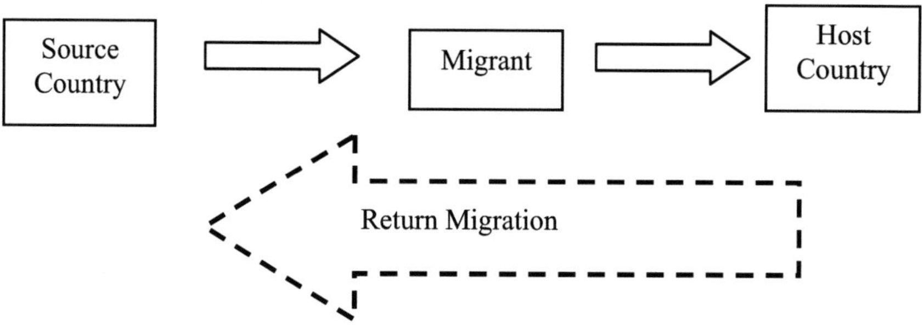

The town versus the country mouse: from rural poverty to urban slums

According to Aesop's fable, the country mouse, seeing the city mouse walking around the countryside, invited him to supper, and he fetched out all his provisions so that he could satisfy the sumptuous expectations of such a distinguished guest. But the city mouse disapproved the poverty of the countryside and he praised the abundance of the city, and he brought the country mouse back with him to town. In the midst of their feasting, however, the country mouse was panicked by the unfamiliar shouts. When he realized that this was a daily danger, he told the city mouse: »your banquets have more bitterness than sweetness. I prefer to be carefree in my poverty, than to be wealthy with your worries«[338].

This classic tale has his well known moral–a simple existence lived in peace is better than one of luxury lived in fear (beans and water in peace are preferable to cakes and wine in anxiety)–but in many cases countryside peasants, comparable to rural mice, are still attracted by the mirage of town, which is able to magnetize their dreams, typically well beyond any realistic expectation.

Internal migration–or sometimes emigration, crossing porous borders–from the countryside to bigger megalopolis, is a mass phenomenon, with disrupting and hardly manageable side effects, especially if it takes place in poor countries with ailing institutions and little public money to spend in integration, affordable housing and social services. Even the psychological aspects of living in a new environment matter, since life in cities is completely different and it can be a real cultural shock for the rural poor, albeit it is often softened by the presence of other members of the native community.

338 See http://aesopus.pbworks.com/barlow017.

Rural migrants, experimenting social and spatial mobility, behave like fearful creatures and they soon become rootless, trying to endure and to resist in a hostile and unknown environment, resulting from a collision between the rural and the urban.

In rural areas networking in its broadest sense (connections from roads to web) is consistently weaker than in more densely populated places, due to their higher difficulty to reach an economically viable critical mass for investments.

And the way back to an increasingly poor and backward native countryside is not–unlike in the Aesop's tale–a typically viable option, since the poor peasants, whether or not completely homeless, often remain stuck for the rest of their miserable life in the quicksand of big slums, where people try to survive packed tightly together.

Such disordered and off-world slums are typically built in unsafe and degraded last-choice places, unfit for living and at the outskirts of historical cities: they are the anteroom of hell–also known as *bidonvilles*, ghettos, *barrios populares*, *favelas*, shantytowns–and they are unplanned and self constructed neighborhoods for the destitute. These dehumanizing shantytowns are characterized by poor quality housing (with leaky roofs, dirt, and uneven floors, outdoor plumbing ...) and lack proper drainage, sewage and sanitation, or safe access to water, with narrow and chaotic roads, little social and health services, poor water and electricity. Lack of any rational housing policy produces an unhealthy environment that is particularly vulnerable to natural disasters, as the dramatic earthquake in Port Au Prince (Haiti) of January 2010 has painfully evidenced.

Overcrowded urban ghettos are historically born out of the decision to keep ethnic groups segregated, like the Jews since the Middle Age in many European towns such as Rome, Venice, or Warsaw. European quarters, with a black–and–white division, were also frequent during colonialism, while postcolonial counterinsurgency favored unprecedented urban growth.

Even historical centers, with old homes that are typically unfit for modern living, are often restructured, but by so doing they tend to expel their poor historic inhabitants, who become unable to cope with high prices and standards–the effect is paradoxical and it may make the poor even poorer. Emigrants keep with them an unconscious desire to rebuild their historical centers elsewhere–especially abroad–to preserve their geographical history and identity within Diaspora communities.

The desperate poor who, leaving their rural straw huts, are attracted in these no end places–with little outward mobility–are often illiterate, since they become street vendors with no permanent job or income and with limited tenure rights, frequently leading to forced evictions within squatter communities. Poor self helping typically does not suffice to solve complex problems, because it needs external enablers, starting from expensive housing redevelopment and infra-

structural upgrading, to cope with sanitation problems, schooling, healthcare, wild motorization, etc.
Proper planning of peripheral areas, which was once represented by greenbelts, is hardened by the irrational and uncontrolled proliferation of mushrooming anarchical suburbs. Landless women escaping the countryside are fatally attracted by often unavoidable choices and, they often end up practicing the … most ancient job, unless they can find a proper and decent shelter, gathering with relatives or clan members already there.
New smelly slums typically spring up disorderly, without any program and especially without invisible but essential recipes as soul or historical memory, and they bring their unlucky densely packed inhabitants to disorientation and lack of cultural continuity. No wonder that despair and violence sprout spontaneously, in such a gloomy environment, where life is hard and rural social ties loosen. As Riccardi (2008), p. 13, points out »the rebellious children of the suburbs are creating an elementary identity for themselves in reaction to their marginalization«.
Law and order administered by the central government or by local institutions is typically weak in the sprawling cities of the Third World, where centre and periphery are relative terms, and the vacuum is easily filled and replaced by criminal gangs, whose slumlordism threatens helpless residents, jeopardizing their daily life – already miserable on its own. Rural feudal landowners often have the economic power to become also city slumlords, where they easily attract their poor peasant ›clients‹. Housing speculation–to buy land for a bargain, to build, and to sell at high prices–is among the best shortcuts to easily make a fortune, but somebody has to pay the bill.
Human rights are not a priority and the poor who live in anonymous slums may be denied the right to vote, should they have no official address – a dangerous clue against clandestine pavement-dwellers, illegally surviving in flophouses or being completely homeless.
Nobody's land titling stands out as a long lasting poverty trap, suffocating development chances[339] and destroying tenure market value. Squatting consists of the grabbing of land without any sale or legal claim.
Solutions for improving the dramatic life of shantytown inhabitants range from ending forced evictions–that simply remove problems, instead of fixing them–to securing tenure rights and assuring basic infrastructures and order. Development is strongly needed, but it has–once more–to be grass-rooted, starting from the bottom of the social pyramid. Unplanned and chaotic urbanization, which is often promoted by wild industrialization, should be prevented improving living standards in the countryside, considering also that social ties tend to loosen in an urban environment, weakening already ailing social safety nets.

339 See Chapter 15.

In 2011, some 165 favelas surround Rio de Janeiro, representing pathologically degraded urban tissues that were improperly built with no prior geological surveys and without considering basic building criteria.
Nowadays more than half of the world's population already lives in towns and this percentage is likely to grow fast–up to 70% in 2050, according to some estimates–mattering also from a qualitative side, due to the concentration in big cities of economic activities and scientific innovation and of the best schools, universities, hospitals, transports, and other facilities.
Our planet is urbanizing fast, hardly remembering somewhat epic Victorian industrialization, and we now live in the age of cities, which are exploding beyond any imaginary boundary. As a consequence, it is now the city that migrates towards rural people, incorporating shrinking and imploding countryside, together with its evicted poor. Unprecedented urban poverty is disorderly mushrooming in unlivable slums which often recall Dante's *Inferno*.
Growing big towns are becoming increasingly interconnected, even physically and geographically, because of the expansion of the world's population. Increasing urban concentration produces continuous conurbation corridors linking several ›globalopolis‹ among them (e.g. San Paolo with Rio de Janeiro in Brazil, Ibadan with Lagos and Accra in Western Africa, Mumbai with New Delhi in India, or Nagoya-Osaka-Kyoto-Kobe in Japan). The impact on poverty of such a trend is not to be underestimated.
Poverty new frontiers are increasingly concerned with unlivable urban ghettos. According to Marx, Stoker and Suri (2013), the global expansion of urban slums - a transitory phenomenon characteristic of fast growing economies - poses questions for economic research as well as problems for policymakers.

Cosmopolitan migration routes

Migration is not geographically limited to South-North routes (from developing to industrialized countries) and, even if the contrarian North-South direction (from rich to less developed countries) is less crowded, South-South migration (between or within developing countries, moving towards the relatively richer and labor-seekers) is also popular, even within countries (eased by shorter distances, an often common language and culture, friendlier legislation)[340]. North-North migration (between industrial countries) has been popular especially within Europe (from Mediterranean countries to Northern ones, such as Germany). Emigration from ex colonies is preferably attracted by former colonizing

[340] For a graphical analysis of migration routes, see http://www.alterinfos.org/local/cache-vignettes/L374xH215/Map-6c722.jpg; http://www.people.hofstra.edu/geotrans/eng/ch7en/conc7en/img/map_globalmigration.gif.

countries, where immigrants might find some survival link (relatives, friend, a common language …).

Migration towards coastal areas is frequent, due the land-locking effect seen in Chapter 2, according to which regions far from the sea are often poorer, and it contributes to explain their overcrowded situation – examples range from China to Maghreb, along the Mediterranean African coast.

International migration is a fact and, to a large extent, it is the result of the lack of sustainable development in home countries, as observed by the Global Commission on International Migration[341]. It is furthermore encouraged by significant ›pull factors‹ that result from the growing labor demands and demographic shortages in the ›developed‹ countries.

In the age of globalization and integration of markets, international migration can therefore be a potentially interesting response for both countries of origin as well as countries of destination. But, even if the economic benefits of migration might be positive, we have to look at the costs and see what the impact is, not only in terms of the economy but also with respect to the social well-being of the people involved.

Kathleen Newland[342] claims that migration remains very much the exception rather than the rule of human behavior, which is predominantly sedentary – random migration, such as that of the Tuareg in the Sahara desert or of gipsy populations in Central and Western Europe is a peculiar exception. An overwhelmingly high number of people become habitués and they prefer to stay at home instead of migrating.

Why then does international migration suddenly loom so large on the international policy agenda? Much of the answer lies in the domestic politics of migrant-receiving countries and part lies in the abrupt demographic transition that the major countries of destination are going through. Another element concerns the consequences of human-capital flight. These and other factors add up to a heightened consciousness about the importance of migration as a force of globalization and economic change.

Understanding the causal relationship between rich country immigration policy and poor country development is a frustrating pursuit, hamstrung by the absence of data, that are frequently inaccurate, and lacking comparables.

If the causal link from poverty to migration is well evident–people irresistibly tend to move, as far as they can, from poor to richer regions–the impact of migration on poverty is less clear cut.

A key point in the understanding of the causal relationship between migration and poverty is represented by the impact of emigration on poor countries. The

341 www.gcim.org/en/.

342 ›*Migration as a Factor in Development and Poverty Reduction*‹, Migration Policy Institute June 2003, http://www.migrationinformation.org/USFocus/display.cfm?ID=136.

two most influential factors concern benefits represented by remittances counterbalanced by implicit costs due to the brain drain.

The remittances traps and opportunities

We have already seen other poverty traps, such as misuse of natural resources[343], the conflict trap[344], being landlocked with bad neighbors[345] or bad governance in a small country[346]. Remittances are part of the game, sharing with natural resources an ambiguous nature. According to how they are used, indeed they can be highly positive but also detrimental and in these cases it pays to be overcautious, examining well the possible outcomes of a phenomenon which is hardly controllable, since in many cases it follows an unofficial pattern.

As anticipated, the real problem about remittances–for what effectively matters here, that is poverty reduction–is how they are used by beneficiaries, in order to detect whether or not they are development catalysts. Remittances are a social obligation that is normally used to finance basic survival and consumption needs, such as children's education, purchase of food, basic healthcare, housing, or–to the extent that these primary needs are already satisfied–even small entrepreneurial businesses, with possible synergies with microfinance.

To the extent that figures are small and the amount per person is tiny (poor are so many ...), it seems unavoidable and realistic that beneficiaries will spend most–if not all–the proceeds for survival consumption, especially if they are very poor. The risk of relying only on remittances is strong and it represents a bad, wrong, and dangerous habit. It's really hard to start again, if bonanza money stops coming in–as it may happen for many reasons, since expatriates are not eternal and they also have their own problems to solve, typically not being particularly rich–and beneficiaries get lazy and stop working. Like a drug, remittances can create dependency and it is not easy to get detoxified from free money. Moreover, they can increase inequalities between the haves and haves not–not everybody has an American uncle ...–and they can encourage consumption of imports.

If, otherwise, money is enough to overcome survival consumption needs, the surplus can be properly invested, allowing also establishing commercial links with the sponsoring country.

Expatriates send money to their birth country and relatives there use it to invest in exportable products, with a commercial link with the foreign country eased by the same expatriates who send the money: such a mechanism can be benefi-

343 See Chapter 3.
344 See Chapter 5.
345 See Chapter 1.
346 See again Chapter 5.

characterized by increasing competition in science and technology. Forward looking hosting countries welcome foreign talents.

Competition to attract the best and smartest researchers is a lucid, forward looking strategy with high yield returns and positive spill over in the hosting country. These brains often come from former colonies with historical and linguistic links – irrespectively of their race, sex, religion, provenance, or other silly discriminatory prejudices. Anglo Saxon countries, traditionally excelling in science and speaking English, the common language–*lingua franca*–of the civilized world, deserve a natural advantage, even if American and British Universities are increasingly challenged by ambitious newcomers, such as India or China, which are well aware of the strategic importance of advanced instruction.

Many developed countries deliberately look for skilled migrants, planning accordingly their immigration policies. Skills and smart brains of whatever nationality are always a precious comparative advantage, if they are properly exploited.

Homesickness or patriotism sometimes calls back ›repented‹ brains, but the original country has to be not only attractive but also smart enough, after the honeymoon, to well exploit these marvelous opportunities.

Studying abroad is a not-to-be-missed chance – the author of this book is a happy and convinced cosmopolitan and learned neither English nor Finance in his marvelous birth country. Also emigration of brains is not necessarily a damage for their native country, provided that there are also foreign brains, properly attracted, that come in (statistics are deceiving and quality is better than quantity) and that the emigrated brains send ›intellectual remittances‹ back home. In this way it is possible to establish scientific links between the host and the native country and to attract young researchers eager to specialize in the best universities. Once again, we shouldn't forget that the world, if it is not flat, it is becoming flatter and science is by definition internationalized, helping itself with scientific discoveries, such as the Web, that are incredibly easing communications and exchange of ideas.

The problem is not brain drain, but more simply brain emptiness of the short sighted and lazy academics, bureaucrats and politicians that stay at home and miss one opportunity after the other meritocracy is a real threat for those who hardly deserve a job.

The loss of skilled brains imposes several different costs on their birth countries, such as the implicit cost of education. To the extent that they spend at home most of their school years and specialize abroad only at the end, after having passed a strict selection in their schools of origin, the obvious consequence is an asymmetric division of investments and proceeds, biased against the poor country. Even if it is difficult to measure, it's a net transfer from the

ing to build up a virtuous cycle, and one's belly doesn't have to be empty – only surplus money, beyond the survival yardstick, may realistically be invested.
The economic power of migrant remittances is affecting millions of households around the world, as a source of capital and support. In Asia, which accounts for more than half of the world's migrants, and in Latin America, remittances have helped to address the most basic needs of migrants' families and their communities. The challenge now rests in further transforming the potential of remittances into a sustainable input to poverty alleviation and development efforts.
The relatively small portion of remittances that are used for investment (apart from human capital investment through education and health spending) reflects not only the immediate consumption needs of poor families, but also the discouraging investment climate for the poor. Until such problems are tackled (as poor infrastructure, corruption, lack of access to credit, distance from markets, lack of entrepreneurial skills, and disincentives to savings), it is unrealistic to expect remittances to solve the problem of low investment in poor communities. In the meantime, remittances lift many recipients out of poverty, if only for as long as their flow up to the point continues.
Unlike foreign aid[348], remittances do not increase or fuel corruption.

Pain from the brain drain?

Whereas remittances are the major benefit of migration from the point of view of the source countries, the loss of human resources–particularly highly skilled and gifted people, the best and the brightest–is the most serious cost.
Brain drain or human capital flight[349] is concerned with emigration of individuals with precious technical skills or knowledge, normally due to conflict, lack of opportunities, political instability, or health risks. It is usually regarded as an economic cost, since emigrants usually take with them the fraction of value of their training sponsored by their native society. The converse phenomenon, within an overall zero sum game, is conversely represented by brain gain, which occurs when there is a large-scale immigration of technically qualified persons. Brain drain, which is common amongst developing nations, can be stopped by providing individuals who have expertise with career opportunities and giving them opportunities to prove their capabilities.
Brain drain is a hotly debated question even in Western countries, such as Italy–sadly among the exporters of brains–and it is gaining momentum in a world

348 See Chapter 14.
349 See ›*Brain drain - Definition and More*‹, Free Merriam-Webster Dictionary, 2010; http://www.merriam-webster.com/dictionary/brain+drain.

poor to the rich country, not exactly what humanitarian aid policies would suggest.

There are also implicit fiscal costs that are associated with the brain drain, since the country of origin loses the tax revenues that these potential high-earners would have paid into the national exhausted coffers, should they have stayed at home. But this apparently simple and intuitive argument is in reality more complex, taking into account the fact that without a foreign specialization, smart expatriated would have had an untrained brain, in an entrepreneurial unfriendly environment.

The net developmental losses of the brain drain are difficult to estimate, according to Migration Information Source[350]. Losses of highly skilled professionals are much more disgraceful where they are scarce. And ailing countries which are weakened by wars, corruption, hunger, and endemic underdevelopment, can easily get to a complete halt of their development, with a disastrous free-fall of the economy, due to the absence of a managing class. Some professional experiences are crucial for development.

But it shouldn't be forgotten that most of the people who emigrate, painfully fleeing their native country, are typically not represented by smart scientists, but simply by poor desperate, who are hardly welcomed by the target country – the secret dream of their sleepless nights, that is so different from the harsh reality that waits for them, but that is still normally better than the hell they leave behind them.

Newland (2003) admonishes that, despite the important numbers of remittances, many experts believe that labor migration does not significantly improve the development prospects of the country of origin. Source countries have had great difficulty in converting remittance income into sustainable productive capacity – but this is a micro problem, to the extent that money directly goes to the beneficiaries, without being intermediated by the government. In addition, most are able to exercise little control over the composition of their labor exports – rather, it is determined by the foreign labor markets, and may bear no relation to ›surplus‹ labor at home.

Successful expatriates often prove to be extremely smart (unsurprisingly even more than most Western students), since they have been able to go studying abroad starting from a very poor background and they have survived a particularly tough Darwinian selection. They just need to be given a chance, within a meritocratic and forward looking context.

As we shall see in the second part of this book, that is mainly devoted to specific microfinance issues related to poverty traps, microfinance institutions (MFIs) are continuously and desperately in need of skilled workers–like any other company or organization–in order to avoid Human Resources bottlenecks, re-

---

[350] http://www.migrationinformation.org/USFocus/display.cfm?ID=136.

membering once again that money, albeit necessary, has to be properly managed and that it is just a mean, not a target.
Skilled brains are consequently highly wanted and the circumstance that they have fled from poor countries is not itself a damage, provided that in their more developed new residences they make precious experiences–hardly ever possible in unsophisticated poor countries–which can be conveniently used in favor of native countries.

Clandestine vulnerability: low skill, low pay and low income

Clandestine routes of desperate poor who are escaping from their unlivable native countries continuously change, in order to circumvent repressive measures of richer destination countries, whose efforts are increasingly coordinated, since they require a shared intelligence system to contrast the phenomenon. The best antidote against uncontrolled migration seems to solve the problem at its root, creating development in poor countries.
Migration is a typically fluid and continuously changing situation and masses of desperate and clandestine ›low cost‹ foreign workers–so different from cheap airlines and representing the weakest ring of the social chain–randomly wander, looking for daily jobs and occasional accommodation in extemporary ghettos, in a deteriorated urban environment–a sort of ›nowhere o nobody's place‹–with little social aggregation and identity. Durable inequalities are by definition hardly left behind by hopeless migrants.
A corollary problem of the poorest migrants, who are often clandestine, is represented by their intrinsic vulnerability, both abroad but even at home: should they go or be sent back to the country they have fled from – when it rains, it pours … The reason of their vulnerability is somewhat obvious but for this reason it is not less painful.
When a clandestine normally arrives in the new country, he has no documents, little or any money, nowhere to go–unless some compatriots give him temporary shelter–and he is jobless, with few but … confused ideas! Since he is hardly part of the ›scientist club‹ of the much welcome foreign researchers–those who concur to cause the aforementioned brain drain problem–his arrival is not typically greeted and it should better happen unnoticed, in order to avoid expulsion.
Low skilled migrants find it harder to assimilate with the local population, due to segmentation factors such as culture, language, socio-economic conditions, residence (typically in the outskirts), closeness of the Diaspora ethnic clan, reminding that separation and discrimination may end up in violence.
Hostility can easily transform into overt xenophobia. Even due to the fact that unprecedented mass migration is nowadays an irrefutable reality, it doesn't pay

anymore to build up barricades and progressive integration. Learning to peacefully cohabit with people that we haven't freely chosen, albeit extremely difficult to put in place, is the only positive and necessary answer to an otherwise destabilizing issue.

When seeking for a home or a job, clandestine are easily blackmailed by landlords or employers who ask for high rents or pay low wages, nourishing a black economy where taxes or social contributions are simply ›forgotten‹. The ›low skill – low pay and low income‹ pattern is a common cliché, which in some countries is contrasted by lowest wage legislation, highly debated, and uneasy to extend to clandestine employment.

Problems come up also when the clandestine needs health treatment or whatever public service or if he is subject to controls. And, being guilty with his original sin of illegal immigration, he hardly can defend himself in a Court where he doesn't dare entering.

If a clandestine succeeds in saving up some money and sending it back home, don't expect that his remittances follow a legal transfer mechanisms, starting from a sending bank where he is not entitled to open an account!

According to the Human Development Report 2009[351] »national and local policies play a critical role in enabling better human development outcomes for both those who choose to move in order to improve their circumstances, and those forced to relocate due to conflict, environmental degradation, or other reasons. Host country restrictions can raise both the costs and the risks of migration. Similarly, negative outcomes can arise at the country levels where basic civic rights, like voting, schooling, and health care are denied to those who have moved across provincial lines to work and live«.

A racist and unwelcoming acceptance of humble and poor migrants is a common feature all around the world: natives are often afraid, intolerant, and suspicious and when the migrants are vulnerable and desperate, they often tend to breach the law. Hidden violence is potentially inside each of us. Cultural integration and assimilation is among the biggest challenges.

History shows that the way governments treat foreigners today will look like the treatment of their citizens tomorrow.

The Diaspora model and transnational networks with motherland

A Diaspora of permanently displaced and relocated collective, forming a stable ethnic group abroad, reminds us the departure of Jews from Palestine, their motherland, but it does not have an always sad meaning. People who meet out-

351 http://hdr.undp.org/en/reports/global/hdr2009/.

side their native country and establish a local community, often have a positive and well trained approach towards life and its challenges.
A land that welcomes and protects them–like the Promised Land for the Jews–is the mirage for many refugees. Disillusion is however frequent, especially if migrants dream up about a distant place they hardly know about, forgetting for a moment that life is hard everywhere. Resentment within renegades is likely to store up in exile.
According to Migration Information Source[352], transnational networks are not a new phenomenon, but they are relatively new as objects of interest to development analysts and policymakers. Jagdish Bhagwati[353] suggests that »a realistic response requires abandoning the ›brain drain‹ approach of trying to keep the highly skilled at home. More likely to succeed is a Diaspora model, which integrates past and present citizens into a web of rights and obligations in the extended community defined with the home country as the centre«.
According to Collier (2013), once a foreign Diaspora is established, obstacles to further immigration diminish, leading to an accelerating number of migrants from the country of origin.
Globalization on one side increases migration and its problems but on the other side it can provide unprecedented and innovative solutions, due to new incessant technological discoveries. Emails, chats and social networks, free intercontinental phone, and video connections through computer are an intangible dream which has become reality, together with faster, easier, and cheaper traveling – in an age of swift and cheap transportation and communication, emigration no longer represents the break with the home country that it once did[354].
Internet communications and social networks are increasingly linking physical with virtual communities, easing contacts and exchanges.
The governments of countries of origin are increasingly seeking to cultivate ties with the Diaspora communities, which are typically connected even among them, seeing them as a source of investment (flowing in money with remittances, capital investments …), overseas market openings, foreign exchange, expertise, and political support (in domestic campaigns as well as vis-à-vis the governments of their new countries of residence). This behavior, that is often opportunistic, proves particularly useful in promoting development in the native country – often members of Diaspora are much richer and skilled than those at home (think about the Jewish community in New York or many Chinese communities around the world.
Successful expatriates, who are proud of their conquered social status, are typically eager to tighten their ancestral bond with the motherland with foreign di-

352 http://www.migrationinformation.org/USFocus/display.cfm?ID=136.
353 ›*Borders Beyond Control*‹, in Foreign Affairs (Jan/Feb., 2003).
354 http://www.migrationinformation.org/USFocus/display.cfm?ID=136.

rect investments, often well beyond (for scale and engagement) remittances, with tourism, charities, fundraising for political candidates backing their Diaspora interests or their native land, consumption, and import of fatherland's products. Italian pizza is everywhere and by now produced locally, even if … not always with tasty results.
There is always a cultural enrichment meeting diversities: networks, relationships, links, exchanges, international trade with imports and exports, ethnic integration, together with a cosmopolitan attitude are small pieces of a unitary puzzle that can greatly contribute to the eradication of poverty in underdeveloped countries. Diasporas are in many cases an efficient form of business community where solidarity plays an important social role, enhancing development.
Should governments spend less energy and money in repression (on both sides, since also emigration is often forbidden, as sadly witnessed during the Soviet domination) and more resources in integration and networking, with development-friendly harmonized migration strategies and policies, we would certainly live in a much happier world, with a reciprocal solidarity and friendship overcoming hostility and diffidence towards what ignorantly we don't know.
According to Collier (2013), at present remittances sent home by migrants more than compensate for the brain drain.

The condensed Chapter

The poorest dream to flee away from the hell-on-earth where they come from, migrating to wealthier places which magnetize their hopes. Educated expatriates produce a brain drain phenomenon, exporting their intellectual knowledge, whereas unskilled workers, who are often clandestinely arriving in Western countries, are hardly welcome wherever they go.
Remittances to native countries soften poverty traps, since they establish useful financial and trading networks, albeit risking creating undue dependence on expatriated relatives, far from the eyes but not from the wallet.

Out of Poverty Tips

Poverty is borderless and wealth magnetizes everybody, especially the underserved. But dreams always have to face crude reality, starting from uneasy journeys and often unwelcome destinations.
Diaspora and social networks of expatriates belonging to the same clan do help desperate settlers.
Cultural assimilation is a cornerstone of mutual development, where immigrants really melt with inmates, paddling in the same direction.

Selected Readings

COLLIER P., (2013), *Exodus: How Migration is Changing Our World,* Oxford University Press, Oxford.

KAPUŚCIŃSKI R., (2001), *The shadow of the Sun*, Penguin books, London.

MARX B., STOKER T., SURI T.. (2013), *The Economics of Slums in the Developing World,* in Journal of Economic Perspectives, 27(4): 187-210.

CHAPTER 13 – Development as freedom: from human rights to economic liberty

> Development requires the removal of major sources of unfreedom: poverty as well as tyranny, poor economic opportunities as well as systematic social deprivation, neglect of public facilities as well as intolerance or over activity of repressive States.
>
> Amartya Sen, *Development as Freedom*

Poverty and unfreedom

Among the many factors that are supposed to interact with poverty, we may wonder if there is a place also for (lack of) freedom. In other words, is misery somewhat linked with unfreedom? If it is, which are the salient aspects of this relationship?
A first spontaneous answer may come from a slightly different questioning: are people in general more productive–and possible happier–when they are free to make their personal unconstrained choices, selecting them from the widest possible range?
The Indian Nobel prize winner Amartya Sen dedicated a book to ›*Development as Freedom*‹ (1999) and from his path-breaking research[355] we can derive useful hints, trying to answer to our preliminary question. Sen's main thesis is that economic development is in its nature an increase of freedom, which represents an enrichment of human life.
Development is deeply concerned with freedom, which enhances opportunities and enables capabilities. People–and especially the disadvantaged poor–deserve freedom and empowerment to be worth what they really value, and they go beyond economic income expectations and follow a holistic approach to liberty. John Rawls, elaborating his celebrated theory of justice[356], accordingly with this

355 See also Prendergast (2005).

356 In ›*A Theory of Justice*‹, Rawls attempts to solve the problem of distributive justice by utilizing a variant of the familiar device of the social contract. The resultant theory is known as ›Justice as Fairness‹, from which Rawls derives his two famous principles of justice: *the liberty principle* and *the difference principle*. The topic has been recently readdressed by Sen (2009).

vision talks about ›the priority of liberty‹ and justice, which is represented by the demand of fairness – fairness principles nicely cohere with a tangible idea of justice.

Empowerment enlarges the freedom of the marginalized poor to make free choices, trespassing social exclusion and enhancing human capabilities.

The intrinsic value of liberty, which is strictly connected with subsequent responsibility (making people accountable for what they do), cannot be overstated. Overcoming poverty is a struggle for freedom[357], which always has to remember the primacy of justice and law: ›*ubi societas, ibi ius*‹ – every society draws up its own system of justice, within its social contract. Even a small plant can become a protective tree of honest justice.

In 1962, the American Nobel Prize and monetary economist Milton Friedman in his book ›*Capitalism and Freedom*‹ makes the case for economic freedom as a precondition for political freedom.

For many aspects, the world we are living in enjoys unprecedented freedom: democracy and dialogue – an increased predisposition to listen to the reasons of the others. Even if with stops and go, such a world is gradually expanding among the some 190 world's countries and, with it, political freedom is gaining momentum.

But democracy (etymologically meaning ›rule by the people‹), as an empty shell, is often degenerating in a zero sum game in which an ethnic coalition wins at the expense of others, following a polarized majority rule – the winners take it all, above all when consensual governance and political compromise are absent. Inclusionary, moderate, and equitable institutions are–once again–greatly wanted but hardly present in young and weak democracies[358]. True democracy is concerned with the deep geography of people.

According to Pritchett and Woolcock[359] »a working democracy is [...] a messy collection of institutions that allocate, delegate, and limit powers«. Democracy, to be kept alive, has to continuously reinvent itself, following a dynamic pattern of innovation and adaptation to the new challenges. When democracy–concerned with men and the equilibrium of their governance systems–breaks down, citizens may suffer from ceaseless spasms of political instability. Hunger for democracy is a powerful spring to reach or recapture it, following the seductive ecumenism of peace.

Human rights issues are debated every day in every latitude and it is a mixed sign: positive since the issue is hot and considered important, but also negative since, should human rights be fully respected everywhere, it would be useless to discuss so extensively about the topic – and they find their cornerstone since

---

357 Khan (2009), p. 25.

358 See Chapter 5 for an analysis of institutions in a conflict environment.

359 In Easterly (2008), p. 166.

1948 in the U.N. Universal declaration of human rights. According to such a declaration, recognition of the inherent dignity and of the equal and inalienable rights of all members of the human family is the foundation of freedom, fair justice and peace in the world. »Everyone has the right to life, liberty, and security of person« (article 3).
Equality, strongly dependent on freedom, has been ironically described in ›*Animal farm*‹ by George Orwell, according to which »all animals are equal, but some animals are more equal than others«.
Poverty and unfreedom derive from lack of basic capabilities, such as freedom to have access to:

- basic education[360];
- elementary medical facilities;
- availability of lands[361] / resources.

Realizations and induced development both come out of given capabilities and freedom to exploit them.
Khan (2009), p. 69, underlines that »it is shocking that income too often determines whose rights are recognized and whose rights are ignored«, with an economic divide between the haves and the marginalized haves not. The poor are hardly autonomous or independent, and this fact typically ends up in lack of freedom, even if also the underserved have vested interests to defend, starting from a fairer allocation of resources. Are the poor, who are often passively obedient to authority, born to serve, following a master–and–slave paradigm?

Freedom is tolerance

Freedom is an uneasy concept to define, first of all in negative terms: it is concerned with the absence of any external restriction, while possibly clashing with others own liberty and so finding a natural limit in the ›no harm principle‹. It was so envisaged by the Victorian philosopher and economist John Stuart Mill, but it was already present in similar forms in the Gospel of Luke (§6:31) »Do to others as you want them to do to you«, following the Golden Rule or ethic of reciprocity or, according to the basic teaching of Confucius »never impose on others what you would not choose for yourself«. Poverty is, in practice, a form of unfreedom–poor liberty–since it doesn't allow people to fully enjoy the fruits of liberty, which is an empty shell if it is deprived of means to reach it.
Freedom is very much concerned with tolerance, which is also a troubled concept: it is well symbolized by Voltaire (as paraphrased by Evelyn Beatrice Hall

[360] See Chapter 9.
[361] See Chapter 15.

in 1906), when he proclaimed that »I disapprove of what you say, but I will defend to the death your right to say it«. Tolerance stands out as a real necessity (more than a form of respect) in a variegated and pluralist world where human diversities necessarily have to find a common synthesis and harmony within differences. Pluralist societies are consistent with ripe democracies. Religious tolerance is among the most difficult achievements, especially for those who are made blind and fanatic by their supposed superiority, especially if challenged by other different creed.

Freedom is actually a synonym of tolerance[362], the attitude of bearing with and being open to different beliefs, commitments, and actions of everybody else in matters of world-view, religion or other topics. Freedom ends where evil begins–subtly being represented by differences, diversity, minorities–and individual liberty finds its limit in other people's freedom. Today tolerance sets the very boundaries of liberty and dignity that every man needs.

Ethnic diversity often brings to unfreedom and intolerance and–as Khan (2009), p. 49, claims–»when migrants, women, or members of certain ethnic, racial, or religious groups are over-represented among the poor, and when they have disproportionately low scores on basic measures of human well being, it is almost certain they are being denied equality of access to rights and opportunities«.

Intolerance is often due to an excess of ethnic (or religious …) identity and it brings to morally repugnant discrimination and exclusion, and this denial of opportunities has a direct impact on poverty. Discrimination drives and deepens misery, especially if addressed to suffering minorities.

In 1995 UNESCO issued the declaration of principles of tolerance[363]: »Tolerance is respect, acceptance, and appreciation of the rich diversity of our world's cultures, our forms of expression and ways of being human. It is fostered by knowledge, openness, communication, and freedom of thought, conscience and belief. Tolerance is harmony in difference […]«[364].

The right to be happy is probably the ultimate human right, representing the difficult synthesis and the final goal of other bare survival rights. Is liberty something worth dying for?

Why democracy helps the poor

We may wonder which is the political form that most suits the needs and aspirations of the poor.

Khan (2009), p. 45, remarks that »giving the people who are affected a real say and genuine control over development options and outcomes is essential«. This

362 See http://www.hyoomik.com/lublin/tolerance.pdf.

363 http://www.unesco.org/webworld/peace_library/UNESCO/HRIGHTS/124-129.HTM.

364 Art. 1.1.

shareable vision is consistent with the grass-rooted bottom-up approach, so useful even to make effective foreign aid strategies[365].

According to Moyo (2009), p. 41, democracy–provided that it really works–offers the poor and disadvantaged the opportunity to redress any unfair distribution through the State. Economic growth is a prerequisite for democracy and not vice versa (p. 43). Under dictatorial rule, people don't need to think – all they need to do is to follow. Lack of freedom and personal and critical thinking hamper inventions and development. Political leaders should always be authoritative rather than authoritarian, since permanent and dictatorial addiction to unchallenged power suffocates democracy and freedom.

In a ruling system driven by democracy, with free and not-gamed elections, a free press and whatsoever, the poor can group together (this being neither a trivial nor a particularly frequent case), can easily reach the majority and rule the country, defending their own interests better than in other gloomier scenarios. But unsuccessful past experiences are gradually teaching to Americans and other Westerners that exporting ›forced democracy‹–an intrinsic contradiction–doesn't pay. People need to carefully prepare the ground for it, and it could take ages to do it, and it is highly advisable to let it grow spontaneously or, at least, endogenously.

Again, these logical passages deserve to be cautiously considered, far from being automatic, especially if the leaders of the underserved are poorly trained for the job, unskilled, overexcited, and populist. It is again the bingo curse: when you conquer something much bigger than you and your dreams, you soon discover to have thousands of previously unknown ›friends‹ and dreams are very likely to become unexpected nightmares.

Somebody considers economic needs more important than political freedoms, but, as Sen argues, the opposition is mostly illusory. He also reminds us that democracy, as well as being an end in itself, plays an instrumental role in giving people a voice and a constructive role in shaping values and norms. The significance of democracy lies in its intrinsic importance, in its instrumental contributions (to development …) and in its constructive role in the creation of long lasting values and norms, to be inherited by our children. Democracy is a cultural value that has to be properly transmitted to future generations.

To the extent that democracy is good for economic growth, it also has a positive effect on poverty eradication. According to Friedman (2009), p. 51 »a world of sustainable markets and environments is a world of abundance, and a world of abundance always favors freedom and democracy. It is much easier to give people the freedom to choose when there is plenty to choose from«.

Experience teaches that democracy can be encouraged and sustained, not artificially imposed.

---

365 See Chapter 14.

Democracy is neither ineluctable nor perfect and its expansion or regress follows alternate historical phases of ups and downs, even if the trend seems encouraging.

Freedoms ... are many

Sen magisterially links the lack of what he classifies as complementary ›substantive freedoms‹ with economic poverty. The first are political freedoms (free speech and elections among competing parties, uncensored press), economic opportunities (for consumption and participation in trade and production), social opportunities (education and health facilities), transparency guarantees (freedom to deal with others under guarantees of fairness and disclosure) and protective security (social safety nets, from pensions to social insurances). The latter (economic poverty) deprives people of the freedom to satisfy hunger or to achieve sufficient nutrition or to obtain remedies for treatable illnesses or the opportunity to be adequately clothed or sheltered or to enjoy clean water or sanitary facilities. What we are used to take for granted in developed countries is often a dream in the poorest areas of the world.
Sen argues for a broad view of freedom, that encompasses both processes and opportunities, and for recognition of »the heterogeneity of distinct components of freedom«. And freedom is much concerned with the possibility of making unchallenged choices in many contexts: political parties, opportunities of employment, residence, kind of instruction, marriage (avoiding weddings ›combined‹ by the relatives, where social interests prevails over love – in contrast with article 16:2 of the Universal Declaration of Human Rights, according to which »marriage shall be entered into only with the free and full consent of the intending spouses«), and so on. Free choice is much concerned with comparisons, in a sort of ›beauty contest‹ where citizens can select case by case the best option, enhancing healthy competition.

Survival liberty

The most elementary freedom is of course the ability to survive[366]–seriously threatened in extreme contexts such as famine–rather than succumb to premature mortality. Basic freedom is threatened and undermined by the persistence of extensive hunger in a world of unprecedented prosperity. This paradox is caused by a mixture of selfishness, indifference, superficiality, and cynicism, which are so diffused in opulent nations, where artificial barriers keep the poor aside from the life of the rich – what the eye does not see, the heart does not grieve over.

[366] According to Article 3 of the U.N. declaration of Human Rights, everyone has the right to life

With adequate social opportunities, even the poor can effectively shape their own destiny and friendly help each other, going beyond deeply rooted social inequalities, especially where castes are strong and social mobility limited, such as in India, and the harsh material limitations of an often cruel environment, individuals – being freed up to take their own choices. Freedom is a principal determinant of individual initiative and social effectiveness, bringing to liberalism. Conversely, deprivation of individual capabilities, due also to unfreedom, has strong links with low income, which can be a major reason for poverty consequences (hunger, illiteracy, illnesses …).

Unemployment is another form of unfreedom, since it brings to social exclusion, as well as an economic deprivation, of the labor seekers, with psychological drawbacks deriving from losses of self-reliance – everybody needs to be felt useful. In the absence of social subsides, unemployment tends to exacerbate poverty, which is often transformed into hopeless misery.

Poverty often brings to social exclusion, exacerbated by the very fact that the poor tend to be shy, ashamed by their condition, and they try to hide and disappear, making hard and underestimated the identification and solution of their problems.

The usefulness of wealth lies in the things it allows to do and it is directly linked with development, although an adequate conception of development goes far beyond a mere accumulation of wealth. Again according to Sen (1999), p. 14 »[…] has to be more concerned with enhancing the lives we lead and the freedoms we enjoy«. Freedoms have an intrinsic value, which is often concealed by that of utilitarian targets such as income and wealth, easier to measure and to reach but far more short sighted and incomplete.

In developing countries, the concept that poverty is simply a shortage of income, conjugated with an absence of stored income (capital) is more vividly understood than elsewhere – and (lack of) income has an enormous impact on what we can (not) do. Inadequate income is a strong predisposing condition for an impoverished life, which is identifiable in terms of capability deprivation[367], influenced also by other factors, such as the age of the person, his/her level of instruction and skills, gender and social roles, location, health, environment, and once again what the ancient Romans used to call the blindfolded Goddess – luck. Poverty is due to both capability inadequacy and to lowness of income, two different but often converging concepts.

Distribution of income within the enlarged rural family clans contributes to complicate the matter, already complex on its own.

As depicted by Sen, freedom, in its largest sense, is both a primary end on itself and the principal means of development.

[367] Sen (1999), p. 87.

Market freedom

Economic freedoms are also concerned with the opportunities of transaction in a free market, which are often subject to arbitrary controls with undue restrictions to competition, which make it opaque, unfair and severely biased.
The role of the market in economic development is necessary but not sufficient, since it is focused on private goods, while the provisioning of public goods goes beyond the market, such as basic health, instruction, and infrastructures, justice and other non tradable primary needs. Far from being an impartial spectator, the market–driven by greedy individuals behind it–is often an active participant to the game, shaping its rules according to the interests of its puppeteers. Private and public goods are of course complementary and empirical evidence shows that private markets are hard to develop without basic public goods: who would invest in a country with no roads, illiterate people and no health coverage? Certainly capitalistic entrepreneurs would not.
Markets interact with liberty and labor: a free market enhances liberty and promotes occasions for employment, since it is not constricted by artificial regulation and impediments but it is also regulated, in order to avoid abuses and rent seeking from Schumpeterian monopolistic positions. The three parameters go together, towards desirable or unwanted destinations, with an undetermined number of possible combinations. Sailing towards safe harbors is difficult and risky, considering that the wind frequently and randomly changes its direction and speed. Continuous repositioning, with trials, errors and corrections, is both advisable and wise.
The role of markets, so important for economic development, depends not only on what they do, but also on what they are allowed to do.
Whereas unfreedom sabotages development, economic liberty is very much concerned with the ›market trap‹, an expression used by Khan (2009), p. 110, in order to describe the expectation that the market is able on its own to get the destitute out of poverty. This may happen, following a liberal *laissez faire* policy, without requiring the intervention of the State, even for what concerns the respect of individual and collective human rights, which is delegated again to the market and to its self regulating forces and mechanisms.
Poverty is also concerned with the inability to develop one's potential. It is a form of unfreedom and deprivation, both physical and cultural, longing for material and intellectual liberty.

Social opportunities

Social opportunities such as education and healthcare are the cornerstone infrastructures of development and we can draw useful lessons from history again[368], which contrast the thesis according to which human development is luxury affordable only by richer countries.

Sen develops the basic idea that enhancement of human freedom is both the main object and the primary means of a long lasting and stable development. Individual capabilities crucially depend on economic, social and political arrangements, among other things.

Freedom is not a dogmatic and fixed concept and it necessarily has to be adapted to various circumstances[369], albeit preserving its core values, considering for instance:

- personal heterogeneities – people have disparate physical characteristics, which are connected with disability, illness, age, or gender[370] and this makes their needs diverse. We are not all the same (… »together we stand, divided we fall«[371]) and we need and deserve, wherever possible, a ›tailor made dress‹, which fits our peculiar and changing situation;
- environmental diversities – climatic circumstances strongly influence needs, expectations, and style of life, as well as the epidemics. It is a concept well depicted also by David Landes (1999)[372], who has long investigated about the by products of nature's inequalities;
- variations in the social climate – the world changes fast and our life continuously try to adapt accordingly. Quality of life is influenced also by social arrangements and by changing environment, considering for instance the impact of globalization, due to which we increasingly share technology, development, but also worldwide pollution and terrorism;
- differences in relational perspectives – it is not the same to be poor in a rich country or in a poor one . The psychological aspects of self confidence and relationship with the others are a cornerstone of human behavior, influenced by experience and shaping for the good or the worse our level of happiness;

---

368 See Chapter 1.
369 Sen (1999), p. 70.
370 See Chapter 11.
371 From ›*Hey You*‹, a Pink Floyd's song.
372 See Chapter 1.

- distribution within the family – intra-family (or within the enlarged clan) sharing and showing solidarity is often a matter of survival, as well as social justice. Atomizing families are increasingly spreading, with the disruption of the patriarchal model, not always for the better, only where individuals can cope with these new social models, in the transition from a rural and poor enlarged family towards a smaller entity, wealthier, and urbanized. Distributional rules within the family are related to social conventions, depending on gender or age or perceived needs and are highly dependent on different cultures and environments.

Freedom becomes an even more delicate issue when dealing with disadvantaged persons (disabled, ill, old, otherwise handicapped), who are hardly able to be productive and too weak to require respect for their rights, which become even more commanding, trying to balance physical misfortunes. The unfortunate link between disability and poverty is often strong (›when it rains, it pours‹), especially where social safety nets are absent or hardly working. Solidarity is highly wanted.

According to Khan (2009), p. 69 »countries with some of the highest inequalities in income are also countries where significant segments of society do not enjoy human rights«.

Global freedom in a www scenario

Freedom is nowadays also greatly influenced by globalization, with a controversial twofold impact: on the one side, globalization, driven by Western ›democratic‹ countries, export free ideas and behaviors (the very essence of globalization is born indeed from freedom to trade, move capitals and travel), even with new powerful devices such as the Web, while, on the other side, its standardizing and centripetal force tend to uniform ideas, unfortunately not always the best ones, threatening native cultures and ›biodiversities‹. As a consequence, the world is becoming more homogeneous but also flatter – ›*The World is Flat: a Brief History of the Twenty-First Century*‹ is an international bestselling book by Thomas L. Friedman that analyzes globalization, primarily in the early 21th Century.

With globalization, human rights' ›quantitative‹ expansion is somewhat fatally diluting their intrinsic quality. The U.N. declaration of human rights is ›universal‹ but its practical application shows important differences and problems from place to place.

Cross-cultural communication and worldwide pollination of new ideas and devices–such as microfinance or so many scientific discoveries–are however incredibly useful and they have a path breaking impact even on freedom. Science is easier to export than ideas, since its universal application, applying the Galilean scientific method of replicability, and reduces the possibility of different outcomes. But problems come out when scientific discoveries and technological devices are used by different populations (we have already seen the perceived dangers of the Web in China but there are many other examples, often concerning genetics, from modified food to even more controversial human manipulations, somewhere accepted and elsewhere abhorred).

Among the most uniform global items, technology commands a premium[373]: it is widely perceived that while languages, religions, or social habits preserve important differences, everybody is universally attracted by the same technologies. We all live in an iPad world and social media have an extraordinary and unprecedented importance in spreading freedom, ideas and, possibly, even democracy. And the Maghreb upheavals of 2011, with their domino effects, are a clear evidence of the importance of real time videos and news, nowadays stronger than any censorship.

From tyranny to demo-crazy?

The idea to export democracy is in itself a good and deserving one, but it is too simplistic and especially it tends to be applied too fast, with little or any graduality, forgetting the lessons of Western history. Such a history should remind us that the walk towards still imperfect democracy has been winding and painful even in now developed countries, taking long centuries of preparation and fine tuning, with ups and downs, as democracy was alternated, in dark moments, with dictatorship – if only we think about Hitler in Germany.

And transition to democracy, following several distinct steps, is proving incredibly difficult even now, as it is painfully witnessed by Russia after the collapse of the Soviet Union, or by Iraq or the ailing and fragile democracies of some South American or Asian countries or, even more, by the puzzle of so many African countries, that are still poised between their historical political rural fragmentation and the painful construction of national identity, eventually phasing out from their colonial troubling experience.

Liberal democracy is a typical Western idea, that is not culturally shared and so it is difficult to adopt elsewhere – and different social contracts between rulers and their citizens are continuously being experimented all around the world. A revised form of the Western social contract[374] should embrace also the poor, moving beyond its original elitist vision, adapting Socrates and the original enlightenment philosophical theories (of Hobbes, Locke, Rousseau) to the nowadays context (as John Rawls and Amarthya Sen has magisterially tried to do).

[373] See Chapter 16.

[374] Social Contract Theory, nearly as old as philosophy itself, is the view that persons' moral and/or political obligations are dependent upon a contract or agreement between them to form society. See http://www.iep.utm.edu/soc-cont/.

Lack of democracy proves as dangerous as its forced and intrinsically contradictory implementation – beware of simple solutions to difficult problems, remembering that shortcuts are seductive but dangerously short sighted.
Democracy is a bit more complicated that a new product–such as a mobile phone device–to be exported, appreciated and used, since it requires a long and painful process of preparation and progressive cultural adaptation, without which it is inevitably deemed to be considered as an artificial system of government, far from the local historical experience and unsurprisingly uneasy to be understood and accepted. Counterweights matter and they are a core constituent factor of democracy, but again they need time to develop as antibodies to tyranny, since they are enabled to flourish where freedom from fear is allowed to spread.
New systems, ideas and lifestyles always need to be culturally digested and assimilated, otherwise they create disappointment and confusion – we instinctively tend to reject what we don't understand. As Machiavelli recalls in his masterpiece *The Prince*[375] »the innovator has for enemies all those who have done well under the old conditions«. Tyrants and their courtiers are unsurprisingly hardly supposed to be enthusiast about what is due to destabilize their autarchic system of power, abolishing their selfish and unjust privileges.
When the country is divided by ethnic rivalries, the matter gets even more complicated, since tribal identities and clashing interests prove incredibly difficult to compose and settle down, for the sake of superior common democratic interests. These ideals do not belong to a cultural heritage of ethnic divisions and local self ruling, and they are atomized in small places, hardly linked among themselves, and each being governed by its own king or village boss, that command an ancestral loyalty.
When democracy is abruptly and artificially imposed from outside, it is often quite far from any ideal model, bringing to confused and instable forms of cohabitation that Paul Collier (2010) has acutely nicknamed ›democrazy‹. Relapses to tyranny, disorder, and chaos are unsurprisingly frequent, and downs often outweigh ups, to the dismay of superficial Western idealists, that are unable to understand why things go wrong abroad even if they shouldn't, mainly because they have forgotten the hard lessons of their own rough history. Long lasting democracy dislikes shortcuts since it is a not ephemeral cultural process and it is never a free ride.

375 http://www.constitution.org/mac/prince06.htm.

Subsidiarity, the third complementary way beyond failing States and missing markets

Imperfect and self-referential markets, which are often dangerously detached from the real economy, are not balanced by perfect governments. Subsidiarity can contribute to freedom, filling at least some of the gaps between the State and the market. Capitalism suffers both from a crisis of accumulation, as a consequence of the barriers to the expansion of surplus value due to the increasing costs of production, resources, and technological limits to production, and from a crisis of legitimacy, due to its intrinsic socio-economic limits.

The issue, dealt with in Chapter 14 for its impact with foreign and domestic aid, is unsurprisingly complex and it still needs to be well analyzed, even if it already shows its benefic potential.

According to Collier (2009), p. 201 »sovereignty is best lodged at the lowest level to achieve its function«, so recalling the principle of subsidiarity, which is much less intrusive and respectful of individual freedom than other decision models and is able to promote local democracy, decentralizing power and getting closer to the microfinance area of intervention.

The main problem concerning the capitalistic vision of unmitigated free market and its irrational exuberance is that in many cases it dramatically fails to serve the poor and to solve their problems, with its greedy and unequal sharing, where immediate and short-sighted profit[376] maximization emerges as the leading target, regardless of other nobler social aims. Market forces are driven by greed, remembering the famous statement of Adam Smith, who in his *Wealth of Nations* conceded that »It is not from the benevolence of the butcher, the brewer, or the baker, that we can expect our dinner, but from their regard to their own interest«, forgetting that consumption is a survival means, not a self explicating destiny.

The celebrated ›invisible hand‹ acts behind self interest that pushes individuals and combines their aggregate efforts and is ideally supposed to bring to overall enrichment, benefiting the society as a whole. But market failures and imperfections, which are so dramatically present in every day's life should make people more conscious and suspicious. The Platonic ideal according to which the market is self-correcting and efficient seems exciting and so difficult to extirpate, albeit proving wrong, as wealthy States if the world typically do.

The border between self interest and pure selfish greed is both subtle and slippery. John Maynard Keynes admonished that »the market can stay irrational longer than you can stay solvent«. And people tend to be predictably irrational.

Market price is the nexus and the equilibrium point between demand and supply, but when both are limited by the inability to pay whatever price–typical of

[376] Looking at its etymology, profit derives from the Latin *pro facere*, meaning ›act in favor of‹.

the poor–the cornerstone of market economics breaks down and something else is needed to fill the gap. In rich countries, the poor witness their contradictory heresy, which testifies the improper workings of market rules.

Again Keynes–who is possibly the most influential and controversial economist of the 20th Century–prophetically used to say that markets are neither perfect nor self-regulating. Even small market imperfections matter[377].

(Failing) markets cannot be faithfully trusted to solve all problems. They fail when the (uninteresting) poorest are excluded or when private aims do not match with the public interest. Mixed economies, combining free market with State intervention, may make it better.

Non-market goals may demand for additional creativity, since they go beyond bare profit maximization strategies and they are hardly measurable in cash terms. And to the extent that the poor are moneyless–by definition–and so unable to pay, they immediately become uninteresting and neglected by the market, magnetized by wealth, not by misery. Impatient markets have other drawbacks, because, for instance, they typically don't immediately reflect ecological and demographic problems, underestimating negative externalities, since they are difficult to detect and reflect in market prices[378].

The State should fill market gaps and go beyond its failures, promoting public good and aligning sustainable development with private interests. But it is evident to everybody–for so many complex and interacting reasons that have been synthetically recalled in Chapter 5–that States, especially in poor and undemocratic countries, are inefficient, corrupted, and often even greedier than the market. While market forces tend to neglect the poor, the State, supposed to help them, often becomes their worst enemy, showing a creeping hostility that the underserved are too weak to contrast. Social insurance is a state function that is mostly needed by the poor and social spending reduces poverty and inequalities, but it is expensive, demanding adequate financial coverage.

According to Sachs (2009), p. 220, public intervention–to be financed with available public funds, issued debt, or foreign help–is linked with the help for the destitute, provision of key infrastructure, sound business environment (with legal and judicial working systems[379]), social insurance (linked to help for the poorest and vital in particular for the underserved), technology, and environmental friendship. The institutional framework, which has been pessimistically examined in Chapter 5 dealing about its failures, is the backbone of public intervention, which ideally resist beyond expiring politicians.

Subsidiarity is an organizing principle according to which matters ought to be handled by the smallest, lowest, or least centralized competent authority. As a

377 See Stiglitz (2010), Chapter 9.

378 Sachs (2008), p. 35.

379 See International Development Law Organization, http://www.idlo.int/.

corollary, functions of government, business, and other activities should be as local as possible. If a complex function is carried out at a local level just as effectively as on the national level, the local level should be the one to carry out the specified function.
The principle of subsidiarity is based upon the autonomy and dignity of the human individual, and it holds that all other forms of society, from the family to the State and the international order, should be in the service of the human person.
The principle of subsidiarity is accordingly defined in Article 5 of the Treaty establishing the European Community. It is intended to ensure that decisions are taken as closely as possible to the citizen and that constant checks are made as to whether action at Community level is justified in the light of the possibilities available at national, regional, or local level. Specifically, it is the principle whereby the Union does not take action (except in the areas which fall within its exclusive competence) unless it is more effective than action taken at national, regional, or local level. It is closely bound up with the principles of proportionality and necessity, which require that any action by the Union should not go beyond what is necessary to achieve the objectives of the Treaty.
Person to person connections are a typical feature of subsidiarity, a concept frequently mentioned in the encyclical letter Caritas in Veritate[380] (§ 47; 57; 58; 60; 67).

From lack of capabilities to poverty

Lack of basic capabilities is a form of unfreedom which prevents development. According to the DAC Guidelines on Poverty Reduction[381], poverty is due to the shortage of core capabilities, that indispensable in order to improve the living standards, such as:

- economic capabilities – the ability to earn a decent income, to consume and to have assets, which are all essential to food security, material well-being, and social status;
- human capabilities, based on health, education, nutrition, clean water, and shelter. Disease and illiteracy are barriers to productive work, and thus to economic and other capabilities for poverty reduction. Reading and writing facilitate communication with others, which is crucial in social and political participation. Education, especially for girls, is considered the single most effective means for defeating poverty and some

380 http://www.vatican.va/holy_father/benedict_xvi/encyclicals/documents/hf_benxvi_enc_20090629_caritas-in-veritate_en.html.
381 http://www.oecd.org/dataoecd/47/14/2672735.pdf.

of its major causal factors, for example illness–in particular AIDS–and excessive fertility[382];

- political capabilities include human rights, a voice and some influence over public policies and political priorities. Deprivation of basic political freedoms or human rights is a major aspect of poverty. It includes arbitrary, unjust, and even violent action by the police or other public authorities that are a serious concern of poor people. Powerlessness aggravates other dimensions of poverty. The politically weak have neither the voice in policy reforms nor secure access to resources required to rise out of poverty;

- socio-cultural capabilities concern the ability to participate as a valued member of a community. They refer to social status, dignity, and other cultural conditions for belonging to a society which are highly valued by the poor themselves. Participatory poverty assessments indicate that geographic and social isolation is the *main* meaning of poverty for people in many local societies. Other dimensions are seen as contributing factors;

- protective capabilities enable people to withstand economic and external shocks. Thus, they are important for preventing poverty. Insecurity and vulnerability are crucial dimensions of poverty with strong links to all other dimensions. Poor people indicate that hunger and food insecurity are core concerns along with other risks like illness, crime, war, and destitution. To a large extent, poverty is experienced intermittently in response to seasonal variations and external shocks – natural disasters, economic crises and violent conflicts. Dynamic concepts are needed because people move in and out of poverty. Today's poor are only partly the same people as yesterday's or tomorrow's ones. Some are chronically poor or inherit their poverty, while others are in temporary or transient poverty.

Poverty and human rights

Poverty is a key problem of human rights. The causal link between poverty and (lack of) human rights is subtler but not less destructive than other more overt breaching such as violence or torture.
According to Khan (2009), p. 3 »current global efforts to end poverty pay lip service to human rights, but include no serious attempt to make rights real«.

[382] See Chapter 10.

Accountability for human rights is a mainstream–albeit neglected–target for development.
Human rights have an important economic side, but they go well beyond it: they are universal. Human rights, strongly related to lack of dignity, refer to the »basic rights and freedoms to which all humans are entitled« and they allow people to be in control–rather than powerless victims–of their own destiny, with a self determination capacity. The 30 articles that the U.N. Universal declaration of human rights can be split into two groups:

1. civil and political rights – They include the right to life and liberty, equality, and expression;
2. economic, social, and cultural rights – They include the right to have access to food and water, the rights to work and education, and other rights that are linked to culture.

The Universal Declaration of Human Rights and the International Covenant on Civil and Political Rights form the so-called ›*International Bill of Human Rights*‹. World War I and World War II atrocities mainly brought governments to establish the United Nations, in 1948 and, secondly, the Universal Declaration of Human Rights. This regulation occurred because governments and institutions, devastated by the war-caused disasters, felt the need to rebuild in a more solid and pacific way what had been destroyed throughout the two world wars.
Precedent documents to the Universal Declaration of Human Rights were the Magna Charta (1215) of Medieval England–a cornerstone in the history of democracy–the Bill of Rights (1689), issued by the English parliament, the American (1776) and the subsequent French (1789) declarations of independence, albeit valid only locally. What was needed was a universal declaration that should have influenced not only a country but all countries, shaping common principles to be shared.
According to the U.S. declaration of independence »we hold these truths to be self-evident, that all men are created equal, that they are endowed by their Creator with certain unalienable Rights that among these are Life, Liberty, and the pursuit of Happiness«.
On December 10, 1948, the Universal Declaration of Human Rights (UDHR) was adopted by the 56 members of the United Nations. The vote was unanimous, although eight nations chose to abstain.
The influence of the Universal Declaration of Human Rights in modern laws has been substantial. Its principles have been incorporated into the constitutions of most of the more than 185 nations that are now in the UN. Although human rights come as a declaration, which is not a legally binding document, they have achieved the status of customary international law because it is considered a

common standard of achievement for all people and all nations. So the idea, on which the universal declaration is built up on, is the consciousness that all governments and institutions must respect individuals' dignity.
In 1966 the UN adopted:

- the International Covenant on Economic, Social and Cultural Rights[383], which commits its parties to work toward the granting of economic, social, and cultural rights to individuals, including labor rights and rights to health, education, and an adequate standard of living;
- the International Covenant on Civil and Political Rights[384], which commits its parties to respect the civil and political rights of individuals, including the right to life; freedom of religion, speech, and assembly; electoral rights and rights to due process and a fair trial.

According to Khan (2009), p. 104, the split of the aforementioned two treaties has puzzled the strategies for spreading human rights: »the categorization of rights has lent credence to the view that some rights can be prioritized over others«, forgetting that only a comprehensive approach can tackle the different aspects of poverty and human rights. »We can create a virtuous cycle of rights to end the vicious circle of abuse« (p. 224). »A human rights plan to end poverty must necessarily look at deprivation and exclusion, insecurity, and voicelessness« (p. 226).
Human rights are formally guaranteed by the international law »designed to give people the means to protect and demand their rights, as claims on those exercising power«[385]. According to the U.N. Initiative on Legal Empowerment of the Poor »the rule of law refers to a principle of governance in which all persons, institutions, and entities, public and private, including the State itself, are accountable to laws that are publicly promulgated, equally enforced, and independently adjudicated, and which are consistent with international human rights norms and standards«[386].

Development is a human right

Human rights are often seen as something detached from development, very often described in terms of income, resources, and consumption – consequently, economic growth is often seen as the only solution to poverty. Growth is doubtlessly essential for development, but not on its own, since it is a necessary com-

[383] http://www2.ohchr.org/english/law/cescr.htm.
[384] http://www.hrcr.org/docs/Civil&Political/intlcivpol.html.
[385] Khan (2009), p. 203.
[386] http://www.undp.org/legalempowerment/.

ponent but not an exclusive one. It needs to be complemented by other soft factors, not always properly measurable, such as human rights.

Human rights need to be put at the centre of the debate on development and they need to be taken in mind when dealing with any development plan, because human rights violations aren't only a consequence of poverty – they are also a cause. Describing poverty only in terms of income means agreeing that the only solution is making income levels increase; respect of human rights is not considered as it should an important element of an ideal ›developed‹ country. However, when people living in poverty are asked to talk about their situation, they insist on the fact that their children don't go to school, on the general situation of insecurity they live in, and not on whether they live with one or two dollars a day.

Scholarship for children is a human right, whereas living with over one dollar a day is not.

The Millennium Development Goals to eradicate poverty within 2015[387], issued in 2000, albeit difficult to fully put into practice, offer a framework and a direction for intervention and consider fundamental values, such as:

- freedom. Men and women have the right to live their life and raise their children in dignity, free from hunger and from the fear of violence, oppression, or injustice. Democratic and participatory governance based on the will of the people best assures these rights;

- equality. No individual and no nation must be denied the opportunity to benefit from development. The equal rights and opportunities of women and men must be assured;

- solidarity. Global challenges must be managed in a way that distributes the costs and burdens fairly in accordance with basic principles of equity and social justice. Those who suffer or benefit least deserve help from those who benefit most;

- tolerance. Human beings must respect each other, in all their diversity of belief, culture, and language. Differences within and between societies should be neither feared nor repressed, but cherished as a precious asset of humanity. A culture of peace and dialogue among all civilizations should be actively promoted;

- respect for nature. Prudence must be shown in the management of all living species and natural resources, in accordance with the precepts of sustainable development. Only in this way can the immeasurable riches

[387] For a full text of the declaration, see http://www.un.org/millennium/declaration/ares552e.pdf; see also http://www.un.org/millenniumgoals/bkgd.shtml.

provided to us by nature be preserved and passed on to our descendants. The current unsustainable patterns of production and consumption must be changed in the interest of our future welfare and that of our descendants;

- shared responsibility. Responsibility for managing worldwide economic and social development, as well as threats to international peace and security, must be shared among the nations of the world and should be exercised multilaterally. As the most universal and most representative organization in the world, the United Nations must play the central role.

Violating poor human rights: a cause and consequence of misery

Some argue that human rights constitute the »core of a universal thin morality« (Michael Walzer), while others claim that they form »reasonable conditions of a world political consensus« (Martha Nussbaum). Still others narrow the concept of human rights »to a minimum standard of well-ordered political institutions for all peoples« (John Rawls).
A context of poverty lacks respect for human rights, which in turn brings back poverty, within a vicious circle, difficult to halt. Here there is an example that shows the interdependence between human rights and how they are strongly linked to poverty: As an example, the context may be that of a poor village in an undeveloped country that has suffered a long civil war and that is now trying to find a way out of the poverty trap. Most of the population has no access to medical treatment. This is a violation of article 25 of the Universal Declaration of Human Rights:

> (1) Everyone has the right to a standard of living adequate for the health and well-being of himself and of his family, including food, clothing, housing, and medical care and necessary social services, and the right to security in the event of unemployment, sickness, disability, widowhood, old age, or other lack of livelihood in circumstances beyond his control.
>
> (2) Motherhood and childhood are entitled to special care and assistance. All children, whether born in or out of wedlock, shall enjoy the same social protection.

The first consequence is that children and adults have no access to medical treatment, so there are no teachers (it is a very common problem in sub-Saharan

Africa – there are very few teachers because of AIDS), and children are not fit enough to go to school. This is a violation of article 26 of the declaration:

> (1) Everyone has the right to education. Education shall be free, at least in the elementary and fundamental stages. Elementary education shall be compulsory. Technical and professional education shall be made generally available and higher education shall be equally accessible to all on the basis of merit.
>
> (2) Education shall be directed to the full development of the human personality and to the strengthening of respect for human rights and fundamental freedoms. It shall promote understanding, tolerance, and friendship among all nations, racial or religious groups, and shall further the activities of the United Nations for the maintenance of peace.
>
> (3) Parents have a prior right to choose the kind of education that shall be given to their children.

Further consequence is that without teachers and schools, there is no education. Children grow up without learning new skills, and illiteracy affects high percentages of the population, making it extremely hard for them to find a job. This is a violation of article 23 of the Universal Declaration of Human Rights:

> (1) Everyone has the right to work, to free choice of employment, to just and favorable conditions of work, and to protection against unemployment.
>
> (2) Everyone, without any discrimination, has the right to equal pay for equal work.
>
> (3) Everyone who works has the right to just and favorable remuneration ensuring for himself and his family an existence worthy of human dignity, and supplemented, if necessary, by other means of social protection.
>
> (4) Everyone has the right to form and to join trade unions for the protection of his interests.

The lack of the scholarship will cause lack of jobs. For example, there will be no teachers and no doctors. The lack of teachers takes us back to the lack of education; the lack of doctors has a negative impact on the sanitation ambit. Working to protect human rights can only be successful if there is a clear image of what is nowadays situation. The list below shows the basic question one must ask himself when reporting human rights topics:

1. Who is responsible for promoting human rights and who is guilty of violating them?
2. Where do human rights violations take place?
3. What does it mean for someone to have human rights?
4. Why do these violations occur?

Responsibility for human rights' violations can be attributed to three main parties: governments, companies, and armed groups. Governments, especially those in the African continent, often lack political will to promote human rights and individuals' dignity. The following table shows a few example of how these three parties can be involved in human rights violations.

Table 13.1. – Examples of human rights violations

GOVERNMENTS	ARMED GROUPS	COMPANIES
Dictatorship – violation of Article 21.1(»Everyone has the right to take part in the government of his country, directly or through freely chosen representatives«.)	Child Soldiers – violation of Articles 3 (right to life, liberty, and security), 4 (freedom from slavery) and 5 (freedom from torture).	Unfair salaries – violation of article 23. 3: »Everyone, without any discrimination, has the right to equal pay for equal work«.
Education denial – Violation of Article 26.1(»Everyone has the right to education. Education shall be free, at least in the elementary and fundamental stages. Elementary education shall be compulsory. Technical and professional education shall be made generally available and higher education shall be equally accessible to all on the basis of merit«.)	Sexual Slaves – Violation of articles 3, 4, and 5 (see above). Education denial	Pollution – Violation of article 25 (according to which »people must live in a healthy environment«.)

Governments are also responsible for many human rights abuses even if they don't make them in first person, because it is their responsibility to promote human rights in their country. An example is the defense and protection of children. The UN 1989 convention on the defense of children's rights' main job is to make pressure on countries for action to protect minors, because it is considered the single country's responsibility to ensure children respect for their human rights.

War and human rights

War creates a vicious circle because atrocities are responded to with other atrocities. It is rare for diplomacy to intervene before the other side has responded to a violent attack with violence, which is the reason why human rights are so often forgotten during conflicts. War doesn't leave any space for individuals' dignity and people feel their hands are tied. Cassese (2008) makes two examples of how governmental armies often avoid violating human rights:

- international norms appoint that soldiers must wear uniform, in order to be distinguished from civilians. Governmental soldiers often do so, whilst rebels and terrorists are often camouflaged within the population;
- troops must be encamped in specialized military areas. This rule is often respected by governmental armies, but the same can't be said for rebel groups, which often camp their soldiers in normal habitations.

This does not mean that governments don't commit atrocities, but only that they are more able to take advantage of serious gaps of the international law to avoid diplomatic problems. The list of the human rights abuses that governmental armies cause, is not shorter than the rebels' one. Let's just think to the responsibility of Sudan's president, Omar Al-Bashir, in the Darfur conflict. He armed the Darfurian Janjaweed rebels and ordered them to exterminate all the ethnically black population of Darfur, so he is responsible of human rights violations (although he continuously denies it!). Instead, it is very rare for rebels to deny their responsibilities. The following list shows some of the most recurring human rights' abuses in modern wars:

- massacres – The act or an instance of killing a large number of humans indiscriminately and cruelly;
- genocide – Intentional extermination of a single ethnic, racial, or religious group. It concerns killing group members, causing them serious bodily or mental harm, imposing measures to prevent birth, or forcibly transferring children, all with the aim to bring the destruction of a group;
- women and girls are often raped by soldiers or forced into prostitution, or they can be subject to sexual assaults (which often involve sexual humiliation and mutilation) and forced pregnancy;

- mass rapes – a group of people are raped, during hostilities, usually to be then exploited or for blackmailing. An example of mass rape took place in the Bosnian Serb campaign for victory in the war in the former Yugoslavia;
- torture, either physical or psychological, aiming at the humiliation or annihilation of the dignity of the person. Physical torture might include mutilation, beatings, and electric shocks to lips, gums, and genitals, psychological torture includes food and water deprivation, sleep deprivation, and being tormented by high-level noise;
- political oppression – which often takes the form of discrimination. When it occurs, basic rights may be denied on the basis of religion, ethnicity, race, or gender. Severe forms of discrimination are not new and, perhaps, one of the most severe forms of discrimination has been the South African Apartheid.

Amnesty International, Human Rights Watch and the role of civil society

Nowadays, civil society–whose foundations are the bedrock of democracy–has achieved an extremely important role in monitoring the human rights' situation worldwide. The civil participation in the battle for human rights can come in two main ›forms‹:

- NGOs, such as Amnesty International and Human Rights Watch;
- Single people, such as the South African leader Nelson Mandela, the Burmese Aung San Suu Kyi, or the Iranian Shirin Ebadi, all Nobel prizes for peace.

NGOs are groups of people working together, independently from the government. Single people are those who have given up on their freedom and their privileges (the three Nobel prize winners mentioned above, for example, have both experienced a long-term imprisonment) to stand up for what they believed is right by contrasting governments and very powerful institutions and, on some occasions, facing death.
Human Rights Watch[388] is an international nongovernmental organization that, similarly to Amnesty International[389], conducts research and advocacy on human rights. The two main areas in which Human Rights Watch works on include discrimination caused by sexual orientation and capital punishment, and it

---

388 www.hrw.org/.
389 www.amnesty.org/.

mainly concentrates on freedom of religion. Human Rights Watch produces research reports on human rights' abuses and it works in contact with the media by drawing international attention to abuses, in order to pressurize governments and international organizations to reform when necessary.

Amnesty International and Human Rights Watch are doubtlessly the two most known organizations working on human rights. They have made a big step in the long way to human rights, because people know what is going on in the world also thanks to organizations like these two. Spreading awareness is an extremely important phase, because there is very little people can do (e.g. pressure on governments) if they are not given an idea of the human rights' situation in the world.

Another institution that is renowned for its focus on human rights is represented by Freedom House, which publishes an annual report[390] on the ›worst of the worst‹ countries.

AMNESTY INTERNATIONAL

Amnesty International is an international nongovernmental organization, funded in 1961 and made up of over 2 million people, that defines itself as an organization working »to conduct research and generate action to prevent and end grave abuses of human rights and to demand justice for those whose rights have been violated«. Amnesty International's main targets are governments, private individuals and non governmental bodies such as companies. It deals in seven main areas, that include women's' rights, children's' rights, torture, death penalty, prisoners of conscience, refugees, and human dignity.

Amnesty International mainly operates by generating diplomatic pressure on governments and companies through appeals, public displays, and raising awareness of human rights' abuses throughout the world. Amnesty International doesn't simply work to promote and protect human rights, but it deals with the close link between world poverty and human rights.

Amnesty doesn't only pressurize the world's most powerful institutions into promoting and respecting human rights, but also into considering them a starting point in the resolution of economic crisis and in development.

»World leaders are focused on economic crisis, we say to them 'it's not just the economy, it is injustice, insecurity, inequality, and indignity. World leaders need to put human rights at the centre of the economic rescue plan, but to be credible leaders they need to fix their own, appalling human rights' record«. (Irene Khan, Amnesty International secretary general, *Amnesty International 2009 report*).

390 For the 2010 report, see http://www.freedomhouse.org/uploads/WoW/2010/WorstOfTheWorst2010.pdf.

The condensed Chapter

Poverty and unfreedom both derive from lack of basic capabilities (education, healthcare, availability of key resources, etc.), whereas freedom, enjoying a democratic and tolerant environment, eases and fosters economic development and social opportunities.
Subsidiarity enhances liberty, complementing the market and the State where these institutions are weak or inadequate.
Development can be rightfully conceived as a human right to be given to everybody, without forgetting the humiliated poor, who are too often unfree to choose their destiny.

Out of Poverty Tips

Freedom is a cornerstone of development, since it unleashes creativity and entrepreneurship, securing also basic human rights.
Democracy, the political byproduct of freedom, helps the poor with its redistributive effects and shared rights, fostering social opportunities.

Selected Readings

ARCHER M.S., (2008), *Pursuing the Common Good: How Solidarity and Subsidiarity Can Work Together*, Vatican City Press.

KHAN I., (2009), *The Unheard Truth: Poverty and Human Rights*, Amnesty International, W. W. Norton & Company, London.

RAWLS J., (1971), *A Theory of Justice*, Harvard University Press, Cambridge.

SEN A., (1999), *Development as Freedom*, Oxford University Press, Oxford.

SEN A., (2009), *The idea of justice*, Penguin Books, London.

CHAPTER 14 – The good Samaritan's paradox: is foreign aid damaging?

> It is time to stop pretending that the aid-based development model currently in place will generate sustained economic growth in the world's poorest countries. It will not.
>
> Dambisa Moyo, *Dead Aid*

The impact of foreign aid in the beneficiary country: a blessing or a curse?

The Good Samaritan is described in the Gospel of Luke[391] as a merciful foreigner who helps a wounded man found on his way and ignored by other heartless travelers. It is among the most ancient and widely known examples of pitiful and successful emergency aid, through the intermediation of a local hospital. The present foreign aid reality, described in this Chapter, is often characterized by similar good intentions (goods are for giving), but its outcomes are hardly so benign and poor achievements are a frequent–albeit unwanted–consequence.

A fiery debated issue is the foreign aid to poor countries, which is a voluntary transfer of resources from richer nations, which is motivated by economic, political, or humanitarian reasons. It is considered either a blessing or a curse, according to the interpretation of its ambiguous nature and questioned efficacy – as Pogge (2008) claims, world poverty cannot be eradicated by ›throwing money at the problem‹. Efficiency, good management, decency, accountability, and fairness are greatly wanted, together with altruism and compassion, which are a necessary but not sufficient perquisite.

The debate is culturally biased by democratic differences of opinion but it rests even on undisputed evidence that while foreign aid in some emergencies or in certain development phases is indeed helping, in many other cases proves a real disaster.

Foreign aid can take several forms. Firstly it can be military aid – possibly in the form of armed humanitarian relief but always considering the threat to national sovereignty posed by disguised ›Troy horse‹ gift. Secondly, it can take the form of debt forgiveness or economic development assistance, and thirdly even disaster assistance money. In any case, foreign aid is an input–not an out-

---

391 Chapter 10, verses 25-37.

put–to development as it shown in Figure 14.1. Aid has to be properly dealt with and managed, and this is an uneasy task which requires much wanted but typically missing professionalism – quality always matters. To donate is principally a question of heart, not of wealth, even if money still matters.

Figure 14.1. – Aid is an input, not an output, to development

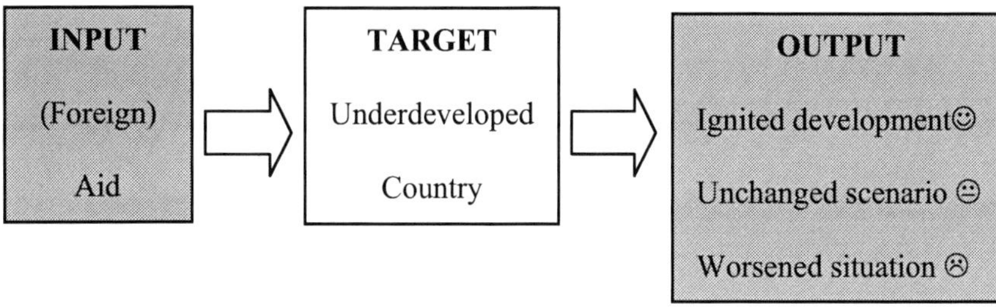

The big question about its effectiveness is whether foreign aid really reaches the poor, instead of getting dispersed before reaching them, and–if so–the extent of its real contribution to their long term development (back to the old habits, still poor and disillusioned, when foreign aid is over?). Donors should act less like charities and more like strategic investors, possibly with an increasing involvement of local capital.

What really matters is education to development, in the awareness that a mistaken approach brings to ephemeral, short-sighted results. Good intentions and spontaneity are not enough in a complex field where professionalism is increasingly wanted.

The meeting between demand and supply of aid is often harder than expected, since aid is often imposed from above, following an egocentric top-down methodology (the one-size-fits-all aid approach described by Paul Collier, 2008), without a preventive shared analysis of real needs and targets. Poverty shows up to be much more than a technical problem, since it is a deceptive and complicated tangle of political, social, historical, institutional, cultural, and environmental problems[392], as we have seen in previous Chapters dealing about the poverty traps. A tailor made approach is deeply needed, and it should be flexibly adaptable to different situations, reminding that »one size does not fit all«. But in any case, aid won't make poverty history.

Calderisi (2006), p. 14 points out that »the tyrants love aid. Aid helps them to stay in power and contributes to underdevelopment«. And again (p. 28): »It is governments, not people, which benefit from global generosity«.

›Do not harm‹ should always be the first commandment, even with foreign aid.

Among the caveats, it shouldn't be forgotten that:

[392] See Easterly (2006), p. 6.

- international aid is culturally shaped by the synthesis of the Western culture, that is always trying to export its ›values‹ (democracy, capitalism …) even where they are hardly understood or perceived as valuable. But to the extent that single human beings are placed at the centre of the attention–in detecting and setting the problems–foreign egocentric attitudes soften;
- financial loans to poor countries pour a lot of money in fragile States where corruption is so widespread that it hardly goes where it should. As a result, even the poor population is liable for loans that have never reached it and so even debt relief, presented as a concession and statistically accounted in the category of foreign aid, is a hoax.

Foreign aid shows some similarities with the natural resources curse described in Chapter 3. Flows of unearned money invade a poor country and they can create a physical and psychological dependency syndrome. Economic drawbacks are a frequent corollary and may be represented by the revaluation of the local currency, which makes exports harder; there may also be rising inflation or crowding out effect of local producers, who may suffer the unwanted competition of donated goods.

The aid curse, which is always suspended between promises and perils, is also likely to be asymmetric, since the poor are seldom part of the club of the happy few who share the pie, whereas they fully bear the unwanted consequences of aid.

The ideals and cultural attitudes behind foreign aid are a peculiar mixture of guilt and historical legacies of colonial exploitation, emotional humanitarianism blended with solidarity and altruism, commercial self interest (to sell one's products, creating new markets), neo colonialist attitudes, and good or bad conscience. The outcome of all this is unsurprisingly mixed, contradictory, and confused. Reminding that idealistic high purposes matter, the divine music of solidarity, properly inspired by unconditional love and sharing ideals, has to be properly incarnated in feasible and effective strategies.

Dangerous aid? Even the Troy horse was supposed to be a gift

Aid is not an automatic synonym of help and local poverty issues cannot be uniformly packaged from abroad or dealt with irrespectively from local habits and needs. It is always important to remind that each poor is simply different from others and he/she deserves specific attention and care, remembering that one-size-doesn't-fit-all. International aid is one of the most powerful weapons in the struggle against poverty – and like all the weapons it may be friendly or harmful, depending on its effective use and proper targeting, rather than on common-

ly good initial intentions. Aid is a form of relational good, which is contrary to egoistic individualism, looking for social added value, beyond selfish utilitarianism. The altruist naturally expects reciprocation, even if gratitude is less frequent than expected.
Among the aid big dilemmas, the trade-off between delivering money or goods and services from abroad is hardly trivial. The choice is limited when goods and services are not present in the recipient country and they are considered necessary. Cash is to be used for foreign purchase of these items, but to the extent that the local country is–at least partially–enabled to produce the goods or to provide the needed services, it would be unfair and counterproductive to cut off local producers and providers, as it often happens, following lobbyist pressures often within the same donors.
In other particularly common states of the world, the dilemma is still unsolved. When emergencies require speediness of intervention, and so they somewhat privilege foreign suppliers, long term development should take more care of local opportunities, to be patiently nurtured and exploited.
Let's consider also that liquidity is easier, safer, and quicker to transfer and that local prices of goods and services are typically much more convenient, especially in poor countries. A provisional conclusion might be the following: buy locally, whenever and wherever you can; so doing you will foster local development and make aid more easily accepted and ›inculturated‹.
Progress brought from abroad is hardly culturally accepted and it is much better if it starts locally, since it participated and shared by the people of the community.
Utopian megalomania–of those who want to save the world (unfortunately ... not from themselves)–and unrealistic expectations due to over-enthusiasm are both inspiring and exciting, but they are hardly effective if they are not counterproductive or unintentionally harmful.
Whenever aid proves effective, it is however often uneasy to scale up, as it happens in the market economy with standardized products. Information asymmetries and intrinsic *ad hoc* peculiarities hamper standardization.
To the extent that results do not matter, it seems difficult to make aid effective. Paradigm shift is largely needed, making interventions recipient-driven, instead of donor-driven. Even the Troy horse was supposed to be a gift[393], in spite of Virgil's admonishment »*timeo Danaos et dona ferentes*« – I fear Greeks, even those bearing gifts.

393 According to the story, Laocoön guessed the plot and warned the Trojans, in, but the sea god Poseidon sent two sea serpents to strangle him, before he could be believed. King Priam's daughter Cassandra, the soothsayer of Troy, insisted that the horse would be the downfall of the city and its royal family but she too was ignored, hence their doom and loss of the war. Since then, the Troy horse is a synonym of a dangerous and deceiving gift.

Banerjee and He[394] claim that »aid can at best help people survive, but it cannot promote development«, while according to Moss, Pettersson and van de Walle[395] »donors should be unambiguously aware that their assistance can have perverse effects on some of the very outcomes they hope to encourage«.
It looks like the above mentioned Good Samaritan's curse, considering also that moral hazard problems worsen the dilemma, since the donor is often unable to distinguish if a poor outcome is due to low effort and poor implementation or simply to bad luck[396]. And time has come to reinvent aid, softening pessimism with undisputed and tangible pro growth results.

Spoiling aid rents

Foreign aid policies and strategies are inspired by ongoing ideologies, which change across time, due to the feedback deriving from successes and failures–learning from their pathological anatomy–and to the prevailing mood of running politicians, who typically lack adequate experience and vision to address these complex issues.
Historical experience tells us that aid rents can be spoiling, with perverse side effect incentives, like natural resources revenues–already described in Chapter 3–since they can disincentive recipient countries from making personal efforts for growth and development. The results will be dysfunctional effects, similar to those of the oil extraction bonanza, bringing to no-developmental discretionary expenditures.
Spoiling aid rents may be softened by the fact that aid is mainly targeting investments, rather than immediate consumption. But diverted and misallocated funds–that are so common in practice–are likely to fuel and satisfy any need of the undeserving recipients, typically with little or any external control and with the complicity of corrupt middlemen that participate in the sharing of the pie.
Aid proves much more effective and longer lasting–so decreasing spoiling rents–when the recipient country has a strong institutional background, as it was the case in many European countries devastated by World War II, such as Germany. This country strongly benefited from Marshall Plan intervention coming from the U.S., a single big donor with no problems of coordination. The way in which institutional development affects the efficiency of aid is however paradoxical, since if the recipient country has strong and sound institutions, it is unlikely to be poor, whereas underdeveloped and poor countries–those more needing help–typically have very weak institutions, undermining the possibilities and the incentives to build State capacity. The depressing conclusion is that aid

394 In Easterly (2008), p. 63.
395 In Easterly (2008), p. 276.
396 See Svensson (2000).

is less effective where it is most needed, because of an inefficient institutional local framework. Aid stimulates growth in countries with good policies and efficient institutions, but not elsewhere or otherwise.

Humanitarian versus development aid

Social conflicts and humanitarian crises are increasingly affecting the unsheltered poorest. Such conflicts are caused by an often irrational interaction of human or natural factors, and as a consequence many poor silently die, while the luckiest who survive wander as homeless vagabonds, desperately looking for safe places.

Emergency interventions may be a symptom of improper planning and they may develop crisis mentality, focused on immediate and tangible results over sounder long-term prevention or reconstruction.

Since the poor have limited resources–insufficient even for bare survival–in emergency situations they can only rely on international supply of basic goods, such as food, water, and drugs. They have to look for external help in due time and hope that foreign agencies don't get tired – don't give up now ... please don't give up. Pride and indignant defense of an empty sovereignty are common reactions to the foreign intrusion, while emergency and compelling needs unconditionally favor immediate intervention.

Uneven development in disadvantaged areas makes humanitarian emergencies increasingly likely and harder to fight, especially if the whole country is underdeveloped. Arbitrage from poorer to richer regions causes imbalances, migrations, and social tensions. Reduction of inequalities stands out as a long term target for development, decreasing the vulnerability of the weakest.

Whenever disasters are foreseeable, prevention–such as peace promotion–represents an unavoidable mitigation measure. And preventing a crisis with early warnings and timely intervention is much cheaper than managing it when it deflagrates. Long term economic deterrence has to cope with short term measures, usually political and military ones, envisaging peacekeeping as a primary option, with the risk of undermining the neutrality of the intervention.

In some cases, international aid, albeit desperately needed–such as the Myanmar's one, facing the disruptive floods of May 2008–may be considered by dictatorial regimes tantamount to foreign invasion, threatening the local autarchic government and, consequently, to be refused.

Conflict mediations and post war reconstructions[397] are an important strategy that is intended to avoid or limit emergencies, considering long lasting physical and psychological drawbacks, such as destruction of infrastructure (bridges considered military strategic points; roads, airports, and railways, but also

---

[397] See Chapter 5.

schools, hospitals, and homes), diffusion of unchecked landmines, but also the trauma of children soldiers coming home or families torn apart by the war.
Relapses from a war to another are unfortunately common and humanitarian crises can be endemic and recurring, getting so deeply rooted to become culturally accepted with sad resignation, especially when it seems difficult to dream for a better world.
The trade-off between humanitarian and development aid is an important distinction between different forms of anyway complementary help.
Humanitarian aid is rightfully driven by principles such as efficacy, legitimacy, (societal acceptance by recipients) and impartiality. It is very much concerned with catastrophes and emergencies, which sometimes are foreseeable like famines and in other cases are unpreventable, such as earthquakes, during which richer and safer countries put in place, often with short notice (in case or unannounced earthquakes or other natural disasters), material and logistical assistance in order to save lives, limit displacements, and alleviate suffering.
Typical characteristics of proper humanitarian intervention are urgency, speed, and effectiveness of intervention, coordination and skill: they are often conducted using airplanes and technological devices imported from aiding countries.
Development aid has completely different, albeit interdependent, targets and it aims at addressing the long term socio-economic natural causes of underdevelopment which may gradually lead to a crisis or emergency, unless they are properly treated.
The history of humanitarian aid is full of heroic successes but also of embarrassing fiascos. They induce some caution and suggest good strategic policies, such as learning from past experience about the necessity of being always prepared, internationally coordinated and able to delegate responsibility in a flexible way, mindfully combining a top-down approach-taking profit of economies of scale and experience–with a grass rooted bottom–up involvement.
The differences between humanitarian versus development aid are evident even considering their complexity and effectiveness: even if it is hard to say which of them is more complex, it seems evident that they are completely different, requiring diverse training, equipment, and strategies. They can both be complementarily useful in alleviating poverty but again on different grounds.

Phasing out emergency

After a humanitarian crisis (earthquake, mass migration due to famine or war …), when the worst is over, and deadly fog slowly fades away thanks also to emergency relief, the development phase has to start, but then the environment changes and a new approach is needed.

During humanitarian crises, local populations are often too weak to give substantial contribution to the solution of their own problems–often a real matter of survival–and so foreign aid is vital. To the extent that the country is facing real emergency, its politicians may behave less greedily than in standard times, easing the rescuing of hit populations. But this phenomenon, if present, is hardly long lasting and when survivors understand that money is pouring in from abroad, many of them inevitably soon try to take profit of it, retaining confusion as a precious ally.

Proper delivery timing, following efficient scheduling, is essential even with aid; food for survival is highly appreciated before harvesting, medicines when epidemics are erupting, and so on. Late intervention is often useless, and petty bureaucratic concerns can sink aid.

Foreign aid usefulness is hardly questionable in emergencies, to the extent that vulnerable populations need immediate help that is unavailable locally. But if it lasts too long, without the domestic cooperation and full involvement of the local population, aid can hardly contribute to sustainable development. Is aid really sustainable and, if so, to what extent?

And when the crisis is over or it slows down, foreign media soon get tired and concentrate on something else: people easily forget what happens elsewhere and they are distracted by their own neighborhood problems. Solidarity of absent spectators, who are not personally involved in the drama, is hardly surviving its ephemeral–short termed–myopic emotions.

Development aid can be granted on a bilateral systematic way–government to government–or in a multilateral way. Antipoverty policies fall into the category of development aid, since poverty is typically structural, with long term debilitating effect caused by deprivation of crucial assets, basic needs and survival capabilities. Temporary interventions and occasional social safety nets can help to sort out emergencies but not to eradicate poverty. Disaster relief is a needed but short-sighted action, unless it is translated to longer term development intervention.

Reconstruction policies, when urgencies are over, are typically aimed at strengthening democratic institutions, rebuilding civil society. Ideology plays an important part in these difficult steps. Top down solutions, aimed at importing Western models in devastated countries, are typically hardly effective and unsuitable, especially if they misrepresent local cultures and historical heritage – it is difficult to accept and put into practice what people don't understand. Remote strategies are imposed from the outside, relying on moral suasion and diplomatic mediation or escalating to stronger measures, such as economic sanctions or military deterrence, whereas hands–on strategies require physical presence of peace–keeping foreign armies, which are more expensive and risky.

Coordination of international aid during emergencies is typically uneasy and competing donors, each willing to arrive first, may transform a catastrophe in a sort of Olympic competition – even if there are no medals to distribute. A strong coordinating leadership is highly wanted, especially if the logistic playground–a strategic cornerstone, as we learn from wars–is difficult to manage.

Bilateral and multilateral aid

The bilateral aid system involves money that is being donated from one nation to another through the government. This sort of donation is very often finalized to increase the receiving country's GDP and it can also come as foreign debt relief. It generally involves program aid (government receiving money and then individually deciding how to spend it).

Most bilateral agencies refuse to hire local experts and they often mistrust them (in spite of their cheaper payrolls and better awareness of local situations than foreigners' ones), preferring their often colluded own nationals. And bilateral aid is also often influenced by colonial legacy, giving priority to countries with historical links.

Bilateral aid programs are typically linked with commercial trade between the donor and the beneficiary country. Even if trade is bilateral, it can be skewed to asymmetrically favor the donor country, in order to rebalance its aid effort, often in a concealed way, since aid is largely publicized, whereas its compensating side effects are typically less evident, or even completely undisclosed.

Government-backed companies which export in poor countries under the umbrella of bilateral agreements are not always a shining example of profitability and competitiveness at home, and they are revamped by protected trading deals between governments, where the recipient country is often unaware of the quality level of imports. Lucrative foreign work for ailing contractors in rich countries can help them to survive to otherwise merciless competition.

To the extent that bilateral exchanges are unbalanced in favor of the Western countries, the developing nation may end up paying low quality foreign companies with its own resources. The result is unduly subsidizing foreign inefficiencies – legitimate perplexities of local rulers are easily softened with bribes, unless there is a competitive democratic system, which is enabled to challenge failures with better alternatives. And embezzled money … has wings and it can easily fly away to safer places, such as tax heavens, just in case of need.

Multilateral aid involves money that is sent to international organizations such as the UN (and its many branches such as UNICEF, FAO, UNCHR, WFP, etc ...), the World Bank and the International Monetary Fund, that are all big bureaucratic institutions with a large inflexible apparatus. These organizations then split the addressed budget to peacekeeping missions (they are expensive and unpopular but often necessary and less anachronistic than military interventions of former colonizers): it is money to be invested in education, food distribution, protection of refugees …

Complex bilateral or multilateral organizations strongly rely on contractors or sub-contractors to carry on their programs, and they so increase the complexity of the delivery mechanism, together with higher transaction and monitoring costs – forgetting about the ›keep it simple and stupid‹ rule. Reliability and accountability are better enforced if the results are easily observable.

Among the positive aspects of multilateral aid, economies of scale, of scope, and of experience are worth to be remembered. Playing with large numbers on a broad multinational spectrum enable indeed supranational aid agencies to benefit from higher scaling, once they have properly reached economic break even point, stronger focus on projects, and better information gathering and sharing.

Bilateral aid can become very hard to manage, as giant sums of money are involved and they end up in the beneficiary country's capital. And the governments discretionarily decide their use. Sometimes the government is corrupted, as it often happens in undeveloped countries. Corruption, when combined to large amounts of capital at disposal, can be a real kiss of death for countries that are already poor.

Beyond State-to-State cooperation: a bottom up subsidiarity approach

Both humanitarian (emergency) and development aid can be government-sponsored or even charity-based (typically to a smaller scale). In the latter case they are funded by private NGOs, foundations, associations, or other institutions.

Private charities, being tinier that big institutions, tend to have smaller economies of scale and scope, a more restricted budgeting and less political power to influence the target country. In comparison to the bigger public institutions, private NGOs may have running expenses with a higher break even point, eroding the percentage of revenues to be allocated to the direct beneficiaries, even if bigger public entities have a high bureaucratic charge and they may be even more expensive and less flexible.

According to Calderisi (2006), p. 8 »people-to-people aid and humanitarian assistance are much more effective in communicating values and shoring up African morale than official assistance«.

Charity-based aid is naturally linked to subsidiarity[398], that is a form of decentralization and contracting out and it is also an organizing principle according to which matters ought to be handled by the smallest, lowest or least centralized

---

[398] See Chapter 13.

competent authority. Nothing that can be done by a smaller and simpler organization should be done by a larger and more complex organization. This principle is a bulwark of limited government and personal freedom. It conflicts with the passion for centralization and bureaucracy characteristic of the Welfare State[399].

Another way of bypassing central governments is to promote single projects rather than providing unconditional funding to support the local budget, writing dangerous white checks.

According to detractors, subsidiarity (peer-to-peer relationship) may undermine State institutions, with an ›amputation‹ of the State's intermediation. But in poor countries with bad governance[400], subsidiary may be the only workable mean of effectively delivering foreign aid, bypassing failed institutions and their corrupted managers.

Sharing the intervention strategy and its implementation with the beneficiaries can increase participation, and feedback may in some cases dilute efficiency, especially in emergency cases.

Being subsidiarity a natural bridge connecting the market and the State–but even enabling to go beyond their failures–it is strongly connected with grass rooted social capital[401], which is the basic element of cohesion, solidarity, and mutuality within an ethnic group or clan.

Subsidiarity is also concerned with the devolution of social protections from the State to the civil society, to the extent that the latter can perform better than the former. The transition from State-led to market-led approach to poverty alleviation has to pragmatically consider that both approaches have their pitfalls, which have to be properly solved with subsidiarity and its not-for-profit actors.

Donor or need driven aid? When the superficial West misunderstands the complex Rest

Rich western countries can do more for the poor than what they now do, using more development: friendly devices, such as smarter and more fine-tuned approaches to fair bilateral trade, safe migration, sharing of technologies, and–last but not least–a more effective deployment of foreign aid[402].

The West represents a relatively rich but often sad world, if compared to poor but sometimes joyful Rest. Because of the globalization effect, the two worlds are increasingly linked, but they are also kept segregated by selfishness and ignorance.

---

399 http://www.acton.org/publications/randl/rl_article_200.php.
400 See Chapter 5.
401 See Chapter 9.
402 See Easterly (2008), p. ix.

People love to donate what they like, much more than what the poor really need and they want to autonomously choose where to put their money and how to manage it. Some trendy projects are over funded, while others do not have adequate coverage, because they are often more strategic but less appealing. Great livers are great givers, but generosity is not enough, unless properly targeted to sustainable projects.

A poor understanding of real problems is a frequent side problem, together with superficiality, arrogance, and laziness – of those who think they can comprehend what they have never seen. Such problems hardly allow people to take effective strategies.

As Easterly (2007), p. 7, points out »poor people die not only because of the world's indifference to their poverty, but also because of ineffective efforts by those who do care«. The projects funded by foreign aid cost too much – much more than would have if it was funded and managed locally. This partly happens because a lot of foreign aid comes with conditions that are imposed by the donor countries. Aid is not intrinsically ineffective, but it can be wasted.

The military option is a simplistic answer to complex problems: sometimes it works, especially to restore order in a country attacked by others (the example of World War II is probably the biggest but there are more), but often–more than expected–it doesn't work and imported use of force triggers hidden violence, in a spiral that can soon get out of control.

According to Calderisi (2006), p. 7 »forty years of foreign aid have established one unsurprising fact. Around the world, successful countries are those that have chosen the right policies for their own reasons and seen foreign aid as a complement to their own efforts rather than a bribe for undertaking difficult reforms«.

Accountability–a synonym of responsibility, answerability, enforcement, blameworthiness, liability, and reliability–is a key function in the governance relationship between donors, beneficiaries, and the intermediary aid entity (NGO, foundation, agency …).

A major consequence of the misunderstanding between the West and the Rest lies in the often arrogant top down approach, according to which a standard and customized approach is indifferently applicable to diverse circumstances, with little or any personalization. Globalization and its corollary–think globally and act locally–naturally favors the top down approach with its pros, easing economies of scale and experience, quicker budgeting and simpler decisions, but the results are hardly positive. They have to be properly balanced with a face-to-face bottom up vision, involving a community as wide as possible and starting from the targeted beneficiaries of aid.

The top down approach is far from being useless and it has positive aspects, such as scaling and sharing of experiences, even if its replication is far from being automatic and what works in a context may well be a fiasco elsewhere. The culture behind the top down approach is influenced and biased by a scientific methodology, according to which experiments should be replicable. In reality, to some extent they are, as we can see from technology (e.g., mobile phones can be used everywhere, in the presence of appropriate telecommunication infrastructures) or medical applications (medicines, cures …), but in most cases they interact with a peculiar environment, with unpredictable personalized results. Culture of foreign aid is hard to change, biased by short term horizons and anxiety about tangible quick results, and it risks making beneficiaries dependent rather than empowered.

A mistaken approach to world's poverty, rethinking foreign aid

By typing the word ›poverty‹ on Google, more than ten million different links are given. Searching on Wikipedia, there are a few paragraphs about poverty reduction. The titles are ›economic liberalization‹, ›capital, infrastructure, and technology‹, ›aid‹ and ›good institutions‹. Nobody can doubt how important infrastructure, technology, and good institutions are in poverty reduction, and the importance of the other two points, aid and economic liberalization, strongly depend on peoples' points of view. However, many people doubt of the efficiency of the West's approach to poverty. Dambisa Moyo's (2009) and Bill Easterly's (2008) theses are just two examples of critiques to the way we are dealing with the matter. Too often we search for and talk about the mistakes of the poor, as if they were the cause of their disgraces. The consequence of this approach is that money, efforts, and resources are invested to impose the solutions we think will work best, such as millions of dollars in aid, funds to protect third world farmers, hospital building …

Despite the fact that in some cases these solutions are well functioning, efforts are often wasted, and priorities are not always clear cut as they should be.

Instead of imposing Western ›solutions‹ and providing governments with unearned money and resources, we should combat the above listed phenomena we are responsible for. »If you are part of the problem, be also part of its solution«, G. K. Chesterton admonished.

There are many aspects in the first world's behavior that are heavily weighing on the poor, as described in Table 14.1.:

Table 14.1. – Poverty traps and consequences on the poor

PROBLEM / POVERTY TRAP	EXAMPLES OF CONSEQUENCES ON THE POOR
Global warming and pollution.	See Chapter 8.
Speculation on food commodities.	Damage to poor farmers.
Obstacles to the access of third world products to international markets.	Poor countries are withheld from economic benefit and missing export does not bring in precious foreign currency.
Weaponry supply in exchange for commodities.	Local wars are fuelled (e.g. China supplying arms, allowing genocide in Darfur in exchange for Sudanese oil).
Multinationals with basements/settlements in poor countries are often responsible for local population exploitation, pollution, and unfair working conditions.	Poverty as a consequence of the various human rights violations.
Waste of resources and consumerism.	Arguments for commodities finding themselves in the poor countries often lead to wars, such as D.R. of Congo's continuous tensions for coltan, mainly used to produce mobile phones, or the 20th Century war in Transvaal, South Africa, between England and the Netherlands.
Links between international and rich countries' criminal organizations.	Foreign women on streets, forced prostitution.

Let's think about some of the positive consequences there could be in world poverty, should we deal with the above listed problems.

Commitment to reforestation, making use of renewable energy, and the various approaches to climate change will alleviate poverty for all of those people who are dealing with the tremendous effects of climate change such as droughts, desertification, floods …

If speculation is forbidden, then national economies would be less damaged by price changes.

If the World Trade Organization changes its rules in order to let the poorer farmers put their products on international markets, they will be able to produce income that will allow them run their life and those of their families.

These points are to help us to understand how influent Westerners are about poverty and how much could be done for the poor without actually giving them anything. We must change our behavior to help them to create an ideal condition for development – less money, fewer resources, more coherence, and more efforts.

Dead aid?

In ›*Dead Aid*‹, (2009), p. ix, Dambisa Moyo claims that the majority of sub-Saharan countries »flounder in a seemingly never-ending cycle of corruption, disease, poverty, and aid dependency«. And they are poor precisely because of that aid. »Aid has been, and continues to be, an unmitigated political, economic, and humanitarian disaster for most parts of the developing world«. In short, aid is »the disease of which it pretends to be the cure«.

Foreign aid is a curse that fuels corruption and conflicts, and at the same time it discourages local development and free enterprise, with a crowding out effect whose damages can be long lasting and they van become visible often after many years, especially if and when aid dries up and little local initiative is still present.

Foreign aid, with its vicious cycle, may be the silent killer of growth while other financial transfers, such as remittances[403], are much more effective, following a bottom-up approach and taking profit from direct acquaintance of the beneficiaries, who are typically relatives of the expatriated workers who send the money.

Governments need cash, especially in resourceless poor countries where the tax revenues are symbolic. In underdeveloped areas, the role of the government is even more crucial, since the private sector is too fragile to foster development, and basic physical and social infrastructures (roads, telecommunication networks, aqueducts, hospitals, schools, courts ...) are weak and they often are present at an embryonic stage.

A growing amount of cash is needed to meet increasing needs of rising populations, while Western donors' money is shrinking or it is increasingly diverted in other directions, mainly military interventions to export or restore democracy.

The puzzle of aid governance: are donors really targeting the poor?

In democratic countries, politics is based on a complex system of checks and balances and popular consensus is constantly monitored. People who vote are the same who receive the services and if they are unhappy, at the soonest occasion they simply change.

Trading markets are also based, albeit to a different extent, on a similar mechanism. Products introduced in the market, to let companies survive and prosper,

---

[403] See Chapter 12.

have to be successful and trustworthy: consumer is the king and he decides what is appreciated and what is not.

Advertising, imitation, need, convenience, attraction, usefulness, competition are all parameters that orient consumer's choices. It is a complex psychological state of mind with enormous economic impacts. Producers who are unable to correctly target consumers are deemed to failure, even if their products are potentially good.

Even if this is quite a trivial scenario, its synthetic description seems however important in order to underline the outstanding differences with aid, where this feedback and accountability loop is broken and foreign donors / sponsors are different from recipients living in underdeveloped countries[404]. The poor hardly have a word on aid, even though they are the ultimate beneficiaries of it, and aid agencies' first task is to please their sponsors, not the beneficiaries. There are no local elections or strong market feedbacks from the poor recipients – similar to consumers. This elementary but powerful distortion has shown to have severe and unfortunate side effects.

In a competitive market-based environment, there is pressure for lowering prices and increasing quality, looking for an optimization of value for money – what you get for what you pay. Within the foreign aid context, competition is strongly hindered by the potentially unlimited extension of the needy beneficiaries and by their low contractual power, with little legitimacy to complain or ›vote with their feet‹, since they are not the funding donors. The unsurprising outcome is that the foreign aid market is hardly competitive and quality is not necessarily the first priority.

The price of a good or service–such as aid–is the synthesis of the demand and supply for it. But not-for-profit interventions may only imply conventional pricing, since the demand is represented by the beneficiaries but also–on a different ground–by the donors, who are often weakly coordinated among them and possibly pursuing different goals. No surprise that performance evaluations are so difficult, requiring qualitative items–traditionally uneasy to quantify–to be taken into account.

Aid agencies have a strong incentive in making donors happy, since such agencies are the middlemen between sponsors and targeted beneficiaries, and they can also have to recur to information asymmetries (target countries are far, impact is difficult to judge and measure, the poor's voice is seldom heard and if you look for a benign witness, it shouldn't be too difficult to give a proper reward, in exchange of his ›political correctness‹ …).

The sponsors, not the poor, are the aid agencies' true clients and this is the necessary clue in order to understand the big conflict of interest that is so damaging for the destitute.

---

404 See Easterly (2008), p. 13.

Donors are often generous and light hearted–their psychology matters and it should deserve deeper attention–and they wouldn't be pleased to know the often shocking reality of wasted and misused aid, but they are unfortunately too far from the playing field to properly watch the ongoing match.

Not all aid agencies are of course so cynic and good intentions are often predominant, but efficacy–without the poor's continuous feedback–is only a mirage, as it would be democracy without free polls or a market economy not taking care of consumers' choices and preferences.

The triangular governance relationship among foreign donors, intermediating aid agencies, and local needy beneficiaries shows an often astonishing difference between theory–idealistic targets–and practice, bringing to ineffective aid implementation.

If aid is misdirected or improperly spent, who is held accountable? Donors, intermediating aid agencies or the poor recipients? This uneasy question and its multiple possible answers realistically summarize many of the unsolved problems concerning foreign aid effectiveness, as it is shown in Table 14.2.

Table 14.2. – Aid governance interactions of donors, intermediaries and recipients

Player	Theoretical aspirations / targets	Practical deviations from ideal behaviors	Converging behaviors, so as to mitigate governance problems
Foreign donors	To save the world, making poverty history. To alleviate misery and sufferance, as an intermediate step. To model the transformation of poor countries according to Western standards (democracy; development; institutional governance …). To avoid adverse selection, i.e. the risk to select the wrong beneficiary.	Egocentric approach, blended with utopian goals and megalomania. Excessive trust in aid agencies, without taking care of accountability, effectiveness, and feedback from beneficiaries. Ignorance about the real needs of the poor, mainly due to geographical and political separation and to cultural differences. Emotion-	Be patient, privilege a bottom up approach, promote local independent audit and unbiased feedback from local beneficiaries, beware of fashionable and short sighted projects, try to be involved in the local culture and problems even traveling and looking at situations with your own eyes. Learn to listen and start to un-

Player	Theoretical aspirations / targets	Practical deviations from ideal behaviors	Converging behaviors, so as to mitigate governance problems
	To ease coordination and sharing of costs and experiences among different donors. Reputational value of agencies is increasingly important for donors.	al approach and overreaction to sensational and trendy happenings, soon forgotten when the immediate emergency is over. Short sightedness and urgency for quick and visible results. Volume of aid may be considered more important than its real impact, consistently harder to measure. Donors' coordination is hindered by ignorance, selfishness, laziness, incompetence.	derstand that generosity is useless without professionalism. Align preferences with those of the beneficiaries, so reducing any intermediary's discretion. Impose result-based conditionality on further aid supply. Dominant donors may ease coordination, decreasing transaction costs, and information asymmetries.
Aid agencies	Acting as brokers, so as to aid agencies to optimize the intermediation between donors and aid recipients, making help effective. Transaction costs and information asymmetries typically make direct donor-beneficiary relationship a hardly	When the beneficiary is not the paying agent, it is the former who needs to be pleased. Information asymmetries can be cunningly exploited, to the extent that distant donors are not fully aware of local situations. Laziness is more than a temptation, when	Accept independent audit and avoid fruitless investments. Impose some minimum governance and transparency conditions on beneficiaries: if the whole aid process has to be audited, quality is about to be checked along all the investment chain and problems

Player	Theoretical aspirations / targets	Practical deviations from ideal behaviors	Converging behaviors, so as to mitigate governance problems
	viable option, motivating the existence of intermediary aid agencies. Aid contracts should ideally be ›complete‹, envisaging and regulating all the possible states of the world. To be a humble learning agency.	there is little competition for results: what matters is raising funds anyways. Discretionary management, that is somewhat necessary, may easily get out of any external control. Overinvestment, even in suboptimal projects, is another possibility: agencies have to invest anyway, in order to justify their very existence and if they don't spend the raised money, they may be less able to get new funds. Accountability has also negative side effects and it can be suffocated by bureaucracy. The agent may have a different objective function, hardly consistent with that of the donor, hindering the detection of his efforts and out-	are more likely to come up at the very end of it – where more money is likely to be spent. Proper training can increase awareness, involving all the stakeholders (donors and, in particular, aid agencies and beneficiaries), respecting their specific role, softening information asymmetries (reducing so damaging misunderstandings) and easing aid delivery and receipt, aligning diverging interests towards more ›culturally‹ shared goals. Confrontation with open and frank discussions, personal acquaintance, sharing of problems and solutions and constant contact are all small complementary components of a tighter and deeper

Player	Theoretical aspirations / targets	Practical deviations from ideal behaviors	Converging behaviors, so as to mitigate governance problems
		comes[405]. Articulated and transaction-intensive services, with an unavoidable discretion, are hard to detect and monitor. Delivery mechanisms are typically characterized by internal accountability. Broken feedback loop produces incentive biases in aid[406] and only donors have political leverage over the decision-making process[407]. Aid contracts are far from being ›complete‹ and the more detailed they are, the higher the risk of not covering unexpected events.	link. The intermediating role of the aid agency, possibly helped by local facilitators is crucial for a successful achievement of these key strategies. Write flexible and easily enforceable agreements, where substance prevails over form and continuous monitoring prevents abuses.
Local (poor) beneficiaries	To be helped in the initial stages of development, up to the point of going on with their own	When donated money rains down from the sky, the first temptation is to get it quickly	Accept conditional aid, respecting transparency rules. Learn to use money for development

405 See Easterly (2008), p. 155
406 Reinikka in Esterly (2008), p. 181.
407 Martens in Easterly (2008), p. 285.

Player	Theoretical aspirations / targets	Practical deviations from ideal behaviors	Converging behaviors, so as to mitigate governance problems
	forces. Not to be tempted by moral hazard–the take the money and run away option, so frequent in financial intermediation[408]–which represent a fraudulent and myopic behavior.	and unconditionally. And unearned money is easy to spend quickly. Long term budgeting and careful use of funds for sustainable development is typically not a priority. Over the counter agreements with aid intermediaries are always possible in order to share the pie, damaging both unconscious donors and powerless targeted beneficiaries. A psychological portrait of the beneficiaries is difficult to figure out and donors often wonder if beneficiaries are naïve or duplicitous.	instead of simply grab and spend it. Try to establish direct feedback with donors, expressing them real needs. Exploit cultural exchanges, which can enrich both parts. Try to limit the influence of local greedy and powerful intermediaries (ruling politicians, the army …) who have strong personal incentives to divert incoming money … to their own endless pockets.

Biased belief on debt relief

High foreign indebtedness, which has been cumulated over years on bilateral or multilateral terms, is a consequence of bad local economic policies, stagnant or recessive economy, possible due to conflicts, or external shocks.

408 For the microfinance implications, see Chapter 18.

Debt relief–partial or total forgiveness of cumulated foreign debt–has become a hot issue since the 1980s, when the economies of the weakest States, located in particular in sub-Saharan Africa, underwent a long period of stagnation, and service of the debt soon became unbearable.

Country defaults are common. As Moyo (2009), p. 86, points out, Spain defaulted on its external debt thirteen times between 1500 and 1900. Since the 19th Century, Venezuela has defaulted nine times, Brazil seven times, Argentina five times (most recently in 2001). World Bank stands out as the biggest global lender, especially for infrastructures and development finance, even in the form of project lending.

Provision of aid and loans, conditional upon budget and macroeconomic stability, is in principle widely welcome. Such a provision has however to be wisely implemented, avoiding draconian cuts in pro growth spending, such as education or healthcare. Since development is also dependent on consumption, repressive measures can be counterproductive. Structural adjustments towards more stable and sounder economic policies are effective only if they are carefully tailored and progressively implemented in feasible scenarios.

Conditional loans are hardly linked to valuable parameters such as improved human rights, lower corruption, or reduced military spending. Adjustments to stricter monetary and budget policies are typically damaging for the poorest that silently pay the bill and hardly participate to the pie's sharing. Debt amnesty may be conditional on the application of tighter economic policies, including privatizations and cuts on excessive public spending, under the (severe) supervision of the International Monetary Fund or other international agencies. Is debt relief able to raise reform efforts?

If foreign debt is kept or cut back to sustainable levels, more resources can be released for development spending, including poverty reduction[409]. Should too many resources be drained to the service of the debt, there would be no residual cash to finance growth projects.

Forgiving (converting to grant), restructuring, or rescheduling sovereign debt–meeting solvency problems–is a complex task with many side effects for the beneficiary country, which are not always positive.

Unconditional debt relief is a dangerous form of help, which can unduly spoil inefficient governments, supporting politicians who would not otherwise deserve to stay in power. To the extent that governments are corrupted and their debt issues have not been used to help the poor, even debt relief is unlikely to be beneficial for the underserved. But if it is considered as a form of aid, it can crowd out other helping measures, even those directly addressed to the poor such as targeted aid or social public spending. It also creates a bad precedent

409 Addison, Hansen, Tarp (2004), p. 3.

and when ›forgiven‹ countries issue new debt, they may think that even these new obligations will be sooner or later deleted by generous and flexible lenders.

The best help comes from oneself: looking for home-grown solutions

The best solutions to local problems are typically–unsurprisingly–home-grown. Put this way, the statement looks both simple and sharable, even if top down standard strategies (imposed from above with little or any country personalization) are particularly frequent and culturally driven by utopian egocentric vision.

Domestic solutions follow both a macro and a micro approach. The former deals with stabilization policies, aimed at bringing inflation and interest rates to manageable levels, as well as reducing foreign trade imbalances and the volatility of the local non convertible currency. On the micro side, policies should accelerate private business and, with it, employment and wealth creation.

Helping the poor to help themselves … sounds intuitively good.

Foreign aid also reduces the need for a system of taxation. And without such a system, it is really more difficult to construct a well-functioning government, and it is less likely that forces for representation take root (historically, the principle of ›no taxation without representation‹ has promoted democracy). When a government doesn't depend on taxes for its revenues, then it will have fewer incentives to seek accountability.

Aid is more than just sending money, needing to be geared up by complementary actions

Donors should check what happens to their money, targeting their funding and bypassing the ›sticky fingers‹ of government as much as possible. To some extent, donors should also make aid conditional on democratic reforms because this is the way to soften aid inefficiency. However, when doing so, they should be careful not to put the cart before the horse. One of the goals of aid is precisely democratization. To the extent that aid is dispersed and grabbed by ruthless politicians and warlords, they would obviously not even notice if aid dries up, failing to reach the targeted poor. Only the undeserving real beneficiaries would complain, using the poor as a pretext for not interrupting the bonanza.

Aid principles and strategies include:

- increasing aid efficiency – ›making more using less‹, maximizing the profit of international aid money without requiring larger amounts of capital. The main areas to work on can be classified in three main points: coordination, transparency, and accountability, coherence;

- coordination, in the form of contact and cooperation between people working on development projects in the same area;
- transparency and accountability – it is extremely important that the use of money that is spent in international aid is monitored and accounted;
- coherence, so as not to destroy a man's house and then help him build a new one. On the one side, the rich nations donate money to the poor ones. On the other side, their commercial and economic politics that developed countries carry out are an obstacle to the development of poor countries.

Improving aid efficiency means also making sure that donors start to consider other ways to help developing nations, without necessarily involving the use of money, but more often changing those politics that maintain the poor in need of asking for further help. To work on this objective, a wider perspective needs to be developed and other institutions like the World Trade Organization need to be involved.

It is important to consider that coherence means the presence of one, clear aim: eradicating poverty. Only once this aim is clear to everyone, it is possible to address various strategies towards its achievement.

Coordination, coherence and accountability are strongly linked to each other. For example, coordination between parties would mean splitting up development objectives and make accountability easier for the development agents, as they would have a more restricted area to work on.

The condensed Chapter

Instead of being a blessing from heaven, foreign aid is often a curse–somewhat similar to the oil curse–that acts as a boomerang against poor countries, weakening their efforts to develop and to self empower, and creating a dangerous dependency on volatile external help.

Humanitarian emergency aid greatly differs from long term development programs, even if they often follow a top down egocentric approach, where wealthier countries impose their views and methods, irrespectively of local particularities. A much more tiring bottom up approach is typically more effective and culturally accepted, starting from the playground of the poorest and gratefully acknowledging a subsidiarity approach. It allows for a better coordination of governance issues, aligning the often divergent interests of donors, intermediary aid agencies and needy beneficiaries. Sustainable development goes beyond a cultural syndrome of aid dependency, a bottleneck that leads to passivity, fatalism, and failure.

Out of Poverty Tips

Give me a fishing rod, instead of a fish. Start from a bottom up approach, close to real necessities and beware that foreign help may have spoiling and destabilizing effects, unless properly shared and conceived.

Selected Readings

CALDERISI R., (2006), *The Trouble with Africa: Why Foreign Aid Isn't Working*, Palgrave Macmillan, London.

EASTERLY W., (2006), *The White Man's Burden: Why the West's Efforts to Aid the Rest Have Done So Much Ill and So Little Good*, Penguin Press, London.

MADDISON T., HANSEN H., TARP F., eds., (2004), *Debt relief for poor countries*, Palgrave, Basingstoke.

MOYO D., (2009), *Dead Aid: Why Aid Is Not Working and How There Is a Better Way for Africa*, Penguin Books, London.

APPENDIX – Foreign aid banana skins

As we have seen above, foreign aid does not automatically help the poor and, in many cases, it is wasted or it can even be harmful. Here there is a list of some of the most common ›banana skins‹ involving aid and development agencies, with some mitigation measures. Many of them come from the provocative book of Dambisa Moyo (2009), a Zambian researcher with smart and nonconformist ideas.

Even if we share most of her ideas, we think that Moyo is sometimes too pessimist and the sub-Saharan African situation, the poorest area of the world, is not comparable to other poor but developing areas of Asia or Central and South America. Bottom-up aid, subsidiarity and micro approach avoiding the corrupt intermediation of rotten governments can do much. And many aid banana skins may be avoided or, at least, softened.

We should always beware of material aid, which is useful but only if it is complemented with consideration and love for the poor.

Table in Appendix – Detecting and mitigating foreign aid banana skills

Banana skin	Mitigation measure
Setting *a priori* unconditional goals is good for motivation, but it may be counterproductive for implementation. Unmet expectations bring to frustration.	Fewer ineffective approaches will survive if only results were more visible[410]. Realism, verisimilitude, flexibility, and better prioritization in setting goals and targets are highly needed. Start solving solvable problems, beginning with the simple and obvious, and look for effectiveness and substance over spectacular and ephemeral outcomes.
The real problem is getting resources to the poor (delivering).	Avoid dispersion and misdirection, more likely where intermediation is complex; many smell and eat the tasty pie before its targeted destination. Try to select and focus on feasible realistic targets. Reaching the poor with the donor's advocacy should be the real target. Respond to the supposed beneficiaries, not to the paymaster.
	When the poor help themselves, being

410 See Easterly (2006), p. 17.

Banana skin	Mitigation measure
It is difficult to receive a feedback from the bottom about aid's effectiveness: top down surveys are hardly useful, feedback works only if somebody listens. The only people whose views seem to matter are foreigners[411] and donors' efficacy is often hard to measure[412], especially in fields such as gender inequalities or human rights. Donors may find it difficult to observe the effort and the outcomes of their agents – aid intermediary agencies.	committed and motivated, and ›it's up to them‹ to sort out problems, they receive immediate feedback, with no information asymmetries or fallacies. The donors first have to understand the real needs of the potential beneficiaries, talking with them and listening, and only later they are supposed to design, implement and manage together with them. Avoid unneeded middlemen, who divert aid and distort information. Listen to warning voices. Always ask the poor how they perceive their needs and beware of faraway investors. Promote ›voice‹, letting the recipients talk and freely express their ideas, aspirations, and concerns. Grass-rooted initiatives make it better and community-driven development, with the participation and empowerment of the poor, are longer lasting.
The poor … by definition have little money and no political power to make their needs known. They are hardly empowered to blame somebody if they requests are unmet and aid does not reach them.	The poor don't have to be passive or fatalistic. Even victimization doesn't help. Democracy, much more that oligarchic autocracy, empowers the poor.
Aid fragmentation, due to the existence of too many donors with multiple objectives and tiny resources, brings to dispersive confusion, lack of coordination, inefficient design, and implementation, overcrowding recipient countries with too many projects uneasy to coordinate and filter. Different donors are typically neither competing nor collaborating and they may just ignore each other. Reputational risk is	Donors should focus and specialize, reaching critical mass below which their intervention is useless or even harmful. Dimension is however not a dogma and even small NGOs can be effective, if properly targeting their aid. Coordination among donors, together with harmonization and alignment of procedures, policies and standards, is highly wanted, allowing to minimize

[411] See Hancock (1989), p. 125.
[412] See Easterly (2008), p. 50.

Banana skin	Mitigation measure
also limited by fragmentation, representing a disincentive for the donors and their efforts, reducing the accountability of the projects. Donor fragmentation brings also to a project multiplication, which is difficult to coordinate, especially within the recipient country. Dispersion eases dissipation and it increases transaction costs, together with duplication and waste. Fragmentation is an obstacle to efficient scaling.	duplications and to share experiences and some cost. Best practice templates can help, at least to address initial problems.
Rich people of the West tend to oversimplify problems they are hardly aware of – big actions for big problems are hardly effective and often bring to irrelevant outcomes.	Acknowledging cultural differences is the first step in order to improve aid efficacy. Avoid unchecked and arbitrary decisions. Beware of poor planning or inappropriate technology.
Benevolent imperialism to spread Western capitalism (a World Bank / IMF approach …) is hardly effective. The West cannot transform the Rest, represented by complex societies with different histories and cultures.	Inculturation of development principles, that have to be adapted to the local needs and understandings, makes them shared and accepted. Arrogance and paternalism are always counterproductive.
A lot of effort is wasted or misdirected. Do not harm is always a golden rule. Improper planning (bureaucratic errors, wastefulness, inappropriateness, lateness …) and bad management (implementation), complemented by involuntary idiocy, are frequent pitfalls.	Try to avoid superficiality and misunderstanding. Triumphalism is counterproductive – daily humble effort is what really matters. Joint planning and on-field coordination are wanted. Cost escalation is a continuous threat, to be timely monitored. Local officials with indigenous capacity have to be empowered, otherwise they fail to learn and just act as passive spectators.
Lack of home grown development.	Homegrown development is more direct and realistic–avoiding utopian goals and reminding that in many cases much can be done with little–and it has lower transaction costs; closeness and face to face acquaintance decrease

Banana skin	Mitigation measure
	information asymmetries; more modest and doable steps are much more effective than hardly manageable macro projects. Long term sustainability, progressively empowering the poor, stands out as a key target. It is often better to accept (sound) proposals from recipient countries, rather than making them.
High levels of foreign aid are often correlated with low levels of democracy. Foreign aid, like the revenues of natural resources, provides an opportunity for governments and leaders to appropriate funds illegitimately, keeping other groups out of power, so as not to share the pie. External resources can exacerbate existing domestic imbalances. Donors risk making recipient States worse, increasing corruption, bureaucracy, dependency on them rather than on their own citizens.	Beware of ›sticky fingers‹, since aid can both foster and breed corruption. Avoid linking aid to political opportunities to establish a privileged relationship with one country, for purposes which are completely different from poverty relief. Corruption can be managed, reduced, or even circumvented. Aid can be–to a certain extent–conditioned by morality. Alignment of donors' interests and targets with those of the ultimate beneficiaries can mitigate funds misallocation or mismanagement.
Undemocratic and illegitimate governments with easy and uncontrolled access to foreign funds are nominally accountable only to foreign donors – and funds may be easily diverted and misspent to finance the army or personal smuggling, in disguised development projects.	Avoiding corrupt governments, averting unnecessary intermediation with direct interventions to the poor is a simple way to improve efficacy and enhance transparency.
Foreign aid also reduces the need for a system of taxation. And without such a system, it's more difficult to construct well-functioning government.	Coordination of foreign aid with domestic budget and fiscal policy. Taxation brings representation and is a fundamental–albeit ›expensive‹–cornerstone of democracy. With development, the tax base naturally grows and the poor should benefit out of it.
Foreign aid can slow down the growth	Avoid crowding out effects, improv-

Banana skin	Mitigation measure
of domestic savings.	ing the financial system and its outreach. Domestic savings are counter cyclical and they provide a shelter in recession.
Foreign aid brings corruption, highly detrimental for growth and development, providing crook governments with fresh money to spend.	Implement proper systems of check and balance, independent audits, and accountability. Patience, enduring commitment and engagement are strongly needed to disrupt culturally rooted corruption.
Material aid often forgets core values such as human rights, environmental sustainability, and gender equality.	Aid has to be carefully targeted and released. Discriminations need to be avoided and aid should be primarily targeted at helping minorities.
A surge in aid inflows–possibly to the tune of several percentage points of a recipient's GDP–presents considerable macroeconomic challenges for the recipient country. How should countries adapt their monetary and fiscal policies? Will inflation result? Will the large inflows boost the exchange rate and make exports less competitive, and should this be resisted?[413]	The impact of aid has to be planned and fine tuned, especially in poor and small countries where it can be consistent, relative to the rest of the economy, and where it can have a shocking effect. Credible impact evaluations are an international public good and successful programs may conveniently be scaled up, while ›unlucky‹ ones are to be abandoned[414].
Loans are hardly distinct from grants.	Avoid long term loans. Don't favor delinquency on scheduled repayments and refuse to send more money if previous loans are not repaid[415].
If recipient countries know that many donors are competing for aid, the threat of unsatisfied donors to withdraw may not worry recipients, to the extent that they can easily find a substitute.	Coordination among donors, setting minimum standards.
Aid tries to respond to market failures,	Strengthen public influence and State

413 Aiyar, Berg, and Hussain (2005).

414 See Duflo, Kremer in Easterly (2008), p. 117.

415 This is a well known and dangerous dilemma: should financiers avoid sending more money, the debtor may be unable to repay his loan, whereas if more funds are given, the debtor can either be rescued or cause an even bigger loss.

Banana skin	Mitigation measure
meeting unsatisfied needs, but it is hardly observable and measurable, to the extent that its real value is not fully and objectively identifiable and it may be biased by subjective judgment.	institutions, to soften market failures. Focus and specialize on specific targets and minimize subjectivity with continuous feedback.
To the extent that foreign aid is considered a permanent, reliable, and consistent source of income, governments of recipient countries have little incentive to find their own and autonomous way to development[416], with a consequent subsidies dependency. Aid flows suffer from high conditionality and are volatile and unpredictable[417] – geopolitical priorities change across time.	Avoid being lazy or short sighted. Make aid conditional on autonomous development. Beware of the lobby of aid, both on the giving and the recipient's side. Aid flows should follow long term pro-growth strategies. If capital is rationed, it is better to keep aid to a lower sustainable level that to boost and then stop it.
A culture of aid dependency makes receiving countries addicted and doped, it weakens local stimuli to grow autonomously and it engenders inlaziness and indolence. When foreign aid dries up, people are unable and unused to react.	Partnership–cooperating to reduce poverty–is better than dead end aid. Support has to be time limited. Active and preventive involvement of the intended beneficiaries improves the probabilities of success of aid projects.
Conditional aid, given setting rules to be followed, is often hardly working and when rules are violated, aid typically continues. Unconditional aid, devoid of any social and environmental covenant, may however be ever worse (see, for example, the cynical Chinese strategy in resource-rich African countries, where human right respect is never an issue). If foreign aid is addressed to key humanitarian targets such as instruction or healthcare, then there may be a dangerous crowding out effect, since bad governments	Conditions and covenants must be simple, easy to control and acceptable. Real outreach of the poorest should always be indispensable cornerstone. A radiography of the overall public spending, albeit intrusive and difficult to make, may soften these problems, making humanitarian aid conditional on the avoidance of improper funds diversion.

416 Moyo (2009), p. 36.
417 Fitzgerald in Nafziger, Väyryen (2002), Chapter 3.

Banana skin	Mitigation measure
may save public money, diverting it to ›unpleasant‹ expenses.	
Aid that consists of often useless import of foreign goods contributes to weaken and destroy local markets.	Don't import a mosquito net and buy it locally if it is available. Local prices are also much cheaper and there are no customs and lower transportation costs.
Aid is much more easily consumed than invested.	Control of unproductive public consumption and readdressing of resources to real investments.
Sizeable money from aid nourishes corruption, destroys merit, and misallocates talent – those who remain principled are driven away[418]. Unchallenged discretionary power favors funds mismanagement.	Fungible aid (in cash or easily tradable goods) is much easier to be smuggled and it has to be kept to a minimum and carefully checked. The crowding out effect of corruption can be conveniently reduced again with monitoring and meritocratic appointments, following international best practices.
Since corrupted countries are poorer and aid is targeted to poor countries, aid primarily goes to poor countries. Aid risks to have a tautological justification and to be given only because needed, irrespectively of its efficacy.	Fair and disenchanted survey of the target country always has to precede intervention. If a country needs help but it is not fit to properly receive it, safe and sound background has to be prepared before intervention. In the meanwhile, emergency / humanitarian aid may conveniently be deployed, so as … to keep the patient alive till he can stand to be cured.
There is a pressure to lend and to grant aid, in order to justify the existence of big Western aid agencies – aid is a business and it has to go on, even if improperly carried on. Big, bureaucratic institutions are ›self–justifying‹ and aid is not their product, but is merely the justification for their existence. And vainglorious bureaucrats tend to interact with ruthless autocrats,	Fairness and accountability–possibly certified by external and independent auditors–should be a primary concern of aid agencies. It is easy to circumvent donors about the real outcomes of far and complex projects. Worthy projects have measurable costs.

418 Moyo (2009), p. 50.

Banana skin	Mitigation measure
typically bypassing the poor. Power and prestige, mixed with corruption, produce a lethal cocktail for the poor.	
Debt relief hardly helps the poor, who are typically not within the beneficiaries of lent money. Donors fear that without pumping new money, debtors are unable to repay old debt[419].	Who is really in need, the donor or the recipient? Debt relief, sometimes necessary, especially after calamities, is not educating in the long run: who will pay, knowing that sooner or later debt will be relieved?
Soft factors such as trust and reliance are basic ingredients for development but in a world of aid, there is no need or incentive to trust your neighbor and no need for your neighbor to trust you[420]. Informal confidentiality destroys accountability.	Even if soft factors–the true glue behind human relations–are hardly detectable, they are indispensable for successful outcomes, especially for what concerns risky projects. Trust and cooperation are harder to establish when cultural differences are substantial.
Conflicts are fomented by competition for the control of resources, including aid. By lowering average incomes and slowing down growth, aid increases the risk of conflicts. Aid may foster a military culture[421].	Try to separate aid from conflicts. During humanitarian crises they can interact, whereas development aid, being less urgent and dramatic, can be more carefully planned and granted. Aid has to be made conditional on good governance and peace keeping, and it does not have to indirectly reward warlords.
Foreign aid, besides having a crowding out effect on domestic savings and investment, in favor of greater consumption, may bring inflation and diminishing exports.	Think globally but buy locally, especially if domestic producers risk being crowded out by imported goods which, being aid driven, are not subject to standard market rules.
Very poor countries have a problem of absorption capacity of aid resources, and of lack of skilled manpower. Much wanted ›technical assistance‹ and expertise can hide military support.	Aid packages have to be reasonably unsophisticated, in order to be accepted and understood by local cultures. Since this point is often impossible or counterproductive with technology, involvement, and proper training of

419 Moyo (2009), p. 55.
420 Moyo (2009), p. 59.
421 Moyo (2009), p. 60.

Banana skin	Mitigation measure
Aid is a double-edged sword and may easily leak into inappropriate military spending, diverting funds from their institutional destination. Where borders are porous, such as in stateless countries, inadvertent aid leakage may easily spread across different nations[422].	local experts is absolutely vital. It may take time, but it's worth trying. Improper understanding about the features of aid packages make them unaccepted or misconceived, often generating a parallel secondary market where aid goods are improperly resold, instead of being delivered to the targeted beneficiaries.
Lack of ownership and participation, with little involvement of recipient countries, concentrated only within intermediaries and local profiteers.	The psychological attitude of aid recipients, hardly neglected, and underestimated, has a tremendous importance in shaping attitude towards help. Involvement and participation strongly improve the success probabilities of the intervention. The poor are often shy and intimidated.
Big sums of aid, and culture of aid-dependency, encourage governments to support large, bulky, and often unproductive public sectors – just another way to reward their cronies[423]. Wasteful efforts create confusion and dismay. Big projects bypass the poor, are often unrealistic; they create market distortions and attract corruption.	To those unused to make mindful budgetary plans and to properly deal with large amounts of money, massive aid can create dangerous dependency. The supply of aid may patiently and conveniently take place on several installments, conditional upon monitoring and proper accountability. Involvement of local beneficiaries is absolutely vital for long lasting projects.
Deceptively seduced by the siren call of aid, governments sink their ships on the rocks of development demise[424]. Broken promises of corrupt governments are easily forgiven.	Should developing governments raise money issuing debt, rather than receiving unconditional loans, they would have to face and to meet financial markets' expectations, which are less forgiving than donor countries.
In an aid scenario, those who are not within the lucky beneficiaries may also suffer from crowding out effect, while in a trade scenario, even if com-	Since aid is not democratically distributed, discrimination between winners and losers can increase and the powerless poorest are more likely to

422 Collier (2009), p. 116.
423 Moyo (2009), p. 66.
424 Moyo (2009), p. 88.

Banana skin	Mitigation measure
petition may be tough, opportunities abound[425].	be part of the latter category. Fairness and anti-discriminatory supply to all the needy ones has to be properly conceived and put in place. If aid divides, it is much more likely to be refused or misunderstood and wasted.
The institutional trap[426], according to which weak institutions are a big obstacle for development, is often neglected by foreign aid strategies, which typically invest even in countries with bad institutions, backing them instead of promoting due changes.	Full consideration of a realistic absorption capacity is a preliminary condition for efficient aid. Bad institutions should be put in front of a tough trade-off: change policy and become democratic and fair or renounce to undeserved aid. Needy institutions may have a substantial stimulus to change and if they don't want to do it, it really means that the money is wasted and counterproductively spent.
Deceptive and emotional fund raising can distort charitable advertising.	Avoid capitalism of mercy and look at the substance. Popular media can distort information and exaggerate disasters.
Lack of coordination among donors, who are all willing to be involved in the same popular and trendy jobs, brings to a wasteful duplication of efforts.	Don't overcrowd with unneeded or uncoordinated help disorganized recipients. Specialize and keep it hard, surviving ephemeral enthusiasm. Consult disaster victims before intervening.
The more bureaucrats spend, the better they are judged, promoting their own careers. Big and fast loans from big donors are easier to conceive and to manage, if compared to numerous smaller ones, but their quality control is weaker.	It is only from careful and preventive on-field surveys that proper amounts of funding have to be selected for suitable and reasonable local investments. Small is difficult. Extravagant projects, carried on misunderstanding the problems that the poor actually face, risk being both grandiose and irrelevant, like cathedrals in the desert. Empathy for the poor is highly want-

425 Moyo (2009), p. 122.
426 Described in Chapter 5.

Banana skin	Mitigation measure
	ed.
Selfish bureaucrats think only about themselves, preserving their privileges, fringe benefits, and payroll and forgetting about the poor. Impermeability to scrutiny and information asymmetries are an obstacle against meritocratic assessments. Aid money has to be spent anyway, so as to justify the existence of the institution and of its bureaucrats.	Ideals and social results need, at least partially, to be accountable and measurable. Payrolls and benefits should be linked to concrete results. Learn from mistakes and painful errors, preserving an institutional memory from the (true) history of the aid agency.
Running and fixing costs of projects are often neglected and underestimated.	Careful and wise budgeting of the longer term project's implications has to properly consider its efficient maintenance, requiring technical assistance and adequate financial coverage.
Projects funded by foreign agencies are typically conceived and designed by foreigners and again they are implemented by foreigners using foreign equipment manufactured in foreign countries.	These projects are largely deemed to be considered a foreign affair, unaccepted by local cultures. Full foreign coverage of the projects make them more popular and accepted at home, but far less effective where they should. Involvement of local workforce and resources is a must for successful projects.
Capital intensive agricultural investments effective in donor countries may not work in underdeveloped areas.	Beware of ›environmental‹ and ›cultural‹ differences even for what concerns investments. Lack of skill, equipment, fertilizers, spare parts, etc., together with different cultivations and climate make the difference. Adaptation to incomparable realities is needed. Some investment strategies can be successfully exported, others can not and shared experience with local farmers can bring to the right decisions. Excessive use of advanced technologies may bring to cultural shocks and refusals.
Those who accept free handouts today	Pay attention to consumerist depend-

Banana skin	Mitigation measure
will become paying customers tomorrow[427], creating economic dependency difficult to eradicate.	ency, that is easy to establish and difficult to eradicate. Foreign sophisticated products, such as genetically modified food, may command a short term competitive advantage, since they are free or subsidized, but in the long term they are likely to be expensive and uneasy to replace with local products, which risk being crowded out from the market. Beware of subtle dumping strategies, especially for what concerns the drug of food aid.
Negative experiences with humanitarian interventions, together with aid fatigues caused by tighter finances, may cause opposition movement in donor countries, especially if humanitarian aid is in the form of military mission with many casualties.	Beware of the Somalia syndrome for the US in 1993, which prevented them for intervening in the Rwandan genocide of Spring 1994. Try to fairly represent to the public opinion the true reasons of the intervention, possibly to be legitimated with multilateral sharing. A welcoming local population makes things easier.
Short term results, which often are needed to give a feedback to impatient foreign donors, are often not compatible with underdeveloped recipient realities and needs, where growth is a long-termed painful goal. Politicians from both sides–within the donor and the recipient country–often have a short time horizon, typically not exceeding their electoral mandate, hardly consistent with the long-term needs of development.	A marathon runner is much more useful than a sprinter. Anxiety for myopic short term results is biased by an impatient Western culture, not taking into account the different concept of time that characterizes other cultures[428].
Aid is typically concentrated in investments, often neglecting maintenance and financial coverage for running costs. Aid beneficiaries, especially if located in Sub-Saharan Africa,	Allocate funds also for monitoring and maintenance. Teach local beneficiaries that careful attention to running problems and costs is a cultural value without which development is hardly

427 Hancock (1989), p. 168.

428 See Chapter 9.

Banana skin	Mitigation measure
are hardly known for their perseverance in maintenance and fixing of infrastructures and properties.	possible. Make further aid conditional on proper maintenance of already existing projects.
Aid agencies are eager to hire the most skilled and talented native workers, often subtracting them to local institutions, since it is possible to pay higher and more stable payrolls and offering them more attractive career possibilities – locals are typically excited by the idea of working for a big foreign institution. The brain drain can be very damaging, especially if key employees are scarce and hard to replace. Their specific knowledge of the country, together with the implicit cost of their training paid by local institutions, brings another systemic implicit cost to the country. Multinational entities, such as the World Bank, the IMF, or UN agencies or big foundations, such as the Bill and Melinda Gates are particularly attractive.	Cooperation between foreign agencies and local institutions is strongly recommended, avoiding costly price competition which pushes salaries high – especially in key functions such as healthcare. Selfish behavior of foreign agencies, worried exclusively about their personal targets, without considering the damaging external impact of their policies, is to be avoided, with diplomatic fair play strategy.
Aid fragmentation brings to too many small projects, which are often misconceived and unable to reach minimum critical mass, with no scale returns, excessive fixed costs, and messy duplication. Coordination becomes problematic, both within donors and their agents and with recipient countries, unable to manage too many countcrparts.	Again, coordination among donors, who may conveniently merge their activities, specializing in specific industries or countries, can allow for an efficient sharing of costs, information, and experiences.
Aid budgets, typically allocated on a yearly basis, are to be spent, anyway, regardless of their utility. Unspent money often reduces future budget disposals, so creating vicious incentive to use funds quickly.	Focus on accountable real outcomes, making future funding conditional on effective results and not automatically or passively linked to past expenses. Make disbursements conditional also on the recipient's actions and performance. Yearly budgeting is hardly

Banana skin	Mitigation measure
	consistent with long term development and creates uncertainties about adequate future funding.
Donors' pride often prevents their exit from ruinous projects, so minimizing waste of money and resources.	Aid conditionality is again needed. Making mistakes is human (›*errare humanum est*‹) but persevering is diabolic.

CHAPTER 15 – Capital for development and the property trap: from the misery of ungrowth to the mystery of growth

The poor inhabitants of [underdeveloped] nations–five-sixths of humanity–do have things, but they lack the process to represent their property and create capital. They have houses but not titles; crops but not deeds; businesses but not statutes of incorporation.

It is the unavailability of these essential representations that explains why people who have adapted every other Western invention, from the paper clip to the nuclear reactor, have not been able to produce sufficient capital to make their domestic capitalism work.

This is the mystery of capital.

Hernando De Soto, *The Mystery of Capital*

Accumulate and innovate, to move out of poverty

Development is enhanced by the synergic interaction of tangible and intangible resources, representing the ›software‹ of an economy (physical and human capital, from equipment to skills and technology), and the main tool in order to reduce poverty, always reminding that development challenges are both daunting and vast.

Productivity, that is the maximization of output for a given input, is very much linked with this interaction–representing a sort of orchestra director–and it is the key propellant behind the much wanted (and possibly vibrant) growth. The dark side of underdevelopment is represented by factors such as the inefficiency trap: a strategy combination with a modest outcome. The latter is very much concerned with limited productivity and little specialization and division of labor, and it was advocated since Adam Smith and nowadays it has become more and more necessary, due to the increasing complexity of manufacturing.

Also the poor need to accumulate human capital through education, networking, and knowledge sharing, so to enter a largely unknown development playfield following an evolutionary adaptation of ›*homo sapiens*‹ to ›*homo oeconomicus*‹. Whether these concepts are relatively known, their complex interaction is far from being clear and their changing features have a great impact on the final output–economic growth–considered both from a quantitative and a qualitative point of view, particularly important for its time consistency and long term sustainability.

The understanding of the interactions between the aforementioned variables–capital combined with labor and intangible knowledge and inventions, with their output influenced by productivity–is of great importance, not only retrospectively but also in prospect, in order to understand what makes some countries rich and other poor.

Spill over of productivity has an effect in softening inequalities, but it requires much time, and the marginal lower utility of incremental wealth can make wealth less concentrated, with incentives from the part of the poorest that are not shared by the richest. It is a movie that has already been seen in developed countries, and it is likely to be played even elsewhere, with a similar painful transition process.

Growth and development, deriving from the ability to master a correct set of priorities, follow a logistic pattern–not an exponential and dreamy one–with a marginal decrease of the upside speed due to a mixture of decreasing returns of capital, lower stimuli, growing inutility of wealth, and environmental constraints. After euphoria and megalomania, wait for decline – it's just around the corner.

According to the Economist[429], " innovation, the elixir of progress, has always cost people their jobs. In the Industrial Revolution artisan weavers were swept aside by the mechanical loom. Over the past 30 years the digital revolution has displaced many of the mid-skill jobs that underpinned 20th-century middle-class life. Typists, ticket agents, bank tellers and many production-line jobs have been dispensed with, just as the weavers were. Even if new jobs and wonderful products emerge, in the short term income gaps will widen, causing huge social dislocation and perhaps even changing politics. Technology's impact will feel like a tornado, hitting the rich world first, but eventually sweeping through poorer countries too. No government is prepared for it. Why be worried? It is partly just a matter of history repeating itself. In the early part of the Industrial

---

429 The Economist, *Coming to an office near you*, Jan 18th 2014, http://www.economist.com/news/leaders/21594298-effect-todays-technology-tomorrows-jobs-will-be-immenseand-no-country-ready?frsc=dg%7Cd

Revolution the rewards of increasing productivity went disproportionately to capital; later on, labour reaped most of the benefits. The pattern today is similar. The prosperity unleashed by the digital revolution has gone overwhelmingly to the owners of capital and the highest-skilled workers. (...)The main way in which governments can help their people through this dislocation is through education systems.

Figure 15.1. – The logistic curve of development

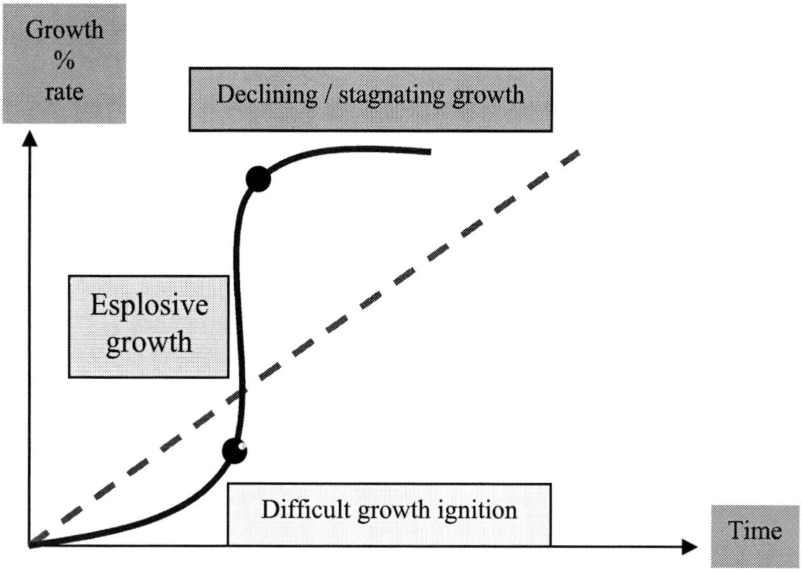

In reducing poverty, the enterprise function, employing people and buying from the surrounding suppliers, plays a fundamental role, rotating around its stakeholders.

Development is a progressive sum of many consecutive and coordinated small acts. And innovation breaks competition, fostering uniqueness–being a powerful differentiator, beyond competitive convergence–and bringing to strategic reengineering of the business process.

Most poor countries develop export strategies that are based upon low labor costs but so acting they create a self-fulfilling cycle. According to Lindsay[430] »in order to compete in their chosen segments, they must keep labor costs at a minimum. It therefore becomes impossible for them to increase salaries, for if they do, they will find themselves with uncompetitive products«. The best strategy–from knowledge to action–is once again raising productivity and, along with it, salaries.

[430] In Harrison, Huntington (2000), p. 286.

According to Helpman (2004), the accumulation of physical and human capital–which interacts also with social and financial capital–is important for growth, together with technological and institutional factors, even if it is just a component of the development process. Asset accumulation reduces ›physical‹ poverty, but much more is required for misery eradication, because of poverty multidimensionality that goes well beyond assetlessness.
Development in poor countries needs to be ignited and taught, mainly from abroad, hoping that, sooner or later, it can become autonomous and self sustaining, in a context where flowers of hope may spontaneously sprout and reminding that personal and collective initiatives eventually matter.
Wealth is–above all–an accumulation of possibilities, which is fueled by creative energy that unlocks opportunities with entrepreneurial spirit, innovation, and increasing competence (following a learning-by-doing pattern).

Combining physical with intangible capital

Virtuous capital accumulation allows to properly store wealth and it is made possible when physical capital (machines, equipment, real estate properties, hardware …) is happily and luckily combined with human capital (stock of education and training embodied in the labor force, with skills, innovation, organization …), responding to economic incentives.
Capital can be subdivided into different categories:

- tangible capital: housing and construction materials; consumer and productive durables; appliances; plant equipment; electronic devices; bikes, motorcycles or cars, cattle and crops, etc.;
- financial capital: cumulated savings, employment payroll, etc.;
- human capital: education (from know why to … know how), skills, motivation, fairness, etc.;
- social capital[431]: belonging to a 'protective' community, etc.;
- natural capital, freely available often also to the poor »includes the stocks of environmentally provided assets such as soil, atmosphere, forests, water, and wetlands«[432]; in urban areas, land is principally linked to housing.

Instruments for growth, such as physical capital and intangibles, do not have a moral autonomy and they cannot be said to be ethical or not, on their own – all depends on their use, which is subject to the man's will. Material greed–so

[431] See Chapter 9.
[432] Osmani in Addison, Hulme, Kanbur (2009), p. 111.

tempting for the rich but even for the poor–makes men slaves of the objects they presume to own, forgetting that we really possess what we are able to renounce to.

Money always has to be complemented by adequate skills, or otherwise it gets soon wasted. The biggest problem in underdeveloped areas is concerned with human capital, deemed to develop and implement appropriate business strategies.

Capital accumulation has an impact on growth and several economic models examined this relationship, starting from Robert Solow's seminal insights. They argue that capital is subject to diminishing returns (this being one of the causes of slower marginal growth traditionally recorded in richer countries) and new capital is more valuable than old (vintage) capital, because capital production is based on known technology and because technology–to be considered as economic fuel behind growth–is improving. Development strategies increasingly depend on breakthrough technologies.

Capital is more productive in capital scarce (i.e., poorer) countries. Convergence (catch up) to richer countries seldom and occurs when it does, it is the result of several causes (innovation, knowledge, good governance, discipline, previously unexploited competitive advantages, and … a bit of luck).

Capital and labor are instinctively attracted by higher productivity, which can provide higher returns. Since productivity cannot grow indefinitely, marginal returns on capital tend to be marginally decreasing, encouraging the search for other unexploited opportunities, even if capital is more likely to flow to areas that are already rich, as Lucas (1990) has pointed out. In places with a high productivity, population density typically increases.

In order to make long term growth possible, capital has to smoothly interact with labor and technology. Productivity is the measure of such an interaction, reminding that it is mostly technology that underpins development through productivity increase, which leads to increased incomes allocated in savings and investments. Conversely, parasitical static accumulation of wealth brings to patrimonialism, which drains development, instead of promoting it.

Initial poverty is very much concerned with lack of capital that is available for investments. The propensity to invest has a cultural background, too. According to Harrison[433] »frugality is the mother of investment–and financial security–in progressive cultures but is a threat to the ›egalitarian‹ status quo in static cultures, which often have a zero-sum worldview«. Lack of public investments (in transports, healthcare, schooling …) brings to infrastructural traps. On the other way, assets like community endowments and public infrastructure facilitate escape from poverty.

433 In Harrison, Huntington (2000), p. 299.

Physical capital is inextricably linked with intangible capital – a close relative of the social capital described in Chapter 9. Physical capital is typically represented[434] by:

- natural endowments (geographical location[435], resource endowments, forests, rivers and lakes, mountains or flat land, climate …);
- financial resources (savings and reserves);
- infrastructures (buildings, bridges, roads, TLC backbones …).

Social capital, which is somewhat more difficult to define and identify since it is an intangible asset, is concerned with institutional capital, knowledge resources, human capital, and culture capital (innovation and creativeness, with their corollary of heuristic insight addressed at problem solving …).

Development is a complex issue that needs proper engineering, following modern managerial techniques, even if many of its features are hardly conceivable in a mechanical and rational way.

Figure 15.2. – Interaction of capital, labor, productivity and growth

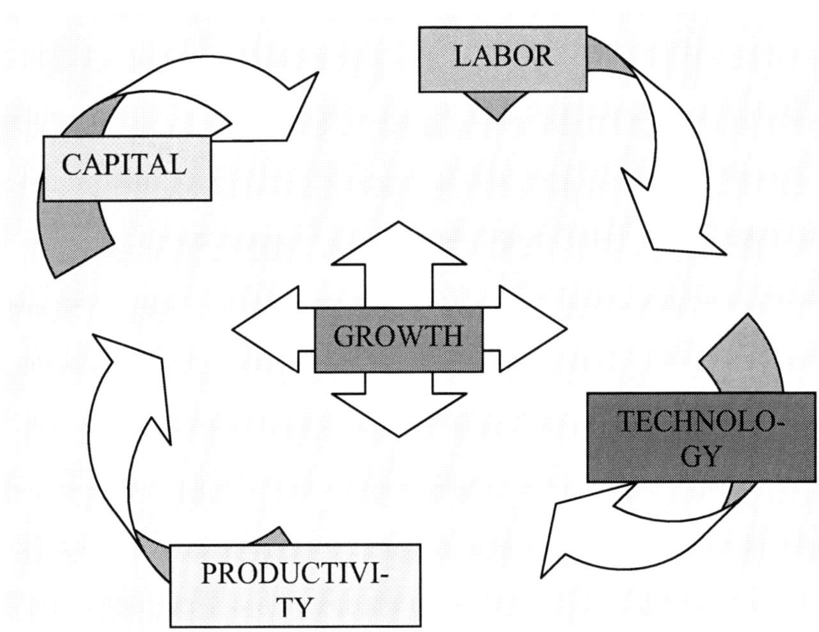

[434] See Fairbanks in Harrison, Huntington (2000), Chapter 20.

[435] For the problem of landlocked countries, see Chapter 2.

When ability complements capital: productivity, innovation and poverty reduction

We have seen above that physical and intangible capital-represented by skills, ideas, or knowledge-have to synergistically interact each with the other, possibly with a bit of creative disorder. Ability has to complement capital, and productivity is the unifying glue. When endowments and opportunities do not meet and match, development becomes impossible and poverty persists. The spirit of this intangible union is hard to detect and to model with a scientific replicable approach – what works in an environment is not automatically deemed to be a success elsewhere.

Science–closely related to technological applications–is based on a replicable Galilean model, typically devised in response to nature's intrinsic complexity, in order to master its secrets for utility purposes, so as to improve human living standards.

Knowledge and information are largely recognized as public goods – scientific knowledge is a scalable and non-rival good, usable by everybody without decreasing others' utility. Only secondarily they can be seen as a private asset and a segregated source of competitive advantage, since everybody can benefit of knowledge capital. The problem in underdeveloped countries is that a weak State is hardly able to protect and to promote public goods, lacking proper incentives and resources. Knowledge is hardly perceived as a valuable ›cultural‹ asset, with its widely recognized positive socio-economic potentialities and implications that are so evident in developed countries but largely underestimated in weaker ones.

Technological scalability, driven by an innovative, challenging, and experimental attitude, underpins prosperity and it peaks with intangible inventions–such as software applications–which can be replicated virtually costlessly, potentially everywhere. Network technologies produce externalities, applying the Metcalfe's property, according to which the value of a telecommunications network is proportional to the square of the number of connected users of the system (two telephones can make only one connection, five can make 10 connections, and twelve can make 66 connections).

Profitability is increasingly linked to ›value for money‹, which expresses the quality that a customer gets for what she pays.

Figure 15.3. – Productivity as a trade off between growth and underdevelopment

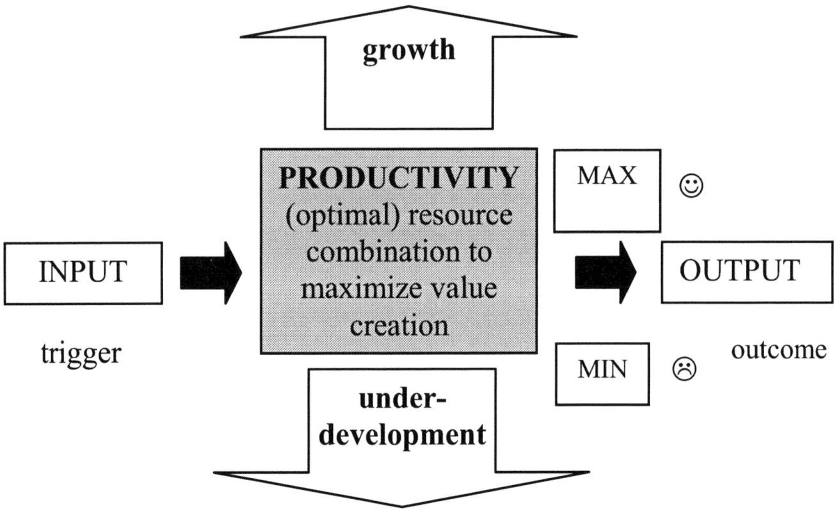

Productivity sets the level of sustainable wages–which follow the popular motto »the more you give … the better I live«–and return to employed capital, which are the basic determinants of income, whose amount is indirectly proportional to the poverty level.
Considering a fixed input, the output can be increased–ideally, maximized–with an innovative combination of production factors, such as labor and capital.

The property trap

Hernando De Soto, the guru of people's neo liberal capitalism, wrote in 1999 *The Mystery of Capital*, a celebrated and original book that tries to explain (as it is reported in its sub title) ›*Why Capitalism Triumphs in the West and Fails Everywhere Else*‹ – a thesis substantially consistent with Landes' historical Eurocentric approach, illustrated in Chapter 1.
Capital is described as the force behind productivity of labor and according to De Soto, p. 5, in underdeveloped countries »most of the poor already possess the assets they need […] but they hold their resources in defective forms: houses built on land whose ownership rights are not adequately recorded, unincorporated businesses with undefined liability, industries located where financiers and investors cannot see them«. Wealth of the poor exists, but it is paradoxically hardly exploitable. When land and property have clear titles, reducing litiga-

tion and frauds, their value and fungibility dramatically increase, easing an otherwise almost impossible intermediation.

The land issue is a core part of geomatics, the discipline concerning land surveying and earth mapping. It is a major topic of litigations in poor countries–both in absolute and in relative terms, since there are not many other economic issues to dispute about–which bears crucial problems, which are often unsolved but anyway particularly important in undermining development. Uses and ownership of lands are differently approached by small farmers, bigger entrepreneurs, or pastoralists, each with their own (conflicting) needs and aspirations.

The issue of landownership and distribution is particularly complicated and paradoxical and it mainly occurs in backward rural places, since everybody's untitled land risks becoming nobody's territory, bringing Wangari Maathai (2009), Chapter 11, to wonder »whose land is it, anyway?«. Uneven titling may however deepen social differences between full proprietors and illegal tenants.

Land property guarantees are the cornerstone of bank lending, above all for what concerns mortgages, as we shall see in the second part of this book, dealing with microfinance topics, where guarantees are absent or unconventional ones can be present.

In Western countries we are used to mortgage-backed loans, to the point that we often tend to undervalue their importance, which is nevertheless daily perceived by the many that can afford to buy a real estate property only if a mortgage bank acts as a provider of finance.

The problem with so many developing countries, especially in scattered rural areas, is that land titling is simply missing and consequently the land and the often poor constructions above it are just unofficially occupied by its informal owners, following ancestral customary rules – and this very land is hardly useable as a guarantee, since they cannot demonstrate to have a real and officially recorded property. Houses can be built either on the sand or on a rocky surface, this being a biblical metaphor for ephemeral versus long lasting investments.

Many developing countries have inherited their legal framework from their colonial past, but since their independence the world has consistently changed and a managing class of trained civil servants is in most cases still missing and highly wanted. Good institutions are needed to protect increasingly complex property rights and private property a right but also a gift to be shared–is a critical institution for fostering economic development. Colonization and then decolonization have brought to erratic and unfair land redistribution, arbitrarily expropriating and recomposing the puzzle of rural entitlements, whereas the interests of poor peasants have always been dominated by more powerful groups of pressure.

It takes many complex steps and significant financial resources to legally start a business or own a house in different parts of the modern world. The records of who-owns-what are often puzzling and, if they are improperly kept, they can bring to long legal disputes. Where the poor are opposed to large landowners, the latter are typically favored by their influence on not always impartial courts. To the extent that the poor mistrust courts, they hardly look for justice, bearing a high cost of abuses from formal authorities and with a huge–albeit hardly visible–social cost.

Tenure security is important and land titling is much desired by farmers, who otherwise are condemned to be mere sharecroppers. Excessive fragmentation of land is however another problem, worsened by demographic booms, which should carefully be avoided, since even in agriculture economies of scale matter.

Systems of land titling greatly differ across the world and land titling is a form of privatization out of collective sharing which creates a property-owning society that can be sadly exemplified by communism, under which people were equal and all poor. Land rights also affect investments, even considering the subject to which guarantees may be granted. It is unsurprisingly mainly the poor those who lack land tenure, being consequently prevented from investing.

The value of land as a guarantee derives also by two predominant characteristics:

- land is more fungible than many other assets – they indeed tend to be highly specific and hardly worthy outside their synergic workings, in a going concern system which disrupts during crises, showing a consistently lower break up value;
- land's value is consistently less volatile than the value of so many other assets – it is a much appreciated quality, especially if considering that when guarantees are used, it's when the outlook is gloomy and their value can be substantially depreciated, so becoming … useless when useful.

The equation ›no real (land) guarantees, no money‹ is so common in Western banking dealings that we are hardly used to understand the importance of its missing presence in developing countries.

Illiterate informal landowners, whose rights to occupy the land are hardly opposable as prescribed, lack any formal title of property, and so they are hardly able to convert their property capital into a working guarantee.

And the fact that little (if any) real estate taxes are applicable to unrecorded properties, may initially sound as good news for lucky tax non-payers, even if no tax collection means lower resources for infrastructures–whose role is decisive even for property value enhancing (a home with no road connections is hardly valuable)–and especially it brings no incentives for cadastral mapping

and checking, with negative impacts on the overall development which go far beyond the land issue.
The creation and progressive (step by step) accumulation of capital–the fuel behind development–would never have been possible in Western countries without the contribution of land injections or other assets in kind (real estate properties, gold or other precious metals, sometimes equipment, and furniture). They form indeed the initial capital and they make the ignition of a wealth multiplying process possible, where capital is successfully combined with labor and skills and cemented by overall synergies and productivity.
The property trap has serious drawbacks which hinder development whereas lack of land property makes it unavailable as collateral, preventing the diffusion of financial products which elsewhere prove useful even for the poor, such as housing microfinance[436], with a progressive build approach. Housing is both a shelter and a commodity, but if land and real estate properties are not properly owned, they become both a precarious shelter and a not negotiable commodity, destroying much if not most of their intrinsic potential value. And the poor typically don't have other valuables – otherwise they wouldn't be destitute. Poor housing may bring to a housing trap[437].

The mystery of hidden capital

It is again De Soto who warns us that capital is surrounded by a shroud of mysteries:

- the mystery of missing information – the world's poor are unable to properly document their endowments (and hardly possessing alternative ones) but also their very … existence, often having no documents or verifiable addresses;
- the ›philosophical‹ mystery of capital – concerning its intrinsic consistence and proper workings;
- the mystery of political awareness – governments hardly recognize the negative impact on development of dead capital;
- the missing lessons of Western history – transition to capitalism is somewhere more painful and less successful than elsewhere, but we hardly investigate the reason, forgetting that this would be a healthy lesson for newcomers;

---

436 See http://www.gsd.harvard.edu/research/research_centers/cuds/microf/cuds_microf.pdf.
437 See http://www.rturn.net/law.php.

- the mystery of legal failure – the legal and institutional framework which is regulating and protecting land in developed countries is hardly working elsewhere, being badly copied or wrongfully customized to local habits.

From each of these interacting and self fulfilling mysteries, we may draw useful lessons about the importance of land titling in capital incorporation.
Private property has also other well-known aspects but anyway complex ones. They strongly contribute to the well being of its owners and they are transmittable and inherited through generations, following an ideal relay race where wealth passes from father to son, accumulates or depreciates if improperly managed and it profoundly contributes to the overall welfare. The right to free inheritance, which was denied by communist regimes but is hardly practicable even elsewhere (even if it is formally allowed), is fundamental to encourage long term investments, beyond one's hopeful life span. According to Ali ibn Abi Talib[438], wealth converts a strange land into homeland whereas poverty turns a native place into a strange land.
A new form of property trap is represented by the rising phenomenon of land grabbing, due to which governments and corporations are buying up farmland in other countries to grow their own food – or simply to make money. Taking profit of their competitive advantages, powerful entities can in reality expropriate the land to the peasants who cultivate it even without being formal proprietors. Powerful foreign or even local institutions possess the liquidity that the poor by definition don't have or a privileged relationship with the local politicians, who also take part in the land partition. To the extent that the land proceeds are taken away and exported to other countries, poor peasants witness another undue appropriation, particularly harmful during recurrent food crises.
Hidden or untitled (real estate) capital is often accompanied by the presence of … invisible poor, whose birth has never been recorded or recognized. Officially non existent poor do not have any certified identity and consequently they are not able to sign contracts with their official name, to have a passport or other documents, including electoral certificates or welfare cards. As a matter of fact, nonexistent poor are marginalized, deprived of their primary rights and exposed to frauds and blackmails (when looking for a job or trying to purchase durable goods …). The biggest census in history is now taking place in India, where a digital passports project is being implemented, involving millions of underserved.

438 Cousin and son-in-law of the Islamic prophet Muhammad.

Land reform

The property issue is often rural, since many poor still live in the countryside, even if urbanization is gaining unprecedented momentum. For rural families, land unsurprisingly represents a shared fundamental asset (the others being their huts, cattle, some working tools, and few savings) and a primary source of income, security, and status. Lack of proper land titling often brings to acute poverty, and related problems of hunger, social unrest, and environmental degradation[439]. Rural landless workers often live under a tough feudal control of landowners, in an environment where exploitation, violence, and abuses of destitute peasants are both common and unpunished.

Even if land titling is normally more diffused in cities rather than in rural areas, the process of undeclared and surreptitious migration from the countryside to towns hardly ever takes place in a regulated manner, by masses of poor desperate fleeing rural areas and looking for whatever job they can. The slums where they live in the outskirts of big towns typically don't have any legal titling and they are seldom connected to aqueducts and a proper sewage network.

Land rights are often subordinated to forced transmigration from resource-rich territories, from where natives are often sent away without any compensation – and local resistance to the illegal takeover of native land is often met with ruthless violence, mixing blood with the smell of money.

Proper land titling is strongly linked with inheritance rights, which are so important and ideologically biased in the Western world but often absent in underdeveloped areas. A central issue for development is collective versus individual property, together with the possibility to transmit it to children and grandchildren – or to keep them within the clan network, following different customary habits. It may give or deny the chance to transform land or real estate properties in invested capital, able to ignite sustainable economic growth.

Land reform is a big issue, likely to ease the formalization of household credit, and potential benefits stemming from it enclose[440]:

- increased crop production and nutritional welfare. Small holdings generally produce more than larger ones. Family-operated farms generally produce more than collective farms and farms largely dependent on wage labor. A cultivator with ownership is far more likely to make long-term capital investment;
- foundation for economic growth. Broadening access to land and strengthening cultivators' land rights can generate increases in overall

---

439 See http://www.rdiland.org/OURWORK/OurWork.html?gclid=CLa4puX-4Z0CFdOJzAodLibcNw.

440 Source: http://www.rdiland.org/PDF/PDF_Reports/RDI_117.pdf.

economic activity. This increased demand stimulates the creation of non-farm employment;

- facilitating democracy. Land reform removes its beneficiaries from the ›power domain‹ of the landlord. Furthermore, as land-reform beneficiaries increase their incomes and become more economically secure and confident, their ability to participate in the political process is strengthened;
- reducing instability and conflict. In traditional developing countries, land reform has reduced political instability by eliminating basic grievances arising from the relationship between tenants or agricultural laborers and erstwhile landowners. Many of the past Century's most violent civil conflicts ensued when land issues were ignored. Land reform can address the most basic rural grievances and increase citizen commitment to a system in which economic and social demands are negotiated peacefully;
- other benefits. Landless families are driven by their poverty into the cities. Effective land-reform measures give landless agricultural families a stake in their village society, reducing pressures that lead to premature and excessive urbanization. Transferable land rights also acquire a predictable market value, and they can be used as collateral, ›cashed out‹ for non-agricultural investment or retirement, or passed on as wealth to the next generation.

Reshaping dead capital, the dowry of the poor

It's unsurprisingly hard for informal poor, who officially do not exist, to raise ›official‹ capital. This point is particularly true for migrants, either clandestine going abroad or inner migrants, often from the countryside to town. Once born illegal, with an undeserved original sin, it is difficult to become legal. In addition, potential financing entities are discouraged by the very fact that it proves hard to enforce ›inexistent‹ borrowers to repay their debt – that's the reason why moneylenders, whose methods are much rougher, are so diffused.

Extra legality naturally grows with uncertainty and lack of parachutes. Hidden capital is often dead capital and invisible resources are hardly useful or much less useful than expected.

Unofficial wealth is unsurprisingly channeled into the black economy, and it is often dangerous, unfair, and difficult to get out from it, with a parallel life always threatened by uncertainty and lack of enforceable rules and rights.

Dead capital needs to sort out of underground, in order to be converted in a self fulfilling growth process, which is able to lock in and take a force on its own.

Initial capital for the poor is represented on the one side by land and properties–with huge differences, considering if and to which extent lands are arable and cultivated and properties are represented by poor huts or bigger and more stable homes–and on the other side by a natural endowment of cattle and livestock.
These forms of capital in kind are very different and complementary: livestock is mobile capital, whereas land or properties evidently aren't. From any of these forms of capital we can extract different returns: from livestock we can get meat, milk, leather, wool, fuel from wastes, enabling the farmer to start up activities and process the outcomes. Arable land is complementary for pasture, yielding fruits and vegetables, and real estate properties can be lent or used for living, storing, and processing, up to the start up of small industrial activities.
Capital starts up with accumulation, to the extent that nomadic people begin to settle down. And capital in kind can start getting transformed into cash, easing intermediation and releasing resources, making assets fungible, networking people, and protecting transactions[441]. When capital is converted to money, it can properly be stored, saved, and moved.
Intangible wealth represented by financial assets can easily be moved in a global world, much more than labor or tangible resources, diversifying risk and being allocated in the most promising areas. To the extent that capital does not properly circulate, it becomes stagnant and unproductive.
Formal property is more than just ownership[442] and it goes beyond the mere system for titling, recording, and mapping assets: it enables the proprietors to free capital and to start up an accumulation process, at the very root of economic growth.
Formalizing land rights has been promoted as a way to encourage agricultural investment and stimulate land markets[443] and land or real estate sales help wealth to circulate and they improve its allocation, making land capital more productive. Land titling secures a hopeful future because it is a powerful catalyst for local capital generation. Clear and enforceable rules of the game are a necessary precondition for investments, even from abroad, all contributing to economic development.

An uneasy catch up, meeting milestone institutions (and avoiding … tombstones)

Many developing countries try to make their best efforts to catch up richer countries and they carefully prepare themselves to be admitted to play the global game. But by the time they feel fit enough to play, to their dismay they dis-

441 De Soto (1999), Chapter 4.
442 De Soto (1999), p. 218.
443 Jacoby, Minten (2007).

cover that the rules of the game are changing and continuously upgrading. The technology frontier advances and gaps between frontrunners and followers are indeed likely to increase, even if long term convergence is uneasy but not impossible and reversals of fortune do occur[444] across centuries.

Institutions–so important for (un)growth–are born following a spontaneous demand for shared interests to be jointly represented and directed, taking profit of economies of scale and experience. Many of them are historically rooted and often date back to ancient times: normally, the more basic and vital the social interest, the older the institution. This is the case for hospitals, schools, tribunals, basic infrastructures and so on towards more complex institutions, which expand both in their industry or scope and geographically, because local problems increasingly share an international or even intercontinental dimension. Transcendent institutions are represented by religious entities that sometimes are dangerously coincident with State running regulations.

Poor nations and individuals are unsurprisingly weakly represented, and they are often unable to share their common interests and to convey them in the institution, where powerful lobbies and groups of pressure are often informally present. The transparent Lobbying Act, regulating and legalizing pressure activities in the U.S., is hardly present in other more hypocrite countries, where lobbies do exist anyway but they are not ›aesthetically‹ presentable (Europeans are often subtler than Americans, this not necessarily being a quality). A clear example of this under representation is given by the Ecological agreements–like the Kyoto treaty to limit carbon dioxide emissions–where poor and not contaminant countries have little influence over big industrial and pollutant nations.

Being the target obstacle constantly moved further, catch up is undoubtedly difficult, but the followers don't have to lose any hope–as the Ancient used to say, ›*spes ultima dea*‹, hope is the last Goddess–always reminding that even frontrunners are human beings and they can make mistakes and fall, especially if betrayed by overconfidence or relaxation, likely attitudes of human psychology.

Nowadays it becomes increasingly difficult to be rich and stupid for more than a generation, this being a simple reinterpretation of Aesop's tale of the grasshopper and the ant, or of Max Weber's protestant and capitalistic ethics, with a healthy lesson about redistributive justice.

The relationship between institutions and poverty is too complex to be properly dealt with as it would deserve – it is suffice here to underline its often underestimated importance.

444 See Acemoglu, Johnson, Robinson (2002).

Praise for homegrown development, overcoming the foreign debt trap

The poor are more resourceful than expected[445] and, to the extent that they can avoid relying too much on foreign aid, they can build up a sounder path towards development, reminding that ambition of progress is a powerful spring for development.

The dangers and malpractices of foreign aid have already been analyzed in Chapter 14 but here they should briefly be recalled so to stress their importance in hindering development.

Victimization, especially in countries with a colonial heritage, is often present, even if nowadays it hardly represents a justifiable excuse for avoiding strong personal engagement, which is the keystone behind self development. It is a matter of persistence, motivation, and zeal.

Productivity can be enhanced even investing in smart individuals, which in underdeveloped areas may tend to be culturally suffocated by a backward minded group. According to Muhammad Yunus »each individual person is very important. Each person has tremendous potential. She or he alone can influence the lives of others within the communities, nations, within and beyond her or his own time«. Self development, engineering domestic solutions, and fostering local empowerment, has many positive aspects, such as:

- reliance on self committed resources;
- lack of information asymmetries;
- pragmatic disaffection from inconstant external sponsors;
- development on a self reliant culture, where results are linked to one's efforts.

According to Easterly (2008), p. 24 »the world's poor will mostly determine their own fate by their home-grown institutions and initiatives, as much historical and contemporary evidence suggests«. Development is hardly working if it is imposed from abroad and it needs to be culturally assimilated as a positive value and worthy target, reminding that societies that do not expand are condemned to painful decline. Modern societies are complex, as well as their development.

To move out of misery, the poor need an external help but they also have to invest their own time and resources strongly cooperating with external donors, who are typically much less committed than the poor themselves. Victimization

445 Easterly (2006), pp. 28-29.

and mourning over colonialist wounds is a hardly working strategy, often used as an excuse for underperformance and little effort.
Homegrown development is possible, cutting the umbilical cord that often inappropriately continues to link poor countries with foreign sponsors, well beyond growth-birthing necessities, overcoming also the slippery foreign debt trap[446].
Foreign debt is actually a seductive form of aid, contracted at top levels–from State to State–which nurtures a culture of dependency, according to which underdeveloped populations prefer to wait for external help instead of unleashing their internal energies to fix problems and foster growth. Money often falls like manna from heaven, filling the empty safe box of corrupted and voracious governments.
Cumulated debt soon becomes a burden that curtails government spending, with the result of suffocating any possibility to meet urgent development needs and imposing stricter conditions on budget spending. Absence of democratic challenging typically makes politicians who contract illegitimate debt, irresponsible and unaccountable of their sinful actions, irrespectively of the country's unchecked creditworthiness, while their long term legacy emerges when damages are already irreparable.
When debt is rescheduled or forgiven, institutions like the International Monetary Fund typically intervene, conditioning this measure upon the respect of tighter fiscal policy measures, impressively called ›structural adjustment policies‹. These measures are likely to depress growth and development, due to their drastic cut back of government expenditure, typically concerning sensitive issues such as welfare and essential services.
Ironically, if the concession of loans is unlikely to be beneficial for the poor, they are much more probably hit by repayments. Renegotiations, irrespective of their needs and conducted on a top level agenda, suffering from an artificially imposed austerity, are inappropriately induced from abroad as a bitter and often poisonous medicine.

Poverty and the inefficiency trap

Efficiency is very much concerned with productivity and with an optimal use of scarce resources. Disorganization, frictions, lack of proper skills or of resources such as capital and other tangible and intangible endowments, are all factors that threaten efficiency and hamper development – especially if they are combined together, often in an unpredictable capricious way.
Efficiency is also a cultural value, and it is very much concerned with time and its consumption in productive activities.

---

[446] See Chapter 14.

On a comparative ground, efficiency has to be confronted with competing agents in similar businesses and environments and any efficiency gain typically brings to a surge in productivity. The poor are typically not an example of efficiency, since they lack its basic ingredients, represented by instruction, skills, capital and other constituents of productivity. Corollaries are unemployment, disempowerment, lack of chances or business opportunities, mistrust, and they are both causes and effects of inefficient and backward environment, where old fashioned habits find it difficult–or merely impossible–to catch up with an evolving world.
Increasing efficiency requires a multidisciplinary approach, since this concept is represented by a synthesis of a wide range of interacting factors – including quality, which is often underestimated, since it is hardly detectable, but nevertheless essential.
Efficiency is a wide concept that can be declined in its micro applications, down to the very core of each entrepreneurial activity, but even–synergistically–at a macro level, concerning the choice of the best and most suitable method or instrument to reach an (efficient) goal. Alternative–and complementary–options can be the market, the State, or a bottom-line subsidiarity approach. Each of them has a different impact on efficiency. The choice of the most suitable instrument, far from being easy or clear cut, poses key institutional questions.
An equitable sharing of resources, merits, and proceeds stands out as the best rewarding system to struggle for improving efficiency, knowing in advance that everybody can benefit out of it.

The condensed Chapter

Growth is ignited and fueled by a happy combination of labor and capital, with productivity depending on adequate skills and innovation, which are hardly present in poor environments.
The property trap, concerned with missing land titling, blocks the poor who are unable either to legally hold their real estate premises, or to transfer and use them as a guarantee. The result is what the Peruvian economist De Soto has nicknamed ›the mystery of hidden capital‹, advocating proper land and housing reforms, which are potentially able to start up much wanted homegrown development.
Storing wealth is difficult in bank-less places, where people try to hold on to their cattle and untitled fields.

Out of Poverty Tips

Would you invest in a home that is not yours? Property rights are a cornerstone of economic development, driven also by productivity and homegrown development, beyond spoiling and ephemeral foreign aid.
True development comes from inside.

Selected Readings

ADDISON T., HULME D., KANBUR R., eds., (2009), *Poverty Dynamics. Interdisciplinary Perspectives*, Oxford University Press, Oxford.

DE SOTO H., (2003), *The Mystery of Capital. Why Capitalism Triumphs in the West and Fails Everywhere Else*, Basic Books, New York.

HELPMAN E., (2004a), *The Mystery of Economic Growth*, Belknap Press of Harvard University, Cambridge.

CHAPTER 16 – Dismantling the poverty traps, lifting all boats: climbing up together the development ladder

> The key to ending extreme poverty is to enable the poorest of the poor to get their foot on the ladder of development. The ladder of development hovers overhead, and the poorest of the poor are stuck beneath it. They lack the minimum amount of capital necessary to get a foothold, and therefore need a boost up to the first rung.
>
> Jeffrey Sachs, *The End of Poverty*

The economic lives of the poor

An understanding of the economic life of the poor proves useful in order to find out the proper solutions for a lasting improvement of their conditions, dismantling the intertwined poverty traps that cause their underdevelopment, in the struggle for getting out of poverty. Development from an initial poor condition is often wild–somewhat looking like Far West-style colonization–and fragile, and it is likely to increase disparities. This fact happens at least in the short run, whereas sustainable development is made possible limiting inequalities, with a non discriminatory tide that sooner or later lifts all boats out of the poverty of nothing.

According to Banerjee and Duflo (2007):

- a typical extremely poor family unsurprisingly tends to be large: when every penny counts, it helps to spread the fixed costs over a larger number of people. A patriarchal family might be a potential target for Microfinance Institutions (MFIs), finding a social guarantee in family ties;

- the poor tend to be very young, due to high mortality as well as fertility rates. They might consequently lack skill and experience–but not enthusiasm, motivation, and willingness to emerge–for entrepreneurship, so slowing or preventing financial access. The poorest never are–by definition–successful entrepreneurs, and it is difficult to detect if this is either due simply to lack of capital and opportunities or to unfitness for such a job;
- the poor allocate slightly half of their budget to food, while spending the rest in ceremonies (following the ancient Roman motto ›*panem et circenses*‹ – what governors basically needed to provide, in order to make people happy and avoid upheavals), tobacco, alcohol, etc.;
- ownership of assets might consist of land property–even if cadastral records are typically missing–and few assets such as radios, bicycles, or televisions (if electricity is available);
- from a psychological point of view, while the poor certainly *feel* poor, their reported levels of self happiness are not particularly low, even if they appear anxious about health problems, lack of food, and death coming next. Micro-deposits and micro-insurance might prove useful solutions to soften these problems;
- realistic acquaintance of the living condition proves good for survival but they might bear to passive acceptance of poor standards, so preventing any effort or desire for improvement;
- the extremely poor spend very little on education, even if attendance to primary school may be often guaranteed by free-of-charge public schools;
- higher levels of education are often jeopardized by school fees, necessity of labor force, lack of family motivation, distance from schools (especially in under populated areas), lack of teachers (especially in sub-Saharan Africa, where AIDS and other illnesses decimate young generations, with an effect somewhat similar to the one experimented two centuries ago in Europe with Napoleonic wars) so preventing socio-economic development and–consequently–making any access to financial institutions and products harder;
- many poor households, especially in backward rural areas, tend to have multiple occupations: they cultivate the land they own (even if without legal title to land–a typical problem in poor areas–the stimulus to invest in it collapses), and they operate in other non-agricultural businesses;

- lack of specialization due to risk-spreading strategies and infrequent migration for job reasons–reflecting the value of remaining close to one's social network–prevent however many poor from grasping the economic opportunities they seek and long for;

- business scalability is typically very small, so preventing economic margins from growing. Should the poor be enabled to raise the needed capital to run a business that would occupy them fully, they might–with the help of microcredit–increase job specialization and productivity;

- the market environment constrains choices: some save little because they lack a safe place to put their money[447]. Availability of basic infrastructures (roads, power and TLC connections, schools, health facilities, water, and basic sanitation …) varies greatly across countries and is higher in urban areas;

- many poor are ›penniless‹ entrepreneurs, not according to a free choice, but since they are forced to do so: with few skills and little capital, it is easier, especially for women, to be a self entrepreneur than to find an employer with a job to offer.

In developing economies and particularly in the rural areas, many activities that would be classified in the developed world as financial are not monetized: that is, money is not used to carry them out. Almost by definition, poor people have very little money, even if in some circumstances they do need to use cash, going beyond an ancestral barter economy. Rutherford (2000) cites several types of needs:

- *Lifecycle Needs*: such as weddings, funerals, childbirth, education, home-building, widowhood, old age;

- *Personal Emergencies*: such as sickness, injury, unemployment, theft, harassment, or death;

- *Disasters*: such as fires, floods, cyclones, and man-made events like war or bulldozing of dwellings;

- *Investment Opportunities*: expanding a business, buying land or equipment, improving housing, securing a job (which often requires paying a large bribe), etc.

Welfare interventions (represented by unemployment subsidies, food stamps, pension schemes, healthcare packages, social insurance programs …) can

[447] See Chapter 17.

greatly contribute to alleviate poverty, smoothing incomes against adversities, but they need to be backed by proper funding and fair allocation. This point proves a difficult task in countries where taxation is too little to provide adequate resources, and fairness is still far from being a culturally accepted concept.
Kim and Loury (2013) show that some social groups are stuck in poverty traps because of network effects and find it difficult to overcome low human capital investment activities.

The survival challenges of the poor

Whereas luxuries–by definition not concerning the poor–variably grow with income, represent are a fixed cost, intrinsically risky and difficult to give up, independently of the income level.
Poverty is an extremely complex and multidimensional issue[448] and the economic life of the poor change substantially according to their social condition – ranging from the chronically vulnerable poorest of the poor, who are daily engaged with hand-to-mouth survival, to those who are painfully approaching, step after step, middle class social status. The environment and a capricious mix of events–the blind Goddess–make the rest.
The output has random and volatile outcomes, even if many of them get permanently stuck in some poverty trap. If life is difficult and volatile, striving towards a painful and timely task (a necessary step for any improvement of one's condition) may seem an useless effort – people build up more when uncertainty decreases, reminding however that uncertainty is a structural living condition for the poor. The poor play with their miserable life every day, knowing that the game may soon be over.
The poor–lacking even basic resources–are also characterized by very low levels of autonomy and empowerment, which are necessary ingredients for entrepreneurship and creativity.
Without a proper incentive for development, self-preservation of one's selfish interests is likely to prevail and a stagnant conservative mindset takes the edge over innovation and entrepreneurial risk.
Poverty is very much concerned with uncertain and insecure life, in a daily struggle for survival. And poor people worry about the lack of control concerning their own life, feeling completely dependent on external unpredictable factors that they are mostly unable to manage and mitigate. The poor often face large fluctuations in their living standards, with a constant feeling of insecurity, knowing that when things go wrong, it is uneasy to readdress them. The poor

448 See, extensively, Addison, Hulme, Kanbur (2009) and the introduction to this book.

disproportionately suffer from insecurity, which is always immanent in their volatile life.

According to Osmani[449] »extreme poverty relates to the notion of depth or intensity of deprivation, whereas chronic poverty relates to the duration of deprivation«.

The poor, who are wounded by a hard and difficult life, are not so because they are illiterate or ignorant or lazy, but rather because they have been denied the opportunity to have a fair access to resources and to combine them with their talents, in order to sort out poverty. Many poor, especially in rural areas, live in communities where sharing is a survival cultural value, while in some cases they are simply on they own, experimenting the loneliness and exclusion of the weakest, a hard economic and psychological condition. But as rivers get larger when they find an obstacle, difficulties are likely to forge and reinforce even the poor's endurance.

Poor people find original and collaborative ways to meet these needs, primarily through creating and exchanging different forms of non-cash value. Common substitutes for cash vary from country to country but they typically include livestock, grains, jewels, and precious metals.

As Ashta (2007) points out, a key problem in developing countries is that there are many poor people who can provide only their work. Since complementary assets require outside financing (being savings not existent or not properly ›stored‹), the lack of finance (together with lack of education, State aid, infrastructures ...) is an obstacle to the birth of entrepreneurship, with negative side effects on employment.

Yunus (1999) shows that if the poor are provided access to finance, they might start up micro enterprises, building up a virtuous cycle and transforming underemployed laborers into small entrepreneurs.

The poor who live in a permanent state of need are different from wealthier individuals, even from a psychological perspective – those who live in the margins, see themselves and the others, while those who live isolated and surrounded by their selfish wealth, just see themselves. Poverty is transcendent and it goes beyond material deprivation, involving states of mind, aspirations, need to be considered and taken care of.

Need of a ›Deus ex Machina‹? The impact of foreign direct investments on economic growth

A *Deus ex machina* (literally, in Latin, ›god from the machine‹) is a plot device, which was typical in ancient Greek tragedies, in which a person timely appears, in order to conveniently solve an otherwise too complicated plot.

449 In Addison, Hulme, Kanbur (2009), p. 249.

The *Deus ex machina* metaphor may be used to represent the much wanted foreign financial intervention in an underdeveloped country where local forces are absolutely unable to kick–start a job–creating growth pattern. This happens in a context where the poor country lacks the skills and resources that are highly needed especially in the beginning, before that accumulation of capital and experience can make the model workable on its own. Ending poverty is a titanic task, which often goes well beyond the capabilities of underdeveloped areas, stuck in their misery. And no growth locks the underserved into poverty.
In many cases, there isn't a lack of skills, but rather of the proper information and contacts to access the job market. This represents an example of relational poverty, increasingly harmful in a more and more interconnected world.
According to Osmani[450] »the very concept of trap implies that a person will never escape poverty unless some exogenous event helps her to break out of the trap«. The chronic poor, who are stuck in his misery traps, need an external *Deus ex machina* to get out of the quicksand of misery. They seriously risk being stuck permanently there, finding it difficult to sort out with their own feet, along their whole life span, and seriously risking transmitting their poor conditions to future generations.
Dismantling the interdependent poverty traps is a painful long term strategy – it indicates how to get there, giving direction and scope. Finding proper ways to gradually unleash market forces–controlling their powerful and destabilizing disequilibria–is a well known strategy for promoting timeline development that, sooner or later, is deemed to lift all boats. In such a context the weakest may take profit of positive spillovers, externalities, and of an unprecedented distributive capacity of a stronger State, backed by growing financial resources collected through taxes.
Among the determinants of economic growth, foreign direct investments (FDI) are a key ingredient: it is the establishment of an enterprise by a foreigner or, more generally, an international investment and, complementary with other important factors, it is vital for successful development in poor countries.
Poverty reduction has to be supported by proper incentives, with both monetary and non monetary benefits, in order to be viable.
In theory, foreign capital should flow from richer to poorer countries, following an arbitrage process. They should be attracted by marginally higher potential returns, due also to the presence of low labor costs and, in some places, of abundant and unexploited natural resources. UNCTAD compiles statistics on foreign direct investment[451].
FDIs are beneficial in terms of growth and development, since they allow countries to create more jobs, with a positive trickle down effect that sooner or later

450 In Addison, Hulme, Kanbur (2009), p. 248.
451 http://www.unctad.org/Templates/Page.asp?intItemID=1923.

indirectly reaches even the marginalized poorest, easing the import of technologies, magnetizing skilled labor and enhancing productivity. A (decent) job is the best road out of poverty.

Investments are a necessary but not sufficient condition for development, since capital constantly needs to be allocated to its most productive uses, taking profit from arbitrage conditions and being attracted by the highest marginal potentials for growth and productivity.

Another key factor behind growth is represented by trade and by its positive impact on exports. Trade is also likely to enhance productivity, not only increasing competition among exporters, but also allowing import of much wanted technology, which has to be shared by local companies. Trade barriers (particularly concerning impediments to the export of traditional goods, such as food or textiles from poor to rich countries) are hardly damaging the underdeveloped regions of the world, often more than counterbalancing aid or other subsidies. This point seems particularly evident if only we consider that poor countries are hardly able to export products or services with high added value. And basic commodities, that are difficult to differentiate, greatly suffer from competitive pressures and international speculation.

Trade barriers are not only a problem between the West and the Rest, but also within poor countries or among them. Tiny internal African trade stands out as an example of another lost opportunity, culturally fueled by ignorance, diffidence and laziness. Even trade begins at home.

Even if distances are shortened by technology, which makes transports cheaper, faster, and more reliable, geography still matters and proper locations–if conveniently exploited–may still represent a competitive advantage.

A big question is whether economic growth causes high or low inequalities, in a world increasingly characterized by extremes of affluence and poverty. Starting from a poor context, initial development normally increases inequalities. And once growth settles, having reached a higher and marginally decreasing level of development, inequalities might be reduced by converging factors, also because of the equitable distribution effect of public spending, fueled by the collection of taxes, negligible in previous stages of development. Countries with higher initial inequalities tend to experiment low growth, stifling progress against poverty[452]. Pro poor growth requires a more egalitarian income distribution[453].

Economic growth is not a zero sum game where winners are counterbalanced by losers. The win-win invisible hand behind self interest is due to have some beneficial side effects for the whole society, especially for the enthusiastic supporters of free market forces.

---

452 Ravallion in Banerjee, Benabou, Mookherjee (2006), Chapter 14.

453 See Guha-Khasnobis, Mavrotas (2008), p. 39.

Unpacking the Pandora box of development, starting from agricultural productivity

In Greek mythology, Pandora's box is a large jar, which unleashed many terrible things on mankind–ills, toils, and sickness–but also hope. (Under)development is like a Pandora box: when you try to ›open it up‹, you hardly know what may come out and the interaction of positive and negative aspects is typically bizarre and unpredictable.

Even the poorest countries are potentially able to join the convergence club as followers, unless they keep stuck in their poverty traps. The key problem is to try to understand the reason why some countries–in spite of their intrinsic potential–are still lagging behind, being unable to unleash convergent development. Only sustainable and long term cumulated development brings to material prosperity, reminding however that spiritual prosperity is an intangible state of mind, mainly unrelated with physical abundance.

Trying to properly address growth, unlocking the door of development, it shouldn't be forgotten that the trend of economic development typically starts with the improvement of agricultural production (with scientific farming and other innovations), scaling then up to manufacturing and after to services and high-margin R&D. And when development soundly takes off, being built brick after brick, it becomes self sustaining. This is the recipe for growth and the dream behind microfinance, whose sustainability is a prerequisite for a long lasting outreach[454]. Time and patience are needed to promote proper evolution, resisting to the temptation to be right too soon.

The key factor is agricultural productivity, which can be enhanced once again maximizing the ratio of outputs to given inputs. The land-to-labor ratio, that is typically small in underdeveloped countries, is the key productivity ratio in agriculture, that goes beyond subsistence farming, a vital condition in which poor peasants daily struggle in order to eke out a living.

When people have enough to eat and–going beyond their survival needs–they are enabled to save something, their demand for nonagricultural goods rises, creating a new market for industrial goods and services[455], in a context of growing labor specialization and technical progress. Emerging social middle-classes are the broadest factor behind mass development.

Any increase in agricultural productivity is directly reflected in growth in family incomes of small cultivators. And once peasants become wealthier, they look for new products and services, creating a demand for new markets and allowing at least some of them to move to urban areas.

---

[454] See Chapter 20.

[455] See, extensively, Eswaran, Kotwal in Banerjee, Benabou, Mookherjee (2006).

Productivity gains raise the land-to-labor ratio, through better job organization and more extensive use of technologies, fertilizers, irrigation, etc. This improvement happens also occupying contiguous and synergic segments of the food value chain, e.g. processing and transforming or packaging agricultural products, making them available even for export.
Productivity and economic marginality can be conveniently increased by proper culture rotation or weeding and shifts towards more lucrative crops, domesticated animals, or agricultural technologies – such as the heavy plow or, lately, mechanical tools such as tractors. Infrastructural investments also matter: proper road connections, construction of irrigation pipelines, use of new fertilizers and in some case of highly debated genetically modified organisms can boost productivity and access to agricultural products, easing trade and labor mobility.

Rural behinders farming out of poverty

Any productivity gain decreases the number of people that need to be occupied in agriculture and it makes workforce available for other destinations, climbing up the development ladder. Business models are typically more scalable, moving from agriculture to industrial activities, and there is more room for diversification and creation of added value.
In the industrial sector, growth is typically faster and outputs are more volatile than in the agricultural field, while capital–unlike land, which is fixed in supply–can be accumulated over time and it can produce incremental wealth, if properly stored and productively combined with workforce and intangible resources. In addition to economies of scale, even economies of experience–learning by doing–are more likely and consistent in the industrial sector, if compared to agricultural occupations.
Agricultural productivity is also linked with demographic trends: high population growth means that each agricultural worker, having less land *pro capite*, is less productive[456]. In the industrial sector, the very fact that capital is not fixed or limited allows workers to higher flexibility and resilience. Should total output grow more than population, the amount of capital per worker can even increase, so avoiding any productivity dilution.
Any population growth, which often occurs in poor rural areas, brings more labor force, which should increase the productivity of cultivated land, but also lower wage rates and increase the land's rental rate, especially if land is owned by big landlords who can take profit of the higher supply of workforce. According to this scenario, capitalists and landlords become richer and peasants poor-

[456] See Eswaran in Banerjee, Benabou, Mookherjee (2006).

er[457]. No wonder that the land issue is so hotly debated, often bringing to disputes, riots, and revolts.
As we have already seen in Chapter 4, demography is closely linked with poverty and when the poor peasants find it difficult to sell their meager crop, it becomes difficult for them to pay the due rent to often merciless landlords.
The industrialization of agriculture is not a self igniting process and some external help is typically needed, importing equipment and technology. If the industrialization process is properly managed, the payoff can be substantial.
The land issue–already seen in Chapter 15–is a key problem even for productivity and on the one hand large estates (*latifondiums*) can have mixed effects, formally raising productivity but also increasing inequalities and uneven distribution of the crop proceeds. On the other hand, even excessive fragmentation of the arable land can be dysfunctional. Lack of proper land titling, disputes, and abuses are a typical scenario of backward areas, while environmental issues[458] are a new problem that can decrease the proportion of arable land, causing concerns especially if it is combined with a growing population.
Export of food products is a must for many developing countries which are hardly able to sell abroad anything else, at least in the first steps of their development. It is seldom an easy process and it exposes fragile economies to the international volatility of prices, driven by speculative reasons. Protectionism of most developed countries, which strongly subsidize their agriculture, stands out as a strong barrier.
Strongly connected with land property there is the construction industry, that is a typical growth enhancing business, which stimulates internal demand for housing and which is labor intensive, attracting a lot of unskilled poor workers, who however need to be properly guided by building experts. The real estate industry is driven in underdeveloped countries by peculiar factors, because of the necessity to rebuild countries that had been destroyed by the war – provided that relapses are not too likely and that the outlook is sufficiently peaceful. Even the housing necessities of a growing population matter, as peasants increasingly move towards cities, abandoning old rural huts possibly for something better to be built soon.
Besides agriculture and the real estate business, a typical occupation of a developing country is the textile industry, which is concerned–like agriculture–with internal consumption but potentially export oriented, if there is a surplus exceeding local needs or a specialization in some interesting niche. Highly labor intensive jobs, where quality and productivity are not a priority, can still command a premium in poor areas where workforce is numerous and cheap, even if it is unskilled and supported by limited investments.

---

[457] Eswaran in Banerjee, Benabou, Mookherjee (2006), p. 144.
[458] See Chapter 8.

Once properly ignited, exit from poverty is sustained by transformation in life styles and growth in consumption, possibly beyond the satisfaction of basic needs.

The alphabet of development: promoting pro-poor equitable growth

Within the anatomy of hope, growth can ideally be illustrated with the metaphor of the stairs, with the poor painfully but progressively succeeding in climbing up the development ladder. The first steps are typically the most difficult and too many poor are unable to start climbing, because they are not enabled at least to try. Some midwifery is needed for development.

The fight against poverty is too complex and multidimensional to be won quickly with a unilateral approach. A progressive strategy–aimed at transforming misery from chronic to transitory–needs to be patiently conceived and implemented, giving it its due time. When growth takes off too rapidly and the living standards rise too fast, people find it difficult to psychologically adapt to a brand new unexpected bonanza. And they tend to waste resources and to take an unbalanced view about wealth – when development becomes an undeserved free lunch, it hardly resists for long.

Equitable and sustainable economic growth is very much concerned with enterprise-led development, even in a context where poverty encompasses different dimensions of deprivation that relate to human capabilities, including consumption and food security, health, education, rights, voice, security, dignity, and decent work[459].

The transition to a market economy is however characterized also by problems that cohabit with opportunities, such as inequalities and social competition, harshly dividing success from failures – an unsuitable context for many, since then used to similar destinies. There are forms of poverty that are resistant to economic growth and so inertial removal of misery is a hard task–lifting all boats–characterized by underestimated unlucky outcomes.

The poverty traps examined in the preceding Chapters embrace historical or geographical factors, or even gender discrimination, demographic uncontrolled expansion, cultural problems, wars and social unrest, health, and nutritional problems.

---

[459] OECD (2001).

Matching endowments with opportunities

Sustainable pro poor growth requires a solution of growing inequalities: economic growth reduces absolute poverty, to a degree depending on how equitable the distribution of income in a society is[460]. Growth is by its intrinsic nature often asymmetric and in poor countries where the role of the State is very limited, redistribution policies are hardly possible, through social security programs and incentives for the development of the destitute. International aid can fill the gap, but only to an extent limited by scarce resources, an often insufficient knowledge of the country's problems and other drawbacks, pointed out in Chapter 14.

High inequalities make growth unbalanced and hardly effective for the poorest and their incomes. The risk of marginalization is high and it may bring to social unrest. When growth opportunities are not shared, a sort of ›far west‹ run may take place, increasing social differences for a long time ahead. Only when the developing country stabilizes and its growth becomes more balanced, inequality is more likely to drop.

When inequality is high, growth reaches the poor only marginally, since it is hardly effective to alleviate their problems, and to the extent that they are left aside, their contribution to the overall growth is limited and dispersion limits the growth's outreach potential. Considering their volume and critical mass, the poor represent an important asset for sustained and sustainable growth, with the likely result of enlarging its base and widening its effects.

From a marketing perspective, the poor represent an endless market of opportunities, ready to be exploited[461]. Since even the poor can save and accumulate capital for growth, a virtuous cycle can be ignited by their involvement in the development process.

Pro poor growth, to be made more scalable and effective, has even other positive side effects, as it can consistently reduce the country risk, by decreasing the possibilities of social unrest and turmoil, hunger, and illnesses that are traditionally linked with extreme poverty and other by products of being destitute.

Instruction and vocational training, which are so crucial for productivity enhancement, are a necessary part of the growth mechanism: since the poor increase their knowledge, they can more easily be part of an economic system where added value is increasingly looked for.

Mitigation measures of economic and social inequalities are mainly government sponsored (promoting public education, progressive taxation[462], minimum wages[463], social security …) or market driven, referring to the decreasing marginal

460 Goudie, Ladd (1999).

461 See Prahalad (2006).

462 Commonly accepted in Western countries.

463 Attractive but dangerous, as interest rate ceilings are in microfinance (see Chapter 21).

utility of wealth (a well known property, hardly perceived by many greedy rich) or wealth dilution forces (the richer are more prone to dissipate … the poor being prevented from having little to dissipate). Encouraging the creation of a middle class is another complementary way to tackle poverty, since it reduces the distances between the extremely poor and the wealthiest and it smoothes unequal class polarization.

Pro poor growth can be strengthened empowering the poor, through the promotion of human rights and a better governance of the limited State's resources. Involvement, democratic participation, and sharing–always putting the individual, with her or his rights and duties at the center of attention and intervention–are forward sighted strategies against marginalization and social exclusion, which are so frequent with the voiceless poor.

Access to capital, resources, education, and training even for the poor is an indispensable prerequisite for poverty reduction.

According to the Human Development Report 2009[464] »human development is about putting people at the centre of development. It is about people realizing their potential, increasing their choices and enjoying the freedom to lead lives they value«.

Globalization can make the poor better off:

- giving them access to the market of capitals (even through microfinance) and to inflows of capital, with a positive effect on wages and productivity;
- enabling them to migrate to richer countries, in search of better wages;
- opening foreign markets to the export of their goods;
- letting technology circulate.

All these opportunities have their drawbacks (capital markets are volatile and bring instability, migration can cause brain drain[465], exports are generally good news but can increase inequalities, and technology is neither neutral nor free …).

Promotion of pro poor growth passes through financial inclusion and admission of the unbanked to the credit market: microfinance is proving an effective device, even if its potential is still enormous and largely unexploited – even small loans can ignite productivity.

The set of available opportunities for growth may go beyond current expectations and imagination and path breaking inventions and intuitions can unpredictably change the scenario. As Friedman (2009) puts it, the Stone Age didn't end because we ran out of stones.

---

464 http://hdr.undp.org/en/reports/global/hdr2009/.

465 See Chapter 12.

Dismantling the intergenerational poverty trap

Intergenerational transmitted poverty is the most enduring form of–typically chronic–misery[466], especially in backward rural patriarchal societies or in urban unlivable slums. Social factors play a fundamental role in the perpetuation of poverty.

The poor face several barriers in transferring wealth, endowments, and bequests to the next generation and their difficulties are mainly due to the malign interactions of poverty traps, such as:

- credit constraints, preventing optimal investments in human capital and assets transfers[467];
- the role of gender inequalities (different schooling, discriminated ability to inherit, distorting marriage market …) in perpetuating uneven lifetime incomes;
- the property trap, with connected inheritance problems and inability to intermediate the assets[468], preventing sales, guarantees, transmission to descendants, etc. – if only we think about the importance of these issues in Western countries, we can shed some light on their absence in poor ones;
- sticky social classes, that prevent mobility, imprisoning individuals in their current social status;
- ancestral cultural backwardness, an intangible badwill fatally transmitted to next generations.

The aforementioned traps are often intertwined. For example, land inheritance is frequently associated with persistent gender disparities and women are often discriminated heirs.

Most intergenerational transfers that take place within the family, strongly contribute to shape the future of their children. They indeed invest or not in their schooling and education, they choose between current consumption and savings or investments for the future, depending also on the family's wealth level, in an interaction of[469]:

- preferences (with possible discriminations against girls or favoring just firstborn children – as it happened also in feudal Europe), which typi-

466 See Hulme, Shepherd (2003).
467 Quisumbing in Addison, Hulme, Kanbur (2009), Chapter 12.
468 See Chapter 15.
469 Quisumbing in Addison, Hulme, Kanbur (2009), p. 268.

cally become more evident and discriminatory when resources are scarce;

- future returns of investments in children (low expected returns incentive mortality or illiteracy), reminding that they typically show (huge) innate differences that bring to different levels of productivity and success;
- constraints to resources, with low budget opportunities and investment limits;
- ›bargaining‹, in order to avoid transmitting resources to (some) children, showing biased preferences or selfishness, even if parents are typically supposed to be altruistic, at least towards their children.

Intergenerational transfers are essential for emancipation, since they enable future generations not only to maintain themselves, but also to look after their parents, with the result of improving the overall family welfare with a parental form of insurance.

The timing of the transfer is typically linked to key moments of life, such as schooling or wedding, which are considered as different kinds of investment. In the latter case, a generous bride price or dowry–in relative terms–may cynically enable the bride or the groom to climb the social ladder. Potential benefits accrue to the whole native family, with social and economic convenience typically suffocating true and disinterested love.

Marriage is a key occasion for intergenerational transfers. If the poor marry the poor, and the rich mate only within them–with a positive assertative mating[470] with similar individuals–social mobility is evidently endangered and inequalities between different social classes increase.

According to Bird (2007) »poverty is not transferred as a ›package‹, but as a complex set of positive and negative factors that affect an individual's chances of experiencing poverty, either in the present or at a future point in their life-course. The factors influencing an individual's likelihood of being poor include both the ›private‹ transmission (or lack of transmission) of capital and the ›public‹ transfer (or lack of transfer) of resources from one generation to the next. These can be positive or negative [...]. Being a poor child increases the chances of being a poor adult but this is not always the case«. Children inherit poverty, rather than creating it.

And it is again Bird (2007) who claims that »agency, status and the social constructions determining roles can combine to result in differentiated access to

470 According to evolutionary theories, positive assortative mating, increasing similarities within couples, has the effect of reducing the range of variation and results in disruptive natural selection.

and control of resources and the returns on those resources, unequal investments in the human capital formation of household members and unequal distributions of leisure and labor time. Other important factors include:

- systematic inequalities within and between households;
- adolescent pregnancy;
- early child care and development practices;
- domestic violence;
- household income;
- household and individual assets;
- household decision-making;
- livelihood and survival strategies;
- service uptake;
- exposure and vulnerability to risk and resilience or ability to cope«.

Intergenerational poverty traps can be dismantled enabling the poor to accumulate survival assets in excess of their expected future consumption, so as to make a surplus transfer to next generations possible. The process should consider both material entity and proper timing – money obviously maximizes its utility when it is most needed, first of all for long term investments in human capital and for consumption-smoothing in emergencies, which are typically endemic for the poor.

The migration from extended family system to more impersonal market economy enables to bypass the poverty traps that are intrinsically present in backward clan boundaries.

Migrating from an extended family system to a market economy

The extended family system–sometimes defined as a kin system–represents a protected environment where shared rights, mutual obligations, reciprocity, loyalty, and gratuity shape the life of the clan members. There are not market rules, since decisions and allocations of time, money and other resources do not follow a strict economic pattern of convenience and self interest.

The kin system is an informal institution that fills the gap of an absent or weak State with an alternative source of power and authority. Its interaction with a changing world can bring to mixed and unpredictable results, either easing the transition towards a market economy (if properly shared and assimilated by its

members), or behaving as an improper isolation factor and involuntarily becoming an instrument of decadence and stagnation. In the latter case, it artificially keeps the clan members out of the current economic trends, especially if they live in backward and isolated rural areas, where time is motionless and the clock of history seems to have stopped.
Solidarity within the family ›kin‹ members forces the community individuals who are successful to share their merits and rewards with the clan, not only diluting their wealth–especially if it is seen as disproportionate from other relatives, remained poor–but also providing job and opportunities to the other clan members, typically irrespectively of meritocracy, fairness, equal opportunities. Sharing of city homes with kin members is also very common – and less damaging.
Collusion and nepotism tend to prevail, since clan identity is culturally stronger than any other (typically fairer) rule, both impersonal and democratic, avoiding the temptation to be biased by ethnic or clan belonging. Societies that succeeded to go beyond these legacies have long commanded economic supremacy on other more traditional and collusive communities.
When the level of sophistication grows and development is characterized by a high intangible component, the damages of nepotism and improper selection increase, too. On the one side, closed societies can hardly make the big jump towards sustained growth and their productivity is likely to keep a competitive disadvantage towards other more open realities. On the other side, competitive edges are mainly concerned with the choice of a strategy that competitors are unable to replicate, exploiting core competences and producing gain from pain.
Dismantling this development bottleneck is a hard task, especially if the clan is considered the basic institution within the society and it finds difficult to comply with the–completely different–rules of the market economy.

To grow or not to grow? Poor countries' development sustainability

Growth and development are the best antidotes against poverty, as it has been shown in Chapter 15, positively solving the Hamletic dilemma.
An analysis of the poverty traps and bottlenecks of developing countries is pre liminary to an understanding of what can be done in order to have sustainable growth. Long term cumulated growth is what really matters and what makes the difference between performing and not performing countries. All countries sooner or later experience short episodes of growth, either strong or modest, but they are not sufficient to get out of the poverty trap – sustained long term growth is necessary.

Growth may start for a variety of causes, which can be deliberately planned or even fortuitous, such as the discovery of natural resources.
Sustaining growth is however a non contingent strategy, requiring investments and budgeting, looking for productivity improvements.
From the beginning of the 21th Century, GDP growth is increasing in most less developed countries (LDCs) at unprecedented levels, considering also their low starting points. Anyway its long term sustainability has to be questioned, considering its intrinsic composition and quality.
According to UNCTAD (2008) »LDCs are still characterized by low levels of domestic resource mobilization and investment, very weak development of manufacturing industries, high levels of commodity dependence, weak export upgrading, worsening trade balances, and rising food and energy import bills. These conditions imply that LDCs are very vulnerable to growth slow-downs, or even growth collapses, arising from external sources«.
Most of LDCs are net food importers, and their exports of agricultural products are mainly represented by coffee, tea, tobacco, or cotton, while edible products are not always sufficient for self consumption, requiring imports from abroad.
Basic products manufactured in LDCs and exported in richer countries, taking profit of the labor cost differentials, hardly incorporate technological advances. Consequently the local demand for technological upgrades is smaller, decreasing the quality of growth and exposing it to obsolescence. Japan, now stagnating but still representing the third country in the world for its GDP, is a remarkable example of growth applied to technology, by far the most dynamic growth segment.
The digital divide and the technological gap between the haves and haves not is often increasing, with a consequent diverging cumulated growth pattern.
Foreign aid[471] can help to fill the gap, with big donors such as the World Bank financing infrastructural projects and small donors, often represented by NGOs, intervening through a complementary bottom up approach.
In order to promote development and poverty reduction, foreign aid and domestic resources have to be targeted to the expansion of labor intensive income earning opportunities, so to raise the *pro capite* GDP of the largest possible amount of population, stimulating consumption, savings, and investments.
Only structural changes targeted at growth development can decrease the LDCs dependence on foreign aid, often represented by debt relief policies which give temporary breath to the poor country, hardly resolving its core problems. And forgiven debt is often unsurprisingly followed by the creation of new debt. To the extent that debt contracted with foreign lenders is still outstanding, it drains resources for its service, avoiding their allocation to development strategies.

---

471 See Chapter 14.

Economies that have well performed over the long term owe their success not to geography or trade, but to institutions that have generated market-oriented incentives, protected property rights, and enabled stability.

Living standards show diverging evolutionary patterns, widening the differences between those who improve their conditions and those who aren't able to catch up, especially if hit by volatile prices of imported primary food. Economic growth can effectively contribute to alleviate poverty, to the extent that it can allow for better income distribution.

The level of poverty within each country is highly dependent on balancing and interacting factors such as:

- kind of exports (commodities versus manufactured goods, with their often low technological contents);
- labor productivity and capital endowment, leading to capital accumulation and technological progress, together with capability building (learning by doing, accumulating, and sharing skills and experience);
- social differences and inequalities;
- import mix (from technology to foodstuff), which may worsen the trade deficit, if exports are not sufficient to fill the gap or they are more volatile than imports;
- ›depth‹ of the education system: whether most children, no matter if poor, are admitted to primary schooling, discrimination grows in subsequent years of education, increasing gender inequalities;
- hunger (and dependence on imported food consumption), little access to safe water, and poor sanitation are another evident obstacle to the well being;
- agricultural policies and reforms, linked with land titling issues. Asymmetric subsides and trade liberalization, exposing poor peasants to unprecedented competition, may prove extremely harmful;
- level and quality of employment, taking into account demographic trends, according to which an increasing number of young job-seekers has to meet a demand for workforce which may follow different evolutionary patterns;
- smooth level of carefully delivered international aid, often wrongly peaking in emergencies and suddenly deflating, with stops-and-goes which hardly allow for careful budgeting. Compliance with international standards and accountability together with monitoring indicators

are highly wanted, in a context of increasing competition for scarcer international funds.

Overcoming the parasitic rent appropriation

Parasitic–unproductive–enterprises are rampant in developing countries[472] and they act illegally:

- providing ›protection‹ to their affiliates, going well beyond the boundaries of a legal State;
- enforcing contracts (in an often brutal and informal way, that bypasses courts and laws);
- acting as unwanted or unnecessary–but unavoidable–intermediaries, to earn up undue margins;
- acting as financial intermediaries (moneylenders …), often in a monopolistic environment;
- being unduly linked to political parties, in order to share the pie of foreign aid and public resources.

Corruption, fraud, embezzlement … are evident corollaries of parasitic enterprises, whose negative impact on the economy goes well beyond these immediately perceivable effects. Indeed it also distorts fair competition, impartiality, and meritocracy, to the detriment of the poor and of the honest smartest individuals.

Parasitic enterprises may represent a sort of … State within the State, if they are properly organized and eradicated in the territory, with ritual affiliations and cultural bondages. They are made possible by the weakness and lack of authority of the official government, typically involved in the deal and looking for hidden intermediaries in order to divert and share flows of public money.

Corrupt institutions and dishonest bureaucrats are both a cause and a consequence of the problem – and parasitism, once in place, is difficult to eradicate.

Lack of governance, unfairness, insecurity, and a bad sensation that the rules of the game are either inexistent or not applied, are factors that immediately reflect in higher perception of the country and political risk; these problems are likely to keep foreign investors away and to block or seriously delay development. The poor are by definition kept out from these illegal power games.

Parasitic rent appropriations are likely to induce stagnation–or vice versa–reinforcing a poverty trap that is difficult to extirpate, especially if parasitic activities are highly profitable, even due to the fact that by definition they pay lit-

[472] Mehlum, Moene, Torvik in Bowles, Durlaf, Hoff (2006), p. 79.

tle or any taxes and they are highly flexible and resilient, since they are free from the application and observance of fair rules. This fact returns in unfair competition with legal and honest enterprises, which pay higher costs, and are discriminated in their activities, often being prevented from entering already ›occupied‹ markets.

Whenever parasitic enterprises are more profitable than legal ones, and the State is unable to readdress fairer rules of the game, a powerful poverty trap spiral gets into action. It proves then difficult to stop this downward spiral, unless its very causes are fully eradicated.

Development is very much concerned with a fair institutional environment, which is enabled to go beyond clan or ethnic links, typically connected with parasitism, which finds its cultural (il)legitimacy in social capital and family or clan ties.

From heaven to hell: escaping poverty ... or becoming poor

Poverty should never be considered a permanent 'death' sentence that is inherited since birth, and many successful examples show that it is possible to sort out the misery trap. Reasons to escape include poverty pathways such as:

- income diversification (potentially eased by recourse to micro-finance), starting from higher yields in the agricultural sector;
- permanent employment in the private or public sector;
- being a beneficiary of a successful aid / assistance scheme;
- win the lottery (and then escaping from greedy relatives and friends, ... eager to share).

It is however also possible to fall into poverty, for many different complementary reasons, such as[473]:

- poor–health and health–related expenses;
- marriage / dowry / new household-related expenses;
- funeral related expenses;
- high interest rate debt (up to personal financial distress);
- environmental / agricultural disasters (drought, flood, land exhaustion, cattle disease, etc.).

[473] Krhisna in Addison, Hulme, Kanbur (2009), pp. 190-192.

Dynamic intergenerational or intragenerational assessment of the poverty conditions keep into account the historical life trend, dividing the poor in four categories[474], enabling us to differentiate between the two polar situations: always remained poor or, respectively, not poor. We can differentiate also the osmotic links between the two, considering either a fall into poverty or a way out from it. The poor are always suspended between different pathways – remaining behind, getting lost or succeeding to catch up. Risk plays a fundamental role in shaping poverty mobility. Social mobility–driven by income, occupation, and status changes–stands out as a key sociological concept.
Another complementary classification is chronic versus temporary (momentary) poverty: such a classification is useful for a better understanding of the misery's degree of persistence, as illustrated in Figure 16.1.

Figure 16.1. – Chronic versus temporary poverty

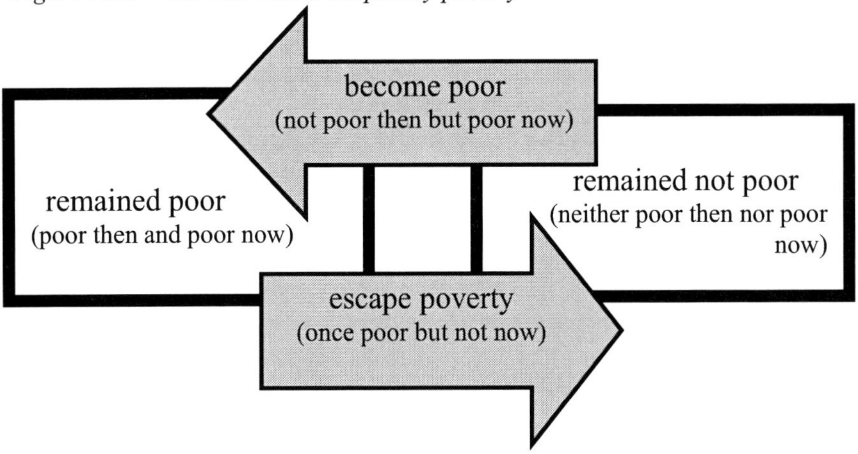

The analysis should not forget that rural areas are different from increasingly populated urban centers, and poverty concentration can show great differences. The poor are unsurprisingly attracted by wealth but the fact that they tend to settle down in urban areas is often a matter of desperation, escaping from a backward countryside which suffers from a long-standing agricultural neglect.
Development governance is a key issue for successful poverty reduction strategies.

[474] Krhisna in Addison, Hulme, Kanbur (2009), p. 188.

Trespassing the poverty line threshold, with a progressive leap forward

In 1958, the Chinese communist dictator Mao Tse Tung launched a strong strategic initiative to speed up the process of industrialization, by suddenly shifting resources from agriculture to industry. The ›*Great Leap Forward*‹, as it was labeled and known, proved to be a real disaster, leading to widespread starvation and famine in the countryside in which more than 20 million people perished, paying a painful tribute to misconceived ideology and irrational planning.

The great leap forward is always tempting, as it promises to solve problems with sudden change of strategy, creating a fracture with the past and readdressing the population towards a brand new target. But it is likely to be difficult and dangerous to put in place, mostly because it lacks any cultural rooting and people find it hard–or even impossible–to assimilate new strategies and, consequently, to make them effective and lasting. Enduring development, with a progressive–rather than sudden–frog leap forward is far less exciting but much more effective and realistic.

The poverty line is the minimum level of income that is necessary to achieve adequate living standard in a given country.

The chronically poor, who experiment a durable misery based on structural deprivation, spend most or often all of their miserable life below the poverty line. Resourceless poor, with limited endowments and little initial assets, can be chronically poor even without being caught in a poverty trap[475]. And it is difficult for them to overcome the poverty line threshold, since they find it hard to accumulate and save. Indeed they are typically prevented from borrowing against future earnings, facing capital rationing constraints.

Inability to invest in human capital is likely to persist across generations–low schooling is typically an inherited problem–and young poor are also likely to face broader inheritance traps because they receive from preceding generations not only little endowment, but also backward cultural legacies, such as the still common practice of combined marriage, with its corollary of little social mobility.

Transient–ephemeral–poverty indicates a periodical state of crisis, different from permanent–chronic–misery, and typically easier to manage.

Civic sense bypassing the ›tragedy of commons‹

The ›tragedy of commons‹ refers to a dilemma described in an influential article of Garrett Hardin (1968), depicting a situation in which multiple individuals, acting independently and solely, and rationally consulting their own self-

475 Addison, Hulme, Kanbur (2009), p. 20.

interest, will ultimately deplete shared limited resources even when it is clear that it is not in anyone's long-term interest for this to happen.

Common property, instead of private one, leads to careless underinvestment in the long term conservation–for example, by over–harvesting forests or over-grazing grassland–and sub–optimal management of shared resources.

Overgrazing common land with too many privately owned animals is a typical example. Thinking about the opportunity to add up an animal, each farmer acknowledges that, although the overall grazing productivity is reduced, he has a marginally positive return, which is higher than the damage that he shares with the collectivity. Every farmer consequently has an incentive to add up an animal, up to a point of no return, where the land is so depleted that everybody risks a common catastrophic loss.

The atmosphere represents the most global and volatile commons, and public ownership of water is another example – and private property rights for water, through water markets, are often useful. Even seawater and the depletion of shared fishing resources are another example of how selfish overexploitation can imperceptibly destroy common good. The tragedy of commons, being linked to the excessive harvesting and overgrazing of shared resources, is intrinsically connected to ecological issues, requiring strong cooperative effort.

Mosquito nets against malaria are an example of positive externality, somewhat reversing the tragedy of commons' paradigm. The personal incentive to utilize nets may look small, even if it isn't, but if most people agree upon using them, malaria is going to be much less diffused, with a benefit–a free ride–also for the lazy ones who do not want to use any protection.

Norms of reciprocity and deep understanding of the values standing behind shared social capital[476] can mitigate the tragedy of commons' undesired side effects, difficult to observe and detect at first glance – and even for that dangerous and long lasting.

Maintenance represents an indirect corollary of the tragedy of commons and upkeep of public goods, that is an apparently easy concept, is however quite far from the mentality of so many Africans. When roads are built but not properly and periodically repaired, they deteriorate up to the point of becoming useless or–even worse–dangerous.

Civic sense and community-based management, establishing common rules, and quotas, are the best antidote against weak institutions and the tragedy of commons. Since good examples of civic sense are a transmittable cultural concept, they are fundamental for the diffusion and application of the civic sense, however always remembering that the devil is within the details.

---

[476] See Chapter 9.

The tragedy of commons is a concept that may conveniently be linked with the prisoner's dilemma[477], a fundamental problem in game theory that demonstrates why two people might not cooperate even if it is in both their best interests to do so.

Overcoming the competitive disadvantage of handicapped nations

A handicap is something that hampers or hinders, representing a disadvantage or a penalty that prevents unlucky nations from catching up–or even from starting up–development. Disadvantages are simultaneously comparative–differential, more than absolute–and competitive, leaving the weakest behind, especially if the rules of the game are those of a pitiless capitalistic system and they are settled by the strongest players.

Growth–the propellant behind development–can be jointly examined from both a macro and a micro level, considering its entity both at an aggregate level and on an individual basis.

Nations tend to have competitive (dis)advantages in comparison to other countries, which address their growth pattern at first on aggregate terms, with a subsequent subdivision at a micro level.

Rich nations with higher productivity and larger capital endowments export capital-intensive goods and tend to import labor-intensive goods from poor countries, where wages are consistently lower.

Porter[478] stresses the importance of the productivity paradigm as the most powerful factor behind growth, enabling to shift from comparative advantage (due to favorable endowments of resource rich countries or to cheap labor) to competitive advantage based on knowledge, investment, insight, and innovation. Macroeconomic policies are less discretionary than in the past, being subject to international scrutiny, but what really matters is the quality of the business environment. It is driven by microeconomic factors of the market (quality of local demand; level of competition, and stimulating rivalry; degree of innovation and differentiation …), which can be aggregated in order to express the overall characteristics of the market. Little competition in poor markets weakens productivity and strategic focus.

Progressive development patterns are followed by successive improving and upgrading in competition, with increasingly sophisticated business models. Again according to Porter, in early-stage development, firms primarily compete on cheap labor–an abundant resource in poor countries–and natural resources, concentrated only in some areas. Development requires much more, being

---

477 See http://plato.stanford.edu/entries/prisoner-dilemma/.

478 In Harrison, Huntington (2000), Chapter 2.

pushed by higher productivity: it requires an upgrade of human capital, an improvement in infrastructure and TLC networks, an opening to foreign trade and foreign investment, a protection of the intellectual property (to incentive copyrighted innovation), an upgrade of the regulation to international standards (in order to comply with the increasingly tougher rules of the game) and–last but not least–a sustainable and environment-friendly path of development.
Short sighted rent or monopoly seeking behaviors are a pathology that is still afflicting many developing countries, where antitrust legislation is not present and where the only strategy is plain exploitation of existing natural or geographical resources. While rent seeking finds a natural limit in not renewable resources, development fostered by intangible components is potentially unlimited. Exploitation of family or clan ties, from recommendations to undeserved help and favoritism or nepotism, is another typical rent seeking strategy, which is highly diffused all around the world but with peaks in undemocratic less developed regions. The damage for productivity and growth is typically substantial and often underestimated.
Wealth is not an immobile fixed concept, as many peasants still believe. With hard work and commitment the pie can grow and its slices should be cut according to merit, with a social safety net for the unluckiest.
As we have already seen in Chapter 9, Lindsay[479] notes that country's comparative advantage (given by the presence of natural resources or low labor costs and duly reflected in the prism of competitiveness) is typically unable of pushing up economic marginality. This effect prevents the creation of high and rising living standards, having little or any effect on innovation and productivity. Much effort is wasted looking for unproductive strategies, being unaware of the circumstance that they simply don't work.
Looking for comparative versus competitive advantages, Lindsay highlights the importance of a competitive mind-set that is naturally oriented towards openness, globalization, and competition, instead of being sheltered in autarchic protected markets. The way towards the achievement of competitive advantage is represented by flexible meritocracy, proactive approach mixed with innovation, shared vision, and involvement, focusing on human capital and extracting productivity out of a symphonic combination and fine tuning of factors. In this way it is possible to avoid culturally rooted development traps such as rigidity and hierarchy, often blended with paternalism and dangerous overdependence on external partners.
The development of more complex businesses, with higher productivity and margins, and entry barriers that keep competitors away, is the key strategy towards the creation of real and sustainable competitive advantage. Simple and unsophisticated countries find it extremely difficult to follow such strategies,

---

479 In Harrison, Huntington (2000), p. 287.

which require basic background of education, infrastructures [...] and prolonged efforts driven by a vision. Uniqueness is a strategic differential asset.
Once the growth process is properly ignited, it can become self fulfilling and it can magnetize new resources (skills and qualified labor, capital ...) but there has to be comparative convenience, which is increasingly harder to find in a global context where competition gets tougher.
Productivity naturally eases the attraction of foreign direct investments, always looking for interesting returns, and it contributes to push up exports: these are two crucial factors for sustained development, as the Chinese or Indian outstanding growth pattern is showing.

Climbing the social ladder from the Bottom of the Pyramid

›*The Market at the Bottom of the Pyramid*‹ is a celebrated book of Prahalad (2006) that is not primarily focused on microfinance, even if many insights can be usefully applied to our topic and they allow us to a better understanding of the social and economic possibilities of the poorest.
The central thesis is that there is a hidden market even for the poorest, which is waiting for being discovered and exploited with unconventional means, since the traditional ones, relying on standard market forces, are hardly working with those who are too poor to pay a price for anything.
Converting poverty from a burden to an opportunity–exploiting the concealed capital, extracting value from the bottom of the social pyramid–is challenging and it requires a mix of solutions, ranging from self esteem to entrepreneurial drive. Money can help–albeit it might hurt too–but the true target lies in reshaping a passive mentality, transforming ancestral problems into unthinkable opportunities. Human potential has unlimited upside and development opportunities are impressive, especially for those who start from the lowest levels. Partnering and sharing with the poor might really bring to a win-win scenario – the dream target of any sustainable microfinance project.
The pyramidal concept can be extended to figure out the ›geometric‹ differences, but also the converging opportunities, between the poor and the rich.

Figure 16.2. – Development is a bottom-up approach, leading to a turned pyramid

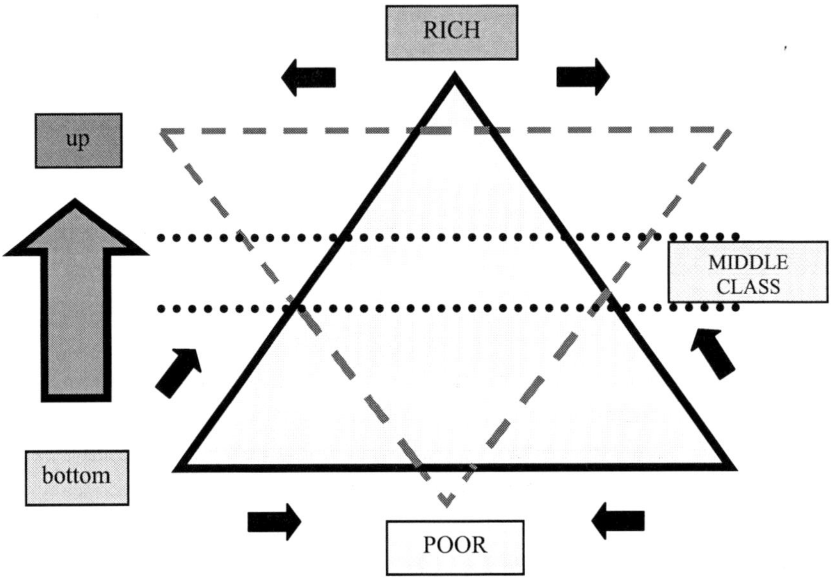

The poor are able to create strategies, weight trade-offs and seize opportunities, which can be incremental, bringing up to a virtuous development pattern. They need a friendly environment, proper counseling, some capital, and … a bit of good luck. People in developing countries are, as De Soto (1999) claims, just as capable of innovation, creativity, and entrepreneurship as those in the West – the poor are not the problem, they are the solution.

The poverty penalty is a result of mixed causes such as local monopolies (prospering out of entry barriers), inadequate access, weak distribution, strong traditional intermediaries (such as moneylenders), lack of democracy and justice, etc., which limit competition, choice, innovation, freedom and–especially–hope of a better future.

Creating the capacity to consume among the poorest is a primary task of charity or philanthropy, which however rarely solve the problem in a scalable and sustainable fashion. In order to overcome this problem–which has many similarities with microfinance, that can simply be seen as a financial product–products have to be affordable (small packages, like small loans, can greatly help), accessible (with a capillary distribution to the poorest, possibly even in underpopulated rural areas), and available (the decision of the poorest to buy is based on the cash they have at that very moment, whereas purchasing decisions are rarely deferred).

New goods and services are strongly needed and they might be as successful as microfinance products. The private sector–on the one side–representing larger firms (often multinationals) which traditionally serve much wealthier clients, and–on the other side–the poorest at the very bottom of the social pyramid, do not traditionally trust each others and they live in distant worlds. However, when the poor are converted into consumers, they acquire the dignity of attention from the private sector and they are entitled to choose – often for the very first time in their lives.

The poor, who are typically considered as uninteresting burden, potentially represent a huge and unexploited market and the static picture of their current situation is unable to capture trendy options. According to these options, people and places with a higher expected growth, albeit starting from a low wealth level (often beyond the survival threshold), are to become an interesting target in the medium to long run, that is possibly to be cultivated and presided from the beginning, so as to command a first mover competitive advantage on latecomers. Competitors benchmarking is a way to reduce misalignments but also strategic differences.

Expected higher growth is concerned with increasing purchasing power and foreign entrepreneurs, such as multinationals, tend to invest more where they expect higher growth. Self confidence and enthusiasm also play a decisive role and what really matters is not the absolute level of wealth, but rather its trend – and the pace of its growth pattern.

The opportunity for the poorest but also for private firms (fighting in an increasingly competitive and global environment and always looking for new clients) is huge and consistently unexploited. Contributing to pro poor growth, multinationals and local enterprises can open up new markets, progressively enabling customers to raise their living standards, buying more durable and consumable goods. Since both are struggling for survival, they should really understand how much they need each other. The sooner they do, the better it is.

Deskilling work is critical in Bottom of the Pyramid markets, which lack technical and learning abilities, suffering from a shortage of talent, as a consequence of unsophisticated and not meritocratic education. Education of clients to new markets and products is strongly needed, primarily focused on survival objectives such as health or nutrition. Illiteracy or media darkness, that are so frequent in rural areas, do not help.

Scale of operations is potentially huge, concerning 4 to 5 billion people. Since unitary margins are low, adequate returns require big volumes. Smart and innovative solutions in order to create a market for the poorest, must be sustainable and ecologically friendly. Design of products and services that are suitable for the destitute must acknowledge that infrastructures, wherever existent, are typically hostile and that first-time customers need simple products with basic characteristics. The distribution system might also prove a bottleneck and trade innovations are as critical as those concerning products or processes.

Corruption is another often undervalued main obstacle to poverty alleviation, being a market mechanism for privileged access, and transaction (contractual) governance–the capacity to guarantee transparent and enforceable economic deals–is strongly needed to set free huge and otherwise trapped economic resources.

As De Soto (2003) points out, poor countries are often asset–rich but capital–poor, since assets cannot become capital–the mostly wanted collateral for microloans–unless the country guarantees an efficient set of laws whereby the ownership of assets is clear and unquestioned, making them fit for being bought, sold, mortgaged, or converted into other assets.

Another hot issue is the local enforcement of contract law, which is often left in the hands of corrupted and ruthless local ›strongmen‹. Property rights violations and unjustified expropriations, often following a coup d'état, are a major source of political and country risk, while democracy provides a safety net from idiosyncratic changes. If the rules of the game are changing and unfair, smart players remain far from it, preventing the creation of any suitable background for microfinance or other market projects.

Development needs the presence–or the creation from scratch, if it doesn't exist–of a middle class of small entrepreneurs with vested economic interests, that can interact with the poor and attract them, offering jobs and giving assistance.

Poverty can become a profitable business, provided that there is a comprehensive understanding of its very causes – and how they can be dismantled. A core question is concerned with what prevents companies doing business with poor people and how these obstacles–bottlenecks–can be modified and removed: adapting the business model and designing innovative ones, widening their scope and outreach, making products affordable, cutting costs with the participation of the customers ... The aim is to match potentially unlimited demand–the poor being so many–with a rigid and diffident supply. The capacity is both enormous and underestimated.

Ignorance, farness, unfamiliarity, and lack of trust towards the poor often bring to a discrimination trap that creates an obstacle between demand and supply. Frictions and information asymmetries destroy huge potential markets.

To the extent that new markets are created by foreign multinationals–especially for non basic products–the real involvement of local small companies can create a cluster (network) of satellite companies that are positioned around the powerful foreign company. This uneasy relationship, if successful, can strongly improve development, especially if wealth is wisely distributed among a wide range of local people, to the benefit also of the poorest, who are typically the last to enjoy the positive impact of a trickle down effect.

An efficient financial system is an indispensable requisite for effective market, since lack of credit can prevent any growth. Whereas big foreign multinationals are traditionally supported by large international banks, their small local suppliers and customers are typically much better served by tailor made microfinance institutions, which typically grow and develop together with their clients.

Shaping a strategic vision for the future and an inclusive growth pattern, together with the poor

Despite the considerable amount of research that is devoted to economic growth and development, economists have not yet discovered how to make poor countries rich. Development can be achieved by the poor countries if only governments allow the market mechanism to function effectively–to get the prices right–and they permit economic agents to fully exploit the available gains from trade. This point requires not just openness and non-distortion public finance, but also the enforcement of property rights and the restraint of predation[480].
While we have stressed many times the importance of economic growth in reducing poverty, we have never analyzed in depth this crucial causal relationship: according to Sen (1999), p. 44, the impact of economic growth depends much on how the fruits of economic growth are used.
Injustice and social differences are highly suspected to increase, due to the diverging impact of growth. It is a pattern that was already observed so many times almost everywhere and at any level:

- from a macroeconomic side, we can directly observe the increasingly divergent development drift between the haves and haves–not, if only we look at the increasing differences among developed, developing, or not developing countries–the common saying according to which the rich become increasingly richer while the poor become poorer is often cynical but unfortunately undisputed[481];
- from a microeconomic perspective, we can observe these differences even within each country, comparing different individuals or groups; success is always an unpredictable mixture of endurance, will and a bit of unavoidable luck, while failure can be often (but not exclusively) attributed to laziness, cowardice but also and sometimes only to bad luck, as those who are permanently disabled or others who live in a difficult environment can sadly witness.

480 Azariadis, Stachurski (2005).

481 Attention should however be paid to deterministic theoretical patterns, described in Chapter 1, according to which economic history follows its projected trend, while in effort in normally doesn't.

Severe social inequalities are frequent even in developed countries – if we only think about the pitiless U.S. welfare model, particularly concerning a merciless health system about to be uneasily reformed. But in poor countries they are even more dangerous, since the poorest living at the bottom of the pyramid can hardly take benefit from the wealth spilling over from the relatively richer, and they lack social safety nets, flying with no parachutes in a turbulent atmosphere. Divergences tend to grow with development, and only later they tend to diminish, thanks to the redistributive effect of public spending – made possible by a higher tax collection. It is a trickle down effect, according to which some wealth inevitably spills over to lower social classes, and to marginal decreasing utility of wealth, making convergence between the haves and the haves not a bit easier.

Growth beyond Inequality

Sustained and long termed economic growth is a key factor of poverty alleviation, as seen in Chapter 1, even if it does not automatically bring to positive scenarios for the underserved. The main reason is that growth may be – and often is – severely unbalanced and polarized, so bringing to suboptimal human development, up to the point of increasing inequalities. The poor stay poor while the rich get even richer.

Converging development towards a common target is a key strategic issue behind development, with a broader distribution of opportunities. In its strictest sense, inequality is very much concerned with lack of chances, a key characteristic of the poor.

Taxation is a double edged sword, in the sense that while it may contrast inequalities, with public wealth redistribution from the richer to the poorer, it is also a major constraint to growth. Proper taxation, with a smart fine tuning of its often undesirable effects, is so a strategic issue to keep well in mind, going beyond biased ideologies.

Market distortions often bias growth and its spillovers, exacerbating elitarian income inequalities, and fostering social differences. Trickle down of increased wealth from the top to the bottom of the pyramid may take time and get dispersed.

Globalization, described in Chapter 11, also plays its part, representing a big opportunity for growth but also an unprecedented challenge.

Inequality is also sourced by the volatility of economic trends, whose effects constantly need to be smoothed and monitored, remembering that the poorest constantly live close or beyond the survival threshold.

Unequal institutions which improperly extract wealth and destroy fair opportunities are another cornerstone of polarized development, which brings to a vicious cycle, unsustainable in the long term. Fair diffusion of prosperity is the key for its long termed sustainability.

The condensed Chapter

The troublesome economic life of the poorest, constantly facing basic survival challenges, needs an external kick to ignite development, starting from basic activities such as agriculture, textile production and housing, up to marginally richer exports of goods and services.
Low wages and job insecurity in the informal sector in developing economies can create and perpetuate destitution among the working poor.
The transition from extended family clan systems to a market economy needs time and proper guidance, helping the poor to progressively climb the social ladder from the Bottom of the Pyramid, a fortunate metaphor of the Indian economist Prahalad, who shows that there is an unexploited market at the poorest level of the society.
Long term sustainable growth is what primarily matters for eradicating poverty.

Out of Poverty Tips

Detecting the economic lives of the poor and their continuous survival challenges is a crucial starting point for any out of misery strategy.
Survival businesses, such as agriculture and clothing, are followed by housing and increasingly sophisticated investment, through an incremental development pattern, farming out rural behinders from atavistic misery.
Changes in technology, education and globalization are a key factor behind productivity and growth.

Selected Readings

ALBERT P.J., WERHANE P., ROLPH T., eds., (2014), *Global Poverty Alleviation: A Case Book*, Springer Verlag, Berlin.

AGHION P., DURLAUF S.N., (2005), *Handbook of Economic Growth*, Elsevier, Amsterdam, in http://elsa.berkeley.edu/~chad/azstach.pdf.

BANERJEE A.V., BÉNABOUR R., MOOKHERJEE D., (2006), *Understanding Poverty*, Oxford University Press, Oxford.

BOWLES S., DURLAF S.N., HOFF K., (2006), *Poverty traps*, Princeton University Press, Princeton.

PRAHALAD C.K., (2006), *The Fortune at the Bottom of the Pyramid*, Wharton School Publishing, Philadelphia.

CALTON J.M., WERHANE P.H., HARTMAN L.P., (2013), *Building Partnership to Create Social and Economic Value at the Base of the Global Development Pyramid,* in Journal of Business Ethics, Issue 4, pp. 721-733.

CHAPTER 17 – Coping with financial exclusion in an informal survival economy

> If you're poor, managing your money well is absolutely central to your life – perhaps more so than for any other group.
>
> D. Collins, J. Morduch, S. Rutherford, O. Ruthven, *Portfolios of the Poor*

The financial life of the poor

In Chapter 16 we have seen some highlights concerning the economic life of the poor and in Chapter 15 we have analyzed the poor's (un)wealth, dealing with the property trap and the mystery of hidden capital. In the current Chapter we argue about a complementary topic, that is concerned with the financial aspects of poverty – poor people are poor first of all because they don't make enough money, even if there are many other less obvious interdependent causes.

When financial and economic flows add up, they are transformed into accumulated capital and wealth, which represent storage for future consumption and starting sources for investments. Long term wealth accumulation, that is so important for igniting development and keeping it alive, is however a target well beyond the capabilities of the abject poorest. This point is due also to credit constraints, which are particularly binding for the poor with no collateral, since they constrain small enterprises development and lock the underserved in their poverty traps.

Both economic and financial flows and accumulated wealth need to be financially intermediated, so to make safe storing possible, to allow people for lending and borrowing, in order to leverage up capital, matching asynchronous financial maturities, hedging against risk and providing emergency capital, in case of need. Proper financial instruments can so soften pervasive insecurity. If these are some of the main basic functions of financial markets, other more sophisticated necessities are sometimes needed, even if they are seldom provided to the poor.

For roughly two thirds of the world population, simply there are not financial institutions and life has to be designed in another–unpleasant–way. When opportunities are denied, it proves difficult to get out of poverty, considering that the world works with money and everybody needs the first coin to catch the second one – in many cases, it is just a starting problem, likely to be solved if only properly addressed.

The poor are often considered being completely unaware of the financial mechanisms, which are so pervasive in the capitalistic culture. On the one side, this point is true regarding the most sophisticated products, which are totally–and luckily–unheard of in most poor environments, but on the other side, through a simpler perspective, many poor are astonishingly very familiar with basic financial aspects, counting every penny they earn and trying to make the most out of it – a matter of survival, under a continuous stimulus of permanent need.

Basic forms of informal saving and borrowing are much diffused, since they are an answer to day-by-day problems for the poor who have the necessity to store up money, in order to normalize and match volatile cash inflows with often unpredictable outflows, in an environment where personal or impersonal emergencies (sickness, injury, unemployment versus natural disasters ...) are endemic. A basic survival strategy becomes coping with risk–traditionally higher in poor environments–and putting in place appropriate mitigation measures against endemic emergencies.

Income shocks, which occur when poor households receive less than expected, are typically combined with disgraceful events such as illnesses, livestock death, natural calamities etc., which derail households from their envisaged accumulation pattern, making the poor even more vulnerable.

Unlucky events may cause a 'last-straw' threshold effect, if they are the last inauspicious event of a long sequence of ominous happenings.

Financial instruments and markets in poor environments–making basic financial intermediation feasible and possible–have huge potential, for a variety of complementary reasons, such as:

- need for simple but vital financial products to manage and intermediate money – saving, borrowing, depositing, preserving, transferring, and repaying;
- lack of suitable financial services, since the existing ones are typically expensive–often unaffordable–unreliable, unregulated, and poorly designed, and they make the poor even more vulnerable and unable to choose among different competitive options;
- need to intermediate funds, in order to match different maturities, to smooth volatility, to mitigate risk and store savings in a safe place. Volatility tends to be negatively skewed, since improvements are typically gradual, while declines are more sudden and severe;
- need for formal and institutional markets, complementary to unofficial financial services.

Financial intermediation, based on money as a conventional system of payment and exchange for goods and services, goes beyond a barter economic system and it allows people to store, transfer, and transform fungible wealth, conventionally represented by a currency. Money is a tangible and psychological metaphor for the price of things, within a set of opportunities represented by the market.

Monetary savings are a cornerstone within the financial system, even in its embryonic phase, and they can help the poor, who live on income that is by definition small, but also uncertain, volatile, and unpredictable. One never knows what may happen tomorrow, especially if living with no safety nets, apart from the solidarity of the family clan. It is astonishing to see how even the poorest can save and intermediate cash – and those who do not have social security nets need to save more.

The poor do need to intermediate, to hold cash reserves and to get survival bridge-financing in the form of little lump sums of money, often with little notice, when cash inflows are late and income patterns are volatile, so as to smooth the ups and downs of household consumption[482]. Such a necessity is carried through with a network of typically informal relations, ranging from the family and the ethnic clan to neighbors, friends, local saving clubs, or greedy moneylenders.

The network may have an increasing pattern of formality, becoming semi-formal or even formal. In such an evolution, microfinance can help. The poorest may however be intimidated by a contact with formal banking institutions, unfit for their needs.

Survival cash flow management

Uneven cash inflows are irregular, unpredictable, typically low, and often seasonal, since they are awkwardly timed, especially in the countryside – peaking in harvest times and drying up in other ›hungry‹ periods. The systematic risk of the businesses (from volatile agricultural outputs to uncertain trading results) has a strong impact on incomes – to be consumed for survival but also stored for deferred use. Financial intermediation is a necessity, not just an option, even if it is unsophisticated and concentrated on short term liquidity management.

Financial products are typically highly flexible and their intermediation can bring to many different possible outcomes, even in unsophisticated and backward environments. Need is a powerful engine behind innovation and creativity whereas the demand for financial products, including microfinance, is particularly strong at the base of the social pyramid, also because of the increasing

482 See Collins, Morduch, Rutherford, Ruthven (2009), p. 14.

purchasing power of the poor. Successful examples may conveniently be replicated over a larger number of poor borrowers and depositors.
Informal reciprocal lending and borrowing among the poor are highly diffused, typically exchanging little sums of money for short time horizons, and they normally take place within the extended family network, being acquaintance, confidence and trust fundamental aspects of unregulated exchanges. Interest rates are often forgiven, to the extent that loans are short termed and reciprocal, balancing fluctuating states of need, where today's lenders are likely to be tomorrow's borrowers.
The poor have unsophisticated primary needs for basic survival and complicated products are not suitable and dangerous for them, even if the world they live in is not less complicated or variegated than that of wealthier households – the problems of the ant are not smaller than those of the elephant.
As the leading economist Raghuram G. Rajan says[483]:

> People, poor and rich, need reliable financing so that their ideas can be brought together with assets to generate long-run sustainable growth. The two key ingredients to a well-functioning market economy are competition and access, competition so that performance keeps improving and access so that everyone has a chance to participate and nobody's talents are wasted […] we will focus on access to finance, for after all, people, poor and rich, need reliable financing so that their ideas can be brought together with assets to generate long-run sustainable growth.

There are human events that are relatively or totally impermeable to the level of wealth, such as births, marriages, or funerals. If little choice is attributed to the last sad event, which democratically occurs to both the rich and the poor, birth and weddings are influenced by the level of wealth only to a very little extent – actually, poor spouses make even more children that richer couples, as we have seen in Chapter 4, whereas most people long for getting married anyway, irrespectively of their financial means and romantically trying to be poor but happy.
The financial life of the poor is very much concerned with these basic choices and happenings and it moves around key and unsophisticated events, following the ordinary life cycle. Wealth matters more–and makes the difference–in other complementary aspects, such as the standard and quality of living or the possibility to build up entrepreneurial activity, for which some initial money is gratefully needed.
Challenges, events, and opportunities always have a financial side, which is important but rarely decisive. The financial psychology of the poor–concerned

---

483 http://www.yearofmicrocredit.org/pages/whyayear/whyayear_quotecollection.asp.

about how they perceive money and attribute a symbolic value to it–also matters, in order to understand their cultural values and to foresee their needs and behavior.

Financial illiterates

Most of the poor have no contact with formal financial institutions, whose standardized products do not fit their needs and qualifications, and consequently they are approximately considered as being completely illiterate, even from a financial point of view. The poor are underbanked, or, more frequently, completely unbanked. Financial literacy matters.

This superficial statement is however in most cases far from being completely true and even the poorest who have no certified identities and are unable to write and read, possess a simple and informal financial background, which helps them dealing with their daily challenges.

Parallel to formal financial institutions, unofficial intermediaries have a pervasive and decisive role in matching some of the basic liquidity needs of the underserved. Their presence is highly welcome, since they are there–while others aren't–and they are flexible, suitable and sometimes even cheap and affordable (if only we consider intra-family interest-free loans) but they also have some nasty features, being in many cases unreliable, expensive up to usury levels, unfair and so on.

Formal institutions conveniently complement informal markets and the first are best suited to accompany the poor, since they wish to transform them into small entrepreneurs along their development road.

Cash flow management is vital for the poor, whose incomes are characterized by their low value and uncertain timing, especially in rural areas where crop returns are seasonal. Jobs are temporary and not always gainful, opportunities are limited and payrolls irregular, notably those deriving from casual or secondary or irregular employments. Short term liquidity management is the first financial concern, in the attempt to match cash inflows with outflows. The time horizon of investments and divestitures typically reflects contingent survival needs, even if the poor are also concerned by longer maturities and they try to match differed financial expenses with savings and loans.

Fungible money, that is divisible and combinable in many ways, is more flexible than barter economy where wealth storage is uncertain and exchanges are imperfectly priced. Synchronization of fragmented money inflows and outflows takes place almost daily, reflecting high ›cash flow intensity of income‹, should cash flows be compared with tiny income returns[484].

[484] See Collins, Morduch, Rutherford, Ruthven (2009), p. 32.

Incomes are small not only from an absolute perspective but also–even more–in relative terms. They are indeed typically shared within an enlarged family, where only some members are money earners, and the others are too young or old and weak to work, or simply they are unable to find a proper job. Among the expedients from which a family builds up a purchasing capacity, there are small business, casual job with intermittent, part time, or multiple occupations, self production, and consumption of food, remittances from working relatives, even from abroad, and sometimes grants. Through them, poor families are likely to be enabled to survive and, in the luckiest cases, to put some money aside, envisaging an uncertain future.

Surviving in an informal economy

Since cash flows are highly volatile (due to precarious jobs, irregular payments from employers, seasonality factors …)–especially considering their relative terms, starting from little amounts–their uneven timing requires some form of rudimental financial intermediation, so to match inflows with outflows. Unpredictability concerns not only irregular cash incomes, but also payments – due to common disgraces such as illnesses, funerals, natural disasters, thefts.

Households financial ups and downs need to be intermediated, smoothing, and synchronizing otherwise unmatched maturities. Even predictable and joyful events, such as marriages, are expensive, due to the dowry system applicable in many developing countries, from India to sub-Saharan Africa. Childbirth, education, home-building, widowhood and retirement are other examples of life cycle events that require adequate cash coverage.

Financial innovation, albeit at informal and basic level, plays its part and it continuously tries to answer unmet demands for intermediation of money, maturities, risk deriving from insecurity, proposing different complementary products. And the ability to properly manage risk exposure is often a vital question for the poorest.

Emergencies are dealt with burning savings and underwriting informal debt with relatives, clan members, or friends – normally with short time horizons and no interest rate charges. Home savings and free borrowing represent the first safe-net against adversities and needy poor try to patch together money from multiple complementary sources.

Multiple collection of tiny loans from many different and complementary sources allows lenders to diversify their risk, but at the expense of huge informal contractual costs. When this method is not enough to meet payable expenses, the poor become desperate and they try to survive reducing their living standards, i.e. burning out their few savings, eating less, moving to even cheaper places, pulling children from school, selling whatever they still consider val-

uable, sometimes even their body, sadly slipping towards prostitution or sale of organs.
Desperation brings to extreme actions, which can go well beyond common expectations. And downward spirals are difficult to halt and reverse. In difficult situations, it is not uncommon to see families falling apart, paying a high tribute to alcohol and other palliatives against a hard existence.
Health problems, in a context where social security is absent, are highly likely to become unpleasant financial issues, creating an urgent need for cash in the short term, while on a longer time span, they may inhibit the ability to work and to earn a decent salary, both for living and repaying cumulated debts at the time of need. Medical emergencies and their probability risk should be covered with adequate insurance products, but the lack of funding means make these diffused instruments hardly available to the poor, who should also discount their belonging to a riskier bracket. The government should encourage health insurance, especially if public healthcare is not available for everybody, but it is again lack of proper financial resources that make both tasks hardly viable.
In an informal economy, most financial transactions are carried out with unofficial counterparts, such as the already mentioned relatives, neighbors, clan members, or friends, using articulated social networks. So mutuality, cooperation, flexibility, and closeness among the poor provide a service that official institutions are both unwilling and unable to give.
No unsubsidized formal financial institution can lend at risk free rates, completely sacrificing intermediation margins. It commonly happens in an informal economy, where equilibrium between occasional lenders and borrowers is found because loans are short termed, amounts are small and gratuity is reciprocal, providing informal social insurance safety net. Help from neighbors can be given even anticipating (discounting) future payrolls, delaying rent payments, giving credit on the purchase of food, sharing costs, and adding up small little interventions and actions, aimed at smoothing adversities of the poorest.
A pitfall of informal social networks is that they provide little shelter against big and shared adversities, commonly referred as systematic risk. When a village is destroyed by floods, solidarity among its unlucky inhabitants is still nice but hardly effective. Diversification and large-scale insurance can help to hedge against shared risk, but it requires more sophisticated tools, which are unavailable to the poorest.
Saving is in many cases more important than borrowing and safe harbors for deposits are highly requested, as it is shown by the success of microdeposits, even more popular than microloans[485].
Differences between informal and formal transactions are often substantial and they are also concerned with bureaucratic accomplishments, which are hardly

[485] See Chapter 19.

present in the first case, where paperwork is rarely required, and so allowing illiterate poor to access the informal financial market.

The (un)rational behind financial exclusion: no guarantee, no history, no money

No guarantee, no history, no money: unless this fairly obvious statement proves wrong, there is little hope for financial inclusion and bankability of the poorest, who are unable to access modern financial services in an appropriate way. The poor with low and volatile incomes, little savings and tarnished or no credit history, are hardly ever given a chance to borrow, according to traditional banking rules.

Exclusion can be declined in many different ways[486], ranging from self exclusion–a prominent, albeit sad, characteristic of many poor, who are so ashamed of their condition that they tend to abscond themselves–to access exclusion, for those who do not comply with the admission criteria or cannot afford the cost of financial intermediation, up to political or social exclusion (for those belonging to the ›wrong‹ clan or who are devoid of civil rights and proper documents).

Conventional banks, which are built around collateral, are traditionally skeptical about those who have no guarantees to offer and they simply consider them not creditworthy. Bankers love to lend money to those who do not need it – think about this simple statement, and you will agree that they are the safest clients! The wealthier they are, the more money they are being lent, forgetting the basic economic principles of marginal decreasing returns. Microfinance, as we shall see later on, tries to reverse the principle, by lending more to those who have less, helping them to start up their economic activities.

Banks or other for-profit financial intermediaries look for positive returns, which are unlikely to sort out from poor clients, whose demand is addressed towards appropriate products, designed to suit their habits, needs, and lifestyle. The differences between standard products and those fit for the poor are so huge that it's something more than a marketing problem of customization.

According to Kofi Annan, former U.N. secretary »The great challenge before us is to address the constraints that exclude people from full participation in the financial sector. […] Together, we can and must build inclusive financial sectors that help people improve their lives«.

The poor, especially if not accustomed to dealing with money, may soon discover that debt is a double edged sword, which is easy to issue–and sometimes to get–but difficult to pay back. Debt may bring to vulnerability and loss of freedom, being an opportunity but also a threat–and a trap–for the poor, which can fall in the spiral of delinquency, if they are unable to meet their obligations.

---

[486] See La Torre, Vento (2006).

In many cases the poor know what they should do and their actual inactivity is due to lack of (financial) means, not of intentions – to the extent that they can't afford to save and invest.

Financial development and inclusion, going beyond the debt trap

According to Natalie Portman »Small loans can transform lives, especially the lives of women and children. The poor can become empowered instead of disenfranchised. Homes can be built, jobs can be created, businesses can be launched, and individuals can feel a sense of worth again«.

Financial development is one of the main determinants of economic growth and prosperity, but the relationship between finance and growth is very weak in low-income countries[487].

Financial development is eased and fostered by:

- financial liberalization (removal of currency controls or impediments to the incorporation of new banks, especially if controlled by foreigners; capital accounts' liberalization; removal of financial restrictions, which allow the authorities to insulate domestic interest rates; integration with international stock and bond markets …);
- bank privatization, softening the governmental control, and the political pressures on the banking system;
- encouraging the presence of a wider spectrum of financial intermediaries, each suitable to a different segment of clientele;
- strengthening the institutional framework (first of all the legal and judicial system);
- setting pro growth political economy, with market liberalizations, no price controls, little or any trade restrictions …

Financial inclusion is both selective (with discriminatory admission rules) and compliant with the stakeholders' interests, following an increasingly formal pattern, with standard rules that are often hardly flexible and unable to meet the poor's needs and possibilities.

The poor are mainly concerned with lack of financial services, or with the unsuitability of the products they are enabled to use in many cases, due to their poor financial literacy or to unfavorable events. So they may fall into a debt trap, being unable to pay back what they have unwisely borrowed. The debt trap can lead to a well known downward spiral, where the poor borrower makes new

[487] See Guha-Khasnobis, Mavrotas (2008), p. 10.

debts to pay back older ones, paying higher interest rates and getting deep into troubles. The more he or she is in danger, the more he or she tends to approach informal and careless intermediaries.
According to Rhyne (2009), p. ix »The success of microfinance movement demonstrates the business viability of financial services for the poor« and the project is to pass from microfinance to inclusive finance, improving the access to more formal institutions.

Getting off a barter penniless economy: from informal lending to inclusive microfinance

In a barter economy, money is simply unknown or not used. The exchange of real goods–a chicken against several bananas, or livestock for land–gives way to an informal market where values are approximate and fair pricing an unneeded option. It is a simple, imperfect but viable world, where survival strategies leave little room for sophistication.
Moving towards a financial economy, physical assets are accompanied by–or transformed into–money and other increasingly sophisticated financial assets. For those who are nostalgic of the gold standard, a good compromise is represented by the precious metal, a real asset with a conventional financial value, which is easy to store, to steal, to intermediate, and to transform. Money is a conventional store of value and it works as a unit of account, providing a simple medium of exchange, whereas liquidity is a measure of how easily an asset may be exchanged for money, fixing a market price – the signal that tells us which is the meeting point of the demand and supply of a product, giving some clue about its upward (if demand exceeds supply) or downward (if supply exceeds demand) trend.
The passage from informal to formal economy is hardly ever clear-cut and in most cases it follows a long and winding evolutionary pattern, with incremental upgrading but also stop-and-go random trends, often without a formal strategy.
Closed clans and family networks play a major role in an informal environment, and their presence is still compatible with an open outset, where the rules of the game are universally applicable, independently of any belonging, and they create a more complex and rational institutional environment, somewhat pitiless but less discriminatory.
The notion of social capital[488] is still valid (it represents the glue which keeps together informal relationships within communities), but it has to be flexibly adapted to a more open environment, which is consistent with a development friendly scenario, where innovation and productivity increases require an open mind and a cultural attitude to accept changes and challenges.

---

[488] See Chapter 9.

Informal lending is traditionally concerned with money-lending, carried through by usurers, while microfinance represents a step forward on the road to a more institutional form of lending, even if its simple philosophy makes it acceptable even from poor clients, out of scope for any commercial bank.
The absence of microfinance–whose presence in poor regions, albeit growing, is still more an exception than a rule–does not mean complete lack of access to simpler and informal sources of financial intermediation. Poor households typically have multiple credit sources in rural economies, as well as unregulated and flexible ways to save–the starting point for self-financing a business–and insure[489].
Many microlending activities are the natural roots of more sophisticated tools such as microfinance and they need to be synthetically described, in order to understand where microfinance comes from and if its characteristics are really ›revolutionary‹–as some enthusiastic supporters might induce to believe–or simply represent a natural evolution and improvement of an existing model.
Informal traditional microcredit is primarily involved with lending by individuals on a non-profit and reciprocal basis, directed by intermittent lending by individuals with temporary surplus, lending by specialized individuals (with proper or intermediated funds), individuals informally collecting deposits, group finance or moneylenders[490].

United we go, divided we fall: exploiting the rationale behind group lending, ethnic loyalty and other solidarity networks

According to a well known African proverb, if you want to proceed fast, go alone, but if you want to go far, walk together with others. Team-centric leadership is embedded within group lending system: it allows a real leader to emerge, differentiating him/herself from others and gaining shared consensus, with the result of instilling within the group sense of purpose, goals, commitment, and confidence.
When the poor help each other, forming a united group, they can find precious synergies, exploiting the potentialities of social capital described in Chapter 9.
Group lending–again not a novelty of microfinance, since it was extensively used in the 19th Century by mutual banks and insurance companies–is a much celebrated idea to overcome the lack of collateral, which represents one of the biggest obstacles to credit access for the poor[491].
The idea to find something within the poor than can replace valuable goods and collective guarantees, considering that they don't have much else, seems smart

489 See Armendariz De Aghion, Morduch (2010), Chapter 3.
490 See Arun (2005); Matin, Hulme, Rutherford (2002).
491 Empirical evidence about group lending is surveyed in Hermes, Lensink (2007).

enough to comply with the requirement of a collateral. Such an intuition appears even smarter if only we consider the cultural and anthropological concept of collectivity within poor rural communities, where microfinance finds its natural habitat. From Chapter 9, we can recall the key concept of social capital and conscious or subliminal tribal loyalty within a homogeneous ethnic group.

The selection of the group–for lending or selling insurance products–is not a trivial passage. And delinquency rates much depend on this initial process, which can conveniently profit from past experience, even if mistakes are frequently recurrent and the general environment may change faster than expected. The key purpose–not only in group lending–is to make the borrower's behavior observable and, possibly, predictable, so to minimize uncertainties and delinquency risk, taking profit of the tight social control that is intrinsically present within ethnically homogeneous teams. This well known problem concerns corporate governance issues–such as moral hazard or adverse selection–that will be examined in Chapter 18. For the moment, it seems enough to remind that apparently a random selection of the group is what should most reduce opportunistic behavior, since otherwise borrowers may be tempted to enter or exit the group at their will, just to get the loan or to subsequently avoid repayment.

An ideally safer random selection of the group components, irrespective of their clan belonging, is however an unviable option. It is true above all in places where communities are small and they belong to the same ethnicity: it is indeed a common situation in the poorest rural areas, where microfinance is most needed in order to contribute to the eradication of misery. But here an often neglected, albeit crucial, characteristic of risky poor rural areas emerges. Ethnic loyalty and the ancestral sense of belonging to the same sharing community is a free-of-charge and effective antidote against shameful and socially unacceptable opportunistic behavior, minimizing its risky outcomes.

Clan solidarity, adapted to local peculiarities, can conveniently be exploited not only for group lending but also for other jointly liable credit devices–mainly illustrated in Chapter 20–consisting of self help groups, credit cooperatives, or other mutual agreements and mechanisms. There the united community can fully exploit its synergies, possibly going well beyond the simple sum of individual poor possibilities and so gearing up poverty to its upper potential. Non monetary values are also part of the jointly liable package.

The problem with ethnic loyalty is that–as Collier (2010), p. 53 claims–it hardly works anymore in a modern economy, where a single group is increasingly close to others, loosing much of its primitive identity and being potentially dangerous, if colliding with the interests of others, without contributing to a common pool of interests. Migration from the countryside to town, the big force behind the worldwide urbanization process, also contributes to loosen clan ties, diluting loyalty and membership values.

Even in order to solve these problems, microfinance needs continuous innovation – and group lending selection and monitoring stand out as one of the industry's biggest opportunities but also one of its dangers.
MFIs typically lend an individual small loan to a household belonging to a group of normally 5 to 20 people, who guarantee for her and intervene in case of delinquency. Should the individual borrower prove reliable, the MFI might extend credit within other members of the group. The essence of group lending is to transfer responsibilities from bank staff to borrowers, who contribute to the selection and monitoring of debtors, helping in the enforcement of contracts. In exchange, customers get otherwise inaccessible loans.
Monitoring takes place with weekly meetings between the MFIs and group members and the repayment status of the borrowers is publicly checked. The consequent advantages are the minimization of screening costs by meeting debtors in groups[492] and the multiplication of savings and loan transactions, with some economies of scale which reduce transaction costs for the microfinance bank and consequent interest charges for the borrowers.
Even group lending has shortcomings, since it mainly works in rural areas where social control is tighter and smart individuals who belong to an unreliable group might be seriously damaged by lack of flexibility (a typical group-loan might be unfit for one of its components, often the smartest).
Stiglitz (1990) argues that the group-lending contract circumvents *ex ante* moral hazard (irresponsible behavior) by inducing borrowers to monitor each others' choice of investments and to inflict penalties to borrowers who have chosen excessively risky projects.
A strong internal incentive for monitoring within the group arises in collective lending, even if this fact cannot prevent all problems. Social sanctions hardly prove effective outside small rural areas where everybody knows others and this problem grows along with the urbanization process which is taking place almost everywhere. But even in small villages, the threat of social sanctions between close friends and relatives is hardly credible[493]. Attending and monitoring group meetings can prove expensive in dispersed areas. Frequency of meetings is another implicit cost. Borrowers' behavior might also prove collusive against the bank, undermining its ability to exploit social links as proper collateral.
Benefits of group lending[494] are counterbalanced by costs. As Madajewicz (2003) points out, costs emerge when borrowers are risk averse and borrowing is expensive. Costs also grow together with the scale of lending, since default amounts rise, and growing businesses suffer from credit rationing problems – with a smart borrower going far beyond his peers.

492 Deutsche Bank (2007), p. 4.
493 See Armendariz De Aghion, Morduch (2010).
494 See Chapter 18.

If the poor succeed to get credit, they can invest, generate profit, and subsequently get more credit. However, cash flows stemming from profits need to be enough to properly serve outstanding debts: it is an unlikely situation in the initial phases of growth, when liquidity is typically burned.
Loan group mechanisms are effective if they are not correlated–since they make possible risk diversification and reduction–but they don't work well when a generalized systematic crisis occurs (such as the periodical floods which devastate Bangladesh and have masterminded the first Grameen bank model).
For many, especially the smartest and wealthiest, individual lending is more flexible, even if it lacks group guarantees and collective monitoring. This approach is however hardly ever available to the poorest and it does not fit rural areas where individualism is not as culturally strong as it is elsewhere, for instance in Western countries. Looking with Western eyes at the financial problems of less developed areas might prove even in this case wrong and dangerous.
Dynamic incentives, such as the threat of not being refinanced if the group defaults (*refinancing threat*), can bring to better group selection, especially for risky borrowers that are obviously more stimulated to have a safe borrower as a peer[495]. This might however not be the case in the absence of any refinancing threat, where risky borrowers have a larger probability of going bankrupt and thus a lower probability of having the repay the debts incurred by his peer, should he/she default.
Strategic alliances within a group lending network represent essential social glue, based on a ›partner or perish‹ model, consistent with a threatening poor environment.

Liberalizing the regulatory framework

Financial liberalization is supposed to affect financial development, which–in turn–has an impact on growth. While the impact of financial development on growth is a fairly shared concept, the causal link between financial liberalization and its development, apparently axiomatic, is not so clear cut; empirical evidence presents mixed results, showing that financial liberalization is a powerful device, with positive but also destabilizing side effects.

[495] Borrowers, if allowed to form their own groups, will sort themselves into relatively homogenous groups of ›safe‹ and ›risky‹ debtors. Without dynamic incentives, a safe borrower will value having another safe borrower as a fellow group member more than a risky borrower will value having a safe borrower as a peer, since a risky borrower - by definition - has a larger probability of defaulting and thus a lower probability of having to pay back the debts incurred by his peer, should he default. See Guttman (2008); Ghatak (1999); Van Tassel (1999).

Even if information asymmetries are somewhat mitigated in informal markets by personal acquaintance, they still persist–and they often grow–in a more sophisticated liberalized context.
Liberalization of financial markets is driven by a liberal neoclassic market approach, according to which free markets, following a *laissez faire* ideology, are most efficient in allocating scarce resources. It began with Anglo-Saxon Western countries such as the U.K. and the U.S., through bank privatizations, removal of restrictions on financial transactions, and reinforcement of the central banks' function of flexible supervision of the market and its players, partially deregulating non core control functions. Since the 1990s liberalization has been translated even to developing countries.
Financial Deregulation is a highly sensitive issue in one of the most regulated segments, due to its recognized intrinsic dangerousness – if there is too much regulation, often following more formal than practical issues, it is hard to be beneficial, bearing extra costs and new useless bureaucratic accomplishments, while if there is too much freedom, it can be highly dangerous, as the smell of easy money has always shown to be. Partial recourse to self regulation has an effect that is proportional to the institutional reputation of associations of financial intermediaries, delegating them many practical and monitoring aspects.
By lowering entry barriers to the market, financial liberalization enhances competition and pressure on profit margins–especially interest rates and commissions–with the result of reducing the cost of collected capital, which is more easily driven to the most efficient institutions, with consequential benefit for consumers, in terms of both higher quality and better pricing.
Capacity building within Central banks supervisory teams has typically been slow and inadequate: it was not able to prevent major banking crises, both born locally and imported from abroad (as it has happened in the worldwide recession of 2008-2009), endangering macroeconomic stability, with particularly harmful effects during recessions, contributing to unemployment and underdevelopment[496].
Central Banks play an essential role, not only in their institutional supervision of the banking system, but also as lenders of last resort, should banks become illiquid as a consequence of poor management or destabilizing run-to-deposits. But in developing countries, Central banks are poorly capitalized and mostly unable to work efficiently, as they are supposed to do. And capitalization mainly comes from public funds, which are again hardly available in poor countries.
Computerized systems of accounting and reporting are now indispensable for careful and real time controls, but they are not ubiquitous within the banking system of developing countries, that are painfully trying to scale up efficiency.

496 See Guha-Khasnobis, Mavrotas (2008), Chapter 1.

Financial intermediaries and banks are the most regulated industry, together with the healthcare sector: the reason is not only their crucial role for the economic development, but also their intrinsic contagiousness – problems since insolvencies are rapidly spread within banks, which are closely linked among them, above all (but not only) through the interbank market.
Unless properly isolated and solved, bank crises can have painful domino effect, rapidly infecting other institutions, together with the real sector.
Market imperfections and improper regulations cause credit constrains, keeping the poor away from the formal financial market, preventing efficient capital allocation, which should be marginally addressed towards the lowest returns.
As we have already seen, even for what concerns Microfinance institutions (MFIs), the biggest regulatory threshold is represented by the permission to collect deposits. In such a case, that is also valid for standard banks, the confidence process is reversed and it is the client (depositor) who has to trust the financial intermediary, whereas if the MFI or the bank simply lends money, it is the borrower and not the institution that needs to be trusted.
The danger is that poorly managed institutions may run out of liquidity, if their assets structure is either illiquid or deteriorating up to the point of causing equity burn out (according to which the market value of liabilities would exceed that of the assets) because of their inability to timely and properly pay back deposits. Cash burn outs may also happen, if liquidity becomes negative, so preventing monetary repayments.
The result is not only run-to-deposit, but also rapidly widespread financial panic, that is potentially highly harmful – it takes hours to destroy credibility and years of painful job to try to restore it.
Experience tells us that too little regulation is useless but too much supervision is damaging, since it suffocates the industry while giving just formal–much more than substantial–protection to citizens. For what concerns the poor, excessively regulated markets would not only transfer to them and to the other customers the costs of overregulation, but also discourage them for trying to access the formal market, pushing them back to moneylenders and informal practices.
Quality of institutions is essential for their effective working, and underdeveloped and low quality financial system is likely to inhibit growth in poor countries where the institutional level is typically low.
With the presence of catalysts such as a common currency–such as the Euro–or strong bilateral and multilateral trading or similar regulatory and compliance standards, financial openness towards foreign countries becomes significant, and financial regulation rapidly tends to become supranational, despite the jealousy of national central banks, forced to delegate part of their beloved power.

The condensed Chapter

The financial life of the poor, facing problematic day-by-day survival cash flow management, is also concerned with financial exclusion, bringing them to a far-West-style informal lending scenario, where rules are arbitrarily missing and fairness is a chimera.
Financial inclusion, going beyond an ancestral barter economy, opens the door to microfinance and other more sophisticated intermediaries, exploiting hidden characteristics of the poor, such as togetherness and solidarity networks.

Out of Poverty Tips

Economic deprivation is strictly linked with financial exclusion. Development ignition comes from cash availability, so as to sweeten adversities and promote incremental and self fulfilling development.
Legality and transparency, within a democratic framework, represent the basic playground for any out of poverty strategy, starting from clean money, accessible even to the poorest at fair (reimbursable) conditions.

Selected Readings

COLLINS D., MURDOCH J., RUTHERFORD S., RUTHVEN O., (2009), *Portfolios of the Poor: How the World's Poor Live on $2 a Day*, Princeton University Press, Princeton.

RUTHERFORD S., (2000), *The Poor and Their Money*, Oxford University Press, Oxford.

SACHS J.D., (2005), *The End of Poverty: Economic Possibilities for Our Time*, Penguin Books, London.

WORLD BANK, (2008), *Finance for All? Policies and Pitfalls in Expanding Access, policy research report*, Washington, in http://econ.worldbank.org/.

CHAPTER 18 – The magic in microfinance: is it a solution for adverse selection, moral hazard, and strategic default?

> My vision for the future?
> Two things: to make credit a human right so that each individual human being will have the opportunity to take loans and implement his or her ideas so that self-exploration becomes possible.
> And second: that it will lead to a world where nobody has to suffer from poverty – a world completely free from poverty.
>
> Muhammad Yunus

What is microfinance? Characteristics and differences with traditional banking

Microfinance is a sort of ›social contract‹ concerned with the provision of financial services to low-income clients. But its real mission goes beyond credit allocation, being concerned with resources to improve the life of the poor, helping them to cross the poverty line.

Traditional sophisticated banking is unfit for the poor – the ›keep it simple‹ golden rule applies even in this context and concerns those who offer them unsuitable products, which may be embarrassing and intimidating for the underserved and troublesome for both parties. Never-buy-what-you-don't-understand is a corollary of the aforementioned rule, even if pressure for selling products at any cost is softened in banking by a risk sharing pattern, where the probability of delinquency and bad repayments hits both parties.

It instinctively sounds as bad news to be refused a loan, even if receiving a loan when the conditions for repayment look improbable depicts a much worse scenario, creating new troubles without being able to solve older ones.

Mark Twain used to say that »a banker is a fellow who lends you his umbrella when the sun is shining and wants it back the minute it begins to rain«.

The poor need and deserve a milder approach to banking, with a progressive adaptation to its advantages and pitfalls, and with an *ad hoc* recipe for their needs. A minimum economic background is anyway necessary, especially for those who are self employed and condemned to be entrepreneurs not as a result of free and meditated choice, but rather as a consequence of being excluded from other opportunities.

Muhammad Yunus says that »I did something that challenged the banking world. Conventional banks look for the rich; we look for the absolutely poor. All people are entrepreneurs, but many don't have the opportunity to find that out«[497].

If compared to traditional banking, in microfinance target clients and products are different and they have to be adapted to their peculiar context. Microfinance enjoys high but vulnerable reputation as socially responsible investment and it benefits from widespread international recognition as a development tool, being promoted by many national governments eager to bridge the financial inclusion gap.

Ad hoc products, tailor made to suit clients needs, have to incorporate even non financial features, following socio-ethical needs. Non monetary objectives are harder to measure and to monitor and the social performance is traditionally more difficult to assess, since it goes beyond quantitative parameters.

The absence of guarantees within the poor brings to wealth deconsolidation, due to which the (almost unworthy) personal wealth of the poor is unsuitable for backing entrepreneurial activities.

For the poorest of the poor, who live in hopeless misery, even microfinance may prove dangerous and unfit, since there is typically little room for more sophisticated development chances in conditions where the struggle for bare survival is the first and often only strategic option. From the title of this book, we derive the idea that microfinance can be effective against the poverty trap, but not always or in any conditions – and in some cases it may even appear counterproductive or, at least, it needs to be accompanied by other complementary actions and measures that make the environment suitable for microfinance intervention. The ground has to be carefully prepared and–looking at the European historical experience–we acknowledge that it may take ages of painful maturation, somewhat shortened in the actual global world, but not beyond a cultural threshold that in any case needs to be carefully assimilated. Poverty is also a state of mind, even if its psychological not measurable dimension is often unperceived and so underestimated.

Due to the United Nations' definition:

---

497 For a video with an interview of Muhammad Yunus, see http://nobelprize.org/mediaplayer/index.php?id=146. For his Nobel lecture, see http://nobelprize.org/mediaplayer/index.php?id=88&view=1.

> Microfinance can be broadly defined as the provision of small-scale financial services such as savings, credit, and other basic financial services to poor and low-income people. The term ›microfinance institution‹ now refers to a wide range of organizations dedicated to providing these services and includes non-governmental organizations, credit unions, cooperatives, private commercial banks, non-bank financial institutions and parts of State-owned banks.

According to CGAP[498] »the Term ›Micro Finance' has two components, namely ›Micro‹ and ›Finance‹. The word ›micro‹ is applied in terms of smallness by and large for representing the poor/ low income people. The word ›Finance‹ which is suffixed with Micro represents small amount of finance matching the needs of the poor/low income people. Since needs of the poor go beyond credit, the word ›Finance‹ here is covering savings, insurance, and other financial and non financial services for their development«.
Heloise Weber[499] indicates that:

> The microcredit approach to poverty reduction is premised on the provision of small loans to individuals, usually within groups, as capital investment to enable income generation through self-employment. Microcredit programs are usually complemented by the extension of micro-financial services, which may include, for instance, options for insurance schemes or savings. Microfinance departs significantly from other approaches to poverty reduction in that it is commercial in a fully-fledged sense.

In the mind of many, microfinance and microcredit are considered synonymous[500]. However, microcredit simply deals with the provision of credit for small business development, while microfinance–sometimes called ›banking for the poor‹–refers to a broader synergic set of financial products, including credit, savings, insurance, and pension benefits and sometimes money transfer, hopefully together with much wanted micro-consulting. Microfinance moves further on than microcredit, even if a big need to push even further comes from the poorest.
As Yunus claims »this [microfinance] is not charity. This is business: business with a social objective, which is to help people get out of poverty«. Microcredit is a »small, short, and unsecured« form of credit[501]. Microfinance programs

498 http://microfinance.cgap.org/2009/06/05/what-is-microfinance/.
499 In Fernando (2006), p. 50.
500 See Bogan (2008) and Chapter 20.
501 See Fernando (2006), p. 9.

have attracted widespread international attention, due to their focus on empowerment, concerning in particular women, and to sustainable and equitable development, able to equitably »lift all boats«.
Additional support services include literacy training, access to health services, and platforms to organize group lending communities.
Microfinance Institutions (MFIs) can be classified according either to their organizational structure (cooperatives, solidarity groups, rural or village banks, individual contracts, and linkage models ...)[502] or to their legal status (NGOs, cooperatives, registered banking institutions, government organizations ...), or even according to their capital adequacy standards (from Tier 1 mostly regulated MFIs to Tier 4 or not ranked start up MFIs)[503].
Microfinance moves one step further, compared to money lending, ROSCAs, ASCAs, credit cooperatives, or informal group lending, even if each new step bears some marginal (additional) complexity, this being the price to pay in order to solve some of the aforementioned problems. No innovation comes for free and increased complexity tends to restrict access to this intermediation form, with consequent social costs due to the progressive exclusion of the destitute and often inverse proportionality with outreach[504].
Microfinance firms are different from traditional banks, since they have to use innovative ways of reaching the underserved and poorest clients, who are not suitable to mainstream institutions, mixing unorthodox techniques such as group lending and monitoring, progressive lending (if repayment records are positive), short repayment installments[505], deposits, or notional collateral, as it will be seen later.
Many wonder if microfinance can really be helpful and, according to some, it seems a useful instrument for new entrepreneurs, while its effects on the general poverty level are questioned[506].

From social capital to group lending and beyond

Group lending (and self regulating solidarity groups, commonly known as self help groups, SHG), follows a collective and jointly liable cultural approach, that is widespread within rural communities. In it, borrowers are mutually accountable for each of the loans extended to the members of the group. It is among the

---

502 See Bogan (2008).
503 See Deutsche Bank (2007), p. 6.
504 See Chapter 21.
505 With possible negative effects, since due to short repayment time, MFIs risk steep deterioration of their portfolio in a matter of weeks only. See Mersland, Strøm, (2007b). Short repayment installments bring to a financial - and cultural - lack of long term planning, which discriminates riskier projects with a longer gestation.
506 See Banerjee, Duflo, Glennerster, Kinnan (2009).

most celebrated microfinance innovations, making it different from conventional banking, even if microfinance goes beyond it[507].

As we have seen in Chapter 9, social capital is concerned with its intrinsic cultural properties, such as mutual cooperation and solidarity, trust, closeness, and friendship, which enhance efficiency within the members of the clan, facilitating cooperation. Social capital is the networking glue within the members of a selected community and its applications can well embrace basic microfinance paradigms, such as group lending, but–as any human aspect–it has its pitfalls, too, which are represented in our case mainly by the problems that are faced by those who are not part of a social community, as a consequence of migration, arbitrary ostracism, racial exclusion, or other causes.

Social bonding, solidarity, mutuality, and associational life generate commonly shared values that can be used as notional and intangible collateral. Single poor are completely asset-less and powerless, but together–forming a moral community–they can get credit. Microfinance can mobilize social capital[508].

Social capital is a mean to first understand and then to alleviate poverty, because it enhances local capacities and focuses them towards common goals, through a grass-rooted mobilization, following a bottom up approach that sounds particularly effective even when foreign aid is concerned[509]. Group gatherings enhance local self-reliance, participatory processes, and development, based on local knowledge and capacity building. Traditional discriminations against women and their children can be overcome considering the whole group as undifferentiated entity, where single members have equal rights, dignity, and opportunities.

The joint accumulation of social capital–meeting microfinance–can ignite a virtuous growth process, strengthening the social framework and fostering sustainable development. The really innovative and path-breaking entrepreneurs, who are individually gifted, somewhat selfishly but rightfully go beyond group lending.

Entrepreneurialism is often a synonym of individualism, at least in its early stages. A resilient empowerment of the poor is greatly wanted, so to combine group lending advantages with a more flexible reliance on individual capabilities.

Other problems may well concern those who are part of the group even without getting any particular benefit out of it. Within the social group, equalitarianism and sharing are survival core values that go far beyond any individual expectation, but when the environment improves and it allows people to think beyond

507 Grameen Bank II model has abandoned this group leading model, recognizing its negative aspects, such as the free rider problem, according to which a bad borrower has an obvious incentive to join safer ones.

508 See Rankin in Fernando (2006), Chapter 4.

509 See Chapter 14.

bare survival, the smartest and the fittest ones may feel imprisoned by their peer's mediocrity.
Creativity may sometimes be a collective characteristic, even if in most cases it belongs to single individuals that are able to distinguish themselves among many undifferentiated members of the community. Rational and utility maximizing individuals (sometimes selfishly moving outside their native clan and going beyond binding group obligations) represent the typical prototype of self made entrepreneur, who is seen with suspicion and envy from his former mates but eventually representing a possible chance even for them.
Women-driven solidarity groups, gathered within loan committees, represent an unprecedented chance against ancestral and deeply rooted gender discrimination, because they favor entrepreneurship, emancipation, and socio-economic development, with positive spillovers on the children, on their health and education – a long term investment against poverty, potentially able to disrupt ancestral hierarchies. Participation is the first form of empowerment.
The very fact that group lending enables borrowers to avoid any tangible guarantee is particularly favorable for asset-less women, who are hardly enabled to inherit anything and are normally dispossessed of any worthy property or asset. This is because men are traditionally favored in actively purchasing, belonging, exchanging, and inheriting, while their spouses are relegated in a passive and deprived dimension. Microfinance is very much concerned with emancipation and a more equal endowment, even if this may be an occasional consequence of rational bias against men, whose delinquency rate is typically higher.
Another smart pragmatic device is represented by frequent repayments (short term installments, starting immediately after disbursement) within the selected group, avoiding balloon payments where the principal is all reimbursed at maturity. Given the financial illiteracy of many poor (who find it hard to understand that ›time is money‹), postponing repayments to years to come would typically end up in a disaster, for them and for the incautious lender.
Financial illiteracy has also a psychological effect on the perception of money, with a misunderstanding of its abuses and dangers. Shortening the repayment period reduces indeed risks for both the lender–this being a rather obvious consideration–but also for the borrower, who is gradually educated to make punctual repayments, earning a good credit reputation, up to the level of being enabled to borrow more for longer periods. Short maturities are meant to set strong incentives for the group to service debt repayments and to avoid opportunistic behaviors, more likely if the time span of the loan is not carefully extended.
The dark side of frequent repayments is that in some cases they might prove unaffordable for the poorest, so preventing outreach. More flexible informal moneylenders typically don't impose regularly scheduled repayments–with an innate capacity to manipulate the poor, well knowing their local habits–and that's

probably the reason why they appear to be thriving even in regions where MFIs are well established[510].

Group lending is a practice that is consistent with the nature of social capital examined in Chapter 9, even if the fact that borrowers belong to the same clan has pros and cons: social bondage can improve repayments but also bring to opportunistic behaviors and limit the possibilities of the smartest people, who are suffocated by an inadequate and backward environment.

According to Rankin[511] »the potential of social capital theory lies in its recognition of social networks and associational life as resources for fuelling development from the bottom-up«.

On an aggregate level, going beyond each single group, microfinance can link different groups of borrowers, synergistically interacting within business clusters, working as developmental districts, and favoring job specialization and trickle down benefits even for the poorest.

The Grameen Bank model

Another frequently unnoticed but important feature of MFIs–not typical of mainstream banks–is the marketing approach to the client. Poor potential customers, especially if living in rural and not densely populated areas, often don't know if a microfinance branch exists and where it is, they cannot afford to travel long distances and they suffer from cultural ignorance about financial matters. Lack of knowledge and motivation does not come out as a surprise.

Going to meet the potential client at his/her home–or, more realistically, barrack–is expensive and time consuming, but it proves effective not only for the possibility to reach him/her and his/her clan, but also to reduce information asymmetries (getting acquainted with her and his family, life, job, and environment), speed transactions, and enforce compliance[512].

Modern microcredit can be classified in different models or categories, which are in constant evolution and more or less popular in different parts of the world, since the experience about the adaptation of a successful model to other contexts is full of difficulties.

Here we summarize the Grameen Bank II model, which is very popular in Bangladesh where the inventor Yunus comes from and where he works:

- it has high gender bias, being focused mainly towards women;

---

510 See Jain, Mansuri (2003).
511 See Fernando (2006), p. 89.
512 See Roodman, Qureshi (2006).

- it does not envisage any sizable guarantee, considering fiduciary agreements and the implicit punishment of not being admitted to further installments as a major incentive for repayment;
- it still lacks financial self-sustainability–and so needs subsidies–due to its ›political‹ decision not to charge high enough interest rates.

The Grameen Generalized System allows some (supposed recoverable) borrowers to remain members of the bank, even when they are unable to pay their loan installments[513].

Another characteristic of recent and more sophisticated microfinance models – always attempting to circumvent the original sin of lack of guarantees – is concerned with progressive loans, according to which loans are divided in regular installments which can be cashed by the borrower only if previous repayments are regular. Even in group lending systems, this sanction might be personal, so relieving the group from the misbehavior of single members[514]. Small and fractionated loans are however unfit for capital intensive projects that require high start up financing or for projects where cash flow gains are irregular and difficult to forecast. The credible threat to deny defaulters' access to future loans, either with group or with individual loans, has proven effective in minimizing delinquency.

Lending beyond collateral

Notional collateral, which is often used by moneylenders, might prove a powerful and surprising form of guarantee, since it is characterized by limited market value–bad news for the lending MFIs–with high personal or affective value for the borrower: if such a value is, in the borrower's mind, higher than that of the loan, the repayment incentive is high. This system seems somewhat cruel but it is effective against intentional misbehavior, even if it proves incapable to prevent involuntary default. Collateral serves to reduce the risk of strategic default when the borrower might be tempted to divert cash flows, while social sanctions (especially within group lending and in more intimate and sensitive rural areas) and denial to further credit are effective punishments to be imposed on defaulting borrowers[515].

---

513 See Gupta (2006).

514 There are several possible combinations, which show how the model is flexible and adaptable to different circumstances: the delinquency of one member can hit either him alone, with no access to further credit installments, or the whole group; in the latter case the monitoring incentive is stronger but the penalty is high and somewhat unfair for the good members. See Becchetti, Pisani (2007).

515 Bond, Rai (2002).

Repayment is difficult to get without adequate pressure and unsanctioned bad examples are very contagious. In the absence of guarantees, no parachutes are available for MFIs: that is the reason why repayment discipline is for them a question of life or death.

The poor often face significant problems in obtaining access to credit services. Microfinance tries to overcome these problems in innovative ways[516]:

- loan officers come from similar backgrounds and they go to the poor, instead of waiting for the poor to come to them, following a bottom up marketing approach (if Mahomet doesn't go to the mountain, it's the mountain that goes towards Mahomet). Direct knowledge of the client represents a plus for moneylenders but also–hopefully–for unsophisticated MFIs;
- group lending models, if applicable (we have already seen that the new Grameen Bank philosophy goes beyond, considering its negative side effects), improve repayment incentives and debt monitoring through peer pressure (particularly effective in rural areas and with women). They also build support networks and educate borrowers with frequent meetings and discussion panels;
- microfinance products include not only credit but also savings, insurance, and fund transfers (internal or remittance);
- development activities, focused on social issues, health, and education, are frequently a corollary to microfinance activities, especially if sponsored by NGOs.

Micro-loans should normally finance micro-enterprises, which play a central role in economic and social development especially in low-income countries, since bigger companies are almost nonexistent, the public sector is underdeveloped and unable to absorb many job seekers, but also the traditional agricultural sector has limited upside in creating employment.

Loans are typically addressed to finance the purchase of fixed assets in order to start up or to expand a business, while they might also finance less creditworthy consumables or working capital. Little if no attention is normally paid to the possibility to provide micro-equity finance, in the form of small business start up grants[517].

Unlike venture capital, micro-equity providers might not be supposed to become shareholders of the financed entity, since social (subsidized) equity is mainly concerned with the socio-economic development of local communities,

---

516 World Bank (2008), p. 12.

517 Pretes (2002).

looking for a sustainability pattern that might make them sooner or later independent from international aid.
Micro-enterprises are firms with typically less than five employees (often, family members), and they are normally unregistered and not paying taxes, being part of the informal sector–well known in developing countries–that gradually tends to emerge and starts paying its toll, in exchange for public services which in the absence of taxes have obvious funding problems[518].
Mechanized businesses are more capital intensive than commercial activities and they normally require bigger financing and additional knowledge. The wealth that is created by manufacturing businesses–the first step of industrialization–might be greater if compared to commercial activities, especially in underdeveloped economies, for which production should represent a starting economic activity, followed by trade and supply of services.
MFIs are consistently smaller than traditional banks–especially if they are start up (›green-field‹) donor-driven institutions–and they have small macro and micro economies of scale, considering their size or the size of their single loans. MFIs start ups typically have a donation (or public) driven equity, while standard banks collect it within private or public placements.
But the business of MFIs and mainstream banks doesn't–or at least, shouldn't–show fundamental differences. Getting money back and earning proper remuneration in order to guarantee survival is–as we shall see in Chapter 21–a quite obvious but not-to-be-forgotten basic point in common. Both look for safe borrowers, both try to keep positive margins containing operating costs with efficiency, scaling. and standardization (whenever possible) and fixing interest rates at profitable levels.
The target for self-sustaining MFIs should normally be convergence to a (normal) banking model. This process has of course to be shared with clients, in order to prove feasible. It is not an easy or quick target, but worth anyway being taken into account, since we go nowhere without clear aims and directions.
Lenders traditionally face:

- financial costs for collecting capital to be lent (with a mix of cost of equity and cost of debt for the remuneration of depositors, bondholders, interbank lenders …); cost of capital grows with risk and is traditionally higher in MFIs, if compared to mainstream banks;
- default costs (for delinquencies in the repayment of interests and principal);

[518] This not being the case only in some Arabic countries, where oil revenues fill the gap, although democracy is similar to taxes - simply not existing - perhaps following the principle ›no taxation without representation‹.

- operational and transaction costs[519], suffering in MFIs from lack of economies of scale.

Small loans have high unitary costs of screening and monitoring, which substantially increase operating costs, without scale benefits that are possible only with larger loans. Unitary costs per loan tend to be similar and irrespective of their size. So, even in this case, the problems of the ant are not smaller than those of the elephant!

Customer retention is a key marketing target for most companies and this basic principle applies to both MFIs and mainstream banks, although it seems somewhat more important for the former, which need to grow with their clients, progressively enlarging lending amounts, in order to reach profitability. If credit grows with positive repayment track records, MFIs normally reach their break-even with a customer after the third or fourth loan, but both need to be ... still alive at that time.

The bridge between (not fully viable) MFIs and commercial banks can be established in both ways, either with organic growth and development of the former, or with ›downscaling‹ of mainstream banks to the microfinance market[520]. This bridge is highly wanted, but the evolution to profitability of subsidized MFIs is a long and difficult process, whereas penetration of commercial banks in the microfinance arena is neither easy nor common. Flexible contamination on both sides seems however useful for the microfinance industry and it might foster financial innovation and outreach.

Different ways for achieving the same result: getting money back!

Standard commercial banks and MFIs have many differences, especially if the latter are informal and unregulated intermediaries, but they tend to have at least a common and basic aspect: they live out of repayments from borrowers.

If ways to get money back show to be different, the ultimate goal does not change, should institutions belonging to one of the aforementioned models desire to survive and, possibly, prosper.

Subsides, as we shall see later on, can soften the ways and methods to claim money back from poor borrowers, but the ultimate goal is unlikely to change – and evidence shows how unwise it might prove.

---

519 Weekly collection of money by credit officers is a high cost, especially in under populated areas.

520 Accion (2003) proposes a service company model, according to which this non-financial company provides loan origination and credit administration services to a bank which can concentrate on the lending activity.

When a potential borrower asks for a loan, traditional bankers demand him/her what he/she needs the money for, how he/she thinks to repay it and, should the answers not be enough convincing, how he/she can guarantee the reimbursement. No convincing answers, no money. This is the standard picture, even if opportunistic behavior such as moral hazard or strategic bankruptcy is always possible, as illustrated in the next paragraph.

In microlending, basic rules might seem different, even if experience continuously shows that favor treatments typically produce disasters in the long run and even if the method has to be adapted to a peculiar context where collateral is typically absent, some basic principles, which are inspired to common sense, still deserve to apply.

The purpose of borrowing is a standard question that has to be linked to a feasible and credible, albeit simplified, business plan: and it's the borrower's duty–if he/she wants to get the loan–to demonstrate how he/she thinks to generate adequate cash flows to service the debt. Simple questions often have difficult answers.

In countries that make use of standard accounting principles, basic cash flow statements normally accompany assets & liability statements and the profit & loss account[521]. For many illiterate poor, these basic compliance requests still look like science fiction.

Higher repayment rates come also as a natural consequence of careful selection of the business to finance and many MFIs are not focused to risky peasants, since they have shifted towards ›non farm enterprises‹ – like making handicrafts, livestock-raising and running small stores[522]. A correct assessment of the volatility of the financed business–albeit difficult to detect–is an important lending parameter even in underdeveloped countries.

Managing microfinance risk is a key task, which can have a huge impact on the stakeholders and their governance problems, as we shall see in deeper detail in Chapter 23.

Information asymmetries traditionally arise since borrowers have better information about their creditworthiness and risk taking than the lending bank. They originate conflicts of interest that might seriously prevent efficient allocation of finance.

The liquidity allocation problem derives from the fact that although money is abundant, it is nevertheless not easy to give it to the right and deserving borrowers.

Relationship lending relies on personal interaction between borrower and lender and it is based on an understanding of the borrower's business, more than to standard guarantees or credit scoring mechanisms, and it represents a key factor

[521] See Chapter 21.

[522] See Cull, Demirgüç-Kunt, Morduch (2008).

in countries with a weak financial system counterbalanced by strong informal economic activity[523]. Multi-period contracts–typical of relationship lending–are an efficient device for dealing with asymmetric information[524].

Corporate governance and conflicting interests between lenders and borrowers: adverse selection, moral hazard, and strategic bankruptcy

Corporate governance is concerned with the set of processes, customs, policies, laws, and institutions affecting the way the MFI is directed, administered, and ultimately controlled, including the relationships among the stakeholders that rotate around it, that are represented by the providers of capital and debt (equityholders and debtholders) versus the clients of microcredit (borrowers), since micro-depositors are considered as debtholders.

Conflicts of interest derive from market imperfections and deviations from theoretical rationality and fairness. Stakeholders may indeed behave opportunistically, with conflicts of interest against other stakeholders, to the extent that they have diverging priorities and objectives. Opportunistic behaviors are of course much more common and tempting for borrowers and that is the reason why lenders typically tend to be overcautious. The corporate governance framework is vitally important in order to understand how the various players are supposed to behave and why, in order to get useful insights about the mitigation strategies against harmful conflicts of interest.

Adverse selection is a typical problem in money lending and it occurs even in traditional banks, when–not knowing who is who–they cannot easily discriminate between good and risky borrowers, who should deserve higher interest rate charges.

Adverse selection problems occur when the lender finds it difficult to discriminate between risky and safer borrowers, so applying to anybody the same interest rates, with unwanted and undeserved implicit subsidy to the worst borrowers, which in many cases disincentives honest ones from asking for loans. Reduction of information asymmetries[525] might contribute to reduce unfair extra charges, with good customers being able to send a believable signal to the MFI about the reliability of potential joiners.

Honest individuals also have a powerful incentive in directly selecting fair partners within the group. Actually groups are encouraged to form on their own,

[523] World Bank, (2008), p. 9.

[524] See Petersen, Rajan (1995).

[525] The standard methods of overcoming adverse selection are to have some kind of increased information in order to improve risk evaluation, as Akerlof (1970) has pointed out in his seminal paper.

even if strong clan or family ties in many rural areas are an obstacle to discrimination according to merit. In case of delinquency, bank officers might be reluctant to sanction good borrowers who have the bad luck to be part of unreliable groups.
Moral hazard is a classical ›take the money and run problem‹, since borrowers might try to abscond with the bank's money or not to fully get engaged in the project for which they have been financed. A milder but highly frequent form of moral hazard is represented by microcredit misallocation, using it for consumption rather than for investment purposes. Multiple borrowing is another frequent possibility, which is eased when computerized banking credit records are missing – typically coordinated by central banks.
Strategic bankruptcy consists in false information that the borrower gives about the outcome of his financed investment, stating that it has failed even if it is not true only in order not to give back the borrowed money. Poor borrowers generally have little or no collateral, so they might have little reason to avoid strategic default.
These classical corporate governance problems are well known in traditional banking and they naturally bring to sub-optimal allocation of financial resources and to capital rationing problems that frequently affect even potentially sound borrowers, if they are not able to differentiate themselves from those who bluff.
Cross-borrowing is another potential conflict of interest between lenders and borrowers, deriving once again from information asymmetries: it is an overlapping strategy, according to which poor clients borrow from an intermediary to pay back older loans contracted with others. It is an evident symptom of repayment difficulty, that is hopefully temporary but in many cases structural. This arbitrage or ›shopping‹ disguising strategy can take place in underdeveloped countries and/or in informal markets where intermediaries are not enabled to cross and check databases with recorded credit histories.
Standard banks in developed countries normally react trying to reduce information asymmetries, using credit scoring analyses, monitoring, and asking for guarantees (in the form of sizeable collateral with intrinsic market value).
Since microfinance borrowers are normally unable to give any worthy guarantee, as we have seen before, these problems normally are even more acute in a context that has also to take care of greater information fallacies and weak judicial systems[526].
As a consequence, it is of crucial importance for the success of microfinance to find any attempt or device to find a solution that can contribute to mitigate these conflicts of interest between the lending bank and the borrower. As we shall see, if microfinance bears higher problems on some aspects, in others it can intrinsically reduce risks, if compared to traditional banks. Specific microfinance

526 See Armendariz De Aghion, Morduch (2010); Chapter 2.

loan contracts are designed with distinctive features (such as joint liability and dynamic incentives) to mitigate these pervasive problems.
The standard agency problem concerns conflict of interests between a potential lender (the principal), who has the money but who is not the entrepreneur, and a potential borrower (the agent), a manager with business ideas who lacks the money to finance them. The principal can become a shareholder, so sharing risk and rewards with the agent or a lender, who is entitled to receive a fixed claim. Agency theory explains the mismatch of resources and abilities that can affect both the principal and the agent. Since they need each other, incentives for reaching a compromise are typically strong, aligning otherwise divergent interests. In microfinance, equity stakes are normally rare[527] and the standard model is concerned with a peculiar form of lending, which tries to overcome the aforementioned problems.
The main differences in dealing with these agency problems between traditional banks and microfinance institutions are the following:

- limited liability companies, where shareholders risk only the capital invested: they are frequently financed by traditional banks, whereas MFIs mainly finance households or small companies with unlimited responsibility. Limited liability protects borrowers who might not be stimulated to repay their debt, especially if it exceeds their equity stake;

- the motto ›no collateral, no money‹ that is traditionally applicable in standard banking undergoes severe problems in poor areas, where the collateral is mostly nonexistent (by definition, those who have valuable collateral are not poor!) or difficult to seize, also due to unclear property rights, a primitive judicial system, and ethical problems (taking resources away from poor households might seriously undermine their chances of survival);

- microfinance loans have very short maturities, if compared with traditional banking loans, which can last even several years, and this point gives the lender big monitoring and enforcing power, checking weekly or monthly the repayment of interest rates, cashing early the lent capital and preventing the borrower from asking new money if he has proven delinquent with the first loan;

- microloans typically consist in very limited amounts, which strongly reduce the magnitude of the lending risk and allow for better diversification;

[527] See Pretes (2002).

- monitoring microfinance borrowers is more expensive and difficult, since normally there are not credit scoring devices, computerized data, credit histories with delinquency rates and proper bookkeeping from the borrower. In addition, weekly meetings between the MFI and the group members (borrowers) allow the creditor to monitor the repayment status of each debtor publicly, increasing the transparency within the group and generating a form of peer pressure which is expected to foster internal monitoring, minimizing debt screening costs[528];

- *ex post* moral hazard, which emerges after the loan is made and when the investment is in process, might lead to the aforementioned ›take the money and run‹ temptation, even invoking fake strategic default[529]. While this well known phenomenon might be present in both cases, in traditional banking guarantees can represent a parachute, while in a microfinance context the absence of guarantees can be counterbalanced by a deeper in site (on field) control on the borrower and lower chances for him to leave his rural area (take the money without knowing where to run away might prove difficult). As a matter of fact, poor have poor chances for escaping repayments … ;

- reputation also plays an important role in preventing opportunistic behavior. Poor borrowers, who at first sight don't have much to lose, in reality are often more concerned about this issue, since the chances they have are very limited and new opportunities strongly depend on a good track record. They also face the aforementioned mobility problems and, in general, these ›problems‹, which can become positive chances for enforcing reputation, are stronger in women, so introducing a gender gap and discrimination–well known in the microfinance experience–according to which at least in some areas[530] women are better borrowers than men. Indeed, women might have stronger incentives to pay back the borrowed money, since they see it as a chance of emancipation (breaking gender-based barriers, typically considerable in underdeveloped countries), taking also profit or their better understanding of basic rural economics, since they–more than men–tend to run the limited resources of the family;

---

528 See Deutsche Bank (2007), p. 4.

529 Dynamic incentives, such as access to additional loans, prove useful in reducing the strategic default option. See Tedeschi (2006).

530 This is the case in Bangladesh, where up to 95% of the clients of Grameen Bank are women, but not elsewhere, for example in Sub-Saharan Africa …

- strong information fallacies and asymmetries which evidently affect poor borrowers are in reality offset by good local information and enforcement mechanism which characterize rural lenders;
- microfinance might soften information asymmetry problems, if relationship lending and peer monitoring–often associated with mutual responsibility–are in place;
- micro savings and microinsurance can be positively linked to microloans, with a double side effect: if they are not available–as it frequently happens–than the whole microfinance circuit is weakened and more exposed to conflicts of interest.

Since continuous access to MFIs matters, poor clients have a strong incentive to avoid any misbehavior, from delinquency onwards, building a sound track record of reliable customers.

Gentle governance for the poor

The lender and the borrower might align their interests, paddling in the same direction–so reducing opportunistic behavior, which is one of the worst and most slippery hidden problems–if the borrower participates to the MFI business, becoming also a depositor and, possibly, a shareholder, as it happens extensively with the Grameen Bank model or within cooperatives. It is a possible solution especially for loyal and not-so-poor customers. Multi-role stakeholdership is a well known device to reduce many conflicts (and to worsen others)[531].

Adverse selection and moral hazard are, as a matter of fact, mutual governance problems, since they might characterize not only the behavior of the borrower towards the MFI, as it is universally known, but also the strategy of the MFI which, for instance, might use its informational advantage in the money market to charge too high loan rates or to take on too much risk with depositors' money[532].

High cost of capital (interest rate charges and banking fees) and short term repayment schedules represent an incentive for proper allocation of loans to cash-flow-producing investments, which are able to ensure the service of the debt, preventing the temptation to address loans to consumables or working capital, which normally act as cash burning devices. The property of small investment

---

531 A multi-role stakeholder simultaneously occupies different positions and he can act as a shareholder, lender, borrower, worker, manager. This context is typical in cooperatives (even credit cooperatives). Corporate governance problems might arise if the multiple stakeholder interest are not properly known outside, due to information asymmetries, and he has an undeclared and hidden prevailing interest, potentially harmful for the other players.

532 See Mersland, Strøm, (2007b).

fixed assets (e.g., cars, agriculture tools …) might sometimes represent a limited guarantee for the lender, so decreasing the overall risk of the loan.
Short term (high-frequency) repayment installments, which are unrelated to the gestation timing of investments and to their ability to generate cash flows, are based on current income and assets of the borrower. The result is a difference with the rigid philosophy of Basel II (or Basel III) principles, now applying to mainstream banks in Western countries, according to which the capacity to generate adequate cash flow to service debt repayment should be the key parameter for lending scrutiny.
Lending is normally cash-flow based or collateral-based but with microcredit this general banking classification seems too rigid and unable to describe its peculiar nature. Poor borrowers with hardly predictable cash flows and unworthy collateral might still get credit, using typical microfinance innovative products. Improving cash-flow forecasting and/or use of effectively worthy collateral might be of great help in reducing interest rates. While such a strategy seems hardly consistent with the poorest real possibilities, it might prove easier–at least to some extent–for the not-so-poor to take individual loans, with an established and growing business.
Focusing on ambitious but realistic scopes is the right strategy, albeit it is difficult to reach, especially for illiterate poor who are not culturally used to targeting.
Progressive lending is a powerful device that has been experimented in particular within group lending, but it might show some drawbacks, which are well known to industrial or trading corporations which increase their sales to clients which have gained a good reputation, but then they start to misbehave, avoiding payments. The risk is that borrowers who lack the increased repayment capacity go to other lenders in search for bridge loans, and they pay old debts making new ones, exploiting information asymmetries and moral hazard techniques, in a well-known spiral of growing indebtedness, concealing and deferring the solution of problems that sooner or later come to final judgment.
Adverse selection is also present, since riskier borrowers have a natural incentive in looking for extreme scenarios, while safer ones are more concerned about their reputation. The social or macroeconomic scenario, should external shocks occur (conflict, natural disaster, and raise in interest rates …) might worsen these governance problems. Offering a borrower lower interest rates on his/her next loan is a financial innovation device which had a huge impact on repayment of the current one[533].
The limited size and short time horizon of loans is however a major obstacle to riskier but higher value-added projects, which become increasingly important with the growth of the economy, and the consequent higher demand for differ-

[533] See the South African evidence analyzed by Karlan, Zinman (2005).

entiation. For these investments other financial intermediaries are more adapt, being represented by bigger MFIs (ranking as Tier 1 institutions) or ordinary commercial banks.
In synthesis, microfinance can in some cases become a ›magic tool‹ to produce new, cheap, flexible, and simple ideas to circumvent information problems and asymmetries that are the main obstacle to optimal allocation of capital, exploiting smart innovations in corporate governance, contract theory, and (flexible) product design. But enchantments soon vanish and they are uneasy to deal with. Microfinance soon reveals to be a difficult instrument, to be managed with care, which needs fine tuning and constant monitoring. So, it is a useful device, although not a miracle or a panacea that comes for free.

Most clients are women, reversing the gender bias: a feminist approach to development?

According to the Genesis book, Adam was created just before Eve and that may be the first evidence of the priority that men tend to command over women. This is unsurprisingly happening also with normal bank credit and it did happen even with microfinance. Looking at the Grameen bank history, it is misleading to say that its founder Yunus preferred to approach women. The reality is that even men were contacted, but they soon showed to have much higher delinquency rates, and so ...
Men are also more arrogant and difficult to deal with, while women tend to be more amenable, docile, and governable, especially in backward areas where machismo is still a dominant ›culture‹ – to the extent that microfinance is an empowerment tool for assertive women, men may get envious and hostile. Microfinance is among the very few devices that can foster the entrepreneurship of vulnerable women.
From another perspective, especially in backward rural areas and in city slums, women typically completely lack the characteristics that would make them attractive for commercial banks, for a number of reasons that are often shared by their male companions but for women are even harder and sometimes specific:

- they lack any valuable collateral, typically being asset-less, since the few resources available to poor families are typically owned or inherited by men;
- literacy and schooling is typically low, both on absolute and relative terms. Lack of proper numeracy is a strong cultural barrier against the management of money and it makes the psychological approach towards credit markets harder;

- they spend a disproportionate part of their life at home, being deprived of any emancipating earning capacity;
- women hardly have any employment history and consequently they do not have any regular income. They also unsurprisingly lack any credit history;
- they are hardly enabled to travel, to find a job outside the family clan and to start up an entrepreneurial business.

But women traditionally have a stronger social collateral than men, bear higher responsibility in children uprising and they are consequently more committed to be present, stable, and loyal – no surprise that their delinquency rates are significantly smaller, if compared to those of their less reliable mates. Social sanctions and peer enforcement are typically stronger and more effective if concerning women.

Gender is a key issue in microfinance, which has a preferential social target towards women–the poorest of the poor–since they tend to spend more of their income on their households and children education, so increasing the welfare of the family, with a positive and longer lasting sustainable effect[534]. Women are typically more vulnerable, since they carry the burden of raising and feeding children more than men and they have also lower mobility (facing cultural barriers that often restrict them to home, for instance following the Islamic *purdah*). The result is higher focus on keeping their original location, with a positive effect on the reduction of opportunistic behaviors (such as the ›take the money and run option‹) and possibilities for emancipation, due also to the participation to credit meetings[535] (which might represent an embryonic form of political gatherings).

In underdeveloped areas, social control on women is high and easy and blame for misbehavior is typically strong. But also empowerment chances, starting from a typically lower level are higher, if compared with men[536]. Women are however often conduits for loans to men, who are the natural target for larger borrowings, in order to finance bigger investments (here the MFI faces a trade-off between higher profitability due to scaling and increased risk, due to gender switch but also–mainly–to increased exposure).

Lack of mobility and few alternatives reduce opportunistic behavior – so damaging in the microcredit market, where trust and fairness are the first requisites

534 See United Nations Capital Development Fund (2002).

535 Attendance to meetings has also other positive side effects and can be seen as a public screening of the conditions of the women (frequency of participation has obviously proven lower in abused women).

536 See Mayoux (2000).

for a stable relationship between lenders and borrowers, with a financial discipline that can benefit both, reducing transaction costs.
The traditional opportunistic behaviors of borrowers against lenders, such as moral hazard, adverse selection, or strategic default are still possible even for women but practically much less likely, especially if women are very poor:

- adverse selection, concerned with the lender's difficulty to discriminate between good and risky borrowers, is typically less problematic with poor women, whose behaviors and possibilities are typically easier to detect and monitor than those concerning men;
- moral hazard–the ›take the money and run problem‹–is again a possible but rarer temptation for women, especially if they have children, they are ›imprisoned‹ at their huts and they need to establish a long term relationship with their lenders;
- strategic bankruptcy–false information that the borrower gives about the outcome of her financed investment–is again possible even with women, but much less likely.

To the extent that the cost of lending is socialized within local communities, women automatically stand out as the main and more stable component, representing most of the social capital, albeit typically hidden and silent.
Participation to solidarity gatherings and group lending is a precious chance for women, enabling them not only to access otherwise unreachable credit, but also to start up a difficult emancipation pattern, generating a collective consciousness, so representing a nice externality. Microfinance can be a ›win-win‹ strategy and a source of women empowerment, if it is properly implemented.
Empowerment is a slow, incremental, and evolving process, to be considered within a proper institutional framework where women can attain better emancipation, properly combining interconnected aspects, concerned not only with gender but also with nationality, social classes, and status, ethnic belonging. Increasing control and enforcement over material assets–easing property rights–has to be properly complemented with intellectual resources (culture, knowledge, information, ideas …)[537], combining … hardware with software.
Unprecedented organized solidarity can transform and reframe gender ideology. So it can foster unthinkable social changes and entrench the hegemony of dominant male interests, going beyond authoritative (under)development models, provided that they prove to be sustainable and viable even in the long run. Backward social hierarchies are easier to be changed if the emancipation process–fostering human rights–is properly financially backed, reminding that so-

[537] See Fernando (2006), p. 189.

cial changes have a material but also an intangible (cultural) dimension. Microfinance can directly influence the former, but also indirectly promote the latter. Since microcredit is focused on (women) empowerment, it is indirectly concerned with the promotion of sustainable and equitable development.
Smart credit programs are supposed to have a long lasting impact in changing social structures, hopefully for the better. Gendering microfinance is–eventually–a cultural issue.

Moral hazard and microinsurance

Insurance is traditionally concerned with moral hazard behaviors, since insured agents may conceal their true intentions or modify their actions, so as to profit from the insurer, getting an undeserved rent. A well known example is given by the behavior of individuals who, after having underwritten health insurance coverage, start neglecting themselves or, in extreme cases, are even prone to get voluntarily ill, to the extent that they can get monetary indemnity from the insurer. In the worst cases, moral hazard falls into the category of outright fraud.
Even the insurer, from his side, can misbehave, should he refuse to reimburse damages, with delays, excuses, or legal cavils. This possibility represents a big threat for illiterate insured poor, who are hardly able to defend themselves, especially in front of smart and astute lawyers, hired by the much more powerful counterpart.
Equilibrium has to be reached and trust has to be shared on both sides, if the common will is to create a market for insurance products. In insurance–or (micro)insurance, not different from this point–trust is differently directed than in (micro)loans or (micro)deposits. In microloans the banker has to trust the borrower, while with microdeposits is the opposite and the poor depositor has to trust the collecting microbank – that's the reason why central bank supervision is compulsory just in the latter case.
Insurance products are uneasy to sell and they appear to be more sophisticated that what is commonly believed – actuarial analysis of risk has to be carefully carried through, creating a reliable database for proper product pricing. That's the reason why informal providers of insurance products find it hard to compete with institutional insurers, who are also better enabled to pool-diversify-risk.

Moral hazard within the banking system

Conflicts of interests and moral hazard problems are not an exclusive of bank's clients, but they potentially involve even the banking sector, with a systematic detriment to the whole community, suffering from a poorly working financial intermediation system, up to the point of being pushed back to obscure informality.

Contrary to financial repression (according to which governments control and unduly influence financial markets), bank liberalization brings competition within the industry, lifting up any artificial protection–from government subsidies onwards–and forcing banks to strive for efficiency, solvency, and profit looking[538].

Undercapitalized banks, artificially kept alive in a protectionist framework, have a natural incentive for taking excessive risks, especially if backed by governmental safety nets, which encourage them to behave imprudently. High leverage always encompasses a risk transfer from the equity holders to debtholders: when little equity is challenged by a potential burn out, the shareholders have a natural incentive in taking risky positions, since returns are asymmetric. So they get most of the pie if the outcome is positive, while they limit their effective risk to the paid in capital if the bank go bankrupt.

Increasing leverage brings to natural risk transfer to debtholders but in the financial sector the risk of default is somewhat mitigated–due to its well known disastrous side effects–by the presence of Central banks, acting as lenders of last resort. An illuminating experience at this regard is the international banking crisis of 2008-2009, with the undeserved rescue of so many banks, especially in the US and UK: it stands out as a possibly unavoidable but still unfair strategic choice, evidencing an implicit blackmail–too big and disruptive to fail?–from the banks to their governments.

History reminds us that weak and corrupted financial institutions inhibit growth, providing a much damaging low-quality finance. The destitute, who are so used to their poor quality goods and services, are living witnesses of these problems – quality, albeit often unnoticed, does make the difference. With its direct approach to the poor, microfinance can simplify the long intermediation chain typical of foreign aid or other subsidies, softening mismanagement and corruption.

On the one side, privatized banks are often fragile and the probability of systemic banking crisis grows up after financial liberalization, but on the other side, public banks have their own problems and they typically suffer from political corruption. They are indeed ›induced‹ to lend money to politically sensitive borrowers, often irrespectively of their soundness or merit, with a consequent crowding out effect for those who would deserve credit but are not in the graces of puppet bank directors. All borrowers are equal, but some are … more equal than others.

When politicians influence credit allocation, they hardly behave as fair entrepreneurs and there can be enormous damages to the economic system, ranging

[538] See Guha-Khasnobis, Mavrotas (2008), Chapter 2.

from waste of precious resources to unfairness – to the dismay of the honest borrowers left unsatisfied.
Since the poor are politically uninteresting, it is not hard to imagine that in the described context, they are typically unfairly excluded from getting the credit they would deserve.
Privatized banks, although fragile, are typically in a better governance shape and they are most suitable for attracting funds, even from international investors, lowering their cost of collected capital, to the potential benefit of borrowers. Financial openness facilitates the economic integration of emerging countries, even if it makes them more exposed to systemic and global crises.
The government's intervention, as we see even in the case of the typically detrimental cap on interest rates, is normally hardly beneficial for financial development, and in many cases it is counterproductive. Institutional and political economy factors, again depending on the political will but not directly dependent on it, can make a far better job in shaping a sounder financial environment, from which even the poor have much to gain.
When a banking system opens up to domestic competition, sooner or later it extends it outside its national borders, and foreign competition is an even bigger threat for weak incumbents, since it is typically sounder, more efficient, and with higher reputational standards. Good news for the clients, not so for the suppliers.
To the extent that collected resources are directly channeled to the poor, microfinance can favor a process of disintermediation, reducing costs, minimizing mismanagement, smuggling, and corruption, and improving efficacy and fairness.

The condensed Chapter

While traditional banking is constitutionally unfit for the poorest with no guarantees, microfinance, using devices such as group lending, is able to overcome traditional corporate governance and information asymmetries issues, such as adverse selection (concerned with the difficulty to choose between good and bad debtors), opportunistic behaviors such as moral hazard (take the money and run) or strategic (false) bankruptcy to avoid repayment.
Following the success story of the Grameen model, women are universally recognized as the best clients, showing low delinquency rates and better discipline, if compared to less trustworthy males.

Out of Poverty Tips

Microfinance is a complementary device for development issues: taken alone it does not work.
Microconsulting is the main cultural background behind strategic investments, teaching how to properly use scarce and expensive resources.

Selected Readings

ARMENDARIZ DE AGHION B., MORDUCH J., (2010), *The Economics of Microfinance*, MIT Press, Cambridge, Massachusetts, 2nd edition.

BATEMAN M., (2010), *Why doesn't microfinance work? The destructive rise of local neoliberalism*, Zed Books, London & New York.

YUNUS M., (2007), *Creating A World Without Poverty*, Random House, New York.

CHAPTER 19 – From microcredit to microfinance: the synergic effects of microdeposits, microloans, and microinsurance

Microfinance recognizes that poor people are remarkable reservoirs of energy and knowledge.
And while the lack of financial services is a sign of poverty, today it is also understood as an untapped opportunity to create markets, bring people in from the margins and give them the tools with which to help themselves.

Kofi Annan

Smart products and nice services, trying to meet the needs of the poor

In Chapter 17, the analysis of the basic aspects of financial exclusion has shown why the underserved, who are trapped in impoverished regions without savings and investments, typically get stuck in underdevelopment. The provision of capital has to follow multidimensional patterns, widening and deepening its granting to the poor and helping to sort out the low income–low saving–low investment triangular trap.

Figure 19.1. – Microdeposits interacting with microloans, microinsurance and financial consultancy.

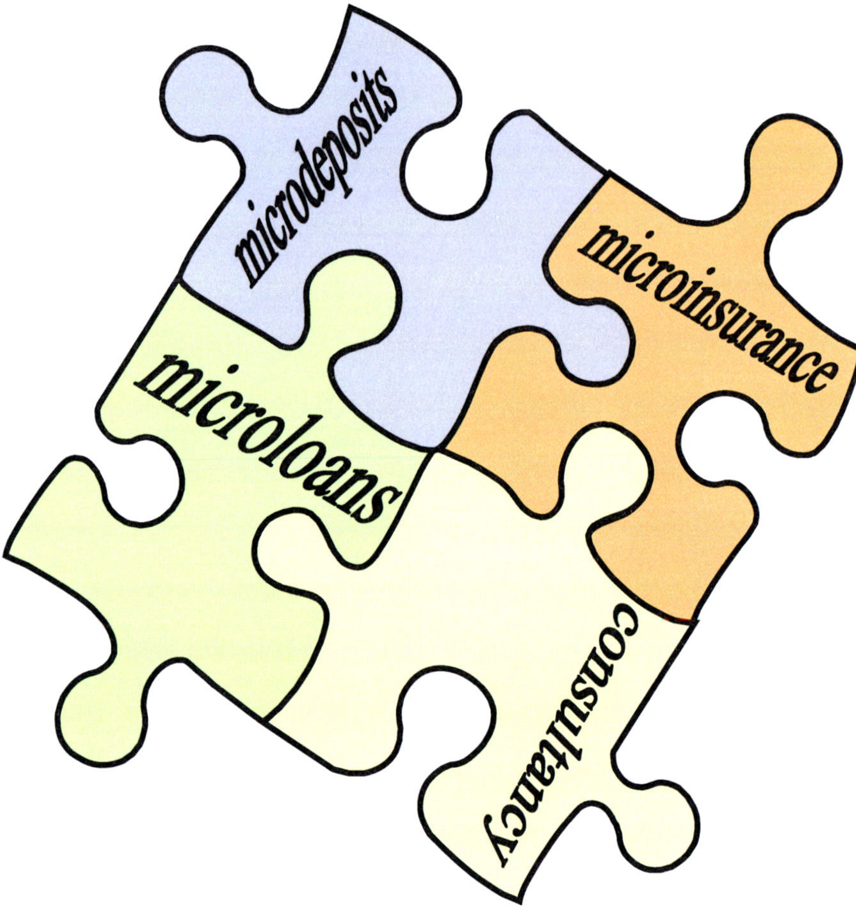

Minding the gap that keeps the poor segregated from formal banking, ›stakeholders‹ of new strategies need to reinvent aid and microfinance, providing a new financial architecture for sustainable development, in order to make poverty a manageable problem.

Financial innovations are proving useful devices to serve the poor and their financial needs, trying to overcome difficulties with a creative approach and smart product design, to fit poor necessities.

Different financial products (each with its peculiar marginality) and institutions can usefully be complementary in serving the demand for credit, which is flexible and segmented, according to the different needs of more or less sophisticated borrowers, duly taking into account also cultural aspects and different stages of development.

Competition, width of choice, specialization, and interaction are just some of the main–normally positive–aspects of the presence of different financial intermediaries. Of course, problems of coordination and potential new conflicts can easily arise and this fact happens especially in the presence of imbalances of regulation between ›far west style‹ unregulated intermediaries and less flexible but more transparent ones.
›Arbitrage circumventive‹ behaviors may easily occur, should intermediaries move from one model to the other, in search of milder rules and higher flexibility (within primitive intermediaries) or wider funding possibilities and more sophisticated products, which can be present in more structured intermediaries.
This trade-off between simplicity / complexity, arbitrary freedom / overregulation, etc., has to be carefully taken into account. On the move towards sophistication, interest rates–representing the price of lending–tend to diminish and if this might seem surprising (since complexity is intrinsically expensive and has to be paid by clients – borrowers, unless somebody accepts to subsidize the intermediary), other factors might explain this phenomenon: more competition, higher efficiency ... This point is of crucial importance, since if it is confirmed it states that borrowers can get better services and products at lower prices, so increasing the quality / price ratio (value for money), that probably is the most important parameter of choice for free consumers.
Imbalances between demand and supply remain however huge and hundreds of millions of potential microfinance borrowers are not able or entitled to have access to fair (regulated) finance. This might seem strange and peculiar in a world which normally faces the opposite marketing problem (abundant supply in a desperate search of new demand, facing subsequent high competition) and where global liquidity has never been so abundant and–consequently–cheap.
Understanding the poor clients and their peculiar and unsatisfied needs is a challenge that can open up unprecedented and still invisible market opportunities, promoting suitable and simplified products, partnering with suppliers of complementary services (e.g. retail shops of mobile phones and cards).

Savings first, credit later: microdeposits and precautionary thrift

Despite significant contrarian evidence, many do not believe that poor people save money, thinking that they are too miserable to be thrifty[539].
The poor, living on a subsistence income, might actually be unable to save, especially in hard times (wars, epidemics and illnesses to humans, livestock, or plants, Biblical plagues such as famine, drought or floods, hail ...) but when they succeed to, they are often unable to find a safe harbor for their savings, that

539 See http://www.microfinancegateway.org/gm/document-1.9.28097/36533_file_04.pdf.

can represent a provision for an uncertain future. As it has been shown in Chapter 17, the financial life of the poor, albeit unsophisticated, is far from being quiet.

Poor people often accumulate non monetary ›in-kind‹ savings (in livestock, sometimes land …), that are uneasy to manage when cash is necessary. The process of saving can take different directions: up when storing monetary and ›in-kind‹ resources, or down to repay contracted loans.

The poor have an incredible potential for saving–with an enormous aggregate impact, due to their large number–if only they are given the chance to find a safe shelter for the money that they painfully succeed to put aside. Actually, the poor–in spite of their meager incomes–save because they must, even if savings and thrift habits may be uneasy to inculcate. Mobilizing savings is a key target for any poverty eradication strategy. Albeit being largely informal and consequently unrecorded, poor people's propensity to save is often neglected.

Among the main problems that the oxymoron represented by ›poor savers‹ constantly face, there are thefts, loans to relatives[540] (often unlikely to be paid back), or erosion caused by shrinking purchasing power in inflated economies. Stashing money inside the pillow or under the floorboard doesn't prove anywhere a safe strategy. Cash safety is a major concern, especially for those who are forced to live in a ruthless environment, such as the proliferating slums of urban conglomerates, where police doesn't care or dare to enter and those who are not strong enough hide themselves, trying to survive unnoticed.

But savings against hard times, which in underdeveloped countries are typically endemic, are in many cases the best insurance for mere survival and they represent the first primordial form of insurance.

Savings help poor households to smooth consumption, keeping it above a survival break-even point. Savings are also helpful when income is volatile, without the stress of servicing debt. Saving facilities much more than loans are critical for the poorest, following a ›savings first – credit later‹ motto. A cardinal parameter in saving is represented by the time horizon, which should be flexible and consistent with the saver's needs, in order to smooth cash requirements with a basic personal financial intermediation pattern.

Informal savings and loan clubs with savings collectors, where each household makes a contribution and makes sure that the others save, allows people to make loans to the contributors on a rotating basis, such as Self-Help Groups in Indonesia or ROSCAs[541] in Africa. Others pay unregulated deposit collectors to

[540] If relatives and enlarged clan members are particularly demanding, borrowing might be a better solution than saving, in order to prevent »expropriation« and to justify refusals to accord them embarrassing loans.

[541] See Chapter 20.

bring the savings to a bank or deposit savings with local money-lenders or credit unions or in the nearest post office[542].

Microdeposits might really represent, in this context, the aforementioned ›safe harbor‹ for savings and they should ignite even in poor countries–as it has happened in more advanced ones–a virtuous financial circle, with an intermediation process from micro-depositors to micro-borrowers. Microsavings should conveniently precede microlending.

Microdeposits are–perhaps surprisingly–often more requested than microlending by the poor and they might well go along together, representing a partial form of guarantee for lenders, especially if linked with insurance products (considering for example health insurance which might prevent ill borrowers from abandoning their job, masterminding paybacks).

Savings are also intrinsically related to borrowing, since they can fuel repayments, teaching borrowers a disciplined way to save and also to behave, for the sake of debt service. Being forced to repay debt might help to prevent wasting money in drinking!

Forced savings are a typical feature of group lending packages, serving as effective cash collateral for loans, and usually they have unattractive characteristics, since they pay no interests and cannot be claimed back until the member exits the group. Micro-loans, which are aimed at financing growth potential, are more requested and diffused than micro-saving[543] products due to:

- regulatory and compliance policies, traditionally harder for the latter;
- trustworthiness, since it is harder for a MFI to persuade potential customers to deposit savings than to collect money;
- timing and entity of cash flows, since debt repayments are set regularly, disciplining borrowers, whereas deposits occur randomly.

In bigger and sounder MFIs, which belong to the Tier 1 or 2 capital adequacy segment, savings collection through deposits might be replaced by cheaper funds (interbank loans; international funds; equity injections …). MFIs should however try hard to attract even the penny savings – small and expensive to collect, but with positive albeit underestimated effects on poverty alleviation.

And those who collect savings obviously need appropriate lending strategies, in order to make proper use of their collected funding.

A further evidence of the vital importance of savings is given by the paradoxical example of savings with negative returns – susus are informal savings accounts and schemes, which are diffused in West Africa or even in the Caribbean. Susu collectors run their businesses from kiosks that are located in the mar-

542 See Banerijee, Duflo (2007), p. 156.

543 See Roodman, Qureshi (2006).

ket place and they act as mobile bankers. Deposits of low but regular value are usually taken on a daily basis over the course of a month. At the end of this period, the susu collector returns the accumulated savings to the client but he keeps one day's savings as commission. Susu collectors may also provide advances to their clients[544]. The practical result is that savers are entitled to claim back less money than the amount deposited, since they pay a commission for safe deposits.

According to CGAP[545] »low usage does not mean low demand. The prevailing perception that poor people do not save may stem from the low penetration of formal savings mechanisms, the most common of which are accounts in financial institutions«.

The huge extent of informal savings is another symptom of the potential request for this kind of financial service. According to CGAP[546] »institutional capacity and incentives are the primary factors behind the inability of formal financial institutions to compete with informal savings approaches«.

Microsavings are naturally related to micropensions, which are a relatively unknown product in many poor countries, where the elderly age is a goal for few and social providence is still to come.

Before developing savings operations, institutions should have the legal authority to mobilize deposits, to have an effective governance, to provide financially sustainable operations and a sound business plan which shows continued viability and indicates where savings can be invested profitably. Institutions should also have sufficient internal controls and technical capacity to manage liquidity and interest rate risks. The physical infrastructure–in a safe and convenient location–and a strong management information system are also required.

Savings are influenced by demographic trends and when fertility is decreasing, the future horizon of generations shortens, reducing the willingness to save if there are little children to grow up.

Interest rate levels may influence savings, as an alternative to consumption, making them more or less lucrative, but when safety needs are compelling and consumption choices limited, savings mostly come out as an independent variable. What matters most are interest rates differentials, between borrowed and deposited money.

According to their versatile dual nature, savings both serve as safety nets and investment backers.

---

544 Jones, Sakyi-Dawson, Harford, Sey, (2000).

545 CGAP (2009a).

546 CGAP (2006).

Savings fuel development

Savings and borrowing are two sides of the same coin and they both need a synchronous and complementary form of financial intermediation.

The cycle of investments is strongly related to savings, which are their financial prerequisite. Accumulated wealth, not to be consumed soon, can be invested in projects and real assets, which should yield positive returns, so to increase the initial wealth and make further savings and consumption choices possible. This well known virtuous circle can be ignited and magnified with microfinance, since MFIs are a suitable mean to intermediate savings and loans within poor communities, allowing the start up of small investments, in the best scenarios up to their self sustainability. Microfinance is so a useful device to unlock the saving's trap, fostering development from a subsistence economy up to a commercial and eventually technology based economy, ideally following a Rostowian[547] growth pattern.

In a basic subsistence economy, with low agricultural productivity, inefficient and weak services and infrastructures, most of the income is absorbed by survival needs, leaving little room for savings, even if–as we have seen in Chapter 17–also the poor save, often more than expected. Wealth redistribution with taxes is a hardly working option, since the taxable base is limited and collection is vastly inefficient. As Sachs (2009), p. 209, points out »many economies remain stuck in the poverty trap of subsistence farming«.

Climbing up the development ladder is the first strategic option of poor countries, starting from agricultural productivity, as we have seen in Chapter 16. Those who succeed to go beyond survival farming sooner or later reach the upper status of a more diversified commercial economy, since they rightfully accumulated savings and other resources to proper investments. This long and painful process of transformation is often asynchronous within the country, typically being slower in the countryside and more accelerated in urban centers, where economies of scale and experience are more concentrated, together with better infrastructures.

Spill over effects of growth sooner or later tend to involve even the remotest areas, even if domestic migration towards towns may harden the differences between not homogeneous zones, likely to develop at a different speed.

In this primordial step of development, microfinance can have its say and it is indeed proving effective, especially if inserted in a virtuous and synergic development pattern.

The following steps, according to Sachs (2009), concern an emerging market economy, where basic needs (infrastructure, education, health services, safe water …) begin to be increasingly satisfied. The next step is represented by a tech-

---

[547] See Chapter 24, with particular reference to table 24.2.

nology based economy, where sophisticated education and investments reshape socio-economic models. In these two final scenarios, the role of microfinance and its scope increasingly narrows and more sophisticated financial intermediaries are needed. They can however cohabit with microfinance, providing different services and products to increasingly diversified clients.
When the economy is technology based, start-up investments are typically financed by venture capitalists, with a high risk attitude and managerial skills to back the company's development. This scenario is hardly consistent with the typical microfinance background, where technology is almost not existent and so venture capitalists are absent, with the consequence that equity investments are missing, while they are so useful for growth ignition.

Microinsurance beyond social networks

The poor have little or no access to formal insurance products, even if social networks, which are particularly strong in rural areas, might provide some basic informal mutual insurance. The poor make use of risk sharing agreements, typically with loan exchanges, whose repayment schedules might however be severely affected by a common systematic risk, so zeroing the insurance when it is most wanted.
A retrospective analysis of risks can give some insight about current and future ones, even if risks are changing and reshaping. Technology can soften atavistic risks–such as many illnesses, now curable–but new ones are emerging as undesired by-products of the same technology (computer frauds; industrial pollution, and related climatic risk …) or as a result of new plagues, such as AIDS or economic and social shocks, nowadays more frequent than before (trade unbalances, currency crises; commodity shocks; demographic uneven shifts and trends …). More secure living conditions–sometimes made possible by microinsurance–are a fundamental prerequisite for sustainable development.
Adaptation to adversities, which severely affect especially the chronic poor, is easier if they are properly insured, but the poor typically lack suitable and affordable products and this fact may substantially contribute to exacerbate risk. Failures in insurance markets and lack of insurance against misery may strengthen and deepen other poverty traps.
Income risk is caused by a variety of factors, including inability to diversify low-pay and unsophisticated jobs. On the one side, idiosyncratic–peculiar–risks can be (even self) insured within the community, while on the other side common risky factors, potentially affecting everyone, cannot be conveniently shared. The link between lack of insurance and debt repayment capacity becomes evident when a common risk–such as a flood–affects all the community

or a subset such as the group lending team. Microinsurance complements microloans, reducing delinquency when risk is devastating.
When risk grows, precautionary savings adjust and consumption declines, even if it hardly declines beyond the survival threshold. Asset holding to buffer consumption is not always an optimal or feasible strategy, since assets' price is often positively correlated with risk (if the negative event is widespread and everybody reacts selling the same assets, the excess of supply drives prices down), leaving little room for diversification.
When the poor undergo economic problems, their ›insurance‹ often means drastic reduction in consumption–such as eating less–or taking children out of school: poor children tend to leave the school in bad years[548].
Informal social insurance–that is typical of a poor environment where most financial products, wherever existent, are not official–might conveniently be complemented by formal and professional tailor-made insurance products, provided by MFIs, with a positive synergic effect, since insured borrowers unsurprisingly have higher repayment records.
Farmers–the majority of poor–find it difficult to insure also as a consequence of typical corporate governance problems–analyzed in Chapter 18–such as moral hazard (insurance reduces the stimulus for avoiding losses) or adverse selection (riskier farmers are the most eager to insure, but it's difficult to discriminate between safe and risky ones).
Obstacles to micro-insurance are typically represented by the high cost for handling each (small) risky position (unless it is part of a standard financial package, allowing for a consistent cost reduction) and by the general problems encountered in micro-lending. Lack of proper intermediaries represents a further problem, considering also the whole risk-handling chain, which needs reinsurance companies.
Credit life insurance is a typical package that is linked to group lending, relieving other members to pay the debt of the dead borrower or to claim it from grieving widows or orphans.
Ignorance is also a primary factor in preventing diffusion of formal insurance policies[549], whereas the social network might be the only source of (informal) insurance available to people.

---

548 Jacoby, Skoufias (1997).

549 Many people, rich or poor, are reluctant to buy insurance because they do not want to think about loss, illness or death. Still, the low-income market may be particularly disinclined to purchase insurance for several reasons:
- the poor often lack familiarity with insurance and do not understand how it works;
- until one actually receives a claim payout, insurance benefits are intangible; it is difficult to persuade someone to part with their limited re-sources to buy peace of mind;
- if the poor do not have to claim, they may believe that they wasted their precious income;
- often the poor have a short-term perspective, only making financial plans a few weeks or months into the future;

Insurance depends on risk and its perception, whereas risk on its turn is linked to a forecast of possible but unlikely events. Those who don't have a time-deep perspective, living and thinking just for the present time, find it difficult to conceive future risky events and consequently they hardly feel the necessity to cover against them. Even insurance is a cultural concept.
Most of the world population cannot afford insurance, hampering vulnerability reduction, whereas it should be properly acknowledged that (micro)insurance goes beyond the extended family system, proving larger and unmet coverage against likely risks.

Designing locally suitable products, beyond a credit-only approach

Financial innovation–like other business innovation–is an ongoing process whereby private parties try to differentiate their products and services, responding to changing needs and new challenges.
The design of suitable products is strongly affected by the local needs of the potential borrowers who demand credit. The local environment is the marketplace where products are conceived, tested, introduced, and challenged. Even if microfinance is not completely assimilated to a market economy instrument, being characterized by a peculiar and outstanding social function, it has nevertheless to follow some basic market rules for its not sponsored survival.
The environment matters and what works in a place may be partially or totally ineffective elsewhere – geographical scalability is a good opportunity, always worth trying even if sometimes unsuccessful.
If the local environment is poor and unsophisticated, even microfinance products have to be designed accordingly and they have to be simple, understandable, practical, and ready for immediate use.
An identikit of the potential microfinance client, considering his/her needs and opportunities, is a fundamental prerequisite for proper product design. When transplanted to richer and more developed countries, microfinance has to be complemented by more sophisticated ancillary products and services, since local market economies are characterized by higher entry barriers. As a consequence, higher per capita loans are necessary, together with a training program that has to teach borrowers how to properly use the money, making appropriate business plans, and complementing them with a realistic system of reporting.
Should a potential poor borrower open up a small grocery shop in his/her rural village in an underdeveloped country, he/she would need just some seed money

---

- if the low-income market is familiar with insurance, they may not trust insurance providers. Source: http://microfinancegateway.org/resource_centers/insurance/focus_notes/_note_1.

and little advice about a job opportunity that he/she probably already knows. On the contrary, the chance to start up a business activity in an affluent country requires many more skills and bureaucratic accomplishments, to be backed with proper advice and counseling. Even if it may seem paradoxical, it is often easier to waste money in rich countries than in poorer ones, where unsophisticated opportunities may be easily at hand and marginal growth is likelier.
The challenge is to overcome a minimalist credit-only approach, going beyond microfinance original orthodoxy, adding value to an already resilient instrument, in order to foster development in an increasingly complex world.
In richer countries, the demand for microcredit is typically more segmented, since local poor cohabit with temporary or permanent immigrants. Discriminating between different potential clients may apparently seem a racist behavior, but in reality it may be a smart and sensible strategy, to the extent that it can enable specialized MFIs to provide more appropriate and suitable products and services to a clientele that is characterized by different social and cultural backgrounds and needs.

The evolutionary and synergic interaction between microloans, microdeposits, and microinsurance

In the synergic interaction between microloans, microdeposits, microinsurance, loans are normally the first product offered, even if the poor often have a priority for savings. Microinsurance typically follows loans and deposits, since it is perceived as a more sophisticated–and less ›primordial‹–service, and it may be provided internally by the same MFI or, more frequently and especially when numbers and complexities grow, by specialized insurance companies, in accordance with MFIs and sharing with them the retail network and facilities.
Looking for a profile of innovative products, the synergic interaction among microdeposits, microloans, and microinsurance is depicted in figure 19.2.

Figure 19.2. – Microloans igniting the microfinance model

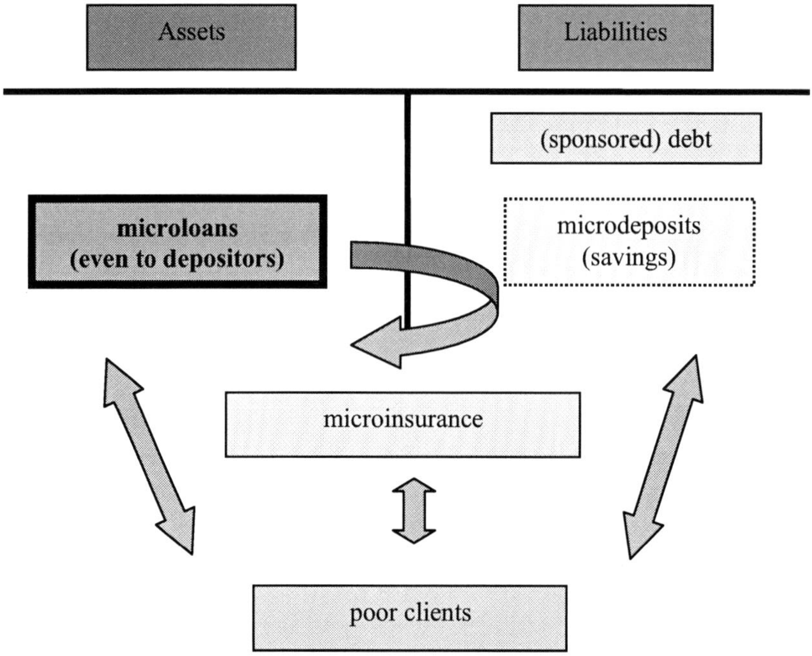

Small not deposit taking MFIs typically get funded with sponsored debt from NGOs or charities.

When the MFI is enabled to take deposits, being supervised by the local Central bank, it is typically large and sound enough to provide more loans, extending its outreach. Larger and bigger sources of funds make the MFI more stable.

Figure 19.3. – Microdeposits igniting the microfinance model

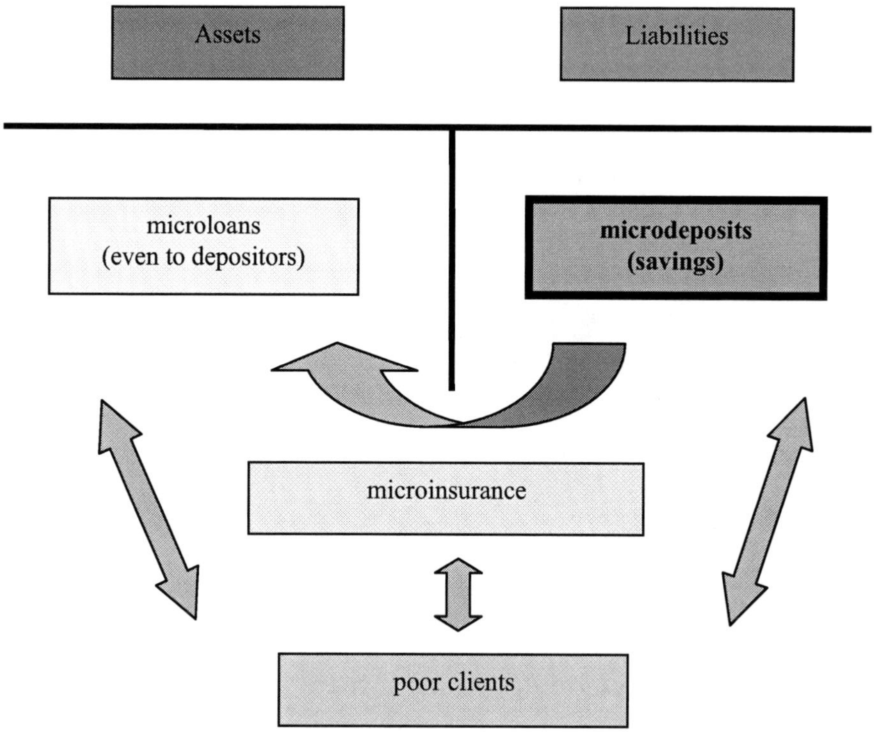

When microinsurance products are available and provided to the poor clients, they synergistically interact with loans and deposits.

Figure 19.4. – Microinsurance interacting with microloans and microdeposits

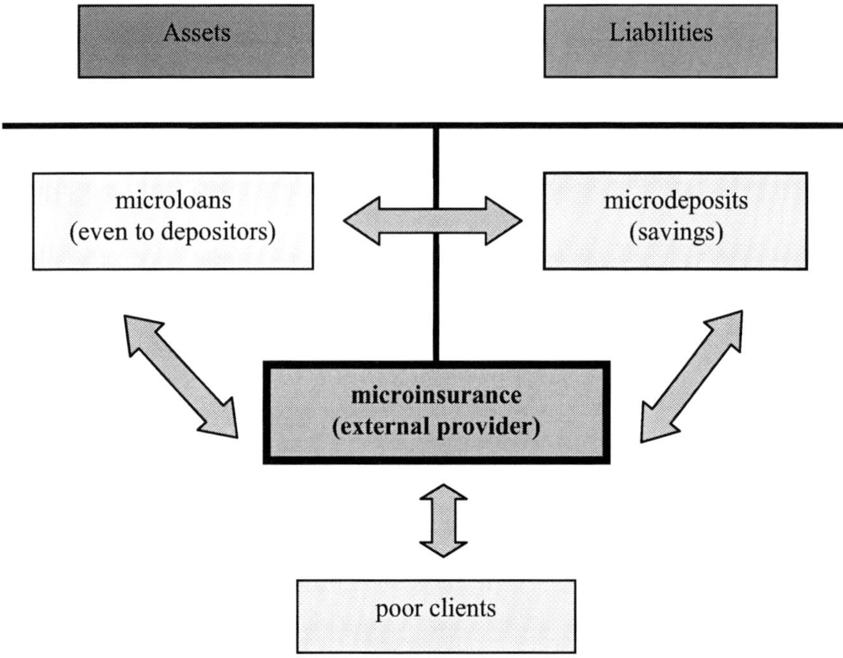

Leveraging up remittances from abroad

Domestic poor typically benefit from remittances, to the extent that they have an ›American uncle‹, who ideally represents a family member emigrated to a wealthier country – as already described in Chapter 11. Remittances often represent a strong financial asset for the survival of those who remain in their native land. But they are also vulnerable to volatile economic trends–due to which when richer countries enter a recession, its immigrants are often the first to be hit–and to potential unwillingness to continue sponsoring their relatives abroad, especially if family ties weaken with new generations.

Remittances are typically transferred in the form of cash, so avoiding official intermediation circuits, even if there is a growing trend for transparent and legal bank transfers, increasing security and anti money laundering controls.

Since remittances are addressed at MFIs, typically in the form of deposits, they can foster credit development, favoring family members and providing the MFI with dedicated liquidity.

The circle may ideally be closed if money is lent from the MFI and backed by remittances deposits, or if it is used by local poor to promote export businesses, favoring fair trade exports to the countries where remittances come from and where expatriates can organize outlet markets for exotic products.

According to CGAP (2005), in order to craft money transfer strategies »financial service providers that cater to the poor have been drawn to the money transfer market because it offers them the opportunity to fulfill their financial goals as well as their social objectives«. And also[550] »As a fee-based product, money transfers can also generate revenues and bolster the bottom line«.

Ancillary products and services

Ancillary products and services may conveniently complement the supply of useful development tools, widening the microfinance intervention perimeter, making it consistent with the complementary nature of poverty traps and remedies.

A holistic ›credit plus‹ approach has considerable attraction in terms of poverty elimination, suggesting that MFIs should offer a range of non-financial services to include: social services such as health, nutrition, education, family planning, business development services, training, social intermediation, organization building.

Microfinance assistance can be credit–led or even training–led, as described in Table 19.1. The latter process–complementary and not alternative–may be considered increasingly important in more sophisticated countries, even if poorer ones start from a less educated background and so they are intrinsically needier than more educated clients.

Table 19.1. – Approaches to microenterprise assistance[551]

	Training Led	**Credit Led**
goal	poverty alleviation	community economic development
clients	welfare recipients and others below the poverty line	low income persons without access to credit and other business services
services	mainly training and technical assistance, client networking, limited lending	mainly credit client networking referrals, limited training, and one to one technical assistance
delivery	group classes, one to one technical assistance	group and/or individual loans

Counseling and consultancy about the use of lent money are gratefully acknowledged, concerning also the business plan design to promote small ini-

550 CGAP (2008g).
551 Source: Burrus, Stearns (1997), p.7.

tiatives, and they may prove substantial in reducing failure and mismanagement, so improving efficacy and repayment rates.
Among the key needs of the poor, proper financing of school fees stands out as a vital pro-growth instrument, even if it goes beyond basic survival means. The fact that instruction is a ›cold‹ project, that is unable to produce immediate cash flows to pay back its financing debt, makes it formally unfit for microfinance, even if it stands out as an evident long term investment. Facilitations to the poor and often prolific clients, may substantially promote education, creating long term development patterns and empowering the underserved.

The condensed Chapter

Microfinance goes beyond basic microloans–microcredit–since it considers also synergic and complementary products, such as microdeposits, microinsurance, and, to a larger extent, ancillary consulting and remittances from relatives abroad.
Microdeposits are a cornerstone of the poor financial needs, enabling them to smooth their volatile incomes and to promptly consume them in case of necessity, fuelling also development, whereas microinsurance allows the poor to hedge against some types of risks, easing repayment and once again readdressing erratic returns.

Out of Poverty Tips

Synergistic interaction of microloans with microdeposits and, when available, microinsurance and microconsulting consistently strengthens the pro growth impact of microfinance, smoothing vulnerability.
But the orchestra has to be properly directed and continuously fine tuned, with lasting developmental targets.

Selected Readings

BANERJEE A.V., BÉNABOUR R., MOOKHERJEE D., (2006), *Understanding Poverty*, Oxford University Press, Oxford.

Chapter 20 – A chaotic supply of financial services: combining informal with institutional intermediaries

> To argue that banking cannot be done with the poor because they don't have collateral is the same as arguing that men cannot fly because they do not have wings.
>
> Muhammad Yunus

A poor informality trap

It has already been shown[552] that the poor typically conduct a hidden–informal–life, since they are often unrecorded at birth and consequently they have no documents and voting rights or healthcare cards, and they are illiterate, with no legal properties of fixed assets (cars, homes …). In other words, many poor are simply officially not existing and the consequences on their life are often unpleasant, especially in a global world where formal identities are a trivial but indispensable passport to everything (traveling and especially flying; moving money from different bank accounts …).

Informality is so a trap that condemns the ›inexistent‹ poor to a clandestine life, parallel to the official one but moving on a lower level, where everything is set by informal rules and so potentially arbitrary and harmful, especially towards those who are unable to defend themselves and their hidden rights.

Formal financial relationships are obviously precluded to the ›phantom‹ poor, especially if they are unable to claim their identity. So microfinance can be a bridge towards formality, at least from a financial perspective, and specialized providers may conveniently act as alternative financial institutions.

Beyond aristocratic banking: informal versus formal financial institutions

Bankers love to lend money to rich people who probably don't need it–the so called High Net Worth Individuals–and to manage their wealthy portfolios, since the risk is limited and the profits can be substantial. Aristocratic banking is by definition not concerned with the poor, who remain a neglected segment of clientele, hardly reached by mainstream traditional institutions.

552 See for instance Chapter 10.

A (formal) financial system should take care of intermediating and mobilizing financial resources between lenders and borrowers, facilitating risk management and allocating liquidity to the most efficient projects, monitoring the (proper) use of cash and providing a payment system that is evidently more efficient than backward barter economy. If these are well known characteristics, their absence is even more evident in informal environments, where these functions are either not existing or poorly managed.

The degree of formality can be declined with different gradations, ranging from totally informal institutions (within the family and ethnic clan; self-help groups; credit associations; occasional or professional moneylenders ...) through semi-formal institutions (ASCAs and ROSCAs; credit cooperatives and small microfinance institutions ...) to bigger and regulated formal institutions (MFIs enabled to collect deposits. formal investment, or commercial banks ...). Evolution to formal banking can hardly miss a full land property titling, described in Chapter 15, since real estate guarantees are a traditional prerequisite for standard loans.

A reversal kind of evolution may conveniently take place when traditional banks downsize and downscale their business model to fit the needs of poorer clients, reaching a larger segment of clientele, often establishing a partnership with retail networks.

Formal and semi-formal providers of finance live together and they often chaotically compete in a variegated and unstable environment, where products, providers, and clients are often improperly differentiated and segmented. Complementarity–like biodiversity–adds up value.

Formal markets are shaped by regulation, audit, and monitoring, often up to the point of suffocating entrepreneurship – a Middle Age of rules blocks the Western world, especially after the financial market crisis of 2008-2009.

Access barriers of many kinds keep the poor excluded from the official credit market, relegating them to informal institutions. Among these barriers we can mention inadequate rules, norms and laws, lack of guarantees, shame, ignorance, and ideological inhibitors, unavailability of suitable products and intermediaries, etc. The informal sector is characterized by little or any entry fees (no authorizations, no taxes, no binding rules ...) but also by small benefits from modern technologies and by an overwhelming degree of opacity that makes intermediation a slippery playground. Access to credit tends to increase the benefits of formality.

The main characteristics and differences between informal and formal financial institutions[553], acknowledging their anyway chaotic nature, are synthesized in table 20.1.

---

[553] Many concepts of this table have been inspired by Collins, Morduch, Rutherford, Ruthven (2009) and World Bank (2008).

Table 20.1. – Informal versus formal financial institutions

Informal financial institutions	**Formal financial institutions**
Paperwork (written contracts) are rarely required, allowing otherwise unbankable illiterate poor to access the financial market. Unwritten agreements are hardly questionable and opportunistic behavior is not sanctioned as it should. Formal justice from an independent court is not a viable option. Transactions are not transparent and fairly priced as they should.	Formal institutions, regulated by investors' protection laws, require discipline and security, on both sides. Contracts are designed to regulate different outcomes and states of the world, disciplining rights and duties. Written agreements may protect also the poor, who are however rarely able to fully understand they meaning, being typically unaware of their complex formal consequences – an unsuitable and unaffordable option for many, if not most, among the poor.
Money is lent and borrowed even in the absence of formal guarantees. Risk is mitigated with short term lending (which favors prompt repayment), small amounts of loans, frequent supervision, acquaintance of the borrower. To start up a business, respecting the decreasing marginal utility of capital, the rule should be ›the less you have, the more you can get‹ – even if in most cases, it isn't.	No guarantees, no history (positive background and delinquency-free track record), no money lent–it is hard to undo skeptical minds. Poor people are not creditworthy (but … are banks ›people worthy‹?) and conventional banks love to lend money to those who don't need it–they are the safest customers! The more you have, the more you can get – the rich become richer and the poor poorer.
Even in informal credit markets, such as self-help groups, proper repayment of initial loans incentives to acquire good credit history, either individually of within the borrowing group. Only informal markets may however trust the unbanked poor, giving them the initial credit to get started. Trust and credit are inseparable companions.	Centralized and computerized credit scoring statistics, supervised by the Central bank, enable banks to stop to finance those with bad repayment history.
Official transaction costs are nonexistent or negligible, due to the informal approach. Sunk costs are	Price is discriminatory for the more affluent clients who, thanks to their status and being enabled to com-

Informal financial institutions	Formal financial institutions
however far from being excluded, involving disputes, uncertainties, biased interpretations, unchallenged frauds, etc. In reality, transaction costs may be higher than those paid by more affluent customers, whose bargaining power grows together with the average amounts intermediated. Tiny intermediated amounts bring to higher explicit or implicit costs.	pare different offers, can choose the most suitable and convenient one. Not so for the poor, who in most cases can't afford to be price sensitive – they would if only they could.
Risk is minimized envisaging the aforementioned *ad hoc* financial packages where loan maturities are short, lent amounts are small and frequent, and lenders are diversified. This process is both time consuming and labor intensive, although typically not remunerated. Small deposits and savings prevent economies of scale, with negative effects on the pricing of money, in the form of higher interest rates.	Standardized products are less flexible, not being adaptable to specific circumstances, but they tend to be cheaper and easier to deliver and to control, allowing for economies of scale and experience, which can ease sophistication. To the extent that positive aspects are fairly shared, borrowers can have good prices for the standard products, provided that enough competition is ensured.
Loans–but also deposits–are typically interest rate free, within the ›friendly‹ informal social network (family or clan members; friends and relatives, pawnbrokers, moneylenders, local landlords, shopkeepers …). In presence of greedy moneylenders, interest rates may reach sky rocket values and reimbursement mechanisms for late payers are typically brutal and they may involve expropriation of valuables. Poor's soundness and bankability is difficult to detect outside their living environment and information asymmetries that are potentially born by external and unaware borrowers have a	Formal banks always charge interest rates – they live on it. But rates are–or should be–transparent, uniform for clients within the same risk class and anyway consistently lower than those charged by moneylenders.

Informal financial institutions	Formal financial institutions
well known credit rationing effect.	
Money may be immediately available, on demand, without formal filing – a nice feature in small emergencies, often involving single households or entire families. Flexibility is typically acknowledged and it eases the reconciliation of transactions with cash flow balances, but lack of convenience, of transparency, and of capacity for bigger requests can severely hurt the needy and resigned poor, rarely treated on equal terms.	Formal providers of finance typically have an added value in their offer of products and services. To the extent that they don't, they remain uninteresting and inaccessible for the poor. Official banks are monitored and supervised by Central banks, especially if the collect deposits.
Informal networks work within fairly closed social communities, where people know each other. If the clan is dispersed, outside its native environment, it may be difficult to be re–established. So context matters. Those who do not belong to a community, may be fully excluded from informal financial intermediation, longing for aseptic formal institutions. Social capital, being the glue among individuals belonging to the same clan, minimizes information asymmetries and the threat of opportunistic behavior, due also to effective social sanctions against misbehaviors. Contractual costs are reduced by acquaintance and trust. Mechanisms of social exclusion are however often unfair, irrational, and not meritocratic.	Banking institutions have formal and often impersonal contacts with their clients, minimizing discriminations but limiting flexibility. Individual loans based on individual guarantees are typically accorded. Standardized contracts may reduce transaction costs, even if self monitoring is not a common feature (while it is typically present in microfinance within the group lending model).
Informal financial intermediaries, belonging to the same network and living in the same place, are all exposed to the same systematic risk (e.g. catastrophe hitting the whole	The poor are intrinsically vulnerable and unable to choose among different competing options. Where informal institutions live together with formal intermediaries and

Informal financial institutions	Formal financial institutions
community), with little diversification options. Similar problems and exposure to common and shared risk are unlikely to be properly diversified.	products, choice is automatically widened and everybody is enabled to compare products and then freely choose what best fits her or him.
Small and informal intermediaries are not professional and often unreliable, failing to keep their promises, often not as a consequence of lack of will but due to their intrinsic fragility. It shouldn't be forgotten that even informal intermediaries are, on their own, typically poor.	Standard banks are formal intermediaries, deemed to be impartial, professional and loyal to enforceable contractual agreements. Reliability, concerned with the effective delivery of what is contractually agreed, is typically higher and enforced under the threat of penalties.
Insecurity is a synonym of unreliability and it mainly concerns unsafe deposits. Lack of privacy and excess of confidentiality can be harmful: individuals may be obliged to reciprocate; shared information about one's financial situation may be embarrassing and intimidating, up to the point that ashamed borrowers may address themselves out of the clan and use relatives only as a last desperate option. It is nice to give and it is embarrassing to ask. Anxiety and dependence are typical consequences of an emotional context.	Privacy is guaranteed by formal contracts and individual needs, outside those of the group or clan, are taken into consideration. Formal intermediation is more aseptic and meritocratic than informal one, normally avoiding ethnic discrimination to financial access.
Sharing and putting resources in common, even savings, is good common insurance against adversities, but it may bring to opportunistic behaviors, if the needy people are simply the laziest ones. Equalitarianism may sometimes be good for bare survival, not for growth and development, since those with superior skills are often curbed by less gifted clan members.	Is individualism a virtue or a social drawback? The truth lies somewhere in the middle. Individualism can foster development, to the extent that their group does not block smarter entrepreneurs, but it can also increase inequalities and selfishness. Loans bundled with insurance products mitigate risk exposure.
To the extent that meritocracy and	Guarantees on real assets and for-

Informal financial institutions	Formal financial institutions
transparency need to be formalized, relying to written impersonal rule–bound agreements, informal markets are not the best example of transparency and objective judgment, being biased by inconstant and moody kindness, common goodwill and mutual obligations.	mal credit scoring policies allow the bank to avoid discriminations among potential borrowers filing for a loan. Impersonal relationship with the bank may be emotionally frustrating but it reduces unjustified discretion and corruption. Public banks under political influence of the ruling parties may be severely biased in their lending policy.
Since informal markets and intermediaries belong to the same background and they live in the same environment, they all share the same seasonality, which is another risk pattern complementary to exposure to similar negative events. Smoothing consumption and investment plans with flexible lending and borrowing requires the existence of timing asymmetric differences between liquid lenders and needy borrowers: if they are either simultaneously cash-rich or cash-illiquid, there is little to intermediate.	Formal and widespread institutions automatically reduce unsystematic risk with adequate portfolio diversification and they may offer more sophisticated products, even linked to insurance devices, in order to mitigate risk.
Informal markets are short term biased. When money needs to be intermediated for longer maturities, the no-interest-rate model is hardly viable.	Balance sheet analysis, that is useful for an asset based approach to lending, relying on guarantees, requires wealth stratification across time. This process is possible only if safe storage is allowed and proper accounting is available.
The property trap[554] makes capital invisible and hardly fungible as a guarantee. Lack of formal property rights is an impediment to capital accumulation. Short term cash flow based approach, with no real guaran-	Real estate properties are the basic guarantee in formal banking, but they have to be properly titled[555]. Asset backed bank loans can foster development and ignite capital accumulation.

554 Described in Chapter 15.

555 See Chapter 15.

Informal financial institutions	Formal financial institutions
tees, stands out as the only viable option, flattening alternatives and choices.	
The way emergencies are treated can really make the difference in hard times, through immediately available loans, penalty-free grace periods for reimbursements or other simple, straightforward, and useful devices. Meager savings are typically burnt out in sad circumstances, provided that they can be safely kept aside in advance. Informal markets may outperform regulated ones, but not in all the states of the world, especially when sophistication and financial soundness are necessary to solve difficult situations.	Specialized instruments, either formal or informal, are urgently needed to deal with emergencies. Living with endemic risk and looking for financial protection is a common request of poor households, hardly satisfied by formal institutions, which are more interested in covering a different client segmentation profile.
Savings are not alternative to loans and poor households can be engaged in both, taking loans at least partially secured against their own savings. This basic principle, manageable in informal finance only to a simple and little extent, may require substantial upgrading for its full implementation.	Only registered banks, under their Central bank's supervision, are allowed to raise deposits and can incentive formal saving plans, even with long term maturities, allowing depositors to earn decent rates and to promptly withdraw the money in case of need.
Informal savers and borrowers are prepared to pay more for financial services, if compared to richer clients. Poor's natural resilience and lack of better options prepare the ground for these uncompetitive extra costs, against which they appear both vulnerable and powerless. Real price of money may be high, due to the short term nature of lending, the small amounts of the principal, lack of compounded interests and flexibility of informal arrange-	Inefficient lending devices, which are highly labor intensive, due to small unitary amounts, may prevent a fairer pricing to the poorest. Delinquency rates are also to be taken into account, even if they are consistently lower in microfinance than in formal banking institutions. And women repay loans better, even if they are largely unrewarded for their greater honesty and punctuality.

Informal financial institutions	Formal financial institutions
ments.	
In an informal environment, time is rarely compounded and–to the extent that interest rates may not be charged or compounded on their own (generating interests over interests)–it hardly enters the poor's mentality, typically short termed, consistently with limited maturities, rarely going beyond some months. The short time horizon of savings clubs is a major problem.	Time is money and the value of time is an essential component of the investment process. With formal market, investors can choose among a variety of options, whose pricing is strongly sensitive to time. Long term loans are possible and frequent, especially if backed by proper collateral.
When interest rates are applied, typically by greedy moneylenders, unsophisticated agreements don't allow adjusting interest rates to take into account early repayments. Unofficial lenders of last resort (with a residual function somewhat comparable to that of central banks, which ensure the ultimate liquidity of banks), such as moneylenders possessing asymmetric information, charge high interest rates to constrained and needy households[556].	Early repayments are rewarded and late payments are sanctioned with delay penalties. Formal regulation may offer flexible options even in the form of switches from fixed to floating rates or vice versa.
Creditworthiness is valuable both in informal and in formal markets, but in the former case it does not follow computerized credit scoring with a written track record.	Clearing systems, under the supervision of Central banks, enable to keep evidence of the credit history of any borrower and to double–check his requests, knowing if he or she is simultaneously asking loans to different banks
High interest rates that are unofficially levied by moneylenders may be a deterrent, keeping unsound potential borrowers away. But if rates are too high and increasing, following a self fulfilling spiral, the bor-	Usury-interests above the lawful rate-is in most developed countries a criminal offence and usury rates, according to the kind of loan, are currently determined and monitored.

556 See Sundaresan (2009), p. 4.

Informal financial institutions	Formal financial institutions
rower may have strong problems, up to the point of being blackmailed and expropriated of his/her poor stuff.	
Improper charges, outside any formal contractual provision and hidden commissions, are frequently levied on the unsophisticated poor, who are hardly able to realize about their existence and even more to negotiate.	Upfront fees and fixed charges are typically negotiated and applicable over a sufficiently long time span.
Flexibility allows for possible multiple uses of lent money, without being forced to disclose its utilization. Even short term consumption needs can be financed. Flexibility is not always a synonym for reliability, this being one of the biggest challenges for informal intermediaries. Informal and general purpose loans are typically not dedicated to specific uses and they leave the borrower free to allocate money where it is mostly needed, for consumption, emergencies, or small entrepreneurial investments.	Formal bank loans are normally dedicated – tell me how much money you want, how you think to repay it (with adequate guarantees) and how you intend to use it. Banks like to see their lent money invested in cash producing activities and they typically don't like it to be spent for consumption needs. Microfinance institutions may be somewhat in the middle and they increasingly tend to be at least partially flexible.
Since cash flows are typically unpredictable and volatile, much wanted regular savings or repayment plans are difficult to put in place.	In a formal environment, cash in– and out– flows may be smoothed by regular deposits and withdrawals, enhancing self discipline (proper financial culture) and reducing volatility.
Unpopulated areas, especially in backward rural regions, unsurprisingly offer little financial options to their destitute inhabitants and unofficial intermediaries may have a monopolistic power, if unchallenged by other competitors.	Financial intermediation is strongly influenced by population density. Unpopulated areas are often branchless, since it is harder for formal institutions to cover their fixed costs. Mobile banking can really make the difference, almost eliminating geographic or temporal

Informal financial institutions	Formal financial institutions
	limits.
Informal intermediaries unsurprisingly raise money unofficially. Funds come from the small savings of million of poor, but even from the proceeds of usury activity (for moneylenders), from monopolistic rents (of landlords …), or from the recycling of dirty money. Cost of informal and untaxed funding, reflecting its opacity, is typically high and it is reflected on large intermediation margins. Links with formal markets (banking system; bond and stock domestic and international exchanges, etc.) are difficult. Microfinance institutions may be a natural bridge in the evolutionary trend towards formality.	Official intermediaries can consistently lower their cost of collecting equity and debt, having access to the interbank market or to capital markets. Tier 1 banks, those with a sounder equity, typically command a competitive edge in raising cheaper funds. To reduce borrowing risk, there is effective need of corporate governance mechanisms, aimed at reducing conflicts of interest among the stakeholders that pivot around the institution, of proper monitoring, of accountability, and performance targets, so lowering the risk cost.

From informal credit markets to cooperative credit, microfinance, and beyond

The United Nations defines an inclusive financial sector as »a continuum of financial institutions that together offer appropriate financial products and services to all segments of the population«[557]. The value chain of different intermediaries accompanies (poor) clients from informality to mainstream products and services. Poor people need an array of financial services to choose from.

Informal credit markets, which have been synthetically described in Chapter 17, have preceded not only microfinance everywhere but also formal banking systems in developed countries. Cooperative credit institutions or Savings and Credit Unions, organized among the rural and urban poor, have been increasingly diffused in Western Europe in particular since the 19th Century and they have been brought to colonies–for example by the English to India or Burma–to provide an alternative to local moneylenders, similar to group lending.

A historical analysis, tracing back the roots of microfinance, can help to better understand its nature and its evolutionary pattern, that is made up of small incremental innovations: once summed up, they have brought to a Copernican

[557] http://www.uncdf.org/english/microfinance/.

revolution, trying to meet an otherwise unmatched demand and supply for financial services.

The idea of rotating credit groups is as old as trade itself, but microfinance and its formal inventor–Muhammad Yunus–have gone far beyond it.

Credit suppliers can be personal (friends, neighbors, relatives, etc.), transactional (relying on moneylenders), or mutual, like ASCAs or ROSCAs. Microfinance service providers are concerned with a wide range of different intermediaries, following an unorthodox and somewhat chaotic evolutionary and environmental pattern and they are characterized by a different level of dimension, formality, scope, and outreach.

Taxonomy of microfinance service providers is useful in order to have a better idea of the framework of the players within a peculiar industry, where formal and institutional banking entities live together with smaller and unofficial credit providers, typically in a chaotic and messy way.

Evolutionary trends and competitive pressures change the very nature of the intermediaries: on the one side the most brilliant informal ones often try to scale up positions, getting sounder and bigger, and progressively migrating towards formality and full recognition from supervising authorities, whereas on the other side many smallest players (if not most of them) find it difficult to survive in the long run and their mortality rate is unsurprisingly high.

A comprehensive picture of the industry has to consider not only its competitors, but also its clients and products. The clients looking for financial products in a poor and backward country are rather undifferentiated, but as soon as development starts, diversities come out like mushrooms and sophistication requires new products and services, tailor made for different segments of clientele.

Figure 20.1. – From the (informal) micro to the (formal) macro financial system

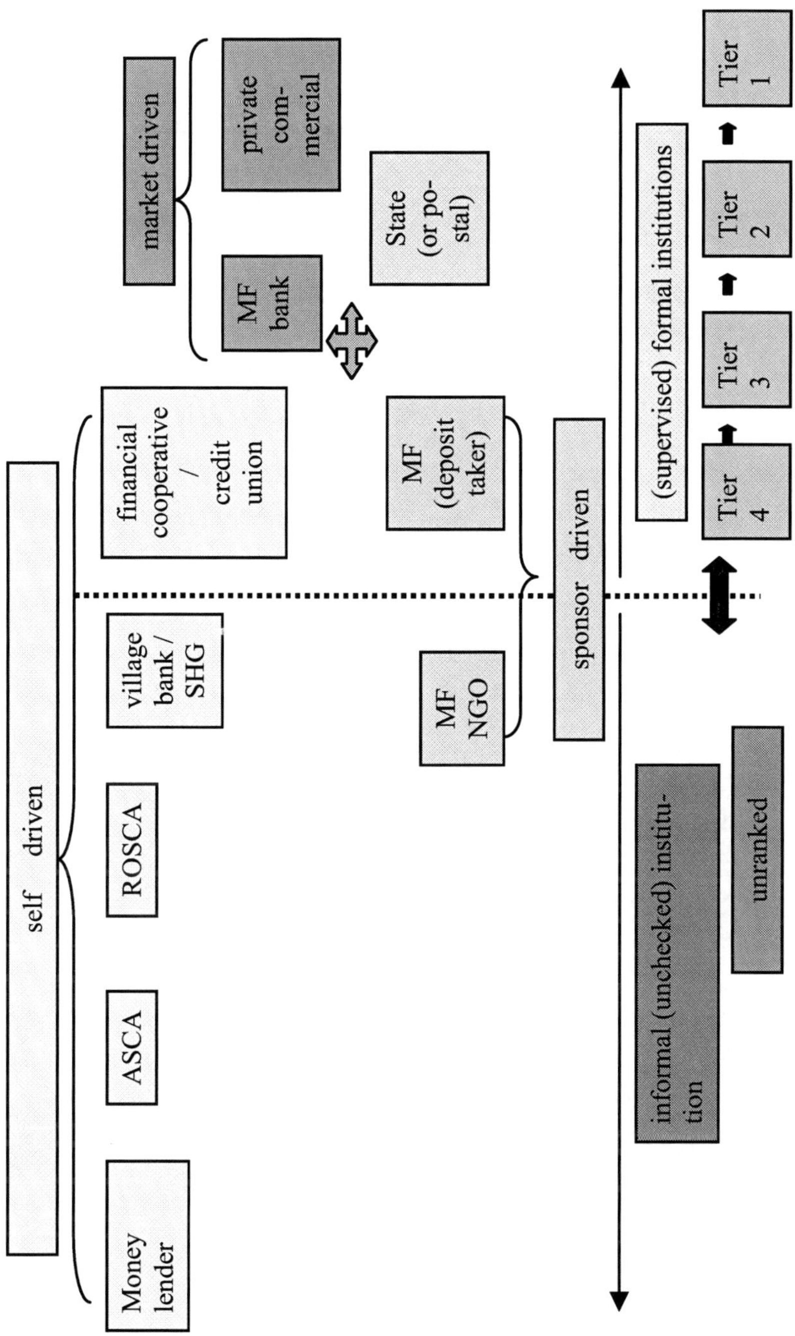

Taxonomy of the main finance service providers, with an increasing degree of formality, ranging from unofficial moneylenders to fully licensed commercial banks, is contained in the following table[558].

[558] Adapted from: Ledgerwood (1999); Deutsche Bank (2007); Ritchie (2007); Khawari (2004).

Table 20.2. – Taxonomy of the main finance service providers

Self driven (community based) informal financial intermediaries			
Type	**Features**	**Advantages**	**Disadvantages**
Money–lender	• It offers small personal loans at high rates of interest. • It is an important source of credit to poor borrowers with no guarantees, which normally are refused by most financial institutions.	• Resilient and flexible. • Easily accessible. • It knows well the debtor. • Available when needed, with a short notice (while other intermediaries typically aren't).	• Interest rates generally too high for investment in business. • It often requires conventional guarantees, with little market value but affectively important for the debtor and may extort repayment: the Poor can end up in debt trap and lose critical livelihood assets, such as land.
Accumulating Savings and Credit Association (ASCA)	• Time-limited informal microfinance groups. Unlike ROSCAs however, ASCAs appoint one of their members to manage an internal fund. Records are kept and surplus lent out. After a pre-agreed period (often 6-12 months) all the loans are called back and the fund, plus accumulated profit, is distributed to the members. • Unregistered.	• Same advantages as for ROSCAs. • More flexibility than ROSCAs for people who want loans. • Members receive a return on their investment.	• Amounts saved are small. • Loans generally are not suitable for agriculture or large investments, due to small loan size and risk. • Savings tied up for the cycle.

Self driven (community based) informal financial intermediaries

Type	Features	Advantages	Disadvantages
	• Time –bound. • Usually a fixed amount deposited each period. • Funds lent to members with interest. • No external funding.		
Rotating Savings and Credit Association (ROSCA)	• It is a group of individuals who agree to meet for a defined period of time in order to save and borrow together. • Variously called susus in West Africa and the Caribbean, tontines in Cambodia, wichin gye in Korea, arisan in Indonesia, xitique in Mozambique, and djanggis in Cameroon, ROSCAs are informal or 'pre-co–operative' micro-finance groups. • Unregistered. • Time –bound.	• It works well in remote rural communities. • Well-known in many countries. • Simple, easy to manage system. • No written records. • It enables people to obtain usefully large sums. • Efficient. It converts small savings into loans instantaneously without paperwork and storage costs. • It is flexible and it can adjust to any group size or kind.	• Amounts saved are generally small. • Inflexible: can't deposit or withdraw funds as needed, so generally not available for emergencies. • No lending. • Savings tied up until member's turn to collect.

Self driven (community based) informal financial intermediaries			
Type	**Features**	**Advantages**	**Disadvantages**
	• Members deposit fixed amount each period. • Each period, one member receives all funds · Rotates until everyone has received funds. • No external funding.		
Village bank and Self-help groups	• Member-based. • Village-based. • They may not be registered. • Small savings collected and intermediated. • They are not ranked, but classified under Tier 4. • A self-help group (SHG) is a village-based financial intermediary usually composed of between 10–15 local women. Most self-help groups are located in India, though SHGs can also be found in other countries, es-	• Varies according to the model – see below for examples.	• Varies according to the model – see below for examples.

Self driven (community based) informal financial intermediaries			
Type	**Features**	**Advantages**	**Disadvantages**
	pecially in South Asia and Southeast Asia. • Members make small regular savings contributions over a few months until there is enough capital in the group to begin lending. Funds may then be lent back to the members or to others in the village for any purpose. • Similar to ASCA, but they intend to be permanent.		
Financial cooperative, including credit unions	• Moving away from informality. • A non profit financial intermediary. • Member-owned: following the one man, one vote principle. • They may be closed bond (e.g. all members have same employer or profession) or open bond (open	• Member-owned and savings–based structure can lead to a strong sense of ownership, which creates incentives for strong management and internal controls. • Federated structure could provide access to services that primary cooperative can't afford such as technical assistance and external audit.	• External finance may lead to borrower domination. • Supervision is often weak. • Board and managers often lack necessary skills, especially financial skills. • Systems may not be adequate for accountability/transparency. • Financial cooperatives in many countries have been used as channel for subsidized services to clientele favored by govt.

Self driven (community based) informal financial intermediaries			
Type	**Features**	**Advantages**	**Disadvantages**
	to all). • Primary focus is on financial services. • Often supervised through govt. ministry or department. • Sometimes federated. • Self-generated capital with retained earnings, members' equity, and little debt. • Lending requires little collateral and is based on character references and cosigning for loans between members. • Usually classified as Tier 3.	• Membership is usually the result of some common bond among members, often through employment or membership in the same community. • Policy-making leadership is drawn from the members themselves.	

Nongovernmental organizations (NGO–MFIs)			
Type	**Features**	**Advantages**	**Disadvantages**
Microfinance NGO (start up; deposit taker; multi-purpose; transformed into a bank …)	• It may be established by local or foreign organization, usually registered as a not-for-profit society or trust. • Principal product is credit. • Set up and managed by outsiders and not the community members. • New entity is often a shareholding company. • NGO is usually one of many shareholders in this new entity. • Usually regulated and supervised. • Set up and managed by outsiders and not the community members.	• Specialization makes it easier to operate a business aimed at long-term sustainability. • It is able to increase capital and finance growth by seeking outside investors. • It is easier to obtain commercial refinance. • Often allowed to offer more services, such as savings.	• Usually not allowed to offer savings services other than ›forced‹ savings. • Difficult to finance growth as it has little access to commercial refinance and no shareholder capital. • Lack of longer-term perspective and strategy. • Product mix is still more limited than a commercial bank. • NGO may be less able to ensure continued focus on poor, as NGO only owns % of company. • Mixed ownership structure can complicate governance.
Deposit taker (NGO) MFI	• It may be established by local or foreign organization, usually registered as a not-for-profit society or trust.	• Multiple services under one roof. • Focus on the poor. • It is close to the target group, in terms of both location and understanding.	• Difficult to operate microfinance using a business approach when other services have a social welfare approach.

Nongovernmental organizations (NGO–MFIs)			
Type	**Features**	**Advantages**	**Disadvantages**
	• Diversified set of services such as health, education, agriculture. • Set up and managed by outsiders and not the community members, outsiders who want to support the poorer people for social, ethical, and political reasons. • Usually classified as Tier 3.	• It helps to experiment with frameworks to develop new microfinance schemes.	• Overly ambitious aspirations with regard to their social relevance. • The limited scale of their operations does not permit them to benefit from elementary economies of scale. • The frequent use of donated funds or soft loans from foreign development organizations. • The influence of people who do not belong to the target group and thus are not subject to peer pressure and are not directly hurt if the institution's money is eventually lost. • Lack of longer-term perspective and strategy.
	• It may be established by local or foreign organization · Usually registered as a not-for-profit society or trust.	• It enables the NGO to retain both social and financial services but develop microfinance using a sustainable business model.	• Difficult to acquire expertise in many diverse subject areas. • Usually not allowed to offer savings services, other than

Nongovernmental organizations (NGO–MFIs)			
Type	**Features**	**Advantages**	**Disadvantages**
	• It may be a separate department or separate legal entity. • Principal product is credit. • Set up and managed by outsiders and not the community members, outsiders who want to support the poorer people for social, ethical, and political reasons. • Usually classified as Tier 3.	• Clients are less likely to get mixed messages. • It is close to the target group, in terms of both location and understanding. • It helps to experiment with frameworks to develop new microfinance schemes.	›forced‹ savings. • Overly ambitious aspirations with regard to their social relevance. • Frequent use of donated funds or soft loans from foreign development organizations. • The influence of people who do not belong to the target group and thus are not subject to peer pressure and are not directly hurt if the institution's money is eventually lost. • Lack of longer-term perspective and strategy.

Formal financial institutions			
Type	**Features**	**Advantages**	**Disadvantages**
Non-bank financial institution	• It includes many different types of organizations: e.g. finance companies, leasing companies and MFIs that have transformed from NGO structure but not become full-fledged banks. • Often regulated and supervised. • Usually classified under Tier 2.	• Finance and leasing companies: focused on a small set of specialized products that may not be available from banks. • MFIs: focused on provision of services to people who cannot get bank access. • Minimum capital requirement lower than for banks.	• Usually not allowed to offer a full range of services, including savings. • Not diversified, thus potentially more risky. than an entity serving a wide range of customers with a diverse set of products and services.
Microfinance bank	• It usually has corporate shareholding structure. • Principal clientele: small and micro –enterprises Often has been transformed from NGO structure. • Regulated and supervised. • These institutions are set up to circumvent the inability of some MFIs to meet commercial bank standards and requirements due to the nature of their lending • Usually classified under Tier 2.	• It has ›double bottom line‹; i.e. profitability and services to lower-income clients. • It may be able to offer the full range of services to clients.	• Not diversified, thus potentially more risky than a commercial bank serving a wide range of customers.

Formal financial institutions

Type	Features	Advantages	Disadvantages
State-owned bank	• It may be a commercial bank, agricultural bank, or development bank. • Regulated and supervised. • Usually classified under Tier 1.	• It may have large branch network, including secondary towns not served by private banks. • State owned institutions understand the local market and benefit from a strong reputation among the poor.	• Often not profitable so must be heavily subsidized to stay in business. • It usually has greater outreach than commercial banks but often does not serve the poor. • It uses standard loan contracts that are not flexible to weekly payments. • Politically influenced.
Private commercial bank	• It usually has corporate shareholding structure. • Regulated and supervised. • Focus on short– and long-term lending to established businesses. • Usually classified under Tier 1. • It is usually ranked on capital adequacy.	• It is able to offer clients a wide variety of financial services, including savings, credit, insurance, and payments.	• Usually not interested in serving low-income people. • Even if interested, difficult to re-orient staff and systems for service provision to the poor. • It has little experience in providing financial service. • Downscaling is costly. • Use standard loan contracts that are not flexible to weekly payments.

In the following paragraphs, the single intermediaries are better described, considering their basic features and characteristics.

Ruthless moneylenders

A moneylender is a predatory and informal financial intermediary–a sort of usurer, ruthless but often indispensable–who is ready to offer to vulnerable poor clients small personal loans at high rates of interest, with a premium over official rates due to prompt and (often) unconditional availability and taking profit of lack of viable alternatives, so exploiting monopolistic rents.

Rural local moneylenders easily approach the poor, (over)lending small amounts of money, with positive side effects but also negative ones that have gained them the reputation of ›loan sharks‹–like the usurer Shylock in Shakespeare's ›*Merchant of Venice*‹–behaving like exploitative cartels:

- moneylenders reduce or eliminate the distance and the information asymmetries with borrowers that they normally known well, being so able to assess their creditworthiness and easing the monitoring during the life of the loan. Since information is expensive to gather, informal credit market is highly segmented and local moneylenders might take profit of competitive barriers, with a consequent monopolistic power (when demand is elastic and supply is rigid, prices–here represented by interest rates–can grow substantially);
- flexibility, informal approach, and quickness are highly valuable characteristics, especially in rural areas where borrowing alternatives do not exist or they are socially and culturally not affordable (this being major and preliminary barriers, often more important than economic ones);
- moneylenders are frequently multi-purpose stakeholders, since in many cases they are not only providers of finance but they might also have other economic relationships with their customers. They can for instance rent them land, houses or tools, and equipment, buy from borrowers some products or hire them as labor force … In such a context, the bargaining power of moneylenders typically grows and they have a ›blackmail option‹ to exercise, should the loan not be repaid on time. This sounds evidently dangerous for the borrower, who can easily become a sort of ›slave‹;
- guarantees do not often exist but when they do, they can be dangerous for the borrower and induce the moneylender to make repayment difficult, should the guarantee be strategic for him (e.g., a bordering piece of land to expropriate). Other guarantees have a notional and affective value for

the borrower much higher than its intrinsic market value: this proves a strong ›psychological‹ incentive for repayment, even if residual value in case of delinquency is low;

- for the moneylender, it is essential to keep clients always in need, in order to maintain his strategic power, so avoiding to emancipate them. A typical strategy consists in financing consumer credit or working capital, instead of entrepreneurial project, naturally focused on longer term value-creating investments. According to the Aesop tale, moneylenders might prefer life–enjoying and short–sighted grasshoppers to hard-working ants!
- moneylenders are comparable to parasites – unproductive firms that improperly feed on productive businesses, extorting and diverting wealth in an illegal and conceived manner;
- even if moneylenders are ruthless, they demonstrate that a market potential is simply there, waiting to be exploited by fairer intermediaries, whose lower prices may well push the perimeter of the potential market even further;
- prices–interest rates and commissions–are neither transparent nor negotiable, due to information asymmetries and monopolistic lack of alternatives, surreptitiously exploiting the ›take it or leave it‹ option.

Moneylenders are often culturally accepted as an icon that is part of the rural landscape, and according to an Indian proverb »a good village is one with a good well and a good moneylender«.

From CGAP (2004a), we draw the conclusion that »abusive lending practices such as lending without prudent regard for repayment capacity, deceptive terms, and unacceptable collection techniques probably cause more damage to poor borrowers than do high interest rates«.

According again to CGAP (2004a) »in many countries, informal lenders are more likely to engage in predatory lending, defined as a pattern of behavior in which an unscrupulous lender exploits or dupes borrowers into assuming debt obligations that they may not be able to meet and uses abusive techniques to collect repayments. The cost of predatory lending can include loss of valuable collateral, transfer of wealth to lenders (especially over time), and / or social and psychological penalties«.

Loans may also take the form of advance against an asset and the intermediaries are typically represented by pawnbrokers in urban areas, which prefer precious metals as a pledge, while in rural areas land mortgage is more popular.

Rotating and Accumulating Savings and Credit Associations

Savings clubs, owned and managed by their affiliates, are established in order to collect individual and segregated savings, whereas in ASCAs and ROSCAs savings are shared.

In the middle between the primitive model of local moneylenders and the more advanced archetype of MFIs, there are financial intermediaries such as ROSCAs[559] (*Rotating Savings and Credit Associations*[560]), ASCAs (*Accumulating Savings and Credit Associations*) or credit cooperatives.

Group lending is another embryonic form of microfinance (being the model for Grameen bank I, now surpassed by the sequel movie ›Grameen bank II – the revenge …‹), again with its advantages and pitfalls. Pros and cons are always worth knowing about for a conscious and careful choice of the fittest model in the best place.

ROSCAs are based on pooling resources with a broad group of neighbors and friends, who especially in rural areas typically belong to the same ethnic clan. Group of individuals agree to regularly contribute to a common ›pot‹ that is allocated from time to time to one member of the group. Each contributor has the chance to win the pot in turn and to use the proceeds to buy indivisible durable goods. ROSCAs' apparent simplicity is however biased by potential conflicts of interests (e.g., participants who win the pot earlier might have limited incentives to make subsequent contributions). In addition, ROSCAs are not very flexible, even if they can help credit constraint households to make simple sharing agreements in order to purchase indivisible goods that anyone might afford only after much time, without knowing where to put his savings in the meantime.

ASCAs are more complex–but also more flexible–institutions, since they allow some participants to mainly save and others to mainly borrow: while in ROSCAs every participant puts in and takes out in rotation the same amount, in ASCAs there is an asymmetry that allows some to use the money.

These primitive forms of financial intermediations rely on simplicity, direct monitoring, and lack of viable alternatives but they undergo severe conflicts of interests and limits of scope.

Village Savings and Loan Associations are saving clubs that represent an institutional evolution of ASCAs and they may conveniently evolve in village banks.

559 See www.gdrc.org/icm/rosca/rosca-resources.html; Bouman (1994); Calomiris, Rajaraman (1998).

560 Local names for ROSCAs range from hui in Taiwan to tontines in rural Cameroon to polla in Chile, tanda in Mexico, chit funds in India, kye in Korea, arisans in Indonesia, susu in Ghana, esusu in Nigeria […].

One head, one vote: credit cooperatives for mutual banking

Cooperatives are universally known for their peculiar governance system, according to which voting rights are not proportional to shares underwriting. This system favors alternative associational voting rights, beyond the standard ›one share, one vote‹ mechanism, easing a model according to which each shareholder is entitled one only vote, irrespectively of her stakeholdership.

In microfinance these well known ›capitalistic‹ features are to be considered less appealing, due to the limited market value and negotiability of unlisted stakes. The governance system pivoting around the fundamental and troubled association of capital and labor, producing a multirole stakeholdership, is on the contrary fully consistent with microfinance's intrinsic nature and mission – hence the popularity of cooperatives within the industry.

According to Branch (2005) »savings and credit cooperatives are user-owned financial intermediaries. They have many names around the world, including credit unions, SACCOs, COOPECs, etc. Members typically share a ›common bond‹ that is based either on a geographic area, or an employer, or a community, or other affiliation. Members have equal voting rights, regardless of how many shares they own. Savings and credit are their principal services, although many of them offer money transfers, payment services, and insurance as well. Sometimes savings and credit cooperatives join together to form second-tier associations for the purposes of building capacity, liquidity management, and refinancing. Second-tier associations also play a useful monitoring role. Donors who want to increase access to financial services, especially savings, often support savings and credit cooperatives«.

Credit cooperatives or unions represent a more advanced instrument, which is closer to MFIs and well known in Europe since the 19th Century (see for instance the German Raiffeisen model[561] since 1864). Credit cooperatives represent group-based ways to provide financial services to the poor, encouraging peer monitoring and guaranteeing the loans of other neighbors. In cooperatives, savers and borrowers are also shareholders of the institution. So they at least partially align their interests with a typical ›one head, one vote‹ mechanism, according to which each shareholder is entitled to one vote, irrespectively of the number of shares he owns, with a consequent peculiar majority rule.

Even credit cooperatives have their problems: first, a much higher complexity than ROSCAs or ASCAs, since they are real–albeit simplified–banks, representing the natural and structured evolution of a permanent ASCA; second, a normally thin capital basis, with a subsequent capital inadequacy in bad circumstances that is worsened also by limited capacity to access to funds to meet liquidity shortfalls[562],

[561] Friedrich Wilhelm Raiffeisen is a remarkable example of social entrepreneur. See Achleiter (2008).
[562] See Armendariz De Aghion, Morduch (2010), Chapter 3.

difficulties diversifying risks (inflation shocks; country or local community risks …).

Branch (2005), considering the advantages of savings and credit cooperatives for increasing microfinance outreach, points out that:

- savings and credit cooperatives reach clients and areas (e.g., rural) that are unattractive to banks;
- they provide savings services to their members, unlike most microcredit NGOs;
- they are often started locally, without major external support;
- their solid base of small savings accounts constitutes a stable and relatively low-cost funding source;
- they have low administrative costs and they may be able to make loans at interest rates that are lower than those charged by other microcredit providers.

Savings and credit cooperatives however suffer from governance weaknesses and inadequate regulation and supervision.

The Darwinian selection from survival to self-sufficiency

MFIs progressively go beyond »a small, close-knit community of institutions offering microloans«[563] and they generally operate according to one of these different evolutionary modes: bare survival, longer-lasting sustainability, or full self-sufficiency[564].

In particular:

- in survival mode, institutions barely try to cover their running expenses, facing a progressive erosion of the start up sponsored capital, which is unable to generate any retained resources for future operations. These institutions, unless they are continuously sponsored, are condemned to death, explaining the high Darwinian selection and mortality of the sector. Mortality burns out not only organizations, but also their goodwill, together with future programs and expectations for the poor, generating dissatisfaction in the donors and dismay in the borrowers. Opportunistic behaviors might also arise, since if borrowers believe that a lender is not

563 Rhyne (2009), p. xiii.
564 See Pollinger et al. (2007).

permanent or unwilling to impose sanctions, delinquency might increase[565];

- sustainability is concerned with the ability to secure longer lasting survival, reaching and keeping a break even point between earned revenues and subsides vs. fixed and variable running costs. Sustainable MFIs earn their cost of capital;
- self-sufficiency is an even higher standard, which gives the possibility to increase the quality and the number of the products-making the big jump from lending–only micro–banks to overall MFIs (with deposits, insurances ...)–while applying market prices that attract non–bankable but potentially viable borrowers. Competition, not undermined by ›addicted‹ subsidized institutions, can also increase, with positive spill-over (and some draw backs[566]). Full self sufficiency facilitates the ability to raise capital from a variety of sources, while market competition prompts MFIs to control costs and to constantly look for efficiency gains.

The institutional life cycle theory[567] of MFIs development describes an evolutionary pattern where most MFIs start up as NGOs with a social vision, funding their operations with grants and concessional loans from donors and international financial institutions[568] that provide the primary source of risk capital.
A big and challenging step forward–a real jump of quality–is represented by the collection of public deposits, before which the MFI has to accept formal banking regulation. This passage is normally accompanied by reduction in subsides and targeted interest rate charges to borrowers which are consistent with the market rate remuneration of deposits and other funding sources, such as interbank loans.
Intensity of regulation is a long debated issue: like a medicine, too much kills the patient and too little is useless. Advantages, costs, and enforceability of regulatory policies constitute a typical trade-off from a theoretical point of view but also from a practical one, considering also the difficulties of less developed countries in effectively controlling unsophisticated intermediaries. The Consensus Guidelines on MFI regulation[569] take a balanced view, arguing that small scale deposit-collecting should be allowed to go substantially unsupervised, especially in a closed context where depositors are only forced-saving borrowers, with a net debt towards the MFIs.
As Bogan (2008) points out, this transition process greatly varies according to the countries where it takes place. MFIs in Latin American countries have made pro-

565 See Schreiner, Morduch (2002).
566 Increased competition reduces margins and decreasing crossed subsidies might harm the poorest.
567 See Bogan (2008).
568 See De Sousa-Shields, Frankiewicz (2004); Helms (2006).
569 Christen, Lyman, Rosenberg (2003).

gress in the transition to regulation and market funding, whereas in other places, such as the Middle East, North Africa, Eastern Europe, and Central Asia, unregulated institutions and social actors such as NGOs still predominate, facing severe limitations in financing options and having no shareholder structure for attracting equity other than donations.

The transition process from a non profit organization or a credit cooperative to a profit oriented firm is strongly advocated and considered ›politically correct‹, since bigger and sustainable institutions have consistent advantages, especially in terms of cheaper and wider provision of capital. In severe imperfect markets, where most MFIs still operate, costs related to market contracts are however generally cheaper for non profit institutions that consequently seem still useful[570].

The macroeconomic context of the country and the development of its capital markets play a major role not only in shaping the regulation framework, increasingly sophisticated in the most advanced countries, but also in the possibilities to have access to financial resources. The better the environment, the easier and cheaper is the funding. National microfinance strategies, bringing the topic to the forefront of domestic development priorities, seem promising in easing the diffusion of MFIs[571].

Banks making small loans need higher–more expensive–capital adequacy, setting aside larger provisions against the higher expected losses from small loans[572], somewhat mitigated by the Microfinance low delinquency rate of micro-borrowers.

Exclusive reliance on donors funding brings to well known capital rationing problems, which prevent MFIs from meeting the enormous unsatisfied demand from the underserved, and it might also avoid pressures to operate efficiently. Commercially-funded MFIs have to survive in the market, coping with daily pressure for revenues enhancing and cost cutting, in order to keep survival margins, flexibly reacting to competitive market shifts (e.g., if market interest rates go down, the commercial institution has to follow the trend, otherwise it will sooner or later be abandoned by the clients).

Donor-backed MFIs may not fully respond to market pressures to operate efficiently or they may deliberately choose to pursue other goals, such as outreach over efficiency, by serving poorer or rural clients with higher delivery costs[573].

Marginal involvement of poorer clients, although they are socially desirable, substantially increases the running costs of the institution, due to concomitant and interacting factors (lower loan sizes with decreasing economies of scale, higher uni-

---

570 See Mersland (2007).
571 See Cgap (2008c).
572 See World Bank (2008), p. 16.
573 Armendariz De Aghion, Morduch (2010).

tary screening and monitoring costs, absolute lack of any worthy collateral, low cultural – entrepreneurial level …).
Cost-benefit analyses are important in order to assess if and to which extent microfinance is effective in respecting its goals and if it can have a better impact that other alternative methodologies or uses of funds. This point is evidently of crucial importance for donors and beneficiaries, with psychological consequences as well as material good or bad ones.
A correct assessment of the right objectives might seem a trivial starting point–although often forgotten or misunderstood–but it is essential since microfinance has never proven to be a remedy for all evils and it is not a suitable tool for the satisfaction of many primary needs.
In order to be sustainable and self fulfilling, at least in the long period, subsidies evidently have to be addressed to projects and investments which are able to generate positive cash flows, ideally consistent enough to repay the debts. But in this context ›cold projects‹, which generate very limited if any cash returns, are automatically excluded, and only ›hot projects‹ can conveniently be selected.
As it happens with many selections, even this choice seems cruel and unfair, since it discriminates not only ›cold projects‹ of primary importance, such as hospitals, education and schools, no-toll infrastructures, etc., but also ›cold poor‹ (the marginal destitute) from ›hotter‹ ones. Also improper use of microfinance, even if with the best intentions, can lead to disastrous results.
Bad but instructing examples concern also government-subsidized agricultural credit, which were considered an appropriate development strategy to reach the poor during post-colonial period. Relaxed requirements for collateral and subsidized interest rates represented a spoiling free lunch for many borrowers (and some cozy lender, often belonging to the same ethnic group), ending up in costly and economically unbearable disaster made of higher transaction costs, interest rate restrictions, corrupted practices, and high default rates. It has unsurprisingly resulted in the phenomenal growth of informal financial markets[574].

How NGOs with a social vision might eventually become commercial banks

Empirical evidence and statistics show that the vast majority of MFIs are very small while very few are large, beyond the deposit-taking threshold. Dimensional growth is often not one of the main concerns–as it is for many companies in other industries–of sponsored MFIs. The paradox is that in order to grow to a sustainable level, they need additional ›fuel‹ (subsidies) but exhausted donors might empty their pockets–pouring money in a bottomless pit–before reaching the magic threshold of profitability.

[574] See Arun (2005).

Scarce donor funding has an empirical evidence of being the principal factor in limiting growth (and consequent positive side effects, such as scaling, increased efficiency, outreach, attractiveness of private investors …)[575] and donor-led models are hardly sustainable in the long run.
The real effectiveness of foreign aid is strongly challenged by a harsh local environment where the cultural distance between donors and beneficiaries requires time and patience much more than money[576]. Money is really a double sided weapon since it eases poverty alleviation but at the same time it corrupts the poor, with the risk of transforming them in permanent beggars.
Self esteem and capability to solve internal problems can break the cycle of dependency for the poor who live at the bottom of the social pyramid[577]. Paternalism driven by a Western-style intellectual trap hardly ever meets the needs of the desperate and when it does, it doesn't last.
Smart coalitions between different NGOs–really too many and too small to survive–are feasible solutions to the problem and if they can hurt the ego of lonely sponsors, they however prove very effective for the sometimes forgotten real objective: sustainable outreach for the poorest!
The transformation of NGOs or other subsidized MFIs to commercial banks does not only require central banks' authorizations, but it is also normally accompanied by the presence of new private and profit-oriented shareholders. Changes in the objectives and in the by-laws of the institutions typically foresee the ability to distribute profits[578], which do not necessarily have to be reinvested in the business. Donors can conveniently act as catalysts for subsequent professional and profitable intervention, ›crowding in‹ funds and preparing the ground for self-sustainable MFIs[579].
Earning survival profits is quite different from earning higher enough profits in order to attract investors who are not concerned with social missions[580]. These investors are maybe heartless and greedy but often necessary for a jump of quality, in order to approach otherwise unreachable international financial markets (like it or not, these are the rules of capitalism and–among others–of listed companies).
Investors in MFIs might be attracted by low correlation to global capital markets[581]. Significant exposure to domestic GDP brings to attractive portfolio diversification for international investors but not for domestic investors lacking significant country risk diversification options.

---

575 Cgap (2004b).
576 See Chapter 14.
577 See Prahalad (2006).
578 See Glaeser, Schleifer (2001).
579 Morduch (2005).
580 Cull, Demirgüç-Kunt, Morduch (2008).
581 See Krauss, Walter (2008); Deutsche Bank (2007).

MFIs can operate as Nongovernmental Organizations (NGOs), credit unions, non-bank financial intermediaries or commercial banks, according to their legal status. This classification might broadly describe the increasing pattern of sophistication that MFIs might follow in their development. The many players in the microfinance industry have different missions and agendas, creating a market segmentation which increases the borrowers' choices, even if the ›not interesting‹ poorest might unfortunately be left aside.

Transformation from NGO to deposit taking MFI bank has a deep impact not only on the dimensions of the institution, but also on its operational management and on its targeted products and clients: the products' portfolio widens, introducing synergic deposits and microinsurance to small loans[582], while the clients' profile may step up, increasing the average loan size and so narrowing the social target.

Stakeholders change with the transforming MFI: funding shareholders may end up their primary mission, divesting their equity and selling shares to the management or other more business oriented investors. Granted capital from sponsors gradually tends to be replaced by commercial equity and debt.

Can microfinance survive in a worldwide debt economy? Opportunities and dangers of leveraged growth

We increasingly live in an addicted economy, which is artificially inflated by debt, where too many citizens tend to live well above their equilibrium survival means, leveraging up artificial growth with tempting short sighted recourse to debt. Overexcited financial markets, with their collapsing paper pyramids, often infect the real economy, typically with negative consequences on the poorest. Paper–financial–economics may suffocate real economics, self fulfilling itself, and influencing it, forgetting its fundamentals. Since debt can indefinitely inflate itself, it fantastically works – like an exciting drug temporarily deprived of any side effect.

When dissipating grasshoppers prevail over thrifty ants, future generations are sooner or later due to pay for their parents' spending attitudes – reminding that there is an old obligation to fulfill ... and desperately looking for who pays their fathers' bill. Structural debt is always a symptom of decadence, leaving a long term badwill to cover. It is relatively easy to leverage up development, letting GDP grow with its fueling debt. But when the speedometer of leveraged growth runs too fast, overexciting the economy, the risks exponentially increase.

Debt can be divided in many different forms, such as:

- public debt, wherever a government accumulates public deficits, as a consequence of public expenses structurally exceeding incoming taxes and other revenues;

---

[582] See Chapter 19.

- banking debt, when financial intermediaries issue loans, underwritten by other intermediaries or, at the latest stage, personally by households;
- personal debt, when single households, living above their current purchasing power capacities, spend more than what they earn, mortgaging future revenues while contracting debt obligations, initially occasional but soon likely to become structural.

In this trendy worldwide environment, which is anyway characterized by huge local differences, we may wonder how MFIs are positioned in such a potentially unfriendly institutional context. Even if MFIs are typically mildly leveraged, as far as they exit their infancy and become adult, their differences with the contaminated and spoiled external world fatally tend to decrease and their originality and virginity weakens, corrupted by the external world and its temptations. Since this fact has already happened with other financial intermediaries–such as credit cooperatives or savings banks, gone far beyond their mutual ideals–it might be likely to occur even with MFIs, especially if temptations, first of all represented by the smell of easy money, look too seducing to be resisted for long.

Leverage temptations are magisterially represented by a famous statement of Frank Modigliani and Merton Miller (M&M), two economics Nobel Prize winners, whose considerations about debt are still alive after their 1958 seminal paper[583]. According to M&M, the market value of a company is completely independent from leverage, whose neutrality has no impact on its wealth's creation or destruction.

Since the market value of a company is represented only by its operating cash flows discounted at the weighted average cost of capital collected to produce them, debt is completely irrelevant. When the difference between the return on invested capital and the cost of debt is positive, capital yields more than the cost of its collection. In such a case leverage, represented by the ratio of financial debts over equity, may initially increase total wealth, acting as a tempting multiplier of this positive difference, but then it may soon become a dangerous boomerang[584].

Whenever addicted growth is improperly fueled by excessive debt, development is artificially boosted, but it is likely to behave as any other speculative bubble, being due to burst when its dimension trespasses any rational equilibrium and decency. A ›debt doctor‹ may be needed to cure ›leveraged‹ poor, who are unused to repay their loans.

Debt is dangerous because sooner or later somebody simply has to pay it back – as it should be obvious even if it doesn't necessarily seem for the silly and short

583 Modigliani, Miller (1958).

584 Especially if real world imperfections, such as bankruptcy potential costs, are included in the model, being offset by the tax advantage of debt (due to the deductibility of negative interest rates) only for mildly indebted companies.

sighted leveraged-grasshoppers. The ways to reimburse debt or to deflate its impact are variegated, even if they share a common denominator. They are all painful, with long lasting negative effects, especially if left growing uncontrolled for a long time, being represented by:

- structural (hyper)inflation – eroding purchasing power for lenders, while the borrowers take benefit of devaluated nominal face value of their debts, sadly remembering war periods and bringing to strong albeit surreptitious wealth redistributions. The real impact of inflation is that of a hidden long lasting tax;
- debtor's default – bringing to a delinquency state of the world where the lender is unable to get his money back, while the moribund borrower (albeit facing an embarrassing reputation drawback) is relieved from meeting his undoable obligations, remembering the Latin proverb ›*ad impossibilia nemo tenetur*‹ – nobody is due to comply with impossible tasks. But as we have already seen in Chapter 18, we should always beware about strategic defaults;
- debt repudiation is a formally sweeter alternative, which is sometimes put in place by new politicians that do not recognize former despotic regimes, claiming that they are different, but often failing to behave so. For creditors, the consequence is however similar, plainly resulting in an ›anyway, no money back!‹ state of the world;
- speculative bubbles – out bursting when prices are over inflated and bringing an hyper inflated and addicted economy back to the ground floor, falling from the sky with no parachute;
- long term austerity – reducing expectations and consumption, with a negative (potentially huge) impact on growth.

MFIs are often too unsophisticated and young to be tempted by these dangerous options, but leverage represents a potentially destabilizing factor also for them, especially if they follow a mission drift pattern, described in Chapter 22.
When debt hinders future growth, the lower pace of growth bursts future income, with a detrimental impact on both expectations and development.
Leveraged financial options exponentially grow with alternative and artificial investment possibilities, with the result of making finance increasingly detached from the real economy, up to the point of seriously destabilizing it, as it has happened during the worldwide recession started in 2008. Is microfinance going to follow the financial mainstream, with its increasingly volatile ups and downs? Not for the moment, due to its limited size, different level of sophistication, and closeness to the real survival economy, even if potential dangers are never to be underestimated.

Contagion threatens MFIs, to the extent that disordered deleveraging in Western banks has an impact on MFIs in developing countries, whenever the latter rely on constrained foreign funding.
Donors and social investors channel larger amounts of funds to MFIs across the globe, generating a significant supply ›push‹ behind the growth story. The abundance of funding has given MFIs greater confidence as well as the capital to grow at a faster pace[585].
Asynchronous austerity policies among different countries may ease softer deleveraging and exit strategies from recession.

The condensed Chapter

In poor but evolving environments, there are typically informal intermediaries, such as ruthless moneylenders, commonly known as ›loan sharks‹, who live aside more established and formal intermediaries, ranging from self driven Rotating or Accumulating Savings and Credit Associations–ROSCAs and ASCAs–to village banks, self help groups, and financial cooperatives.
On a complementary side, sponsor driven institutions comprise microfinance NGOs, up to the point of becoming deposit taking regulated institutions, or fully market driven microfinance banks or fully licensed traditional commercial banks.
A variety of complementary intermediaries is important for development, especially in an increasingly sophisticated world economy.

Out of Poverty Tips

Darwinian evolution of different financial intermediaries may accompany the poor out of their starting misery, providing increasingly sophisticated devices. Choice and availability of different products, following market segmentation attitudes, can make the difference.

Selected Readings

DEUTSCHE BANK, (2007), *Microfinance. An Emerging Investment Opportunity,* in http://www.dbresearch.com/PROD/DBR_INTERNET ENPROD/PROD000000 0000219174.pdf.

585 http://www.cgap.org/gm/document-1.9.42393/FN61.pdf.

CHAPTER 21 – Can microfinance be both sustainable and affordable, without forgetting outreach?

> Microfinance stands as one of the most promising and cost-effective tools in the fight against global poverty.
>
> Jonathan Morduch

Dreams for the present and goals for the future: combining outreach with sustainability

The success of microcredit–and, in a broader sense, microfinance–does not imply that it can solve all the existing socioeconomic problems which affect the poor. Such a false and simplified conviction is both dangerous and deceiving, as it generates exaggerate expectations that are going to remain largely unsatisfied. Microfinance is neither the philosopher's stone nor the Columbus' egg and it is also not what the poorest primarily need, reminding that not everybody is a potential entrepreneur waiting for proper funding.

As a matter of fact, it has already been underlined that microfinance is not the right device to provide direct financial coverage to ›cold‹ investments, which cannot repay themselves generating adequate cash flows. Examples range from hospitals to schools to tribunals or toll-free infrastructures. But linkages with ›hot‹ projects, such as businesses that are (at least potentially) able to generate enough cash to service the debt, are so strict and evident that they cannot be simply dismissed or underestimated (illiteracy and illnesses are major obstacles to economic activity and might inhibit survival … an obvious physical perquisite for repayment). So a systemic and micro-macro approach to the problem is highly wanted.

MFIs, according to their current tide, are actually limited in their ability to serve the poorest (this being a major practical but also theoretical obstacle to optimal outreach), for many complementary reasons such as the poorest natural unwillingness to borrow–life is already risky enough without taking on debt–or exclusion (often self-exclusion) from group lending members. The poorest also desperately need primary goods and services such as food, grants, or guaranteed employment before they are in a position to make good use of financial products.

Highly subsidized safety net programs are what the destitute at the bottom of the economic ladder primarily need. MFIs can cooperate and interact beyond a certain level, even if their job is different and confusion doesn't help in an already messy environment.

Microfinance business is often unprofitable or–in the luckiest cases–it offers only decent returns and consequently it does not easily attract ambitious and profit-maximizing managers, unless they have charitable background and they are looking for ›values‹ beyond money and success. Larger and well established MFIs, transformed into formal banks, might typically be more seductive, but the problem is to let them arrive to such a level. Good strategic management is strongly needed even in this complex field, where poor management is often offered to poor clients, creating a vicious circle difficult to sort out.

The key for a feasible and progressive solution of the main microfinance target maximizing outreach and impact while preserving long term, possibly unsubsidized, sustainability–is to insist on the search for financial innovation, in order to find smart and unconventional solutions to unorthodox problems. This strategy has proved successful in the past, allowing to reach unthinkable results, and it has to be followed even in the future.

Some hints can derive from growing on–field experiences and research, which are increasingly showing that even if some main features are replicable in different environments[586], flexibility and adaptation to local conditions are strongly wanted, since what is successful in a particular context might not be conveniently exported and replicated elsewhere.

Among the different interchanging examples of financial flexibility and innovation, there are changing sizes in target groups, different loan maturities, individual rather than group lending, feasible *ad hoc* forms of guarantee (forcing deposits from retained earnings; pledging notional assets psychologically worthy for the borrower …), frequency of repayment installments, synergies between financial products (e.g., loans linked with deposits and insurances), specific methods of monitoring (from basic rural supervision to technology-driven devices).

There is an enormous market potential for deposit services among poor clients, who are subject to outreach bonds that are not only profoundly different from those envisaged for microloans, but also synergic to them. In other words, while microdeposits are risky for the poor depositors, microloans are specularly risky for the MFI.

Outreach and sustainability, that are much concerned with risk that may affect already tiny margins, are evidently more difficult targets for lending institutions and MFIs which are enabled also to collect deposits that can conveniently reduce their risk profile. This may happen both on an aggregate basis, matching assets (credits towards borrowers) with liabilities towards depositors, and on a single basis, since

[586] Environmental factors are a key issue in explaining variations among countries and include the regulatory environment; macroeconomic stability (country and political risk) ; competition from other financial intermediaries (subsidized by the government; private …); income level of clients, etc. See Roodman, Qureshi (2006).

many depositors are also borrowers, partially counterbalancing their overall exposure towards the MFI.
Deposit taking MFIs are also more likely to survive, not only for their normally bigger dimension, but also because their liability structure is typically cheaper–with a lower cost of collection–and more stable than other institutions which are not allowed to collect savings. Deposit taking MFIs aren't subject to the potential disaffection of bored and discouraged donors or to the volatile mood of international investors.
Tailor-made *ad hoc* products are highly requested in different social, economic, and especially cultural contexts, considering that the segmentation factors between different kinds of poor tend to be greater than those normally affecting wealthier borrowers around the world. The latter are certainly more sophisticated than the first, responding and adapting more quickly to converging standards, driven by globalization pressures and incentives[587].
Cultural changes and improvements are by far the most difficult and longest to look for, since they entail a change of mentality process that needs plenty of time–often measured by generations–to develop solid roots. The frantic and increasingly interlinked world we live in might speed up the process, but velocity tends to go along with superficiality whereas long lasting deepness requires its due time. The tortuous and painful evolution of the European cultures might teach us something–*historia magistra vitae*–about this hard process. No durable results are possible without grieving perseverance.
Client education might represent something more than the standard marketing device for customers' attraction. Client-retention and business training[588] in order to teach entrepreneurship, is a strategy that a growing number of NGO-driven MFIs is trying to follow. It is an interdisciplinary approach to a complex and interacting problem, such as poverty alleviation has shown to be.
The pitfalls and problems of subsidies are too well known not to raise a simple–somewhat embarrassing–question: are they really necessary for a better and deeper outreach of the poorest?
The available empirical evidence does not provide clear-cut answers[589], even if it seems to suggest that sponsorship is unavoidable for start-ups and it is useful for deeper and wider outreach of the destitute[590], which do not represent an attractive target for commercial banks.

---

587 E.g. international accounting standards or European directives, which aim to harmonize legislation, in order to favour comparison-driven competition. The risk for those who do not comply with international standards is to be emarginated from a global market, which sets for everybody the rules of the game: those who don't accept them, are simply not admitted to play.

588 See Karlan, Valdivia (2006).

589 See for instance Cull, Demirgüç-Kunt, Morduch (2008).

590 Subsidies are generally beneficial when assuming a non flat distribution of social weights, a demand of credit which is elastic to interest rates, adverse selection effects and positive spill over of microfinance credits on other lenders, as Becchetti, Pisani (2007) point out.

For-profit institutions normally target wealthier clients–from the not-so-poor onwards–and they are typically able to increase the average size of their loans, so decreasing operating costs and consequent interests charged to the clients (who become increasingly demanding and have a wider set of opportunities, stimulating competition from the supply side). But client selection is unfortunately strongly linked with discrimination, and unprofitable women are frequently left aside, even though they record better repayment rates than men.
Accounting and financial indicators such as the ›financial self-sufficiency ratio‹, which calculates the ability to generate enough revenues to cover running and fixed costs, can measure the threshold to profitability[591]. Institutions serving especially poor customers charge higher interest rates and have fewer default rates than those serving better-off clients, even if operating costs are consistently higher, as it is their effective cost of collected capital.
Igniting growth from scratch, sustaining and outreaching development are the three key moments of a comprehensive pro growth strategy, to be carefully balanced with proper timing and coordination.

Deep, broad and lasting

The trade-off between outreaching depth and financial sustainability strife has given rise to a debate between the *financial systems approach* (which emphasizes the importance of financially sustainable microfinance programs) and the *poverty lending approach* (focused on subsidized credit to help overcome poverty)[592]. Most recent microfinance paradigm seems to favor the financial systems approach, since it is the only one with long term sustainability[593].
A subtler discussion might embrace the kind of MFI and, in particular, its product design. Individual based MFIs seem to better perform in terms of profitability (envisaging a mission drift from poor to richer clients), whereas group-based institutions better serve the poorest (and the most discriminated, such as women)[594].
Goals to be pursued and–possibly–achieved are focused around the aforementioned trade-off and they might consider the following hints:

- in order to improve outreach, one of the key drivers is to reduce cost of debt (interest rates), with a market–unsubsidized–progressive approach. Improving cash flow predictions, insuring borrowers, easing deposit collection for collateral and saving purposes, building data banks for credit and delinquency records are just examples of what MFIs should hardly try

[591] For an analysis of microcredit sustainable (break-even) interest rates, see the appendix of this Chapter.
[592] See Robinson (2001).
[593] Hermes, Lenskin (2007).
[594] Hermes, Lenskin (2007).

to do, together with their clients, while environmental and macroeconomic issues–essential to provide the right framework for development–go beyond their forces but can receive a push from the bottom of the social pyramid;

- MFIs can conveniently reduce the cost of their collected capital, so as to be able to cut their personal borrowing costs and to transfer at least part of the benefit to clients. In addition, they can achieve the goal with dimensional growth, easing economies of scale and reaching a regulated standard, in order to be enabled to collect deposits and to access cheaper sources of funds from domestic and international capital markets;

- improvements in corporate governance issues (transparency, accountability, minimization of conflicts of interest ...) are fundamental for any MFI which wants to collect funds, either from sponsors or private investors or from clients-depositors (or even shareholders, applying the effective model of credit cooperatives). No trust, no money;

- technological improvements can be of great help, easing communication and circulation of information. Wireless devices can cut physical distances, computerized records can ease delinquency and market statistics, etc. Nowadays, operational efficiency and cost cutting cannot be pursued without appropriate technology;

- subsidies can undercut both scale and efficiency and smart grants should always be transparent, rule–bound and time–limited[595], possibly following donor guidelines[596];

- targeting the model of mainstream banks, even if difficult and somewhat inappropriate to the peculiar context, is however an important strategic goal, that is to be followed with common sense, realism, and flexibility, adapting the business model to changing circumstances. Progressive compliance to international standards is a necessary condition for access to international capital markets, especially in an increasingly global and competitive world. Competition needs comparability and those who live in an Ivory tower are definitively out of the game;

- measuring the social impact of microfinance is still a hot and mysterious issue: does it really contribute to alleviate poverty and to promote development and emancipation? The answer to this question–embarrassing for the microfinance enthusiast fans–is hopefully positive, but empirical evi-

---

595 Morduch (2005).
596 See CGAP (2006b).

dence is mixed[597] and further research, using more computerized data bases, wherever available, is strongly needed;

- love for the poor–an invisible state of mind and heart–is not part of a pure capitalistic Decalogue, but it seems essential in a field where even the most successful MFIs hardly prove really lucrative. Intangible benefits can compensate some economic sacrifice, at least for the luckier ones who understand that they need the poor at least as how the poor need them. Easy-money-making objectives should more conveniently be addressed elsewhere, real happiness maybe not.

The classical trade-off between outreach and sustainability stands as a real key point in microfinance issues. Maximum outreach and potential involvement of as many as possible between the poorest is obviously a primary goal, and sustainability is an unavoidable element for its persistence over time (length of outreach). Wideness / breadth and depth[598], quantity. and quality are different sides of the same coin.

The joint maximization of outreach and sustainability is probably every Microfinance practitioner's secret fancy. But the dream might soon become a nightmare, since these key parameters / objectives often prove antithetical, since outreach is an uneasy self-sustained process, which might need severe subsides, at least during its uneasy start up. A typical microfinance dilemma is decreasing repayment marginality, driven by growing outreach. Stamina and endurance to pursue these goals are highly wanted.

According to Rawls (1971), the well-being of a society coincides with that of its unluckiest individual – a demanding inspiration for the good-hearted who are looking for the extreme boundaries of outreach.

Who pays the bill? The more you give … the better I live

An evening in San Francisco, while pleasantly walking on the pier with my wife and children, I was about to take a picture of a folksinger, who made the following preventive request: »If you use the flash, give me some of your cash«. He deserved it.

A big question, involving not only microfinance, is concerned about who … pays the bill, providing the capital and the other resources which are necessary to start up the activity and to keep it going profitably.

The problem is strongly debated and it is essential for the success of any initiative to find a good balance between initial sponsors–mainly foreign–and followers or newcomers.

---

[597] See for example Cull, Demirgüç Kunt, Morduch (2008).

[598] See Mersland, Strøm, (2007a).

Money is strongly needed, at least initially and till it is self producing, and the amount of dedicated funds may have an important impact on outreach–the more you give, the further you can reach–even if this is just a part of the game, necessary but not sufficient and with money alone nobody won't go far.
On the one side, MFIs would have to charge to their (poor) clients' full market rates, following a fully-fledged commercial approach, if they are willing to reach and keep sustainability, represented in accounting terms by the break even point where revenues at least match costs, and from a complementary financial perspective by the equilibrium between cash inflows and outflows.
On the other side, they would need somebody to cover the balance, in order to be able to continue to pay the bill (a precondition for not-ephemeral survival) if they follow idealistic social goals, willing to lower their rates in order to promote outreach and to reduce the socio-economic cost of access to credit. In a market economy, underpricing needs a sponsor to fix unmet costs.

Microfinance scalability

The concept of scalability is concerned with the ability for a business or technology to accept increased volume without impacting the contribution margin (given by the difference between revenues and variable cost) and possibly increasing it. A scalable business with ›last mile‹ suitable features enables to reduce costs, which is an always welcome strategy, particularly important in microfinance, where the small and dispersed size of accounts and transactions bring to fixed costs uneasy to be matched, so endangering sustainability.
The operating leverage is a measure of how revenue growth translates into growth in operating income. It is a measure of how risky (volatile) a company's operating income is. Operating leverage can also be measured in terms of change in operating income for a given change in sales (revenues). The Degree of Operating Leverage can be computed in a number of equivalent ways: a way is defined as the ratio of the percentage change in Operating Income for a given percentage change in Sales.
The operational leverage illustrates the impact of an increase of the sales on the operational margin (Earning Before Interests and Taxes–EBIT–expressed by the difference between the sales and the fixed and variable operational costs). If the MFI has prevalent fixed costs and negligible varying costs, once it reaches its breakeven point, any increase of the sales is mostly reflected in an increase of the operational result (EBIT).
The operational leverage expresses the relationship among the variation percentage of EBIT and the variation percentage of sales:

$$Operating\_Leverage = \frac{\Delta EBIT / EBIT}{\Delta Sales / Sales}$$

The elements that influence the operational leverage are:

- prices and volumes of sales,
- variable costs,
- fixed costs.

Scalability, linked to viable profitability, can improve if fixed costs are offset by a larger amount of revenues and if technological innovations let intermediation and commissioning costs to be cut, as we shall see later on.
Scalability is among the main bottlenecks of microfinance. Many small loans partitioned over huge structural fixed costs per operation indeed squeeze margins, often up to the point of making them negative, so requiring higher compensative interest rate charging or external sponsorship, till the much wanted autonomous sustainability is reached and kept. The poor are many … but hardly scalable, and leveraging up development is a painful task.
The two best strategy drivers to promote scalability and marginal growth are represented by:

1. cutting operating unitary costs, mainly using technology, such as IT, starting from mobile banking applications;
2. increasing unitary loans, so compensating invariable costs per operation with higher lent amounts.

It greatly helps not only to cut down operating costs, so increasing margins and making interest rates charges softer, but also to boost outreach, since microfinance products become cheaper and more easily available, through technology driven IT devices such as mobile branchless banking.

Sustainability accounting metrics: from economic to financial flows

Is microfinance business sustainable and affordable? If it is so, outreach may be pushed, provided that economic and financial positive marginality is not diluted up to the point of turning the business into an unprofitable adventure.
Considering a deposit taking MFI, the basic model can be described in table 21.1.

Table 21.1. – MFI asset & liability statement

ASSETS & LIABILITIES STATEMENT	
Assets	**Equity & Liabilities**
Cash & Bank (liquidity)	
Loans to clients (accounts receivable)	Paid in Capital
– Current	Reserves (cumulated profits and capital contributions)
– Past-Due	Net Profit/(Loss) current year (L)
– Restructured	**Total Equity (D)**
Net Outstanding Loans	
Intra-bank loans	Deposits
Other Current Assets	Short-term Borrowings*
Total Current Assets (A)	**Total Current Liabilities (E)**
Participations and Long-term Investments	Long-term Debt*
Fixed assets	**Total Long-Term Liabilities (F)**
Net Property and Equipment	
Total Long-Term Assets (B)	
Total Assets (C) = (A) + (B) = (G)	**Total Liabilities (G) = (D) + (E) + (F) = (C)**

** in domestic or foreign (hard) currency, creating in the latter case a forex mismatch with mainly domestic assets.*

The starting point in order to answer this key question is accounting metrics of economic and financial flows, together with their assets and liability structure[599]. The answer should possibly be not static, following an evolutionary pattern where different scenarios may be envisaged and tested.

MFIs can reach their economic equilibrium only if revenues exceed costs and they can reach financial equilibrium only if cash inflows are higher than cash outflows. A positive cash flow balance is essential in order to maintain the capacity to cover the expenses in the medium to long term.

The main costs of a MFI are concerned with staff and infrastructural amounts and with the payment of negative interests to depositors, should the institution be enabled to collect funds from savers. We already know that the business model of a MFI is hardly scalable, especially if its dimensions are small and the clients are poor, with limited *pro capite* loans that are time and human resources consuming.

599 See http://www.cgap.org/gm/document-1.9.8956/accounting%20course%20summary%2008%20final.pdf.

In the understanding of the MFI metrics, it is necessary to make a comprehensive integrated analysis of the assets & liabilities statement, the profit & loss account and the cash flow statement, in order to link the structural dimension of the MFI assets and liabilities (with its equity emerging as a differential) with its economic marginality and the cash flow balance. To the extent that the MFI is profitable, its net result increases the equity and it is likely to produce a positive net cash flow, whereas a negative result erodes the equity and absorbs cash, typically demanding capital contributions or liquidity injections. This is the metrics that quantitatively defines sustainability and–with it–the possibility of extending the MFI's outreach.

The assets & liabilities statement, with its variation from one year to the other, is to be linked to the profit & loss account, so as to generate automatically the cash flow statement[600].

Cashed-in incomes and cashed-out expenses are recorded in the profit & loss account and then reported in the cash flow statement.

Survival liquidity is a key indicator both for the MFI and its clients; when cash burn outs occur, rapid intervention is needed; the problem is particularly challenging if it concerns a deposit taking MFI, with a potential systematic impact on the market that Central Banks accurately have to monitor and, eventually, solve as a lender of last resort.

Sources of cash for the MFI are also to be considered, together with their different origin: domestic sources, not linked to foreign fund raising, are more stable during international crises and do not bear any currency risk, whereas they are more exposed to local shocks.

[600] See for instance IAS 7 for an International accounting standard.

Table 21.2. – MFI profit & loss account and cash flow statement

PROFIT & LOSS ACCOUNT	CASH FLOW STATEMENT
Positive Interest and fees on loans	Intermediation margin (J)
Positive Interest from investments	Depreciations and amortizations (non monetary costs)
Total income (H)	
	Δ accounts receivable
Negative Interest on debt	Paid advances
Negative Interest on deposits	Interests receivable
Provision for loan losses	Short-term liabilities
Administrative expenses	Tax liabilities
Staff costs	**Net Cash Flow from operating activities (N)**
Depreciation, Amortization and other	
Sundry operating charges	
Total operating expenses (I)	Δ tangible and intangible fixed assets
	Net Cash Flow from investment activities (O)
INTERMEDIATION MARGIN (J) = (H) – (I)	
	Δ Intra-bank and other short-term loans
Non-operating income	Δ Long-term loans
Grants and donations	**Net Cash Flow from financial activities (P) = = (N) + (O)**
Profit/(loss) before taxation (K)	**NET CASH FLOW (Q) = (S) – (R)**
Profit tax (L)	Cash Balance at the beginning of the year (R)
	Cash Balance at the end of the year (S)
NET RESULT (M) = (K) – (L)	

The Profit & Loss account of the MFI has to go along with that of the poor clients, with positive margins acting as a safety net for both. In any other state of the world, subsidies are deadly needed to make ends meet.

Table 21.3. – Profit & loss account of the MFI and its clients'

(Microfinance's) client P&L account		**Microfinance P& L account**
Revenues from economic activities		
– (running) costs		
– (negative) interest rates on loans	⟷	Positive interest rates on lent funds
+ positive interests on deposits	⟷	– (negative) interest rates on deposits
		– staff and other operating costs
= net income		
– living costs (consumption)		= net income (if positive, making the MFI sustainable and allowing for outreaching new investments)
= net savings		
– borrowed funds		
+ deposits		
Free cash flow (available for savings and investments)		

Balancing loans with deposits: asset and liability management

An asset-liability mismatch occurs when the financial terms of a MFI's assets and liabilities do not correspond. Consequent financial risk can erode their differential, represented by net equity, through a profit & loss imbalance producing a net loss. When volatility is high and liquidity shrinks, the issue becomes even more important, as it happens during crises and recessions.

Due to their predominant financial nature, assets and liabilities of a MFI are highly sensitive to interest rates differentials, as well as foreign exchange fluctuations. Some examples may better illustrate the concept:

- if a MFI issues debt denominated in (hard) foreign currency, whereas all its assets (mainly represented by loans and cash) are in the (weak) local currency, any local currency depreciation along the life of the foreign debt reflects in a currency loss that decreases the net profit (or increases the loss), eroding the equity;
- any imbalance in interest rates sensitivity between assets and liabilities produces losses if liabilities are hit more than assets.

Traditional hedging strategies consist of careful balancing of assets and liabilities exposure to common risk factors, so as to make them elastically synchronized to external shocks, with little or any impact on the profit & loss margins.
Exposure to interest rate and currency risk emerges first of all as a result of the imbalances in the assets and liabilities sensitive to risks. For instance, when interest rate sensitive assets correspond to 80 US$ whereas interest rate sensitive liabilities amount to 100 US$, any increase in interest rates produces a negative imbalance. Duration gap is the difference in the sensitivity of interest-yielding assets and the sensitivity of the MFI's liabilities to a change in market interest rates (yields).
But even mismatched maturities matter, since their uneven renegotiation follows different pricing pressures. Immunization against interest rate and / or currency risk can be achieved with duration matching, creating a zero duration gap, so ensuring that a change in interest rates will not affect the value of the MFI's equity.
Within the microfinance industry, currency risk–analyzed in Chapter 23–is one of the major sources of concern, severely affecting the MFIs that rely on foreign funding, since weak local currencies are likely to devaluate (reflecting higher inflation rates; loss of competitiveness …). Hedging is both expensive and uneasy, typically with a roll over every six months, with risky repricing schedules.
According to Karla Brom (2009)[601]:

- as MFIs diversify their funding sources, sound asset, and liability management (ALM) is critical to help MFIs assess and manage financial risk;
- the crisis has also underlined issues around leverage: increased borrowing can help institutions increase their returns, but it also exposes institutions to greater risk;
- by examining the structure of the balance sheet, MFIs can identify, measure, and manage financial risks arising from the mismatch of asset and liability currencies (foreign exchange risk), maturities (liquidity risk), and repricing (interest rate risk). Once these risks have been identified and measured, usually through gap analysis, MFI managers can decide what level of risk is acceptable and set limits to maintain asset and liability mismatch at an appropriate level;
- effective ALM is especially important for deposit-taking institutions since the variety of liabilities available to them is, by definition, more complex than those available to no deposit-taking institutions;
- in their early phases, MFIs are often financed by a combination of grants and concessional funding, so liability management is not crucial. As MFIs

[601] CGAP (2009a).

grow and expand their funding sources to include commercial sources of funding, such as deposits, commercial loans, bond issuance, and equity, professional liability management becomes a necessity;

- we typically emphasize active liability management for MFIs, rather than active asset management, and for example, focus on negotiating terms with funds providers or diversifying the liability mix rather than changing the terms of loan products offered to clients or adding a lot of new client products.

Cash and equity burn-outs, in an evolutionary growth pattern

A sad and frequent phenomenon that happens to many new companies is concerned with their inability to prosper or, at least, to survive after the first months or (few) years from their incorporation. MFIs are hardly an exception, even if their initial sponsor may make the agony longer and softer, continuously and generously pouring cash where they probably shouldn't.

Cash burn-outs happen when the MFI becomes illiquid, after complete drying up of its financial resources. No liquidity left to pay creditors and–among them–sometimes even depositors, is always a serious problem to front. In addition, also it is important to consider well known sequential side effects, due to which unpaid creditors may be induced by loan losses not to honor their personal debts, igniting a delinquency spiral often uneasy to be stopped, with potential escalating contagious effect. If large banks are too big to be left failing–as the worldwide financial crisis of 2008-2009 has taught us–small MFIs may be abandoned to their destiny, leaving problems unsettled and a bad example that others may follow, especially if left unpunished.

When the coffer is empty, somebody should refill it and new liquidity is desperately needed to honor overdue payments and to start again the machine – if it doesn't happen, the game is simply over. If left untreated, burnings may be … burying.

Equity burn-out is a parallel situation, where the MFI has completely set to zero its capital and reserves, as a consequence of cumulated losses, because costs systematically exceeded revenues. Net losses are normally accompanied by cash burnings, even if this is not an automatic relationship – especially in the presence of many non monetary costs, such as depreciation and amortization[602].

Economic and financial equilibriums are both essential in an evolutionary growth pattern, where the MFI increases the number of its clients and the magnitude of its services, ideally following an outreach-maximizing strategy, albeit compatible

[602] To the extent that costs are non monetary and don't bring to any cash outflow, their presence doesn't affect the liquidity of the MFI. Monetary costs, such as payrolls, purchases, interests to be paid to depositors or to other debtholders, taxes, etc., are however typically the biggest part of the total expenses.

with its resources. The aim is to prevent any cash or equity burn-out, a highly likely situation, especially if the business expansion is accompanied by typical deferral and overestimation of revenues and cash inflows.
Cash and equity burn-outs are evidently a deadly risk, the former even more than the latter.
Indicators such as the debt service cover ratio (the proportion of cash available for debt servicing to interest and principal payments, that is commonly used to assess the MFI's ability to produce enough cash to cover its debt payments) or the leverage, expressing the ratio between financial debt and equity (the higher, the riskier), are useful companions of any professional business plan, where stress tests (in order to find the economic and financial breakeven point) and different scenarios should consciously be simulated.

Outreaching retail microfinance: synergic partnership for the last mile

The ›last mile‹ is a common expression that has been taken from the ICT industry, meaning the final leg of delivering connectivity from a communications provider to a customer. The actual distance of this leg may be considerably more than a mile, especially in rural areas.
In microfinance, the expression can be paraphrased to mean the link between a central structure–the MFI main seat and its core backbone, represented by the key branches–and further potential extensions to typically poorer and more distant places.
Last mile outreaching may also theoretically soften the dogmatic differences between the top down (centralized) approach and the bottom up peripheral solutions (that were illustrated in Chapter 14).
Failure to provide last mile delivery is a common organizational and structural bottleneck that severely hampers outreach, with mixed impact on profitability and sustainability: when the marginal clients are profitable, due to good scaling and efficient minimization of marginal costs to reach them, then outreach is profitable, whereas if still not reached ›last mile‹ clients produce negative margins, further outreach threatens overall sustainability. Service delivery with proper network of outlets in low-income neighborhoods is a strategic cornerstone even for microfinance.
In microfinance, the possible economic outcomes of ›last mile‹ outreaching have to be carefully outweighed, considering the expected returns of any potential branch expansion, which may depend on several interacting parameters such as concentration of possible customers, their wealth level, existence of competing sources of finance, distance, etc.
Since economies of scale are difficult to reach within the microfinance industry, especially if the social target is challenging, further outreach often increases economic

losses and imbalances, up to the point of undermining (even subsidized) sustainability.
Economic marginality is so the key factor behind ›last mile‹ outreach. Cost cutting is the first strategic target, even more than trying to maximize returns, since marginal ›virgin‹ clients are typically poorer and relegated in more distant places and it may take ages before they become profitable. The risk is that by that time the daunting MFI is dead, after bleeding and draining.
Cost cutting devices include two main alternative options–optionally and hopefully complementary–such as:

- branchless (wireless) branching, typically referring to Mobile banking;
- strategic partnership (synergic networking) with other complementary intermediaries already present in ›last mile‹ locations.

M-banking features are going to be synthesized in the following paragraphs, whereas strategic partnerships mainly involve multi-firm subjects such as retailers, banking agents, or insurance companies, with possible cross-selling of complementary products (e.g., standard insurance products with ad hoc microinsurance packages).
The fact that presiding agents already know the place and the local customers, allows them to wash out most of (or even all) the fixed costs and to benefit from the much wanted economies of experience, scope, and scale.

No fuel, no growth: liquidity constraint implications for expanding MFIs

From the aforementioned accounting metrics, we can infer that liquidity is essential for the survival of any company, but in particular for MFIs. They need indeed the necessary cash not only to guarantee financial coverage to their monetary expenses (payroll and overhead costs, interests to depositors …), but also to pay back deposited money, if they are enabled to collect deposits.
Expanding the business traditionally requires consistent cash surplus, since growth shows a natural tendency to burn-out cash and to release it only in the medium to long run. Strongly growing MFIs, which try to ease the tumultuous development of emerging economies, may suffer from severe cash imbalances and they have to duly take into account the necessity to smooth them, in order to reach and keep financial equilibrium, which is indispensable for their survival.
Liquidity shortage is a typical capital rationing issue, especially in a highly growing evolutionary pattern. Economic fluctuating cycles make rationing a softer or harder problem, respectively in boom and in recession periods. Capital rationing causes more troubles in fast growing markets than in mature ones, since the former are more fuelled by leverage and more sensitive to changing risk premiums, which may substantially increase the cost of collected debt.

The necessary ›fuel‹ for growth is typically given to MFIs by its shareholders, who are often represented by foreign investors or donors (especially if the MFI originates as a NGO, possibly to be transformed later on in a profitable and self sustainable institution).
Transformation to more formal institutions catalyzes growth in the MFI's outreach and product offerings. Alarmingly, there is however a decline in the percentage of women clients who are served after transformation and scaling up.
Foreign banks, either directly financing MFIs located in poorer countries or present in the capital of investors / donors, instinctively prefer to concentrate on domestic markets during crises, with a de-multiplying leverage effect that may severely hit growing MFIs, especially if they are hardly enabled to diversify with short notice their funding sources. When debt is shrinking and unable to cover assets, downsizing may have huge collateral effects.

Hot versus cold investments: lessons from project financing

According to a standard classification that is particularly used in project financing[603], we can distinguish between ›hot‹ and ›cold‹ projects, even if only the first are able to generate spontaneous cash flows, ideally beyond the point of being able to service debt.
Cold projects, which generate little or any cash flows, are neither self sustainable nor self bankable and cash for their financing has to be provided by the government or by international sponsors. Cold projects may however be synergistically linked with hot–self repaying–ones.
Microfinance only fits hot projects, since cold ones are not bankable and they must be financed by the government or by international aid organizations. Hot and cold investments are however synergic.
The distinction, even if apparently simple, is far from being clear and many combinations are possible, considering hybrid investments (e.g., a public ›cold‹ hospital where there are also commercial non core ›hot‹ activities).
For what concerns microfinance, the question pivots around the use of loans from the beneficiaries, who are typically due to invest them in ›hot‹ activities, but they are often likely to use the money for personal consumption, a strategy that may put repayment at risk.
The complementarities of hot and cold investments should not be underestimated, considering that we all need both. For instance, even if housing, school attendance, and medical care are ›cold‹ investments that do not produce any cash, they are evidently linked to any entrepreneurial initiative.

603 Project finance is a long term financing of infrastructure and industrial projects, based upon the projected cash flows of the project rather than the balance sheets of the project sponsors; it fosters economic growth and this effect is strongest in low-income countries, where financial development and governance is weak. See Kleimeier, Versteeg, (2009).

Microloans should be strictly addressed to ›hot‹ investments, while other precious complementary products, such as microinsurance devices, are institutionally designed to cover risky occurrences (illnesses, death, damages …) that typically absorb cash and represent an impediment to the development of ›hot‹ entrepreneurial projects.
The fact that ›hot‹ investments can develop in an environment where basic ›cold‹ needs are satisfied is consistent with the idea that microfinance can be only a partial solution to poverty issues that need to be accompanied by complementary interventions.
The synergies between ›hot‹ and ›cold‹ investments, strengthening the infrastructural network, are likely to substantially increase the productivity, with positive effects on growth and development.
The literature on microfinance may well dedicate more attention to the different uses of loans, going beyond the classical distinction between investments and consumption. Lenders tend to address their funding only to the former, which are more likely to generate cash for repayment, while borrowers naturally prefer immediate consumption, especially if it is needed for their bare survival. A balanced view should prevail and money should be targeted principally to cash flow producing investments, even if borrowing small entrepreneurs should consume enough … to stay alive.
Small loans–those provided by MFIs–are consistent only with small projects, unless the latter become so self sustainable and profitable to be able to generate larger amounts of liquidity on their own. Microfinance is typically likely to ease the start up of development, then leaving the jump of quality to larger and more sophisticated intermediaries, unless small MFIs can grow up together with their clients, as we shall see later on in this Chapter.

Technology enhancing outreach

Technology enhances productivity and it may greatly help in fostering outreach, even if it should never be forgotten that proper management and ›human software‹ stay always behind–and above–it.
Outreach is strongly threatened by unsustainability. When the business model is not self sustainable, the MFI is condemned to death, sooner or later reaching cash burn out situation, out of which it is uneasy to recover.
Technology is not a panacea and alone it cannot solve all problems, but it can help to do it, especially if it is synergistically backed by a favorable environment. Operating costs can be reduced using technological devices, such as:

- mobile banking;
- access to Internet cafés;

- biometric technology (to obtain loan approval and credit history), for example applied to Automated Telling Machines and barcode–reading point–of–sale (POS) terminals;
- satellite navigators, to map clients' residences.

Internet dramatically reduces the necessary time to match borrowers and lenders; it virtually eliminates geographical distances, allowing remote banking applications without needing physical branches and enabling customers to access the service at any time, even beyond job hours.
Technology can help to lower the breakeven point and extending the MFI's survival threshold and consequently its outreach, making the business more scalable – this being one of the weakest points of microfinance, whose labor intensive business model absorbs most of the available cash and resources, leaving little or even any margin for the rest.
To the extent that technology can reduce intermediation and transaction costs–or even eliminate them–substantial margins are being saved, to the benefit of both the MFI and its clients. Lower costs have a strong beneficial impact on both sustainability and outreach. As a matter of fact, IT can lower intermediation costs especially in businesses with a virtual component, where physical (hardware) production and distribution are not necessary. This can be the case with virtual branches, transfer of dematerialized money, and so on – young and innovative business models are at hand.
A rough but impressive idea of the outreach potential of technology can be given comparing the number of people who have a mobile phone but not a bank account: »Banks and cell phone companies are taking advantage of new handset technology and the expansion of cell phone use in developing economies to extend financial services to roughly 2 billion people who use cell phones but lack bank accounts«[604].
M-payments are expanding everywhere and they have enormous scaling potential.
IT also has a profound impact on the MFI's organizational model. And a computerized e-government of resources–beyond an old fashioned ›brick and mortar‹ pattern–changes the equilibriums between different stakeholders, easing the management process. In order to conveniently leverage up the full power of new IT devices, e-governance has to be service-oriented, addressing its efforts to clients and the market needs (with new e-governance driven marketplaces), so to ease their direct participation to a shared adventure, creating a working virtual community.
According to Sachs (2008), p. 307, contributions of ICT to sustainable development are represented by:

- connectivity, bypassing geographical obstacles;

[604] Source: Global Envision, Microfinance Goes Mobile, http://www.globalenvision.org/library/4/1708/.

- division of labor, among connected communities within the production chain;
- economies of scale, minimizing variable costs, due also to almost costless replication;
- accountability, due to the easiness of monitoring electronic transactions;
- matching buyers and sellers with B2B or B2C web intermediation;
- building social networks;
- easing education with distance learning.

Synergic branching to outreach clients

Branch penetration, especially in remote rural areas, is a fundamental cornerstone behind outreach. Branching accelerates growth, efficiency, and competition, improving capital allocation and channeling finance to the poor. Mobile banking and other IT devices can foster intangible branching, so providing new services, which matter even more than the institutional framework.

Partnerships between MFIs and insurers can make joint sale of products possible and affordable. MFIs are typically good retailers, since they are close to their clients and able to push for incremental outreach–the demand being almost limitless–should they have enough resources to offer attractive products to a wider set of potential customers.

We have already seen that microdeposits, microloans, and microinsurance policies are highly complementary products–deposits coexist with sustainable loans, and insurances decrease the borrower's risks–and also the distribution channels should be complementary.

It takes pain, money, and time to set up a profitably working distribution network for MFIs, establishing branches in strategic places and coordinating them with a centralized management system, both flexible and hierarchically sound. Fixed costs eat up most of the distribution pie and it makes sense to try to offset them with growing potential revenues, which are consistently translated to positive economic margins (such as the operating income, EBITDA), once the break-even point between operating revenues and costs has been reached and conveniently trespassed.

Adding up a new complementary product, it becomes possible not only to new money out of it, but also to have extra gains from the increased appeal of other already sold products.

Client monitoring with a regular–labor intensive–contact is another cost, that is partly fix, which can conveniently be shared adding a new item, such as a microinsurance product.

The interest rate paradox: why cheap credit might harm the poor

People might wonder why it is easier to buy toothpaste than to buy (borrow) money, since–according to basic economic rules–prices adjust so that at market equilibrium supply meets demand[605]. As a consequence, when demand for toothpaste exceeds the supply for it, price will rise until equilibrium is reached. If the price is too high, some might stop buying toothpaste but those willing to pay the high market price would not have any access problem.

Credit markets are somewhat similar, but they also show important differences, as the Nobel Prize Joe Stiglitz explains in a seminal paper[606]. Even in this case if demand for money exceeds supply, the price (represented by interest rates) grows till it reaches market equilibrium, but here an access problem might arise anyway and information problems can lead to credit rationing even in equilibrium. This fact happens because banks are concerned not only about the interest rate they charge on the loan, but also about its risk.

Interest rates represent the price for lending money, and they are influenced not only by the demand and supply for cash, but also by its intrinsic risk, as seen above, and by its temporal dimension – the longer, the riskier. Short repayment schedules, so common with microfinance schemes, reduce the risk of time and they are also consistent with the short sightedness of many poor, who are culturally unable to program their future and unused to deal with debt issues.

High interest rates have twofold implications and they are a dangerous weapon in the hands of the lender: providing bigger returns to banks that cushion themselves against lacking collateral, they increase the risk of loans. So it might prove too expensive and unbearable for borrowers, giving them opportunistic incentives and leading to moral hazard and in general being associated with higher probability of failure. As a sad paradox, the poorer are those who pay the highest interests.

This general framework applies also in the microfinance arena, which however unsurprisingly shows some peculiar aspects, if it is compared to a standard credit market. A short historical excursus might explain how interest rates have changed from primitive credit markets to modern ones – a pattern that is being followed also by microfinance institutions.

In the beginning there were single, local, and informal moneylenders, providing liquidity and charging high interests, often at usury rates. In case of no repayment, ruthless actions were routinely applied against borrowers. Shylock in Shakespeare's ›*Merchant of Venice*‹ is a bright example of how a usurer might behave, even if happy ends such as that in the drama are unfortunately exceptions more than a rule.

---

605 This example is taken from World Bank (2008), p. 31.

606 Stiglitz, Weiss (1981).

It is not surprising that usury, before becoming a criminal offence as it is now in most Western countries, was strongly condemned by the ›*Book Religions*‹[607]: both Jews and Christians find their source in the *Deuteronomy's* book of the Bible, while Muslims follow what is written in the *Koran*, with consequences that are still present in Islamic Finance[608], according to which conventional interest is not allowed.

Middle Age finance, represented by Florence and the Medici's family in the 15th Century, evolved into company scale and individual lenders were replaced by banks, with rules and costs that began to justify interest rates. Modern banks have consistently refined the model, intermediating liquidity between lenders and borrowers and providing–not for free–many other increasingly sophisticated services.

The origins of microcredit might be set back to the Italian *Monti di Pietà* at the end of the 15th Century, established by religious orders to provide some sort of credit to the poor. At the end of the 16th Century, loan cooperatives and saving banks were established in Europe in order to provide finance to small enterprises. Microcredit was so born long before the prominent Grameen Bank (›bank of the village‹) funded by Mohammed Yunus in Bangladesh in the early 1980s.

In this historical evolving context, interest rates find a rational economic and also ethical explanation, even if they still undergo strong discussions and the right ›price‹ of interest rates is among the hottest monetary questions.

In microfinance, interest rates show almost everywhere in developing countries–albeit with consistent differences–an astonishing high level, generating scandal among those who ideally consider that microfinance should be affordable even for the poorest. High rates particularly affect females, also as a consequence of the fact that in underdeveloped countries the labor market, characterized by significant unemployment and segmentation, is for most of the women essentially nonexistent[609]. Gender discrimination unfortunately still appears difficult to eradicate.

Normal interest rates might vary from 1.5 % to 4 % and more. If this rate apparently sounds cheap to Westerners, it should not be equivocated that the rate is calculated per month and not per year[610]! And interests are frequently paid monthly, with a compound mechanism that substantially raises the toll.

The immediate explanation that these skyrocket rates are due to very high inflation does not hold, since even real rates are consistently higher in Bangladesh–the country where microfinance was born and is stronger–or even more in Bolivia[611], another well established place for microfinance, than in OECD countries. Else-

607 See Mews, Abraham (2007).

608 See www.islamic-banking.com/. For an analysis of Islamic Microfinance, see Segrado (2005); Karim, Tarazi, Reille (2008).

609 Emran, Morshed, Stiglitz (2007).

610 According to Krauss, Walter (2008), the annualized percentage rate of MFI loans is usually between 20% and 60%. See also the reported statistics on MicroBanking Bulletin, www.mixmbb.org.

611 For market price conditions and setting standard comparisons within the MF industry around the world, see http://mftransparency.org/.

where–not surprisingly in Sub-Saharan Africa, the less developed area in the world–both nominal and real rates may be even higher.
The deep presence of moneylenders who charge much higher rates shows a somewhat surprising relative insensitivity of poor households to interest rates. The main reason seems that they strongly need access to finance and in many cases they are forced to accept bad conditions because they lack better choices. Widening the offer, easing the depth and outreach of finance, is a key point for economic development. Lower rates will naturally follow, due to increased competition, as it has happened even in Western countries. Access to finance is (for the moment) more important than its price. Not taking profit of such a situation of need is a delicate ethical problem, of which not-for-profit institutions, such as NGOs in particular, should be concerned about.
How can we conciliate good purposes–helping the poor giving them affordable access to finance–with usury interest rates? Difficult question, with some astonishing answers.
Before trying to answer this embarrassing question, we might try to detect the reasons why interest rates empirically show to be so high in the microfinance arena. The reasons are many:

- the unitary amount of the loans is very low and since each loan has to be instructed, dealt with and monitored, fixed costs are typically very high, preventing economies of scale, due also to the fact that weekly on field collection proves expensive. As a consequence, survival strategies require rates to be high enough to cover their running costs;
- MFIs find it difficult to collect deposits, especially if they are not in the Tier 1 or Tier 2 capital adequacy ranking. Inter-bank deposits are also expensive – the lower the ranking of the MFI, the higher its cost of collected capital;
- MFIs also bear other fixed costs (set up and working of branches …) that have to be repaid by borrowers …;
- since relationship lending–typical of a microfinance context, where customer's creditworthiness is hard to detect and monitor–is costly for the lender (not being a standard product, so preventing economies of scale), it requires high spreads or large volumes to be viable and economically profitable[612]. Since often there are not large volumes for unitary loans (with other barriers to cost cutting economies of scale), high interest charges seem unavoidable.

[612] See World Bank (2008), p. 9.

Empirical evidence shows however that subsidizing microfinance in order to lower interest rates is hardly ever a good policy, since it weakens borrowers, creating an artificial and segmented market. Interest rate ceilings[613]–like those existing in Western countries to prevent usury–have frequently shown to have severe negative side effects: failing to provide adequate consumer protection against abusive lending and weakening lender responsibility. Cheap credit makes borrowers irresponsible, polluting them with free money.

Boomerang interest rates ceilings

According to CGAP (2004a), high interest rates charged to the poor might seem a contradictory policy, especially from NGOs, and they might result in predatory and unscrupulous lending, strongly damaging the poorest and keeping most of them outside an unaffordable credit market.

The introduction of mandatory interest rate ceilings, which are historically and currently used by many governments to address these problems, often hurts the most vulnerable–rather than protecting them–by shrinking their access to financial services, since they typically discourage the provision of tiny loans by making it impossible to recover their high administrative costs. Among the many interacting reasons for such problems, the following are of particular interest:

- when faced with interest rate ceilings, MFIs often retreat from the market, grow more slowly and / or reduce their presence in rural areas or other more costly market segments, if unable to cover their operating costs;
- not-for-profit MFIs might be discouraged from transforming into fully licensed financial intermediaries. On the other side, subsidized MFIs are often embarrassed by informal fees (bribes) requested by dishonest credit officers;
- MFIs might try to circumvent the ceiling–in order to cover their costs–imposing new ›cunning‹ charges and fees, which are often hard to detect;
- the implementation of a transparent and effective ceiling policy might prove difficult, due to different definitions of the interest rate (nominal, real, effective, annual percentage …), different terms and repayment schedules;
- interest rate ceilings are often difficult to enforce, particularly when it comes to softly regulated or unregulated intermediaries, such as many MFIs. The responsibility for enforcement is not always clear or it is placed with agencies without proper technical expertise.

[613] See World Bank (2008), p. 16.

Cheap credit has long been a problem. Lenders charging interest rates which are lower than the average market level tend to be inefficient, misdirecting, and often facing low repayment rates.

»When subsidized credit is much cheaper than loans available elsewhere in the market, getting hold of those loans is a great boon. Loans meant just for the poor are thus frequently diverted to better-off, more powerful households. Even when the loans go to the poor, the fact that highly subsidized loans have typically come from State-owned banks (and the fact that the loans are so cheap) make them seem more like grants than loans, and repayment rates fall sharply as a consequence«[614].

Adams, Graham and von Pische (1984) were among the first to state that too low interest rates can undermine microfinance. On the other side, high rates can obstacle outreach to the poorest and they might bring to shocking situations such as the Compartamos IPO. In April 2007, Banco Compartamos of Mexico got successfully listed and the company was considered promising and profitable, even because it charged its clients interest rates of 94% per year on loans, becoming a micro-loan shark![615].

Interest rates are in part rationing and discriminating mechanisms, determining who chooses (or can afford) to borrow and who doesn't[616].

Subsidized rates such as those normally provided by NGOs consequently have ambiguous results and even though they might prove useful in the short run, they can be dangerous if too protracted. Even from State-run banks we get a negative example, since many of them for ›political‹ reasons charge interest rates well below market standards, showing also weak repayment rates from intrinsically risky agricultural lending. No surprise that they are costly, inefficient, and not particularly brilliant in outreaching the poor[617].

The level of interest rates is however less dramatic than it might seem at first sight. Projects of the poor normally show high rates of return, which are normally consistent with the service of the debt, leaving a positive economic and financial margin that can be reinvested or directed to savings, creating a virtuous circle.

Technology can help to bring down transaction costs and interest rates, to the benefit of poor customers.

High interest rate charges do represent a limit to the ability of MFIs to serve poorer potential clients and they represent a competitive disadvantage against those who are entitled to much cheaper access to credit, even if market segmentation tends to keep a distinction for different classes of borrowers, who are typically not competing in the same markets (should this happen–and the probability is becoming in-

614 Armendariz De Aghion, Morduch (2010).
615 See Rosenberg (2007).
616 Armendariz De Aghion, Morduch (2010).
617 For an example, see Conning, Udry (2007).

creasingly concrete, due to globalization–then the problem might be worth considering and dealing with).

Consumer protection laws, including mandatory public disclosure on total loan costs (often partially hidden to unaware borrowers), might provide desirable safeguard without the negative side-effects of interest rate ceilings[618].

Microfinance is timely-time–dependent–and interest rates follow inexorable chronological quantification, puzzling the poor who are unused to the Western concept of cardinal and unique time[619]. The ›if-You-cannot-pay-today-pay-tomorrow‹ rule is nice but hardly practicable in microfinance.

The (affordable) level of interest rates is a key parameter in microfinance, and it has a deep impact on sustainability, scalability, and outreach, as it is widely known that small loans–albeit being socially desirable, since they may outreach even the poorest–are much less scalable that bigger ones, so endangering long term sustainability. The perverse economic conclusion is that the poorest, being more expensive, should be overcharged than more affluent clients.

The competitive upper limit to interest rate charges is represented by the rates that are applied by moneylenders, even if microfinance differentiates itself not only with its pricing but also–hopefully–with a different and more sensitive approach to the poor. Excessive charging, beyond the threshold of reasonable sustainability, may either cover operational inefficiencies or be a typical mission drift temptation, described in Chapter 22.

Constrained NGOs versus flexible moneylenders, in a slippery institutional environment

NGOs are hardly to be considered a perfect substitute for informal lenders and in spite of their evident advantages–being a fairer, more transparent and cheaper intermediary–potential borrowers suffer their rigidity (concerning the size, timing, and release of the loans, lack of grace period for beginning loan repayment, capital rationing on available funds …). So potential borrowers continue to refer also to moneylenders or other more flexible finance providers; this especially happens in emergency times of cash shortage, when money is immediately needed, regardless of its price.

The real commitment of NGOs is also another hardly detectable soft component, especially in the long run – will they still be here five years from now? Sad to be said, the moneylenders yes, the NGOs may be not.

Much of the NGO's rigidity is not due to their bad will, but to external circumstances, such as the target of being sustainable at any cost, or the will of their worried foreign sponsors to behave overcautiously or even environmental challenges

---

618 CGAP (2004c).

619 For a cultural analysis of the different concepts of time, see Chapter 9.

that NGO managers may be ill prepared to face. On the contrary, moneylenders are much more used to live with endemic problems, typically taking profit of high volatility: in emergencies, they simply react raising prices (interest rates), knowing that if they are able and willing to lend, they will always find desperate borrowers with no other viable alternatives.

In addition, NGOs are young and often unskilled, whereas astute and effective moneylenders are probably as old as humanity and they were born in the same playfield of their poorer clients – knowledge of the territory and information asymmetries matter. Even in Western countries where the offer of financial services is wide and diversified, usurers are unfortunately still popular and difficult to eradicate.

The experience of more developed nations teaches that various forms of financial intermediaries–formal, informal, and even illegal–tend to cohabit and sometimes to interact in a porous and unstable environmental framework, each occupying a different segment of the market. The trend towards formality is typical of increasingly-developed nations, but in recession periods and credit crunches, the unofficial economy tends to grow, mainly using informal financial intermediaries, while recorded transactions, tax payments, and regulated institutions are increasingly avoided. The black economy is perceived as both simpler and cheaper than the official one, even if the poor hardly benefit out of it, their rights being systematically neglected. Crises, cash, and corruption are self sustainable interacting forces.

To the extent that NGOs are regulated or supervised by local Government (which may ask them to be licensed and may argue about their legal status) and Central Bank (especially if they are allowed to collect deposits), the regulatory framework can be seen as a protection for the poor borrowers, but also as a form of political control, especially in illiberal countries where potentially destabilizing foreign NGOs are seen with suspicion. Once again, local moneylenders are not supervised at all, and they are free to act and to make damages.

Should NGOs operate as a substitute of the State (which may withdraw or reduce its subsidies due to budget constraints or other priorities – such as channeling more funds in the army, a vital resource for ailing dictators), then the poor would experiment social welfare losses that are somewhat due to be compensated.

Are NGOs better providers than the State? Much depends on the country's democratic standing and institutional strength. In undemocratic countries there is a weak and illegitimate governance system, together with frequently diverted resources, with the result of discriminating most of the poor, especially the marginalized ones who do not belong to the ethnic clan in power: in such a context, NGOs normally make it better, even if their relationship with local authorities may be likely to be conflicting, raising hot political issues.

An analysis of the interest groups behind NGOs, concerning their stakeholders, can help us in the understanding of their ultimate strategies, which are a result of the synthesis of potentially conflicting interests between donors, intermediaries, and poor recipients[620].

Foreign NGOs have an exit strategy, because they can abandon troubling local activities, addressing elsewhere, whereas local governments don't have such a way out.

Subsidiarity, suspended between market and State forces, can be put in place using NGOs and other not-for-profit organizations for credit delivery, but it seems evident that its challenges are enormous, especially if the playing field is a tough one. The boundaries between NGOs, the State, and markets are controversial and blurring[621] and they put at stress their respective identity, legitimacy, and efficacy.

The poor represent the synthesis of these interacting forces that are sometimes cooperating and in other cases conflicting, and the big question to be asked is if these combined or counter posed forces at the very end make them better off or not. From the empirical evidence, we get mixed results, which are sometimes encouraging but more often marginal or even ineffective.

Financial institutions and intermediaries–from the informal money sharks to NGOs and further on, up to fully licensed commercial banks–are not always soundly competing in imperfect markets. High interest rates are a consequence not only of the imbalance between potentially unlimited demand of credit and insufficient supply, but also of other interacting factors, such as the intrinsic industry risk of lending money and other market imperfections and asymmetries, due to which there is overcrowding in some segments and no offer in others.

Sustainable partnership, from fair trade to social tourism, based on mutual convenience

In order to be lasting, MFIs have to be convenient and rewarding for all their stakeholders, starting from equity and debt holders and finishing with poor beneficiaries (borrowers but also lenders and in many cases even stockholders).

Sustainable partnerships are so unsurprisingly based on mutual convenience, after a start up period when the investment costs are still looking for future break even, as wise and patient capital is supposed to do.

Mutual convenience is also likely to overcome most of the governance issues concerned with the conflicts of interest between foreign aid donors and recipients, already seen in Chapter 14. Reaching and keeping mutual convenience is hard but highly rewarding.

Fair trade and sustainable tourism are just two basic examples of a possible positive partnership, as they link developed with underdeveloped countries. They can both be considered forms of direct export (trade) or indirect one (tourism), and

620 See Chapter 14 for an analysis of the governance problems of foreign donors.
621 See Fernando (2006), p. 36.

precious hard currency payments are the desirable outcome. The real benefit goes however well beyond money and it is represented by non monetary outcomes, concerned with cultural understanding of ›exotic‹ products or places – that are also frequently and synergistically interacting, since people are more incline to buy products from places they have personally visited. And when other investments or foreign aid are associated with already known countries, traditional cooperative problems tend to soften while togetherness improves. Basic investments can just represent a starting point, to be followed by more sophisticated and incremental entrepreneurial activities, if a virtuous growth pattern is first ignited and then adequately fuelled.

Sustainable tourism, bypassing the big multinational networks that often exploit local populations, should benefit also and mainly the poor, respecting their environment and their cultural habits. Mass tourism in relatively unexploited destinations is seen as a major opportunity for economic development and it may lead to the presumably most desirable form of economic growth, i.e. pro-poor growth, either directly or with a weaker trickle down impact.

Even remittances can be positively involved in the game, since fair trade needs somebody to organize the deal on both ways, and expatriates are likely candidates to handle the import, well beyond their personal self consumption needs. Sustainable tourism also needs marketing network abroad–and growing Internet investments–and emigrants are still in a privileged situation, knowing both countries better than anybody else, in a context where information asymmetries, albeit softened by globalization, still matter.

The impact of craft exports and social tourism on the maintenance of local cultures is another important by-product towards holistic forms of sustainability that is once again well beyond its monetary expression.

Local culture preservation is a key target for sustainable development: it follows a bottom down approach according to which the poor have to find the forces to start up durable development first of all within themselves and their unexploited possibilities, reminding that what is artificially imposed from the outside is normally hardly working, if it is not properly assimilated and locally acculturated.

After the failure of so many development projects and aid interventions, the idea that joint business can fix the problem of poverty is gaining momentum and it has strong rationale behind itself. But business is not panacea for all the poverty issues and it can just tackle some of them, contributing to their solution, but only together with other complementary measures.

Clustering microfinance

Development needs to reach critical mass in order to become effective in reducing poverty. Industry clusters, where similar and complementary business activities are

located, enable to reach synergies that are otherwise unthinkable and to set up infrastructures and facilities that make the place attractive, even for much wanted foreign investors, giving competitive advantage to places where economies of scale and experience may start working.
The impact on the local economy, starting from employment, can be substantial, igniting and maintaining development and spreading the wealth among a larger number of individuals, with positive spill over even outside the cluster.
Microfinance is a much needed complementary product that is able to accompany development of small activities, gradually scaling up, specializing in the cluster business, and providing *ad hoc* products.
The diffusion of microfinance branches–increasingly intangible, with mobile banking–is important in order to guarantee financial infrastructural network, providing a basic service.
Clustering microfinance is so a cornerstone of any strategy trying to increase outreach in all its main constituencies–starting from breadth and depth–and to make it longer lasting.
At the beginning, single initiatives and MFIs can play a vital and pioneering role in the start up of development; then a larger number of institutions, possibly specialized to serve different segments of an increasingly diversified clientele, become necessary in order to make a jump of quality.
The presence of several MFIs can also increase competition among them and other financial intermediaries along all the intermediation value chain–from informal moneylenders up to full commercial banks–to the benefit of local individuals, who are enabled to choose among different options, probably for the very first time in their life.

Microfinance and taxes

The topic of microfinance sustainability is, sooner or later, to be related also to its impact on taxation. At least some MFIs are able to become viable and to earn positive taxable base, having an excess of taxable revenues over deductible costs, and so they start contributing to the country's tax revenue, this being an unusual–in poor countries–but particularly important source of public funds, whose metaphoric meaning goes well beyond its material contribution.
Institution after institution, MFIs can contribute at a micro level (that on aggregate has a macro effect), to increase the country's public spending capacity, with positive systemic effect even on taxpaying MFIs.
As a matter of fact, tax payers are not passive shareholders of the State and they command ›voice‹ option, demanding accountability improvements and a fairer representation of how the money is spent. Embezzlement and corruption, albeit

still possible and actually frequent, increasingly become more difficult to put in place.
Among the beneficiaries of these tax revenues, the public Central bank is possibly the closest to the MFI, not only for its supervising activity–especially concentrated on deposit taking institutions–but also for its ancillary functions. The most extreme is concerned with the activity of ›lender of last resort‹, should the insolvency of a banking institution and run-to-deposits panic reaction need to be cooled down, before having a systematic impact, often comparable to financial tsunami.
Taxes are also the soundest way to collect public money, if compared to Government borrowing–to be covered, sooner or later, by a difficult public surplus or, more likely, by deferred taxation–or to volatile and conditional international aid.

Detecting and overcoming microfinance bottlenecks, stepping up even the poorest

Bottlenecks represent a damaging situation where a narrowing obstacle is found along the road and the strategic process gets stuck or severely hampered. In order to solve these severe problems–or at least to mitigate them–early detection is unsurprisingly fundamental, playing a key role in promoting the instrument.
The main microfinance bottlenecks–that hinder development, making sustainability harder and downsizing outreach–are strongly linked with its risk factors and banana skins, which will be examined in Chapter 23.
Prerequisites for any serious detection of the actual and potential microfinance bottlenecks are on-field experience, shared knowledge, and deep understanding of the industry, with sound theoretical background blended with practical implementation.
The most brilliant and widely recognized peculiarity of microfinance is its well known capacity to overcome apparently impossible problems–how to lend money to the poor with no guarantees or regular incomes, possibly getting it back–with smart and effective solutions. Muhammad Yunus is a recognized genius not because he has invented from scratch something completely new or never heard of, but rather because he has made some path-breaking incremental innovation, understanding the reason why traditional banking was unfit for the poor and finding out feasible and working strategies to solve the problem.
But since the challenges that microfinance has to face are still enormous, new ideas are continuously and desperately wanted, in order to expand its outreach, trying to marginally involve even the poorest underserved (for which microfinance is, to a large extent, still ineffective and sometimes even dangerous) and to make it viable and self sustainable.
The most ambitious goal is reaching and successfully serving in a sustainable way also the poorest, till now largely untouched by this revolutionary lending device.

This represents the biggest and most complex bottleneck, strangling microfinance deepest aspirations but also suffocating the underserved, many of which have no further time to wait, since in the meanwhile they continue to die.

Technology can greatly help to reduce bottlenecks, decreasing the break-even point of MFIs and so increasing both sustainability and outreach. According to Moro Visconti and Quirici (2014) "the impact of technology may be measured with differential analysis on MFIs, considering their accounts before and after the introduction of innovative devices; to the extent that technology can reduce fixed costs and improve the scalability and flexibility of the business model, economic margins are likely to expand and cash flows should increase, with positive side effects on both sustainability and potential outreach. For MFIs, technological upgrade is to be considered a key strategic issue in the next years, with a likely digital divide between haves and haves not".

Assessing microfinance social impact

An analysis of the different possible ways to deepen the impact of microfinance starts from considering its social performance:

- managing for results;
- understanding real client's needs;
- reporting to the different stakeholders (clients such as borrowers, depositors, and/or insured poor; shareholders; bondholders and other debtholders; the government and the local community …);
- assessing the impact of microfinance on development and poverty reduction;
- making a poverty scorecard.

According to Richard Rosenberg[622] »funding agencies' microfinance interventions produce better results when design, reporting, and monitoring focus explicitly on key measures of performance that are measured and reported regularly. The more transparent the results, the more likely founders are to learn from successes and failures and to take corrective actions when needed«. Basic tools to measure performance in a few critical areas, analyzed in the paper, are represented by:

1. Breadth of outreach – How many clients are being served?
2. Depth of outreach – How poor are the clients?
3. Loan repayment (portfolio quality) – How well is the lender collecting its loans?

[622] CGAP (2009b).

4. Financial sustainability (profitability) – Is the MFI profitable enough to maintain and expand its services without continued injections of subsidies?

5. Efficiency – How well does the MFI control its operating costs?

The condensed Chapter

The greatest challenge for microfinance is to be self sustainable–so being sooner or later able to cope without money from sponsors–but also affordable for its poor clients, optimizing efficiency in order to save up costs.
To the extent that a MFI is profitable, it can extend its perimeter, coherently with its social mission, reminding that the ideal strategy of any sensitive institution consists in igniting development from scratch, sustaining it in the long run and outreaching new marginally poorer clients, as far as possible.

Out of Poverty Tips

Fine tuning the traditional tradeoff between lasting sustainability and socially desirable outreach.
Making microfinance understandable and affordable of both sides. Deep broad and lasting.

Selected Readings

MATHINSON S., (2007), *Increasing the Outreach and Sustainability of Microfinance through ICT Innovation*, in http://www.fdc.org.au/Electronic%20Banking%20with%20the%20Poor/1%20Mathison.pdf.

MORO VISCONTI R., QUIRICI M.C., (2014), *The impact of Innovation and Technology on microfinance sustainable governance,* in Corporate Ownership and Control, in press

APPENDIX – A pricing formula for assessing affordable and sustainable interest rates

Fairly pricing interest rates is a key strategy for MFIs.
According to a CGAP study[623], a correct pricing formula has to take into account that the annualized effective interest rate (*R*) charged on loans will be a function of five elements, each expressed as a percentage of average outstanding loan portfolio: administrative expenses (*AE*), loan losses (*LL*), the cost of funds (*CF*), the desired capitalization rate (*K*), and investment income (*II*):

$$R = \frac{AE + LL + CF + K - II}{1 - LL}$$

MFI managers have control over (most) elements of the formula.
The CGAP paper offers an explanation of the key parameters:

- Administrative Expense Rate – MFIs tend to capture most of their economies of scale by the time they reach about 5,000–10,000 clients;
- Loan Loss Rate – This element is the annual loss due to uncollectible loans. The loan loss rate may be considerably lower than the MFI's delinquency rate: the former reflects loans that must actually be written off, while the latter reflects loans that are not paid on time – many of which will eventually be recovered. The institution's past experience will be a major factor in projecting future loan loss rates;
- Cost of Funds Rate – The here computed figure is not the MFI's *actual* cash cost of funds. Rather, it is a projection of the future ›market‹ cost of funds as the MFI grows past dependence on subsidized donor finance, drawing ever-increasing portions of its funding from commercial sources;
- Capitalization Rate – This rate represents the net *real* profit–over and above what is required to compensate for inflation–that the MFI decides to target, expressed as a percentage of average loan portfolio (not of equity or of total assets);
- Investment Income Rate – The final element to be included in the pricing equation–as a deduction, in this case–is the income expected from the MFI's financial assets other than the loan portfolio. Some of these (e.g., cash, checking deposits, legal reserves) will yield little or no interest, while others (e.g., certificates of deposit) may produce significant income.

[623] CGAP (2002).

CHAPTER 22 – Philanthropic versus greedy returns: mission drift towards socially irresponsible investments?

> To give away money is an easy matter and in any man's power. But to decide to whom to give it and how large and when, and for what purpose and how, is neither in every man power nor an easy matter.
>
> Aristotle

The seductive smell of money

Money is a conventional unit of measure, account, and trade that delivers from primitive barter economy, which was highly inefficient in its function of storing, promoting, and circulating wealth.
With its seductive smell, money symbolizes possession, while its accumulation measures material wealth. The perception of the value of money greatly changes across different cultures and places, even if greed is an instinctive feature of human nature and money is its tangible icon. Accordingly, Benjamin Franklin recalls that »money never made a man happy yet, nor will it. The more a man has, the more he wants. Instead of filling a vacuum, it makes one«. Since money is measurable and storable, it is primarily concerned with the obsession of quantitatively measure life, in order to objectively assess its alleged value.
Money corrupts ideals and it tempts microfinance players, up to the point of surrender to mission drift – there is a hardly resistible attempt to earn more money abandoning poor clients in favor of wealthier ones, increasing scalability through a paradigm shift that forgets comprehensive development, even through a change of the stakeholders' mix …
According to the encyclical letter Caritas in Veritate (§40):

> What should be avoided is a speculative *use of financial resources* that yields to the temptation of seeking only short-term profit, without regard for the long-term sustainability of the enterprise, its benefit to the real economy and attention to the advancement, in suitable and appropriate ways, of further economic initiatives in countries in need of development.

Responsible MFIs that are able to blend reason with sentiments are well aware that growing commercialism and mission drift have a direct impact on the most vulnerable clients' bracket, with the result of forgetting women.
The delicate equilibrium between outreach and sustainability, described in Chapter 21, is strongly influenced by potential mission drift: greed should favor sustainability but excessive outreach may undermine survival chances.
Sustainability can be reached and optimized increasing both economic margins–maximizing the differential between returns and costs–and financial net inflows. Unitary higher margins are a consequence of minor unitary costs and/or bigger unitary revenues, which can be obtained scaling up loans–extending their average amount, to the detriment of smaller and poorer clients–and decreasing operating costs with technological devices and efficiency gains. Whenever the portfolio risk composition is reduced, in order to increase sustainability, the less better off are typically selected out. The concerning question is how microfinance institutions adhere to the social mission of reaching the poor while scaling up, reminding that increased profitability tends to worsen outreach. Mohamad Yunus remembers that less poor clients crowd-out poorer clients in any credit scheme – without subsidies, hopefully temporary, there is simply no match.
According to Pim Engels[624]:

> Within the micro-finance sector, tension between the financial sustainability and social performance advocates is rising. Rapidly commercializing MFIs, subject to increased competition, show signs of mission drift, whereby the average loan size of an institution increases as a result of a shift in the composition of their new clients. The commercial consideration is that thriving micro entrepreneurs are more profitable: they use larger loans and need less cash, and pay off their debts in shorter time. Reaching out to wealthier clients, while crowding out poorer clients, enhances profitability. The more profitable a MFI is, the less poor micro-entrepreneurs that MFI reaches: supporting poor micro-finance clients is intensive and expensive.

Alternative Financial Institutions have a ›double bottom line‹: in addition to their financial objective, they also have a developmental or social objective. Both financial and social performance matter and need each other: on the one side, without financial sustainability, MFIs dry up their resources and eventually die, unless being kept artificially alive by donors, whereas on the other side if social issues are abandoned, MFIs lose their soul and simply become something else. Tailored social metrics matters in the achievement of non financial targets, in order to fit the

[624] http://www.pensiondevelopment.org/350/mission-drift-micro-finance.htm; http://www.pensiondevelopment.org/documenten/Mission%20Drift%20in%20Microfinance%20%20Pim%20Engels.pdf.

characteristics of each MFI, properly measuring efficiency and efficacy of intervention.
All types of Alternative Financial Institutions, including MFIs, share certain common characteristics. They are generally aimed at lower-income clients and they are not profit-maximizers[625]. Sooner or later, microfinance should be addressed to provide capital for investments in activities where competitive advantage is concentrated, but this does not have to take place to the detriment of the poor.

The temptation to abandon social objectives

Even though MFIs have founding ideals and a strategic mission, their social objectives, put under stress by environmental challenges, may easily shift towards commercial seductions. MFIs so risk betraying the ›double bottom line‹ paradigm where (hybrid) financial and social returns try to peacefully cohabit. Profits are seen as means to an end–outreach-oriented sustainability–establishing a bridge between business and society and integrating corporate social responsibility within the core business strategy.
The temptation to abandon social targets, in order to divert funds or resources to other more lucrative objectives, is always a threat for the poor, used to be neglected.
Disillusion about capitalism and its meager results (especially after the great recession of 2008-2009) may slow down this temptation, even if greed is intrinsically ingrained with human nature, being not emphatic and careless of the needs of the others, especially if economically uninteresting.
According to Hishigsuren[626], the specific strategies that enable MFIs to maintain their mission are:

1. likeminded board;
2. loyal staff and management;
3. participation of members (clients);
4. keeping the platform for development;
5. member responsive assessment and monitoring system.

The key to avoid mission drift temptations is represented by a synergic effort of all the stakeholders to keep alive the MFI's founding principles, adapting them to current threats and changes, but not up to the point of surreptitiously modifying the MFI's core constituencies.

625 See http://www.cgap.org/gm/document-1.9.2701/OP8.pdf.
626 http://www.snhu.edu/files/pdfs/Hishigsuren.pdf.

Efforts to reach significant scale by securing financial sustainability may lead to a tendency to provide larger loans to less poor clients and to employ stricter loan screening procedures. The result can be a reduced attention to the so-called riskier and poorer clients.
Mission drift occurs when the MFI leaves its poor customer segment: it tends to increase when the MFI seeks higher profitability and its average costs become higher. Customer centricity may be replaced by product–and growth–centricity and MFIs may be tempted to drift away from their poor customers.
Mission drift is also a surreptitious answer to inefficiency. Bad managers who are unable to serve the poor may be strongly tempted to hide their mismanagement by increasing the MFI's investment profile, abandoning the poor in order to look for extra returns elsewhere, in marginally richer segments. If the MFI becomes more efficient, it is able to uphold lending to the poorest customers, fostering outreach in a sustainable way.
More focus should be placed upon cost aspects of MFIs and higher cost efficiency should be attainable as the MFI gains experience and fine-tunes its business model. It is a titanic effort, both theoretically and practically, to balance microfinance's social and commercial mission, with a consequent trade off between social and financial performance. Since commercial microfinance is increasing scale and scope, its trendy tide should be cared with concern, especially if its last mission–to reduce poverty, fostering the development with a human face–is replaced by other less inspiring targets.
Mission drift–a social danger–is a hotly debated issue: are MFIs losing sight of their social goals, changing their job and forgetting about unworthy poor clients? Is social lending going to be replaced by commercial lending? Are rural poor going to be discriminated in favor of more promising urban realities? These are key questions and even if in the 2009 ranking of microfinance banana skins[627], mission drift has gone down–as a consequence of other more contingent priorities, induced by worldwide recession–this ›philosophical‹ question about the industry, about its mission, and about identity stands out as a prominent one that is not to be underestimated or taken for granted.
A new paradigm of financial inclusion needs to be shaped, in order to refocus outreach, trying to consider also the underserved poorest and helping MFIs to concentrate on their poverty-reduction mission.
According to Armendariz and Szafarz (2009), mission drift for MFIs is an increasingly common tendency to extend larger average loan sizes in the process of scaling-up. This phenomenon is not driven by transaction cost minimization alone. Instead, poverty-oriented MFIs could potentially deviate from their mission by extending larger loan sizes because of the interplay between their own mission, the

[627] See Chapter 23.

cost differentials between poor and unbanked wealthier clients, and heterogeneity of their clientele.
To the extent that neoliberal approaches to developmental issues discourage subsidies, fiscal austerity, and commercialization strategies may force MFIs out of their ideal social pattern.

Moving towards a segmented, wider, and more sophisticated microfinance market

In developed countries, the financial market is increasingly sophisticated and diversified, while in poorer nations the supply is much simpler, leaving little choice to the potential consumers. But this was the case even in richer countries, where market sophistication is a rather recent and growing phenomenon.
The segmentation among the poorest, the poor, and the not-so-poor may create discriminatory differences: each of these categories requires specific financial intermediaries, and it uneasy to fill the differences, risking leaving behind the uninteresting poorest.
The market naturally increases and it differentiates its offer if there is a pushing demand behind it. It may seem a futuristic scenario in many poor countries, but a static photography of the current situation should not forget to take into consideration that things are changing–quickly–and stereotypes soon become out of fashion. People, even and mostly the poor, change, upgrade and simply desire better services, increasing–and above all improving–the offer.
If we retrospectively look back at the (young) history of microfinance, we soon realize how it has branched out in terms of services rendered, expanding its perimeter and significantly improving its breadth, depth, and outreach – not an easy or foregone task in a difficult underdeveloped environment.
The landscape of microfinance is dramatically changing – not always for the better, since greed and mission drifts are more than a simple temptation, especially if the business and the market are perceived as potentially attractive and lucrative.
MFIs are increasingly segmented between top Tier institutions, which are more and more attractive for international capital markets, and lower ranking–or unranked–entities, which are mostly backed by foreign NGOs and daily struggling for bare survival, in a Darwinian selective scenario.
Indistinct poor borrowers are now increasingly separated in two or more diverging classes, either referring to NGO-backed MFIs, if they are extremely poor, or alternatively being approached by larger institutions, increasingly similar to standard commercial banks.
The selection is caused by several and often casual interactions, ranging from the demand and supply uneven balancing, to environmental factors, and contingent happenings. The outcome is hardly predictable and a growing confusing market is

intrinsically volatile, but the effects of this variability on the poorest are–as depicted in Chapter 17–hardly benign, since they fly with no parachute and they are desperately looking to smooth their uneven incomes, on a daily basis. Even small changes or problems that elsewhere would be considered trivial, for most of the poorest are simply unaffordable.

Funding sources and lending structures: should finance for the poor be subsidized?

Empirical evidence shows that provision of financial services to the very poor requires subsidy (soft financing, consisting of subsidized loans) at least for the start up of simple and often informal banking activities, which can progressively become regulated MFIs, following a virtuous evolutionary path. Subsides might well include grants for capacity building, audit, staff recruiting, office building, ICT investments, etc., as well as the financing of the transaction from NGOs to licensed banks. This was the case even for the well known Grameen Bank paradigm, which is still subsidized[628], in order to charge soft interest rates.

Subsidizing is an unavoidable but dangerous start up mechanism[629], not only because it can spoil and humiliate the poor, but also since it may damage and distort the regular and market-oriented workings of the microfinance industry for the not-so-poor, with side effects (corruption, circumventive and opportunistic behavior generating well known problems such as rent-seeking or round-tripping, lack of transparency, and meritocracy …) that eventually damage also the real poor.

Even subsidized equity has an implicit (shadow) cost, since the shareholders acting as sponsors have to collect the money they put in the MFI, bearing effective market costs and taking care of the loss for the missed potential return in alternative profitable investments. The opinion that capital in sponsored MFIs is free of charge is so wrong and deceiving. And transformation to profitable institutions is consequently less expensive that it might seem, provided that it is properly measured by the real difference between sponsored and profit-oriented cost of equity capital[630].

Like for any young corporation, mortality rate for new MFIs is high. A particular feature of sponsored entities is the impossibility of their survival without grants, especially in the first years. Mismanagement and improper use of funds are however very common, particularly if sponsors are far away from a country they superficially know and check, and these disappointing problems tend to have a cata-

---

628 In the mid-1990s, the bank started to get most of its funding from the central bank of Bangladesh. More recently, Grameen has started bond sales as a source of finance. The bonds are implicitly subsidized as they are guaranteed by the Government of Bangladesh and still they are sold above the bank rate.

629 The subsidy trap is a well known and documented danger. See for instance Morduch (2000).

630 See Chapter 23.

strophic impact on donors that feel cheated and betrayed and often react stopping further subsides, so condemning the institution to an inglorious death.
The link and the interactions with people who belong to different social classes have a great impact in depicting socio-economic conditions. This is true even following the ›trickle down theory‹, which describes economic policies perceived to benefit the wealthy and then ›trickle down‹ to the middle and lower classes[631]. As a consequence, even if microfinance is at first targeting the not-so-poor, there can be positive marginal side effects even for the poorest, who can eventually benefit from a general bettering of economic conditions, which creates new jobs and entrepreneurs.
Credit is not however the only or the main financial service that is needed by poor[632]. Subsidies might be better spent on savings and payment systems, creating a sound financial environment where savings can represent a parachute even for borrowers and an internal funding source for local banking intermediaries. It may so be followed–albeit on a simpler and reduced scale–the simple mechanism of a standard bank that collects money from depositors and intermediates it with selective lending.
Since local financial markets are underdeveloped and poorly regulated, it may occur that the funding source and the lending structure are unbalanced[633] (above all for small MFIs which find it difficult to collect money at home) and so then the whole system appears weak and exposed to currency risk and asymmetric shocks. An example can be a local crisis (that is highly frequent in places where country risk is substantial and unpredictable), which might seriously damage the collection of funds from abroad, suddenly interrupting the source of finance.
International markets have an elephant memory: it takes a long time to build up a respectable reputation, while few weeks are enough to destroy it for ages.
The relationship between donors (from individuals to organized NGOs) and the poor is very complex[634], not only due to evident capital rationing problems–since resources typically fall short of the poor's endless needs–but also to motivational and psychological issues, somewhat harder to measure and detect but probably even more important.
The heart of donors sometimes goes beyond their pockets and a rational analysis of the situation often shows negative consequences that can overwhelm even the best intentions, damaging the poor and creating ephemeral dependence. Some smart donors are thinking to use subsidies sparingly and only in the start up phase, when institutions are too young to be able to walk with their own legs.

---

631 See Basu, Mallick (2008).

632 See World Bank (2008), p. 17.

633 Mismatch may concern even the assets and liability structure, to the extent that some debts are denominated in foreign (hard) currencies, whereas assets, equity and other liabilities are all denominated in domestic currency. See Chapter 21.

634 As it has been shown in Chapter 14.

Easy money and spoiling rents

Everybody knows–especially in richer countries–that children and teenagers cannot properly survive and develop without family ›subsidies‹ (education, keeping, incentives …), which however in the long run can severely spoil and affect them, with everlasting consequences on their adult life. And hardly anybody can afford to be rich and stupid for more than a generation, this being a lesson that Western countries are painfully beginning to discover. Bad Western habits are not really welcome to be exported to poorer countries, as it unfortunately frequently happens. In addition, free and easy money humiliates the poor, transforming them in permanent beggars, with no rescue possibilities. The psychological effect is frequently underestimated by distracted and superficial donors and it is amplified by the natural shame of the poor, who often don't care to ask and they feel attracted but also humiliated by Western living standards. There is no motivation without hope. And free money to the poorest–not used to it–is a particularly dangerous drug, which makes them addicted, keeping them artificially far from their real world.

Even if it is difficult to find a monolithic and inflexible solution to a wide range of problems, a general consideration, inspired to common sense, might prove useful. Starting a self fulfilling system–of a MFI or something else–is often harder than providing immediate subsidy and it proves more time consuming, with no or few short term results that are so important for the psychology of impatient and unwise donors.

The real key issues of mental and cultural changes are education to development, responsiveness and accountability, rational use and sharing of resources. They need time–often measured in generations–and much more effort to grow with solid roots.

Once a donor begins to understand that he/she is receiving more that what he/she gives and the poor understands that he/she can be useful even to the donor, the quality of the relationship consistently strengthens and the results are astonishingly better and longer lasting.

Donors can act as private sponsors and they might be willing to accept a reduction in their expected returns in change of the satisfaction stemming from the financing of projects with high social value, where the poor borrowers are actively involved, with positive psychological and motivational side effects (acquisition of self-confidence, dignity that prevents the poor to be ashamed of their condition, possibility to rescue from the misery trap …).

In microfinance sustainability is permanence[635] and unsustainable MFIs tend to inflict far greater costs on the poor in the future than the gains they may enjoy in the present. MFIs' sustainability is driven by a combination of factors such as a high

[635] Khawari (2004).

quality credit portfolio, coupled by the application of sufficiently high rates of interest–allowing for a reasonable profit–and sound management[636].

Financial sustainability is effective for outreach because permanency leads to a structure of incentives and constraints that, if carefully dealt with, stimulates all the stakeholders (sponsors, MFIs, borrowers and their families …) to increase the difference between social benefit and social cost[637] and to align their interests, so reducing information asymmetries and governance problems.

Unsustainable MFIs might be particularly dangerous–especially if they collect deposits and interbank loans–since they are part of banking and financial institutions that is a very delicate sector where insolvencies propagate rapidly and they can easily undermine even sound institutions.

Subsidized institutions might not harm market-driven intermediaries only if the financial market is well segmented and the former serve extremely poor clients, who in any case would not have access to formal credit. When subsidized funds are available to micro-borrowers on a large scale, they might however practice a dumping policy which discourages unsubsidized institutions, creating entry barriers[638].

Another key issue is the weakness of banking regulation systems in underdeveloped countries, with macro and systematic consequences on the overall day-to-day working and sustainability of MFIs, which really need to reach a sufficient critical mass, this being an easier task within a favorable environment. Even the relationship with financial and banking institutions of donor countries is greatly–positively or negatively–affected by the overall quality of the domestic financial and credit market. Transparency and accountability, good and effective regulation, and compliance to international standards are increasingly important in a global economy, and these golden rules apply also to the poorest, being–if missing–a major factor of marginalization.

Donations from Western countries are pro-cyclical and they might sharply diminish in recession periods, when they are most wanted (since recessions are increasingly global). From this undesired effect we might understand even more the importance of a properly rooted self-sustainability, which is really the best parachute during hard times that in underdeveloped areas tend to be more frequent–if not permanent–and worse, due to local problems such as drought, famine, ethnic clashes, wars, or epidemic illnesses.

Cross subsidies occur when the MFI is able to segment its clientele, discriminating between those who can afford to pay market rates and those who can't. Subsidizing can prove effective, even if it might have some potential drawbacks: the MFI

636 Ayayi, Sene (2008).

637 Navajas, Schreiner, Meyer, Gonzales-Vega, Rodriguez Meza (2002).

638 See World Bank (2004).

should be able to keep a safe and sustainable equilibrium, otherwise the game might once again be not long lasting.
When competition[639] between MFIs eliminates rents on profitable borrowers, it is likely to yield a new equilibrium in which poor borrowers are worse off. With a greater number of lenders who compete in the same (not segmented) market, ›impatient‹ borrowers have an incentive to take multiple loans, that are not always detected by a centralized interbank computerized system (with a track record of exposures, repayments, and delinquencies), since it still doesn't exist in many developing countries. Screening can become more expensive, together with the growing unwillingness of competing MFIs to cooperate and share information.
The passage from unregulated NGOs to public deposit collecting institutions subject to banking regulation, might originate hybrid institutions, where–on the one side–subsidized funding coexists with market collection of capital (public deposits, interbank loans, issues of bonds, or Certificates of Deposit …) and–on the other side–subsidized lending to the very poor can cohabit with market priced loans to those who can afford.
To be or not to be a regulated entity is an Hamletic doubt that has to carefully consider pros and cons. Regulation is expensive and it requires rigorous liquidity, capital adequacy, and reporting standards, bearing extra operating costs that might not always be fully recovered with efficiency gains and lower cost of collected capital. This holds true especially for small MFIs in contexts where savings pool is small and caps on lending rates are set by the local Central bank.
Cross subsidizes might play a role in such a situation, and it requires constant monitoring, due to its delicate and intrinsically unstable mixture of non-profit and for-profit objectives. It is important to take in careful consideration also collusive behavior of borrowers who might get advantage of this somewhat ambiguous subdivision (trying to jump on the cheapest side …) and corruption within the lending staff.
Transition to regulated bank might prove challenging and expensive in the short run[640], requiring additional capital, technical requirements, compliance adequacy, and professional staff. NGOs typically accompany the growth and the transformation of the MFI to a regulated bank, providing the necessary capital and skills.
Regulated institutions can raise funds at lower rates, so reducing their capital cost, with positive side effects on lending costs. Deposits are generally the cheapest and most stable source of financing for MFIs with banking licenses[641] and access to capital markets can further reduce financing costs, prolonging the maturity of debt and strengthening the financial structure of MFIs.

639 McIntosh, Wydick (2005).
640 See Bogan (2008).
641 See Krauss, Walter (2008).

Gains in efficiency and cost cutting, if achievable, might conveniently be transmitted to clients (who might otherwise address themselves elsewhere), reducing interest rates and being able to readdress subsides, if they are still existent, to particular targets, segmenting the clientele (the poorest from the relatively wealthier …) or the products (e.g., business loans might be charged market interest rates, while school fees loans could be subsidized).

The soft and patient (foreign) capital of NGOs

Igniting development from scratch is a daunting task and in poor countries internal resources are missing by definition. Foreign NGOs can fill the gap with their patient capital and social commitment. Focusing on social returns, sponsor driven NGOs need to guarantee either sustainable funding from abroad, or they sooner or later have to pursue financial sustainability in the host countries. The last target seems reasonable and appealing, while problems come up when the NGOs' managers start to perceive that sustainability is a complex task, which in many states of the world may be accomplished only sacrificing at least part of the social objectives, starting from outreach.

As NGOs are generally managed by foreigners, they are typically neutral from a political point of view and consequently they can be an important and effective approach to democracy. But sometimes NGOs can receive economic support from governmental donors and this causes politicization of the organization which, consequently, will lose its political and social impartiality – as it happened in Afghanistan, some NGOs became terrorist aims after the government got involved in their works.

To the extent that the local population is (meant to be) involved in the projects, there is more transparency in the use of money, as the donors can easily see what their capital has been used for. There is however an ›elite capture‹ risk, since in some cases NGOs are controlled by rich locals who use them to get money from the aid system.

Even if in some cases NGOs manage to develop self sufficiency and, at this point, they no longer need economic or professional support from abroad (since they are successfully managed by local people), in most times there is a continuous need to ask for further money and resources, and the locals aren't able to manage the project self-sufficiently.

A practical aspect of external subsidizing is that capital–in the form of equity or debt–comes from abroad and it is so denominated in a foreign currency, so creating opportunities but also problems. Indeed, the capital cost may be consistently lower in richer countries with sound sponsors and liquidity constraints. Other impediments are more easily solved, whereas foreign exchange risk seriously to threaten the NGO-driven MFI, either if it is born by foreign donors or even, as a

double edged sword, if it be endured by local beneficiaries. Chapter 23, which is devoted to microfinance banana skins, deals both with foreign exchange risk and with its impact in shaping the cost of collected (debt or equity) capital.
To the extent that foreign risk is born by external sponsors, it may prevent them from refinancing the MFI, especially if the local currency sharply devaluates, evidencing a loss of competitiveness that may dangerously be added to decreasing foreign aid. Should currency risk be born by local stakeholders–e.g., if the MFI collects debt denominated in hard foreign currency–then the risk would be formally domestic, even if the inability to repay debt and interests may endanger even foreign creditors.
According to CGAP[642]:

> Foreign investment brings important benefits for microfinance institutions (MFIs). It can provide longer term debt maturity and risk capital that often is not available in the local market, but it can come with a significant string attached: foreign exchange risk. Seventy percent of cross-border, fixed-income investments are denominated in foreign currencies (meaning currencies other than the currencies in which the MFIs are operating), leaving MFIs with significant foreign exchange exposure. During the most recent global financial crisis, some MFIs that depend on foreign currency-denominated debt have suffered heavy foreign exchange losses that threaten their overall viability.

Heavier reliance on domestic funds, starting from local deposits, reduces foreign exchange risk but it stands out as a viable option only when MFIs are big and sound enough to collect deposits and to diversify their funding sources–but this is not a likely condition for small and still fragile NGOs.

Lords of microfinance: Microfinance Investment Vehicles, ranging from philanthropy to bare profit maximization

Microfinance landscape is rapidly changing and portfolio growth, product diversification, and institutional transformation are increasing its complexity. To manage this change effectively, MFIs must adapt their governance structures.
Professional foreign donors typically intervene through *ad hoc* investment vehicles, which help to concentrate and convey foreign funds, intermediated through professional investors.
The size of the demand for finance in underdeveloped countries is so big that even microfinance, despite its astonishing merits, is far from getting to optimal outreach and probably only the commercial mainstream will be able to meet it[643].

---

642 CGAP (2010a).
643 Brugger (2004).

Commercial viability (financial sustainability) of MFIs is a precondition in order to attract not-for-philanthropy investors. They can choose to incorporate from scratch their own MFI (following a pattern similar to most NGOs), while a typical, quicker, and safer solution is to invest in different and already viable MFIs, through a specific investment vehicle.
Microfinance Investment Vehicles (MIVs) are special purpose vehicles raising funds[644] from commercial, private, institutional, or even social investors (endowment or pension funds[645], foundations ...). They are run by professional managers in order to invest them in microfinance assets, creating an otherwise unthinkable bridge between international capital markets and financial entities located in underdeveloped countries. MIVs represent a privileged instrument for international commercial bank investments in the microfinance business.
According to CGAP (2008d), MIVs might be classified in six categories:

1. *registered mutual funds*, mainly concerned with fixed income investments in MFIs;
2. *commercial fixed-income investment funds*, providing senior debt to high-growth MFIs;
3. *structured finance vehicles,* which pool and repackage loans towards MFIs (mainly Collateralized Debt Obligations), placing them as marketable securities;
4. *blended-value fixed-income and equity funds*, the most heavily mission driven MIVs, offering a mix of social and financial returns;
5. *holding companies of microfinance banks*, established by leading microfinance consulting companies and Development Finance Institutions (DFIs) in order to provide subsidized start up equity finance;
6. *equity funds,* represented by private equity and venture capital firms, offering a blend of equity and convertible debt to high-growth MFIs in emerging markets.

---

644 The funds are classified into three major categories based on a study by the MicroBanking Bulletin (The MicroBanking Bulletin, *Special Edition on Financing, the Scope of Funding Mechanisms*, issue no. 11, August 2005, Bulletin Highlights - Supply of Funding, Isabelle Barres, page 47.). Those three categories include i. Commercial Funds; ii. Commercially-Oriented Funds; and iii. Non-commercial Funds. A commercial fund is defined as one that »seeks financial return«, while a commercial-oriented fund is one that »eventually seeks financial return«, and finally, a non-commercial fund »does not seek financial return«. In addition, funds in the third category are then divided further into three sub-categories, which are development fund, development agency, and foundation/NGO.

645 Pension funds are long term investors which aim to guarantee to their beneficiaries a rent, so looking for safe investments. Philanthropy might so be present to a very limited extent and bond investments with market returns, free of local currency risk, are typically the right product, if consistent with the fund's investment criteria.

Investment funds might also soften–with appropriate guarantees–MFIs' access to domestic capital, free of currency risk[646], easing linkages with local commercial banks or deposit mobilization from clients. Provision of equity and subsequent capital adequacy are required for safe leveraging. In equity investments, local currency risk is born by (foreign) shareholders, while in bond underwriting the risk is typically assumed by local MFIs. The fact that local currencies are typically non-convertible in a higher inflation environment[647] does not help, since hedging becomes more difficult (especially if the currency is not pegged to the US$ or other strong currencies) and international coordination of monetary policies is harder and less effective.

Other complementary investment options for MIVs are underwriting of bonds issued by MFIs and securitization of the existing portfolios of MFIs, while funds of funds can create further portfolio diversification for investors, albeit with increasing transaction costs.

Apart from money, MIVs can also provide highly wanted expertise, easing the adoption of new technologies and outreaching / cost cutting innovations (such as Automated Telling Machines, computerized credit scoring systems ...)[648], together with helping to face industry typical risks, such as credit risk, country/political risk, currency risk, operational risk, reputational, and liquidity risks.

Most MIVs are debt vehicles but it is only when they provide highly wanted equity that they can strengthen the MFI's financial structure, and then they can also actively participate to its governance, being enabled to appoint directors that represent the fund.

A minimum break-even size is essential for the fund's profitability[649] and it is also critical for attracting underwriters[650], easing the development of upward share distribution–to investors–as well as downward investment distribution to the selected MFIs.

Effective reporting, considering economic and social returns, and using standard key performance ratios is essential, although difficult, for adequate compliance and transparency towards investors, which might otherwise mistrust this unconventional form of investment, addressing their savings elsewhere.

646 Most foreign debt for MFIs is denominated in hard currencies (mainly the US$), so creating a currency risk (due to the imbalance between foreign currency liabilities and domestic currency assets) against which hedging proves difficult and expensive.

647 Inflation and exchange rates are linked by the purchasing power parity theory, which uses the long-term equilibrium exchange rate of two currencies to equalize their purchasing power. Developed by Gustav Cassel in 1920, it is based on the law of one price: the theory states that, in an ideally efficient market, identical goods should have only one price and consequently price changes (inflation) and currency rates are linked.

648 See Brugger (2004).

649 Goodman (2004).

650 Pouliot (2004).

›Double-bottom line‹ institutions such as MFIs attract Socially Responsible Investments and a key move towards sustainable outreach–the optimal goal of microfinance–is balancing social and financial returns.
A key question is concerned with the nature of the ultimate shareholders behind any MIV. Actually, thy can be very diversified, ranging from single households–from small retail investors, up to high net worth individuals–to institutional investors of various nature and dimension, even big sovereign funds of emerging countries with huge trading surpluses, having at their disposal enormous cumulated foreign reserves and already acting as the world's bankers.
The bottleneck is represented by the fact that few MFIs are listed or belong to the Tier 1 capital adequacy bracket, whereas the vast majority is represented by a myriad of small and illiquid institutions, which are continuously struggling for survival. Only dedicated funds, with venture capital attitude, can approach this market, whose big potentialities are counterbalanced by a high level of risk.
Equity valuation of MFIs is a key target for MIVs, whose net asset value depends on the underlying assets performance.
According to CGAP »investors should not value MFIs the same way they value traditional banks. We highlight five characteristics that differentiate MFIs from traditional banks, and justify a slightly different valuation approach: a double bottom line that aims for both social and financial returns, excellent asset quality, high net interest margins, high operating costs, and longer term funding available from developmental investors«[651].

The rich need the poor, learning from the Selfish Giant

According to Walter Bagehot »poverty is an anomaly to rich people. It is very difficult to make out why people who want dinner do not ring the bell«. And also, following John Berger »the poverty of our Century is unlike that of any other. It is not, as poverty was before, the result of natural scarcity, but of a set of priorities imposed upon the rest of the world by the rich. Consequently, the modern poor are not pitied but written off as trash. The 20th Century consumer economy has produced the first culture for which a beggar is a reminder of nothing«.
Richness and affluence are more than a state of mind and they materially indicate abundant wealth accumulation that is a vanity gallery well beyond any reasonable sustenance threshold, which characterizes a significant–but in percentage tiny–number of people, representing a–happy?–minority of the world's population. Poverty and wealth live no more in segregated and exclusive planets, which look like Berlin after the collapse of its infamous wall.
On the one side, the privileged rich, who are imprisoned in their spiritual desert, tend to have an arrogant and illusory sense of superiority, leading to unjustified

651 CGAP (2009c).

pride and ignorant prejudice. The rich throw their insecurity to the poor, fearing to become like them and cowardly discharging their problems on the weakest. For the rich, poverty is concerned with the lost memory of their (poor) ancestors, forgetting the biblical admonishment of Qoheleth[652]: »Vanity of vanities, all is vanity«. Self interest is the very fabric of human nature, whereas unshared wealth over a confident level of subsistence hardly gives any sense to life.

On the other side, poverty is a much more diffused situation concerned with deprivation, deviance, destitution, discrimination, poor health, and hunger, up to the extreme limit of irreversible starvation. When the winner takes it all, the pie is even more unfairly distributed.

The rich and the poor represent two polar extremes and so they fatally touch themselves with continuous contacts, which are often unwanted by the rich, who are afraid of losing their privileges and forget that all ends up into nothing. The underserved are materially magnetized by wealth and unconsciously irrationally driven by their costless dreams.

In the ›*Economic Possibilities for our Grandchildren*‹, 1930[653], John Maynard Keynes reminded that »the love of money as a possession–as distinguished from the love of money as a means to the enjoyments and realities of life–will be recognized for what it is, a somewhat disgusting morbidity, one of those semi criminal, semi-pathological propensities which one hands over with a shudder to the specialists in mental disease«.

Many poor are improperly dressed, they may also stink and bother, embarrassing and sometimes threatening the happy few. But going a little beyond these differences, we progressively start to discover that not only the poor need the rich–this being a materially evident statement, driven by survival necessities–but also the rich may need the poor much more than they may superficially think, even if their are not particularly goodhearted.

Is it the case that all the rich–even the selfish and greedy ones–need the poor?

The ›*Selfish Giant*‹[654], a masterpiece tale of Oscar Wilde, tells the sad and paradigmatic story of an egoistic giant, who was motivated only by self interest and flagrant avarice, living alone in his garden, prisoner of an endless winter that prevented any flowering, freezing also his lonely heart. When, by chance, a poor little boy entered the garden–previously forbidden to the children–and flowers started blossoming, the Giant discovered that real happiness could be reached only sharing and from that time on children were welcome in his property and there was no more winter in his heart.

The epic tale ›*The Buddenbrooks*‹, a masterpiece of the German Nobel price novelist Thomas Mann, published in 1901, was based on the sad experience of the au-

---

652 Ecclesiastes 1:2.

653 http://www.eco.utexas.edu/facstaff/Cleaver/368keynesgrandchildren.html.

654 Freely downloadable from http://classiclit.about.com/library/bl-etexts/owilde/bl-owilde-selgi.htm.

thor's own family: it has transmitted us a superb fresco of the progressive and almost ineluctable decline of a merchant family in Lübeck, over the course of three generations – somberly remembering that nobody can afford to be rich and lazy for more than a few generations … As Louis-Ferdinand Celine says »the honest poor can sometimes forget poverty. The honest rich can never forget it«.
Like it or not, as a consequence of globalization and other related issues, the poor and the rich have much more in common than they used to. So sharing is becoming, more than an altruistic choice, a cohabiting necessity, well beyond one's subjective will.
Practical implementation of these principles may well include microfinance interventions, where richer investors pool some of their resources with the poor, combining strategies and efforts for shared and mutually convenient sustainable outcomes.

The condensed Chapter

Serving poor clients is a good hearted strategy, albeit not enabling to make money, since economies of scale are uneasy to get and bare survival seems the most ambitious target, making microfinance institutions sustainable.
The greedy temptation to shift to richer clients, with higher margins, forgetting social targets, is always present and it proves difficult to resist to.
Patient capital is gratefully acknowledged, as through foreign investors, often conveyed into Microfinance Investment Vehicles, even if it may create parasitism and addiction to external help, whereas local stakeholders have sooner or later to learn to rely mainly on domestic sources.

Out of Poverty Tips

Microfinance can attract not only the poor, but even financial investors, looking for acceptable returns with low volatility and ethical background.
Win win strategies should be coordinated through common targets, aligning the interests of the different stakeholders pivoting around MFIs.

Selected Readings

ARMENDARIZ DE AGHION B., SZAFARZ A., (2009), *On Mission Drift in Microfinance Institutions*, http://ideas.repec.org/p/sol/wpaper/09–015.html, Université libre de Bruxelles, Working paper CEB 09.015.RS.

CHAPTER 23 – Beware of banana skins, detecting and softening microfinance risk

> The policy of being too cautious is the greatest risk of all.
>
> Jawaharlal Nehru

A risky stakeholdership

Microfinance is a risky activity for all the stakeholders that pivot around an institution (the MFI shareholders and bondholders; employees, borrowers, depositors, the Central Bank …) and an analysis of the main elements of uncertainty is useful both for their detection and their mitigation–you may indeed avoid just what you really know. Life with no risk is however similar to a soup with no salt–according to Jeanette Winterson, what you risk reveals what you value and vicissitudes can be lived as a turmoil or as an opportunity.
The optimistic statement of Brad Swanson, according to which »when properly conducted, microfinance is a profitable, low-risk, and expanding financial activity«[655] can be shareable only beyond a certain threshold that is uneasy to be reached, where the MFI is sufficiently sound and organized to become sustainable. Risk has an asymmetric impact on the different stakeholders:

- shareholders, being residual claimants, accept to put completely at risk their capital, whose value has unlimited upside potential even if it is the last claim to be paid back, and only to the extent that some funds are still available. Shareholders, if foreigners, are also exposed to currency risk. The patient capital money is limited and unwillingness to refinance a MFI after its equity burn out seriously threatens its survival. The exchange rate is not only a synthetic measure of the local currency's purchasing power against other countries, but it is also a numerical symbol of soft values, such as country's international reputation and a comparative barometer of its standing;
- debtholders are fixed claimants, who are entitled to receive back their credit and periodic interests before the shareholders but typically after other creditors such as workers. If the loan to the MFIs is denominated in a foreign hard currency, it is the MFI which is exposed to foreign exchange risk, while if the investor has invested in the local currency of the MFI the risk–potentially mitigated by appropriate coverage–belongs

[655] In Sundaresan (2009), p. 25.

to the investor. To the extent that the risk is born by the MFI, it can affect even the same debtholders, if the institution burns the money kept for their repayment, and in most cases it has a major impact on residual equityholders[656];

- employees may not receive regular payroll from an ailing MFI and their risk exposure is likely to increase if they have also invested in the institution (being depositors, bondholders, or equityholders ...), without a safer diversification strategy;

- depositors may have their funds at risk, if the MFI is unable to pay them back–triggering a run-to-deposits panic strategy–and if the local Central Bank does not properly intervene as a lender of last resort. Partial insurance of the deposited money is frequent, as a percentage of the total or up to fixed amounts, and it should cover most of the lent funds, especially if their nominal amount is small and fragmented;

- borrowers do not risk their own money, since they are in the condition to pay back what they owe to the MFI, but it may be asked to return the funds with little or any notice–depending on their contractual agreements–with potentially destabilizing effects. They also may lack a future source of funding, being forced to choose an alternative that is hardly viable if the crisis is systemic;

- the government is formally an external stakeholder, interested in the tax revenue that it may get from the MFI–and in this sense, it is a privileged creditor–but in reality it is concerned also about the social impact of the MFI's potential distress. The Central Bank, depending on the State, is even more directly involved in the matter, especially if the ailing institution is deposit taking and/or if it has commercial links (debts and credits) with other banks, reminding how likely and devastating a domino effect may be.

Among the biggest microfinance risks there are over-lending to delinquent clients, lack of adequate IT processes, excessive geographical concentration, and exaggerate product concentration.

The microfinance risk matrix

The microfinance risk matrix considers not only the contingent impact of adverse events on the different stakeholders seen above, but also the type of risk that is originated by different states of the world. Risk is typically misunderstood and of-

[656] Forex risk may conveniently be mitigated. See CGAP (2006d).

ten underpriced–since the likelihood of events is neglected and underestimated–unless when calamities really occur.

To the extent that professional and specialized intermediaries deal with risk–and MFIs are better candidates than their poor clients–an essential step towards risk mitigation is its transfer to those who can better diversify it. This trivial statement holds true in particular for what concerns microinsurance.

One of the main questions for microfinance–as for any other market product–is concerned with its costs, specifically referring to the cost of accessing microcredit. These costs, which can be explicit or implicit, depend on several factors–such as the nature of contracting and the intrinsic characteristics of the market and its players–which contribute to shape the microfinance industry risk. Access to credit depends on many complementary factors, consisting of hard issues such as the product's price–interest rates–but also related to less evident aspects such as effective availability and necessity of funds that all contribute to shape the market's demand and supply.

Different contracting methods are legally deputed to mitigate risk, even if a substantial part of it rests untouched by market frictions and imperfections, such as poor governance, weak institutions, and a primitive and ailing judicial system. They all contribute to the overall systematic risk, which shapes the environment where MFIs are located and deemed to prosper, survive, or simply die.

Country and political risk are the first factors to be considered by any potential foreign investor, whose asset allocation is influenced by their perception about a target country, possibly never underestimating the probability that investment funds may not be (fully) repatriated. Ailing and undemocratic governments, with weak governance, love indeed to attract foreign funds but also to keep them indefinitely.

Examples of country risk are both painful and frequent and they range from the country defaults recalled in Chapter 14[657], which are likely to sweep away also financial institutions (MFIs included) to specific policies aiming to block or limit repatriation of funds or to attack the microfinance industry. An example refers to 2009-2010 in Nicaragua, where the microfinance sector was put under siege by a politically motivated group of borrowers who call themselves the No Payment Movement (*Movimiento No Pago*), pushing for a moratorium law and causing big systemic problems to foreign investors and other stakeholders.

Risks can also be macro–or micro–economic, being reflected again in overall political or country risk and ranging from strong and hardly controllable volatility of key economic parameters–such as foreign exchange or interest and inflation rates,

[657] Country defaults are common: as Moyo (2009), p. 86, points out, Spain defaulted on its external debt thirteen times between 1500 and 1900; since the 19th century, Venezuela has defaulted nine times, Brazil seven times, Argentina five times (most recently in 2001).

linked among them by well known arbitrage relations[658]–to smaller micro effects (operational or credit risk …). Country risk can be very disturbing for foreign investors, up to the point of discouraging them from coming in or inducing them to exit. It is a fly to quality strategy that may endanger many developing countries, which are even unrelated among them, if the whole segment is indiscriminately perceived as dangerously unstable.

Country risk is also relevant in order to detect the environmental context within which any MFI operates, raising some delicate questions when sharp contrasts come to evidence: can good MFIs survive and prosper in an ailing country? The contrary may not be disturbing, since small inefficient MFIs are too tiny to have a country-wide impact, while the macroeconomic national context is likely to be more troubling, especially in the long term or if the MFI largely depends on foreign funding. Local funding with deposit collection stabilizes MFIs, reducing dependence on volatile and humoral foreign capital.

Information asymmetries, which are enhanced by distance and difficulties of comprehension of different realities, substantially bias the foreign perception of country risk, while locals simply know it better.

Like in a shanghai game, where an improper movement of one stick may cause uncontrollable effect on the others, in risk analysis an unwanted occurrence may have sequential effects that are hardly foreseeable. Early detection and mitigation may have a substantial impact on limiting unwanted perverse effects and their always dangerous contagion.

Since banks and financial institutions are closely linked among them–and tied together by a further systemic reputation risk–this domino effect may well affect MFIs, especially if they are of big dimensions and deposit taking. Smaller and informal institutions are less contagious, even if their higher number makes them hard to check and monitor – and most of them live totally unsupervised. International contagion is also damaging, especially if it concerns sophisticated institutions with complex synthetic products – such as highly leveraged derivatives as the global recession of 2008-2009 has shown. Small MFIs located in developing countries are typically poorly integrated in international financial markets, so benefiting from a natural shelter[659], even if the credit crunch has affected all the economies, with a damaging growth downturn – market economies tend to shrink as credit dries up.

A theoretical example of an interactive risk matrix is represented in figure 23.1., whereas table 23.1. contains a detailed description of the main risks.

---

[658] Such as the Purchasing Power Parity, according to which exchange rates adapt to inflation differentials, or the interest rate parity, which recognizes the positive effect of higher (real) interest rates on a currency appreciation or the spot forward parity, linking the spot with the forward market.

[659] See Moro Visconti (2009).

Figure 23.1. – Interactive risk matrix

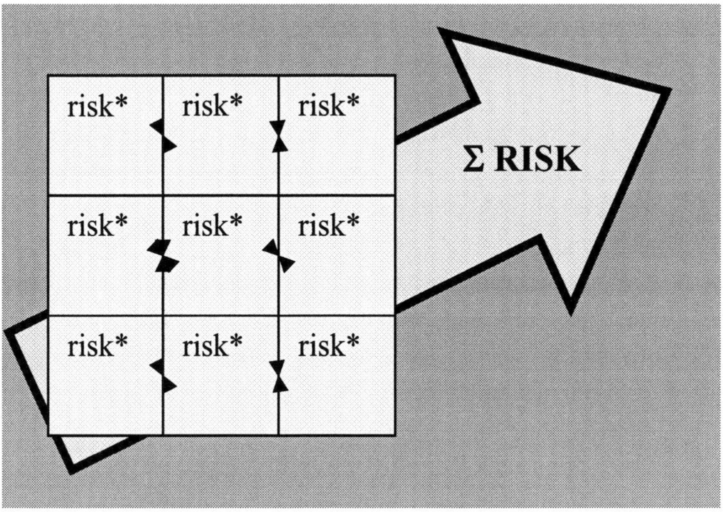

Table 23.1. – The microfinance risk matrix

Type of risk	Description of risk
Country risk	It is the likelihood that changes in the business environment will adversely affect operating profits or the value of assets in a specific country. Country risk includes threat of currency inconvertibility, expropriation of assets, currency controls, devaluation or regulatory changes, institutional corruption or instability factors such as mass riots, civil war, and other potential events. Failing States with bad policies and governance, especially if landlocked[660] by bad neighbors unsurprisingly have a higher and persistent country risk. Successful MFIs show flexibility and resilience from economic volatility and since MFIs are not strongly correlated to the country's GDP and macroeconomic situation, they are most likely to experience less country risk[661]. If international business is unwilling to be present in a place, then country risk is likely to be high – companies tend to cluster and go where other businesses are already operating.

660 This expression is taken from Collier (2007), according to who countries are ›landlocked‹ if they have no direct access to the sea and heavily depend upon their coastal neighbor for transport costs. Each country benefits from the growth of neighbors and this is particularly true for landlocked countries, even if wireless devices somewhat soften this dependence. Land-locked countries could serve as labor resource pools, rather than develop as independent national economies. See Chapter 2.

661 See Krauss, Walter (2006).

Type of risk	Description of risk
Political risk	Closely linked to country risk, political risk is a consequence of the complications that businesses and governments may face as a result of what are commonly referred to as political decisions or any political change that alters the expected outcome and value of a given economic action by changing the probability of achieving business objectives. This is the risk of a strategic, financial, or personnel loss for a firm due to such non-market factors as macroeconomic and social policies (fiscal, monetary, trade, investment, industrial, income, labor, and developmental) or events related to political instability (terrorism, riots, coups, civil war, and insurrection). Political risk is most likely to increase if there are instability factors–such as a recession or a conflict or a natural disaster–and MFIs are always affected by the political crisis in a country. However unregulated MFIs are less correlated to macroeconomic policies and therefore they suffer less political risk.
Financial Market risk	It is the risk that the financial conditions will be adversely affected by changes in market prices or interest rates, foreign exchange rates, and equity prices. During a financial crisis, market risk for MFIs remains low since they are less dependent on the international capital markets (and domestic ones, if they are not in the upper Tier ranking). Institutional risk (due for example to Central banking or stock market regulations) can be a consequence of overreaction to the crisis by policymakers, with regulation becoming more conservative (about new licenses for deposit taking, capital requirements, or branch expansion) [662]. This consequence is good for quality and sustainability, but not for growth and outreach.
Foreign exchange risk	It is the risk of losses due to unstable currency exchange rates and adverse scenarios, such as devaluation of the local currency (if debt is denominated in reevaluating hard and foreign currencies). MFIs face foreign exchange risk only to the extent that debt is denominated in hard foreign currencies, and this is hardly ever being the case in small institutions. Weak currencies are likely to devaluate against harder currencies and an economic downturn might speed up this process, if local inflation is higher and country risk worsens. Credit crunch and bank crises dry up foreign funds, so limiting new sources of risk.

662 See CGAP (2008c).

Type of risk	Description of risk
Interest rate risk	It is the risk that changes in interest rates might affect operating and net margins of the MFI. Interest rates increases raise the cost of collected capital and they are not always transmittable to more expensive loans, since borrowers might be unable to pay higher rates and their default risk might increase. During an economic crisis, basic interest rates (fixed by central banks or within inter-bank loans) normally decrease, since limited pressures on prices typically cool down inflation. Risk premiums conversely tend to increase, due to a general higher default risk. The net effect often brings to an overall increase of interest rates and, consequently, to a higher risk of non–repayment from borrowers. The opposite is likely to happen when the economy is expanding: Central Banks are likely to increase interest rates, in order to cool down inflation.
Operational risk	This is a risk that arises from execution of a company's business functions. It is the risk of losses that arise directly from services and product delivery, resulting from human or systems errors. It involves fraud risks, legal risks, physical or environmental risks, risk of compliance, etc. It's associated with human resources, governance, and information technology. In general, it considers the risk that operational costs are higher than revenues, with consequent negative margins (borrowing and running costs are higher than lending profits). MFIs face less operating risk due to the relationship they have with their clients who closely monitor their MFIs. Operational margins squeeze, due to creeping costs of funding and higher delinquency of borrowers. Growth is hindered and fixed costs have an evolutionary higher break-even point.
Credit (repayment or delinquency) risk	Credit risk applies to lending and investing activities and it considers the risk of financial losses resulting from borrowers' delay or nonpayment of loan obligations. MFIs are institutionally more directly concerned about risk than other Western financial institutions, such as mainstream banks or–even more–hedge funds and other sophisticated and not-so-transparent intermediaries or products. Since repayment installments are weekly or monthly for MF clients, and the loan amounts are small, credit risk is typically lower than in normal banks. Credit risk is likely to increase when the economic growth is slowing down, due to increased cost of capital (higher interest

Type of risk	Description of risk
	rates), higher repayment difficulties, and probabilities of default. If MFIs are increasingly unable to meet the borrowers' needs, then eagerness to repay debt might decrease and opportunistic behavior might increase. Additional clients might be marginally less trustworthy. Repayment rates might fall off during recession[663]. Remittances from Western countries consistently slow down, to the detriment of the poor relatives indebted with local MFIs. Emergency consumption dries up savings, so eroding guarantees and ability to match obligation from the poorest. Credit risk is a fundamental parameter for assessing the bank's soundness and it may be estimated as a function of the expected loss times its probability[664]. When MFIs, especially if licensed as banks, lend money each other, a counterpart risk arises, with a potential systematic impact, even beyond national boundaries. Scoring can soften credit risk, albeit this practice is difficult to implement within the poorest.
Guarantee (collateral) risk	It is strongly linked with credit risk, since the lack of adequate guarantees can undermine the borrower's capacity or willingness to honor his debt. Since guarantees are typically limited or non existent in MFIs, from this point of view they are safer than mainstream banks and they have a competitive advantage. Collateral risk is growing when the economy slows down, especially if it is based on listed securities when stock markets are bearish or on real estate properties with falling prices. In recessions this risk is pro-cyclical, exacerbating the negative trend, and it adds up to a worsen cash flow outlook of the borrower. Both assets based and cash flow based lending become riskier, commanding higher interest rates premiums.
Gender risk[665]	A traditionally hot question concerns gender risk: are women more discriminated when asking for money? It shouldn't be so in microfinance, even if for small loans empirical evidence shows that women are more trustworthy than men and they have better repayment records. Being at the very bottom of the social ladder, women are the unfortunate and natural candidates to suffer more

663 Contrary evidence is given by the empirical case of Bolivia, concerning a former local recession. See Velasco, Marconi (2004).

664 This is a typical parameter used in Basel II rating system.

665 The opinion of the authors - both males - might be biased about this key problem. Bob Marley used to sing ›*No woman, no cry*‹ but microfinance evidence states the contrary and women seem much more trustworthy then men, even if the gender distinction is often more formal than real, being also the men among the beneficiaries of the loans to the women.

Type of risk	Description of risk
	the lack of protection and social safety nets.
Corporate governance risk	Corporate governance sets the rules of cohabitation and of the behavior of the different stakeholders that pivot around the MFIs (borrowers, lenders, shareholders, supervisory authorities …). Typical banking and specific microfinance risks include adverse selection (the difficulty to discriminate between good and non trustworthy borrowers), moral hazard (the ›take the money and run‹ option) and strategic bankruptcy (false information that the borrower gives about the outcome of the financed investment, to elude repayment). Information asymmetries are also part of the game. Corporate governance is also concerned with legal and compliance risk, which involves losses arising from failure to follow relevant legal and regulatory requirements. In unregulated MFIs, the risk–if existent–is low but even the benefits of regulation are low and good governance is missing. Relationship lending and continuous monitoring of unsophisticated and small borrowers reduce the risk of information asymmetries in MFIs, if compared with mainstream banks. When life becomes more complicated, simplicity pays.
Competition risk	Commercial banks have started downscaling in order to access the microfinance market. The informal sector (money lenders) is most likely to provide a stiff competition to microfinance, as it is not affected by the economic turmoil. Competition typically grows in hard times, eroding margins, since the market is shrinking and the players become more aggressive, struggling for survival.
Mission drift risk[666]	Not-for-profit MFIs targeting the poor might transform in for-profit institutions aimed at maximizing returns.
Reputational risk	It is the risk of earnings and capital arising from negative public opinion, which may affect the institutions' ability to sell products and services or access other funding. Trust normally decreases during hard times for material and psychological reasons (pessimism). Will this hurt especially those who already been trusted, often without deserving it or those who have never been, such as the poor? MFIs are well known for loan repayment record but recession might increase repayment defaults, with a negative impact on MFI's stability

[666] See Chapter 21.

Type of risk	Description of risk
	and reputation. It takes years of hard job to build up a reputation but only few minutes to destroy it. On an aggregate side, reputation affects country risk.
Liquidity risk	The risk of losses that arise from the possibility that the MFIs may not have sufficient funds to meet their obligations or be unable to access adequate funding. During hard times, funding is most likely to squeeze as donors hold back their subsidies and due to increased interest rates on the capital markets, MFIs will reduce acquisition of more debt financing. However MFIs should mobilize other sources of funding in the form of local savings and local debt. If MFIs are linked with ailing banks, their liquidity investments in both directions might be halted and interest rates in the interbank market grow. Money is scarcer and more expensive to get.
Strategic risk	It is the risk to earnings or capital, arising from adverse business decisions or improper implementation of strategies, due to mismanagement or organization fallouts. Reliable strategic goals, development of proper business actions and deployment of adequate resources and the quality of management reduce the risk. Strategic risk increases in hard times as targets are more difficult to be reached. Mission drift might be a consequence of high strategic risk and subsequent fight for survival.
Inflation risk	It is the probability of loss that results from erosion of an income or in the value of assets due to the rising costs of goods and services. That is the possibility that the value of assets or income will decrease as inflation shrinks the purchasing power of a currency. Surge in inflation levels might bring to deposit withdrawals for survival needs. The growth of food prices, now finished but still painful, has increased inflation and caused recessive problems in poor countries. In hard times, inflation risk might decrease, since price pressure and salary expectations cool down, unless there is a particular stagflation scenario. Extreme commodity and oil price volatility can increase inflation. Inflation is a hidden form of taxation (from credit holders to debtholders).
Capital adequacy risk	Capital adequacy risk refers to the possibility of losses resulting from the firm's lack of sufficient capital to finance business operations. With under-capitalization, small adverse shift in circumstances can impair the solvency of the MFI, if bad loans erode the capital. Capital adequacy of most MFIs might decline

Type of risk	Description of risk
	during hard times and it may render some MFIs insolvent. The cost of raising capital grows when there are liquidity constraints and lack of confidence in the inter-bank loan market and in the capital markets.
Funding risk (credit tightening)	It is the risk of not finding adequate supplies of financial resources to meet borrowers' needs. Hard times are normally accompanied by credit crunches and higher loan risk. Funding becomes more difficult and expensive, especially for MFIs depending on foreign sources of funds, which are mostly affected by recession and Western banking restraints. Refinancing risk is higher and liquidity constraints to growth can exacerbate gloomy economic perspectives. Money from domestic and international banks is tighter, slower, more conservative, and more expensive[667].
Savings risk	Strongly linked with funding risk, this risk has a direct impact on the licensed MFI's ability to collect deposits, which also represent a guarantee for loans to the same depositors. The attitude to save in hard times is psychologically higher but physically much more difficult, since revenues are falling, affecting households' income. Survival consumption (cash needs) and lower remittances burn savings.
Concentration risk	On the one side, diversification of funding and lending sources improves the MFI's stability. On the opposite side, concentration risk involves in particular small MFIs or NGOs, which do not collect deposits and which rely only on a partner, who acts also as a depository bank, intermediating funds on behalf of the NGO. Diversification is a key strategy especially in hard times, which might hit the unique funding source, with the result of making it difficult to find an alternative in an increasingly difficult competitive scenario. Risk diversification strategies investing in conglomerate activities, so popular some decades ago, are now seen as unproductive, since they prevent synergies, they ease dispersion and lack of focus, and they may be more easily carried forward by the shareholders, directly and not through the inefficient intermediation of the MFI.
Default risk	It is the inability of the MFI to meet its obligations, unless occasional, and it may bring MFI to bankruptcy. The risk can be con-

667 See CGAP (2008c).

Type of risk	Description of risk
	sidered an unlucky combination of some of the other risks described above, with particular reference to operational, credit, and liquidity risk. In hard times risks are typically higher and their combination might be more frequent.

Assessing industry risk: microfinance banana skins

The Microfinance Banana Skins surveys explore the risks that the worldwide microfinance industry faces, considering both the current hazards and their trends (fastest rising risk factors).

A table with the 2011 microfinance banana skins can help to have a first glimpse on the issue:

Table 23.2. – Microfinance banana skins 2011 (2009 position in brackets) [668]

Biggest risks	Fastest risers
1 Credit risk (1)	1 Competition (3)
2 Reputation (17)	2 Credit risk (1)
3 Competition (9)	3 Reputation (11)
4 Corporate governance (7)	4 Political interference (7)
5 Political interference (10)	5 Mission drift (13)
6 Inappropriate regulation (13)	6 Strategy (–)
7 Management quality (4)	7 Staffing (20)
8 Staffing (14)	8 Unrealisable expectations (17)
9 Mission drift (19)	9 Profitability (9)
10 Unrealisable expectations (18)	10 Inappropriate regulation (22)
11 Managing technology (15)	11 Corporate governance (12)
12 Profitability (12)	12 Management quality (18)
13 Back office (22)	13 Ownership (16)
14 Transparency (16)	14 Liquidity (5)
15 Strategy (–)	15 Product development (24)
16 Liquidity (2)	16 Macro-economic trends (2)
17 Macro-economic trends (3)	17 Managing technology (23)
18 Fraud (20)	18 Interest rates (10)
19 Product development (24)	19 Fraud (14)
20 Ownership (17)	20 Transparency (21)
21 Interest rates (11)	21 Back office (19)
22 Too much funding (25)	22 Too much funding (25)

[668] Source: http://www.cgap.org/gm/document-1.9.49643/Microfinance_Banana_Skins_2011.pdf.

Biggest risks	Fastest risers
23 Too little funding (6)	23 Too little funding (6)
24 Foreign exchange (8)	24 Foreign exchange (8)

Even if risk factors greatly change from year to year (for example, credit risk was ranked n. 10 in 2008 but sadly reached the first position in 2009 and kept it in 2011, due to the credit crunch that has accompanied the worldwide recession) a taxonomy of their main components is both possible and useful, not only to describe the microfinance dangers, but also to shape the main features of an evolving industry.

The ranking comes from interviewing the following players:

- practitioners – people who run or work in MFIs;
- investors in MFIs;
- regulators;
- deposit takers.

These players are the core stakeholders, even if this short list doesn't specifically include depositors (somehow similar to investors), the government (being the regulator but also the tax collector …), the surrounding community, etc.

The risks also have an unsurprising different geographical variety that represents an obstacle to ubiquitous scalability–the attempt to indistinctly apply a standard business model everywhere, irrespectively of its needed local personalization–but also a diversification factor for investors which can reduce their overall risk through a geographical subdivision of their portfolios which is mostly effective when correlation among different countries (and their intrinsic risk factors) is limited.

The aforementioned ranking changes from year to year and, in an attempt to generalize this issue, what really matters is the kind of risk and its links with the others risks, rather than its changing position, due to contingent priorities that may overestimate some factors, underestimating other ones (e.g., credit risk ranks high in a recessionary environment such as that of 2008-2009, but this does not mean that management quality is a less risky factor and it seems evident that the two are strongly related, since a good management is absolutely necessary to downsize credit risk).

Going beyond the definition of risky factors contained in table 1.–somewhat super imposable to this more analytical ranking–the top 25 risks of 2011 can shortly be described in the following way:

1. credit risk – the risk of loss when loans are not repaid, with a systemic impact if delinquency is generalized, as a consequence of a common risk factor (recession; natural calamity …). The fable that microfinance is almost a default-free industry is a nice and politically correct tale, nowadays less likely than in the past;

2. reputation, linked to transparency and other related factors (accountability, corporate governance, fairness …). It concerns both the microfinance industry and the single institutions. Greedy investors (who are always looking for the best destination of their funds and hardly in love with microfinance or any other particular industry) rank reputation higher than practitioners, probably because they have wider global choice. The reputation of the industry, that is subject to volatile fashionable trends, may overwhelm the regulation of single institutions, making the crucial discrimination between sounder and weaker institutions more difficult and less meritocratic, to the detriment of microfinance poor final users;

3. competition, traditionally seen again as a double edged weapon in the banking industry, due to its positive impact on fair pricing, strive towards quality and customer satisfaction. It is often counterbalanced by its potential systemic threat, due to the destabilizing effect of defaulting institutions (especially in the presence of a weak institutional framework, with unsophisticated central banks hardly able to intervene), which are unable to cope with the Darwinian selection but nevertheless potentially contagious. In microfinance, links among informal and small intermediaries are weaker, but the protective countermeasures are also much less sophisticated. Competition between different intermediaries–such as that of commercial banks versus MFIs–may encourage irresponsible lending from vulnerable MFIs;

4. corporate governance, concerned not only with the good management quality seen above, but also–more generally–to the set of regulations, agreements, processes, customs, and policies that affect the way a MFI is directed, administered, or controlled, pivoting around its stakeholders;

5. political interference, related to country risk, is unsurprisingly stronger in countries with weaker democratic institutions. There the dirigiste temptation to influence the economy brings to corruption, mismanagement, waste of public resources and abuses, humiliating meritocracy, all in order to buy consensus and limit freedom. Cap on interest rates, undue subsidizing of ailing institutions, with an unfair impact on competition or demagogic support to ›non-repayment groups‹ (as it has happened in Nicaragua in 2009) are just a few of the many examples of the damages that

governments can make, often with the interested sponsorship of foreign allies;

6. inappropriate regulation. As it happens with medicines, too much regulation is oppressive and too little is ineffective. Proper dosage is essential but difficult to conceive, put into practice, and monitor. Regulation fallacies in the sophisticated global banking & finance industry are under accuse for their unwanted contribution to the big recession of 2008-2009. Regulation becomes a particularly delicate issue for MFIs that become deposit takers, since poor savers and depositors are much more vulnerable than other bigger and stronger financiers;
7. management quality, since even MFIs are deemed to be successful only if proper blending of physical and human capital is possible ... together with a bit of luck. In backward areas which are more sheltered by global macroeconomic volatility factors, lack of adequate skills and proper training is more acute, due to local poor schooling and inability to attract smart workers from richer places;
8. staffing, a human resources risk that is strongly related with management quality and declined at a lower organizational level. Staff shortages are eased in recession times, and they remain acute in poorer regions, such as Africa. Development of adequate skills has to proceed together–harmonically–with the development of the industry. Proper academic theoretical background, wisely blended with on field grass-rooted experience, is greatly wanted and often missing;
9. mission drift-a social danger described in Chapter 22-is a hotly debated issue. Are MFIs losing sight of their social goals, changing their job and forgetting about unworthy poor clients? Is social lending going to be replaced by commercial lending? Are the rural poor going to be discriminated in favor of more promising urban realities? These are key question and even if the 2009 ranking has gone down–as a consequence of other more contingent priorities–this ›philosophical‹ question about the industry, its mission, and identity, stands out as a prominent one, not to be underestimated or taken for granted;
10. unrealizable expectations, concerned with the human moody and humoral psychology, are particularly daunting for a fast growing industry, where the potential is unlimited but the reality proves much harder than fancy dreams;
11. managing technology is another key factor. It is sufficient to see how ICT has changed the banking industry, to understand its current–and potential–impact on the less sophisticated–but increasingly similar–

microfinance industry. Small loans to many poor clients are among the main economic weaknesses of the microfinance industry, bringing to low marginality and inability to implement economies of scale. So technology becomes crucial to cut staff costs, making the business less labor intensive and to foster outreach (with mobile banking, computerized data bases for credit scoring, back office efficiency with proper computerized bookkeeping, etc.);

12. profitability, represented by economic marginality at the operating or bottom line level (net income) is strongly linked to interest rate marginality but also to productivity and management quality. According to the 2009 report[669] »few MFIs earn their cost of capital once donations are removed from the picture«. When profitability is missing or insufficient, self sustainability and so–consequently–outreach are endangered. Lack of profitability may go beyond mission drift–the hardly resistible attempt to earn more money abandoning poor clients in favor of wealthier ones–bringing to ... mission failure. Without an adequate profitability, the game is simply over;
13. back office operations, the humble and dirty job behind the counter, represent a risky factor that is strongly linked with management and staff quality and ICT technology;
14. transparency, concerning the real cost of microfinance loans and, more generally, the accountability of the business. It is closely linked with confidence and fair corporate governance relationship among stakeholders with potentially diverging interests. Shortage of funding increases competition and incentives towards better transparency;
15. strategy, concerned with business focus and its practical implementation; technology (M-banking ...) greatly influences new strategies, whereas their perimeter, including product selection, has an impact on mission drift;
16. on the one side, lack of liquidity to make loans or to meet deposit withdrawals – it is somewhat comparable to the ›running-out-of-stock‹ problem for other industries, even if illiquidity linked to withdrawals is a much more serious issue. On the opposite side, overabundance of capital can trigger irresponsible actions or undue risk-taking on the part of invested companies;
17. macroeconomic trends, showing that the industry is less and less insulated from its economic environment, even from an international perspective;

669 http://www.csfi.org.uk/Microfinance%20Banana%20Skins%202009.pdf, box in page 27.

18. fraud – it is always a threat, likelier in recession times, when money is mostly needed, by any mean. It is strongly linked with other risk factors, such as transparency, reputation, corporate governance, etc., representing the darkest and nastier side of the business. Political interference is often related to bribing and corruption. Fraud is difficult to fight not only in simple environments, where lack of controls and absence of procedures transform temptations into easy realities but also in sophisticated contexts, if controls privilege form over substance or have design fallacies, easy to be exploited by smart and careless insiders;

19. product development. Even if the risk associated to this item is small, the item itself is far from being a secondary one. Most MFIs understand their clients' needs, being in close and physical contact with them, better than anybody else (maybe except moneylenders). To know, to choose, to select, to propose, to make available and to deliver the most suitable financial products, and to promote new ones is not a trivial task;

20. ownership, concerned with the composition of the MFI's equityholders, is not a trivial risk, even if it is considered as a declining risky factor, as it shapes the MFI's structure and mission. Which is the most appropriate form of ownership? Should equityholders be represented by philanthropic organizations or by for-profit investors? A balanced–and tasty–cocktail of the two elements is hard to get, and different objectives and ideals often bring to diverging behaviors. The MFI may lose its focus and mission purpose, unless a viable compromise is reached and maintained;

21. the interest rate level, being a big concern for practitioners, less for investors. Even if the poor show a surprising resilience to economic conditions and they are more threatened by lack of money–and incapacity to find a safe harbor for their savings–price of money is still important. Fixing a suitable level of interest rates is a key issue for both MFIs–whose capacity to survive and expand their business largely depends on the marginality kept aside after subtracting operating costs from interest rate revenues–and their clients, who are unable to survive when money is too expensive but at the same time needing a long term relationship with sound institutions;

22. too much funding-over-funding-is related to its specular feature, represented by too little funding, which in the 2009 survey was ranked as number 6. risk. Too much funding may be as dangerous as too little, even if this statement is far from being obvious, since abundance is always better than scarcity. But too much money, concentrated in few top MFIs, typically with a Tier 1 background, can be dangerous, bringing to overin-

vestment, lack of efficiency and proper stimuli, mission drift, overconfidence, irrational excitement, hubris, megalomania, etc.

23. too little funding, dangerous like its contrarian over-funding (which can bring to a mission drift, wasting the excess of liquidity in no core investments, with a dangerous and uncontrolled managerial discretion). If the MFI is provided with too little cash, its expansion is severely biased and it may be prevented from reaching self sustainable equilibrium;
24. foreign currency, a double edged weapon, since it can affect both foreign investors (especially equityholders), if they convert their hard domestic currency in devaluating local ones, and the MFI and its local stakeholders, to the extent that risk is born by them. Currency imbalances between assets and liabilities (e.g., when loans are in local currencies and funding in foreign ones) increase this potentially destabilizing risk and it may threaten investors, keeping them away and exacerbating already seen problems, such as illiquidity or refinancing;

Risk, resilience and coping

Resilience–adaptability, and flexibility–is concerned with the positive ability to cope with adverse and risky events, recovering from shocks and calamities, which are highly likely to affect the poorest. Risk management is concerned with both the detection and the mitigation of risky factors that affect the MFI, often interacting among them, with potentially catastrophic synergic combinations.

A good accounting and reporting system is fundamental in order to assess risk – together with an operational efficiency system. The level of sophistication of risk monitoring is typically consistent both with the MFI's intrinsic nature and with the external controls. Small Tier 4 or unrated MFIs, operating in poor countries and not supervised by Central Banks, are typically unlikely to have a good risk measurement system, while formal and bigger institutions, especially if audited, rated, supervised, or even more listed–this being a rare case–have an increasing level of sophistication and a consequent better risk assessment system.

Risk management is expensive and it has to be consistent with the dimension and scope of the MFI, balancing its costs (even in terms of bureaucratic accomplishments) with the expected pay-offs. In countries with a weak system of governance and compliance, a proper risk management strategy also has an instructive impact– with both an internal and an external control system–and it may be particularly effective in repressing fraud or mismanagement. Pressure from local institutions and controlling authorities, such as the Central bank, are unsurprisingly proportional to the local degree of sophistication and governance – this being a basic institutional framework for any economic activity.

When a risky situation occurs, a recovery management strategy has to be properly put into action, so to soften effects of such a situation and repair the damages. The bottleneck, here and elsewhere, is typically represented by weak and unskilled management.
The risk matrix, representing a map of all the possible negative outcomes–malign states of the world–has a fundamental diagnostic importance in detecting and assessing the risky features. Such features accompany the underserved along all their life, with different intensities, according to their poverty degree–chronic or temporary–and to their variable exposure to different dangers. Prevention is always the best mitigation strategy, together with proper intervention, positive adaptation, and endurance in coping, all aiming at maximizing resilience.
The timing of risk is also an important factor, considering not only its uneven occurrence during the life of the poor but also the possibility that different risk factors may come out simultaneously, with a potentially devastating multiplier effect. Multiple resilience and coping is often a hard necessity.
Defense mechanisms can be put in place at different levels–individual, familial, clan, communal, institutional, etc.–and they can conveniently correlate and reinforce one another[670]. Systemic shocks–such as natural calamities hitting vast communities–are more difficult to withstand and they may necessitate international emergency aid[671].
Microfinance can improve resilience and adaptability, softening risk with *ad hoc* microinsurance packages.
Risk, if properly detected and constantly monitored, can be significantly reduced and–to some extent–even insured. The problem is that only some kinds of risk can be–totally or partially–insured, both from the side of the MFI and from that of the stakeholders pivoting around it, starting from borrowers and depositors. Even if each player has his personal risk, a part–or most–of it is shared. As an example, should the MFI default, its depositors–if uninsured and not protected by the Central bank–would suffer huge losses, but even its borrowers would be asked to pay back immediately what they owe, being prevented from asking further loans. From the side of the clients, their personal problems affect also the institution and personal delinquencies increase the costs born by regular payers.
If compared to bigger and more sophisticated commercial banks, MFIs typically have a higher diversification risk, since they serve a narrower range of similar clients and they provide a more limited set of products and services. In order to fight against enduring poverty, microfinance has to be complemented by other instruments and measures, starting from a pro-growth environment, oriented towards sustainable development.

670 Boyden, Cooper in Addison, Hulme, Kanbur (2009), p. 292.
671 See Chapter 14.

The impact of risk on the MFI's cost of capital

The cost of collected capital is the cost of a MFI's funds (both debt and equity). Conversely, from an investor's point of view, the opportunity cost of capital depends on the expected return of the MFI's issued debt or equity, compared to other possible investments and similar foregone opportunities, with a consistent risk / return profile, always reminding the evident principle according to which higher risk–represented by more volatile returns–has to be adequately remunerated with a bigger expected return. Awareness of financial risk, concerning also the effective cost of collected capital, has increased within MFIs.

Opportunity cost is a key concept in investment finance, referring to whether someone's time or money or other limited resources may be better spent on something else. It is done after a comparison of different chances and alternative uses, in order to optimize value for money and value for time.

The cost of capital is used to evaluate the minimum return that investors expect for providing sources to the MFI, considering also possible alternatives. A correct assessment and pricing of risk is essential for a fair estimate of the cost of capital, even though it is easier to say than to make, as the frequent speculative bubbles driven by risk-addiction teach us.

Capital markets are one of the strongest segmentation factors between the few elected top MFIs and the numerous rest. This because a little sample of the living MFIs is eligible for investors' overcrowded attention and care–bringing to too much money invested in too few institutions–while others are relegated into an ambiguous limbo, out of which few are allowed to sort out and most are condemned to stay, sometimes indefinitely and mostly till their close premature disappearance, remembering that only the strong survive. Risk is always a present albeit uninvited guest and choices between deserving versus unfit MFIs are intrinsically hazardous – only time will tell.

Maximization of return on the invested capital may not be (and typically is not) the first target of equityholders or debtholders, since they also normally pursue social goals[672], nevertheless it still represents a key benchmark, to be used each time the MFIs needs to raise extra funds to finance its investments, typically in loans to poor clients.

Being equityholders residual claimants, even if compared to debtholders, whose claims are fixed (either senior or subordinated, depending on their legal provisions), the former always command a higher risk premium. To the extent that equity investors have to take care of a mismatch between their domestic currency and the local one, their overall risk profile grows, unless they can properly cover themselves against unwanted currency fluctuations. As we have already seen, whereas foreign equity-holders are nearly always exposed in the local currency, foreign

672 For a critical analysis, see Chapter 21.

debt-holders may make loans either in their native hard currency or in the local one. It is the MFI which bears foreign exchange risk if there is a mismatch between (part of) its debts denominated in a hard foreign currency and its assets in domestic currency. This contingency exposure affects not only the MFI, but also its stakeholders, whose interest in the company may be endangered by its own fragility.

Currency risk is a problem that can be mitigated strengthening the local country's macroeconomic soundness. Nations with better economic fundamentals have a less volatile currency and they are increasingly able to raise internally the funds they need to back MFIs, either limiting access to international financial markets or making it more efficient and cheaper. As a matter of fact, currency risk reflects much of the country's risk determinants. Currency hedging techniques are hard to put into practice with weak and odd currencies, especially if they are not pegged to the US$ or the Euro or other hard and sound currencies.

The expected return on capital, adjusted for its intrinsic degree of risk, must evidently be greater than the cost of capital, for any investment to be worthwhile. In the presence of social investments absolute financial returns are just a part of the whole decision process.

The cost of capital can be subdivided into three basic components:

- the cost of issued debt;
- the cost of paid in capital, considering also cumulated reserves (cost of equity);
- the weighted average cost of (debt + equity) capital.

Since the cost of capital is concerned with investment returns, it is normally conceived and calculated referring to listed companies, an unlikely situation for most MFIs, since only some of the biggest Tier 1 institutions are quoted in an official stock exchange. In order to consider both the returns and the weights of debt market or, respectively, of equity market–and not book value–figures have to be taken into account. In listed companies, the market value of equity is represented by its stock market capitalization (the current market value of its outstanding shares). Since the market value (represented by each day's stock exchange share price) exceeds the book value of equity, the price-to-book-value ratio is above the unity, so incorporating an implicit goodwill.

For what concerns debt, its market value can be easily calculated if debt is listed, a frequent situation for what concerns corporate issued bonds but an unlikely occurrence in most other cases. From a practical perspective, in most cases the difference between the market and the book value of debt is not supposed to be significant and the book value may (typically slightly) exceed the real market value, especially if debt has a long maturity and it is not discounted.

It seems evident that, in the case of microfinance, the theoretic definition of ›cost of capital‹ has to be adjusted to the fact that the MFI is typically unlisted and so a proxy of the market value of its equity and debt has to be used.
The cost of issued debt is composed by the ratio of the rate of interest paid, divided by the (market) value of the outstanding debt. If the interest rate is a tax deductible negative component, then the interest rate burden has to be considered net of the fiscal benefit deriving from its deductibility. It is the case, that happens in most countries, of MFIs that have a positive taxable base, with revenues in excess of their costs (an unlikely situation for many if not most MFIs, especially donor-backed start ups).
So, if the gross negative interest rate is 100, the corporate tax rate is 25% and the outstanding (interest-producing) debt is 1,000, the tax-adjusted cost of debt is:

$$\frac{100*(1-0.25)}{1{,}000}=\frac{75}{1{,}000}=7.5\%$$

while without considering the tax shield, the cost of debt would be 100 / 1,000 = 10%.
In practice, the interest-rate paid by the MFI is represented by the risk-free rate (i.e., the domestic rate at which riskless debt, with no bankruptcy cost, is issued) plus a risk component (risk premium), which incorporates a probable rate of default. On the one side the risk free rate component is fixed for all the debtholders, while on the other side the spread is assessed according to the intrinsic risk degree of the MFI.
Remembering also the Stiglitz, Weiss (1981) model, the consideration that the higher the risk, the higher the premium (expected revenue) is not boundless, since an excessive risk premium may only formally remunerate the higher risk and represent a further element of uncertainty – can the debtor afford to pay such a high premium, especially if compared to sounder competitors? When the risk is excessive, debtors are unlikely to find loan underwriters and capital rationing problems are likely to occur, making repayment harder and going concern maintenance a tougher challenge.
If the cost of debt is relatively straightforward to estimate, the cost of equity is more challenging to calculate, since equity does not pay a contractually predetermined return–fixed claim–to its investors. In analogy with the cost of debt, the cost of equity may be broadly defined as the risk-weighted expected return required by potential underwriters of the MFI's capital, always comparing the target company with similar ones, considering their market risk/return profile.
The cost of equity can be estimated using the Dividend Discount model, according to which the Expected Return equals the dividend yield (i.e. dividend per share divided by the market price per share) plus the growth rate of dividends.

If the MFI is listed, the Capital Asset Pricing Model may conveniently be used to estimate its cost of equity and in such a case the expected return E(r), is given by the risk-free rate of return (r_f) added to the β coefficient (expressing the sensitivity of the asset to market fluctuations), multiplied by the risk premium of the stock market (r_m) over the risk free rate:

$$E(r) = r_f + \beta(r_m - r_f)$$

Once the cost of debt (k_d) and the cost of equity – k_e = E(r) – have both been estimated, the weighted average cost of capital (WACC) becomes a straightforward calculation:

$$WACC = k_e * \frac{E}{D+E} + k_d(1-t)\frac{D}{D+E}$$

Where D is the market value of debt, E is the market value of equity, t is the corporate tax rate. The WACC can be used as a discount rate for a project's projected cash flows.
The cost of capital is strongly influenced by the MFI's intrinsic risk level.

Microfinance rating

To the extent that the MFI, albeit unlisted, has an independent rating issued by an external agency, the calculation of its cost of capital is strongly eased.
»MFIs face a distinct challenge when trying to encourage prospective donors and financial markets to back their activities. Although evaluations and assessments are available to MFIs from credible agencies, these tend to be expensive, and lack a common standard that can be applied to the entire industry. Most of the evaluations have not been made public, leaving the methodology and/or results unknown to other potentially interested parties. What is required is a credit rating system that takes into account the nuances of the field, and sends a clear signal to donors and investors of their sustainability«[673]. »A common understanding on the reporting, measurement, and evaluation of MFI performance has not been reached – no surprise given the diversity of the providers«[674].

---

673 http://www.gdrc.org/icm/rating/index.html.

674 Efforts in place to develop rating and certification systems include:

1. PEARLS rating system. This is a rating system, whose acronym stands for Protection, Effective financial structure, Asset quality, Rates of return and costs, and Liquidity and Signs of growth, developed for credit unions by the World Council of Credit Unions (WOCCU). The rating system includes a certification process called Finance Organization Achieving Certified Credit Union Standards (FOCCUS);
2. ACCION Camel. The evaluation guideline for MFIs developed by ACCION International;
3. Girafe rating system. Developed by PlaNetFinance;
4. MicroRate. Developed by Damian von Stauffenberg of MicroRate;

The rating of MFIs is also concerned with their assets' consistency and their equity – the net differential between assets and liabilities; liabilities typically have a market value close to the book value, since debts should never be underestimated, while assets' quality is much harder and questionable to evaluate, as standard commercial banks have shown during the 2008-2010 recession. Deleveraging and stress tests are nowadays standard measures: the former in order to reduce debt exposure and decrease the debt to equity ratio, and the letter to assess the real market value of assets with engaging assumptions. They are uneasily applicable to unsophisticated MFIs but they still represent a benchmark and an ideal example, especially if the MFIs are growing and converging towards bigger banking standards.
Risk management and financial performance assessment influence both the rating and the MFI's evaluation[675], giving an essential feedback to investors and other stakeholders that pivot around the MFI.

Lessons from recessions and depressions

The age of endemic instability we live in seems hardly ephemeral and so we might be forced to get soon used to it, learning how to cope and survive. Near-death experiences force to reevaluate values and priorities.
The global recession of 2008-2009 has proved an unprecedented perfect storm and the financial crisis has affected also the real economy, creating widespread social unrest.
MFIs in developing countries are less affected by the worldwide turmoil, due to their segmentation and resilience to external shocks. If contagion is milder, the biggest risk is probably becoming out of scope, being unable to collect the much needed foreign capital at competitive costs.
Recession has a big impact on corporate governance mechanisms, altering the equilibriums among different stakeholders and increasing the risk of investment returns. In such a context, any governance improvement is highly welcome and recommended. No governance, no money for growth or bare survival.
According to Wellen, Mulder (2008), although microfinance did not feel the impact of some of the past financial crises, the current global financial crisis has brought tough times for most MFIs, first because of their greater integration within

5. MicroBanking Bulletin/ MicroBanking Standards Project. Funded by the Consultative Group to Assist the Poorest (CGAP);
6. The Philippine Coalition for Micro-finance Standards. Developed a set of performance standards to serve as guidelines or benchmarks to assess the operations of Philippine NGOs involved in Micro-finance:
7. CGAP Microfinance Rating and Assessment Fund;
8. Institutional Performance Standards and Plans Developed by the Committee of Donor Agencies for Small Enterprise Development and Donor's Working Group on Financial Sector Development, United Nations Capital Development Fund.

[675] See Isern, Abrams, Craig, Brown (2008).

the larger financial markets, and second because the economy itself is suffering a hit due to rising inflation and reduced remittances. For the microfinance sector, it means that the capital funds will dry up, there will be shorter-term credits, and the demand for microfinance may eventually diminish. The authors suggest that in order to withstand the crisis, MFIs will have to diversify the sources of their funds, to get a clear picture of their capital costs, to develop a workable liquidity plan, to diversify their portfolio, and to increase operational efficiency.

Krauss, Walter (2008) argue that microfinance, supported by donor agencies and nongovernmental organizations, is traditionally recognized as a self-sustainable tool for alleviating poverty. In recent years, the access to funding by MFIs has diversified, for example, client deposits, refinancing via interbank deposits and commercial loans, and raising funds in capital markets.

Risk is the other hot issue and, since international investors have consistently mispriced risky Western assets, we wonder if they are enough lucid and capable to fairly price and assess the risk of MFIs in developing countries – a completely different case, increasingly looking for specialized investors.

As we have seen, MFIs operating in developing countries are bound to face some impact during the ongoing global recession despite profiting from the double safety net of both being only partially correlated to their domestic financial markets, which in turn are often segmented from international markets. Bad and good news are blended and they interact in many possible combinations, with so many potential outcomes that forecasts are difficult to make[676].

The condensed Chapter

All the stakeholders that pivot around the microfinance institution (borrowers, depositors, equityholders, debtholders, employees …) bear some part of risk, due to uncertain future outcomes.

Microfinance banana skins rank industry risks, according to the consensus of practitioners.

Risks often interact in a dangerous self fulfilling spiral and they may run out of control, unless they are properly monitored and mitigated.

Out of Poverty Tips

Proper risk detection and understanding is a cornerstone of any mitigation strategy. Hedging tools may help, even if they are hardly tailor made for microfinance issues, so demanding further research.

---

[676] See Moro Visconti (2009).

Selected Readings

MORO VISCONTI R., (2012), *Is African Microfinance Different? Evidence from Banana Skins,* in African Journal of Microfinance and Enterprise Development, 2, 2, 25–45.

CHAPTER 24 – I have a dream: banking the unbankable, softening the poverty traps with microfinance mitigation chances

> Give a man a fish, he'll eat for a day.
> Give a woman microcredit, she, her husband, her children and her extended family will eat for a lifetime.
>
> Bono Vox (adapted from an ancient Chinese proverb)

A road map for sustainable development, lifting away poverty

Sustainable development, a catalyst for visionary economic growth, that is potentially able to catapult the bottom billion out of poverty, is emerging with increasing consciousness as a long term target. It can be declined in practical and complementary issues which pivot around renewable resource exploitation strategies, protecting the environment and rebalancing its overexploitation with a stabilization of the world's population.

As we have seen in previous Chapters describing the poverty traps and microfinance, sustainable development is the best contraceptive, that is able to lift all boats with a balanced economic trajectory, realizing the vision of ending extreme poverty and, eventually, narrowing the distances between the rich and the poor. Social justice blended with environmental stewardship is the real key behind sustainable development, and incentives and goals are the background of any human worthwhile effort. In order to be sustainable, development also has to be equitable, with the active and encouraged participation of all its stakeholders.

Long term sustainability–investing in the future–commands a premium over short sighted instant gratification and expedient present. The concept of time, analyzed in Chapter 9, helps in the understanding of cultural differences and their practical implications.

According to Areti (2007):

> Sustainable development is often an over-used word, but involves a number of inter-related global issues such as poverty, inequality, hunger, and environmental degradation, etc. People tend to think that we have to make a choice between environmental protection and development. Development that is sustainable and not

> damaging to the natural resources is very much possible. To achieve sustainable development the three pillars–economic, social and environmental–must be integrated in a balanced way. [...] The idea of sustainable development grew from numerous environmental movements in earlier decades and ultimately defined as: development that meets the needs of the present without compromising the ability of future generations to meet their own needs.

›*I Have a Dream*‹ is the title of the celebrated visionary speech of Martin Luther King during his 1963 epic march on Washington, where he raised public consciousness of the civil rights movement.
Banking the unbankable is another worthy and eccentric dream, that is apparently completely different from racial segregation issues, but in practice it represents another form of discrimination, with profound side effects on the civil rights of the poor[677]. Examples of useful tools for sustainable development are renewable energy loans, examined later on in this Chapter, and education loans–an investment in the future, improving the income–generation potential, albeit without short term monetary returns. Human development theory tries to merge different ideas coming from ecological economics, sustainable development, welfare economics, and anthropology.
This book is dedicated to the poor, who are stuck in their destituteness by many interacting misery traps; it is a sad and destructive description of the poverty's causes and consequences, which is optimistically blended with a possible solution–or, at least, mitigation factor–to poverty, represented by a celebrated and by now popular instrument called ›microfinance‹ and its innovative financial paradigm, being able to understand previously neglected poor clients.
Since the author is skeptical about miracles, especially if conceived and managed by human beings, his opinion is that microfinance may help to reduce poverty, but not in any case or at any cost – microfinance is not, alone, the motorway to development: it is only a key component of a wider paradigm shift.

Looking for a creative integrated approach, complementarily tackling the poverty traps

Imagine that all the five fingers of one's hand–each one symbolizing a poverty trap–are aching and that with microfinance one can just treat the thumb. Is one's hand going to be better off? Probably not, whether it is much likelier than even one's cured finger may soon or later be contaminated by the other still aching fingers and get worse off once again.

677 See Chapter 13.

This is how microfinance should be considered: a tool to tackle poverty traps complementarily with other measures and instruments – together they may sinergistically work, while alone they are condemned to failure. Putting wrong expectations on microfinance–unwisely thinking that it acts like a magic wand to solve all the poverty traps–brings to disappointment and despair, while its matched use with other instruments has shown to be much more rewarding and longer lasting. Microfinance is part of a holistic development process which anthropologically puts human development at its center. According to the encyclical letter Caritas in Veritate (§30):

> The theme of integral human development takes on an even broader range of meanings: the correlation between its multiple elements requires a commitment to *foster the interaction of the different levels of human knowledge* in order to promote the authentic development of peoples.

Any attempt to solve the poverty traps should conveniently be anticipated by a careful ›market‹ analysis, so to have a comprehensive acknowledgement and a mapping of the interacting poverty traps, consistent with each environment's peculiarities.

It has already been shown in the introduction that in order to rightfully address the misery issue, we need a holistic approach, deriving from the fact that poverty is a complex and multidimensional topic.

Looking for inspiring solutions, a creative holistic and integrated approach to the poverty issues is characterized by curiosity, open-mindedness, love of learning, persistence, vitality, perspective, social intelligence, temperance. They are all synergic qualities that need to be jointly exploited, finding new ways to address old problems, in order to design environmental friendly products and services and to create economically and socially sustainable added value, reminding that economic development is peace promoting. A realistic approach to the poverty issues is however always needed, given the available resources.

Microcredit schemes, to be managed to achieve economic viability, appear as a popular poverty reduction policy, using social funds. Microfinance, consistent with aid's bottom up approach, is gender inclined towards women, favoring advocacy for sex equality and standing out as a human right and a social movement, going beyond market driven financial development.

The keys for microfinance and development are self fulfillness and self fueling, overcoming inequalities with incremental improvements and becoming a viable alternative to the standard foreign aid model.

Albeit the interaction between poverty traps and economic development is difficult to model and it should require a sophisticated econometric analysis, well beyond the target of this book, its likely trend may not differ too much from the one depicted below. It may show an inverse relationship that is roughly represented by a

hyperbole where poverty traps asymptotically converge to zero beyond a certain ideal threshold of sustained development. The lower the development rates–up to a much damaging negative growth–the higher the impact on self fulfilling and synergic poverty traps.
The interactions between poverty traps and microfinance are synthesized in table 24.1.

Table 24.1. – Poverty traps and (microfinance) mitigation strategies

Poverty trap	**Description**	**Connections with other traps**	**Mitigation strategies**	**Impact of Microfinance**
Landlocked-ness	Characteristic of countries with no direct access to the sea, hampered in their development by isolation, bad neighbors, high transportation costs.	The conflict trap, fixing borders and blocking trade, exacerbated problems of landlocked countries.	Airplane connections. ICT, and other technological and virtual communications. Friendship treaties with bordering coastal countries.	Negligible, since microfinance cannot reshape borders. It may soften micro problems of claustrophobic economies, as it is positively showed in landlocked countries such as Bolivia.
Natural resources curse	Due to improper and unfair exploitation of oil, gas, or mineral resources, to the advantage of local crooks and foreign multinationals, but to the detriment of poor indigenous.	The conflict trap, since oil revenues may finance wars and cause conflicts for geopolitical reasons.	International treaties and Western and domestic public opinion pressures. Competitive ›beauty contest‹ among different exploiters. Fair and democratic disclosure and subdivision of proceeds.	Negligible, since extractive industries are highly capital intensive and so intrinsically unfit for microfinance schemes.
Demographic growth	The poorest tend to over reproduce themselves, sometimes beyond the survival threshold.	Illiteracy trap, especially concerning women: the more they are illiterate, the more they are induced to procreate.	Literacy and instruction, emancipation and job opportunities.	Being a pro-women instrument, microfinance can greatly contribute to their emancipation, with an indirect impact on limiting excess

Poverty trap	Description	Connections with other traps	Mitigation strategies	Impact of Microfinance
				fertility.
Conflict trap	Civil wars and conflict, with likely relapses, block development, destroying the economy.	Natural resources, even exploitation, overpopulation, unfreedom may all interact, igniting or prolonging conflicts.	Foster development, squeezing inequalities, promoting pluralism and reconciliation.	Fostering micro-development, microfinance may give a (small) contribution to appeasement. »Supporting microfinance in devastated and fragile communities can be successful when donors work in concert, select qualified partners, are patient, are willing to take risks, and are prepared to pay higher costs. Effective microfinance can create the foundation for a fully integrated financial sector and fuel reconstruction«[678].
Hunger and malnutrition	The poor are often hungry; undernutrition and/or bad food quality brings to illnesses, up to death.	It reduces school attendance and learning capacity (illiteracy trap), hampering employment possibilities, especially for discriminated girls, who are overexposed to ill-being, rising child mortality.	Improve agricultural production; educate people upgrading hygienic standards; stress the importance of better nutrition.	Economic progress, thanks also to microfinance, improves economic capacity and softens revenues volatility.

678 CGAP (2004d).

Poverty trap	Description	Connections with other traps	Mitigation strategies	Impact of Microfinance
		It brings to desperate and unsustainable depletion of natural resources, reducing capacity to address market opportunities.		
Water shortage	Limit or block economic activity, up to death.	It may bring to conflicts. Lack of regular rainfall exacerbates hunger, illnesses, and child mortality.	Development and improvement of distribution systems.	Implementation of small economic activities, backed by microcredit, can soften these typical underdevelopment problems.
Illiteracy	Analphabetism completely blocks instruction, keeping the poor segregated from a knowledge economy.	Demographic overgrowth.	Capillary investments in education, from basic levels to academic ones.	Social gatherings such as group lending and microfinance returns may promote development and resources for school fees.
Climatic changes	Increase of the world temperature, with more extreme and volatile weather.	Both draught and floods become more common, with potentially severe side effects on health and nutrition.	Cutting CO_2 emissions and deforestation, using renewable sources of energy.	Microfinance, like everything else, will not be spared. The increasing emphasis on responsible finance has added environmental impact to the factors considered as measures of success for a microfinance institution[679].
Language	Languages	Being a lin-	Education, in-	No impact.

[679] See Rippey (2009).

Poverty trap	Description	Connections with other traps	Mitigation strategies	Impact of Microfinance
trap	spoken by small and isolated ethnic groups, isolating them from the rest of the world.	guistic landlockedness, it can interact with the geographical one, increasing isolation.	troducing a second spoken language, possibly English, acting as a lingua franca.	
Property trap	The poor live in properties with no legal titling, so being unable to sell them, inherit or transmit and use as a guarantee for mortgages.	This invisibility trap is linked with the educational trap, since illiterate poor are likely to have no real estate properties.	Expand the cadastral system and record property borders, solving land disputes with equanimity.	Housing microfinance can soften the problem.
Educational trap	Illiterate poor are trapped in a growing misery status, especially in a global knowledge economy.	Illiterate poor typically don't have any property titling and are subject to the demographic trap, especially if illiteracy concerns fertile women.	Invest in education, a long term strategy with no immediate proceeds.	Proceeds from activities backed by microfinance can be conveniently spent in education.
Foreign debt trap	Underwriting of debt financed by foreign countries.	Interacts with aid for development, being a part of it when debt is forgiven. Its rescheduled repayment or cancellation is conditional upon strict fiscal measures to cut the deficit, so shrinking public expenditure	Avoid over-indebtedness, relying on internal funding and developing a taxation system that allows public expenditure to be covered locally.	While foreign debt is a macro country-to-country arrangement, microfinance works on a micro level. While being mostly unable to affect foreign debt choices, it can help making dependence on foreign funding less impellent.

Poverty trap	Description	Connections with other traps	Mitigation strategies	Impact of Microfinance
		for the poor.		

Development is intuitively inversely proportional to the poverty traps, as ideally represented in Figure 24.1.

Figure 24.1. – Development is inversely proportional to the poverty traps

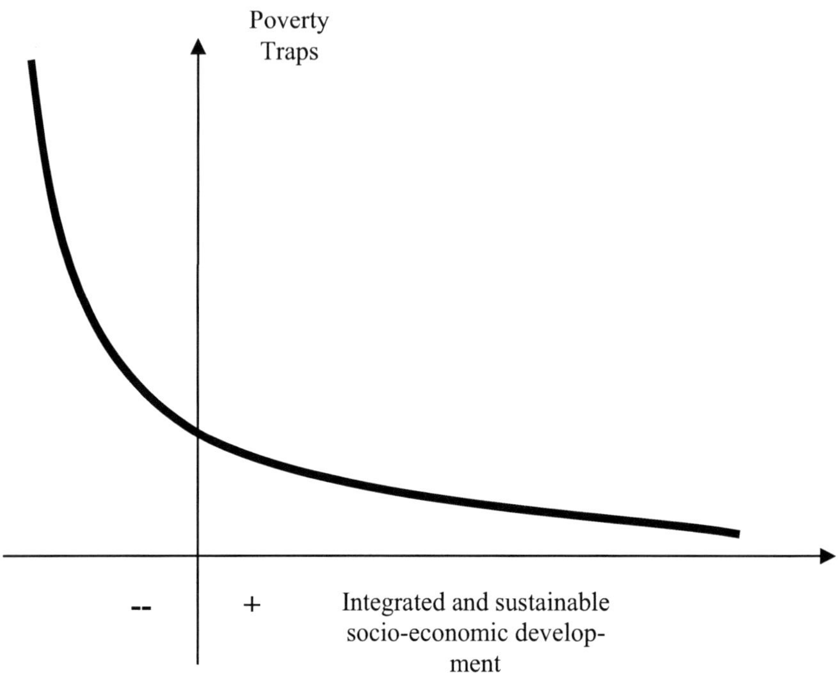

Poverty traps are interacting, as symbolically represented in figure 24.2.

Figure 24.2. – The interacting poverty spiraling wheels

Microfinance within an integrated development pattern

Microfinance is a friendly tool to accompany economic transition out of underdevelopment, following a progressive growth pattern and avoiding the so common mismanagement of development priorities, since it operates within sustainable and inclusive economies.

The take-off model developed by Walt Whitman Rostow is one of the major historical models of economic growth, and it indicates that economic modernization from early stages up to maturity and mass consumption occurs in five basic stages of varying length, following a linear pattern where key socioeconomic indicators (such as investments, savings, consumption, and social trends) interact in different ways.

Rostow's historical and mechanical model is based on the Western experience, being so biased by potentially different pattern alternatives and, dating back to 1960, not being adequately influenced by technological innovation, according to which development may jump beyond single stages of growth, with an unprecedented discontinuity. Alexander Gerschenkron, beyond David Ricardo's theory of comparative advantages, has elaborated a ›backwardness‹ model postulating that the more backward an economy was at the outset of development the more certain conditions were likely to occur during growth: consumption would be squeezed in

favor of investment (*i.e.,* savings) and investment enhancing entities (banks, the State …) would have greater importance.
Sachs (2009) depicts a different pattern and the two models are provocatively compared, in order to show the possible impact of microfinance within each stage of development.
A comparison between the models of Rostow and Sachs is contained in table 24.2.

The controversial utility of microfinance

Development models may conveniently embody microfinance and its impact.

Table 24.2. – Development models and the role of microfinance

Rostow (1960)	**Sachs (2009)**	**Key features** ⟺	**Microfinance**
Traditional society	Subsistence economy	Low agricultural productivity and subsistence farming, poor infrastructure, low schooling.	Microfinance may be started up with seed projects, even if it may be unfit for the poorest.
Preconditions for take-off	Commercial economy	Due to sufficient savings, public expenditure is enabled to back development and trade, starting from agricultural exports, improves, together with infrastructures. Foreign aid does little to equip nations for the transition from poverty to industrialization. Agriculture is complemented by housing and textile production.	Microfinance may substantially contribute to preparing the background for economic development from subsistence to commercial scenario, where increased trade fosters further growth.
Take-off	Emerging market economy	Transition economy, with growing trade, consolidation of exporting activities in specialized areas and increased purchasing power. Industrial activities, starting from unsophisticat-	In its more advanced transitional phase, the economy is eventually taking-off and the role of MFIs should grow accordingly, accom-

Rostow (1960)	Sachs (2009)	Key features	Microfinance
		ed labor intensive ones, begin to be introduced in the development framework.	panying the development with stronger institutions (licensed deposit taking MFIs, up to fully viable microfinance banks).
Drive to maturity	Technology based economy	The level of instruction has to accompany the economy to a consistent jump of quality and sophistication. Productivity gains, maximization of added value, and comparative advantages are necessary to reach the maturity stadium of development. From that peak on, decreasing marginal rates of growth begin to appear.	Sophistication of financial intermediaries grows and MFIs decrease their marginal role, living together with other bigger commercial intermediaries. Mass consumption has a strong financial impact, concerning the savings ratio and the level of debt.
Age of high mass consumption			

A theoretical as well as a practical issue concerns the utility of microfinance. Is it effective as it is widely advertised?

According to Richard Rosenberg[680] »scientific testing of the impact of microcredit is surprisingly difficult. If we find that people who got microloans are doing better than those who didn't, does this mean that the loans caused the improvement? Maybe not. There are several other plausible explanations – for instance, that the people who apply for and get the loans may have more drive and ambition, in which case they would probably tend to do better than others whether or not they get the loan«.

Among the key problems of economics, with huge impacts on social sciences and on microfinance issues, there is the basic assumption that agents (individuals) behave rationally, and so they are risk adverse, profit maximizers, etc. The problem arises not because economists are naively unaware that many–if not most–individuals are irrational, but rather since it proves hard, if not impossible, to mod-

[680] CGAP (2010b).

el irrationality, describing the infinite potential outcomes of illogic behavior with a mathematical handset of equations, theorems, and models.
Behavioral finance, going beyond rigid rational assumptions, softens these problems and it gets somewhat closer to reality, trying to model complexity in innovative ways.
With microfinance, the problem is somewhat mitigated, from the theoretical side, by its apparently unsophisticated mechanisms, although empirical evidence is biased, contradictory, and tricky, with an uneasy definition and testing of cause – effect mechanisms (e.g., are the poor really better off thanks to microfinance?).

Sustainable microfinance, beyond market and State failures?

The market economy has been inspired by the capitalistic system that is now economically and culturally dominating our world, since the end of the cold war: albeit being a powerful engine and stimulus behind an unprecedented development in human history, it is however unable to solve most of the dramatic poverty issues that still trap in misery so many underserved.
State interventions play an important complementary role, softening the market's intrinsic harshness and greed and providing some basic services to its citizens, irrespectively of their economic value.
The synergic effect of the intervention of both the State and the market is difficult to cover all the complex human needs, starting from those of the misrepresented poor, and it has to take into account its uneasy blending and coordination.
We have already seen in Chapters 13 and 14 that subsidiarity connects individuals at the lowest possible level and avoids both State and market imperfections. It is a feasible way to bypass some of the most evident failures of a polarized State versus market model, accompanying its action with gratuity, mutuality, and a cooperative attitude that are immanent and innate in most poor clans.
In some cases, microfinance can trespass myopic market failures and negative externalities, overcoming stateless fallacies, that are particularly common in many underdeveloped countries where market rules–not being fully assimilated by local cultures–and interventions of fragile and institution-less States are hardly present and seldom effective. Investment opportunities need proper financing and microfinance can play its part in development ignition.
Within this complementary triangular system, microfinance may well act as a connecting point among the market, the State, and subsidiarity:

Figure 24.3. – Microfinance as a bridge between the State, the Market, and Subsidiarity

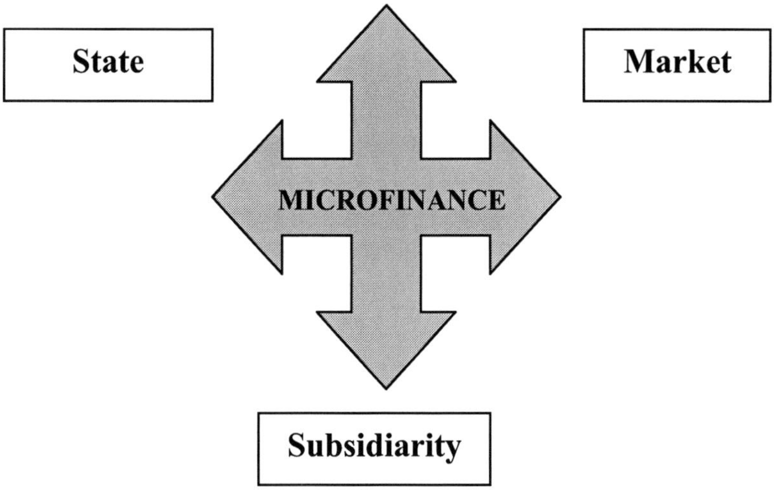

As a matter of fact, in underdeveloped countries where both the State and the market economy are hardly effective, subsidiarity is already albeit unconsciously present, even if in an embryonic and confused form, as well as its bottom up approach that informally links individuals at the lowest possible level of intermediation. The lack of the State authority, mixed with the market's nonexistence or its failures, poses however other challenging issues, resulting in a lack of power, guidance, and opportunities that strongly limit any growth potential.

Informal subsidiarity, which is represented in the financial sector by moneylenders or other unofficial intermediaries, prepares an ideal background for cooperative microfinance. When cooperative microfinance has to pass from its infancy to an adult age, it needs to be complemented by the intervention of both the State (proving an institutional and supervisory framework) and the international and domestic financial markets.

Microfinance complements both the State role and the market one since it is based on a private relationship, not being indiscriminately addressed to everybody, going however beyond the market utilitarian goals. Whereas microfinance needs the State and the market, as we have seen above, it can also give its support to both, strengthening the purchasing power of the poor–and so creating a new market–and improving the poor condition with a positive side back effect on State institutions.

MFIs sustainability has to be properly declined considering not only its capacity to economically survive along time, but also its environmental friendly approach.

Renewable energy loans, in order to substitute polluting combustibles such as charcoal or kerosene, can help poor clients to face the upfront costs of solar home lighting systems or other environmental friendly technologies.
To be effective, microfinance has to be complemented by a sound institutional framework, where public expenditure is addressed to long term infrastructural projects concerning transportation, healthcare, education, administration of justice.

Renewable energy and microfinance, beyond the natural resources curse

Fossil fuel exploitation is likely to generate the natural resources curse already seen in Chapter 3, backing those who are nicknamed ›petrodictators‹ by Thomas Friedman. Furthermore, the exploitation of big natural resources requires huge investments, which are far beyond the financing possibilities of microfinance industry, which simply doesn't fit. Wealth distribution is often uneven and highly biased by divertive measures and corruption. The impact of this often ruthless exploitation on the environment and on its poor inhabitants is in many cases devastating, leaving everybody worse off – except the happy few admitted sharing the pie. And natural resources are typically not renewable (except water of forests, which however have to be safeguarded) and once they are wasted and wrongfully exploited, they cannot be replaced – when oil is gone and its wells dry up, the game is simply over and forever.
Non-renewable fossil fuel is also polluting and unduly warming up the world's temperature. A growing attention towards renewable energy, that is wisely down scaled to local needs and it is able to overcome big infrastructural investments, can help to mitigate these problems, at least in the long run. A technological gap is still to be overcome, and it will painfully take time, but the long term target is hardly rebuttable.
Microfinance is intrinsically involved with a small scale bottom up approach, starting from the poor and their basic financial needs: it increasingly looks as a useful device to accompany long term sustainable development. Sustainability is now conceived–and here comes an upgrade of the past ideology–not only as the ability of the MFI to survive, possibly increasing its outreach (as we have seen in Chapter 21), but also as the possibility to conceive and put into practice an environmental friendly development model, where access and use of renewable sources of energy is incorporated in the model – taking it from the sun, the wind, sea tides, recycling waste …
Solar energy can help to produce enough electricity–especially in hot and sunny places–to charge mobile phones batteries or PCs or to light up, to cook and to refrigerate on a small scale. It is enough to radically change the life of potentially

billions of poor, raising up their living standards and enabling them to grasp new opportunities, markets, products, and lifestyles.
Microfinance can soften and mitigate the energy trap, which is so dramatic for many poor, enabling them to have an affordable access to renewable sources, this being a fundamental precondition for a not-ephemeral development.
The potential market for small–and possibly cheap–technological devices is potentially unlimited and largely unexploited. It can produce the needed energy, taking it directly from Mother Nature.
Since the poor have neither the initial resources nor the proper technology to buy solar panels or other devices to capture energy, they do need seed sponsorship to start up. So philanthropic investment has to be part of the game, possibly with a joint entrepreneurship, according to which the sponsors go beyond the old fashioned and abused model of passive contributor, sharing with the MFI clients the business risk and becoming partners for development.
In places with no electricity, life dies with the sunset and microfinance can foster the use of renewable sources of power, going beyond darkness.

Incredible mission: outthinking and experimenting new solutions

New innovative and smart solutions are deeply wanted, with their imaginative diversity, in order to envisage a development framework, which ought to be:

- sustainable (self fulfilling; environmental friendly …);
- socially and economically equitable, promoting and egoless unselfishness;
- open to innovation and cost cutting;
- able to fully exploit the potentialities of human talent.

When the underserved are stuck in the quicksand of interacting poverty traps, they need an external help, which typically comes from abroad if the native country is intrinsically backward. The problem with this apparently trivial reasoning is that foreign aid is hardly neutral and it can affect development in many different ways, not necessarily benign, as we have seen in Chapter 14 analyzing one of the most controversial issues concerning development.
Introducing microfinance within the ›aid for development‹ debate and reminding that anyway in any business, access to credit is just one of the many critical factors for development, some apparently trivial questions come out:

- can microfinance backed by foreign investors avoid the traditional aid banana skins?

- Is foreign aid backing microfinance effective? And is there an alignment of conflicting interests when donors are transformed into investors / sharing partners, noticing that there is no crowding out effect sending money instead of foreign goods?

Sustainable and equilibrated shared development is the ultimate goal, reminding that beauty of life is harmony of things – and it may be symbolized by music, whose task is harmonizing dissonance.
The main reason why microfinance is proving neither decisive nor particularly effective in taming poverty is due to the very circumstance–widely documented in this book–that poverty causes are many, with multiple and interacting impacts, well beyond a single factor.
Men intrinsically tend to be selfish, but they should learn that some sharing is necessary and even convenient, replicating a sort of Pareto optimality context where nobody can improve his position without damaging another's one. Sharp inequalities are sooner or later disruptive for everybody, the poor but also the rich.
Looking for holistic and zero gravity sustainability, concerning our very human existence and Mother nature, it may gratefully be acknowledged that microfinance, once properly ignited and managed, may be a renewable device–somewhat resembling renewable energy–for banking the poor and so it deserves its place within a synergic orchestra of complementary instruments. But microfinance is not a panacea for all the problems concerning the poor, since it is just one of the many instruments – and instruments are always subordinated to the orchestra director behind and above them.

The condensed Chapter

The multifaceted and interactive poverty traps, which were examined in the introduction and in particular in the first part of this book, have to be carefully analyzed putting Man at the very centre of any investigation about feasible development strategies – with a human perspective. Technicalities and managerial programs, if mechanically applied irrespectively of local immanent conditions, have proved to be a complete fiasco.

Out of Poverty Tips

Poverty traps are deeply interactive, within their smelling melting pot. Interdisciplinary assessment, looking for unforeseeable shanghai interactions, is an increasing must, to be undertaken with proper cultural openness and pragmatic approach.

Selected Readings

AZARIADIS C., STACHURSKI, J., *Poverty Traps?*, in AGHION P., DURLAUF S.N., (2005), *Handbook of Economic Growth*, Elsevier, Amsterdam, in http://elsa.berkeley.edu/~chad/azstach.pdf.

BOWLES S., DURLAF S.N., HOFF K., (2006), *Poverty traps*, Princeton University Press, Princeton.

CHAPTER 25 – How to prepare a sustainable business plan with Excel

By failing to prepare, you are preparing to fail.

Benjamin Franklin

Introduction

In June, 2011, I was teaching Microfinance in Nairobi, Kenya. I was excited about this new didactic experience but my students, mostly Africans, seemed a bit distracted and worried.
I so investigated about the reasons of their mood and they told me frankly that it was nothing personal with me or my lectures, but rather with their deadline of the following week: much feared presentation of a real business plan!
This is the simple and unoriginal starting idea behind this practical chapter and, especially, an Excel tutorial template concerning a business plan. Students are the main characters of this "didactical patchwork" and they should be aware that passive assimilation is completely useless here.
Microsoft Excel is the best known spreadsheet software and it may well exemplify how IT applications can be conveniently used, in order to figure out strategic pathways for the development of new business adventures. Economic value added is increasingly intangible-driven and so software applications, intrinsically scalable, may greatly contribute to sort out poverty, following trendy patterns.
Plain description of poverty traps and microfinance tools, which occupies most of this book, still misses practical applications and the very target of this chapter is to try to present a toolkit for practical business planning. The original idea, as mentioned above, starts with a bottom up solicitation. Traveling throughout still developing countries, I am increasingly convinced that proper planning–business planning–is a fundamental starting point for any sound development pattern.
I discussed about this key issue at first with my worried but helpful students and then with my colleagues and we decided to go through it, trying to transform a problem into an opportunity. This because students (practitioners-to-be) need a practical, flexible and mostly comprehensive framework where to model their management strategies, synthesizing their theoretical knowledge, which would otherwise seriously risk becoming completely useless.

Another useful aspect of an Excel Business plan is that, from a didactical point of view, it is possibly the most suitable tool for synthesizing many different interdisciplinary concepts, which mostly pivot around business administration topics, ranging from Accounting, to Banking, Corporate Finance, Management, Strategy, Marketing … Some complementary macroeconomic, statistical, mathematical, and computer science concepts are always necessary.
This chapter is not going to provide any tutorial about how to use Excel; this is taken for granted and students or practitioners with spreadsheet problems should address themselves elsewhere. A basic understanding of how Excel works is necessary for starting, even if more advanced skills (considering how to make formulas, macros, etc.) are more than welcome. In the increasingly competitive world we are living in, English-Excel-Internet are three basic cornerstones for bare survival or, hopefully, better job prospects.
Also, some basic "double-entry" accounting background is necessary, starting from general ledger; some basic accounting notions will be summarized in the appendix.
In synthesis, two background skills are necessary for proper business planning:
basic accounting (in order to prepare the balance sheet, income statement and cash flow account)

1. basic Excel knowledge (so as to transform ideas into IT numbers).

A business plan is a formal accounting statement which numerically describes a set of business goals, the reasons why they are believed attainable and the strategic plan and managerial steps for reaching those goals. Decisions have to be number driven. Hypotheses and visionary ideas of game changers have to be transformed into numbers and need to be backed by reasonable and verifiable assumptions about future events and milestones.
Microsoft Excel© stands out as the most popular spreadsheet software and for that reason the whole chapter will move around Excel applications, even if other more sophisticated software programs may be conveniently used, considering also that data are typically importable from or exportable to Excel sources. Numbers are a mental discipline of ideas and Excel is a key instrument to play with figures.
Even if this topic is not original or innovative, and has already been extensively investigated, as it appears from many sources, even freely available from the Web, it seems however potentially useful to go through it again, providing some further tips to both students and practitioners, especially to visionaries and challengers.
A link to a free Excel file connects this explanatory chapter to a more practical device. YouTube tutorial videos accompany this chapter and the Excel model.
This Excel file derives from a joint work, coordinated by the author and anybody is welcome to freely copy / download / modify this open source file; the only condition kindly asked is to report any improvement, sending the amended file, together with a list of the modifications to roberto.morovisconti@morovisconti.it.

Enjoy our creative intervention and contribute to upgrade the model, making it "viral" on the Web!
A video with the presentation of this chapter may be downloaded from: http://www.youtube.com/watch?v=Dpd0YQM3Rac, while another video with the presentation of the related Excel file template may be downloaded from: http://www.youtube.com/watch?v=Awdf4L5UiJ8.
Basic Excel explanations go beyond the boundaries of this chapter, but readers may find helpful sources (and web tutorial videos) in the Videos listed after the References.
This software is also perfectly consistent with an e-Learning flexible program, eliminating all space and time differences, being available everywhere and at any time, so breaking barriers and creating virtual classrooms.

Playing with numbers: budgeting and the business plan backbone

Budgeting lies at the foundation of every perspective economic and financial plan, not only for start ups. According to http://en.wikipedia.org/wiki/Budget#Budget_types, budget types include:

- Sales budget – an estimate of future sales, often broken down into both units and Euros. It is used to create company sales goals.
- Production budget – an estimate of the number of units that must be manufactured to meet the sales goals. The production budget also estimates the various costs involved with manufacturing those units, including labor and material. Created by product oriented companies.
- Cash flow/cash budget – a prediction of future cash receipts and expenditures for a particular time period. It usually covers a period in the short term future. The cash flow budget helps the business determine when income will be sufficient to cover expenses and when the company will need to seek outside financing.
- Marketing budget – an estimate of the funds needed for promotion, advertising, and public relations in order to market the product or service.
- Project budget – a prediction of the costs associated with a particular company project. These costs include labour, materials, and other related expenses. The project budget is often broken down into specific tasks, with task budgets assigned to each. A cost estimate is used to establish a project budget.

- Revenue budget – consists of revenue receipts of government and the expenditure met from these revenues. Tax revenues are made up of taxes and other duties that the government levies.
- Expenditure budget – includes spending data items.

Budgeting and "power to predict" have to be properly incorporated within a wider system of business planning.
It should be made immediately clear that the accounting backbone of any business plan–with its consequent Excel formulation–is first of all represented by the interactive matching of the three basic balance sheet documents:

1. the balance sheet, with a representation of assets, liabilities, and differential net equity;
2. the income statement (profit & loss account), with a coherent matching of revenues and costs;
3. the cash flow statement, showing the quantity (and quality) of liquidity created or absorbed.

The cash flow statement is automatically derived combining balance sheet variations (from the previous year) with the income statement of the year under investigation and so no new information are given, since they are already existing, just needing to be reclassified and extracted from their originating somewhat hidden sources.
In the Excel file, input data in the "Balance Sheet" and "Income statement" worksheets are automatically linked with consequential sheets (starting from "Balance sheet variation"), in order to output the much welcome "Cash Flow statement", represented in a separate sheet.
This IT steps faithfully follow the accounting principles which are behind the preparation of the business plan.
Among the major mistakes in preparing a business plan, the mere forecast of expected revenues and costs over a conventional multi-annual time horizon, accompanied by a rough and unsupported estimate of cash flows, stands out as a mostly likely banana skin.
To those who look for shortcuts, avoiding to derive the cash flow statement from the necessary comparison of two consecutive balance sheets, matched with the income statement, it may suffice mentioning that if they so behave (completely ignoring the necessity to prepare a balance sheet, which is the company's cumulated "backbone"), they are likely to undergo unsolvable problems, such as for example:

- how to calculate the impact of a changing net working capital (due to modifications in accounts receivable and payable, in the inventory …);

- how to determine any modification in the net financial position (i.e., financial debts net of financial credits).

The balance sheet and, in particular, the expected income statements along the whole useful life of the investment horizon, are the true backbone behind any business plan. Anything else (break even analysis; financial ratios; market evaluation …), albeit useful or even necessary, is just complementary.
Try to transform your vision into feasible numbers, blending imagination with concreteness.

How to write a business plan … step after step

The main questions concerning the start up phase of a business plan preparation are the following:

- How to conceive and prepare a business plan?
- Which are the consequential steps?
- How to be simultaneously effective and comprehensive?
- How to properly combine hard and soft skills?

These are just a few of the many questions that every practitioner has to face. And even if You are not a business plan expert and You may never be asked to prepare a business plan, You are extremely likely to be in the position to evaluate, assess or just read somebody else's business plan. So, it is always useful to know how to read it and, in order to do so, any potential user should have at least a basic knowledge about how to prepare a business plan; not everybody is due to become an expert, but we are all likely to be somewhat involved in some business plan issues, so … it is better to start approaching them, at least in a broad and intuitive way.
Many sources exist for finding information for your business plan. Your local library and the internet are always helpful sources. If you live near a university, you may be able to schedule an appointment with one of the college's professors. The professor may be able to give insightful tips.
Make sure you cite your information. This way you will have support for any statistics you put into your business plan.
Soft skills are concerned with creativity, imagination, "immaterial" and pioneering entrepreneurship, stamina, flexibility and resilience (...), willingness to create new unexploited value, beyond simple quantitative data entry or numbering: never stop opening up your mind, progressively and continuously!
Remember that business planning is always a work in progress: never stop refining, fine tuning, upgrading, updating ... Never be satisfied: only enthusiasm can light up the fire of changing !!!

Introduction

There are two key questions that define how you will write the plan. Before beginning to write anything, identify exactly who the audience is and what you want their response to be. Do you want the reader:

- To invest in your new idea or in an existing business?
- To buy your business?
- To enter a joint venture?
- To carry out a contract?
- To give you a grant or a regulatory approval?
- To help you to run your own business?

Different types of readers will look for different information in a business plan. If you are clear about who your readers will be, then you can provide them with the information they consider most important.

You get one chance to make a good first impression. Grab that chance. Present a document that:

- is persuasive;
- looks good;
- is free of spelling, grammatical and numerical errors;
- covers the key issues;
- contains the necessary supporting information.

It's obvious that for NGO and social enterprises, the focus on social aspects is very relevant.

The structure of the business plan

You have to capture your reader's attention. You are telling the story of your business and what you propose to do with it is a fascinating story: tell it that way.

It has a beginning, a central part and an end:

- the beginning tells the background to your business and how you got here, outlining the business, management, market, etc. ;
- the middle explains what is special about your ideas and sets out the proposal itself;
- the end ask for what you need to carry out the plan, points to the risks but explains how they will be dealt with and highlights the rewards.

The exact items in a structure plan will vary from business to business but, broadly, they will be:

1. cover page and table of contents;
2. executive summary;
3. business description;
4. business environment analysis;
5. industry background;
6. competitive analysis;
7. market analysis;
8. marketing plan;
9. operations plan;
10. management summary;
11. financial plan;
12. funding request;
13. appendix.

The order will depend upon how it projects the story best. You may merge some sections or you may have extra sections that are not mentioned above.

A huge tome can be very intimidating to your reader, so try to keep the plan itself to a manageable size and put detailed data or evidence in the appendices.

1. Cover page and Table of Contents

Preparing the cover page

The cover page is the first thing your audience will see; it's like a newspaper headline that gives readers the quick information they need.

To ensure a positive first impression, your cover page should:

- have a clean, professional appearance;
- include the name of the business or project;
- give your name and contact information;

Developing the table of contents

The next page of the plan, the table of contents, let the readers know which topics will be covered.

They will also note the maneuverability of your plan – that is how easy it is to flip through the plan and quickly find the sections they want to read.

2. Executive summary

An executive summary may be the only section a reader uses to make a quick decision to the proposal, so it should fulfill reader's expectations.

It is a concise presentation of the main points of the business plan; it is a kind of abstract that gives a brief overview of the business venture. It should describe:

- the mission and the vision;
- the industry and market environment in which the opportunity will develop;
- the business opportunity – the costumer problem(s) your product or service will be solving;
- the key strategies – what differentiates your product or service from competitors' offering and, especially for social ventures;
- the financial aspect – the anticipated risk and reward of the business;
- the management team – the people who will achieve the results;
- the resources or capital being requested – a clear statement to your readers about what you hope to gain from them, whether it is capital or resources.

The executive summary is a formal statement presenting the NGO / Company fact.

Executive summary as mission statements
The purpose of the executive summary is to give the reader a quick understanding of the proposal, but it can also serve to capture the reader's interest in the business. One component that can capture a visionary sense of the business is the mission statement. It should express the opportunity, the business-social philosophy in one brief sentence.

3. Business description

Introducing your business
The business description gives you the chance to introduce your business in terms of its qualities, of positive business environment existing and, very important for social ventures, of social aspects linked to it.
Here you can give pertinent background information that makes it clear way why your concept is interesting and you can express your commitment and capacity for making it successful.
The purposes of the business description are:

- express clearly your own understanding of the business concept (and its social impacts);
- meet readers' expectations by providing a realistic picture of the business venture and social aspects linked to it.

Incorporating the right detail
Include information about the business, such as:

- what the history of the concept or business it is;
- what market the business will serve;
- what product or service is;
- what problem will the product or service solve for customers and possible social implications;
- what the financial status is;
- who will manage the business;
- where the business will be located.

4. Business Environment Analysis

Understanding industries and markets

The industry is the group that produces and sells products or services to the market; it defines your competitors.

The market is where your product or service will be sold; it determines your opportunity and your customers.

The area of intersection represents your business opportunity.

Asking the right question:

- what is the industry? What characteristics define the industry?
- Who are your competitors within the industry? Who sell the same or similar products or services to customers within your market?
- What is the market? – For example it could be defined geographically, demographically, etc. ;
- Who are your customers within the market?

5. Industry background

Defining existing products and services:

- what is the range of products or services encompassed by this industry?
- Is it electronics, or manufacturing, or food, or cereal-making industry?

Sizing the industry

What is the size and shape of the industry? Ask questions such as:

- what is the industry's production capacity, its unit sales and its overall profitability?
- Is the industry spread out geographically, or is it concentrated near the sources of row material or near the end user for efficient distribution?

Identifying important trends

- What is the predicted growth rate?
- What new patterns of growth are emerging?
- What factors might contribute to future growth?
- Is the industry fragmented, consisting of many small competitors?
- Are there major competitors controlling the industry?
- Is it traditional industry offering stable products or services, or is it moving on the edge of technology?

Anticipating barriers to entry
What are the obstacles that could block you from entering this industry? Ask:

- what resources, knowledge, or skills does it take to enter this industry?
- Are there restrictive federal or international regulations, large capital requirements or sophisticated technical knowledge associated with providing the products or services?

6. Competitive analysis

Identifying your competitors
Who solve the same problems for the customer that you intend to solve?
Identify major competitors, their products and services, and their strengths and weakness.

Distinguishing your business from the rivals
What differentiates your product or service from competitors' offering?

Assessing threats from the competition
How much of a threat are your competitors to your venture? Could they have a reaction?

7. Market analysis

Assessing the market's size and growth
Indicate how large the market for your offering is and how fast the market demand for your products or service growths.

Defining your target market
Who are your target customers? What characteristics describe them? – Consider different points of view, such as geographic location, demographic features and behavioral factors.

Articulating your value proposition

Why will customers in your target market purchase your product or service? What are your solutions to customer problems? What are the benefits of your offering for them and the society?

8. Marketing plan

After to have analyzed the business environment, to have studied the competitors and discovered the opportunity, to know your target market, to have a product or service to sell, now you have to think how you will bring your product and your market together.

Using your marketing plan as a road map

Your marketing plan serves as kind of road map describing how you intend to sell your product or service.
The plan should reflect the mission and basic business philosophy of your NGO / Company.

Developing your marketing plan

Start to by looking the key factors affecting the marketing of your product or service. Specifically:

- concentrate on the opportunity – the customer problem that your product or service is solving (keep the perspective of the customers);
- review your marketing objectives – At what level of sales will you reach the breakeven point? (The point at which your sales cover your costs);
- focus on costumers' buying behavior – when, where, why and how do costumers buy this product or service?

Defining your marketing mix

It describes the way you will achieve your marketing objectives. Think about:

- price: at what price you will offer your product or service. Will there be an established place, or will it be tiered on variable depending on consumer demand?
- Place (distribution): the physical movement of the products – how the product will arrive to the end users.

9. Operations plan

The operation plan gives an overview of the flow of the daily activities of the business and the strategies that support them; it is the transforming of the ideas or the row materials into products or services to be sold to the customers.
It should show how the NGO / Company creates value for all its stakeholders. For example:

- breakeven point;
- advantages in sourcing materials;
- innovations in production or distribution (lower costs or increase productivity);
- geographic location;
- access to skilled employees or inexpensive labor;
- how the business produces social advantages.

10. Management Summary

The management team is what makes a business work. It's the glue that brings the pieces together into a finely formed, dynamic unit.
Without the right peoples, anything will move from concept to reality. So, the management summary is an important section of the business plan, one that many of your readers will turn to first.

Describing your team members' qualifications

- What have they accomplished? What are the team members' achievements? Do they have a record of successfully projects?
- Are they realistic about the business's chances for success? Are they capable of recognizing risks and responding to the problems that will inevitably occur?
- What knowledge, skills and specific abilities do they bring to the business?
- How committed are they to this venture? Have they worked together before on project?
- What are each member's motivations? What do they hope to achieve?

Introducing the team as a unit

Show how this is the right to manage the business and the risks by:

- affirming the team's strength;
- addressing the team's perceived weaknesses;
- expressing the team management philosophy.

Relationship

If there are other institutions (public or private) involved in managing, introduce them and explain how they will participate to your task.

- who are them? Are they private or public institutions?

- Are they national or institutions?
- How are they involved to your venture? are there partnerships? How will they participate to your task?

11. Financial Plan

This is a critical section of your business plan because it translates all the other parts of the business into anticipating financial results.

Anticipating readers' concerns

Different readers of your business plan will have different points of view as they approach the financial plan.

This section is where you show your readers the current status and future projections of the NGO / Company's financial performance.

The financial picture you paint here represents your best estimate of the risks involved and the return on investment, the tangible evidence of commercial success.

Specifying your business's capital requirements

The readers of your business plan will want to know what capital investment is required.

How much money do you need to rise, how much do you expect from them, and how do you intend to use the money?

Providing financial projections

In this section, you should highlight and explain the importance of the significant figures (revenue, gross contribution, operating result, net income) from the pro forma income statements over a period of three to five years. State when you expect the NGO / Company to become profitable.

The *pro forma* financial statements are projected statements; they represent your most honest analysis of the financial progress of the business:

- the income statement shows the profit margins;
- the balance sheet provides a picture of the business's assets, equities and liabilities at a specific point in time;
- cash flow statement (how your business produces/uses cash), including a section showing the times of peak need and peak availability

Articulating your assumptions

State your assumptions about the estimated industry and market growth rates. Than give your assumptions about the internal variables of the business, such as the variable and fixed costs, growth rate of sales, cost of capital and seasonal cash flow fluctuations.

Your assumptions are the underpinnings of your financial plan. They should be realistic, within the bounds of industry experience; be sure to document them, including a more detailed set in appendices.

Conducting breakeven analysis for sales

The breakeven point is the time when the business is neither losing nor gaining money. This is the pivotal moment when the business begins to be profitable.
The reader of your business plan will want to know when and at what level of sales the breakeven point will occur.

It's calculated as follows:

Breakeven= Fixed Cost / ((Sales – Variable Costs)/Sales)

Where fixed costs are those costs that don't change as sales go up or down, and variable costs vary in proportion on sales.

Assessing risk and reward

There is real risk in any venture. Your readers will want to know your assessment of the level of risk. They want to know how you plan to avoid the risk of failure and how you plan to increase the chances for success. Depending on the fundamental riskiness of the venture, the investor will require different rates of return to balance the possibility of loss.

Anticipating financial returns

Investors also want to know the expected financial returns – typically either the return on investment (ROI) or internal rate of return (IRR). For a risky business, investors generally require a higher return to compensate for the higher level of risk of loss:

ROI=net operating income / total investments

The higher the ROI, the more efficient the NGO / Company is using its capital to produce a profit.
To attract the investors, The ROI has to be higher than the rate of a free risk investment.
To calculate an IRR of 50 per cent (the return an investor might expect for a risky investment), use the following formula:

$$FV = \text{investment x } (1+0.5)^n$$

Where FV is future value, investment is the dollar amount of the investment, and n is the number of years to receive the return.
The complete set of financial information–assumptions, income statement, cash flow statement, balance sheets, statement of sources and uses–should be included in the appendices.

12. Funding Request

Highlight key aspects (economic and social) of your success strategy, focusing on your future self-financing, always considering that you need funds to begin.

An introduction to the model: a ... »complicated but simple« device

The Excel spreadsheet is divided into two main interacting parts:

1. INPUT - the first part, with red sheets consisting of the income statement and balance sheet, is the data entry of the tool. Data included in these pages will then be automatically shown in the following sections.

2. OUTPUT - the second part with blue sheets concerns the financial and economic analysis: cash flow, key evaluations, etc...

This Excel template is flexibly conceived as a simple but potentially comprehensive and analytical tool for business planning; students should so avoid any unnecessary data entry and should not worry about specific input data, which may well be useless for their investment planning.
The model is so like an oxymoron: "complicated but simple"!
The connected spreadsheets in the Excel file are the following (their number may grow up, together with the degree of sophistication):

Contents:

Colours indicate **Red – INPUT**, **Blue – OUTPUT** or neutral **Yellow – CONTENTS**.
Each sheet normally contains some tutorial tips and, occasionally, some interactive Web link. The key **INPUT** sheets are:

3. balance sheet
2. income statement

Confronting consequential balance sheets, we get as an **OUTPUT**:

5. balance sheet variation

And eventually:

7. cash flow statement

The cash flow statement is, together with the income statement, the most important part of the business plan, representing its real backbone.

Upstarting and forecasting a new business

Starting up a new business, any entrepreneur is surrounded by initial excitement and following frustration, with ups and downs, and hope to take off, eventually. Soft skills have to be carefully blended with entrepreneurial spirit and ... a bit of good luck. And it should always be remembered that there are no self igniting businesses.
Preparing a business plan from scratch, after a tiring brainstorming, the entrepreneur needs to transform ideas and dreams into feasible numbers.
A projection of the income statement along the useful life of the project or, at least, its starting phase, has to consider a time span of some 3 to 5 years: the longer the forecast, the lower its accuracy; but forecasts do not even have to be too short termed: financial supporters are anxious to know about their payback.
This income statement forecast has to be accompanied by a projection of pro forma balance sheet; the first balance sheet may be the photography of the company's assets and liabilities at time zero, whereas successive balance sheets may be conceived mainly on an incremental / developmental basis, considering the impact of yearly income statement on the starting balance sheet:

Balance sheet T_0 → Income Statement T_1 →

$\rightarrow$**Balance sheet T_1 $\rightarrow$Income Statement T_2**
$\rightarrow$
$\rightarrow$**Balance sheet T_2 ...**

If You are blocked and You feel frustrated, not knowing where to start from, You may find here some shortcuts:

1. First concentrate on Your initial balance sheet, which is typically very simple, just containing the starting investments, covered by your own pocket money or some other equity / loan injections; for the moment, there are no stocks, no credits, no structured debt, no working capital ... it is so not too difficult to make the initial photography;
2. Then You have to **concentrate on the income statement forecast** for a sufficiently long period of some 3 years; this is the core part of your projections and assumptions. Again, to soften problems, You may concentrate on operating revenues and costs, trying to divide fixed from floating costs; an example may be the following:

	T_0	T_1		T_2	
			growth T_0-T_1		growth T_1-T_2
revenues	100	150		200	
			50%		33%
fixed costs	-50	-50		-50	
variable costs (20% of revenues)	-20	-30		-40	
EBIT	30	70		110	

It is so important to estimate initial revenues, their likely growth and the portion of costs necessary to reach these revenues.
Incremental balance sheet forecasts have to consider some peculiarities and sensitive items, such as the net working capital, whose variation is represented by:

CASH FLOW FROM WORKING CAPITAL
Δ of commercial credits (accounts receivable)
Δ of other credits
Δ of Prepayments and accrued income
Δ stock
Δ of Accruals and deferred income
Δ of Other debts
Δ of amounts owed to trade creditors
Δ OF NET WORKING CAPITAL

Operating or commercial (not liquid) net working capital is mainly represented by the three aforementioned key items: accounts receivable + stock – debt towards suppliers.
Two fundamental aspects of Net Working Capital should be remembered:

1. if economic margins grow–as they should–across time, then revenues grow more than operating costs and also stock tends to increase; so Net Working Capital grows;
2. any growth in Net Working Capital, representing an Asset increase, has to be properly backed by raised capital, in the form of Debt and / or Equity; NWC increases are so cash absorbing and have an implicit financial cost (often uneasy to sustain, especially for still fragile young companies).

In all this process, the entrepreneur should not particularly care about cash flow projections, not because they are not to be considered important–they are vital–but only since, from an accounting point of view, they automatically derive from a comparison of two consecutive balance sheets, matched with the income statement. So, Excel can calculate the cash flow statement directly, as a simple output.
A graph with the life cycle of companies, consistent with business planning hypotheses, may be like the following:

Figure 25.1. – Life cycle of companies

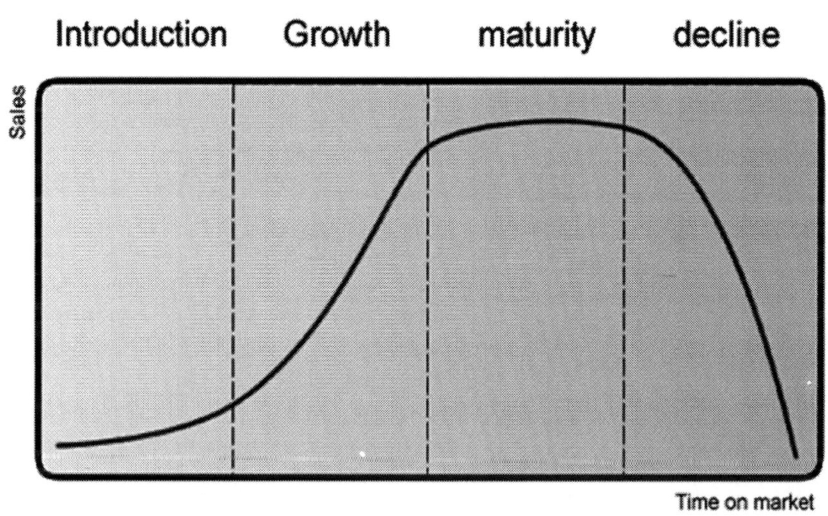

In any projection, be aware than forecast may be cloudy and fragile and that dreams not always come true, having to face brutal reality and unexpected complexity of real life.

Frameworking the business plan scenario

The business plan may be properly frame-worked using PESTLE and SWOT analysis.
Political, Economic, Social, Technological, Legal, Environmental (PESTLE) analysis is a strategic methodology for reviewing the macro environment, with its external forces that impact on ability to plan. This macro environment may well be described considering the poverty traps analyzed in the first part of this book (Chapters 1-16).
A reformulation of Table 24.1., adapted for PESTLE analysis, is synthesized in table 25.1.

Table 25.1. – Poverty traps and PESTLE analysis

Poverty trap	Description	Connections with other traps	Impact on PESTLE variables
Landlockedness	Characteristic of countries with no direct access to the sea, hampered in their development by isolation, bad neighbors, high transportation costs.	The conflict trap, fixing borders and blocking trade, exacerbated problems of landlocked countries.	Political – the issue is typically political / institutional, being concerned with statehood Economic – landlocked countries are typically poorer Environmental – continental climate
Natural resources curse	Due to improper and unfair exploitation of oil, gas, or mineral resources, to the advantage of local crooks and foreign multinationals, but to the detriment of poor indigenous.	The conflict trap, since oil revenues may finance wars and cause conflicts for geopolitical reasons.	Political – instability, corruption Economic – volatile scenarios, with violent ups and downs Technological – alternative renewable resources may be competing Legal – drilling and exploitation rights may be unfair Environmental – pollution is a typical byproduct of fossil resources
Demographic growth	The poorest tend to over reproduce themselves, sometimes be-	Illiteracy trap, especially concerning women: the more they are illit-	Political – demography may be planned Economic – impact on development is important Social – demographic drift and

Poverty trap	Description	Connections with other traps	Impact on PESTLE variables
	yond the survival threshold.	erate, the more they are induced to procreate.	changes have huge social impact Environmental – exploitation of resources greatly depends on population
Conflict trap	Civil wars and conflict, with likely relapses, block development, destroying the economy.	Natural resources, even exploitation, overpopulation, unfreedom may all interact, igniting or prolonging conflicts.	Political – politics causes conflicts but may also solve them Economic – war destroys the economy, suffocating development Social – terrific impact, to be properly detected
Hunger and malnutrition	The poor are often hungry; undernutrition and/or bad food quality brings to illnesses, up to death.	It reduces school attendance and learning capacity (illiteracy trap), hampering employment possibilities, especially for discriminated girls, who are overexposed to ill–being, rising child mortality. It brings to desperate and unsustainable depletion of natural resources, reducing capacity to address market opportunities.	Political – famine is a political issue Economic – no money, no food Social – hunger disrupts social ties Technological – innovation may help to downsize problems
Water shortage	Limit or block economic activity, up to death.	It may bring to conflicts. Lack of regular rainfall exacerbates hunger, illnesses, and child	Economic – strategic issue for development, starting from bare survival Social –discrimination between haves and haves not Technological – innovation and

Poverty trap	Description	Connections with other traps	Impact on PESTLE variables
		mortality.	proper water distribution may greatly help Environmental – water is an environmental cornerstone
Illiteracy	Analphabetism completely blocks instruction, keeping the poor segregated from a knowledge economy.	Demographic overgrowth.	Political – voting rights and representation become difficult Economic – analphabetism is a major source of underdevelopment Social – exclusion is a typical byproduct of illiteracy
Climatic changes	Increase of the world temperature, with more extreme and volatile weather.	Both draught and floods become more common, with potentially severe side effects on health and nutrition.	Economic – impact on agriculture and other activities may be huge Environmental – number 1 issue
Language trap	Languages spoken by small and isolated ethnic groups, isolating them from the rest of the world.	Being a linguistic landlockedness, it can interact with the geographical one, increasing isolation.	Economic – limited communication may severely hamper development Social – different languages divide
Property trap	The poor live in properties with no legal titling, so being unable to sell them, inherit or transmit and use as a guarantee for mortgages.	This invisibility trap is linked with the educational trap, since illiterate poor are likely to have no real estate properties.	Political – it represents a key institutional issue Economic – no titling, no development Social – discriminates between title holders and informal dwellers Environmental – illegal housing spoils the environment

SWOT analysis is a structured planning method used to evaluate the Strengths, Weaknesses, Opportunities, and Threats involved in a project, in order to consider if the objective is attainable and, if so, how.

An example of SWOT analysis, related to the microfinance environment, may be like the one depicted in Table 25.2.

Table 25.2. – SWOT analysis and microfinance

Strengths	**Weaknesses**
• feasibility of pro poor lending strategies • understandable business model • affordability	• limited funding • high operational break-even point
Opportunities	**Threats**
• Potentially unlimited number of clients • Scalability with new technologies • Economies of experience • Viral marketing	• Mission drift • Banana skins (see Chapter 23) • Competition of money-lenders

A matrix for risk metrics

Risk is a concept that identifies and - possibly - measures the expected probability of specific eventualities (possible states of the world). Technically, the notion of risk is independent from the notion of value and, as such, eventualities may have both beneficial (*upside risk*) and adverse (*downside risk*) consequences. Lenders intrinsically have particular downside sensitivity.

However, in general usage the convention is to focus only on potential negative impact to some characteristic of value that may arise from a future event.

Risk can conveniently be measured with the probability that the effective *ex post* outcome is different (lower) than the envisaged one. Pricing risk, cutting through complexity, is often more difficult than expected and unforeseen events are an additional and by definition unpredictable source of risk. Microfinance risk has broadly been defined in chapter 23.

A graphical representation of risk is depicted in Figure 25.2.

Figure 25.2. - Upside and downside risk, as a consequence of revenues' volatility

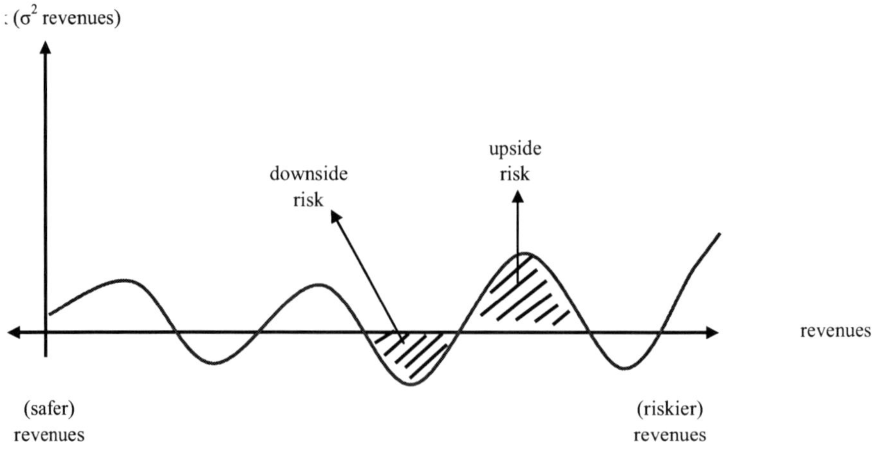

The main risks can interact within the risk matrix, with many possible outcomes often difficult to model and forecast; in many cases, the interaction follows a sort of shanghai model, according to which each stick can randomly hit the others, causing a chain effect with unforeseen results.

Risk - due to uncertain events - is extremely hard to detect and measure.

The most straightforward method is to estimate the statistical probability that a (negative) event occurs, associating to it a measurable cost (or cash outflow). But this is hardly possible in many cases, due to the difficulty to detect the risk source, to forecast the possible outcomes / states of the world and to associate to each of them a weighted cost according to its probability of occurrence. Also, in a changing scenario, many risky factors simultaneously interact among them, within a wide and interlinked risk matrix.

Risk assessment and scoring is a key step in a risk management process, consisting in the determination of quantitative or qualitative value of risk related to a concrete situation and a recognized threat (also called hazard). *Quantitative risk assessment* requires calculations of two components of risk[681]:

- the **magnitude** of the potential loss;

---

[681] An example of risk measurement can be given by the Probability of Default used in Basel II credit scoring systems. It is the likelihood that a loan will not be repaid and fall into default. This Probability of Default will be calculated for each company which have a loan. The credit history of the counterparty and nature of the investment will all be taken into account to calculate the Probability Of Default figures. The probability of default of a borrower does not, however, provide the complete picture of the potential credit loss. Banks also seek to measure how much they will lose should a borrower default on an obligation. This is contingent upon two elements:

- first, the magnitude of likely loss on the exposure: this is termed the Loss Given Default (and is expressed as a percentage of the exposure);
- secondly, the loss is contingent upon the amount to which the bank was exposed to the borrower at the time of default, commonly expressed as Exposure at Default.

- the **probability** that the loss will occur.

Risk assessment consists in an objective evaluation of risk in which assumptions and uncertainties are clearly considered and detected. Part of the difficulty of risk management is that measurement of both of the quantities in which risk assessment is concerned - potential loss and probability of occurrence - can be very difficult to identify or measure.
Risk can also derive from corporate governance problems and conflicts of interests between the public and the private part or within the private stakeholders. The first step, *hazard identification*, aims to determine the qualitative nature of the potential adverse consequences of the risky situation.
Quantitative risk assessments include a calculation of the single loss expectancy of an asset.
Risk is a holistic system, like the human body.

Sensitivity and scenario analysis

Sensitivity analysis is conducted changing a parameter at a time (e.g. interest rates; the time span of the project ...), seeing what happens to the rest, whereas with scenario analysis, two or more parameters change simultaneously, and this effect may be uneasy to model.
Business plans need to be flexible and resilient to external shocks, changes, adaptation, etc. And so sensitivity / scenario analysis, albeit bringing a certain level of sophistication, may be welcome.
The usefulness of sensitivity / scenario analysis derives also from its expected impact on break-even analysis (which may be well combined with the iterative research of the Internal Rate of Return, i.e. the return that makes Net Present Value of projected cash flows equal to zero), asking questions such as:

- which is the most pessimistic scenario (growing rates / costs; lowering returns ...) which may still allow to reach break-even?

Statistical binomial models, such as those depicted in Figure 25.3., may be applied to debt service patterns, in order to ascertain which is the break even (minimum) that may avoid cash burn out, keeping proper cover ratios:

Figure 25.3. – Example of Binomial Model

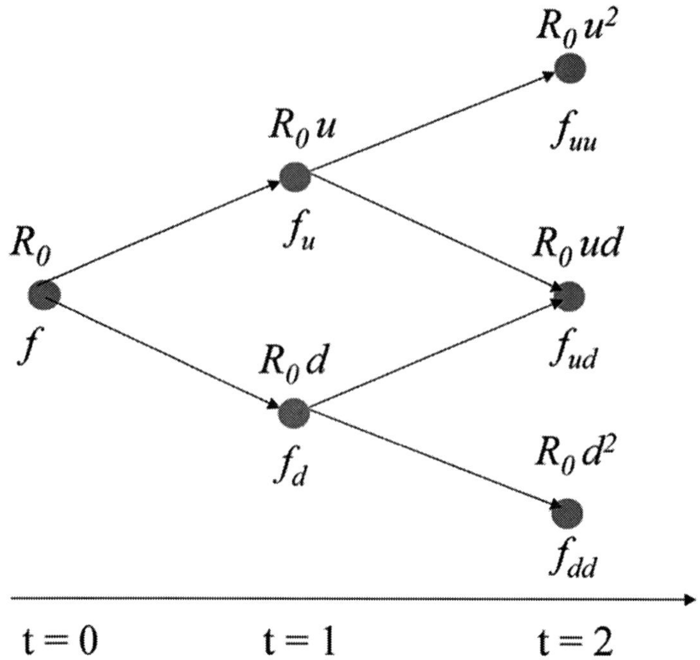

Lenders may well be interested in having an idea about this issue and even more pessimistic disaster cases may be conveniently tested, wondering about the recoverable value of a business when going concern is no more a viable option.

Break-Even Business Planning stands out as a key information, trying to estimate and fine tune likelihood of events.

A more sophisticated risk analysis can make use of Monte Carlo simulations[682].

Risk Mitigation represents a benefit for all the parties and follows several complementary steps:

[682] Monte Carlo methods are useful for modeling phenomena with significant uncertainty in inputs, such as the calculation of risk in business. Monte Carlo methods in finance are often used to calculate the value of companies, to evaluate investments in projects at corporate level or to evaluate financial derivatives. The Monte Carlo method is intended for financial analysts who want to construct stochastic or probabilistic financial models as opposed to the traditional static and deterministic models. For its use in the insurance industry, see stochastic modeling. In finance and mathematical finance, Monte Carlo methods are used to value and analyze (complex) instruments, portfolios and investments by simulating the various sources of uncertainty affecting their value, and then determining their average value over the range of resultant outcomes. The advantage of Monte Carlo methods over other techniques increases as the dimensions (sources of uncertainty) of the problem increase. See www.emeraldinsight.com/10.1108/01409170810920620.

1. **identification** - a trivial but fundamental and uneasy task: one can't avoid what he doesn't know - and a quick look to the risk matrix can give a rough idea of the problem;
2. **selection** - of the most suitable risk bearer and contractual insurance regulation;
3. **measurement** - with probability and severity quantitative estimates;
4. **monitoring** - during the tender and afterwards in the building and management phase;
5. **management** - risk mitigation has a strong impact on corporate governance conflicts among different stakeholders[683]: the lower the risk, the higher the harmony and convergence of interests.

A traditional risk scoring matrix is the one described in Figure 25.4.

Figure 25.4. - Risk scoring matrix

(Severity) Consequences		Probability of occurence (likelyhood)	Rare - 1	Unlikely - 2	Possible - 3	Likely - 4	Almost Certain - 5
	1	Negligible	1	2	3	4	5
	2	Minor	2	4	6	8	10
	3	Moderate	3	6	9	12	15
	4	Major	4	8	12	16	20
	5	Catastrophic	5	10	15	20	25

Legend:
Blue - Low risk
Grey - Moderate risk
Yellow - Significant risk
Red - High risk

impact of risk mitigation

Fixing the sustainable bottom line: how to avoid cash or equity burn outs

Sustainability is a key concern for every stakeholder, in particular for employees or external providers of finance, which did not underwrite any risky capital issue and may not benefit for potential upsides.

Due to its intrinsic importance–a matter of life or death–sustainability needs to be constantly investigated: entrepreneurs and other stakeholders should periodically check and monitor ongoing results and continuously reengineer / fix the model, looking for strategic goals / milestones achievement.

Continuous monitoring is so necessary, always looking for Business Plan release 2.0 or xx.0...

[683] See ZENNER (2001).

The main threats to sustainability are represented by cash and/or equity burn outs; synthetically reconsidering the balance sheet projection, we may have a representation of equity burn outs in Figure 25.5 and a complementary illustration of cash burn outs in Figure 25.6.

Figure 25.5. – Equity burn out representation

BALANCE SHEET	Start Up Phase		Management / Consolidation Phase		
	Year 1	Year 2	Year 3	Year 4	Year 5
Assets					
Total Current Assets					
Total Long-Term Assets					
Total Assets					
Equity & Liabilities					
Total Equity					
Current Liabilities					
Long-term Debt					
Total Liabilities					

Potential EQUITY Burn Out

And for what concerns the cash flow:

Figure 25.6. – Cash burn out representation

CASH FLOW STATEMENT	Start Up Phase		Management / Consolidation Phase		
	Year 1	Year 2	Year 3	Year 4	Year 5
Operating Cash Flow					
Net Cash Flow					
Cash Balance at the beginning of the year					
Cash Balance at the end of the year (S)					
Cash & Banks (= Liquidity) Variation					
Cumulative Cash Flow					

Potential LIQUIDITY (CASH FLOW) Burn Out

Looking for suitable funding: from venture capital to micro-finance

Financial coverage and proper funding of investments is one of the key worries of entrepreneurs. The problem is concerned also with appropriateness of funding, since the proposed investment has to be matched with suitable sources of finance. Standard bank financing is often difficult to get, since the company has no history or track record, its rating is difficult to estimate, physical guarantees of the company are still not existent and personal guarantees of the entrepreneur are often missing, inappropriate or insufficient.

Venture capital, especially in presence of highly risky–but potentially highly rewarding–investments, is an appropriate instrument, albeit its diffusion is still limited, especially in developing countries. The advantage of venture capital, which represents the "patient money of capitalism" (even if greed is far from being out of scope), is that it typically consists of equity underwriting of risky capital, with no fixed rewards.

When venture capital is unfit (due to insufficient growth potential, unsuitable industries, etc.) and banks stay far away, microfinance (in the form of microcredit + micro-consultancy) may be a suitable instrument, even if its funding capacity may be limited and, often, insufficient, if considered alone.

But financiers may, somewhat involuntarily, cause a "snowball" effect, where first comers attract new underwriters.

Entrepreneurs often acknowledge that it is very difficult to exclusively rely on self funding from the beginning; almost any business start up needs some initial equity backing and/or debt sponsoring. The problem with self financing is that it is (obviously) missing when mostly needed, in the beginning of the adventure. Later on it represents a precious source of financing, even considering the Pecking Order Hypothesis, according to which firms tend to prefer self financing, and then issue unsecured debt, and then secured debt and eventually they raise capital.

Traditional banks may well charge customers their huge operating costs and inefficiencies, with a sort of tax on growth financing, whereas other intermediaries may be more suitable for start up investments. Looking for new immaterial lenders, you may think about web P2P lending (is it like online music?).

When resourced are provided by NGOs or other not for profit institutions, they are typically granted as non returnable capital injections, which on one side lower the break even point, avoiding any cost concerned with debt servicing, whereas on the other side they may bring to opportunistic behaviours, avoiding proper monitoring (which is typically associated with debt servicing). A mixed solution with some debt may so be optimal, in order to soften problems related to underachievement or mismanagement, so common especially with new entrepreneurs.

Time horizon of repayment is longer in equity backing venture capital (where cash flow matching is less binding) and consistently shorter in microfinance.

Periodically monitoring and upgrading the model and its underlying miscalibrated expectations

Dreams always differ from ex post historic reality and miscalibrated expectations, which may prove overoptimistic and unrealistic or difficult to meet. And dreams traditionally prove difficult to model and to put into numbers: hypotheses have to be duly backed by realism, with transparent and straightforward strategies which enable to avoid arbitrary assumptions and to check if and to which extent expectations have been met, continuously fine tuning the model.

Inefficient implementation and improper monitoring (due also to late periodical checks which do not timely represent the ongoing situation and its likely trend) are two likely situations which represent an obstacle to problem solving of dysfunctions, with a consequent risk of being out of touch with grass root reality.

Monitoring is mostly performed with an accounting comparison between forecast and historic balance sheets, income and cash flow statements; and differences between reality and expectations have to be duly analyzed, considering their impact and–mostly–their likely incidence on future occurrences.

And early stage projections, made before starting the game, need to be continuously updated and upgraded, facing reality and incorporating its feedbacks in the numerical model.

The purpose of *International Standard on Assurance Engagements* (ISAE 3400)[684] is to establish standards and provide guidance on engagements to examine and report on prospective financial information including examination procedures for best-estimate and hypothetical assumptions.

Mentorship, human capital incubators and microconsulting

Mentorship, incubators and microconsulting may greatly help, together with feedback from investors, potential customers, friends, etc.

There is one problem with consultancy: is it going to be free of charge? Bank intermediaries may charge consultancy commissions, which may be even higher then interest rates; consultancy on this side is even a form of monitoring; "certified" external consulting may be appreciated by lending institutions but again it is normally not for free.

We learn from Wikipedia that Business incubators are programs designed to support the successful development of entrepreneurial companies through an array of business support resources and services, developed and orchestrated by incubator management and offered both in the incubator and through its network of contacts. Incubators vary in the way they deliver their services, in their organizational structure, and in the types of clients they serve. Successful completion of a business in-

---

684 http://www.ifac.org/sites/default/files/downloads/b013-2010-iaasb-handbook-isae-3400.pdf.

cubation program increases the likelihood that a startup company will stay in business for the long term.

Most common incubator services include[685]:

- Help with business basics
- Networking activities
- Marketing assistance
- High-speed Internet access
- Help with accounting/financial management
- Access to bank loans, loan funds and guarantee programs
- Help with presentation skills
- Links to higher education resources
- Links to strategic partners
- Access to angel investors or venture capital
- Comprehensive business training programs
- Advisory boards and mentors
- Management team identification
- Help with business etiquette
- Technology commercialization assistance
- Help with regulatory compliance
- Intellectual property management

Involving stakeholders with a comprehensive corporate governance perspective

»Corporate governance deals with the ways in which suppliers of finance to corporations assure themselves of getting a return on their investment«[686]. In synthesis, it is essential to give investors legal protection from expropriation by managers, limiting self dealing. In a broader sense, corporate governance sets the rules of cohabitation and the behavior of the different stakeholders that pivot around the start-

[685] http://en.wikipedia.org/wiki/Business_incubator.

[686] Shleifer, A., Vishny, R.W. (1997), "A Survey Of Corporate Governance", Journal Of Finance, June.

ing up company (borrowers, lenders, shareholders, employees, suppliers, clients, supervisory authorities …).
To the extent that stakeholders are properly involved and feel themselves as a part of the project, their efforts may be better aligned, minimizing conflicts of interest or information asymmetries, which are so damaging for the company's survival. Good governance may also strongly contribute lowering the cost of collected capital, from both shareholders and debt underwriters.
Proper team building greatly helps to achieve goals and develop fruitful synergies.

Out of poverty business planning

Developmental business planning is characterized by huge constraints, such as capital rationing, atavistic poverty and consequent few resources, lack of sophistication, little infrastructure, etc. But there are also big and unexploited opportunities and growth rates are typically much more appealing, somewhat mitigating intrinsically higher risk.
Marketing analyses focused at targeting customers' unsatisfied needs may consider their lifestyles, usefully referring to publications and videos such as the financial diaries of the poor[687]
Reference to the Bottom of Pyramid's celebrated book of Prahalad is also insightful.
To the extent that the underserved, especially in rural areas, tend to live within enlarged families or ethnic clans, proper marketing strategies should address groups rather than individuals.
If purchasing power is limited by poverty, new ways of carrying on with alternative business plans targeting the poor may well consider, at least partially, non-monetary payments, up to a sort of ancient "barter economy" or payments in kind, even in the form of cooperatives where ideas, (some) money, cheap labour force and other basic input factors may strategically interact.

Concluding recommendation: make it >viral< with social media!

A business plan template for students and practitioners is here described.
The link to a free Excel file is the following:

www.ibidem.eu/downloads/9783838205625.xls

This link connects this explanatory PDF file to a more practical device.
Using new **social media** and technological devices, You may well:

- Tweet and Facebook your business plan;

[687] See Collins, Morduch,Rutherford , Ruthven, (2009).

- Make a YouTube video, even for complementary presentations;
- Create an APP and make it available on M-phones, IPad ..;
- Make extensive use of Smartphones and tablets

Enjoy our creative intervention and contribute to upgrade the model, making it "viral" on the Web!

The Condensed Chapter

A business plan is a formal accounting statement which numerically describes a set of business goals, the reasons why they are believed attainable, and the strategic plan and managerial steps for reaching those goals.
Hypotheses and visionary ideas of game changers have to be transformed into feasible numbers and need to be backed by reasonable and verifiable assumptions about future events and milestones.

Out of Poverty Tips

Proper business planning, providing strategic guidance to otherwise undefined and hardly checkable hypotheses, is an indispensable starting point for any forward looking out of poverty strategy.
Planning also provides an indispensable mental discipline, with a timely stratification of consequential steps that constantly needs proper market confrontation.
Careful and increasingly sophisticated IT-backed project management, by now routinely taught in Business Schools, is an indispensable "fishing rod" for development.

Selected Readings

MCKEEVER M.P., (2011), *How to write a business plan*, Delta Printing Solutions Inc., Valencia.

OSTERWALDER A., PIGNEUR Y., (2010), *Business Model Generation*, Wiley & Sons, Hoboken, http://www.businessmodelgeneration.com/book/.

PINSON L., (2004), *Anatomy of a Business Plan: A Step-by-Step Guide to Building a Business and Securing Your Company's Future*, Dearborn Trade, Chicago.

SHALMAN W.A., (1997), *How to write a great Business plan*, Harvard Business Review, Boston, http://serempreendedor.files.wordpress.com/2008/09/how-to-write-a-great-business-plan.pdf.

Videos[688]

http://www.youtube.com/watch?v=tf_QAQ5-smQ *Excel Finance Class 11: Finance Cash Flow From Accounting Information*
http://www.youtube.com/watch?v=x9B3Ubl61CM&feature=fvwrel
http://www.youtube.com/watch?v=UrIGIGVx7co
http://www.youtube.com/watch?v=yG6_6UbprFw
http://www.youtube.com/watch?v=C9bnzetcD68&feature=related
http://www.youtube.com/watch?v=nRWeEASWmOI&feature=relmfu
http://www.youtube.com/watch?v=QwlClWaR7DI&feature=related
http://www.youtube.com/watch?v=y5I_cnpP99U&feature=related
http://www.udacity.com/overview/Course/ep245/CourseRev/1 - How to Build a Startup
http://www.howcast.com/videos/271321-How-To-Write-a-Business-Plan
http://www.youtube.com/watch?v=G50fFT4xQlw

Websites

http://pages.stern.nyu.edu/~adamodar/
Downloads Free Template for Excel http://www.excelfreesheets.com/
Free Excel Spreadsheet and Templates for Project Managers:
http://itdiscover.com/links/free_excel_spreadsheet_and_templates_project_managers
Free Excel Spreadsheets - http://www.exinfm.com/free_spreadsheets.html

688 Warning: some videos may not be any more available on the Web; for further videos, look for instance on YouTube; then search: Business Plan …

APPENDIX 1 - A guide to the business plan Excel template

Balance Sheet
The balance sheet uses information from all of the financial models (Income Statement and Cash Flow) of the business plan. It is more or less a summary of all the preceding financial information broken down into three areas:

- Assets
- Liabilities
- Equity

ASSETS	31/12/X	31/12/X+1	31/12/X+2	31/12/X+3	31/12/X+4
FIXED ASSETS					
Tangible					
Land & Buildings	220.500	171.500	239.300	267.500	311.500
Plants & Machinery					
Industrial and commercial fixtures	69	421	1.869	2.862	5.420
Capitalized costs					
Subtotal	**220.569**	**171.921**	**241.169**	**270.362**	**316.920**
Intangible					
Subtotal	**0**	**0**	**0**	**0**	**0**
Total fixed assets	**220.569**	**171.921**	**241.169**	**270.362**	**316.920**
CURRENT ASSETS					
Stocks					
Subtotal	**0**	**0**	**0**	**0**	**0**
Receivables					
From trade debtors	0	0	0	0	0
For Projects from:					
-Private Individuals	456	2.736	12.406	17.493	28.029
-Governamental Agencies	0	0	0	0	0
-International Organizations	0	0	0	0	0
From tax authorities	56.821	21.430	0	0	0
From other debtors	0	0	0	0	0
Subtotal	**57.277**	**24.166**	**12.406**	**17.493**	**28.029**
Cash availability					
Money and cash values		49.997	441.685	950.908	2.024.795
Subtotal	**0**	**49.997**	**441.685**	**950.908**	**2.024.795**
PREPAYMENTS AND ACCRUED INCOME					
Subtotal					
Total current assets	**57.277**	**74.163**	**454.091**	**968.401**	**2.052.824**
Total assets	**277.846**	**246.084**	**695.260**	**1.238.763**	**2.369.744**

Assets are classified as current assets and fixed assets (long-term).
Current assets are assets that will be converted to cash or will be used by the business in a year or less.
Current assets include:

- Cash availability: the cash on hand at the time books are closed at the end of the fiscal year.
- Receivables: the income derived from credit accounts. For the balance sheet, it's the total amount of income to be received that is logged into the books at the close of the fiscal year.

- Stocks: this is derived from the cost of goods table. It's the inventory of material used to manufacture a product not yet sold.
- Total current assets: the sum of cash availability, receivables, stocks, and prepayments and accrued income.

LIABILITIES and OWNER'S EQUITY	31/12/X	31/12/X+1	31/12/X+2	31/12/X+3	31/12/X+4
CAPITAL AND RESERVES					
Subscribed capital	10.000	10.000	10.000	10.000	10.000
Grant/Donations					
Legal reserve	130.000	65.836	67.473	483.149	1.047.913
Other reserves					
Profit (loss) of the last financial year before					
Profit (loss) for the financial year	-64.164	1.637	415.676	564.764	1.080.459
Subtotal	**75.836**	**77.473**	**493.149**	**1.057.913**	**2.138.372**
FUNDS FOR LIABILITIES AND CHARGES					
Subtotal	**926**	**7.222**	**24.259**	**48.556**	**81.889**
SEVERANCE INDEMNITY FOR EMPLOYEES					
Subtotal	**0**	**0**	**0**	**0**	**0**
DEBTS					
Amounts owed to banks	200.802	159.678	118.554	77.429	36.305
Amounts owed to trade creditors	282	1.711	7.600	11.637	22.402
Amounts owed as taxes	0	0	51.698	43.228	90.776
Other debts	0	0	0	0	0
Subtotal	**201.084**	**161.389**	**177.852**	**132.294**	**149.483**
ACCRUALS AND DEFERRED INCOME					
Subtotal	**0**	**0**	**0**	**0**	**0**
Total liabilities and owner's equity	**277.846**	**246.084**	**695.260**	**1.238.763**	**2.369.744**

check list (OK if = 0)	**0**	**0**	**0**	**0**	**0**

Debts

All expenses derived from purchasing items from regular creditors on an open account, which are due and payable as well as taxes that are still due and payable at the time the books are closed.

Accruals and deferred income

All expenses incurred by the business which are required for operation but have not been paid at the time the books are closed.

Equity

Once the liabilities have been listed, the final portion of the balance sheet-owner's equity-needs to be calculated. The amount attributed to owner's equity is the difference between total assets and total liabilities. The amount of equity the owner has in the business is an important yardstick used by investors when evaluating the company. Many times it determines the amount of capital they feel they can safely invest in the business.

Income statement

The Income statement is a scorecard on the economic performance that reflects when sales are made and when expenses are incurred. The income statement illustrates just how much your company makes or loses during the year by subtracting cost of goods and expenses from revenue to arrive at a net result (a profit or a loss).

The income statement is divided into two parts: the operating section and non-operating section.

The first section discloses information about revenues and expenses directly resulting by regular business operations.

The non-operating items section discloses revenue and expense information about activity not directly link to the core business.

	year X	year X+1	year X+2	year X+3	year X+4
PRODUCTION VALUE:					
REVENUE FROM SALES AND SERVICES	44.825	269.163	1.220.214	1.720.665	2.756.964
CHANGE IN WORK IN PROGRESS AND FINISHED GOODS					
OTHER OPERATING INCOME					
TOTAL	**44.825**	**269.163**	**1.220.214**	**1.720.665**	**2.756.964**
PRODUCTION COSTS:					
PURCHASES OF GOODS					
RAW MATERIALS	-2.737	-16.617	-70.813	-100.609	-172.970
OTHER OPERATING EXPENSES	-1.872	-11.224	-44.795	-68.333	-125.553
TOTAL	**-4.609**	**-27.841**	**-115.608**	**-168.942**	**-298.523**
CONTRIBUTION MARGIN	**40.216**	**241.322**	**1.104.606**	**1.551.723**	**2.458.441**
OTHER COSTS:					
SERVICES	-15.000	-15.075	-45.225	-60.300	-90.450
RENTS	-40.330	-76.392	-273.474	-402.898	-540.424
PERSONNEL COSTS	-13.426	-91.296	-247.037	-352.296	-483.333
OTHER NOT OPERATING EXPENSES					
TOTAL	**-68.756**	**-182.763**	**-565.736**	**-815.494**	**-1.114.207**
EBITDA	-28.540	**58.559**	**538.870**	**736.229**	**1.344.234**
LEASING CAPITAL					
AMORTISATIONS AND DEPRECIATIONS (tangible assets)	-24.500	-49.000	-78.000	-104.800	-142.000
AMORTISATIONS AND DEPRECIATIONS (intangible assets)	0	0	0	0	0
ACCRUALS					
EBIT	-53.040	**9.559**	**460.870**	**631.429**	**1.202.234**
PROCEEDS FOR PROJECTS from:					
PRIVATE DONORS	0	0	0	0	0
GOVERNAMENTAL AGENCIES	0	0	0	0	0
INTERNATIONAL ORGANISATIONS	0	0	0	0	0
TOTAL PROCEEDS FOR PROJECTS	**0**	**0**	**0**	**0**	**0**
OUTLAY FOR PROJECTS					
PROJECT 1	0	0	0	0	0
PROJECT 2	0	0	0	0	0
PROJECT 3	0	0	0	0	0
TOTAL PROCEEDS FOR PROJECTS	**0**	**0**	**0**	**0**	**0**
FINANCIAL INCOME AND EXPENSES					
FINANCIAL INCOME FROM INVESTMENTS					
INCOME FROM BANK ACCOUNT'S INTERESTS					
INTERESTS AND OTHER FINANCIAL EXPENSES	-11.124	-7.922	-5.977	-3.914	-1.724
GAINS AND LOSSES ON FOREIGN CURRENCY TRANSLATION					
NET FINANCIAL INCOME (expenses)	**-11.124**	**-7.922**	**-5.977**	**-3.914**	**-1.724**
NET ADJUSTMENTS TO CARRYING VALUE OF FINANCIAL ASSESTS					
NET EXTRAORDINARY GAINS AND LOSSES					
Net income before income taxes (EBITDA+INCOME AND FINANCIAL CHARGES+PROCEED FOR PROJECTS)	-64.164	**1.637**	**454.893**	**627.515**	**1.200.510**
CURRENT AND DEFERRED INCOME TAXES			-39.217	-62.751	-120.051
NET INCOME (LOSS)	-64.164	**1.637**	**415.676**	**564.764**	**1.080.459**

Production Value

- Revenues from sales and services: includes all the income generated by the business.
- Change in work in progress and finished goods:
    - Changes in inventories (including work-in- progress) consist of changes in:
    - 1 stocks of outputs that are still held by the units that produced them prior to their being further processed, sold, delivered to other units or used in other ways;
    - stocks of products acquired from other units that are intended to be used for intermediate consumption or for resale without further processing; they are measured by the value of the entries into inventories less the value of withdrawals and the value of any recurrent losses of goods held in inventories.
- Other operating income: includes all the other miscellaneous income.

Production Costs

- Purchases of goods: includes all the costs related to the sales of products.
- Raw materials: includes all the costs related to the sales of products in inventories.
- Other operating expenses: operating expenses include all overhead and labor expenses associated with the operations of the business.

Contribution Margin
It is the difference between production value and costs. Contribution margin can be expressed in absolute value, as a percentage, or both. As a percentage, the Contribution Margin is always stated as a percentage of revenue

Other Costs

- services: costs related to contracts for work, procurement, transportation, office, agency, shipping, etc. generally under obligations to do;
- rents: rental costs paid to third parties;
- personnel costs: Personnel costs are defined as the total remuneration, in cash or in kind, payable by an employer to an employee in return for work done by the latter during the reference period. Personnel costs also include taxes and employees' social security contributions retained by the

unit as well as the employer's compulsory and voluntary social contributions.

- other not operating expenses: not operating expenses include all overhead and labor expenses not associated with the operations of the business
- earnings before interest, taxes, depreciation and amortization (EBITDA): it is the difference between production value and costs;
- leasing capital;
- amortizations and depreciations: depreciation reflects the decrease in value of capital assets used to generate income;
- accruals: accounts on a balance sheet that represent liabilities and non-cash-based assets used in accrual-based accounting. These accounts include, among many others, accounts payable, accounts receivable, goodwill, future tax liability and future interest expense;
- Earnings before interest and taxes (EBIT): it is a measure of a firm's profit that excludes interest and income tax expenses. EBIT shows the capacity of a business to repay its obligations.
- Proceeds for projects from:
    - Private donors: income from private donors;
    - Governmental agencies: income from public agencies;
    - International organizations: income from international organizations.

Outlay for projects
It is necessary to split the expenses into the different project:

- financial income and expenses;
- financial income from investments: financial income is the revenue generated by the temporary surplus cash invested in short-term investments and marketable securities. it also includes foreign exchange gains on debt and write-backs on provisions and charges related to financial operations;
- income from banks account's interests: interest includes all interest payable for debts, both short-term and long-term;
- interests and other financial expenses: the amount reported for expenses for borrowed money;
- gains and losses on foreign currency translation: gains and losses resulting from the translation of the functional currency into local currency;

- net adjustments to the carrying value of financial assets;
- net extraordinary gains and losses: gains and losses resulting from extraordinary activities;
- net income before income taxes;
- current and deferred income taxes: taxes includes all taxes on the business;
- net income or loss: net profit after taxes shows the company's real bottom line.

Loan repayment schedule

This sheet has to be completed only if the company is financed with debt (= levered).

Total amounts owed to banks	200.802		
Facility fees	0,50%		1.004
Insurance fee	1,00%		2.008
Interest	2,40%		4.819
Period of repayment (years)	5	annual stock debt amount	40.160

First of all it's necessary to complete the preliminary information:

- Total amounts owed to banks: insert the total amount received form banks. This is the base value to calculate interests and the other charges;
- Facility fees: bank charges (in percentage of amount received) to pay only the first year (x). This amount will be transferred automatically in the income statement (account: interests and other financial expenses);
- Insurance fees: insurance costs (in percentage of amount received) to pay only the first year (x). This amount will be transferred automatically in the income statement (account interests and other financial expenses);
- Interests: interest rate to recognizer for the loan (the period is set up in the next field). This amount will be transferred automatically in the income statement (account: interests and other financial expenses);
- Period of repayment (years): length of the loan necessary to calculate the interest charges and the repayment plan.

LOAN REPAYMENT SHEDULE	31/12/X	31/12/X+1	31/12/X+2	31/12/X+3	31/12/X+4
Amount owed to banks	200.802	159.678	118.554	77.429	36.305
Annual Interest	964	964	964	964	964
Total loan facility	**201.766**	**160.642**	**119.517**	**78.393**	**37.269**
Repayment	41.124	41.124	41.124	41.124	41.124
Closing balance	**160.642**	**119.517**	**78.393**	**37.269**	**(3.855)**

The Cash Flow Statement

The Cash Flow Statement is a document which provides the information we can intuitively recognize in its name: a report on cash inflows and outflows over a given accounting period.

It mustn't be confused with the income statement: this because there may be a time span that separates the moment when an income or expense is recorded and when the cash inflow or outflow referred to it is made.

It may also be defined as a financial statement that shows how changes in balance sheet accounts and income affect cash. This derivation is extremely important for business planning, using in particular Excel; as it has been shown in the Excel model (see in particular the file, for a practical example), a comparison of two consecutive balance sheets, giving the variation of assets, liabilities and equity from one year to the following one, matched with the income statement of the second year, gives as an output, duly reclassified, the cash flow statement.

CASH FLOW FROM OPERATING ACTIVITIES	year X	year X+1	year X+2	year X+3	year X+4
Net income (loss)	-64.164	1.637	415.676	564.764	1.080.459
Current and deferred income taxes	0	0	39.217	62.751	120.051
Net extraordinary gains and losses	0	0	0	0	0
Adjustment and accruals	0	0	0	0	0
Net financial income (expenses)	11.124	7.922	5.977	3.914	1.724
Leasing capital stock	0	0	0	0	0
Amortisations and depreciations	24.500	49.000	78.000	104.800	142.000
EBITDA	**-28.540**	**58.559**	**538.870**	**736.229**	**1.344.234**
Movements of net working capital	-56.995	34.540	69.347	-9.520	47.777
Δ severance indemnity for employees	0	0	0	0	0
Δ funds	926	6.296	17.037	24.297	33.333
Changes in CAPEX less-accumulated depreciations	-245.069	-352	-147.248	-133.993	-188.558
Operating cash flow (UNLEVERED CASH FLOW)	**-329.678**	**99.043**	**478.006**	**617.013**	**1.236.786**
Net financial income (expenses)	-11.124	-7.922	-5.977	-3.914	-1.724
Net financial liability	200.802	-41.124	-41.124	-41.124	-41.124
Movements in equity	140.000	0	0	0	0
Net extraordinary gains and losses	0	0	0	0	0
Adjustment and accruals	0	0	0	0	0
Current and deferred income taxes	0	0	-39.217	-62.751	-120.051
LEVERED CASH FLOW	**0**	**49.997**	**391.688**	**509.224**	**1.073.887**
Starting net cash availabilities	0	0	49.997	441.685	950.908
Final net cash availabilities	0	49.997	441.685	950.908	2.024.795
CASH FLOW variation	**0**	**49.997**	**391.688**	**509.224**	**1.073.887**

check list (OK if = 0)	**0**	**0**	**0**	**0**	**0**

The cash-flow statement is one of the most critical information tools for the business, showing how much cash will be needed to meet obligations, when it is going to be required, and from where it will come. It shows a schedule of the money coming into the business and expenses that need to be paid. The result is the profit or loss at the end of the month or year. In a cash-flow statement, both profits and losses are carried over to the next column to show the cumulative amount. If there is a loss on the cash-flow statement, it is a strong indicator that the company will need additional cash in order to meet expenses. The information are taken directly from the income statement and the balance sheet variation.

Assets variations are the following:

ASSETS	X+1/X	X+2/X+1	X+3/X+2	X+4/X+3
FIXED ASSETS				
Tangible				
Land & Buildings	-49.000	67.800	28.200	44.000
Plants & Machinery	0	0	0	0
Industrial and commercial fixtures	352	1.448	993	2.558
Capitalized costs	0	0	0	0
Subtotal	**-48.648**	**69.248**	**29.193**	**46.558**
Intangible				
Subtotal	**0**	**0**	**0**	**0**
Total fixed assets	**-48.648**	**69.248**	**29.193**	**46.558**
CURRENT ASSETS				
Stocks				
Subtotal	**0**	**0**	**0**	**0**
Receivables				
From trade debtors	0	0	0	0
For Projects from:				
-Private Individuals	2.280	9.670	5.087	10.536
-Governamental Agencies	0	0	0	0
-International Organizations	0	0	0	0
From tax authorities	-35.391	-21.430	0	0
From other debtors	0	0	0	0
Subtotal	**-33.111**	**-11.760**	**5.087**	**10.536**
Cash availability				
Money and cash values	49.997	391.688	509.223,8	1.073.887
Subtotal	**49.997**	**391.688**	**509.224**	**1.073.887**
PREPAYMENTS AND ACCRUED INCOME				
Subtotal	**0**	**0**	**0**	**0**
Total current assets	**16.886**	**379.928**	**514.311**	**1.084.423**
Total assets	**-31.762**	**449.176**	**543.504**	**1.130.981**

Liabilities and owner's equity variations are, instead, the following:

LIABILITIES and OWNER'S EQUITY	X+1/X	X+2/X+1	X+3/X+2	X+4/X+3
CAPITAL AND RESERVES				
Subscribed capital	0	0	0	0
Grant/Donations	0	0	0	0
Legal reserve	-64.164	1.637	415.676	564.764
Other reserves	0	0	0	0
Profit (loss) for the financial year	65.801	414.039	149.088	515.695
Subtotal	**1.637**	**415.676**	**564.764**	**1.080.459**
FUNDS FOR LIABILITIES AND CHARGES				
Subtotal	**6.296**	**17.037**	**24.297**	**33.333**
SEVERANCE INDEMNITY FOR EMPLOYEES				
Subtotal	**0**	**0**	**0**	**0**
DEBTS				
Amounts owed to banks	-41.124	-41.124	-41.124	-41.124
Amounts owed to trade creditors	1.429	5.889	4.037	10.765
Amounts owed as taxes	0	51.698	-8.470	47.548
Other debts	0	0	0	0
Subtotal	**-39.695**	**16.463**	**-45.557**	**17.189**
ACCRUALS AND DEFERRED INCOME				
Subtotal	**0**	**0**	**0**	**0**
Total liabilities and owner's equity	**-31.762**	**449.176**	**543.504**	**1.130.981**

check list (OK if = 0)	0	0	0	0

The details of calculations are the following:

CASH FLOW FROM WORKING CAPITAL	year X	year X+1	year X+2	year X+3	year X+4
Movements of commercial credits in current assets	0	0	0	0	0
Movements of other credits	-56.821	35.391	21.430	0	0
Movements of credits for projects	-456	-2.280	-9.670	-5.087	-10.536
Δ "Prepayment and accrued income"	0	0	0	0	0
Δ stocks	0	0	0	0	0
Δ "Accruals and deferred income"	0	0	0	0	0
Δ **debt for taxes**	0	0	51.698	-8.470	47.548
Movements of Other debts	0	0	0	0	0
Movements of mounts owed to trade creditors	282	1.429	5.889	4.037	10.765
MOVEMENTS OF NET WORKING CAPITAL	**-56.995**	**34.540**	**69.347**	**-9.520**	**47.777**

CASH FLOW FROM INVESTING ACTIVITIES	year X	year X+1	year X+2	year X+3	year X+4
Movements of Intangible fixed assets	0	0	0	0	0
Movements of tangible fixed assets	-220.569	48.648	-69.248	-29.193	-46.558
Amortisations and Depreciations	-24.500	-49.000	-78.000	-104.800	-142.000
Leasing capital stock	0	0	0	0	0
MOVEMENTS OF FIXES ASSETS	**-245.069**	**-352**	**-147.248**	**-133.993**	**-188.558**

CASH FLOW FROM FINANCIAL ACTIVITIES	year X	year X+1	year X+2	year X+3	year X+4
Movements of Amounts owed to banks	200.802	-41.124	-41.124	-41.124	-41.124
MOVEMENTS OF NET FINANCIAL LIABILITIES	**200.802**	**-41.124**	**-41.124**	**-41.124**	**-41.124**

CASH FLOW FROM OWNERS' EQUITY	year X	year X+1	year X+2	year X+3	year X+4
Movements of Subscribed capital	10.000	0	0	0	0
Movements of Donations	0	0	0	0	0
Movements of Reserves	130.000	-64.164	1.637	415.676	564.764
MOVEMENTS IN OWNERS' EQUITY	**140.000**	**-64.164**	**1.637**	**415.676**	**564.764**

Ratios

Definitions of principal ratios are the following:

Liquidity	
Current ratio	Current assets/Current liabilities
Quick ratio	(Total current assets-inventory)/Total current liabilities
Capital Structure	
Equity financing	Fund balance/Total assets
Total debt/total assets	Total liabilities/Total assets
Interests expenses/debts	Interests expenses/debts
Debt service coverage	(Net Income + Amortization/Depreciation + Interest Expense + other non-cash and discretionary items) / (Principal Repayment + Interest payments + Lease payments)
Leverage	liabilities/Net Worth
Activity	
Total asset turnover	Total operating revenue/Total assets
Fixed asset turnover	Total operating revenue/Net fixed assets
Current asset turnover	Total operating revenue/Current assets
Overall Efficiency Ratios	
Sales-To-Assets	Sales/Total Assets
Gross Margin	Gross Profit/ Sales
Net Margin	Net Profit / Sales
Return on Sales	Operating result/Sales
Return On Equity	Net Profit / Net Worth
Return On Investment	Net Profit / total assets
Specific Efficiency Ratios	
Inventory Turnover	Cost of Goods Sold/Inventory
Inventory Turn-Days	360/Inventory Turnover
Accounts Receivable Turnover	Sales/Accounts Receivable
Average Collection Period	360/Accounts Receivable Turnover
Accounts Payable Turnover	Cost of Goods Sold/Account Payable
Average Payment Period	360/Accounts Payable Turnover
Social utility	
Allocations to total projects	Total Projects Outlay / (Total operating revenues + Total Projects Proceeds)
Allocations to project 1	Outlay for Project 1 / (Total operating revenues + Total Projects Proceeds)
Allocations to project 2	Outlay for Project 2 / (Total operating revenues + Total Projects Proceeds)
Allocations to project 3	Outlay for Project 3 / (Total operating revenues + Total Projects Proceeds)
Proceeds from Donations On Total Revenues	Total Projects Proceeds / (Total operating revenues + Total Project Proceeds)
Proceeds from Donations On Total Projects Outlay	Total Projects Proceeds / Total Projects Outlay
Capital Donated on Net Worth	Donations / Neth Worth
Others:	
Native people employed	Number of native people empolyed / total numeber of employees
Woman employed	Number of women empolyed / total numeber of employees
Other Ratios	
Net financial position	Difference between cash, credits and banks
Capital raised	Equity + Finalncial liabilities

In the present case, main ratios are:

	31/12/X	31/12/X+1	31/12/X+2	31/12/X+3	31/12/X+4
Liquidity					
Current ratio	0,28	0,46	2,55	7,32	13,73
Quick ratio	0,28	0,46	2,55	7,32	13,73
Capital Structure					
Equity financing	0,27	0,31	0,71	0,85	0,90
Total debt/total assets	0,73	0,69	0,29	0,15	0,10
Interests expenses/debts	-5,5%	-5,0%	-5,0%	-5,1%	-4,7%
Debt service coverage	-2,57	7,39	83,60	172,07	710,08
Leverage	2,66	2,18	0,41	0,17	0,11
Activity					
Total asset turnover	0,16	1,09	1,76	1,39	1,16
Fixed asset turnover	0,20	1,57	5,06	6,36	8,70
Current asset turnover	0,78	3,63	2,69	1,78	1,34
Overall Efficiency Ratios					
Sales-To-Assets	0,161	1,094	1,755	1,389	1,163
Gross Margin	89,72%	89,66%	90,53%	90,18%	89,17%
Net Margin	-143,14%	0,61%	37,28%	42,79%	48,76%
Return on Sales	-118,33%	3,55%	37,77%	36,70%	43,61%
Return On Equity	-84,61%	2,11%	92,24%	69,59%	62,86%
Return On Investment	-23,09%	0,67%	65,43%	59,43%	56,72%
Specific Efficiency Ratios					
Inventory Turnover	0,00	0,00	0,00	0,00	0,00
Inventory Turn-Days	0	0	0	0	0
Accounts Receivable Turnover	0,00	0,00	0,00	0,00	0,00
Average Collection Period	0	0	0	0	0
Accounts Payable Turnover	16,34	16,27	15,21	14,52	13,33
Average Payment Period	22	22	24	25	27
Social utility					
Allocations to total projects	0,00%	0,00%	0,00%	0,00%	0,00%
Allocations to project 1	0,00%	0,00%	0,00%	0,00%	0,00%
Allocations to project 2	0,00%	0,00%	0,00%	0,00%	0,00%
Allocations to project 3	0,00%	0,00%	0,00%	0,00%	0,00%
Proceeds from Donations On Total Revenues	0,00%	0,00%	0,00%	0,00%	0,00%
Proceeds from Donations On Total Projects Outlay	0,00%	0,00%	0,00%	0,00%	0,00%
Capital Donated on Net Worth	0,00%	0,00%	0,00%	0,00%	0,00%
Others:					
Native people employed	100%	100%	100%	100%	100%
Woman employed	50%	50%	50%	50%	50%
Other Ratios					
Net financial position	-118.098	-24.697	417.785	968.401	2.052.824
Capital raised	276.638	237.151	611.703	1.135.342	2.174.677

Break-even point

The Breakeven Point identifies the point where the total revenue is just sufficient to cover the total cost.
The formula for break even point is:

QBP = fixed costs / Contribution Margin per Unit

If we consider the structure of costs of this venture:

	31/12/X	31/12/X+1	31/12/X+2	31/12/X+3	31/12/X+4
Product price=	60	60	60	60	60
%of Variable costs on Product Price =	-10%	-10%	-9%	-10%	-11%
Fixed costs=	-93.256	-231.763	-643.736	-920.294	-1.256.207
Contribution Margin per Unit=	66,17	66,21	65,68	65,89	66,50

We consider a fixed operative cost all operative costs that are not included in the contribution margin (all costs between Contribution Margin and EBITDA):

	31/12/X	31/12/X+1	31/12/X+2	31/12/X+3	31/12/X+4
Revenue (p x q)	44.825	269.163	1.220.214	1.720.665	2.756.964
- Variable costs	-4.609	-27.841	-115.608	-168.942	-298.523
Contribution Margin	**40.216**	**241.322**	**1.104.606**	**1.551.723**	**2.458.441**
Degree of Operating Leverage	**-0,8**	**25,2**	**2,4**	**2,5**	**2,0**
Breakeven Quantity	**-1.409**	**-3.501**	**-9.800**	**-13.967**	**-18.891**

Contribution margin is the same as calculated in the Income Statement.
Quantity to breakeven increases as time passes because Contribution Margin for single product remains constant, while fixed costs grow exponentially.

Operating leverage

Is a measurement of the degree to which a firm or project incurs a combination of fixed and variable costs.

1. A business that makes few sales, with each sale providing a very high gross margin, is said to be highly leveraged. A business that makes many sales, with each sale contributing a very slight margin, is said to be less leveraged. As the volume of sales in a business increases, each new sale contributes less to fixed costs and more to profitability.
2. A business that has a higher proportion of fixed costs and a lower proportion of variable costs is said to have used more operating leverage. Those businesses with lower fixed costs and higher variable costs are said to employ less operating leverage.

The higher the degree of operating leverage, the greater the potential danger from forecasting risk. That is, if a relatively small error is made in forecasting sales, it can be magnified into large errors in cash flow projections. The opposite is true for businesses that are less leveraged. A business that sells millions of products a year, with each contributing slightly to paying for fixed costs, is not as dependent on each individual sale.

For example, convenience stores are significantly less leveraged than high-end car dealerships

Cost structure	31/12/X	31/12/X+1	31/12/X+2	31/12/X+3	31/12/X+4
Variable costs on Revenue=	-10%	-10%	-9%	-10%	-11%
Fixed costs=	-93.256	-231.763	-643.736	-920.294	-1.256.207
Product price=	60	60	60	60	60
Revenue (p x q)	44.825	269.163	1.220.214	1.720.665	2.756.964
- Variable costs	-4.609	-27.841	-115.608	-168.942	-298.523
Contribution Margin	**40.216**	**241.322**	**1.104.606**	**1.551.723**	**2.458.441**
- Fixed costs	-93.256	-231.763	-643.736	-920.294	-1.256.207
EBIT	**-53.040**	**9.559**	**460.870**	**631.429**	**1.202.234**
Degree of Operating Leverage	**-0,8**	**25,2**	**2,4**	**2,5**	**2,0**

What happens when there is a change in quantity sold?

	31/12/X+1	31/12/X+2	31/12/X+3	31/12/X+4
? Quantity Sold=	**500%**	**353%**	**41%**	**60%**
Revenue (p x q)	269.163	1.220.214	1.720.665	2.756.964
- Variable costs	-27.841	-115.608	-168.942	-298.523
Contribution Margin	**241.322**	**1.104.606**	**1.551.723**	**2.458.441**
? Contribution Margin				
	500,06%	**357,73%**	**40,48%**	**58,43%**
- Fixed costs	-231.763	-643.736	-920.294	-1.256.207
EBIT	**9.559**	**460.870**	**631.429**	**1.202.234**
? EBIT	**-118,02%**	**4721,32%**	**37,01%**	**90,40%**
With a ? Quantity Sold of	**500%**	**353%**	**41%**	**60%**
a DOL of	**-0,8**	**25,2**	**2,4**	**2,5**
allows a ? EBITDA of	**-118,02%**	**4721,32%**	**37,01%**	**90,40%**
? EBITDA=? Quantity Sold X Operating Leverage ?	-379,47%	8920,17%	98,30%	148,01%

A flexible structure of costs is less profitable but is best suited for unforeseen events.

The presence of high variable costs, which grow with the increase in sales, reduces EBIT and consequently the Operating Cash Flows.

A rigid structure is more profitable than a flexible structure, but it carries an increased operating risk.

The fixed costs are not linked to changes in sales volume and revenue growth: after reaching the breakeven point, a fixed structure of costs produces more Cash Flow from core business operations than a variable structure.

REFERENCES

ACCION (2003), *The Service Company Model: a New Strategy for Commercial Banks in Microfinance*, InSight paper n. 6, September.

ACEMOGLU D., JOHNSON S., ROBINSON J.A., (2002), *Reversal of Fortune: Geography and Institutions in the Making of the Modern World Income Distribution*, in Quarterly Journal of Economics, 117, November, pp. 1231–1294.

ACHLEITER A.K., (2008), *Social Entrepreneurship and Venture Philanthropy in Germany*, Centre for Entrepreneurial and Financial Studies, Technische Universität München, TUM Business School.

ADAM B., (2004), *Time*, Polity Press, Cambridge.

ADAMS G., VON PISCHE J.D., (1984), *Undermining rural development with cheap credit*, Westview Press.

ADDISON T., HANSEN H., TARP F., eds., (2004), *Debt Relief for Poor Countries*, Palgrave Macmillan, London

ADDISON T., HULME D., KANBUR R., eds., (2009), *Poverty Dynamics. Interdisciplinary Perspectives*, Oxford University Press, Oxford.

ADELMAN M., (1973), *Economic growth and social equity in developing countries*, Stanford University Press, Stanford.

AGHION P., DURLAUF S.N., (2005), *Handbook of Economic Growth*, Elsevier, Amsterdam, in http://elsa.berkeley.edu/~chad/azstach.pdf.

AGOLA N.O., AWANGE J.L., (2014), *Globalized Poverty and Environment,* Springer Verlag, Berlin.

AIYAR S., BERG, A., HUSSAIN M., (2005), *The Macroeconomic Challenge of More Aid*, in http://www.imf.org/external/pubs/ft/fandd/2005/09/aiyar.htm.

AKERLOF G.A., (1970), *The Market for "Lemons": Quality Uncertainty and the Market Mechanism*, in Quarterly Journal of Economics, August.

ALBERT P.J., WERHANE P., ROLPH T., eds., (2014), *Global Poverty Alleviation: A Case Book*, Springer Verlag, Berlin.

ALTMAN D., (2008), *Microfinance seems fairly insulated from credit turbulence*, February, in http://www.iht.com/articles/2008/02/12/business/glob13.php.

ARCHER M.S., (2008), *Pursuing the Common Good: How Solidarity and Subsidiarity Can Work Together*, Vatican City Press.

ARETI K.K., (2007), *Understanding Sustainable Development*, January 10, in http://ssrn.com/abstract=956240.

ARMENDARIZ DE AGHION B., SZAFARZ A., (2009), *On Mission Drift in Microfinance Institutions*, http://ideas.repec.org/p/sol/wpaper/09–015.html, Université libre de Bruxelles, Working paper CEB 09.015.RS.

ARMENDARIZ DE AGHION B., MORDUCH J., (2010), *The Economics of Microfinance*, MIT Press, Cambridge, Massachusetts, 2nd edition.

ARUN T., (2005), *Regulating for Development: the Case of Microfinance*, in Quarterly Review of Economics and Finance, 346–357.

ASHTA A., (2007), *An Introduction to Microcredit: Why Money is Flowing from the Rich to the Poor*, working paper, in http://papers.ssrn.com/sol3/papers.cfm?abstract_id=1090195.

AYAYI A.G., SENE M., (2008), *What Drives Microfinance Institution Financial Sustainability*, working paper, March, Audencia School of Management, Nantes.

AZARIADIS C., STACHURSKI, J., *Poverty Traps?*, in AGHION P., DURLAUF S.N., (2005), *Handbook of Economic Growth*, Elsevier, Amsterdam, in http://elsa.berkeley.edu/~chad/azstach.pdf.

BANERJEE A.V., BÉNABOUR R., MOOKHERJEE D., (2006), *Understanding Poverty*, Oxford University Press, Oxford.

BANERJEE A.V., DUFLO E., (2007), *The Economic lives of the Poor*, in Journal of Economic Perspectives, Winter.

BANERJEE A., DUFLO E., GLENNERSTER R., KINNAN C., (2009), *The miracle of microfinance? Evidence from a randomized valuation*, in http://econ–www.mit.edu/files/4162.

BANFIELD E., (1958), *The Moral Basis of a Backward Society*, Free Press, Chicago.

BARRO R., (2000), *Inequality and Growth in a Panel of Countries*, in Journal of Economic Growth, 5.

BASU S., MALLICK S., (2008), *When does growth trickle down to the poor? The Indian case*, in Cambridge Journal of Economics, 32, pp. 461–477.

BATEMAN M., (2010), *Why doesn't microfinance work? The destructive rise of local neoliberalism*, Zed Books, London & New York.

BECCHETTI L., PISANI F., (2007), *Promoting Access to Credit for Small Uncollateralized Producers: Moral Hazard, Subsidies and Local Externalities under Different Group Lending Market Structures*, Working Paper, University of Rome Tor Vergata.

BECK T., DEMIRGÜÇ KUNT A., LEVINE R., (2007), *Finance, inequality and the Poor*, Journal of Economic Growth, pp. 27–49.

BENEDICT XVI, (2009), *Caritas in Veritate*, Encyclical Letter, in www .vatican.va/holy_father/benedict_xvi/encyclicals/documents/hf_benxvi_enc_20090 629 _caritas–in–veritate_en.html.

BEVAN P., (2004), *Exploring the Structured Dynamics of Chronic Poverty: a Sociological Approach*, University of Bath, in http://staff.bath.ac.uk/hsspgb/Time%20and%20Poverty%20Final.pdf.

BEYARAZA E., (2000), *The African Concept of Time: A Comparative Study of Various Theories*, Makerere University Press, Kampala.

BHARADWAJ A., (2014), *Reviving the Globalization and Poverty Debate: Effects of Real and Financial Integration on the Developing World*, Advances In Economics And Business 2(1): 42-57, 2014 http://www.hrpub.org doi: 10.13189/aeb.2014.020107.

BIRD K, (2007), *The intergenerational transmission of poverty: An overview*, ODI Working Paper 286; CPRC Working Paper 99, in http://scholar.google.it/scholar?hl=it&rlz=1W1ADBF_it&q=author:%22Bird%22+intitle:%22The+intergenerational+transmission+of+poverty:+An+overview%22+&um=1&ie=UTF–8&oi=scholar.

BLOMBERG B.S., HESS G.D., THACKER S., (2000), *Is There Evidence of a Poverty-Conflict Trap?*, Wellesley College Working Paper No. 2000–06, May, in http://ssrn.com/abstract=232383.

BOGAN V., (2008), *Microfinance Institutions: Does Capital Structure Matter?*, in http://ssrn.com/abstract=1144762.

BOND P., RAI A., (2002), *Collateral Substitutes in Microfinance*, Working Paper, in www.econ.yale.edu/seminars/develop/tdw02/rai–021118.pdf.

BORDIEU P., (1977), *Outline of a Theory of Practice*, Cambridge University Press, Cambridge.

BOUMAN F.J.A., (1994), *ROSCA and ASCA: Beyond the Financial Landscape*, in BOUMAN F.J.A. and O. HOSPES (eds.), *Financial Landscapes Reconstructed: The Fine Art of Mapping Development*, Boulder, Westview Press.

BOWLES S., DURLAF S.N., HOFF K., (2006), *Poverty traps*, Princeton University Press, Princeton.

BRAINARD L., JONES A., PURVIS N., eds., (2009), *Climate change and global poverty*, Brookings Institution Press, Washington.

BRANCH B., (2005), *Working with Savings & Credit Cooperatives*, August, in http://www.cgap.org/gm/document–1.9.4396/DB25.pdf.

BRANCH B., KLAEHN J., (2002), *Striking the Balance in Microfinance: A Practical Guide to Mobilizing Savings*, PACT Publications, Washington.

BRUGGER E.A., (2004), *Micro-Finance Investment Funds: Looking Ahead*, KfW Financial Sector Development Symposium.

BURRUS W., STEARNS K., (1997), *Building a Model: ACCION's approach to microenterprise in the United States*, ACCION International, Washington.

CALDERISI R., (2006), *The Trouble with Africa: Why Foreign Aid Isn't Working*, Palgrave Macmillan, London.

CALDWELL C., (2009), *Reflections on the Revolution in Europe: Immigration, Islam, and the West*, Allen Lane, London.

CALLAGHAN I., GONZALEZ H., MAURICE D., NOVAK C., (2007), *On the Road to Capital Markets*, in Journal of Applied Corporate Finance, pp. 115–124.

CALOMIRIS C., RAJARAMAN I., (1998), *The role of ROSCAs: Lumpy Durables or event insurance?*, in Journal of Development Economics, pp. 207–216.

CALTON J.M., WERHANE P.H., HARTMAN L.P., (2013), *Building Partnership to Create Social and Economic Value at the Base of the Global Development Pyramid,* in Journal of Business Ethics, Issue 4, pp. 721-733.

CARTER M.R., BARRETT C.B., (2005), *The Economics of Poverty Traps and Persistent Poverty: An Asset-based Approach*, January, in http://ssrn.com/abstract =716162.

CASSESE A., (2008), *International Criminal Law*, Oxford University Press, Oxford.

CASTIGLIONE D., VAN DETH J.W., WOLLEB G., (2008), *The Handbook of Social Capital*, Oxford University Press, Oxford.

CGAP, (2002), *Microcredit Interest Rates*, Occasional Paper, November, in http://www.cgap.org/gm/document–1.9.2696/OP1.pdf.

CGAP, (2004a), *Interest Rate Ceilings and Microfinance: The Story so Far*, Occasional Paper, September, in www.cgap.org/p/site/c/template.rc/1.9.2703.

CGAP, (2004b), *Annual Report*, in http://www.cgap.org/gm/document–1.9.41932/CGAP_Annual_Report_2004.pdf.

CGAP, (2004c), *The Impact of Interest Rate Ceilings on Microfinance*, Donor Brief, n. 18, May, in http://www.cgap.org/p/site/c/template.rc/1.9.2376/.

CGAP, (2004d), *Supporting microfinance in conflict-affected areas*, Donor Brief, December, in http://www.cgap.org/gm/document–1.9.2362/DonorBrief_21.pdf.

CGAP, (2005), *Crafting a Money Transfers Strategy*, Occasional Papers, in http://www.cgap.org/gm/document–1.9.2704/OP10.pdf.

CGAP, (2006a), *Graduating the Poorest into Microfinance: Linking Safety Nets and Financial Services*, Focus Note n. 34, February, in http://www.cgap.org/gm/do cument–1.9.2586/FN34.pdf.

CGAP, (2006b), *Good Practice Guidelines for Funders of Microfinance*, in http://www.cgap.org/gm/document–1.9.2746/donorguidelines.pdf.

CGAP, (2006c), *Safe and accessible: Bringing poor savers into formal financial system*, Focus Note N.37, September, in http://www.cgap.org/gm/document–1.9.2578/FN37.pdf.

CGAP, (2006d), *Foreign Exchange Risk Mitigation Techniques: Structure and Do cumentation a Technical Guide for Microfinance Institutions,* October, in http://www.cgap.org/gm/document–1.9.3001/TechnicalTool_ForeignEx.pdf.

CGAP, (2008a), *The U.S. Subprime Crisis: Five lessons for microfinance*, July, in http://www.cgap.org/p/site/c/template.rc/1.26.2705/.

CGAP, (2008b), *Banking on Mobiles: Why, How, for Whom?*, n. 48, June, in http://www.cgap.org/gm/document–1.9.4400/FN48.pdf.

CGAP, (2008c), *Microfinance and the Financial Crisis*, Virtual conference, November 18–20, in http://www.cgap.org/gm/document–1.9.7439/CGAP%20Virtual%20Conference%202008%20Summary.pdf.

CGAP, (2008d), *National Microfinance Strategies*, June, in http://www.cgap.org/gm/document–1.9.4349/BR_National_Microfinance_Strategies.pdf.

CGAP, (2008e), *Foodflation*, July, in www.cgap.org/p/site/c/template.rc/1.11.1909/1.26.2715.

CGAP, (2008f), *Foreign Capital Investment in Microfinance. Balancing Social and Financial Returns*, Focus Note n. 44, February, in http://www.cgap.org/gm/document–1.9.2584/FN44.pdf.

CGAP, (2008g), *Making Money Transfers Work for Microfinance Institutions*, March, in http://www.cgap.org/gm/document–1.9.3003/Technical%20Guide%20Money%20Transfers.pdf.

CGAP, (2008h), *The Early Experience with Branchless Banking*, n. 46, April, in http://www.cgap.org/gm/document–1.9.2640/FN46.pdf.

CGAP, (2009a) *Asset and Liability Management for Deposit-Taking Microfinance Institutions*, June, in www.cgap.org/gm/document–1.9.34818/FN55.pdf.

CGAP, (2009b) *Measuring Results of Microfinance Institutions: Minimum Indicators That Donors and Investors Should Track*, July, in www.cgap.org/gm/document–1.9.36551/ Indicators_TechGuide.pdf.

CGAP, (2009c), *Shedding Light on Microfinance Equity Valuation*, Occasional Paper, February, in http://www.cgap.org/gm/document–1.9.9021/OP14.pdf.

CGAP, (2010a) *Microfinance Foreign Exchange Facilities*, Occasional Paper, May, in http://www.cgap.org/gm/document–1.9.43712/OP17_rev.pdf.

CGAP, (2010b) *Does Microcredit Really Help Poor People?*, in http://www.cgap.org/gm/document–1.9.41443/FN59.pdf.

CHRISTEN R.P., LYMAN T.R., ROSENBERG R., (2003), *Microfinance Consensus Guidelines: Guiding Principles on Regulation and Supervision of Microfinance Institutions*, July, in http://www.cgap.org/gm/document–1.9.2787/Guideline_RegSup.pdf.

COLLIER P., (2007), *The Bottom Billion: Why the Poorest Countries are Failing and What Can Be Done about It*, Oxford University Press, Oxford.

COLLIER P., (2009), *Conflict, Political Accountability and Aid*, Routledge, London.

COLLIER P., (2010), *Wars, Guns & Votes. Democracy in Dangerous Places*, Vintage, London.

COLLIER P., (2013), *Exodus: How Migration is Changing Our World,* Oxford University Press, Oxford.

COLLINS D., MURDOCH J., RUTHERFORD S., RUTHVEN O., (2009), *Portfolios of the Poor: How the World's Poor Live on $2 a Day*, Princeton University Press, Princeton.

CONNING J., UDRY C., (2007), *Rural Financial Markets in Developing Countries*, in EVENSON R., PINGALI P., SCHULTZ T.P., eds., *Handbook of Agricultural Economics*, Elsevier, Amsterdam, vol. 3, chapter 15.

CORDOVA J. and C., (2006), *Chasing Windmills*, in http://www.quotationspage.com/quotes/Jadelr_and_Cristina_Cordova/.

CULL R., DEMIRGÜÇ KUNT A., MORDUCH J., (2008), *Microfinance Meets the Market*, in Journal of Economic Perspectives, 23, pp. 167–192, in http://financialaccess.org/sites/default/files/G4_Microfinance_Meets_Market_0.pdf.

DE SOTO H., (2003), *The Mystery of Capital. Why Capitalism Triumphs in the West and Fails Everywhere Else*, Basic Books, New York.

DE SOUSA–SHIELDS M., FRANKIEWICZ C., (2004), *Financing Microfinance Institutions: The Context for transitions to Private Capital*, micro Report #8, Accelerated Microenterprise Advancement Project, USAID, Washington, in www.microfinancegateway.org/content/article/detail/23657.

DEUTSCHE BANK, (2007), *Microfinance. An Emerging Investment Opportunity,* working paper, December, in http://www.dbresearch.com/PROD/DBR_INTERNET_ENPROD/PROD0000000000219174.pdf.

DHARAMSI K., (2008), *Global credit crunch affects microfinancing*, September, in http://sify.com/.

DIAMOND J., (1997), *Guns, Germs, and Steel: The Fates of Human Societies*, Random House, New York.

DICHTER T., eds., (2008), *What's Wrong with Microfinance?*, Malcolm Harper, London.

EASTERLY W., (2001), *The Elusive Quest for Growth: Economists, Adventures and Misadventures in the Tropics*, MIT Press, Boston.

EASTERLY W., (2006), *The White Man's Burden: Why the West's Efforts to Aid the Rest Have Done So Much Ill and So Little Good*, Penguin Press, London.

EASTERLY W., ed., (2008), *Reinventing Foreign Aid*, MIT Press, Boston.

EMERSON E., (2007), *Poverty and people with intellectual disabilities*, Mental Retardation and Developmental Disabilities Research Reviews, Volume 13, Issue 2, pp. 107–113.

EMRAN M.S., MORSHED A.K.M., STIGLITZ J.E., (2007), *Microfinance and Missing Markets*, in https://editorialexpress.com/cgibin/conference/download.cgi ?db_name=NAWM2007&paper_id=427.

EVANS P., (1995), *Embedded Autonomy*, Princeton University Press, Princeton.

FERGUSON N., (2011), *Civilization: The West and the Rest*, Penguin, London.

FERGUSON N., (2013), *The Great Degeneration*, Penguin, London.

FERNANDO J.L., (2006), *Microfinance perils and prospects*, Routledge, London.

FOFACK H., (2008), *Technology Trap and Poverty Trap in Sub-Saharan Africa*, World Bank Policy Research Working Paper Series, in http://ssrn.com/abstract=11 49085.

FRIEDMAN T.L., (2009), *Hot, Flat, & Crowded*, Penguin Books, London.

FUKUYAMA F., (1995), *Trust: The Social Virtues and the Creation of Prosperity*, Free Press, New York.

FUKUYAMA F., (2005), *State building. Governance and World Order in the Twenty-First Century,* Profile books, London.

GANGOPADHYAY P., SHANKAR S., RAHMAN M.A., (2014), *Working poverty, social exclusion and destitution: An empirical study*, in Economic Modelling, Volume 37, February, pp. 241–250.

GARMAISE, M. J., NATIVIDAD, G. (2013), *Cheap Credit, Lending Operations, and International Politics: The Case of Global Microfinance*, in Journal of Finance, 68, 1551–1576.

GHANI A., LOCKHART C., (2008), *Fixing Failed States*, Oxford University Press, Oxford.

GHATAK M., (1999), *Group Lending, Local Information and Peer Selection*, in Journal of Development Economics, October.

GLAESER E., SCHLEIFER A., (2001), *Not-for-profit Entrepreneurs*, in Journal of Public Economics, pp. 99–115.

GOLD M., (2002), *Life & Life Only: Dylan at 60*, in Judas! Magazine, April.

GOLEMAN D., (1996), *Emotional intelligence*, Bloomsbury, London.

GOODMAN P., (2004), *Micro-finance Investment Funds: Concepts, Objectives, Actors, Owners, Potential*, in KfW Financial Sector Development Symposium, Zurich.

GOUDIE A., LADD P., (1999), *Economic growth, poverty and inequality*, in Journal of International Development, 11, pp. 177–195.

GUHA–KHASNOBIS B., MAVROTAS G., (2008), *Financial development, institutions, growth and poverty reduction*, Palgrave, Basingstoke.

GUPTA I.P.V., (2006), *Grameen Bank of Bangladesh – The Grameen General Credit System*, ICFAI Center for Management Research, India, in www.asiacase.com/ecatalog/NO_FILTERS/page–BIZSTRA–640131.html.

GUTTMAN J.M., (2008), *Assortative Matching, Adverse Selection, and Group Lending*, Jin ournal of Economic Development, pp. 51–56.

HANCOCK G., (1989), *Lords of Poverty*, the Atlantic Monthly Press, New York.

HARDIN G., (1968), *The Tragedy of the Commons*, Science, Vol. 162, No. 3859, December, pp. 1243–1248, in www.sciencemag.org/cgi/reprint/162/3859/1243.pdf.

HARRIS G.T., (1999), *Recovery from armed conflict in developing countries*, Routledge, London.

HARRISON A. ed., (2007), *Globalization and Poverty*, NBER, University of Chicago Press, Chicago.

HARRISON L.E. (1985), *Underdevelopment Is A State of Mind: The Latin American Case*, University Press of America, Lanham.

HARRISON L.E., HUNTINGTON S.P., eds., (2000), *Culture Matters*, Basic Books, New York.

HAWKING S., MLODINOW L., (2005), *A Brief History of Time*, Random House, New York.

HECKSCHER E.F., OHLIN B., (1991), *Heckscher-Ohlin Trade Theory*, MIT Press, Cambridge.

HEINSOHN G., (2003), *The "Youth Bulge" Phenomenon*, in www.hudson–ny.org/221/the–youth–bulge–phenomenon.

HELMS B., (2006), *Access for All: Building Inclusive Financial Systems*, Consultative Group to Assist the Poor, Washington, in www.cgap.org/p/site/c/template.rc/1.9.2715/.

HELPMAN E., (2004), *The Mystery of Economic Growth*, Belknap Press of Harvard University, Cambridge.

HERMES N., LENSINK R., (2007), *The Empirics of Microfinance: What Do We Know?*, in Economic Journal, February.

HIRSCHLAND M., ed., (2005), *Savings Services for the Poor: An Operational Guide*, Kumarian Press Inc., Bloomfield.

HOFF K., SEN A., (2005), *The Kin System as a Poverty Trap?*, April, World Bank Policy Research, Working Paper No. 3575, in http://ssrn.com/abstract=719141.

HULME D., SHEPHERD A., (2003), *Conceptualizing chronic poverty*, in World development, March.

ISERN J., ABRAMS J., BROWN M., (2008), *Appraisal Guide for Microfinance Institutions. Resource Manual*, CGAP, March, Washington, in www.cgap.org/gm/document–1.9.4394/MFIAppraisalTechnicalGuide.pdf.

JACOBY H.G., MINTEN B., (2007), *Is Land Titling in Sub-Saharan Africa Cost-Effective? Evidence from Madagascar*, The World Bank Economic Review, Vol. 21, Issue 3, pp. 461–485, 2007, in http://ssrn.com/abstract=1146045.

JACOBY H.G., SKOUFIAS E., (1997), *Risk, Financial Markets, and Human Capital in a Developing Country*, in Review of Economic Studies, pp. 311–335.

JAIN S., MANSURI G., (2003), *A little at a Time: the Use of Regularly Scheduled Repayments in Microfinance Programs*, in Journal of Development Economics, pp. 253–279.

JEWKES R., (2002), *Intimate partner violence: causes and prevention*, The Lancet, April.

JONES H., SAKYI–DAWSON O., HARFORD N., SEY A., (2000), *Linking formal and informal financial intermediaries in Ghana: conditions for success and implications for RNR development*, ODI, Natural Resource perspectives, No. 61, November.

KAHN B., JANSSON T., (2007), *Tough Enough: Microfinance Defies Recession*, December, Inter American Development Bank.

KAPUŚCIŃSKI R., (2001), *The shadow of the Sun*, Penguin books, London.

KAPUŚCIŃSKI R., (2003), *A reporter's Self portrait*, SIW Znak, Kraków.

KARIM N., TARAZI M., REILLE X., (2008), *Islamic Microfinance: An Emerging Market Niche*, August, in www.cgap.org/gm/document–1.9.5029/FocusNote_49.pdf.

KARLAN D., VALDIVIA M., (2006), *Teaching Entrepreneurship: Impact of Business Training on Microfinance Clients and Institutions*, Yale University Discussion Paper.

KARLAN D., ZINMAN J., (2005), *Elasticities of Demand for Consumer Credit*, in http://papers.ssrn.com/sol3/papers.cfm?abstract_id=838406.

KHAN I., (2009), *The Unheard Truth: Poverty and Human Rights*, Amnesty International, W. W. Norton & Company, London.

KHAWARI A., (2004), *Microfinance: Does it hold its promises? A Survey of recent literature*, Hamburg Institute of International Economics, Discussion Paper No. 276.

KIM Y.C., LOURY G.C., (2013), *Social Externalities, Overlap and the Poverty Trap,* in Journal of Economic Inequality, pp. 1-20.

KLEIMEIER S., VERSTEEG, R.J., (2009), *Project Finance as a Driver of Economic Growth in Low-Income Countries*, February, in http://ssrn.com/abstract=134 0903.

KRAUSS N., WALTER I., (2008), *Can Microfinance Reduce Portfolio Volatility?*, in http://papers.ssrn.com/sol3/papers.cfm?abstract_id=943786.

LA TORRE M., VENTO G., (2006), *Microfinance*, Palgrave Macmillan, Basingstoke.

LANDES D.S., (1998), *The Wealth and Poverty of Nations: Why Some Are So Rich and Some So Poor*, Norton & Company, New York.

LE BILLON P., (2006), *Fuelling War: Natural Resources and Armed Conflicts*, Adelphi Paper 373, IISS & Routledge.

LEDGERWOOD J., (1999), *Microfinance Handbook*, World Bank, Washington, in http://www.microfinancegateway.org/p/site/m/template.rc/1.9.30882/.

LITTLEFIELD E., (2008), *Microfinance and the financial crisis*, November, in http://microfinance.cgap.org.

LUCAS R., (1990), *Why doesn't capital flow from rich to poor countries*?, in American Economic Review papers and proceedings, 80, pp. 92–96.

MAATHAI W., (2009), *The Challenge for Africa*, Pantheon, New York.

MADAJEWICZ M., (2003), *Joint-liability contracts versus individual-liability contracts*, Working Paper, Columbia University.

MADDISON A., (2001), *The World Economy: A Millennial Perspective*, in www.mtholyoke.edu/acad/intrel/ipe/oecd1.htm.

MADDISON T., HANSEN H., TARP F., eds., (2004), *Debt relief for poor countries*, Palgrave, Basingstoke.

MAIMBO S.M., RATHA D., eds., (2005), *Remittances: Development Impact and Future Prospects*, The World Bank.

MARX B., STOKER T., SURI T.. (2013), *The Economics of Slums in the Developing World,* in Journal of Economic Perspectives, 27(4): 187-210.

MATHINSON S., (2007), *Increasing the Outreach and Sustainability of Microfinance through ICT Innovation*, in http://www.fdc.org.au/Electronic%20Banking%20with%20the%20Poor/1%20Mathison.pdf.

MATIN I., HULME D., RUTHERFORD S., (2002), *Finance for the Poor: From Microcredit to Microfinancial Services, Policy Arena on Finance and Development*, in Journal of International Development, pp. 273–294.

MAYOUX L., (2000), *Microfinance and the Empowerment of Women. A review of the Key Issues*, in www.ilo.org/public/english/employment/finance/download/wpap23.pdf.

McGILLIVRAY. M., CLARKE, M., (2006), *Understanding human well-being*, Chapter 6, UNU Press, in http://ssrn.com/abstract=1443089.

McINTOSH C., WYDICK B., (2005), *Competition and microfinance*, in Journal of Development Economics, December.

McKEEVER M.P., (2011), *How to write a business plan*, Delta Printing Solutions Inc., Valencia.

McKINSEY & COMPANY, (2007), *Sustainable Markets for Microfinance*, in Market Overview Document, June.

McLINTOCK A.H., (1966), *An Encyclopedia of New Zealand*, 3 vols, Wellington, NZ:R.E. Owen, Government Printer, vol. 2, pp.67–75.

MERSLAND R., (2007), *The Cost of Ownership in Microfinance Organizations*, in http://papers.ssrn.com/sol3/papers.cfm?abstract_id=9705100.

MERSLAND R., STRØM R., (2007a), *Performance and Trade-Offs in Microfinance Organizations – Does Ownership Matter?*, inhttp://papers.ssrn.com/sol3 /papers.cfm?abstract_id=970513.

MERSLAND R., STRØM R., (2007b), *Performance and Corporate Governance in Microfinance Institutions*, in http://papers.ssrn.com/sol3/papers.cfm?abstract_ id=996283&rec=1&srcabs=1004109.

MERTON R.K., (1968), *Social Theory and Social Structure*, The Free Press, New York.

MEWS C.J., ABRAHAM I., (2007), *Usury and Just Compensation: Religious and Financial Ethics in Historical Perspective*, in Journal of Business Ethics, pp. 1–15.

MICROCAPITAL, (2008), *How Far Will the Credit Crunch Affect the Microfinance Industry?*, October, in http://www.microcapital.org/microcapital–story–how–far–will–the–credit–crunch–affect–the–microfinance–industry/.

MICROFINANCE INSIGHTS, (2008), *What does the Subprime Market's Devolution mean for Microfinance*, in http://www.microfinanceinsights.com/.

MODIGLIANI F., MILLER M.H., (1958), *The Cost of Capital, Corporation Finance and the Theory of Investment*, The American Economic Review, Vol. 48, No. 3, in www.his.se/PageFiles/17648/modiglianiandmiller1958.pdf.

MOORE K.A, REDD Z, BURKHAUSER MBWANA K,, COLLINS A., (2009), *Children in Poverty: Trends, Consequences, and Policy Options*, Child Trends Research Brief, Washington.

MORDUCH J., (2000), *The Microfinance Schism*, in World Development, n. 4.

MORDUCH J., (2005), *Smart Subsidy for Sustainable Microfinance*, in ADB Finance for the Poor, December.

MORO VISCONTI R., (2009), *Are microfinance institutions in developing countries a safe harbor against the contagion of global recession?*, in International Finance Review, Volume 10.

MORO VISCONTI R., (2012), *Is African Microfinance Different? Evidence from Banana Skins,* in African Journal of Microfinance and Enterprise Development, 2, 2, 25–45.

MORO VISCONTI R., QUIRICI M.C., (2014), *The impact of Innovation and Technology on microfinance sustainable governance,* in Corporate Ownership and Control, in press

MOYO D., (2009), *Dead Aid: Why Aid Is Not Working and How There Is a Better Way for Africa*, Penguin Books, London.

MYHRVOLD–HANSSEN T.L., (2003), *Democracy, News Media, and Famine Prevention: Amartya Sen and the Bihar Famine of 1966-67*, June, in www.disasterdiplomacy.org/MyhrvoldHanssenBiharFamine.rtf.

NAFZIGER E.W., VÄYRYEN R., eds., (2002), *The prevention of humanitarian emergencies*, Palgrave, Basingstoke.

NAPOLEONI L., (2008), *Rogue economics*, Seven Stories Press, London.

NAUGHTON B., (2007), *The Chinese Economy. Transitions and Growth,* MIT Press, Cambridge.

NAVAJAS S., SCHREINER M., MEYER R.L., GONZALES–VEGA C., RODRIGUEZ MEZA J., (2002), *Microcredit and the poorest of the poor: Theory and Evidence from Bolivia*, in ZELLER M., MEYER R.L., *The Triangle of Microfinance*, John Hopkins University Press, Baltimora.

NOVAK M., (1993), *The Catholic Ethic and the Spirit of Capitalism*, Simon & Schuster Adult Publishing Group, New York.

OECD, (2001), *The DAC Guidelines on Poverty Reduction*, in http://www.oecd.org/dataoecd/47/14/2672735.pdf.

OSTERWALDER A., PIGNEUR Y., (2010), *Business Model Generation*, Wiley & Sons, Hoboken, http://www.businessmodelgeneration.com/book/.

PAGE J., ADAMS J.R., (2003), *International Migration, Remittances, and Poverty in Developing Countries*, December, World Bank Policy Research, Working Paper No. 3179, in http://ssrn.com/abstract=636598.

PETERSEN M.A., RAJAN R.G., (1994), *The Effect of Credit Market Competition on Lending Relationships*, NBER, Working Papers No. 4921.

PICK S., SIRKIN J.T., (2010), *Breaking the poverty circle*, Oxford University Press, Oxford.

PINSON L., (2004), *Anatomy of a Business Plan: A Step-by-Step Guide to Building a Business and Securing Your Company's Future*, Dearborn Trade, Chicago.

POGGE T., (2008), *World Poverty and Human Rights: Cosmopolitan Responsibilities and Reforms*, Polity Press, Cambridge, 2nd ed.

POLLINGER J.J., OUTHWAITE J., CORDERO–GUZMAN H., (2007), *The Question of Sustainability for Microfinance Institutions*, in Journal of Small Business Management, pp. 23–41.

POULIOT R., (2004), *Governance and Accountability in MFIFs*, in KfW Financial Sector Development Symposium, Zurich.

PRAHALAD C.K., (2006), *The Fortune at the Bottom of the Pyramid*, Wharton School Publishing, Philadelphia.

PRENDERGAST R., (2005), *The concept of freedom and its relation to economic development–a critical appreciation of the work of Amartya Sen*, in Cambridge Journal of Economics, Vol. 29, November, Issue 6, pp. 1145–1170, in http://ssrn.com/abstract=904706.

PRETES M., (2002), *Microequity and Microfinance*, in World Development, n. 8.

RAIFFEISEN F.W., (1970), *The Credit Unions*, The Raiffeisen Printing & Publishing Company, Neuwied on the Rhine.

RAWLS J., (1971), *A Theory of Justice*, Harvard University Press, Cambridge.

RAY D., (1998), *Development economics*, Princeton University Press, Princeton.

RHYNE E., (2009), *Microfinance for Bankers and Investors*, McGraw Hill, New York.

RICCARDI A., (2008), *Living Together*, New City, London.

RIPPEY P., (2009), *Microfinance and Climate Change: Threats and Opportunities*, in www.cgap.org/p/site/c/template.rc/1.9.34043/.

RITCHIE A., (2005), *Typology of Microfinance Service Providers*, World Bank, in http://siteresources.worldbank.org/INTCDD/Resources/mftype.pdf.

ROBINSON M., (2001), *The Microfinance Revolution: Sustainable Banking for the Poor*, World Bank, Washington.

ROODMAN D., QURESHI U., (2006), *Microfinance for Business*, ABN–AMRO Centre for Global Development, November.

ROSENBERG R., (2007), *CGAP Reflections on the Compartamos Initial Public Offering: A Case Study on Microfinance Interest Rates and Profits*, CGAP Focus note 42, Washington D.C., in http://www.cgap.org/gm/document–1.9.2440/FN42.pdf.

ROSENBERG R., (2010), *Does Microcredit Really Help Poor People?*, January, in www.cgap.org/p/site/c/template.rc/1.9.41443/.

ROSS M., (2004), *How Do Natural Resources Influence Civil War? Evidence from Thirteen Cases*, International Organization.

RUTHERFORD S., (2000), *The Poor and Their Money*, Oxford University Press, Oxford.

SACHS J.D., (2005), *The End of Poverty: Economic Possibilities for Our Time*, Penguin Books, London.

SACHS J.D., (2008), *Common Wealth: Economics for a Crowded Planet*, Penguin Books, London.

SCHREINER M., MORDUCH J., (2002) *Replicating Microfinance in the United States: Opportunities and Challenges*, pp. 19–61, in CARR J., TONG Z.Y., eds., *Replicating Microfinance in the United States*, Woodrow Wilson Center Press, Washington.

SEGRADO C., (2005), *Islamic Microfinance and Socially Responsible Investments,* University of Torino, in http://www.gdrc.org/icm/islamic–microfinance.pdf.

SEN A., (1999), *Development as Freedom*, Oxford University Press, Oxford.

SEN A., (2009), *The idea of justice*, Penguin Books, London.

SHALMAN W.A., (1997), *How to write a great Business plan*, Harvard Business Review, Boston, http://serempreendedor.files.wordpress.com/2008/09/how–to–write–a–great–business–plan.pdf.

SHLEIFER A., VISHNY R.W., (1997), *A Survey of Corporate Governance*, Journal of Finance, June.

SHLEIFER A., VISHNY R.W., (1998), *The Grabbing Hand: Government Pathologies and Their Cures*, Harvard University Press Cambridge, Massachusetts.

SMICK D., (2008), *The World is Curved. Hidden Dangers to the Global Economy*, Penguin Books, London.

SMITH A., (1776), *Of the Origin and Use of Money. An Inquiry into the Nature and Causes of the Wealth of Nations*, in www.econlib.org/LIBRARY/Smith/smWN.html.

STIGLITZ J., (1990), *Peer Monitoring and Credit Markets*, in World Bank Economic Review, pp. 351–366.

STIGLITZ J., (2007), *Making Globalization Work: The Next Steps to Global Justice*, Penguin, London.

STIGLITZ J., (2010), *Freefall: Free Markets and the Sinking of the Global Economy*, Penguin, London.

STIGLITZ J., WEISS A., (1981), *Credit Rationing in Markets with Imperfect Information*, in The American Economic Review, Vol. 71, No. 3., June, pp. 393–410.

STOLPER W.F., SAMUELSON P.A., (1941), *Protection and Real Wages*, in Review of Economic Studies, 9, pp. 58–73.

STULZ R.M., (1999), *Globalization of Equity Markets and the Cost of Capital*, Working Paper Ohio State University, Dice Centre Working Paper no. 99–1, in http://ssrn.com/abstract=153669.

SULLIVAN A., SHEFFRIN S.M., (2003), *Economics: Principles in action*, Prentice Hall, New Jersey.

SUNDARESAN S., (2009), *Microfinance emerging trends and challenges*, Edward Elgar, Cheltenham.

SVENSSON J., (2000), *When Is Foreign Aid Policy Credible? Aid Dependence and Conditionality*, in Journal of Development Economics, pp. 61–84.

TEDESCHI G.A., (2006), *Here Today, Gone Tomorrow: Can Dynamic Incentives Make Microfinance More Flexible?*, in Journal of Development Economics, pp. 84–105.

UNCTAD, (2008), *The Least Developed Countries Report 2008*, United Nations, New York and Geneva, in http://www.unctad.org/en/docs/ldc2008overview_en.pdf.

UNITED NATIONS CAPITAL DEVELOPMENT FUND, (2002), *Supporting Women's Livelihoods – Microfinance that Works for the Majority*, in http://www.uncdf.org/english/microfinance/uploads/thematic/gender_supporting.pdf.

ÜNVER I.H.O., GUPTA R.K., KIBAROGLU A., eds., (2003), *Water Development and Poverty Reduction*, Kluwer Academic Publishers, Dordrecht,

VAN DOREN C., (1991), *A History of Knowledge,* Ballantine books, New York.

VAN TASSEL E., (1999), *Group Lending Under Asymmetric Information*, in Journal of Development Economics, pp. 3–25.

VELASCO C., MARCONI R., (2004), *Group Dynamics, Gender and Microfinance in Bolivia*, in Journal of International Development, April.

VON BRAUN J., GATZWEILER F.W., eds., (2014), *Marginality. Addressing the Nexus of Poverty, Exclusion and Ecology,* Springer Verlag, Berlin.

VON PISCHKE J.D., (2002), *Microfinance in Developing Markets,* in CARR J., TONG Z., eds., *Replicating Microfinance in the United States*, W. Wilson Centre Press, Washington.

VON STAUFFENBERG D., (2007), *Survey of Microfinance Investment Vehicles*, in www.gsb.columbia.edu/null/download?&exclusive=filemgr.download&file_id=646439.

WADO W.A., (2013), *Education, Rent Seeking and the Curse of Natural Resources,* in Economics and Politics, November.

WAGH S., PATTILLO C., PATTILLO A., (2007), *Impact of Remittances on Poverty and Financial Development in Sub-Saharan Africa*, February, IMF Working Papers, pp. 1–43, in http://ssrn.com/abstract=967879.

WEIL D.N., (2004), *Economic Growth*, Addison–Wesley, Boston.

WELLEN L., MULDER M., (2008), *Influences of the financial turmoil on MFIs*, Unpublished notes, October, World Bank.

WITTFOGEL K., (1957), *Oriental despotism; a comparative study of total power*, Random House, New York.

WORLD BANK, (2004), *Financial Sector Policy and the Poor*, 15, Working Paper, in http://info.worldbank.org/etools/docs/library/128759/Financial%20Sector%20Policy%20and%20the%20Poor.pdf.

WORLD BANK, (2008), *Finance for All? Policies and Pitfalls in Expanding Access, policy research report*, Washington D.C., in http://econ.worldbank.org/.

WRIGHT G.A.N., (2000), *Microfinance Systems: Designing Quality Financial Services for the Poor*, The University Press, Dhaka.

YAIR M., (1992), *Agricultural Productivity and Economic Policies: Concepts and Measurements*, Working Paper No. 75, OECD Development Center, August, in http://miranda.sourceoecd.org/vl=4172647/cl=20/nw=1/rpsv/cgi–bin/wppdf?file =5lgsjhvj7g21.pdf (13–16).

YAMADA T., (1984), *Causal Relationships Between infant mortality and fertility in Developed and Less Developed Countries*, December, NBER Working Paper Series, in http://ssrn.com/abstract=254882.

YUNUS M. (with JOLIS A.), (1999), *Banker to the Poor: Micro-Lending and the Battle against World Poverty*, Public Affairs, New York.

YUNUS M., (2007), *Creating A World Without Poverty*, Random House, New York.

YUNUS M., (2008), *Microfinance unscathed by financial crisis*, October, in www.zimbio.com.

ZHEN N., FU B., LU Y., WANG S., (2014), *Poverty reduction, environmental protection and ecosystem services: A prospective theory for sustainable development*, Chinese Geographical Science, February 2014, Volume 24, Issue 1, pp. 83-92.

WEBSITES and e-SOURCES

http://crisistalk.worldbank.org/2008/11/microfinance-an.html.
http://devdata.worldbank.org/atlas-mdg/.
http://geo.worldbank.org/.
http://hdr.undp.org/en/reports/global/hdr2009/ Human development report.
http://hdr.undp.org/en/statistics/ Human Development Index.
http://knowledge.wharton.upenn.edu/article.cfm?articleid=1147.

http://papers.ssrn.com/sol3/papers.cfm?abstract_id=1064261.
http://rru.worldbank.org/businessplanet/.
http://web.worldbank.org/WBSITE/EXTERNAL/DATASTATISTIC, World Bank Development indicators.
http://www.earth.columbia.edu/.
http://www.globalissues.org/issue/2/causes-of-poverty.
http://www.globalpolicy.org/social-and-economic-policy/poverty-anddevelopment/general-analysis-on-poverty-and-development.html.
http://www.globalsecurity.org/military/world/war/index.html.
http://www.happyplanetindex.org Happy Planet Index.
http://www.iht.com/articles/2008/02/12/business/glob13.php.
http://www.miseryindex.us.
http://www.nationmaster.com/graph/eco_eco_fre-economy-economic-freedom.
http://www.nationmaster.com/graph/eco_ent_get_cre_cre_inf_ind-entrepreneurship-getting-credit-information-index.
http://www.nationmaster.com/graph/eco_hum_dev_ind-economy-human-development-index.
http://www.nationmaster.com/graph/eco_pop_bel_pov_lin-economy-population-below-poverty-line.
http://www.nationmaster.com/graph/eco_pov_sha_of_all_poo_peo-poverty-share-all-poor-people.
http://www.oecd.org/dataoecd/47/14/2672735.pdf.
http://www.oecd.org/dac. (The Development Assistance Committee, DAC, is the principal body through which the OECD deals with issues related to co-operation with developing countries).
http://www.productsofslavery.org/.
http:// www.seepnetwork.org.
http://www.unicef.org/statistics/index_countrystats.html.
http://www.who.int/en/.
http://www.cia.gov/library/publications/the-world-factbook/.
hdr.undp.org/en/statistics/indices/hpi/ Human Poverty Index.

VIDEOS

Video Dr. Muhammad Yunus: http://mitworld.mit.edu/video/289/;
MIT World: http://nobelprize.org/mediaplayer/index.php?id=146;
for his Nobel lecture: http://nobelprize.org/mediaplayer/index.php?id=88&view=1.
http://www.youtube.com/watch?v=n3kzzVP2c7w, Sachs End of Poverty.
http://www.youtube.com/watch?v=o_H0g30YwQ8, Bill Easterly White man's burden.

http://www.youtube.com/watch?v=jbkSRLYSojo, Hans Rosling's 200 Countries, 200 Years, 4 Minutes – The Joy of Stats – BBC Four.

***ibidem*-Verlag**

Melchiorstr. 15

D-70439 Stuttgart

info@ibidem-verlag.de

www.ibidem-verlag.de
www.ibidem.eu
www.edition-noema.de
www.autorenbetreuung.de